Heritage of Canada

Heritage of Canada

Published by
the Canadian Automobile Association
in conjunction with
The Reader's Digest Association (Canada) Ltd.

Acknowledgments

Chapter essays by John Aitken, A. W. (Tony) Cashman, Robert Collins, Dr. Graeme Decarie, Hector Grenon, Paul Grescoe, Douglas How, William Kilbourn, Omer Lavallée, Paul Minvielle, Mario Pelletier, Charles W. Smith, John Swettenham, Prof. Richard Wilbur, Douglas Wilkinson.

Closeup features researched and written by Patricia Derrick, and Philomena Rutherford.

Highlight features by the editors and researchers and by Dr. Graeme Decarie, Lynda Dickson, and Michael Ballantyne, Clell Bryant, Kenneth Conoley, Charles W. Smith, Dusty Vineberg-Solomon, William Wigle, Jack Williams.

Thanks is expressed to the Public Archives of Canada, the National Historic Parks and Sites Branch of the Department of Indian and Northern Affairs, the National Museums of Canada, the provincial departments responsible for historic sites and monuments, historical societies and museums across Canada, and the following individuals and organizations:

Agnes Etherington Art Centre
Jim Burant
Corporate Archives, Canadian Pacific
R. C. Cardwell
Archives of the City of Montreal
Michel Gaumond
Glenbow-Alberta Institute
Conrad Graham
Ruth Grattan
Walter Haldorson
Edna Hall
Heritage Park Society
Historical Resources Administration,
    Province of New Brunswick
Stanley W. Horrall
Hudson's Bay Company
Prof. William James
Dr. Robert R. Janes
Kingston Historical Society
Robert Lapenna
John Leefe
Dr. Jules Lévesque
McCord Museum
McGill University Libraries

Eileen McIlwaine, C.N.D.
R. M. McPherson
Montreal Military and Maritime Museum
Eric W. Morse
Le Musée du Royal 22ᵉ Régiment
Niagara Parks Commission
Nova Scotia Museum
Office of the Commissioner of the
    Northwest Territories
Old Fort William
W. J. Patterson
Mary Peck
Robert S. Pilot
Prince Edward Island Heritage
    Foundation
Royal Canadian Mounted Police
Royal Ontario Museum
Isabel St. John
Service d'Archéologie et d'Ethnologie,
    Gouvernement du Québec
Simcoe County Archives and Museum
Victor Suthren
Debbie Trask
Westmount Library

EDITOR: Hugh Durnford
ART DIRECTOR AND DESIGNER: Jacques Lavigne
ASSOCIATE DESIGNERS: Lucie Martineau, John McGuffie, Lyne Young
ASSISTANT EDITORS: Ian Walker (Heritage Sites), Julie Bayliss, Mary Ricard, Herb Rutherford, Philomena Rutherford, and Douglas R. Long
DESIGN ASSISTANT: Robert Gaboury
EDITORIAL RESEARCHERS: Eileen McKee (research editor), Horst D. Dornbusch (assistant research editor), David L. Dunbar, John R. F. Gillis, Natalie J. King, Michèle McLaughlin, Barbara Peck, and Patricia Derrick, Alice Farnsworth, Lynda Leonard, Deena A. Soicher
PICTURE RESEARCHERS: Viki Colledge (picture editor), Rachel Irwin, Susan Wong
COPY PREPARATION: Gilles Humbert (chief), Lynne Abell, Joseph Marchetti, Margot Weinreich
COORDINATOR: Anne A. Racine
CARTOGRAPHY: K. G. Campbell Corporation Ltd., Ottawa, and Mary Ashley
INDEXER: Carolyn McConnell
PRODUCTION: Holger Lorenzen

BOOK DEPARTMENT
DIRECTOR: Louis Hamel
MANAGING EDITOR: George Ronald
MANAGING ART DIRECTOR: Jim Hayes
PRODUCTION MANAGER: Mark Recher
ADMINISTRATOR: Denise Hyde-Clarke

Foreword

H. M. MacDougall
Chairman of the Board of Governors
Heritage Canada

Pierre Berton
Vice-Chairman of the Board of Governors
Heritage Canada

By Heritage Canada, the charitable national trust

*By heritage, Heritage Canada means the work
of man and of nature whose character enriches
the quality of Canadian life today;
works which illuminate our past or which
reflect the excellence of Canadian achievement;
or examples of Canada's natural beauty which
have survived into our time.*

Every Canadian may have his own definition of heritage; some would say simply that it is everything remaining from yesterday, and that is reasonable. For Heritage Canada, the charitable national trust, independent of government, the focus of heritage lies in places which we see, hear, touch; great public buildings, log cabins, mountains or open places. These are the part of our heritage which the trust seeks to protect, for they enrich our lives or tell us who we are.

Such also is the focus of this book from the Canadian Automobile Association. Ambitiously, it unfolds our past and relates it to places which the reader can visit: places which, while they remain, give a third dimension to the written word. *Heritage of Canada* therefore contributes to our understanding of past and present. Heritage Canada welcomes this book as a contribution to the conservation of our heritage, a responsibility which we share with every Canadian who cares about this country.

Contents

How to Find Heritage Sites

This book tells the story of Canada and directs you to 591 places that are part of that story. Thirty-three chapters, ending with the First World War, unfold historic events through narratives, highlights (in buff-colored boxes) and pictures. Text and pictures emphasize the places where history was made. Each chapter focusses on one historic site which is illustrated on its opening pages. This main site and other sites related to the chapter are mapped and described at the end of the chapter. Interspersed among the chapters are seven double-page closeup features (bordered in buff) portraying daily life at different times and places. An epilogue brings the story of Canada to the present.

Maps on the Heritage Sites pages which end all chapters use white symbols to represent main sites, black symbols for other sites. These are the symbols:

* ✳ Four or more heritage sites
* ♠ Historic building or buildings
* ◤ Museum with exhibit or exhibits pertinent to chapter
* ♥ Commemorative statue, cairn or plaque
* ♠ Fortification (trading post, citadel, etc.)
* ▪ Ruins, including ghost towns
* ● Historic route by land and/or water
* ● Otherwise unclassified attraction such as a ship, mountain or annual event
* ■ Historic site at which there is no commemoration or visible remnant

Most sites are in or near communities, and the community names appear on the maps. Geographical features and remote parks which are sites go by their own names.

Heritage Sites pages also note what can be seen at each site—first the main site, then the others in alphabetical order. A number after a site name matches a number in that site's symbol on the Heritage Sites page map: numbers on maps read roughly from left to right and/or top to bottom. Sites are accessible by road except as indicated.

Historic sites are to be enjoyed—and shared. All historic sites and artifacts, including those not officially classified as such, are protected by law. There are heavy penalties for disturbing sites, or removing or damaging artifacts.

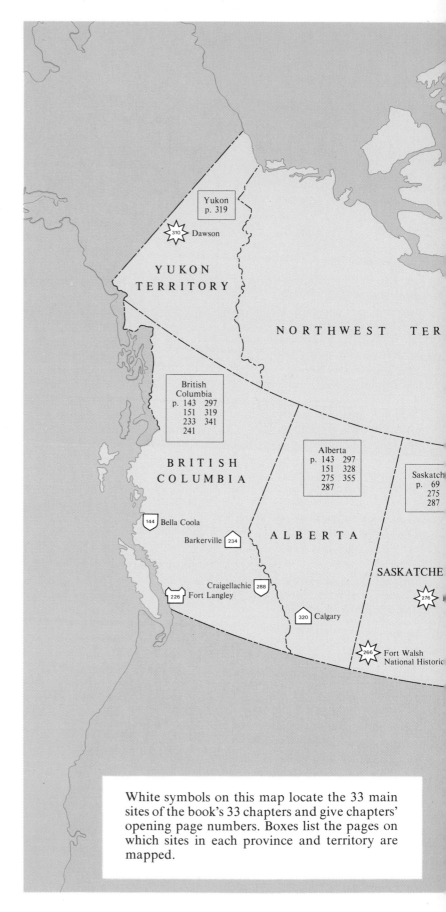

White symbols on this map locate the 33 main sites of the book's 33 chapters and give chapters' opening page numbers. Boxes list the pages on which sites in each province and territory are mapped.

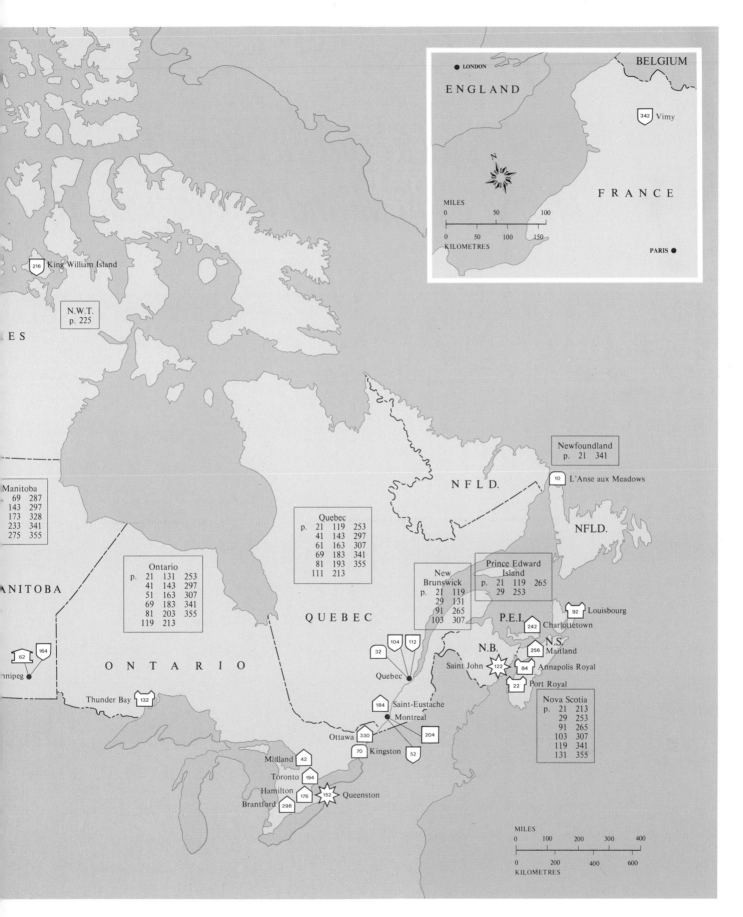

ENGLAND

● LONDON

BELGIUM

342 Vimy

N

FRANCE

MILES

0   50   100

0   50   100   150
KILOMETRES

PARIS ●

216 King William Island

N.W.T.
p. 225

Newfoundland
p.   21   341

10   L'Anse aux Meadows

N F L D.

NFLD.

Manitoba
69   287
143   297
173   328
233   341
275   355

Quebec
p.   21   119   253
41   143   297
61   163   307
69   183   341
81   193   355
111   213

Prince Edward
Island
p.   21   119   265
29   253

Ontario
p.   21   131   253
41   143   297
51   163   307
69   183   341
81   203   355
119   213

New
Brunswick
p.   21   119
29   131
91   265
103   307

92   Louisbourg

MANITOBA

62

164

nnipeg ●

QUEBEC

P.E.I.

242 Charlottetown

N.S.

256 Maitland

N.B.

84   Annapolis Royal

ONTARIO

Saint John   122

22   Port Royal

Thunder Bay   132

104   112

32

Quebec ●

184   Saint-Eustache
● Montreal

Nova Scotia
p.   21   213
29   253
91   265
103   307
119   341
131   355

204

Ottawa   330

70   Kingston

52

Midland   42

Toronto   194

Hamilton   176   152   Queenston

Brantford   298

MILES

0   100   200   300   400

0   200   400   600
KILOMETRES

9

A Voyage Ends, a Story Begins on Newfoundland's Northern Tip

Almost a thousand years ago, after a long passage from Greenland, a stocky blond man armed with a broad battleaxe stepped onto a pebbly beach at the northern tip of Newfoundland. He looked with satisfaction across lush, grassy meadows: plenty of forage here for sheep and cattle. Beyond the meadows were rolling, wooded hills: here would be firewood, and timber for building huts and boats. Offshore in four *knorrs,* watching him, were several dozen men and women. They were Norse, come to establish what may have been the first European colony in North America.

The voyage from Greenland, in seas sometimes shrouded in fog, sometimes whipped by gales, had been cold and dangerous. Each *knorr* had carried a square sail of coarse wool stiffened by strips of walrus hide. Each captain had stood at the stern, steering with a rudder over the right (steerboard) side. But the course had often been guesswork: the high bow, 100 feet ahead of the captain, had been hidden in fog and the black of night and the blown spray. The ships had bent and worked with every wave, for the planking was of thin oak strips lashed and nailed to oak ribs. It flexed in seas that would have smashed a rigid ship. Water had been everywhere—mist, spray, rain and the cold Atlantic. The only shelter had been crude tarpaulins over undecked holds.

But when at last the wind had dropped and the fog had cleared, the crews swung out long oars to row the last few miles to a line of green that hung on the horizon. These *knorrs* began recorded Canadian history.

Each new sunrise at L'Anse aux Meadows is a reminder that here shimmered the dawn of Canadian recorded history. Norsemen such as this Viking settled here at the northern tip of Newfoundland late in the 10th century A.D. Remains of the settlement were not discovered until the 1960s. Above: archaeological excavations at the site.

11

A Long Walk From Asia in the Search for Food

Human beings apparently came to North America by the Bering Land Bridge, a great plateau that now lies beneath the shallow waters of Bering Strait and the Bering Sea. Canada's Indians and Inuit are descended from Asians who gradually moved across this plain that archaeologists call Beringia. For thousands of years at a time it connected Siberia and northwestern North America.

Man may first have crossed the land bridge about 40,000 years ago. Certainly he crossed it some 25,000 years ago and again some 12,000 years ago. He was neither explorer nor discoverer; he simply followed his food supply. From 28,000 to 23,000 years ago the people we now identify as Paleo-Indians moved into the Yukon and Northwest Territories. Gradually some went down the Rocky Mountain Corridor, and from there east and south to populate much of North, Central and South America. Inuit seem to have arrived between 13,000 and 10,000 years ago.

The last ice age ended about 10,000 years ago, the sea covered Beringia and there was no more movement from Asia: the Paleo-Indians and the Inuit had become North American natives.

Burial ridges raised 2,000 years ago by Indians of the Point Peninsula Culture are in Serpent Mounds Provincial Park near Keene, Ont. One of seven mounds is 6 feet high, 200 feet long and shaped like a serpent. An excavation in another (right) has been preserved behind glass.

They were sisters—but broader and heavier—of the Viking longships that had terrorized the river valleys of Europe. Now they were anchored off a new land, each with 15 crew members and 20 passengers with all their implements, food, cattle and fodder.

As the man on shore (we do not know who he was) raised his battleaxe, a cheer went up from the ships and the Norse splashed ashore. Beside a stream now called Black Duck Brook they began a settlement whose remains can still be seen—at present-day L'Anse aux Meadows.

By autumn there were seven turf houses. Women daily gathered driftwood for two fire pits, each six feet across and two feet deep, in which quarters of caribou and chunks of whale were roasted. Men dug holes in the sand to trap tender flounder when the tide ebbed. Along the beach were boat sheds with low turf walls and timber posts supporting turf roofs. Sheep grazed behind the sheds, and women gathered berries in the distant corners of the meadows.

On a massive stone anvil in a hut by the creek, a smith shaped implements of iron and copper.

The Newfoundland coast at L'Anse aux Meadows, little changed in the thousand years since Norsemen gathered driftwood here and cut turf with tools smelted from bog iron.

Were Africans Here 1,500 Years Before the Norse?

Stones in Quebec, paragraphs in Plutarch, and an Irish saint's search *(right)* for a paradise beyond the sea . . . all are tantalizing hints that Africans and Europeans reached North America long before the Viking settlement at L'Anse aux Meadows around A.D. 1000.

Two pieces of limestone discovered in the early 1700s near Sherbrooke, Que., are said to bear Libyan inscriptions—carved perhaps by members of an expedition that sailed up the St. Lawrence and St. Francis rivers some 500 years before Christ. The inscriptions have been deciphered: "Thus far our expedition travelled in service of our revered Lord Hiram to conquer land" and "This is the record of Hanta who attained the great river and left these words cut on stone."

Plutarch, the Greek biographer, wrote in about A.D. 75 of pilgrims sailing from Britain to a shrine beyond the Atlantic. Some scholars say their route may have been via Greenland, Davis Strait and the Labrador coast and that the shrine may have been on Cape Breton Island or on Anticosti Island in the Gulf of St. Lawrence.

St. Brendan, a 6th-century monk, is said to have searched seven years for a "land of promise" across the Atlantic. On the basis of an account written three centuries after his death, Brendan is reputed to have reached the Azores and the Madeiras, perhaps even the Caribbean.

Irish monks may have lived somewhere along the St. Lawrence toward the end of the 9th century. Micmac Indians seem to have come in contact with Christians long before the arrival of French missionaries in the 1600s. The French called the Micmacs the Porte-Croix (Bearers of the Cross)—for they used two fingers to make a sign like the sign of the cross.

His helper toiled a few hundred yards upstream, digging into the spongy soil for bog iron ore. It was heated over a charcoal fire; hot coals were added to the ore until it melted into a soft, glowing iron that could be hammered into shape.

One day, we can imagine, a woman watched from the doorway of her hut and in her hand was a pebble with a hole bored through its centre—a flywheel for the spindle she used to spin wool. The pebble slipped from her grasp and was lost in a hole at the base of the turf wall. There it lay hidden for almost 10 centuries, to be found in 1964. (A replica is in the interpretive centre at L'Anse aux Meadows National Historic Park.)

Norwegians, Swedes and Danes had begun their voyages about A.D. 800, driven largely by overpopulation. The Swedes and Danes struck only through Europe but some Norwegians pointed their dragon-prowed ships into the North Atlantic. They settled in Iceland about A.D. 900 and with their Irish slaves became the Icelandic people.

An Icelander named Erik the Red murdered a man in 982 and was exiled for three years. He spent his exile exploring the forbidding shores of Greenland, and there he established two colonies.

Men from these settlements sailed farther yet, beyond Baffin Island to Melville Peninsula, trapping falcons and polar bears for the courts of Europe. One ship in the arctic trade was driven off course in 986 and sighted strange new wooded lands—apparently Labrador and Newfoundland. This was the first clear recorded European discovery of America south of the Arctic.

Leif Eriksson, son of Erik the Red, heard of the discovery. Attracted by the possibility of timber close to Greenland, he sailed (about A.D. 995) and landed at a fertile spot he called Vinland. He remained there for a year.

Archaeologists have proved beyond doubt that there was a Norse settlement at L'Anse aux Meadows. But was that Eriksson's Vinland or

was L'Anse aux Meadows settled by Norse who came after him? That question has tantalized scholars for years.

The Vinland story was preserved in two Norse tales, the *Saga of the Greenlanders* and the *Saga of Erik the Red*. Both mention Vinland but neither locates it in terms that can be understood. (A stone found in 1812 at Yarmouth, N.S., 860 miles southwest of L'Anse aux Meadows, bears an inscription that some scholars suggest is early Norse.)

For 200 years the sagas were passed on by word of mouth; only then were they written down. They differ on the number of settlements and on incidents in those settlements, but they agree on the timing of voyages and in their description of lands the Norse discovered. They also suggest why the settlements disappeared: the expeditions were marred by misunderstanding, distrust and bloodshed.

One account tells how a group of natives—Skraelings, the Norse called them—came to trade. A bull which the Norse had brought from Greenland charged bellowing out of the forest. The terrified Skraelings, never having seen such an animal, ran for shelter in the Norse huts. The Norse, thinking this an attack, barred their doors and fought the Skraelings off. Three weeks later, when other Skraelings approached the settlement, the Norse assumed they were a war party seeking revenge, and attacked with axe and sword.

Now it was the turn of the Norse to be terrified, for fearsome winged objects flew through the air at them, killing and wounding several men. Un-

East coast fishermen still weight their nets with killicks, anchors such as the Norse used a thousand years ago. A killick is made of supple tree branches bent and tied around a long, heavy stone, then secured to crossed wooden flukes.

Fifteen crew members, 20 passengers and up to 40 tons of cargo were transported on a knorr *(below). In rainy weather, humans sheltered with cattle, sheep and goats under tarpaulins rigged over an undecked hold between foredeck and afterdeck. Food was eaten cold except when fires could be lit on a stone hearth on the afterdeck. Knorrs were flat-bottomed for easy beaching. The bow and stern rose high and a single mast rose from the centre. The hull's overlapping planks were caulked with animal hair dipped in tar.*

A Landmark, a Star . . .

How did the Norse—who had no compasses—navigate on the open sea? As men had done for thousands of years, they sailed from one landmark to another, and from atop a 50-foot mast a lookout could spot a 7,000-foot peak up to 125 miles away. They could sail from Norway to North America and never be more than 200 miles from land.

In northern latitudes, shadows point north at noon. Thus, once a day, a bearing dial *(right)* made an effective compass: the shadow of its upright centre pin was aligned with a mark on the dial's edge pointing north. Navigators calculated latitude at night by estimating the height of the North Star above the horizon; the farther north one sails, the higher the star appears.

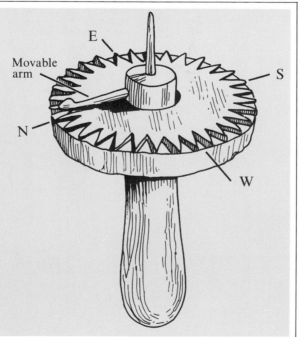

This painting by Christian Krohg represents Leif Eriksson sighting North America. The Norse sagas describe his voyage about A.D. 995 to a hospitable land whose natural abundance included wild grapes—for which he named it Vinland.

15

able to get close enough to the Skraelings to use hand weapons, the Norse males fled, leaving their women and children to catch up as best they could.

One woman was Freydis, daughter of Erik the Red. Pregnant and unable to run, she struggled along behind the men, screaming her contempt for their cowardice. She grabbed the sword of a fallen Norseman, turned on the Skraelings with a wild battle cry, and ripped away her dress, presumably to whet the iron blade on her breast. This seemed no woman to trifle with: the Skraelings turned and ran.

The Skraelings had, in all likelihood, been on a sealing expedition. The winged objects that demoralized the Norse were harpoons to which the Skraelings attached the inflated bladders of animals—to keep the harpoons afloat when seals were speared. They were the Skraelings' only means of defence.

Some years after the fight with the Skraelings, Freydis commanded an expedition of Greenlanders in an uneasy partnership with Icelanders. Because of their mutual distrust, it was agreed that each group should be limited to 30 fighting men. Freydis brought five extra. On reaching Newfoundland she had her followers murder the Iceland men and steal their ship. Her men refused to kill the Iceland women, so Frey-

The historic voyage of John Cabot in 1497 was in the barque Matthew *(above: a model in the Newfoundland Museum at St. John's). His landfall on June 24 may have been near Cape North, N.S. (below).*

dis herself snatched up an axe and butchered them.

By the 15th century domination of the northern seas passed to English, French and Portuguese fishermen. Precisely where they went is uncertain—they kept their fishing spots secret—but English ships from Bristol are known to have explored the North Atlantic by 1480, 12 years before Columbus. At least one voyage by Bristol men probably reached North America before 1492.

But Columbus that year seemed to prove that Asia—the land of spices and silks and, so it was believed, all the world's precious stones—could be reached by sailing west. Henry VII of England, like most kings of the time, was chronically short of money, so when the Italian navigator and mapmaker John Cabot approached him in 1496, he was receptive.

Cabot had been active in the spice trade in the eastern Mediterranean. Now Henry authorized him to sail westward and to claim for England any lands he discovered that were hitherto "unknown to Christians." The king would get one-fifth of the profits of Cabot's trade monopoly; Cabot would retain the rest.

On May 20, 1497, he left Bristol in the barque *Matthew*, apparently less than 75 feet long, with canvas that included a triangular lateen sail such as Arab spice traders used. A lookout sighted land June 24—perhaps Newfoundland, perhaps Cape Breton; the exact spot has never been established. Certainly it was no land of silks and spices. Cabot recorded that "the inhabitants . . . weare beasts' skinnes, and have them in as great estimation as bowes, arrowes, pikes, darts, wooden clubs and slings. The soile is barren in some places, & yeeldeth little fruit, but it is full of white beares, and stagges farre greater then ours."

But there was good news for Bristol men: "It yeeldeth plenty of fish . . . there is a great abundance of [cod]."

Still, Cabot was looking not for fish but for the kingdoms that Marco Polo had visited. He planted a cross claiming the land for England, then continued along what he thought at first was the coast of Asia. Finding no sign of Asia's riches, he turned back to England.

The king, encouraged, gave £10 "to hym that found the new Isle" and sponsored a second voyage. Cabot sailed in May 1498 with five ships.

Three years later, probably in Newfoundland, natives showed Portuguese explorers an Italian sword and earrings that may have been Cabot's. There never was any other trace of the explorer, his crews or his ships.

Cabot found no shining cities but he did show

A Killer Disease and the Cure Cartier Lost

A baneful disease, as Jacques Cartier called it, ravaged the 110 Frenchmen living in icebound ships near Stadacona (Quebec) in the winter of 1535-36. They knew neither what it was nor how to combat it.

Cartier wrote that "a pestilence . . . wholly unknown to us" spread among the French: ". . . their legs became swollen and puffed up . . . . Then the disease would creep up to the hips, thighs and shoulders, arms and neck. . . . the flesh peeled off down to the roots of their teeth while the latter almost all fell out in turn." They had scurvy, caused by a lack of vitamin C, which is found mainly in citrus fruits, fresh vegetables, and raw or lightly cooked fresh meat.

The French offered prayers and performed an autopsy for clues to the cause of the disease. At one time, "on all our three ships there were not three men in good health." Twenty-five died; some were buried in snow, for "the ground was frozen hard and we were too feeble and exhausted to dig into it."

Cartier and his men were "in desperate fear lest the Indians should realize our plight and helplessness." But from the Indians, in early spring, they learned of a cure: "They told us how to strip off the bark and leaves from a certain tree, boil them in water, and drink the liquor every other day while placing the dregs on swollen and afflicted legs." The tree, which Cartier called the annedda—it was the eastern white cedar *(right)*—"did us so much good that all those who consented to use it were cured and recovered their health, thanks be to God."

And then the cure was lost—for Cartier never told *how to identify* the annedda.

A century later Champlain wrote of "the disease which preyed upon us as fiercely as it had preyed upon him." He knew of Cartier's annedda but not what it was. Nor, apparently, was the cure known to the Indians whom Champlain encountered in 1604. Because of scurvy, the king refused to finance colonization between 1609 and 1612.

What's in This Name?

Jacques Cartier apparently took the Indian word *kanata* (village, community) to be the name of the land he had discovered. That is one (and perhaps the best) explanation. Two of many others:
• Spaniards sought gold around the Baie des Chaleurs, found none and said: *"Aca nada"* (Here is nothing). Indians repeated the phrase to French explorers—who thought the words were the country's name.
• French settlers were allowed only one can of spruce beer a day and "every moment articulated 'can a day.'" This in 1811 from the *Kingston Gazette,* which added: "It would be ungenerous in our readers to desire a more rational derivation of the word CANADA."

that North America was a continent, not a peninsula of Asia, and he established an English claim that would shape the destiny of the new land.

England was not the only country interested in the territories across the Atlantic.

On April 20, 1534, a man in his mid-forties stood on the quarterdeck of a small ship in the harbor of Saint-Malo in the north of France. A letter bearing the seal of François I, king of France, instructed Jacques Cartier to take two ships to discover "certain isles and countries where, it is said, there must be great quantities of gold and other riches."

Fair winds carried Cartier's two ships over the northern seas but his heart sank when on the 33rd day, after sailing through the Strait of Belle Isle, he sighted what apparently was Labrador. He found nothing but rock and stunted shrubs. "I did not see one cartload of earth," he wrote. "I believe that this was the land God gave to Cain."

Cartier's ships hauled south to explore what he thought was a large bay. It was the Gulf of St.

Jacques Cartier first saw the St. Lawrence River on Aug. 10, 1535, and named it for the saint whose feast day that was. With skills learned as a North Atlantic fisherman, he sailed 800 uncharted miles up what he thought was a waterway to the Orient. Théodore Gudin's painting (right) of that historic voyage to Hochelaga (Montreal) was commissioned in 1839 by King Louis-Philippe of France for the Musée du Château de Versailles.

Lawrence and Cartier is recorded as the first European to enter it. He sailed past the Magdalen Islands and on June 29, 1534, went ashore to a charming land with sandy beaches and rich meadows, "the best-tempered region one can possibly see"—present-day Prince Edward Island. But there was no gold, so the ships coasted north off what now is New Brunswick, paused at a huge warm-water inlet that Cartier named Baie des Chaleurs, and on July 14 sailed into the Baie de Gaspé.

Indians who looked up from their fishing as the French ships dropped anchor were Iroquois, members of a sophisticated agricultural nation that ruled the St. Lawrence Valley and the lower Great Lakes. This was a fishing expedition from a village the Iroquois called Stadacona (at present-day Quebec).

Their chief, Donnacona, greeted the French with gifts and feasting. But the Iroquois became uneasy when—on what now is called Pointe de Penouïl in Forillon National Park—Cartier erected a 30-foot cross bearing the arms of Fran-

çois I. In sign language Cartier assured them it was simply a marker to guide future voyagers.

He took two of Donnacona's sons to France to be trained as interpreters, and François agreed to a second expedition of three vessels. They left Saint-Malo in the spring of 1535 led by the flagship *La Grande Hermine* (a replica of which is in Cartier-Brébeuf National Historic Park at Quebec). The Iroquois interpreters guided Cartier past Anticosti Island and up the broad river. Suddenly it narrowed. There on a great fist of rock stood the settlement called Stadacona. Donnacona greeted them.

But the warm reunion soon chilled. Over the objections of Donnacona, who wanted to monopolize Indian contacts with the French, Cartier travelled upstream to another Iroquois village, Hochelaga, where eventually Montreal would grow. Hochelaga welcomed Cartier with dancing and so much food that he said it seemed to rain corn bread and fish. Behind the palisaded village was a mountain that Cartier named for the cardinal of the Medicis, once bishop of Monreale in Sicily. Monreale in French became Mont Royal. From atop the mountain Cartier scanned the river and glimpsed a flash of white from the Lachine Rapids. Beyond, he was told, lay a freshwater sea.

Cartier wintered along the Saint-Charles River near Stadacona. His ships and his huts were coated inside with several inches of ice; the river froze to a depth of 12 feet. And scurvy struck: men's arms and legs became swollen, gums rotted, teeth fell out, and 25 men died. The Indians saved others by showing them how to brew a remedy from the bark and leaves of the eastern white cedar.

Cartier wanted Donnacona replaced by a friendlier chief. In the spring, as the expedition prepared to return to France, he invited Donnacona and other Iroquois to a ceremony at a fort his men had built—and took them prisoner. He promised the Indians their chief would be returned in a year.

But, because of war between France and Spain, Cartier did not come back for five years—in 1541—and by then Donnacona and the others were dead, presumably of European diseases for which they had no immunity. Cartier lied and said they were living in luxury in France. Few of the Iroquois believed him; the new chief, Agona, was—if anything—less friendly than Donnacona had been. He and his people sensed that Cartier had come to stay. He had. This time, in five ships, there were more than 400 Frenchmen.

Cartier had instructions to found a settlement as well as to explore, and he built a fort he called Charlesbourg-Royal at Cap-Rouge, eight miles up the north shore of the St. Lawrence from Sta-

This replica of Jacques Cartier's La Grande Hermine, *in Quebec's Cartier-Brébeuf National Historic Park, was built in 1966 with 16th-century tools and methods. The 78-foot wooden original led two other ships from Saint-Malo, France, in the spring of 1535, on Cartier's second expedition to the New World.*

dacona. But Cartier was disgruntled: command of the expedition had been given not to him but to a soldier-courtier-pirate named Jean-François de Roberval, and Cartier was to await his arrival at Charlesbourg-Royal in the spring of 1542.

But all through a hard winter the embittered Iroquois kept the French in a state of siege, and in June Cartier sailed for France.

As Cartier's five ships headed home, Roberval with 200 settlers in three ships was en route to Charlesbourg-Royal. They met in Newfoundland. Roberval said he had arms with which to cow the Iroquois and he ordered Cartier to accompany him. But Cartier had had enough of Canada and he slipped away the next night and returned to France. He had with him several barrels of what he thought were diamonds and gold, hoping that treasure would help the king to overlook his disobedience.

Roberval had raised money for the expedition by selling his property, borrowing from friends and returning briefly to his old trade of piracy. Unable to recruit enough volunteer settlers, he got the king's permission to scour French prisons for thieves and debtors willing to buy their freedom by becoming colonists. A few lords and ladies of the court joined him on agreement that they would become the aristocracy of the colony. Roberval's 200 were a mixed lot.

The winter of 1542-43 at Charlesbourg-Royal was one of terror. The colonists suffered from hunger, filth, cold and scurvy. (Cartier had not told Roberval of the scurvy cure; now the Iroquois withheld it from him.) Roberval used the lash freely on rebellious men and women who refused to work or otherwise "failed in their duty." In the depth of that winter nightmare, Canada saw its first execution as Roberval ordered one Michel Gaillon hanged for theft.

In the spring the survivors straggled down to their ships. Contemptuous Iroquois eyes followed their retreat downriver. Charlesbourg-Royal had failed, and in Paris Cartier's gold and diamonds had proved to be worthless iron pyrites and quartz—introducing a new phrase into the French language: *faux comme diamants de Canada* (as false as Canadian diamonds). Not for half a century would French colonists return to the St. Lawrence.

Roberval was murdered one night as he left his church in Paris. Cartier fell from royal favor but lived to age 66 with a reputation as a congenial tippler with a fund of tall tales. Whatever his faults, he had discovered one of the great entrances to North America and had established a French presence in the New World.

The failure of Charlesbourg-Royal marked a pause in the exploration of Canada. But only a pause. Five hundred years after Norsemen landed at L'Anse aux Meadows, Canada had been brought into the orbit of Europe. The North Atlantic was no longer a barrier but a pathway.

An Island of Demons, Her Penalty for Love

It was spring and they were in love, Marguerite de Roberval and her young man. For three weeks in June 1542, as the ships took on water and supplies at present-day St. John's, they roamed the Newfoundland hills, picking berries, fishing for salmon, making love—as Marguerite's servant stood guard. When her uncle Jean-François de Roberval learned of the affair, he was furious. En route to the St. Lawrence to command a colony in the land Jacques Cartier had discovered, he marooned Marguerite and the servant on uninhabited Ile des Démons (possibly Fogo Island off the northeast coast of Newfoundland, or an island in the Strait of Belle Isle). The young man, whose name is lost to history, chose to be with his beloved.

They built a cabin. Game, fruit and bird eggs were plentiful. Christian faith sustained them amid the fearful screams of the island's demons—perhaps the cries of birds and animals. But after eight months they had seen no ship, hope of rescue was fading—and Marguerite was pregnant. The young man took ill and died. Marguerite buried her lover and had their child.

She became a skilled hunter and again there seemed hope. But after some 17 months on the island the servant died. Then Marguerite's child. After a year of utter loneliness, two years and five months after Roberval had put her ashore, she was rescued by Breton fishermen. She returned to France. Whether she saw her uncle is not recorded.

Jean-François de Roberval's colony at Cap-Rouge, upstream from Quebec—the first French attempt at settlement in Canada—had been a tragic failure. Marguerite de Roberval's very survival had been a superb triumph.

Heritage Sites

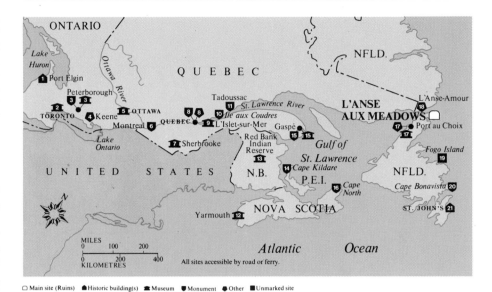

□ Main site (Ruins)   ● Historic building(s)   ▲ Museum   ▼ Monument   ◆ Other   ■ Unmarked site

L'ANSE AUX MEADOWS, Nfld. A Viking settlement, possibly the Vinland of the Norse sagas, took root near here about A.D. 1000. Remains of seven turf buildings, two cook pits and a smithy have been unearthed in L'Anse aux Meadows National Historic Park. Displays in the park interpretive centre include a floorboard of a Norse boat, iron rivets excavated at the site, a stone lamp and a soapstone flywheel used for spinning wool.

Other sites

Cape Bonavista, Nfld. (20) A statue of John Cabot marks where he may have landed in 1497.

Cape Kildare, P.E.I. (14) A statue of Cartier in Jacques Cartier Provincial Park, three miles southwest, commemorates his landing in 1534.

Cape North, N.S. (16) A cairn and a bust of Cabot are at nearby Cabot's Landing. A trail leads to the summit of Sugar Loaf, which some think was Cabot's landfall in 1497.

Fogo Island, Nfld. (19) This may be the Ile des Démons where Marguerite de Roberval was marooned in 1542.

Gaspé, Que. (15) A 30-foot granite cross commemorates the wooden cross Cartier erected in 1534 on Pointe de Penouïl, across the Baie de Gaspé, to claim the land for France. A nearby museum and interpretive centre depicts early exploration.

Ile aux Coudres, Que. (10) A 20-foot granite cross at Saint-Bernard commemorates the first Mass in Canada, celebrated Sept. 7, 1535, the day Cartier landed here.

Keene, Ont. (4) A grassy knoll 6 feet high and 200 feet long, shaped like a serpent, is an Indian burial mound believed about 2,000 years old. It is in Serpent Mounds Provincial Park.

L'Anse-Amour, Nfld. (18) A burial mound in the shape of a circle—2 feet high and some 80 feet in circumference—was built of cobblestone by Early Maritime Archaic Indians about 5500 B.C.

L'Islet-sur-Mer, Que. (9) Ribs from the bow of one of Cartier's ships, *La Petite Hermine,* are in the Bernier Maritime Museum.

Minton, Sask. (not shown) A 135-foot-long stone turtle effigy near Big Muddy Lake is centuries old.

Montreal (6) A plaque on a boulder at McGill University marks the site of the 16th-century Iroquoian village of Hochelaga.

Ottawa (5) The National Museum of Man has reconstructed a Prince Rupert, B.C.,

This stone lamp used by the Norse at L'Anse aux Meadows a thousand years ago is displayed at the national historic park there.

archaeological excavation that yielded tools, stone carvings, and skeletons from 5,000 years of habitation by the Coast Tsimshian Indians.

Peterborough, Ont. (3) A marker locates a 2,000-year-old Point Peninsula Indian grave uncovered during excavation for a parking lot. The Peterborough Centennial Museum displays a gorget and a scraping tool from the grave.

Port au Choix, Nfld. (17) Burial sites uncovered in Port au Choix National Historic Park tell most of what is known about "red paint people" who lived 4,000 years ago. Dorset Inuit lived on nearby Pointe Riche about A.D. 100. An interpretive centre displays relics and skeletons from the burial sites.

Southampton, Ont. (1) Relics in the Bruce County Museum reflect the way of life of 14th-century Petun Indians. Their palisaded village stood in nearby Port Elgin.

Quebec (8) In 16-acre Cartier-Brébeuf National Historic Park, facing the Saint-Charles River where Cartier wintered in three ships in 1535-36, is a replica of *La Grande Hermine,* his flagship on voyages to Canada. A 25-foot granite cross commemorates the cross Cartier erected in 1535. A cairn on the east bank of the Cap Rouge River is at the site of the colony of Charlesbourg-Royal (1541-43).

Red Bank Indian Reserve, N.B. (13) Artifacts in the school here date from about 400 B.C. and include Adena Indian spear points and copper beads recovered from the Augustine burial mound.

St. John's, Nfld. (21) The Cabot Tower on Signal Hill commemorates Cabot's discovery of Newfoundland in 1497.

Sherbrooke, Que. (7) Inscriptions on two pieces of limestone preserved at the Séminaire de Sherbrooke may have been made by pre-Viking explorers of this area.

Tadoussac, Que. (11) A cross beside the Tadoussac Church commemorates Cartier's landing in 1535.

Toronto (2) Artifacts, reproductions and dioramas in the Royal Ontario Museum depict prehistoric life in Ontario.

Viking, Alta. (not shown) The Ribstones, on high ground nine miles southeast, are two quartzite rocks in which, an estimated 1,000 years ago, Indians scraped lines to represent buffalo backbones and ribs. Plains Cree hunters left sacred offerings on the rocks.

Yarmouth, N.S. (12) A 400-pound stone at the Yarmouth County Museum may have been inscribed by Norsemen 1,000 years ago.

The First Frail Settlement, a Foothold in the Wilderness

Jean de Poutrincourt: Port Royal seemed the perfect place to make his dream come true.

It was Nov. 14, 1606, and they were back, a score of weary Frenchmen who had spent 10 discouraging weeks searching to the south for a likelier site for a colony. Their little pinnace slipped slowly in from the stormy Bay of Fundy, then skirted the shore of what Nova Scotians would one day call the Annapolis Basin. Soon Port Royal was in sight, the tiny fort they and others had so recently hacked out of the wilderness. The pinnace anchored and a boat put off for shore, Jean de Poutrincourt in the bow.

Out to meet them came a boat, a dinghy and a canoe. The boat's oarsmen were in costume, half-men, half-fish. In the canoe were four painted men who looked like Indians. And in the dinghy stood a bearded, blue-clad figure carrying a trident—Neptune! When this king of the sea spoke, he spoke in verse—and Poutrincourt grinned as he recognized Marc Lescarbot, a young Parisian lawyer who had abandoned his unprofitable practice to come to Acadia (most of today's Maritime Provinces and part of Maine). Neptune's oarsmen and attendants were French soldiers. Lescarbot had recruited them to be a welcoming committee. But they were more than that: his script and the roles they played made this North America's first theatre.

Poutrincourt laughingly shouted his approval and, once ashore, embraced his friend. They walked arm in arm to the fort and, as they entered, trumpets blared and four cannon fired.

It was a fitting welcome for Poutrincourt. Two years earlier, on a voyage from France with Pierre de Monts, governor of Acadia, he had fallen in love with the sheltered basin. With its wooded hills, fertile soil and sparkling waterfalls, it seemed the ideal place for a colony. But de Monts, holder of a new fur-trade monopoly for Acadia, decided differently. He took his carpenters, stonemasons and soldiers to Saint Croix Island in the St. Croix River (now the New Brunswick-Maine border).

As the summer of 1604 waned, a palisade rose at the northern end of the island, enclosing dwellings, a barracks and a storehouse. Poutrincourt sailed for France in late September with a rich cargo of furs. He left behind de Monts, Samuel de Champlain and 77 other men; apart from some Spaniards in Florida, they were the only Europeans in North America.

Snow fell Oct. 6 and by December the river was filled with churning ice floes, making passage to the mainland impossible. Saint Croix was now a prison where fresh food and water were a memory. The island's trees were fed into the fires, only a row of cedars being spared as a windbreak. Everything froze: the men's Christmas drink was rationed by the pound.

Then: scurvy. Teeth loosened and limbs swelled painfully. De Monts and Champlain were unaffected but 35 men died. Another 20 were near death at the end of March when Indians arrived with fresh meat. Gradually the suffering eased. On the morning of June 16 a boat arrived with some provisions and news that a supply ship was approaching with Poutrincourt on board. Sick men crawled out to help fire a cannon in celebration.

A 6½-week voyage south in the summer of 1605 located no good site for a colony. Another winter on the island was unthinkable, so de Monts ordered the colony moved to Poutrincourt's sheltered basin off the Bay of Fundy. There the settlers erected a bigger, stronger fort—the first successful white settlement north of Florida. They named it Port Royal.

The reconstruction (left) at Port Royal, N.S., is a replica of the fort that Poutrincourt, de Monts and Champlain knew. In every detail (above), from fieldstone fireplaces to heavy beams, the reconstruction is faithful to the style of 1605.

The French had neighbors—a band of about 100 Micmacs led by a tall, bearded chief named Membertou who revelled in attention from the French and returned unswerving loyalty.

In October, with the fort complete, Poutrincourt and de Monts sailed for France to try to preserve the fur-trade monopoly from envious rivals in the court of Henri IV. In July 1606, Poutrincourt, now lieutenant-governor of Acadia, returned without de Monts, but with more Frenchmen eager for adventure. Among them were his 14-year-old son Charles (de Biencourt) and his lawyer-poet friend Marc Lescarbot. On Sept. 5 Poutrincourt set sail in a pinnace with about 20 men to comply with de Monts' wishes—to seek once more a site farther south.

Lescarbot was left in charge of Port Royal. It was now that he conceived the Neptune Theatre with which he welcomed back Poutrincourt and his party that fall. That voyage too had been a failure and the French lost interest in the coast south of present-day Maine. Fourteen years later the English Pilgrims claimed it.

Perhaps the success of Lescarbot's Neptune Theatre gave Champlain the idea for his *Ordre de Bon-Temps.* He bartered with the Indians for moose, caribou and deer, joined them in hunting partridge and duck, sent his men to gather shellfish and to fish for trout. Then he announced the formation of the Order of Good Cheer, with himself as its first grand master.

On that first day, with the shadow on the sundial close to noon, Poutrincourt and Membertou sat expectantly at the head of the massive table in Port Royal's great dining hall. Seated on the floor were Membertou's family, and at the door stood soldiers and tradesmen downing their daily three-pint wine ration. At a signal from Poutrincourt, Champlain strode into the hall, staff of office in hand, chain around his neck, a napkin on his shoulder. Behind him came the 13 other men who dined at Poutrincourt's table, each bearing a steaming dish of food.

Poutrincourt banged the table and the men at the door cheered. The Order of Good Cheer was off to a boisterous start. Thereafter the 15 men took turns, each responsible for the feast on his day as grand master.

Again the winter was mild. As the last snow was disappearing in the spring of 1607, carpenters built Canada's first water-driven grist mill (on what is now called the Allains River). Crops were planted. Poutrincourt awaited with confidence the arrival of the yearly supply ship. But when it came on May 24, it brought bad news: de Monts had lost his fur-trading monopoly. Port Royal was now no longer profitable. It had to be abandoned.

Amid the wails of the sorrowful Micmacs, the main party left for France. Poutrincourt, Champlain and seven others stayed to harvest the crops (evidence of Acadia's agricultural potential). On Aug. 11 they too set out for France, leaving Membertou to watch over Port Royal in return for 10 barrels of flour.

Acadian Governor Pierre de Monts founded the first successful French colony in the New World—Port Royal in Nova Scotia.

Sable Island: Mutiny and Murder and a Colony Dies

Sable Island, a treeless, windswept crescent of sand 190 miles east of present-day Halifax, was no place for a colony. But in 1598, after 26 years' preoccupation with civil war, France turned actively again to the New World—and chose Sable. Troilus de La Roche, a court favorite, was named lieutenant-general of Canada and recruited 40 colonists for the island—although only convicts, beggars and vagabonds would go.

They built huts and a storehouse with timbers from a wrecked ship. They planted vegetables among the dunes, to eke out a diet of fish, berries and meat from game that included wild cattle—descendants of animals shipwrecked or abandoned by earlier visitors. La Roche sailed for the Newfoundland fisheries leaving a commandant and 10 soldiers as a garrison. He had promised to return but a violent storm drove his ships to France. Nonetheless, furs and sealskins were waiting when, the next spring, a relief ship brought more colonists. Each year La Roche sent supplies from France and the colony returned its harvest of furs and skins.

But in 1602 no ship came and that winter the settlers mutinied. The commandant and the storekeeper were butchered. The storehouse was ransacked. More murders followed. By spring, when a ship arrived, only 11 men were alive. Back home, in shaggy furs and beards, they told Henri IV their story. To La Roche's astonishment—he considered them murderers—the 11 were pardoned and each was compensated with 50 crowns and a share of the pelts they had brought back.

No more colonists were sent to Sable Island. Since then a third of it has been claimed by the sea, and more than 200 ships have perished on this graveyard of the Atlantic.

There but for Poutrincourt the French attempt to settle Acadia might have ended. De Monts never returned to North America, and Champlain, acting as de Monts' lieutenant, turned his attention to the St. Lawrence (see p. 32). But Poutrincourt gave Henri IV grain and wild geese from Port Royal and convinced the king to give him the Port Royal concession de Monts had held and to let him revive the colony. It took two years, however, to find financial backing, and there was a new problem—the Jesuits wanted to send missionaries. Poutrincourt, a devout Roman Catholic, was suspicious of the ambitious Jesuits despite the support they had from Queen Marie. He consented to take two priests to Port Royal, but on Feb. 26, 1610, on the pretext that he had first to build them suitable lodging, he sailed without them. With him went his son Charles and Poutrincourt's personal priest, Jessé Fléché. Membertou met them, pointing out that Port Royal's buildings were intact.

On June 24, the feast day of Saint-Jean-Baptiste, Abbé Fléché baptized Membertou and his family on the shore in front of the fort. They were the first Indian converts to Christianity in what became Canada. Membertou adopted the king's name, Henri; his wife became Marie after the queen; 19 other members of his family took the names of French nobility. Now Poutrincourt had evidence for the queen that the Lord's work was being done—without the Jesuits.

A month after Membertou's baptism the younger Poutrincourt sailed for France, hoping to use the conversions to obtain greater financial and political support for Port Royal. He found Queen Marie agreeable to providing more money—but only if Jesuits Pierre Biard and Enemond Massé went on the next ship. When its Huguenot owners learned of this condition, they refused to outfit the vessel. Finally, the Marquise de Guercheville, wife of the governor of Paris and a strong advocate of the Jesuits, paid off the Huguenots. Charles and the priests reached Port Royal on May 22, 1611. By fall he and the Jesuits were in open conflict.

The first serious dispute came when Membertou fell ill. He received the last rites of the church and asked to be buried among his fellow Micmacs. Charles approved this (he was only 19 but was in command in the absence of his father, who was in France seeking financial aid for the ailing colony) but Father Biard balked because the

Saint Croix Island (now part of Maine) was Pierre de Monts' first choice as a site for a settlement. Thirty-five of the 79 colonists perished the first winter (1604-05) and the exposed island was abandoned in favor of a sheltered site on the Annapolis Basin.

'Savage' Wisdom Saved 'Civilized' Europeans

When food ran short one winter, Jean de Poutrincourt sent some of his Port Royal settlers to live among the Micmacs—and saved the Frenchmen's lives. "Without the assistance of these same Savages," a Jesuit priest wrote, "I do not know but that they would all have perished miserably."

Most 17th-century Frenchmen held Indians in contempt for their "savage" ways. But French dependence on the Indians of the eastern woodlands was nonetheless frequently if unintentionally acknowledged. Explorers, fur traders and settlers relied on Indian hospitality for food and shelter—and medical help: balsam gum for wounds, red ochre for insect bites, hemlock tea poultices for bruises and sprains.

The Indians, on the other hand, scorned French medical care and other practices. Marc Lescarbot described how one Micmac

at Port Royal, treated for a badly cut foot, returned jauntily two hours later, "having tied round his head the bandage in which his heel had been wrapped." Indians ridiculed the French for blowing their noses on linen handkerchiefs. One asked: "For what purpose do they preserve such a vile thing?"

What made the Indians so incomprehensible yet so vital to the French was their closeness to nature. Life matched the seasons: in winter most tribes hunted (deer, caribou, moose); in spring and summer they ate fish, seal, beaver and the flesh and eggs of birds, and gathered shellfish, roots and berries, drying and storing the surplus for periods of shortage; in the fall they returned to hunting.

Indians made good use—and taught the French how they could make good use—of materials at hand: clay, wood and bark for cooking utensils; birch bark for dwellings, canoes and dishes; rushes for mats and bags. The French recorded that Indians used almost 275 species of plants for medicines, 130 for food, 27 as smoking "tobacco," 25 for dyes. Each spring they tapped trees for what the Jesuits called "maple water" and made syrup and sugar.

Some tribes, such as the Hurons, depended heavily on agriculture and grew maize, squash and beans. Indian cultivations sometimes were accidental, as in Prince Edward Island where raspberry, cranberry and wild rose seeds discarded by Micmacs grew to be the "Indian orchards" around Malpeque Bay and Rustico Bay.

Success on the hunt was vital to survival. Hunters honored dead creatures to ensure a plentiful supply of animals. They burned or buried animal bones, believing that the

Wigwams such as this one in the Micmac villa near Fort Amherst National Historic Park Rocky Point, P.E.I., were made of birch bark.

creatures of the forest would not let themselves be easily trapped or killed if they knew their bones would be thrown to hunters' dogs. They decorated their cloth out of respect for animals whose meat tained the tribe.

Game was often scarce and fasting unavoidable. Fatalistically, the Indians cepted the possibility of famine; real cally, they feasted when food was plenti A hunter who returned laden with ga shared his wealth with the entire villag although only males were invited to feast and women and children got the l overs. Each guest provided his own b dish; meat was served from a hollowed-tree stump that served as a kettle. Chunk fat were often eaten as a first course. men wiped greasy fingers in their hair o the back of the nearest dog.

Such were the "savages" whose ha and superstitions disgusted the Jesuits the Poutrincourts—but whose very attu ment to nature saved French lives and haps New France itself.

Through visions when fasting, every Indian male adolescent acquired a guardian spirit. It protected him all his life and, appearing in dreams, directed his actions. In this painting, one of 36 by Lewis Parker and Gerald Lazare at Sainte-Marie among the Hurons, near Midland, Ont., Huron dancers re-enact a sick man's dream—that he was cured by the incantations of hunchbacks wearing wooden masks and carrying sticks.

This map shows the distribution of Indians and Inuit in southeastern Canada around 1600, based on language. The Iroquois were a confederacy of five nations: Seneca, Cayuga, Onondaga, Oneida and Mohawk.

☐ *Algonkian language group*
■ *Iroquoian language group*
☐ *Inuit language group*

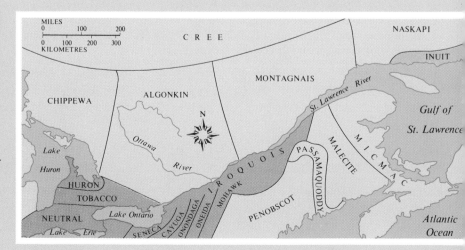

How Indians Made a Bark Canoe

Gunwale and thwarts of split white cedar were lashed together to make a frame. It was placed on a levelled bed of earth. Thirty-to-50-inch-long stakes of sapling driven into the ground marked the canoe's shape.

Frame and stakes were removed and overlapping sheets of bark from the paper birch were laid on the bed. Then the frame was placed on the bark and weighted with stones atop other pieces of wood.

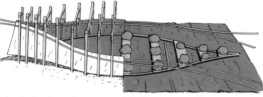

As the bark was bent around the frame, the stakes were reset. Battens were lashed to them to hold the sides firm. Gores or slashes were made in the bark so that it took on a canoe's curved form.

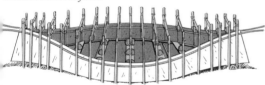

When all the bark had been shaped, the frame was raised to its proper height and the bark sewn to it. The long thin roots of the black spruce were used to sew or lash the canoe together.

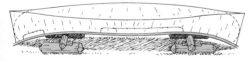

The canoe was removed from the bed and placed on supports. The pieces of bark were sewn together and the ends of the canoe closed. Curved pieces of cedar were lashed inside each end. Then the canoe was righted.

When all seams had been waterproofed inside with spruce gum, the canoe was lined with planks of white cedar. Ribs were fixed over the lining and the canoe was turned over to be waterproofed on the outside and perhaps decorated.

Micmac burial ground was not hallowed. It was Membertou who compromised: when he died, he was buried apart from his people.

The feuding continued. Biard irritated Charles by suggesting that Indian conversions had been rushed through for political reasons. Charles retaliated: he refused to let any of the priests—Biard and Massé had been joined by a third Jesuit, Gilbert Du Thet—cross the Bay of Fundy to preach to the Malecite Indians. Massé went anyway. Tempers were so hot when he returned that the Jesuits decided to return to France.

Charles denied them permission; they had arrived under the queen's orders and would have to leave the same way. The priests boarded a ship. Charles ordered them off. Biard said he would excommunicate anyone who touched him—and did excommunicate Charles and the ship's captain when they put the Jesuits ashore.

Months later, in June 1612, a truce was reached. Du Thet was allowed to return to France. He hurried to Paris and told the Marquise de Guercheville of Port Royal's troubles.

Her personal representative, René de La Saussaye, was in charge of the ship *Jonas* that arrived at Port Royal in May 1613 with more colonists and with horses, goats and supplies of all kinds—everything the elder Poutrincourt had been unable to procure. But La Saussaye stopped only to pick up Biard and Massé, then sailed away to start a new colony, with Jesuit support, which would surpass Port Royal.

La Saussaye landed on what now is called Mount Desert Island, off the Maine coast some 40 miles southeast of present-day Bangor. In July, while he and his men were arguing about where to build a fort, they were attacked by a raiding force led by Capt. Samuel Argall, "Admiral of Virginia." With 60 men in a 14-gun ship, he had sailed from Jamestown, Va., carrying orders from the governor of Virginia to destroy all

In the reconstructed fort at Port Royal, N.S., is a replica of the hall where the Order of Good Cheer—North America's first social club—gathered daily during the winter of 1606-07. Its members feasted on beaver tails, salmon, caribou, moose pie and breast of goose—delicacies they believed would have delighted even the most demanding of French gourmets.

French settlements on land claimed by England. That included Acadia.

Argall easily captured the French and their ship. La Saussaye, Massé and another 13 accepted Argall's offer of a pinnace to take them to French territory. (They were picked up off the coast of Nova Scotia by a French ship and returned to France.) But Biard and 13 others—fearful of shipwreck—accompanied Argall to Jamestown. There, through Argall's intercession, they escaped hanging and agreed to return to Acadia with him on a new raid of destruction.

Argall now levelled La Saussaye's unfinished settlement and the remains of the habitation on Saint Croix Island. In November he descended on Port Royal. Finding the fort empty (Charles de Poutrincourt and all his men were in the fields) the raiders stripped Port Royal bare within minutes, taking even the locks from the doors. Some animals were herded aboard Argall's ship, others were slaughtered. Then the buildings were set afire. Argall, with Father Biard at his side, led his men to the fields where the helpless French had been watching. Biard tried to persuade his countrymen to desert. "Be-

gone," one replied, "or I'll split your head with this hatchet."

Argall's raiders departed.

Jean de Poutrincourt had succeeded in his last attempt to get backing for the colony. He returned to Port Royal on March 27, 1614, to a scene of destruction. The great hall where the Order of Good Cheer had met was no more; the charred remains of the head table were just visible in the ruins. The fields lay barren.

A figure came out of the forest. A Micmac, Poutrincourt thought. Then he recognized his son Charles who, along with the other survivors, had spent a miserable winter with only roots and lichens to eat.

Sadly the older Poutrincourt acknowledged defeat. He returned to France with most of the settlers and transferred title to his Port Royal concession to his son Charles. He died two years later. Charles, who remained to develop the fur trade, partially rebuilt Port Royal. But more and more he turned to the forest life of the Indians, and the settlement became just a tiny collection of huts. The fields returned to the wild.

The Fur Trade: A Matter of Fashion

1500s: copatain hat

1600s: cavalier hat

1700s: tricorne hat

Europeans did not want furs for warmth or luxury: under a pelt's long, glossy guard hairs lay a short, woolly undercoat that made the best kind of felt cloth—and Europeans *did* want felt hats *(left)*. Indians wanted iron pots and tools. From all this came the fur trade.

The undercoat of the beaver was particularly valuable because of its thickness and durability. Adult beaver were big (averaging 50 pounds), plentiful (numbering some 60 million in North America in the 1600s) and relatively easy to catch *(see below, right)*.

To make felt, the inch-long undercoat was removed from the pelt, rolled or pounded flat, then bonded with shellac so it could be shaped. Microscopic hooks that covered each hair helped hold the felt together and reduced the amount of bond needed.

The first traders were European fishermen who often bartered for furs off the Indians' backs. Such furs were prized because, before sewing pelts into robes, the Indians scraped the underside of each skin to loosen the roots of guard hairs. Most fell out and, as the robes were worn, fur side in, the remaining guard hairs were rubbed off, exposing the soft undercoat.

Fur-bearing animals were scarce in Europe by 1600 but a new merchant class was hungry for luxury goods. Henri IV saw the fur trade as a means both to ease France's tax burden and to

build an American empire. Port Royal was one result. Settlement along the St. Lawrence was another. Since the finest furs came from the north, French trade and French influence moved in that direction.

By the late 1600s nearly 100,000 beaver pelts were being traded each year. A beaver hat cost 20-30 livres, almost one-third the monthly pay of a French army captain. Traders made up to 2,000 percent profit but nobody told the Indians.

How Beaver Were Trapped

The best beaver pelts were taken in winter when the fur was thickest and the animals, snug in their lodges, were easiest to catch. Before steel traps came into use in 1797 (see p. 138), various techniques were used. Some hunters built deadfalls: an animal trying to take a bait triggered a device that dropped a log on its neck. Others cut holes in pond ice to attract beaver to fresh air—and to put them within reach. At other times of the year, dust dropped through a lodge's air vent stampeded beaver into underwater nets. Or dams were broken to eliminate the deep ponds in which beaver could hide.

Heritage Sites

PORT ROYAL, N.S. A reconstruction of the first successful European settlement north of Florida (1605) stands in 20-acre Port Royal National Historic Park. Its buildings surround a courtyard and are fortified by a palisade and a cannon platform. They include the governor's residence, the banquet room where the Order of Good Cheer met, and a fur-trading room.

Other sites

Advocate Harbour, N.S. (6) Pierre de Monts found copper here in June 1604.
Annapolis Royal, N.S. (4) A monument with a bronze bust of de Monts is in Fort Anne National Historic Park.
Lequille, N.S. (5) A replica of a 17th-century French mill, housing a power plant, is on the Allains River where Jean de Poutrincourt built North America's first waterpowered grist mill (1607).
Liverpool, N.S. (8) A cairn in Fort Point Park commemorates the first landing in Acadia (May 6, 1604) by de Monts and Poutrincourt.
Pictou, N.S. (10) The Mic Mac Museum displays 17th-century French trade goods from two Indian burial sites. They include beads, textiles, axes and copper pots.
Port Mouton, N.S. (7) The de Monts expedition of 1604 spent May in this bay, waiting for a supply ship. The harbor was named when a sheep jumped overboard.

All sites accessible by road or ferry except where noted in text.

⌒ Main site (Fort) ♠ Historic building(s) ▲ Museum ♥ Monument ■ Ruins ■ Unmarked site

Rocky Point, P.E.I. (9) A reconstructed 16th-century Micmac village near Fort Amherst National Historic Park shows tribal life before the arrival of white men.
Sable Island, N.S. (11) A plaque marks the site of a colony established by 40 ne'er-do-wells in 1598 and abandoned in 1603. *Not accessible to the public.*
Saint Croix Island, Me. (1) A plaque marks the remains of the habitation where

de Monts, Champlain and 77 other men spent the winter of 1604-05.
Saint John, N.B. (2) A monument near the harbor commemorates Champlain's landing here on Saint-Jean-Baptiste Day, June 24, 1604. The Saint John River was named after the saint.
St. Mary's Bay, N.S. (3) Traces of silver and iron were discovered along the shore by the de Monts expedition of 1604.

In 1607, after six men at Port Royal died from the exertion of grinding grain by hand, Jean de Poutrincourt had North America's first water-driven grist mill built on the Allains River. This replica of a 17th-century French mill marks the site, at today's Lequille, N.S.

Cod and Conflict in a Newe Founde Lande

Detail from a 1690 map of eastern Canada at the Newfoundland Museum in St. John's.

Codfish were so thick and so easy to catch that a weighted basket let into the sea would come up full: so reported explorer John Cabot of his "Newe Founde Lande" in 1497. Fishing fleets flocked in each spring from England, France, Portugal and Spain, but it was more than 100 years after Cabot that the first settlers perched houses around Newfoundland's rocky bays.

John Guy took 39 Englishmen to present-day Cupids in 1610. English fishermen, however, saw all settlers as interlopers who usurped shore areas needed for drying fish. They burned settlers' houses, damaged mills and ruined crops. Some settlers retaliated, "tempting [the fishermen] by wine and women" and destroying their gear. Eventually London prohibited settlement within six miles of the shore and the first captain to arrive in a harbor each year became its all-powerful "fishing admiral." The settlers stayed nonetheless and by 1677 there were dozens of communities on the Atlantic side of the Avalon Peninsula.

France, meanwhile, had fortified Plaisance (present-day Placentia) on the west side of the peninsula. There, in November 1696, Pierre Le Moyne d'Iberville took command of a 120-man Quebec force of soldiers, militiamen and Indians. His objective: to drive the English from Newfoundland. Iberville marched some 70 miles across the peninsula and took Ferryland from the rear. Then, joined by 300 French soldiers who landed at Ferryland, he swept up through St. John's to the northern tip of the peninsula, burning and looting as he went. He destroyed 36 settlements, killed 200 persons and uprooted hundreds more before quitting Newfoundland in March 1697.

That summer 2,000 English troops reached St. John's. The settlers returned to their villages and started over again. In 1713 the Treaty of Utrecht gave the island to England.

French "wet" fishery ships were anchored on the Banks from April to June. To combat the sea and the cold, workers stood in barrels and wore leather aprons. Men behind wind barriers (right) caught one fish at a time; the catch was dressed on deck and dumped into the hold with thick layers of salt.

For two years, handsome Peter Easton was the terror of Newfoundland's fishermen and settlers. A veteran of the English navy, he turned to piracy in 1604 and arrived in Harbour Grace about 1611 with 10 armed ships. He built a fort (left, under attack in a fanciful painting). Then he recruited—or pressed—fishermen into his service, and plundered fishing ships. In Conception Bay he took two ships and 100 men; in St. John's he pillaged 30 ships; in Ferryland he looted other vessels. (The colony at Cupids was spared after giving the buccaneer two pigs.) Easton, often accompanied on shore by minstrels and trumpeters, became known as the Pirate Admiral. Pardoned and invited back to England by James I, he decided instead to move his freebooting to the Mediterranean to rob Spanish treasure ships, and soon settled in Savoy as one of the world's richest men. He bought a palace, married a wealthy woman, became a marquis and spent the rest of his life in luxury and splendor. The Conception Bay Museum at Harbour Grace stands on the site of his Newfoundland fort.

Red Indians Became Prey

Newfoundland Beothuks adorned themselves with red ochre (as at right) and Europeans' descriptions of them led to use of the term Red Indian.

Peaceful and friendly by nature, the Beothuks were gradually exterminated by white fishermen and settlers. The slaughter began with a misunderstanding. In November 1612 John Guy and a party of settlers met some Beothuks at Trinity Bay. Settlers and Indians ate, drank beer and laughed together, and arranged to meet the following year. But an armed fishing ship arrived at the meeting place before Guy. Its crew fired a cannon at the excited Beothuks. The Indians fled and Beothuks would never meet with whites again. They began to take Europeans' fishing gear. Fishermen pursued what they now called the "nuisance" Indians and killed them. They began wiping out villages to steal the Indians' furs. Finally, killing Beothuks became a sport.

The butchery was outlawed in 1769 but went on nonetheless, and the last of the Beothuks, a young woman named Shanawdithit, died in St. John's in 1829.

English fishermen (above), lacking much salt, had to dry their cod on shore—sometimes for months—to preserve it. This "dry" fishery was a gruelling race against autumn and bad weather. Men fished all day for cod, and netted herring for bait every second night. At landing stages (sheds and wharves), where the workday might last 22 hours, cod were gutted and split in about four seconds before being washed and thinly salted. They were then put out to dry on open-air flakes—wooden racks like those still found in Newfoundland outports, particularly along the south shore. The men's reward was a small share of the profits from the dried cod they called "Poor Jack." The lowest-paid men sometimes ended up with a few pennies.

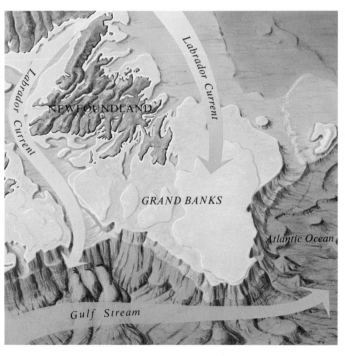

Left: The cold Labrador Current meets the warm Gulf Stream, stirring undersea minerals on the vast plateau called the Grand Banks. Sunlight, penetrating the relatively shallow (180-foot) water, helps the minerals to fertilize a mass of microscopic life that supports billions of cod.

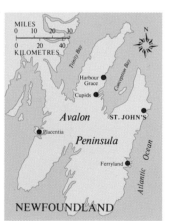

Seeing 'the Strange Things of the World'

The first tourists came to the New World in 1536. Their cruise ended, according to a survivor, in cannibalism and piracy. Richard Hore, a London leather dealer, chartered a ship to take 30 gentlemen to Newfoundland "to see the strange things of the world." They coasted south and east of the island and went sightseeing ashore, but trouble started when the ship ran out of food. Ignoring the fish around them, the men grew desperate with hunger, drew lots and began to kill and eat one another. "If thou wouldst needs know," one admitted later, "the broyled meat that I had was a piece of man's buttocke."

Hore and the surviving tourists were saved by the arrival of a well-provisioned French fishing ship. They captured it, left its crew to an unrecorded fate, and sailed home.

A Valiant Man and Wise, and His Beloved Colony

Unaware of mutiny brewing in the warm July of 1608, Samuel de Champlain watched joyously as walls and roofs and a palisade rose from a shelf of land lapped by the St. Lawrence River. He called it all the Habitation. It was to be a storehouse, a jumping-off place for fur traders going upriver, a stronghold against the implacable Iroquois. Above all it would be the fulfilment of a dream; here in the abounding wilderness Champlain planned to found a community from which would spring a mighty empire. In his own lifetime the Habitation would know famine, defeat, neglect and betrayal—but it would survive as the first continuously occupied white settlement north of Florida. Betrayal would come first.

Weeks earlier Champlain and his 30 men had leapfrogged past Basque whalers trading for furs at Tadoussac, at the mouth of the Saguenay River, and had come farther up the St. Lawrence. On July 3 he stepped ashore at a "place where the river narrows" (a *kébec* in Algonkin)—where Quebec City now stands. He had seen this place on his first voyage to Canada in 1603, had found it beautiful, its soil good, the setting, with its great shadowing rock, excellent for defence. Now, on the site of the present-day Church of Notre-Dame-des-Victoires, his small band of men were building a settlement.

Champlain drove them hard. In the heat, under siege from mosquitoes and blackflies, and sluggish after idle months at sea, they began to grumble. One, a locksmith named Jean Duval, stirred their resentment and urged them to throw off tyranny. With four other malcontents he plotted to assassinate Champlain, sell the Habitation to the Basques at Tadoussac, and return to

Europe rich. On the day set for the murder, however, one of the plotters confessed. Champlain sent him back to work, then arranged for a friendly sailor to invite all the plotters to enjoy some wine on board a ship that evening.

While drinking below decks Duval and his accomplices were suddenly surrounded by sailors loyal to Champlain. The man who had confessed was set free but a jury of ships' officers and sailors found the other four men guilty. Three were sent home in chains. Duval said he deserved death, and got it. His severed head was impaled on a pike and placed in full view of the workers. From then on Champlain and the colonists lived in amity.

But in February scurvy and dysentery struck. Every man fell ill. The doctor died. Others died. By June, when long-awaited ships arrived from France with supplies and more eager colonists, only eight men at the Habitation were alive.

All around, amid the resurgent beauties of spring, lay reminders of a winter of despair. Champlain's response—a calculated risk and one of the most decisive acts of his life—was to plunge upriver into the land of the ferocious and powerful Iroquois. A handful of Frenchmen went with him. In 1603 the French, to gain fur-trading allies, had pledged to support the Algonkins, and through them the Hurons, against the Iroquois (a confederacy of the Seneca, Oneida, Onondaga, Cayuga and Mohawk nations). Now, in the summer of 1609, Champlain lived up to the promise and in doing so set the stage for nearly a century of battling between the French and the Iroquois.

At present-day Batiscan, 70 miles up from Quebec, he met several hundred Algonkins and Hurons. French and Indians together moved south along "the River of the Iroquois" (the Richelieu). Champlain was forced to abandon his light boat at the seething rapids at Chambly and all but two of his French companions turned

Samuel de Champlain, "father of Canada." This bronze statue by Vernon March is in Couchiching Beach Park at Orillia, Ont.

The sail comes down, the oars go out, and Samuel de Champlain waves a greeting on his return to the Habitation at Quebec in the fall of 1608 after a voyage of exploration up the St. Lawrence. The Habitation, made of butternut, was constructed by Champlain and 30 men in only three months.

The first use of firearms in tribal warfare—Ticonderoga (in modern New York) in 1609—was recorded in this drawing by Champlain. He is in the centre between the Algonkins and Hurons (left) and the Iroquois.

back. The three remaining Frenchmen and about 60 Indians paddled in canoes to "a very large lake, filled with beautiful islands, and a large, beautiful region near the lake, where they [the Indians] had represented to me their enemies lived." Champlain gave the lake his own name.

Now they moved cautiously, travelling by night and hiding by day. Late on July 29, as they approached a cape on the westward shore, probably the rounded promontory below modern Ticonderoga, N.Y., shouts came out of the darkness—from a war party of Mohawk Iroquois heading north. The Mohawks went ashore. There was a parley and an agreement to fight (part of the protocol of the warpath). "They said," wrote Champlain, "that as soon as the sun [arose] they would attack us, and our Indians agreed."

At first light, Champlain's allies, in war paint, landed unhindered. Hidden among them were the three Frenchmen, armed with arquebuses. They took up battle positions and watched as some 200 stalwart Mohawks advanced.

Champlain recounts: "They came slowly to meet us and at their head were three chiefs. Our Indians likewise advanced and told me that those who had the three big plumes were the [Mohawk] chiefs, and that I was to kill them. My white companions went [unnoticed] into the woods. Our Indians divided into two groups, and put me ahead some 20 yards, and I marched on until I was within some 30 yards of the enemy, who as soon as they caught sight of me halted and gazed at me and I at them. When I saw them make a move to draw their bows upon us, I took aim with my ar-

Did Champlain have long hair and sport a Van Dyke? Perhaps, but the only painting claimed to be of Champlain (top) is a fraud, copied in 1854 from a 17th-century portrait of a French civil servant. The sole likeness of Champlain (above) is by himself, from his drawing of his encounter with the Iroquois at Ticonderoga (top of page).

Brûlé, First to Live as a Coureur de Bois

On a June day in 1611, at the Lachine Rapids near Montreal, Champlain met a French youth of about 19 just returned from a year in Indian country far to the west. Like his Indian friends, he was nut-brown and dressed in skins. And he spoke their dialect fluently. He was Etienne Brûlé, the first coureur de bois and Champlain's agent in the wilderness.

Brûlé was the first white to see lakes Ontario, Erie, Huron and Superior, and may also have discovered Lake Michigan. He was first to see the sites of present-day Ottawa and Toronto, and to tread the soil of what became Ontario. He was also the first European to shoot the Lachine Rapids—and the first to live as an Indian.

He was of French peasant stock and arrived in New France in 1608. After two years at Quebec he asked to be allowed to live among the Indians. Champlain, eager to train interpreters and anxious for information about the beckoning lands to the west, entrusted him to the Algonkin chief Iroquet for a year. It is likely he paddled to Iroquet's home, 240 miles up the Ottawa River, and to Huronia, south of Georgian Bay, before returning to meet Champlain.

From then until his death at 41 he lived mostly among the Hurons. He once fell into Iroquois hands and (the story goes) used a ruse to save himself from torture. When one of his captors snatched at a religious medal Brûlé wore around his neck, the sky darkened and peals of thunder split the air. Brûlé pretended the storm signalled divine intervention and persuaded the fearful Iroquois to release him.

In 1629 he turned traitor and served the English who captured Quebec—and Champlain—that year. When Champlain returned to New France in 1633 he found that the Hurons had tortured, killed and eaten Brûlé. Nobody knows their reasons, but the Indians had probably resented Brûlé's betrayal of their friend Champlain. They would not be punished, the French leader assured them, because the traitor was no longer considered a Frenchman.

Brûlé left no records, no journals, no letters. He is occasionally glimpsed in the writings of Champlain and of the Jesuit fathers—who felt his licentiousness mocked their teachings. He flits through history like a brave through the primeval forest—enigmatic and almost invisible.

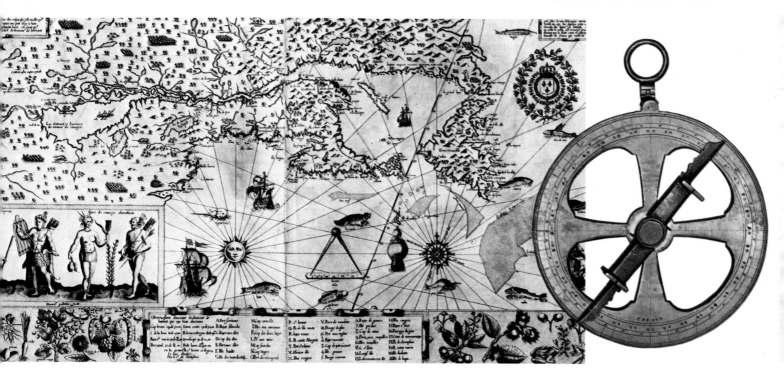

This map of New France was made by Samuel de Champlain, perhaps from data gained using this astrolabe (inset), now in the New York Historical Society Museum in New York. An astrolabe enabled explorers to calculate latitude (the distance from the equator). This one, made of brass and inscribed "Paris, 1603," was found in 1867 near Cobden, Ont., by a farmer who thought it worthless and sold it to an American visitor for $5. Champlain's diary makes no mention of the loss of an astrolabe but in 1613 the explorer did travel up the Ottawa River past the future site of Cobden. A replica of the astrolabe is in Ottawa at the National Museum of Science and Technology.

Champlain (in red) bids Etienne Brûlé farewell near the Huron capital of Cahiagué in 1615. Brûlé and 12 Huron warriors travelled through Iroquois territory to enlist the aid of the Susquehannahs in Champlain's attack later that year on an Onondaga fort near present-day Syracuse, N.Y. The painting is by Rex Woods.

quebus and shot straight at one of the three chiefs, and with this shot two fell to the ground, and one of their companions was wounded. This frightened the enemy greatly. One of my companions fired a shot from within the woods, which astonished them again so much that, seeing their chiefs dead, they lost courage and took to flight. I pursued them and laid low still more of them."

Whether Champlain realized it, this encounter at Ticonderoga was momentous. It had been the Indians' first exposure to firearms in battle. From then on every Indian wanted a gun. As some did acquire them, confrontations of massed men would soon yield to surprise raids, ambushes, guerrilla warfare.

Among Champlain's Indian allies Ticonderoga strengthened the French leader's reputation for courage and dependability. But in Iroquois minds it spawned a tradition of French treachery they would never forget— Champlain had taken sides in a tribal war and New France would pay the price in blood and terror.

Champlain was eager to explore the wilderness to the northwest and to see the great body of water (Lake Huron) near which his Huron allies lived. But there were delays. He started for Huronia in 1613 but abandoned the trip. The Hurons muttered that the French leader was not honoring his pledges of support. Fewer and fewer furs were brought to the Habitation.

Finally, in the spring of 1615, Champlain met the Hurons at Sault Saint-Louis (the Lachine Rapids, at Montreal Island) and promised to go to their country and join them in an attack on the Iroquois heartland to the south. He set off July 9 with interpreter Etienne Brûlé and another Frenchman and 10 Hurons.

They ascended the Ottawa River, passed the site of Canada's future capital, struggled through rapids and across tangled portages, crossed Lake Nipissing, and descended the swift French River into Lake Huron. They turned their canoes south along the east shore of Georgian Bay and on Aug. 1 landed about four miles north of present-day Penetanguishene, Ont. On Aug. 3, at Carhagouha (near modern Lafontaine, Ont.), Champlain and his party met 12 French soldiers who had arrived in Huronia a week earlier. (There Champlain helped the Recollet Father Joseph Le Caron celebrate the first Mass in what became Ontario.)

Across the folding hills and through the rich forests of Huronia, Champlain went from village to fortified village. At each he exhorted the chiefs to hurry their attack on the Iroquois. In mid-August, at Cahiagué, on Lake Simcoe near today's Warminster, a council of war came together to plan the great campaign against the Onondaga tribe of the Iroquois.

It was September before 500 Hurons and 14 Frenchmen departed. Brûlé and 12 Hurons had left two days earlier to enlist the aid of the Susquehannahs, a tribe living south of the Iroquois in modern Pennsylvania.

The canoes of the main party worked south, past Orillia and Peterborough, down the Trent River into the Bay of Quinte, then across Lake

"Hudson's Last Voyage" by John Collier. In the spring of 1611, mutineers cast Henry Hudson, his son John and seven men adrift on James Bay in a small boat. They were never seen again—unless by Nicolas de Vignau (see box this page). The mutineers sailed Hudson's ship Discovery *to England. There they were tried for murder—not mutiny—and acquitted.*

Did He See Henry Hudson or Did He Lie?

"I have been to the northern sea," interpreter Nicolas de Vignau told Champlain in the fall of 1612, "and I have seen the wreckage of an English boat."

Vignau had spent the previous winter with the fierce Algonkin Indians of Allumette Island in the Ottawa River, near present-day Pembroke, Ont. With them, he said, he had visited what is now James Bay. The Indians had killed some starving, shipwrecked Englishmen (Vignau had seen their scalps) and taken a boy prisoner.

Determined to see "the northern sea" for himself, Champlain set off with Vignau in March 1613. They got no farther than Allumette Island. There the Indians, old acquaintances of Champlain's, warned him of hazardous rapids and portages and hostile tribes ahead. And they turned angrily on Vignau, denying his whole story. Champlain questioned the shaken Vignau sharply and the interpreter confessed he had

never made the trip. "The most impudent liar that has been seen for a long time," said Champlain.

But Vignau may have told the truth. His only lie may have been his "confession." One group of Englishmen probably was on James Bay as Vignau said—explorer Henry Hudson and eight members of his crew, set adrift by mutineers the previous summer and never heard of again. The wrecked boat could have been theirs, and the prisoner Hudson's 19-year-old son. And the Allumette Island Indians had reason to contradict Vignau's story: as middlemen in the fur trade they did not want the French venturing north and dealing directly with other Indian tribes.

Vignau and Champlain returned down the Ottawa. At the Lachine Rapids, near Montreal, Champlain left Vignau "in God's keeping." There is no further record of this "most impudent liar" who may not have lied at all.

Paresseux Falls in Ontario's Mattawa River Provincial Park is one of many obstacles on the rocky, rugged Mattawa River, up which Champlain canoed in 1615 en route to Georgian Bay and Huronia. The 30-foot waterfall (paresseux means lazy) is by-passed by the Paresseux Portage (below), one of several along the 35-mile-long river.

Ontario. They entered Iroquois country somewhere near Stony Point, N.Y., and headed inland on foot toward an Onondaga fort near present-day Syracuse. Their plan was to attack at dawn.

But as they neared the fort that October day, Onondaga braves ambushed some of the Hurons. Surprise was lost. Only a siege would do now and, as an angry Champlain soon saw, it would be a tough one.

The Onondaga fort was protected on three sides by a lake and streams, and walled with 30-foot palisades topped by fighting galleries. Champlain harangued the chiefs and, through them, their braves.

They must, he said, "construct a cavalier, a movable tower overtopping the walls of the fort, from which we may fire down on the defenders. At the same time we shall make wooden mantelets, or screens, impervious to arrows, and we shall move them forward against the fort. With such protection we shall be able to set fires along their palisade, and thus make a breach."

The Indians wanted to wait for Brûlé and the Susquehannahs. Champlain said no. So the

Canada's First Farmer

Only the year before there had been virgin forest almost everywhere below the cliff. Now, in 1618, rows of wheat, corn, peas and beans stretched away from the Habitation. What Champlain saw that June day as he returned to New France was the work of Louis Hébert, pharmacist, doctor—and Canada's first farmer.

With an axe, a pick and a spade—and the help of a servant—Hébert had created a 10-acre kitchen garden for the tiny colony. Later he was given two pieces of land—one where the Basilica of Notre-Dame and the Quebec Seminary now stand in Quebec's uppertown, the other along the Saint-Charles River.

All of Hébert's lands have been swallowed by urban development. But in Montmorency Park is a statue of the good farmer, who died in 1627—a year before the first plough arrived in Canada from France.

Hurons went to work with hatchets, knives and stone clubs, and built his cavalier.

On Oct. 11, under a rain of arrows and stones, 200 men carried it forward. Three Frenchmen mounted it and opened fire, compelling the Onondagas to flee their gallery and fight from cover. But then everything went wrong. Champlain found himself in charge of men "who do what they like," who shouted so much that "one could not make oneself heard." Indians advancing to set fires abandoned their shields; when they did get a fire going, the wind was against it. Champlain ordered the French to fire as best they could, but after three hours the Hurons gave up.

The French and Hurons withdrew with their wounded and waited a week for the Susquehannahs. During that time Champlain tried—without success—to get them to attack again. On Oct. 18, two days before their Susquehannah allies did arrive, they turned back, for home.

It was a black day. Champlain bore not only the taint of defeat but also two leg wounds which forced him to travel in a wooden frame on an Indian's back.

At Lake Ontario, Champlain asked for a canoe and paddlers to head for the St. Lawrence. No men could be spared, said the Indians. He found four volunteers, then was told no canoe could be spared. Champlain capitulated: "Their plan was to detain me with my [13] comrades in their country, both for their own safety and out of fear of their enemies, and that I might hear what took place at their council and meetings, and decide what should be done against their said enemies."

En route to Huronia the Indians engaged in a deer hunt and Champlain, hobbling in fascination after a strange bird, got lost in the woods for three days. By the time they reached Cahiagué it was Dec. 23, and a long, hard winter lay ahead. Champlain spent much of it in the lodge of his friend, the chief Darontal. He also spent many hours talking with Father Le Caron, and making copious notes about Indian life, and visiting neighboring villages.

It was May 20, 1616, before he left for the St. Lawrence. He reached the Habitation in early June. To the tiny settlement he seemed like a man back from the dead.

Champlain's explorations were over. But his dream found elaborate expression in 1618 when he proposed to Louis XIII and the Paris Chamber of Commerce that Quebec be built up to a large fortified community. The St. Lawrence, he argued, was the short route to "the Kingdom of China and the East Indies, whence great riches could be drawn." Quebec's customs duties on goods passing to and from the Orient would far surpass those collected in France.

This is Champlain's sketch of the assault on an Onondaga fort near modern Syracuse, N.Y., in the autumn of 1615. The defeat of Champlain and his Huron allies showed that a strong fort could withstand gunfire—even from a cavalier overlooking the palisade.

The plan won the support of both king and chamber. When Champlain sailed for Canada in 1620 he bore the credentials of the Duc de Montmorency as viceroy, of himself as Montmorency's lieutenant, and an order from the king to maintain the country ". . . as closely in conformity with the laws of my kingdom as you can." For the first time, he took to Canada his wife, Hélène, now 22.

Then: reality, the results of his two-year absence. Louis Hébert, the only man trying seriously to farm at Quebec, was being harassed as an enemy of the fur trade. Firearms were being sold to the Indians. Worst of all: the Habitation, Champlain found, was in "an abandoned and ruinous condition."

So he did what he always did: he put people to work to repair, to build, to clean, and when that was done he began to build a fort called Saint-Louis up on the rock. From then on Champlain devoted himself largely to running the colony which 12 years after its founding still needed annual aid from France to survive. He persuaded Indians to settle near Quebec and till the soil, smoothed out quarrels among the tribes, unsuccessfully sought peace with the Iroquois, coped with the jealousies of traders, built roads, supervised at downriver Cap Tourmente the construction of a habitation for men raising cattle and hay. And in 1624 he built a new Habitation at Quebec, this time of stone, on the site of the old one. But even the new Habitation could not keep his wife at Quebec. On Aug. 15, 1624, accompanied by Champlain, she left for France and did not return. He did, two years later—to his greater love, the colony.

A new danger loomed—an English attack. There had been rumors of France and England warring, and Champlain worried particularly in the spring of 1628 when no supply ships came from France. Instead, in July, six English ships under David Kirke ravaged Cap Tourmente, blockaded the St. Lawrence, captured three French supply ships and forced a fourth back to France. From Kirke came a demand for surrender.

A Child Bride Named Hélène—and Faith, Hope and Charity

The groom was in his early forties, a man of renown just returned from New France and victory over the Iroquois. The bride was a child of 12. And when Hélène Boullé, daughter of a wealthy Calvinist secretary to Louis XIII, was married to Samuel de Champlain Dec. 27, 1610, it was with the understanding that the union would not be consummated until Hélène reached 14.

But Champlain's affections for his little bride (for whom in 1611 he named St. Helen's Island, just off the Island of Montreal) were probably paternal, reflecting a repressed desire for fatherhood. Hélène remained in Paris for 10 years, arriving in Quebec (right) in 1620 as a spirited woman of 22, when her husband was in his fifties.

Champlain's humble Habitation must have dismayed her—as did the lack of compatible company in the small community. The Indians were drawn by her beauty and kindness and she became their teacher. She wore a mirror on a chain; gazing at themselves in its silvery depths, her naïve pupils believed she carried their images in her heart.

But she stayed only four years before returning to France forever. A convert to Catholicism, she became an Ursuline nun in 1645, 10 years after

Champlain's death, and later founded an Ursuline monastery at Meaux, France. She died Dec. 20, 1654.

There had been no children of the marriage, and four years after Hélène's departure, Champlain adopted three Indian girls of 11, 12 and 15, presented to him by Indians in gratitude for food he had given the starving band. He named the girls Faith, Hope and Charity, and loved them like daughters.

Faith soon returned to her people, but Hope and Charity remained with Champlain until he went to France in 1629 after surrendering Quebec to the English. He begged in vain to be allowed to take the girls. He made provisions for their care, but when he came back to Quebec in 1633, they had reverted to the Indian life. The father of Canada was not to know the gratification of even an adopted family.

QUEBEC

A. Le Fort
B. les Recollets
C. La plate forme
D. Les Jesuittes
E. La Cathedralle
F. Le Seminaire
G. l'Hostel Dieu
H. L'eveché
I. La Redoute
K. Le magasin a poudre

Quebec as seen from the St. Lawrence—in a 17th-century sketch and a 20th-century photograph.

Champlain had only a few barrels of biscuit, some dried peas and beans, and not enough gunpowder to defend the colony. He wrote a courtly reply. He had soldiers and plenty of food, he lied. "Were we to surrender . . . we should not be worthy of the name of men in the presence of our king."

Kirke and his two brothers, confident the colony could not survive a winter of agonizing hunger, sailed for England. Unknown to them, 11 French sailors had slipped by the blockade and had come upriver in a small boat with momentous—and ironic—news: Cardinal Richelieu, first minister to the king, had formed a new Company of One Hundred Associates, with Champlain as a partner. From now on, Richelieu pledged, 200 to 300 colonists would be sent each year. It was news Champlain had yearned to hear but it had come too late. The Kirkes returned in July 1629 to a starving colony. Champlain surrendered.

On the 24th he left his beloved settlement, a prisoner. But he vowed that if he returned he would build a church and name it Notre-Dame-de-la-Recouvrance. His home, his Habitation, his work of more than 20 years were gone—and Quebec had surrendered *after* the peace between England and France.

Champlain was hardly back in France before he was beseeching the king and Richelieu to demand the return of New France. He extolled again its potential, but he reported something else from brute experience: there should be an obligation "to cultivate the land, before all things, in order to have the basic foodstuffs on the spot." Finally, under the 1632 Treaty of Saint-Germain-en-Laye, the colony was restored to France.

It was 1633 before Champlain returned to Quebec. Now he was undisputed commander of New France. Having given to his wife all he owned in France—an indication that he never expected to return—he immersed himself in his work, in what were to be the happiest years of his life.

He set men to work at once to build the promised church on the site of today's Basilica of Notre-Dame. By August 1634 he had again rebuilt the ruins of Quebec, including the Habitation. He enlarged the fortifications, constructed an island fort upriver at Deschambault and started another habitation at Trois-Rivières. He felt "new courage" as more settlers arrived.

Although the Iroquois threat was worse than ever, he was optimistic. He treated his Indian allies as equals and they revered him. "Our sons shall wed your daughters," he told them, "and henceforth we shall be one people."

But Champlain's happiness was not to last long. In October 1635 he was stricken with paralysis and put to bed in the fort he had built. He died on Christmas Day, and was buried with all the pomp the little colony could command. Indians came in the hundreds. Jesuit Father Paul Le Jeune pronounced a funeral oration "for which I did not lack material." When the Hurons came down in trade the next summer they brought presents to help the French "wipe away their tears."

Champlain died without reward or even compliment from France. He died when the population of his colony numbered barely 200, far less than the Dutch and English populations to the south. But his colony had taken root. It would survive, and his legend would grow with it.

"No other European colony in America," historian Samuel Eliot Morison has written, "is so much the lengthened shadow of one man as Canada is of the valiant, wise and virtuous Samuel de Champlain."

Heritage Sites

QUEBEC Champlain's 1608 Habitation stood on what is now called Place Royale, the main buildings approximately where Notre-Dame-des-Victoires Church is today. Stone foundations from Champlain's second Habitation (1624) have been excavated in front of the church: beneath them are the remains of a 2,000-year-old Algonkian village.

Also in Quebec (12)

BASILICA OF NOTRE-DAME This church, in Canada's oldest parish, is on the site of Notre-Dame-de-Recouvrance Church, constructed by Champlain in 1633.

CHAMPLAIN MONUMENT A marble base topped by a bronze statue of Quebec's founder marks the site of Fort Saint-Louis, built by Champlain in 1620.

LOUIS HÉBERT MONUMENT A statue of Canada's first full-time farmer (1617) is in Montmorency Park. At the base are sculptures of Hébert's wife and their son-in-law Guillaume Couillard, Canada's first permanent settler (1613).

Other sites

Batiscan, Que. (10) Champlain met with Algonkins and Hurons here in the summer of 1609 before invading Iroquois territory.

Cobden, Ont. (6) A cairn three miles east commemorates the discovery of an astrolabe believed lost by Champlain in 1613.

Deschambault, Que. (11) The ruins of a small fort built by Champlain in 1634 are on an island in the St. Lawrence River.

Lachine, Que. (8) Champlain was the second white man, after Etienne Brûlé, to shoot the churning rapids at this Indian/French rendezvous.

Lafontaine, Ont. (1) A 20-foot stone cross marks the site of Carhagouha, the Huron village where Champlain met Father Le Caron in August 1615 and helped celebrate the first Mass in what is now Ontario.

Mattawa River Provincial Park, Ont. (5) A plaque marks the historic Paresseux Portage, one of several Mattawa River portages taken by Champlain while journeying by canoe to Huronia in 1615.

Orillia, Ont. (3) In Couchiching Beach Park a fine bronze statue of Champlain by Vernon March overlooks where the explorer passed on his way to fight the Onondagas in 1615. Figures at the base of the monument are of Indians and a fur trader.

Ottawa (7) The National Museum of Science and Technology has a replica of Champlain's astrolabe. At Nepean Point a statue of Champlain stands above the Ottawa River, which the explorer ascended in 1613 and 1615.

Main site (Ruins) □   Historic building(s) ▲   Museum ▲   Monument ▼   Ruins ●   Other ●   Unmarked site ■

Tadoussac, Que. (13) The fortified house that Pierre Chauvin built in 1600—Canada's first trading post—has been reconstructed at the mouth of the Saguenay River. Champlain first set foot in Canada at nearby Pointe-aux-Alouettes in 1603.

Ticonderoga, N.Y. (9) A plaque on the shore of Lake Champlain below present-day Fort Ticonderoga marks the site of Champlain's fateful 1609 battle with the Iroquois.

Toronto (4) An inscribed boulder at Discovery Point near the mouth of the Humber River honors Etienne Brûlé, the first white man to see Lake Ontario. A stone plaque commemorating Brûlé is at the Old Mill in Humber Park.

Warminster, Ont. (2) Near here is the site of Cahiagué, the principal village of the Huron nation, where Champlain wintered in 1615-16.

A replica of a fortified house built in 1600 by the fur trader and colonist Pierre Chauvin stands on what is believed the original site, at Tadoussac, Que. Chauvin traded successfully that summer, and left 16 men—the first colonists in the St. Lawrence Valley since Roberval abandoned Charlesbourg-Royal in 1543—to winter in the house. Only five survived. They were rescued the following year and the colony was abandoned.

In a Haven of Piety, a Hunger for Martyrdom

After 800 miles of paddling and portage, of blackflies and bad weather, of sleeping on hard ground and often going hungry, travellers from Quebec came at last to a little river that runs into Georgian Bay near the present-day town of Midland, Ont. They steered their birchbark canoe into a man-made channel that ran from the river to a gate in a palisade of logs. Inside was the mission of Sainte-Marie, an island of French civilization, of Roman Catholic order and piety, deep in the territory of the Huron Indians.

Sainte-Marie among the Hurons, built in 1639 on the east bank of what now is called the Wye River, was for 10 years the home of black-robed Jesuit missionaries. Other Frenchmen had passed that way before. Etienne Brûlé, probably in 1610-11, was the first European to travel the region between Georgian Bay and Lake Simcoe. Samuel de Champlain spent the winter of 1615-16 at the Huron settlement of Cahiagué (near today's Warminster, Ont.). And then came scores of fur traders and coureurs de bois. Frenchmen to whom survival and trade meant more than piety and who often lived the uninhibited life of the Hurons. The Jesuits were Frenchmen of a different kind.

The devout of France saw the discovery of the New World as a command from God to convert the heathen. Members of the Recollet order came to Huronia first, in 1615. But the Recollets were poor and few. The Jesuits had rich and powerful friends who supported their missions.

Sainte-Marie among the Hurons has been reconstructed in meticulous detail beside the Wye River near Midland, Ont. The original, headquarters of a Jesuit mission to convert the Hurons to Christianity, survived only 10 years; the priests destroyed Sainte-Marie in 1649 to keep it from falling into heathen hands. Above: an artificial waterway enabled canoes to be paddled from the Wye into the stockade.

Jesuit Chronicles of 17th-Century Canada

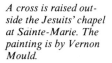

The Jesuit order's annual *Relations* (reports) from Canada fascinated French readers and stimulated immigration to New France in the mid-17th century.

Interest in Canada had been sparked by Champlain's several volumes and by Recollet missionary Gabriel Sagard's *Le Grand Voyage au Pays des Hurons* (1632). But the *Relations* on activities at Quebec and Trois-Rivières and in Huronia aroused widespread support for Jesuit efforts to convert the Indians and to encourage immigration. The *Relations* of 1635 said: "Why cannot the great forests of New France largely furnish the ships for the Old? Who doubts that there are mines of iron, copper and other metals? . . . all those who work in wood and iron will find employment here."

But the *Relations*' main purpose was to gain support for missionary work. At first the Jesuits concentrated on converting Indian children—through them they hoped to reach adults. Readers of the *Relations* donated toward the establishment of a mission near Quebec—it soon grew to include a hospital, chapel and school—and a boarding school for Indian children at Notre-Dame-des-Anges. This school failed: some pupils took ill and died; many deserted. The school was closed.

Again with support from readers impressed by the *Relations,* the Jesuits founded missions at Sillery, three miles from Quebec, in 1637 and at Trois-Rivières three years later. By 1640 hundreds of Indians had been baptized and these missions were flourishing.

The *Relations* of the early 1630s concerning Huronia were also optimistic. They inspired donations for the establishment of mission stations and, in 1639, the mission-fort at Sainte-Marie. But the *Relations* of the 1640s tell of Iroquois attacks, destruction of the satellite missions around Sainte-Marie and the martyrdom of eight of the Jesuit missionaries.

The *Relations* from New France (produced yearly from 1632 to 1673) became—and remain—one of the finest prime sources of Canadian history of the period.

A cross is raised outside the Jesuits' chapel at Sainte-Marie. The painting is by Vernon Mould.

They came to Quebec—the first of them in 1625—eager to embrace any hardship, even martyrdom, for the spread of Christianity. They believed that "the blood of the martyrs is the seed of the Church."

From 1625 to 1629 the Jesuit Jean de Brébeuf worked alongside the handful of Recollets, living and travelling with the Indians and learning their language. The Recollet Gabriel Sagard wrote: ". . . one must make up one's mind to endure and suffer more than could be imagined, from hunger, from sleeping always on the bare ground in the open country, from walking with great labor in water and bogs, and in some places over rocks, and through dark thick woods, from rain on one's back and all the evils that the season and weather can inflict, and from being bitten by a countless swarm of mosquitoes and midges, together with difficulties of language in explaining clearly and showing them one's needs, and having no Christian beside one for communication and consolation in the midst of one's toil."

In 1634 Brébeuf and two other Jesuits, fathers Antoine Daniel and Ambroise Davost, took over the mission to the Hurons from the Recollets. Year by year the number of blackrobe fathers increased. In 1635 came Pierre Pijart and François-Joseph Le Mercier; in subsequent years, Isaac Jogues, Paul Ragueneau, Pierre Chaumonot, Jérôme Lalemant and many more.

They found Indian life very different from the discipline and order of a Catholic mission. The Hurons lived in longhouses, many families in one building. Jérôme Lalemant wrote: "If you go to visit them in their cabins—and you must go there oftener than once a day, if you would perform your duty as you ought—you will find there a miniature picture of hell, seeing nothing ordinarily but fire and smoke, and on every side naked bodies, black and half-roasted, mingled pell-mell with the dogs, which are held as dear as the children of the house, and share the beds, plates and food of their masters. Everything is in a cloud of dust and, if you go within, you will not reach the end of the cabin before you are completely befouled with soot, filth and dirt."

The Hurons cleared land by burning off trees and underbrush. The women planted and tended corn, beans, pumpkin, tobacco, sunflowers and hemp among the stumps. When the soil and wood supply became exhausted, the village moved, built new longhouses and cleared another patch of forest.

A museum employee portrays a Jesuit priest reading from the missal in the Church of Saint-Joseph in the Huron compound at Sainte-Marie among the Hurons, near Midland, Ont. Another, dressed as a donné (a lay missionary), tends the fire in the Jesuit cookhouse.

Jean de Brébeuf worked among the Hurons for more than two decades, then died a martyr in 1649 as the Iroquois decimated the Huron nation. His death at the stake fulfilled a recurring dream of himself bound to a post with his hands tied behind. Brébeuf was proclaimed a patron saint of Canada in 1940.

This conception of an Iroquois massacre of Hurons is by Joseph Légaré (1795-1855), Canada's first historical painter.

The staple food was *sagamité,* a porridge of cornmeal often seasoned with fish, sometimes rotten fish. It was cooked in clay pots or birch-bark bowls by dropping heated stones into the mixture, and replacing them when they cooled, until the porridge came to a boil. The missionaries put up with *sagamité* but far harder to bear were the nakedness, promiscuity and religion of the Indians, whose lives were ruled by messages received in dreams (see p. 26) and whose chief sport seemed to be torture.

Undaunted, the Jesuits preached their faith. And increasingly, they tended the sick and dying. European diseases were now ravaging the Hurons: a survey of 32 villages in 1639 counted only 12,000 where there had been 30,000. It was easy for the Indians to blame the blackrobes. They were in the habit of baptizing the dying (for

The Feast of the Dead: Huron Ritual at a Fur-Lined Pit

Every 12 years the Hurons converged on Ossossané (eight miles northwest of modern Elmvale, Ont.) to reinter their dead. They believed every Indian had two souls. Both lived in the body until the Feast of the Dead, then one went to the land of the spirits, the other remained in the bones.

A week before the ceremony the bodies of relatives were taken from temporary graves. Intact bodies were cleaned, then adorned with feathers and beads and wrapped in beaver pelts; bones were enfolded in beaver. A feast followed.

At Ossossané the remains were taken from their beaver wraps and placed in a fur-lined pit 10 feet deep and 30 feet wide. Then all were covered with beaver robes and mats; earth, stone and logs were scattered over the mass grave. The skins in which the souls had been wrapped were cut into pieces and tossed to the mourners as mementos of the dead.

then there was no danger of recantation) and their rites became associated with death.

Sharing Huron village life, the Jesuits found it almost impossible to maintain their daily routine of devotions—which they never considered abandoning any more than they would their black habits. They longed to establish a Christian community as an example of civilized life. In 1639, at the Huron village of Ossossané (eight miles northwest of modern Elmvale, Ont.), they met and planned a permanent establishment to be called Sainte-Marie.

The outer palisade of the mission surrounded two enclosures, one for Frenchmen, the other for Indians. On the French side were residences and stables, a granary, workshops and a chapel for the Jesuits. On the Indian side were more residences, the hospital, a cemetery and the Church of Saint-Joseph. The hospital was well removed from the priests' quarters so that women could be treated there as well as men and children. Outside the palisade were cultivated fields.

Most of the time only a few Jesuits were at Sainte-Marie, resting from tours at outlying missions. Soldiers and fur traders also found lodging. The farmers and artisans of Sainte-Marie were *donnés*—from the French "give"—devout laymen who donated their skills and years of their lives to the service of God. By March 1649 there were three priests at Sainte-Marie—with four assistants, 23 *donnés*, seven hired men, four boys and eight soldiers—and 15 priests at outpost missions elsewhere in Huronia.

Homesick Frenchmen must have loved the reassurance of a life regulated by the ringing of bells and by the seasons and festivals of the church, especially after the rigors of a missionary tour.

The Indians loved Father Jean de Brébeuf. He was a large, powerful man interested in all aspects of Huron life. He learned the language easily, as did Gabriel Lalemant. For others the language seemed impossible. Father Paul Le Jeune sadly wrote: "I learned conjugations, declensions, a little syntax, vocabulary with unbelievable toil, for I must ask 20 questions to have cognizance of a single word, so much would my unskilled teacher vacillate."

At first, the Jesuits believed that the Indians' religion was evil and that their shamans (medicine men) were the agents of Satan. All the old beliefs had to be driven out to leave room for the true faith. But as the blackrobes understood more of the language and culture, they saw that the Hurons believed in an all-powerful God and in an afterlife, although they had no concept of

Openings in the roofs of Huron longhouses let smoke out and sunlight in. Dwellings like this replica at Sainte-Marie among the Hurons were windowless and covered with rough bark. Some were 200 feet long. Fires inside, every eight feet or so, were for cooking and warmth. Each fire was shared by two Huron families.

Among artifacts displayed at Sainte-Marie among the Hurons, near Midland, Ont., are (left to right) a reproduction of a Huron wampum belt, a medicine man's turtle-shell rattle, Indian corn, beads of shell and clay, and clay pots.

quickly become dependent on the metal tools and cooking pots and other trade goods that the Europeans brought.

However uneasy the relationship between the blackrobes and the majority of Indians, the enemies of the Hurons were the enemies of the Jesuits. Throughout the existence of Sainte-Marie, the Hurons were under attack or threat of attack by the five Iroquois nations: Seneca, Onondaga, Cayuga, Oneida and Mohawk. The Iroquois wanted to control the fur trade: the Huron nation stood in the way. Hurons were frequently ambushed for their furs, then enslaved or tortured to death. The first martyr, the *donné* René Goupil, was en route to Huronia in 1642 when ambushed near Sorel, Que. He was taken, along with Father Isaac Jogues, to Iroquois territory and killed. Jogues was tortured and mutilated but eventually was rescued by the Dutch, only to die a martyr four years later.

In 1645, to gain relief from Iroquois attacks, the Hurons signed a tentative peace treaty with the Iroquois. But within a year the Iroquois were on the warpath again, hitting deeper and deeper into Huronia and laying waste entire villages.

Sainte-Marie was relatively secure, protected by its palisade and with food enough for several years. The outlying missions were vulnerable.

The onslaught began early one morning in July 1648. Father Antoine Daniel, in charge of the mission of Saint-Joseph II at Teanaostaiaë (about 16 miles west of Orillia, Ont.), had just finished Mass when Iroquois raiders struck. At the first war cry there was panic. Some Hurons ran for weapons, some tried to flee. With death imminent for many, Father Daniel baptized those he could by sprinkling holy water from a bowl. He was riddled with arrows, then shot. His body and the bodies of his followers were consumed in the flames of his church.

An Iroquois army of 1,200 spent the winter of 1648 near the Huron frontier. During the night of March 15, 1649, the Iroquois stole undetected through the forest to Saint-Ignace II (near Waubaushene, Ont.) and attacked before dawn. The village was taken with only 10 Iroquois casualties but many Hurons were captured or killed. Now the Iroquois moved swiftly to launch an assault early that same morning on Saint-Louis (near Victoria Harbour, Ont.). It too was overcome, then set ablaze. Among the prisoners were Brébeuf and Gabriel Lalemant; they were taken to Saint-Ignace II.

That afternoon the Iroquois reconnoitered Sainte-Marie and burned more Huron villages. Then they retired to Saint-Ignace II to lick their wounds and to deal with prisoners.

Brébeuf and Lalemant died at the stake after appalling tortures. Renegade Hurons among

hell. The priests tried to build on whatever beliefs were not in conflict with Christianity and to eliminate the rest. It was not easy.

"Do they hunt in heaven, or make war, or go to feasts?" a Jesuit was asked. Told that there was nothing earthly in the Christian heaven, the Huron replied: "Then I will not go. It is not good to be lazy."

Heaven must have seemed a lonely place to the Hurons. They believed that after death, without exception, they would be reunited with departed members of their families. But the Jesuits taught that heaven was an exclusive place: only the baptized could enter. One priest, trying to save the soul of a dying woman whose children had not been converted, asked which would she choose, heaven or hell? "I choose hell," she replied quickly, "if, as you say, my children are there."

The fur traders were living proof that not all Frenchmen were scrupulous Christians. If chastity was a good thing, the Hurons asked, why did not all Christians practise it?

European crafts and farming methods struck the Hurons as funny. They could not understand why anyone would house animals and give them corn that *people* could eat. But they had

Isaac Jogues: On an Ear of Corn, the Raindrops of Salvation

Father Isaac Jogues suffered such torture at the hands of the Mohawks, for so long, that he came to long for death. But in every magnificent moment of his ebbing life he strove to serve the creatures of the God he loved.

One day in August 1642, at Teonontogen (near present-day Schenectady, N.Y.) after being beaten and mutilated and burned, Jogues was tossed an ear of corn to eat. On it were a few raindrops—with which he baptized two Huron fellow prisoners, preparing them for death. The frail, outwardly timid Jesuit, then 35, would not himself meet death until 1646. But his martyrdom had begun.

Jogues had been with a Huron trading party that Mohawk raiders ambushed near Sorel. They were taken to Teonontogen, where Mohawks gnawed the prisoners' fingers and an Indian woman was forced to cut off Jogues' left thumb. René Goupil, a *donné* (lay missionary), suffered similar mutilation.

Most of the Hurons were slain but the Frenchmen remained prisoners. While the Mohawks argued over putting them to death, Jogues baptized dying infants and Goupil taught children the sign of the cross. For this, one day as he walked with Jogues, Goupil was stalked by two angry braves. One pulled a hatchet from a blanket and killed Goupil—the first of the eight Jesuit martyrs. Jogues knelt for his deathblow. None came. From then on he served the Mohawks as a slave.

The forest was his chapel. Through the winter of 1642-43 he knelt ragged and frozen before a cross he had carved. He absolved and baptized Christian and pagan victims of the endless torturing.

After 13 months he escaped and returned to France. With his mutilated hands, he was not allowed to celebrate Mass. But in Paris the queen regent kissed the stumps of his fingers and later the Pope restored Jogues' priestly privileges. He returned to Canada in 1644.

His superiors denied his requests for a Mohawk mission until 1646. But the Mohawks turned against Jogues and *donné* Jean de La Lande, blaming them for a caterpillar infestation of their corn. At Ossernenon (present-day Auriesville, N.Y.) they seized Jogues and La Lande, stripped and beat them. Flesh was cut from Jogues' back and arms. That night, Oct. 18, an Indian buried a hatchet in Jogues' brain, then hacked off his head. La Lande was slain the next morning.

Now there were three Jesuit martyrs. There would be five more—in Huronia—before the decade ended.

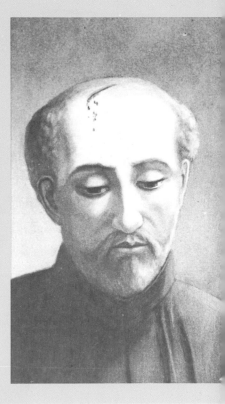

The martyrdom of Jesuits Jean de Brébeuf and Gabriel Lalemant, as imagined by the Spanish painter Francisco Goya.

Scalping: White Men Taught the Indians How

Scalping started not with the Indians but apparently with a governor of New Netherlands who wanted Indians killed.

He paid for scalps, which were easy to handle and (he thought) good proof of death. The Indians took up the practice. By the 18th century, the French paid for British scalps, the British paid for French scalps, and each paid for scalps of the other's Indian allies.

This custom of removing all or part of an enemy's scalp went back at least 2,500 years to the Scythians of southern Russia. But many historians say scalp-taking was virtually unknown to North American Indians before the arrival of Europeans. To most tribes, if not all, scalping was a white man's custom.

The Indians learned it well. In some tribes taking the scalps of enemies became a requirement for warrior status, in others a ritual to placate the dead. Scalps were decorated and carried by braves or worn by women in dances to celebrate their men's battle victories. Scalps were usually cut from the dead. But prisoners could be scalped and yet live; sometimes victims were allowed to return home as a warning or a challenge to their fellows.

This reliquary in a museum in Hôtel-Dieu Hospital at Quebec contains some bones of three Jesuits martyred in 1649: Jean de Brébeuf, Charles Garnier and Gabriel Lalemant.

their tormentors "baptized" Brébeuf with boiling water, saying: "You told us that the more one suffers on earth, the happier one is in heaven. We wish to make you happy; we torment you because we love you and you ought to thank us for it." He died after four hours of agony. Lalemant was tortured all through the night until, wearying of the sport, an Iroquois split his skull.

On March 19, the Iroquois, inexplicably fearful of a Huron attack, withdrew as swiftly as they had come. Prisoners who could not walk were tied to stakes in the longhouses, which then were set on fire.

At Sainte-Marie the Jesuits had seen smoke rising from Saint-Louis and they knew what it meant. The Iroquois had the advantages of surprise, numbers and weapons. The Hurons panicked. Through the summer they burned and abandoned their villages. Some sought refuge with other tribes only to be slaughtered or enslaved by marauding Iroquois. It was during one of these raids that two more Jesuit fathers—Charles Garnier and Noël Chabanel—were killed.

The missionaries and staff of Sainte-Marie and those Hurons who had remained fled to St. Joseph's Island (now Christian Island) in Georgian Bay. There they established the mission Sainte-Marie II. But of the original Sainte-Marie

one Jesuit wrote: "That spot must be forsaken which I call our second fatherland, our home of innocent delights, since it had been the cradle of this Christian church; since it was the temple of God, and the home of the servants of Jesus Christ. Moreover, for fear that our enemies, only too wicked, should profane the sacred place, and derive from it an advantage, we ourselves set fire to it, and beheld burn before our eyes, in less than an hour, our work of nine or 10 years."

Between 6,000 and 8,000 fugitives crowded onto barren St. Joseph's Island for the winter. They had few supplies and by spring there were only a few hundred Hurons alive. They asked the Jesuits to take them to Quebec.

Early that summer, 40 well-armed Frenchmen set out from Montreal hoping to save Huronia. They met on the way the remnants of the once proud Huron nation seeking refuge far from their ravaged homeland.

Of North America's eight martyr saints, five died in Huronia: Brébeuf, Garnier, Lalemant, Daniel and Chabanel. The other three—Jogues and the *donnés* Goupil and Jean de La Lande—were killed in what now is New York State. The relics of Brébeuf and Lalemant are in Quebec City. The Martyrs' Shrine at Midland overlooks the Wye River and a reconstruction of the Jesuits' beloved Sainte-Marie among the Hurons.

Heritage Sites

MIDLAND, Ont. Sainte-Marie among the Hurons, the outpost from which Jesuits directed their Huronia mission in 1639-49, has been reconstructed beside the Wye River. Visitors enter through a lobby lined with C. W. Jefferys illustrations of events in Huronia history, then see a film on life in 17th-century New France. Inside the palisade are residences, a hospital, a forge, a cookhouse, a longhouse and a chapel containing Jean de Brébeuf's grave.

Also in Midland (3)

HURON INDIAN VILLAGE This reconstruction of a palisaded 17th-century settlement is in Little Lake Park. A longhouse is lined with bunks; roots, dried corn and herbs hang from the rafters; in the centre are fireplaces. Also within the palisade are a medicine man's lodge, a sweat bath and food-storage pits.

HURONIA MUSEUM Exhibits include a Nativity diorama of Huron chiefs presenting furs to the Christ Child.

MARTYRS' SHRINE Near the twin-spired church, constructed by Jesuits in 1926, is a small grotto dedicated to Our Lady of Huronia, patroness of Sainte-Marie and the martyred Jesuits.

Other sites

Christian Island, Ont. (1) A plaque marks the stone ruins of Sainte-Marie II, the mission in which Jesuit and Huron survivors of Iroquois attacks took refuge in the winter of 1649-50.

Elmvale, Ont. (5) The Ossossanë bone pit where Hurons reinterred bodies during the Feast of the Dead, held every 12 years, was eight miles northwest. There is a marker at the site. Nearby was the Huron village of Ossossanë where Jesuits met in 1639 to plan Sainte-Marie.

Lafontaine, Ont. (2) A 20-foot stone cross identifies the site of Carhagouha, a village where Recollets, and later Jesuits, lived and ministered to the Hurons.

Minesing, Ont. (not shown) Huron artifacts in the Simcoe County Museum and Archives include 17th-century pottery, clay pipes, arrowheads and knives.

Quebec (not shown)

CARTIER-BRÉBEUF NATIONAL HISTORIC PARK A 10-foot granite monument commemorates Jean de Brébeuf, believed to have built a house near here in 1626.

HÔTEL-DIEU HOSPITAL MUSEUM A reliquary contains half of Jean de Brébeuf's skull and bone fragments of Charles Garnier and Gabriel Lalemant. The other half of Brébeuf's skull and more bones of the others are in the Jesuit Chapel.

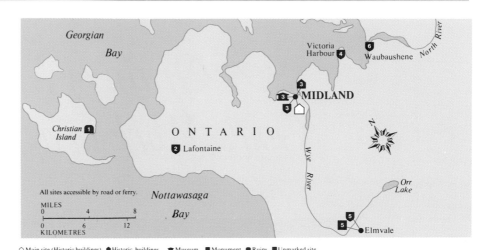

All sites accessible by road or ferry.

MILES
0   4   8
0   6   12
KILOMETRES

⌂ Main site (Historic buildings)   🏠 Historic buildings   🏛 Museum   ▮ Monument   ▪ Ruins   ▪ Unmarked site

OLD JESUIT HOUSE In front of a two-storey stone house (c. 1700) are the foundations of the 1637 Jesuit House where six of the Canadian martyr saints once lived. The house is a museum of the history of the Jesuits in North America. Exhibits include a weather vane from the Jesuit College (1635) and axes forged for the order in the 17th century.

Victoria Harbour, Ont. (4) Saint-Louis, a Huron village and Jesuit mission where Iroquois captured Jean de Brébeuf and Gabriel Lalemant in 1649, was two miles south. A cairn is at the site.

Waubaushene, Ont. (6) A marker four miles south identifies the site of Saint-Ignace II, where Jean de Brébeuf and Gabriel Lalemant were tortured and killed.

'A ragged robe of rabbit skin . . .'

About 1640, Father Jean de Brébeuf wrote a carol in the Huron language, telling of the Nativity in terms the Indians understood. Brébeuf's manuscript of *Jesous Ahatonhia* (Jesus Is Born) was lost but the carol became part of Huron tradition. It was sung in Quebec by Hurons who fled there after the Iroquois attacks in Huronia in 1649, and 100 years later it was written down, then translated into French and English. The second verse of J. E. Middleton's English version (1926) is reproduced here.

Within a lodge of broken bark
The tender Babe was found,
A ragged robe of rabbit skin
enwrapp'd His beauty round;
But as the hunter braves drew nigh,
The angel song rang loud and high—
Jesus your King is born, Jesus is born,
In excelsis gloria.

A Grain of Mustard Seed: God's Work in a Hostile Land

Plaques at the base of this 40-foot obelisk in Place Royale carry the names of some of Montreal's first colonists: Gorry, Hébert, Godé, Panie, Caillot, Laimery, Damien . . . and of de La Dauversière and members of La Société de Notre-Dame de Montréal who financed the mission of Ville-Marie. In the background is a former customs house (1838), now an office building.

PREMIÈRE MESSE À VIL

Champlain had named it Place Royale in 1611. Now, after 31 years, other Frenchmen landed at this likely spot for a settlement, on the south shore of a great island in the St. Lawrence River, 160 miles upstream from Quebec. These were settlers—40 farmers and craftsmen, six women, a few children, some 60 souls in all, led by Paul de Chomedey, Sieur de Maisonneuve, and protected by a few soldiers. Confident they were doing God's work, they had determined to live in this hostile land. At the edge of the forest, in the shadow of the island's greening mountain (which Jacques Cartier in 1535 had called Mont-Réal), they fell on their knees.

Later that day—Saturday, May 17, 1642—Mass was said at a simple altar adorned with cherry blossoms. Then the first trees were felled for a palisade. Tents were pitched. Arms, implements and provisions were unloaded. Throughout that first historic day the Host consecrated at the Mass was left exposed—a mighty reminder that Christ did indeed share the wilderness with them. And the altar lamps that night were flickering vials of fireflies.

At a High Mass next day, the Jesuit Barthélemy Vimont spoke words that in time would seem to ring with prophecy: "What you see is only a grain of mustard seed, but this small seed will produce a tall tree that will bring forth wonders."

The first desperate quarter-century would bring constant Iroquois harassment and one massacre after another. But one day de Maison-

Two famous representations of de Maisonneuve are Philippe Hébert's 10-foot statue in Montreal's Place d'Armes and in T. A. Lafuengruen's stained-glass window, First Mass at Ville-Marie *(de Maisonneuve, in blue, kneels behind the priest). The 68-inch-wide window is above the entrance to the chapel at Hôtel-Dieu Hospital in Montreal. "Your work is the work of God," Father Barthélemy Vimont told the founders of Ville-Marie. "Your children shall fill the land." Artistic licence is evident in the figures at the altar; the colonists waited two months before encountering the Indians they had come to Christianize.*

Jeanne Mance, Ville-Marie's Angelic Nurse

Jeanne Mance was by calling a nurse, by nature a businesswoman, by temperament an adventurer—and by reputation an angel.

She had no doubt that God wanted her in New France and found funds with which to build a hospital in Ville-Marie in 1642, rebuild it in 1645. Now here she was nine years later, mistress of a fortified hospital, coaxing a fire to thaw a cup of wine for a badly wounded Indian enemy.

The Mohawk chief known as La Barrique (the big barrel), shot during a skirmish and abandoned for dead by his band, improved under intensive care. Jeanne Mance won the Indian's confidence. He wondered at the radiance of her face as she described, in Mohawk, the Frenchmen's God. He recognized the courage and strength beneath her china-doll beauty.

In the little hospital (some distance from the fort, at today's Saint-Paul and Saint-Sulpice streets) Jeanne Mance and the surgeons tended the victims of Iroquois attacks—Indian and French alike.

The "murder" of La Barrique—as his followers thought—provoked a barrage of attacks by his brother. Day after day the crippled chief saw wounded brought in. On a day when the alarm had sounded four times, he asked to be carried to the fighting and cried: "This is your brother, and you would kill my best friends!"

The fighting ceased. The angel Jeanne Mance had won Ville-Marie a precious respite from Iroquois attack.

Pierre Le Ber's portrait of Marguerite Bourgeoys, painted hours after her death in 1700, is the only known true likeness of Montreal's first schoolmistress. It is in the Montreal motherhouse of La Congrégation de Notre-Dame, which she founded.

neuve's settlement on Champlain's Place Royale below Cartier's mountain would be Montreal.

Religious zeal flowered into holy passion in 17th-century France. Ardent souls, their fervor fanned by the Jesuit *Relations* (see p. 44), yearned for evangelization of New France's Indians. A penniless tax collector, Jérôme Le Royer de La Dauversière, felt divinely inspired to plant a mission at Cartier's Mont-Réal.

A country abbé, Jean-Jacques Olier, gave de La Dauversière 100 silver *pistoles* ($5,000) and in 1640 they founded La Société de Notre-Dame de Montréal. In the next 25 years its wealthy members would contribute 600,000 livres ($3 million). Most of the initial 75,000 livres bought food and implements for the society's newly acquired seigneury on the island of Montreal. De Maisonneuve, a 30-year-old nobleman-soldier, was chosen to lead the expedition.

De La Dauversière scoured Anjou, Aunis and Normandy for unmarried men who for wages, food and lodging would defend the mission and clear the land—after three years they could return to France. But one volunteer was the beautiful, 34-year-old Jeanne Mance. She arrived at La Rochelle on horseback as two small ships were loading. In her purse was a benefactress' 1,200 livres for a hospital.

The expedition put to sea in May 1641, de Maisonneuve and 25 men in one vessel, Jeanne Mance and 12 men in the other. A third ship had sailed from Dieppe with 10 men, two accompanied by their families, and a young girl. All three vessels reached Quebec in late summer.

Governor General Huault de Montmagny resented the newcomers' autonomy. He berated an undertaking that would put French settlers at the mercy of the Iroquois and offered instead the fertile and defensible Ile d'Orléans near Quebec. De Maisonneuve replied he would go to Montreal "even if all the trees on that island were to change into so many Iroquois."

That winter in Quebec the Montreal-bound group was joined by Marie-Madeleine de La Peltrie, wealthy benefactress of Quebec's Ursuline Convent. They sailed for Montreal May 8, 1642, in a pinnace, two barques and a barge. Nine days later they were ashore at Place Royale.

Outside the 320-foot-square palisade they built was a moat; inside, corn and peas were planted and dwellings and a chapel were erected. Artillery pieces were put in place.

On July 28 the settlement welcomed its first Indian visitors, friendly Algonkins. Twelve more colonists arrived in August, bringing a tabernacle for the Host, various church vessels, food, arms, beds, dishes, medicine, two oxen, three cows, 20 sheep—and word that the society had met in Notre-Dame de Paris to ask the Virgin to protect the settlement. On Aug. 15, the Feast of the Assumption, they celebrated with pomp and cannon fire and formally named the little outpost Ville-Marie.

As the echo of the last salvo died, an old Indian turned to de Maisonneuve and said through an interpreter: "Behold the places where once there were villages flourishing, whence our ancestors were driven by our enemies." Said another Indian, crumbling soil in his fingers: "The corn grew well then. See the richness, how good it is."

Soon snow drifted over the good earth. The

The 100-foot illuminated cross erected in 1924 on Montreal's Mount Royal was financed by $10,000 in commemorative stamp sales and a $26,000 donation from the Société Saint-Jean-Baptiste de Montréal. An herb jar (above) brought from France by Jeanne Mance is in a museum at the Hôtel-Dieu Hospital in Montreal.

settlers huddled in one large and four small houses within the fort, living a communal life, finding "in Jesus Christ a single heart and a single soul." There was no sickness—something "never before remarked in new settlements," the Jesuit *Relations* recorded, attributing Ville-Marie's health to divine protection.

But on Christmas Eve the ice-jammed St. Lawrence flooded low-lying parts of the settlement. As the waters rose, de Maisonneuve raised a cross and on it nailed a promise that he read aloud: if they were spared, he would plant a cross on Mount Royal. At the Nativity hour the waters subsided.

De Maisonneuve ordered a trail cut, a cross built, and on Jan. 6, 1643, the Feast of the Epiphany, he carried it on his shoulders to the mountaintop. More than three centuries later there would still be a cross on Mount Royal.

Montreal Island had been Iroquois in Cartier's time, with Hochelaga a town of 3,000. In the 1500s the Iroquois abandoned the island and settled to the south, in present-day New York State. The Hurons lived to the west, south of Georgian Bay; east and north of Montreal were Algonkins. Hurons traded at Montreal, Algonkins at Trois-Rivières and Quebec.

The Iroquois wanted mastery of the St. Lawrence, their link to western tribes whose furs they exchanged at Fort Orange (Albany, N.Y.) for Dutch muskets and implements. They determined to rout the French and destroy the Algonkins and Hurons.

On June 9, 1643, 30 Iroquois jumped six foresters at Ville-Marie, scalping three. Two others

The Lone Wolf Killer, Fearsome Pieskaret

He hid in a huge pile of wood near a Mohawk village. He was Pieskaret, an Algonkin chief, a living legend in New France in the mid-1600s. He had sneaked hundreds of miles south into Iroquois country. That night he entered a longhouse and slaughtered all its occupants as they slept.

Pieskaret slew the occupants of another lodge the second night, then returned again to the woodpile. The third night he found sentries ringing the village, killed one, then ran, Mohawks at his heels. After many hours they gave up, exhausted. As they slept, Pieskaret killed them too.

Many such forays made the Iroquois respect and fear Pieskaret. In 1647, hunting alone near Trois-Rivières, Pieskaret met six Iroquois carrying a peace flag. Pieskaret, off guard, conversed with his old enemies and apparently told them of two Algonkin villages on the St. Lawrence River (near present-day Nicolet). Some distance away one Iroquois rushed Pieskaret from behind and killed him.

The six were scouts for a party of nearly 1,000 Iroquois. At dawn next day they attacked the Algonkin villages. Most of Pieskaret's people were slain or taken prisoner because—only once—he had trusted the Iroquois.

Madame de La Peltrie, whose dog Pilote stood guard at Ville-Marie, is believed to have exchanged this clock for a steer to feed the Quebec Ursulines and their pupils. The clock is in the Montreal Museum of Fine Arts.

were burned next day and the third escaped. A 22-year siege had begun.

All that summer, Iroquois warriors harassed workmen clearing the fields. De Maisonneuve sent men out in groups, under armed guard, the chapel bell signalling their departure and return. Men started each day with Holy Communion that might be their last. Military engineer Louis d'Ailleboust arrived in September with 40 farmer-soldiers, and reinforced the fort. Dogs were trained to sniff out the enemy.

On into the second winter Iroquois marauders hindered and taunted the French. Many colonists wanted to counterattack, but de Maisonneuve said no: they were "only a handful of people with little experience of the woods." Some scoffed that de Maisonneuve was more pious than courageous.

On March 30, 1644, the baying of Pilote, Madame de La Peltrie's dog, again betrayed the presence of Iroquois. To demonstrate his authority, de Maisonneuve led 30 men through deep snow to a hill which later became known as Place d'Armes. There they fired volley after volley at some 200 Indians who were on snowshoes and slipped elusively from cover to cover. Two colonists were killed, another was wounded, two were captured. Powder ran low, de Maisonneuve ordered a retreat—and the settlers turned and ran. De Maisonneuve, a pistol in each hand, faced the enemy alone. An Iroquois chief attacked. De Maisonneuve fired and missed. As the Indian

tore at de Maisonneuve's throat, the Frenchman emptied his second pistol into the chief's head. The Indians recovered the body and fled. De Maisonneuve's courage was questioned no more.

The Jesuit *Relations* and other records tell how the Iroquois, thirsting for revenge, "lay for entire days, each one behind a stump" or in tall grass so that "a man 10 feet from his door was not in safety." Colonists carried muskets everywhere and cut gun slots in the walls of their homes against enemies "behind a tree, under a pile of leaves or in a ditch, waiting for hours on end." The register of the dead was "marked in red letters" by warriors who "came like foxes, fought like lions and stole away like birds." Once-friendly Hurons, to curry Iroquois favor, sometimes enticed unsuspecting Frenchmen out from the ramparts—to be murdered and scalped by hidden Iroquois. With prayer and fasting Ville-Marie besought God to end the horror.

A truce was declared in 1645 when Governor General Montmagny at Quebec negotiated a prisoner exchange. But the Iroquois, inflamed by Huron tales of priestly witchcraft, renewed attacks in 1646. Now "at night a man dare not open his door and in daytime he dare not go four feet from his home without musket, sword or pistol." Most settlers lived outside the fort; de Maisonneuve ordered them inside the stockade at night. Jeanne Mance's hospital, founded in 1642 and relocated in October 1645, was outside. Now it was fortified with cannon. An adjoining chapel served as an ammunition store with gun slots and an armed guard.

But still settlers were felled by Iroquois bullets and tomahawks. Several colonists left and by midsummer 1651 the settlement consisted of about 150 persons; de Maisonneuve knew he must recruit more trained fighting men. Jeanne Mance urged him to use a 22,000-livre donation from her hospital benefactress. He left for France Nov. 5, 1651, knowing that Ville-Marie would be doomed if he failed.

He would not return for two years. Somehow Ville-Marie would survive but there would be two more years of bloodshed and terror.

Quebec believed Ville-Marie's days were numbered, that the settlement would be wiped out just as the Iroquois had decimated the Huron nation and forced the destruction of Sainte-Marie among the Hurons (see p. 42). By the spring of 1653, Quebec was virtually certain that the fragile colony on Montreal Island had been obliterated. A ship was sent, its commander under orders not to land unless Ville-Marie was seen to be in French hands. It anchored offshore in dense fog, the jittery crew barely able to make out the fort, the Frenchmen ashore peering at an eerie shadow that some took for a ghost ship. None of those who insisted it *was* a ship would risk a tomahawk to investigate. The vessel retreated and Quebec was convinced Ville-Marie was dead. For the colonists it was "a little something to laugh about."

But there were two encouraging events. One of the five Iroquois nations, the Onondagas, finding war too costly, made peace with Ville-Marie in June 1653. And even Quebec held a church service to rejoice when de Maisonneuve and 105 five-year recruits landed Sept. 22. Raising and outfitting this contingent had taken the hospital's 22,000 livres, *another* 20,000 from Jeanne Mance's benefactress, and a further 35,000 from La Société de Notre-Dame de Montréal. (There would be trouble later over the original 22,000 livres.)

The Mohawks, fiercest and most warlike of the Iroquois, continued their attacks, as did the Oneidas and even some Onondagas. In March 1658 de Maisonneuve ordered that settlers were to go into the fields only if absolutely necessary, and then to work only where retreat would be easy. He built a fortified house at each end of the settlement and had a well dug in the courtyard of the fort; it was now dangerous to draw water from the river. In 1659 another well was dug at the hospital, and a windmill for grinding wheat was built and fortified.

What Ville-Marie longed for seemed at hand in May 1663 when four Iroquois invited peace, offering themselves as hostages. But in the night they split one man's head, brained two women, abducted three little girls, and escaped.

Martine Messier Primot, attacked in a raid on Ville-Marie, grabbed at her assailant and held on—until he ran howling for the woods. When a Frenchman hugged her for joy at her escape, he was slapped. "I thought he wanted to kiss me!" said the lady. The sculpture is by Philippe Hébert.

Radisson Plans a Party—and a Mass Escape

The 50-odd Frenchmen at the mission of Sainte-Marie-de-Ganentaa were surrounded by hostile Iroquois in the winter of 1657-58. They would be spared until spring, they expected, then slaughtered when French settlements on the St. Lawrence would be attacked.

They could anticipate no help; the mission was deep in territory of the Onondaga tribe of the Iroquois (near modern Syracuse, N.Y.), some 200 miles from the nearest French settlement at Montreal and 120 from the Dutch at Fort Orange (present-day Albany).

Two years before, during an uneasy peace, French soldiers and Jesuit priests had established the mission at the request of the Onondagas. The tribe hoped that a French fort would provide a refuge from their enemies. But now the Mohawks, another Iroquois tribe,

were out to disrupt the peace. They had started by turning the Onondagas against their French visitors.

All winter the French secretly planned an escape. At night, in a loft above the mission building, they built two boats and eight canoes. Then, on March 19, at the suggestion of Pierre-Esprit Radisson (see p. 63), a young Frenchman who had lived among the Mohawks, they invited all the male population of the Onondaga village to a great feast around a fire outside the mission gate. The hosts would eat nothing; the French hoped the Indians would gorge themselves into stupor.

They were fed dish after dish of pork, fish, game, chicken, turtle, corn. "They stuffed themselves till they could eat no more," says a contemporary account. ". . . flutes, trumpets and drums were

played so that the Savages could dance and to charm away the tedium of so lengthy a feast. The French brought down the boats and loaded them . . . so secretly that none of the Savages perceived it. Then Radisson said: 'I am going to have a soft instrument played to make you sleep. Do not get up till very late tomorrow. Sleep till someone comes to wake you for prayers.' At these words someone played a guitar, and the barbarians fell at once into profoundest slumber."

They awakened to find the French gone, the manner of their going hidden by a fresh snowfall.

Three Frenchmen were drowned as the party fled north to Lake Ontario but the rest reached Montreal on April 3, two weeks after the gluttony at Sainte-Marie-de-Ganentaa.

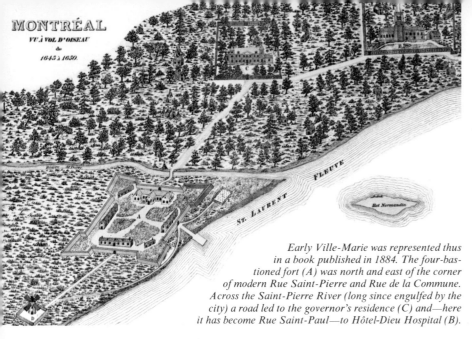

Early Ville-Marie was represented thus in a book published in 1884. The four-bastioned fort (A) was north and east of the corner of modern Rue Saint-Pierre and Rue de la Commune. Across the Saint-Pierre River (long since engulfed by the city) a road led to the governor's residence (C) and—here it has become Rue Saint-Paul—to Hôtel-Dieu Hospital (B).

Traces of gold remain on the Virgin's robe in this ivory statue that may have been de Maisonneuve's. According to tradition, he bequeathed it to the Sulpician Seminary when he left Ville-Marie in 1665. The statue, in a Gothic case, is in Notre-Dame Church Museum in Old Montreal.

Amid all the terror Ville-Marie clung to its missionary raison d'être, instructing and baptizing Indians who sheltered there. Priests speaking Huron and Algonkin languages taught men one day, women and children the next.

To encourage settlement, land was allotted near the fort from 1648. But the major inducement was resident bounties of 100 to 1,000 livres—magnificent sums where master tradesmen earned two livres daily.

Women were few and girls as young as 12 married. Some brides were imported from France. By 1664 there were 60 dwellings between the St. Lawrence and present-day St. Antoine Street, from modern McGill Street on the west to the vicinity of Bonsecours Market and St. Denis Street.

As the outpost became a true settlement, it gradually acquired a new name—Montreal.

As elsewhere in New France, furs were the currency. Whenever the Iroquois intercepted Algonkin and Huron flotillas bound for the midsummer fur market, Ville-Marie went without the food and implements that furs could buy.

By 1665 its population of 500 equalled Quebec's. Toolmakers, millers, coopers, carpenters and farmers cleared one another's land and built one another's houses. They had free medical care—and from 1658 they had a school.

There was but one school-age child—other than prospective brides—when teacher Marguerite Bourgeoys arrived in 1653. So, instead of teaching, she washed and ironed for the sick poor and shared her food with them. The Iroquois had pulled down the cross on the mountain; Marguerite Bourgeoys had it rebuilt. She had a chapel to the Virgin erected outside the fort (Notre-Dame-de-Bon-Secours chapel is on the site). Finally her school was opened in a renovated 18-by-36-foot stable.

Montreal-born Marie Barbier joined Marguerite Bourgeoys and her French postulants in the Congrégation de Notre-Dame, the first reli-

Dollard: Was He Hero or Mere Glory Hunter?

Seventeen Frenchmen, four Algonkins and 40 Hurons left Ville-Marie on April 20, 1660, to look for Iroquois up the Ottawa River. Their leader was 25-year-old Adam Dollard des Ormeaux. On May 1 they camped by an old Algonkin fort at the foot of the Long Sault Rapids near present-day Carillon, Que. The next day 200 Onondagas came down the river en route to an army of fellow Iroquois massing for assaults on Ville-Marie, Trois-Rivières and Quebec.

Shots were fired and the French and their allies took refuge in the little fort *(below)*. Two Onondaga assaults were repulsed but for six days the defenders were pinned down by Onondaga musket fire. Water ran out, food and ammunition dwindled. On the seventh day 500 Mohawks and Oneidas arrived and new assaults began. Twenty-six Hurons deserted. Dollard's desperate men hurled two pistols, their barrels packed with powder, as grenades. But the defenders' final weapon, a powder keg with a lit fuse, fell back and exploded among them. The Iroquois swarmed in to find Dollard and all but five of his men dead. One survivor escaped but was never seen again. The other four were tortured to death.

Dollard was proclaimed a hero and a martyr who went to certain death to deflect Iroquois forces trying to wipe out Ville-Marie. But some historians have claimed he was an ambitious hotblood, that he stumbled on an Iroquois war party when he was merely seeking glory and fortune by ambushing small Indian bands taking furs to the Dutch.

Whatever their motives, the 17 Frenchmen fought well and died bravely. The Iroquois did not attack Ville-Marie.

A monument to Dollard and his men stands at Carillon.

gious community founded in Canada. They sheltered *les filles du roi* (prospective brides from France—see p. 83) and prepared them "to make a family." On the convent door was a sign: Girls To Marry. (The congregation moved in 1668 to Saint-Gabriel Farm in what now is Montreal's Pointe Saint-Charles district.)

Murder, arson and theft were common downriver in Quebec. Not so in Ville-Marie. The settlement's pervading holiness reformed many a recruit, "changed as clothes are after you put them in the wash." Not to say, as a Sister Morin wrote, that there were "no public sins."

From 1664 Ville-Marie elected police magistrates. Until then the final arbiter of civil and criminal cases was the sometime Solomonic de Maisonneuve. He ordered brawlers to pay their victims' medical bills and slanderers to publicly declare each other honorable. In 1648 he ordered a soldier executed for "immorality." (The Jesuits intervened and the man was reprieved on condition he become executioner at Quebec.) A man who accosted a married woman was stripped of 3½ acres—which was divided between the woman's children and the church. A soldier was cashiered, banished and fined 200 livres for immoral advances to "decent women."

Ville-Marie's greatest scandal was the adultery—at the Sunday vesper-hour—of the wealthy trader Jean Aubuchon and Marguerite, wife of surgeon Etienne Bouchard. De Maisonneuve's sentence was as sensational as the infidelity. Aubuchon was fined 600 livres and

The windmills of New France (such as this one, built in the late 1600s, at Windmill Point on Ile-Perrot near Montreal) were used primarily for grinding grain. But the massive stone towers—some were 25-30 feet high—served also as forts during Indian raids. The four-foot-thick walls often had small windows or loopholes through which settlers could fire on attackers.

He Frowned, Quarrelled, Raged, Fought—and Made the Church Grow

Quebec's first bishop, François de Laval, lived like a saint and expected New France to follow his example.

He slept in a hard, flea-filled bed, ate food grown mouldy and wormy. He frowned on entertainments and railed against drunkenness, carnal pleasures and pretty clothes. Even the governor's daughter was forbidden to dance except with girls—and then only if her mother would be present. But the colonists admired Laval's generosity to the poor and never doubted his sincerity or his devotion to what *he* thought was his duty.

The 36-year-old nobleman arrived in New France in 1659, tight-lipped under a large nose, bishop of Quebec in fact but not in title. The Pope had named the Jesuit-trained Laval vicar apostolic (titular bishop) but the Sulpician Gabriel de Queylus had been appointed vicar-general by the Archbishop of Rouen. Until Laval's appointment was confirmed by Rome in 1674, his authority was in question and he fought fiercely against slights real and imaginary. Once two schoolboys were whipped for saluting the governor and not him.

He quarrelled bitterly with four governors, and with the Sulpician and the Recollet orders. He raged against those who traded brandy to the Indians, threatening excommunication and demanding the harshest civil penalties for some of the wealthiest and most respected citizens. He had few friends in high places.

But during his 23 years of leadership the church grew. Quebec had five parishes when he arrived; he established 30. A church was built at Quebec and several schools and convents were founded. Missionaries preached and baptized from the Atlantic to the Lakehead and south to the Mississippi Valley. A tithing system was introduced to support this holy army.

Nearest to Laval's heart was the Quebec Seminary he founded in 1663. It is still a teaching institution and part of the present building dates from 1678, the middle of Laval's era. His bones are buried in the crypt under an outer chapel.

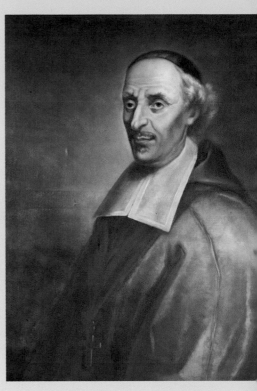

banished from Ville-Marie. Madame Bouchard's husband was told he could keep her "locked up for the rest of her life or give her back to her father and mother." But the Bouchards were reconciled and had several children.

In 1665 de Maisonneuve returned to France to try to resolve a dispute with Bishop François de Laval of Quebec.

At the root of the dispute was the 22,000 livres—donated by Jeanne Mance's benefactress—which had been used to recruit men in the early 1650s. La Société de Notre-Dame de Montréal gave its Montreal property to the Sulpician Order in 1663 and Laval ordered the Sulpicians to refund the 22,000 livres to the hospital. A Paris court found the claim unjustified but the stubborn Laval refused to accept the verdict. Hoping to appease the bishop whose demands he had repudiated, de Maisonneuve resigned his governorship in 1669 and retired to a humble Paris apartment. He died in 1675, aged 64.

Meanwhile, the crack Carignan-Salières Regiment—100 officers and 1,000 musketeers, pikemen and grenadiers led by the Marquis de Tracy—had landed in Quebec in June 1665. Fifteen months later, some 300 boats carried 600 of the soldiers, 600 habitant volunteers (110 from Montreal) and 100 Hurons and Algonkins up the *Rivière des Iroquois*—the Richelieu—to Lake Champlain. The Iroquois saw the army approaching in full war panoply. They fled.

Tracy put their villages to the torch and destroyed their harvest. A cross and the arms of France were planted in the ruins of the main village—a four-bastion fortress with 20-foot-high triple palisades. The next summer Iroquois envoys came to Quebec.

In the 20-year peace that followed, Ville-Marie blossomed. Some of Tracy's own men swelled a population that reached 1,720 by 1685. Only a year after the campaign to the south, the once-austere mission station was the prospering fur-trade capital of New France. To its gala fur fairs (see p. 72) great canoe flotillas swept down the Ottawa River each summer.

Outside the weathered palisade, near the common where de Maisonneuve had knelt that day in 1642, where Père Vimont had seen a mustard seed take root, now each year there were parleys and peace pipes, officials and black-cassocked priests, and merchants and habitants in grey doublets and colored breeches. And Indians. Iroquois among them.

Maison Saint-Gabriel, Marguerite Bourgeoys's convent at Pointe Saint-Charles in Montreal, is almost as old as the city itself. It was rebuilt in 1698 on the 1668 foundations.

Heritage Sites

MONTREAL A 40-foot stone obelisk in Place Royale stands approximately where on May 17, 1642, de Maisonneuve founded Ville-Marie, the missionary centre that became Montreal. A plaque lists the names of some of the original settlers. Plaques just north of the monument mark the sites of the community's first market place (1657) and de Maisonneuve's residence (1663-65).

Also in Montreal

AUBERGE LE VIEUX SAINT-GABRIEL (6) The remains of a two-storey dwelling built toward the end of the 17th century are part of the south wing of this restaurant. Also preserved are a 17th-century fieldstone fireplace and a tunnel where women and children hid during Iroquois raids.

CONGREGATION OF NOTRE-DAME (8) In the Centre Marguerite-Bourgeoys (a museum) are a portrait of the order's founder (painted by Pierre Le Ber hours after her death in 1700), and some of her writings. Marguerite Bourgeoys's remains are preserved in a marble chest in a nearby room, and a tablet north of the building commemorates her beatification in 1950. Two stone towers just to the east are the remains of a fort where Marguerite Bourgeoys and her disciples are said to have taught.

FIRST HOSPITAL (4) A plaque marks approximately where Hôtel-Dieu, founded in 1642 by Jeanne Mance, was relocated outside Ville-Marie's fortifications in 1645.

FIRST SCHOOL (5) A bas-relief of Marguerite Bourgeoys surrounded by children identifies the site of the stable in which she began teaching in 1658.

HÔTEL-DIEU DE MONTRÉAL (10) This hospital was re-established on its present site in 1861. A museum contains an herb jar owned by Jeanne Mance, medicine jars from 1663, and a prayer bell used to warn of Iroquois attacks. A stained-glass window in an adjoining chapel depicts Montreal's first Mass (May 17, 1642). At the Pine Avenue entrance to Hôtel-Dieu is a bronze sculpture of the hospital founder supporting a wounded settler.

MAISON SAINT-GABRIEL (7) Rebuilt in 1698 on the 1668 foundations, the two-storey house in which Marguerite Bourgeoys established Montreal's first convent is now a museum. Exhibits include the 1668 fireplace and a table that belonged to Marguerite Bourgeoys.

MOUNT ROYAL CROSS (9) A 100-foot-high illuminated cross, visible for 40 miles, commemorates the erection of a wooden cross by de Maisonneuve in 1643 after Ville-Marie was spared from a flood.

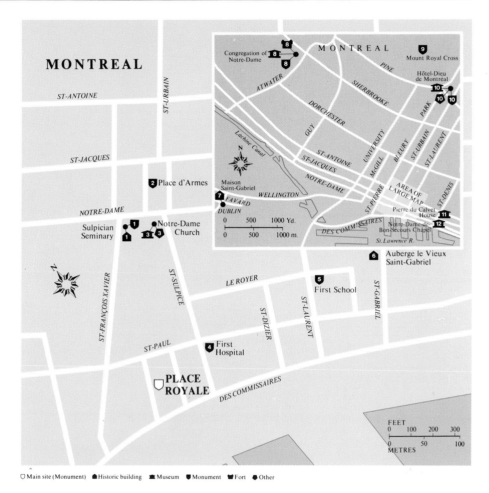

MAIN SITE (Monument) ▲ Historic building ■ Museum ▼ Monument ◆ Fort ◆ Other

NOTRE-DAME CHURCH (3) One of Canada's largest churches has 11 nine-foot-high stained-glass windows depicting the history of Montreal. Seventeenth-century silver tableware and other Canadiana are in a museum at the rear of the church.

NOTRE-DAME-DE-BON-SECOURS CHAPEL (12) Constructed in 1773 on the foundations of a chapel built in 1657 by Marguerite Bourgeoys, the chapel has paintings and wall mosaics of Marguerite and of de Maisonneuve. Costumed dolls in a basement museum depict events in Marguerite's life.

PIERRE DU CALVET HOUSE (11) Built in the first half of the 18th century, this three-storey fieldstone home typifies the architectural style of historic Montreal. It is closed to the public.

PLACE D'ARMES (2) A 40-foot granite and bronze monument featuring a statue of de Maisonneuve stands approximately where Montreal's founder repelled the Iroquois on March 30, 1644. At de Maisonneuve's feet are statues of Charles Le Moyne (the founder of Longueuil), Lambert Closse (de Maisonneuve's lieutenant), Jeanne Mance and an unidentified Iroquois. Beside Le Moyne is Pilote the watchdog.

SULPICIAN SEMINARY (1) A plaque commemorates Jérôme Le Royer de La Dauversière, the first person to urge settlement of Ville-Marie. (The seminary dates from 1685 and is closed to the public.)

Other sites (not shown)

Carillon, Que. A 12-foot stone monument to Adam Dollard des Ormeaux and his 16 French companions stands at the reputed site of their 1660 battle with the Iroquois. Concrete monoliths in nearby Parc Carillon commemorate the battle.

Ile-Perrot, Que. A stone windmill similar to windmills built near Ville-Marie stands at the eastern end of the island. The mill and a nearby house date from the late 1600s.

Quebec A tomb in a chapel of the Quebec Seminary contains the bones of François de Laval, first bishop of New France and founder (1663) of the seminary.

A Century of Conflict
on the Great 'Bay of the North'

Excitement gripped the Frenchman standing at the prow of the English ketch *Nonsuch* as she scudded down the east coast of Hudson Bay. A hunger for revenge against New France churned inside Médard Chouart, Sieur des Groseilliers. For days he had scanned the bleak shore for some sign of human life. Now, on Sept. 22, 1668, his eyes gleamed as he spied a wisp of smoke curling above the tips of the spruce trees. That meant Indians—and furs.

The 36-foot ketch shuddered as its cannon roared a greeting. Then it hove to. Indians emerged from the bush and some of *Nonsuch*'s men went ashore; Capt. Zachariah Gillam recorded that they "had some small Commerce." As Groseilliers returned aboard, his glance settled lovingly on furs stashed against the bulwarks—furs these Indians had traded cheaply.

Groseilliers was a Frenchman working for the English. He and his furs had twice saved New France from financial ruin—but he had been rewarded with fines and seizure of his pelts. Furs brought down the Ottawa and St. Lawrence rivers to Montreal and Quebec were easily intercepted and taxed. A sea route for the fur trade—such as Groseilliers suggested—was rejected by New France officialdom for fear it would mean loss of tax revenue. Disgusted, Groseilliers had sought other backers—and found them at the court of England's Charles II. New France would pay dearly for its high-handed treatment of Groseilliers—*how* dearly he never dreamed. Nor did he foresee that this voyage of *Nonsuch* would launch an empire almost as large as Europe—the Hudson's Bay Company.

With stories of the New World, Groseilliers, 47, and his brother-in-law, Pierre-Esprit Radisson,

25, had charmed the English court in 1666. In London taverns, financiers listened long to the two adventurers. There was a wealth of furs to be taken in the lands that bordered a great uncharted bay in North America. It could be reached by a northern sea route that would bypass the French territory along the St. Lawrence.

Groseilliers told prospective backers that, 10 years before, on a trading expedition, he netted furs worth 15,000 livres ($37,500). They rescued Quebec from disaster but taxes considerably diminished Groseilliers's personal profit.

He learned from Cree Indians of a "Bay of the North" that might be accessible by sea and in 1659 he and Radisson tried to reach it. They were unsuccessful, he said, but they returned with 60 canoes laden with furs. Radisson and Groseilliers, however, were rewarded with abuse, fines and jail. As soon as they were released they started the hunt for backers.

By March 1668 the London businessmen were convinced by the French pair. They bought the 43-ton *Nonsuch* and outfitted her and a sistership, *Eaglet* (borrowed from Charles II). The ships slipped their London moorings June 5 and sailed (Groseilliers aboard *Nonsuch*, Radisson in *Eaglet*) up the east coast of England, and into an Atlantic storm that sent *Eaglet* limping home.

But *Nonsuch* sailed across the ocean, along the coast of Labrador, through Hudson Strait and into Hudson Bay. After the encounter with the Indians on Sept. 22 she went on to James Bay.

"The 29th we came to the River on the East side," wrote Captain Gillam. He named it Rupert River after Prince Rupert, one of the expedition's patrons. *Nonsuch* was hauled ashore and made ready for winter. A log house with a stockade was built and it was christened Charles Fort after Charles II. (It was later renamed Fort Rupert: the Hudson's Bay Company trades there still.) Groseilliers roamed inland to contact Indians. In spring some 300 came to trade.

On an historic voyage in 1668, the HBC ketch Nonsuch *became the first vessel to trade in Hudson Bay. This replica, built in England in 1968, is now on permanent display inside the Manitoba Museum of Man and Nature, in Winnipeg.*

Pegs inserted in a traverse board (this one is on the Nonsuch *replica in Winnipeg) recorded a ship's course and speed. Holes in the compass rose (top) are in circles representing the eight half-hours of a four-hour watch; a peg was used to indicate the course each half-hour. Pegs in the rectangular section showed distance in fathoms (left) and speed in knots (right). All pegs were removed at the end of the watch and the information entered in the ship's log.*

Solemn Ceremony and Boisterous Nights: The Ritual of HBC Trade

It was brandy, tobacco, muskets and food that brought the Indians each summer. They signalled their approach—in waves of up to 50 canoes, often in line abreast—with a scatter of musket fire. So began the annual trading ritual at Hudson's Bay Company forts.

Before any trading, chiefs and HBC officers sat in solemn ceremony. None spoke until each man had smoked the calumet, the pipe of peace and fellowship. Then talk was initiated only by the most respected of the Indians.

To identify an Indian leader as an HBC trading partner, the company gave him a complete outfit: breeches, stockings, a lace shirt, cloth coat, feathered hat and colorful sash. (This painting by Adam Sherriff Scott is of the pageantry that preceded trading at York Factory. The chief, walking beside the governor of the post, is in scarlet with one red stocking and one blue.)

With the words "Come and trade," a company officer began the dialogue. "Open the window" was the Indian reply; to which: "The window is open." The window, or "hole in the wall," was a wicket in the wall of the trading room.

For several days the fort sold only brandy. That fueled boisterous nights of singing, dancing and quarrelling. After two or three days the brandy was cut off and the revels ended.

Indian leaders and company officers met again, the Indians bearing a gift of beaver pelts. Then, sitting in a circle, whites and Indians again smoked the calumet.

The ceremony ended, it was back to the hole in the wall for two weeks of bartering furs.

A replica of the Hudson's Bay Company ship Nonsuch, *in Manitoba's Museum of Man and Nature—at Winnipeg—was built in 1968 with 17th-century methods and tools. Like the original* Nonsuch *of 1668, it has an oak hull, pine masts and 2,000 square feet of sail.*

Nonsuch sailed for home Aug. 12, 1669, with a fine cargo of furs, proof that the bay route was not only navigable but also profitable. The following May "The Governor and Company of Adventurers of England trading into Hudson's Bay" received a royal charter giving it power of life and death over its subjects in "Rupert's Land," the right to maintain a navy and make war—and a trade monopoly in the bay forever.

Quaker Charles Bayly was fearless, honest, stubborn, zealous—and a prisoner in the Tower of London for refusing to swear allegiance to Charles II. But the Hudson's Bay Company, sensing in him the qualities needed by a governor, secured his release, and in September 1670 he landed at Port Nelson—the estuary of the Nelson and Hayes rivers on the west side of Hudson Bay. Bayly built posts in James Bay at the mouths of the Albany and Moose rivers and Indians flocked to them. Montreal and Quebec were losing the fur trade.

Paris turned for help to . . . Groseilliers and Radisson. They were persuaded, by appeals to their patriotism and promises of greater profits, to abandon the HBC.

The French scouted the English posts along the bay and learned they were built to "resist the cold and not the arms of those who might attack from the land." Radisson in the vessel *Saint Pierre* and Groseilliers and his son, Jean-Baptiste Chouart, in *Sainte Anne,* set out in 1682 from Quebec for Port Nelson. They knew that if they captured the estuary for France's newly formed *Compagnie du Nord* they would have a base from which to try to control the bay.

Two other expeditions were en route to Port Nelson: the HBC vessel *Rupert,* captained by Zachariah Gillam, and a Boston ship, *Bachelor's Delight,* commanded by Gillam's son Benjamin. (Probably neither Gillam knew the other was bound for the bay.)

On Aug. 18 or 19, *Bachelor's Delight* arrived at the Nelson River. On Aug. 20 Radisson and Gro-

Radisson (standing) and Groseilliers canoed north in search of the Indians' "Bay of the North," found furs instead—and were punished for their enterprise. They turned their backs on France, won support in England, and helped found the Hudson's Bay Company. This painting is by Frederic Remington.

seilliers sailed into the mouth of the Hayes River, a few miles to the south. The French did not see *Bachelor's Delight* anchored upriver.

Radisson heard cannon fire Aug. 26 and discovered *Bachelor's Delight*. He lied to Benjamin Gillam, telling him that he had 50 men and a commission from France to build a fort and keep out foreign traders. Benjamin believed him.

Radisson later spotted *Rupert* heading for the Nelson and intercepted the ship to keep Zachariah Gillam from finding his son. Again Radisson lied. He assured the HBC captain that he had 300 men and two ships—and expected a third. This alarmed Gillam and his passenger, John Bridgar, who had instructions to build a company post on the Nelson. It was too late in the season to turn back, so Zachariah dropped anchor at the river mouth.

On Oct. 21 a storm drove *Rupert* into the bay and she sank, taking Gillam and nine crew members to their death. Bridgar and 14 other survivors camped all winter in a makeshift fort. Radisson maintained his deception. When Benjamin Gillam visited the French post in the spring and discovered how he had been tricked, he was imprisoned and Radisson seized his fort. Bridgar, meantime, had learned of Benjamin Gillam's presence up the Nelson but when he marched to the fort he was seized by Radisson.

Radisson and Groseilliers, with their prisoners, sailed for Quebec in *Bachelor's Delight*, leaving Groseilliers's son in charge at Port Nelson. Quebec taxed their cargo for a third time.

Moose Fort (later Moose Factory, Ont.) was built by HBC Governor Charles Bayly in 1673. The arrival of the first white women, 10 years later, is portrayed in this painting by Will Davies.

Groseilliers never returned to Hudson Bay. He went back to his home at Trois-Rivières, where he died in about 1696. Radisson rejoined the HBC in 1684. He returned to the bay the same year and tricked his nephew Chouart—who thought Radisson was still in the employ of France—into relinquishing the post and its furs. He stayed on the bay until 1687 when he went to England. The coureur de bois who had lived and hunted with the Indians died there in the summer of 1710.

How Muskets Fired

Within a generation of the Hudson's Bay Company supplying them with firearms, Indians forgot their ancient skills with the bow and arrow. Three types of musket, each with a different firing mechanism, were used during the 1600s and 1700s.

The primitive matchlock required a slow-burning fuse—and dry weather—to spark the priming charge in the flashpan (A).

A stone scraped by a wheel in the flashpan (A) sparked the charge of the complicated wheel-lock. It fired in wet weather but was difficult to repair.

The flintlock (full view below) fired when a flint striking serrated steel raised the flashpan cover (B), sending sparks into the pan (A). It was reliable in wet weather and was easily repaired.

The Battle in the Bay, Sept. 5, 1697—from a painting by Norman Wilkinson. Iberville's 44-gun Pélican *(centre) engages the English* Hampshire *at close range off York Fort.*

It was two years before the French retaliated against the HBC—with an attack overland. On a stormy March 30, 1686, Chevalier Pierre de Troyes set off from Montreal with more than 100 men in 35 canoes for the south end of James Bay. There was a reward for Radisson's capture.

The early going was hazardous. They were slowed by the Long Sault Rapids (near present-day Carillon, Que.). Pierre Le Moyne d'Iberville and his brother Sainte-Hélène plunged waist-deep into the icy river to pull their canoes upstream, all the while bullying and encouraging the others to follow. Wet and cold, the troops pushed on, sometimes up to their necks in swirling water, frequently blinded by sleet and snow.

They moved up the Ottawa River to Lake Abitibi, then into the Abitibi River, a tributary of the Moose. On June 18, at the mouth of the Moose, they sighted the HBC's Moose Factory. Toward evening Iberville and two others reconnoitred the fort, getting close enough to push a ramrod down a cannon to determine whether it was loaded. It was not. And no guards had been posted.

At dawn June 21 de Troyes's force attacked and a nightshirted HBC garrison surrendered. On July 3 they took Charles Fort (modern Fort Rupert) and a company supply vessel.

Next the French headed for Albany Fort—without knowing its exact location (at the mouth of the Albany River). HBC sentries spotted the flotilla of canoes and, mistaking the Frenchmen for Indians coming to trade, fired cannon in welcome. The French landed unopposed. The HBC governor, Henry Sergeant, would not surrender but he did nothing to stop the French from digging gun emplacements and landing cannon.

The French attacked July 25 while Sergeant and his wife were at dinner. (One shot hurtled past Mrs. Sergeant's nose and she fainted.) The shelling was resumed next morning. An hour later it stopped and the French yelled a chorus of "*Vive le roi!*" Up from a cellar came the English. The fort gates opened and Sergeant emerged, proffering port and surrender.

Now the French ruled all of Hudson Bay and James Bay except for Port Nelson. But when the English retook Albany Fort in 1693, the French abandoned Moose Factory and Charles Fort.

Twice the English had been routed—and twice France's foothold on the bay had been lost. Now, in 1697, Pierre Le Moyne d'Iberville returned, in the 44-gun *Pélican*. He led four other ships into Hudson Strait but one sank and the others were separated in a fog. He was anchored at Port Nelson (where the HBC had established York Fort, now York Factory) on Sept. 5 when three English ships appeared: HMS *Hampshire* (52 guns) and two HBC vessels, *Royal Hudson's Bay* (32 guns) and *Dering* (30 guns). Iberville attacked, disabling *Dering*, then for two hours blazed at the other vessels as their gunfire raked his ship.

Pélican's sails fell blazing, her bridge crumbled, her prow was shot away, her decks were bloodied with 90 dead and wounded. As *Hampshire* prepared to ram, Iberville swung his battered craft onto a parallel course. As the ships passed, *Hampshire*'s captain raised a flagon of wine to his foe; Iberville returned the toast. Seconds later, her bottom ripped on a shoal, *Hampshire* foundered with all hands. *Royal Hudson's Bay* surrendered.

The outer walls of Fort Prince of Wales (near Churchill, Man.) have been restored, conveying a sense of the massive strength of the great HBC bastion in the wilderness. It was attacked only once, by a French fleet in 1782. The garrison of a mere 39 men, commanded by Governor Samuel Hearne, surrendered without firing a shot.

Iberville: Savage Master of *La Petite Guerre*

On a crisp February night in 1690 some 210 French soldiers and Indian warriors—one of their leaders Pierre Le Moyne d'Iberville, a ruthless guerrilla fighter—crept into the sleeping English settlement of Corlaer (now Schenectady, N.Y.). They had marched 200 miles to wage *la petite guerre* against the English as revenge for the Iroquois massacre at Lachine (see p. 77).

The 400 settlers and 24 soldiers inside the Corlaer palisade were confident of their safety and the gate had been left open. The raiders swept in, slaughtered the garrison in its blockhouse and set buildings afire. The settlers were cut down with guns and axes. "The cruelties committed," wrote one contemporary, "no pen can write nor tongue can express; the children alive thrown into the flames, and their heads dashed in pieces against doors and windows."

Iberville, whatever atrocities were committed, has been called the first Canadian hero. He was the third and most famous of the 12 sons of Charles Le Moyne (who came penniless to New France in 1641, made a fortune in the fur trade and died in 1685).

Iberville, born at Montreal in 1661, was "unusually handsome"—a savage fighter who was also a heartless lover. He was 25 when a court found him guilty in a paternity suit. But he was not obliged to wed the woman and disregarded an order to support his daughter.

In 1696 he led an expedition that ravaged Newfoundland (see p. 30). He commanded his last and largest expedition in 1706, capturing the British-held Caribbean island of Nevis in March. He died four months later in Cuba, not by the sword but from yellow fever.

When Montreal fur "pedlars" set out to break the Hudson's Bay Company monopoly in the Northwest, the HBC built Cumberland House. The fort (above: its construction, in a painting by Franklin Arbuckle) is gone but Cumberland House lives on as the oldest settlement in Saskatchewan.

Three days later *Pélican* and her prize were wrecked in a storm. But Iberville's three ships that had been lost in the fog arrived; York Fort was taken Sept. 13 and renamed Port Bourbon.

The French had regained Hudson Bay but it was an empty victory: Hudson Strait was sealed by the Royal Navy until 1713. That year the Treaty of Utrecht returned Hudson Bay to the English for good.

The company controlled the bay and it had built a great stone fortress, Fort Prince of Wales (at present-day Churchill, Man.). But stone walls were useless against a new threat, the Montreal "pedlars"—independent fur traders who later formed the North West Company (see p. 132).

Joined after 1763 by New England businessmen who were angered by the HBC monopoly, the pedlars struck westward, establishing posts to intercept fur flotillas bound for the HBC at bayside. The effect was devastating.

What furs the Indians brought were "the refuse of the Canadian pedlars," complained a factor at York Fort. From a previous annual average of 30,000, his 1768 trade slumped to 18,000 made-beaver (a unit of exchange equivalent in value to one prime beaver pelt).

Yet the company was reluctant to establish posts in the interior. Its only inland settlement, Henley House, built in 1743, had taken trade away from Albany Fort, 100 miles downriver.

When HBC officials went inland to trade with the Indians their efforts were futile. In 1772, two agents rounded up 160 canoes full of furs bound for York Fort, only to see the Indians all desert to the pedlars at Cedar Lake (north of Lake Winnipegosis).

By 1774 the company's survival was at stake. It was decided to establish a second permanent inland trading post and Samuel Hearne (see below) reconnoitred along the Saskatchewan River before deciding on a site at Pine Island Lake (about 50 miles west of present-day The Pas, Man.). Cumberland House, as the post was called, was located farther west than the traders had ventured and was decisive in changing HBC fortunes. It lay where three tribal territories met and it had access to several great waterway systems.

The company was ahead of the pedlars and strove to keep its lead, pushing ever westward as the pedlars caught up or forged ahead. The paternalistic, unadventurous "baysiders" became fiercely enterprising businessmen. A half century of cutthroat competition with the pedlars lay ahead as the new-style company men battled their way to the Pacific.

Long Walk to the Coppermine—and Massacre at Bloody Fall

Copper lay "all in handy lumps" beyond the Barren Grounds—where a mighty river that no white man had seen emptied into an icy sea. So said the Chipewyan chief Matonabbee in 1768 as he presented a chunk of copper ore to the Hudson's Bay Company at Fort Prince of Wales (near present-day Churchill, Man.).

Samuel Hearne, a 24-year-old clerk, was sent to travel 900 miles northwest through one of the most desolate regions on earth to locate the river. Twice

he started from the fort but was forced to return after Cree guides robbed and deserted him.

He set off again Dec. 7, 1770, this time with Matonabbee. Along the way scores of Indians joined the trek. Hearne was horrified to learn that they wanted to make war on their enemy the Inuit.

On July 13, 1771, 30 miles from the Arctic Ocean, they reached the Coppermine River. Two days later a camp of about 20 Inuit was sighted near a

waterfall. Hearne watched helplessly as the Indians massacred the sleeping Inuit. He called the place Bloody Fall.

Now the Indians took him to the copper but hours of searching produced only a few chunks—riches perhaps to the Indians but of no use to the HBC. He returned to Fort Prince of Wales.

Hearne's great achievement, the discovery of the Coppermine River, was doubted until 1821, when Sir John Franklin (see p. 216) found Inuit skeletons at Bloody Fall.

Heritage Sites

WINNIPEG A replica of the ketch *Nonsuch*, first trading vessel into Hudson Bay (1668), nestles beside a re-creation of London's Deptford Dock in the Manitoba Museum of Man and Nature. Quayside buildings open for visits are the Boar's Head Inn and a warehouse with a sailmaker's shop.

Other sites

Churchill, Man. (2) Stone ramparts, the remains of the fort from which Samuel Hearne journeyed overland to the Coppermine River in 1771, are in 60-acre Fort Prince of Wales National Historic Park. On a rock half a mile from the fort is his carving: "Sl. Hearne, July ye 1, 1767." *Accessible only by train.*

Cumberland House, Sask. (1) A cairn commemorates the Hudson's Bay Company's first successful inland post (and Saskatchewan's oldest white community), founded by Samuel Hearne in 1774.

Fort Albany, Ont. (4) Traces of an HBC fort built in 1684 have been uncovered here. *Accessible only by air (charter).*

Fort Rupert, Que. (6) *Nonsuch* anchored here in September 1668. The crew built Charles Fort (later Rupert House) and wintered in it. A cairn commemorates the *Nonsuch* visit. *Accessible only by air.*

Lachine, Que. (8) The Lachine Historical Museum is in one of Canada's oldest buildings; its foundations were laid about 1670 by Charles Le Moyne, founder and first seigneur of Longueuil.

Longueuil, Que. (9) The Charles Le Moyne Historical Museum, modelled after a fort that Le Moyne built near here in 1685, exhibits muskets and portraits of the Le Moyne family, and a manuscript

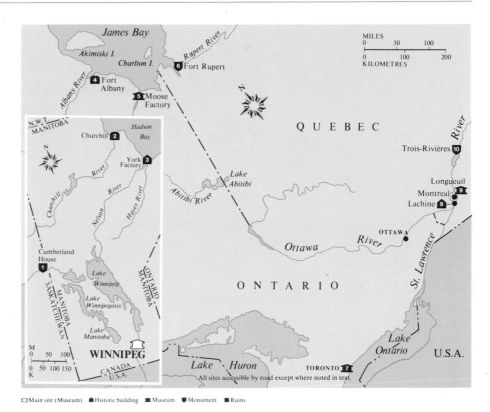

granting direct descendants of Charles Le Moyne use of the seigneury of Longueuil.

Moose Factory, Ont. (5) Early life in this HBC trading post (Ontario's oldest white settlement, founded in 1673) is chronicled at an interpretive centre in Centennial Park. A slide show traces the development of the Hudson Bay fur trade. *Accessible only by train.*

Toronto (7) The Royal Ontario Museum

exhibits such HBC artifacts as brass trade tokens, muskets, axes and glass beads.

Trois-Rivières, Que. (10) Pierre-Esprit Radisson and Médard Chouart des Groseilliers of the HBC lived here. A plaque marks where Groseilliers's house stood.

York Factory, Man. (3) A fur warehouse (c. 1835) on the site of the HBC's most important post, established in 1682, is a national historic site. *Accessible only by air.*

Construction of this manor (now the Lachine Historical Museum) at Lachine, Que., was begun around 1670 by fur trader Charles Le Moyne, then the richest man in New France.

A Flamboyant Governor Wins Lasting Peace for New France

In the heat of mid-July a magnificent spectacle unfolded against the improbable backdrop of the wilderness. Canada had never seen anyone quite like the man who dominated this scene of pomp and splendor. He was Louis de Buade, Comte de Frontenac, aristocrat, courtier and soldier, the fractious, flamboyant governor of New France.

He had come to New France in 1672. Now, a year later, on a small bay where the Cataraqui River flows into Lake Ontario (the site of Kingston), he was fulfilling a twofold purpose: to control the fearsome Iroquois and to build a fortified base for the fur trade west of the St. Lawrence Valley.

France had ordered Frontenac to strengthen the St. Lawrence settlements but he defiantly reached west instead. He offended the colonial administrators with his pomposity, irked Montreal fur traders by giving political support (and often public money) to his favorites, and angered the ordinary folk he took from their farms to labor on his Cataraqui expedition.

He came with a cavalcade of European splendor and the trappings of power, and throughout the spectacle all eyes were on him. He was a vain man and would have it no other way.

Some 400-500 Iroquois waited, impressed, as French canoes filled with shouting scouts and woodsmen approached the western shore of the Cataraqui. Next came two big barges, painted red and blue, armed with cannon and loaded with supplies; then canoes carrying Frontenac and his attendants, their swords and breastplates

Governor Frontenac, in this painting by Adam Sherriff Scott, arrives at Cataraqui (Kingston) in 1673 to awe the Iroquois and to build the first—wooden—Fort Frontenac as a fur-trade outpost. Above: the remains of the second Fort Frontenac, built of stone by La Salle in 1677. It was partially destroyed by the French in 1689 to prevent its capture by the Iroquois, then was rebuilt in 1695 by Frontenac. It fell to the British in 1758.

The Fur Fair: A Time for Trade and Revelry

Les canots s'en viennent! The canoes are coming! The news would race through Montreal on a midsummer day: the annual fur-trade fair—two weeks of avarice and revelry—was about to begin.

Before 1678 trading had been haphazard: Indians appeared irregularly at the settlement or bartered with coureurs de bois deep in the forest. Then, to assure supplies, the fair was established.

Several hundred Algonkins, Hurons and Ottawas beached their pelt-laden craft at a muddy common called Place Royale, and were greeted by the governor of New France, seated in a large wooden chair. Traders had stalls displaying knives, axes, muskets and colorful clothing.

Trading began the next day. There was much bargaining and bartering: eight knives or two axes might buy one beaver pelt; a greatcoat, two pelts; a musket, six. From stew pots in the Hôtel-Dieu courtyard Indians were treated to a ragoût of boiled dog, beaver, bear and corn, seasoned with fruit. They drank the brandy that helped lure them to Montreal. At night they roamed the town waving tomahawks and guns, tearing off their clothes, singing, whooping, fighting. Heads were staved in, noses bitten off. Finally the Indians left, taking their new possessions—and sometimes measles, smallpox and cholera.

But Iroquois attacks made the trip dangerous and after a few years most of the trade went to Fort Frontenac on Lake Ontario and to Fort St. Louis on the Illinois River.

The Canadian Land Forces Command and Staff College at Kingston is on the site of Cataraqui, where Frontenac established a base in 1673. Fort Frontenac had access to all the river systems that fed into or rose near the Great Lakes— the vital canoe routes of the westward expanding fur trade.

glittering in the sun. Still more canoes (there were 120 in all) carried more colorfully dressed woodsmen and Indians and armed and helmeted soldiers.

The Iroquois had said they would meet Frontenac in their council houses. His imperious reply: "It is for the father to tell the children where to hold council." Frontenac dubbed himself Onontio, "the common father of all nations."

He set men to work building a wooden fort. It would bear his name and be an example of French strength and purpose, a miracle of quick construction to awe the savages. Politics and negotiation could wait until the right setting had been created.

In only four days Fort Frontenac was completed. Over the governor's spacious pavilion flew a great French flag of heavy white silk adorned with a golden fleur-de-lis—the white signifying peace, the gold representing wealth and power. On the appointed day Frontenac sat outside on an ornate chair under a canvas canopy.

It was French custom to call Indian chiefs brothers but again, through an interpreter, Frontenac addressed these chiefs of the five Iroquois nations as his children. He expressed joy that they had come "with all the proofs of submission that children owe their fathers." He rebuked

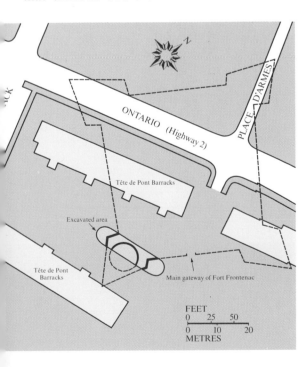

Three-hundred-year-old foundations of the stone Fort Frontenac built by La Salle (broken line) lie beneath streets and buildings of modern Kingston. In the courtyard of red-roofed Tête de Pont Barracks (opposite page), home of the Canadian Land Forces Command and Staff College, ruins of the southeast bastion have been excavated. All archaeological work on the site has been done by the Canadian Armed Forces.

Frontenac's Comtesse Stayed Home in Paris and Handled His Debts

Anne de la Grange, Comtesse de Frontenac *(above),* never saw New France.

The only child of a wealthy member of the French king's Privy Council, she was a beautiful 16-year-old when she fell in love with the future governor in 1648. Frontenac was then 26, a well-connected but spendthrift army officer, and Anne's father swore she would never marry a penniless fortune hunter. He put Anne in a convent but it was too late: the couple had married in secret hoping he would relent. He did not. Anne was disinherited.

Frugal domestic life appealed to neither and they ran up enormous debts. Their son, François-Louis, born in 1651, was brought up by servants.

During Frontenac's two terms in Quebec, Anne remained in Paris to manage his salary and ward off creditors. She enjoyed court intrigue and was acclaimed for her wit. She whispered Frontenac's projects in the proper ears and mended the frayed edges of his reputation.

The marriage lasted 50 years but was increasingly one more of convenience than of love. In 1699, when she received news of Frontenac's death in Quebec the year before, she is said to have been handed a silver chest containing the heart of the old warrior. Stiffly, she refused it: "I do not want a dead heart which, when beating, did not belong to me."

This pine armoire in the Montreal Museum of Fine Arts was made in New France in the late 17th century. It is nearly seven feet high and is in the Louis XIII style that developed in France in the early 1600s.

them for "treachery and cruelty" toward the Hurons, allies of the French. He exhorted them "to become Christians, by listening with respect and submission to the instructions the Black Gowns [priests] will give you . . . to observe strict peace on your part, as I shall do on mine." Goods at the fort would be traded "at the cheapest rate possible, as I do not intend that you be treated otherwise than as Frenchmen."

The Iroquois watched and listened, hostile to those who moved into territory they wanted to control. From strongholds in what now is New York State, and armed with muskets provided by the English, they had for years fought the French, the Hurons and other Indian allies of the French. But now the English were on the verge of surrender to the Dutch at New York (City). The Iroquois, their source of muskets and ammunition gone, could not afford to fight the French as well as their enemies the Susquehannahs and the Mohicans. So they smoked the peace pipe with Frontenac. In four long days of talk, they suited their words to the hour.

If they were Frontenac's children, they said,

Iroquois warriors usually went into battle wearing only breechcloth, moccasins and red ochre body paint.

Joseph-Antoine Le Febvre de La Barre (below) replaced Frontenac in 1682. He led 1,250 men against the Iroquois but, with food and water scarce and many men sick, he was forced to come to humiliating terms with the Indians.

surely he would fight at their side. They would consider becoming Christians as he had urged. They welcomed a trading post on the Cataraqui, to save them travel to Montreal, but they pressed for good prices.

It was Frontenac's first exposure to the skilled diplomats of the Iroquois confederacy, and he found himself parrying and sidestepping. To his superior in France he wrote: "You assuredly would have been surprised, my lord, to see the eloquence, the shrewdness and the finesse with which all their deputies addressed me."

Frontenac would have greater cause to appreciate Iroquois talents. Years of mortal conflict with the Iroquois lay behind the ceremony at Fort Frontenac in 1673. Years more lay ahead.

Frontenac was the grandson of one secretary of state, the grandnephew of another, and the godson and namesake of Louis XIII. Well educated, he joined the army in his teens, fought in several campaigns in the Thirty Years' War, became colonel of a regiment at 20 and the equivalent of a modern brigadier general at 24.

When not on active service, he lived at the court in Versailles. There he ran up huge debts and eventually owed 36 persons up to 24,000 livres (about $60,000) each. In an extravagant era this was less a stigma than evidence of his charm. Biographer W. J. Eccles wrote that "anyone who could borrow that much money from that many people must have had great persuasive powers." However, at 50, by assuming the governorship of New France, he was able to evade his creditors.

When Frontenac arrived at Quebec in 1672 a 20-man guard preceded him down the gangplank. A curled wig covered his thin hair and his plumed, wide-brimmed hat was lined with scar-

Hoping to cut down on drunkenness in Quebec—by having the colonists drink beer instead of brandy—the intendant Jean Talon had built one of Canada's first breweries in 1668. Its vaults, owned by the city of Quebec, are now a museum containing 17th-century guns and antique furniture.

La Salle Discovered Not *La Chine* But Lachine (and Louisiana)

He was called mad, an arrogant fool, but René-Robert Cavelier de La Salle believed passionately that he could find a way across North America to China and its riches. Land he was given near Montreal when he arrived in New France in 1667, aged 23, was jokingly named *La Chine* (China). He sold it to finance an ill-equipped expedition to the Ohio River, which he thought led to the Orient. He drove his men hard but he was no woodsman or navigator and turned back near the eastern end of Lake Ontario.

La Salle became a fur trader to raise money for new explorations. He built a fort at Niagara and replaced Frontenac's wooden fort at Cataraqui (Kingston, Ont.) with a stone structure. In 1678, with 30 men and the blessing of Louis XIV, he set out to claim the Great Lakes and the Mississippi River for France—and to expand his trading operations. On Lake Erie in 1679 he built the 45-ton *Griffon (right),* the first ship launched on the lakes. At Fort Crèvecœur (near today's Peoria, Ill.) in 1680 he learned *Griffon* had disappeared in Lake Huron. He canoed and snowshoed to Niagara and confirmed there was no trace of her or her cargo of furs. He did learn that another ship bringing him supplies from France had been sunk in the St. Lawrence. In Montreal he was told his men at Crèvecœur had mutinied and destroyed the fort.

The indefatigable La Salle organized a new expedition in 1681, followed the Mississippi to its mouth and found not China but alligator-infested swamps. Nonetheless on April 9, 1682, he claimed the territory, which he named Louisiana, for France and, to the sound of hymns and musket fire, erected a cross bearing the arms of France. The king wrote: "Completely useless." La Salle was called to France in disgrace.

But by lies and exaggerations he persuaded the king to send him back, this time by sea, to colonize the Mississippi delta. He bickered with his men and could not find the mouth of the river. He landed in what now is Texas and set out on an overland search. His men had had enough. On March 19, 1687, one shot him in the head and he died in the wilderness he had claimed for France.

let silk. His damask coat was of levantine grey cloth. His dress, his bearing, his swarthy face all bespoke courage, confidence and strength. He ignored Versailles's instructions that his authority was limited, and sought instead to rule—in his words—as a "high and mighty lord."

He soon installed a friend, René-Robert Cavelier, Sieur de La Salle, at Fort Frontenac, as a seigneur tapping the western fur trade. New France became split between two trading factions, Frontenac's favorites and his enemies.

Frontenac arrested François-Marie Perrot, governor of Montreal, for defying his authority. He arrested François de Salignac de la Mothe-Fénelon, the Sulpician abbé, who had castigated him for forcing habitants to labor and for oppressing those who opposed him. The colony's Sovereign Council (see p. 82) referred the cases and sent the accused to the king. Perrot was reinstated and eventually made peace with Frontenac. Fénelon never returned to New France; the king found Frontenac and Fénelon both at fault but his severest censure fell on the governor.

A new intendant, Jacques Duchesneau, was made president of the Sovereign Council. After three years of trying to bully and dominate its members, Frontenac had so little influence that he was responsible for not much more than military affairs. But he continued to tyrannize the clergy, make arbitrary arrests and judicial decisions and to impose his will in such matters as orders of precedence.

One notable feud was with Bishop François de Laval. When the bishop decreed it a mortal sin to sell brandy to the Indians, Frontenac accused the clergy of encroaching on royal authority, of seeking to control the fur trade. Supported in France by the anticlerical Jean-Baptiste Colbert, minister responsible for colonies, Frontenac argued that brandy was vital to the trade, that if denied it, the Indians would go to Albany to get cheaper, better English goods—and rum.

To debate the issue, the king in 1678 established what became known as the Brandy Parliament. Frontenac guided the choice of members and Colbert gave them biased instructions. The majority ruled that prohibition would substitute English rum and Protestantism for French brandy and Roman Catholicism.

A year later, however, a royal edict limited the sale of liquor to Indians in French settlements and forbade the transport of liquor to Indian villages. Frontenac did little to uphold the order; liquor *had* become an integral part of the fur trade and his objective was fur-trade profit. His construction of Fort Frontenac at Cataraqui had been the first step toward creation of a network of trading posts and forts on the Great Lakes and the Mississippi River.

Colbert believed that a strong, diversified economy in the St. Lawrence Valley was more important than the fur trade in the west. He established fur-trading fairs in Montreal to attract Indians and to discourage farmers from becom-

A building that dates from 1683 and was the home of explorer Louis Jolliet now houses the lower terminus of a funicular between Lower and Upper Town in Quebec. In 1673, with Jesuit missionary Jacques Marquette, Jolliet travelled down the Mississippi River to present-day Arkansas. In 1694 he explored the coast of Labrador.

In a petite guerre *raid on Deerfield, Mass., one winter night, some 200 Canadians and 140 Indians from a reserve near Montreal killed 69 and took 111 prisoners.*

barricaded his house in what Frontenac claimed was an act of rebellion. Bishop Laval attempted to make peace but the boy, who had gone to stay at the bishop's palace, was taken and locked up for a month, although the king had forbidden Frontenac to imprison anyone except for sedition or treason.

Soon afterward, Frontenac arrested a councillor on a charge that, without a passport, he had sent a ship to his own property in the Gaspé. The governor had no right to demand that the man hold a passport or to imprison him. The king, his patience exhausted, ordered Frontenac and Jacques Duchesneau home.

Frontenac left New France late in 1682 after 10 turbulent years.

Frontenac contended the excellence of his administration had kept the Iroquois in check. He said it often at the French court and apparently believed it, but he exaggerated.

Iroquois hostility had grown in the Frontenac years. The Five Nations had made peace with the Mohicans and Susquehannahs and now were free to make war on the French. A struggle for control of the west became inevitable. The English, having retaken New York in 1674, were eager for furs and encouraged the Iroquois.

Frontenac had been warned that the vital system of Indian alliances was crumbling; when the time was ripe the Iroquois would again descend on New France. But, accepting Iroquois protestations of peaceful intentions, he had done nothing to help his Indian allies or to build the defences of the struggling colony. His successors reaped the harvest of his neglect.

The first, Joseph-Antoine Le Febvre de La Barre, made a disastrous attempt to attack the Iroquois and was recalled a year later.

The second, the Marquis de Denonville, led a raid on the Iroquois in 1687. Indians continued to harass fur-trade outposts and the settlements near Montreal but peace hopes grew nonetheless. On Aug. 5, 1689, Denonville was in Montreal awaiting Iroquois leaders he expected would agree to a treaty. As he waited, 1,500 Iroquois raided Lachine, only nine miles west, in one of the bloodiest massacres in New France's history.

Denonville was exhausted after four years in office and asked to be replaced because of his health. Frontenac, now 67 and again in financial difficulty, used his influence to regain the post of governor in 1689. He was convinced, as before, that he could win Iroquois favor and bring about peace. But New France reeled under Iroquois at-

Jacques-René de Brisay de Denonville came to New France as governor in 1685 and worked hard to make the colony prosperous and law-abiding. He took the unruly sons of seigneurs into the army and started a school to train river pilots. After four years of striving for peace with the Iroquois, he thought they were about to sign a treaty. Instead they butchered scores of settlers at Lachine, near Montreal.

ing coureurs de bois. But he agreed that the French could look to the west to block other powers and to seek a route to the south. Frontenac paid lip service to the St. Lawrence policy and exploited Colbert's exception.

He foundered on his own disobedience. Infuriated by his lack of power, by Intendant Duchesneau's councillors who hounded his favorites, he demanded that the Sovereign Council recognize him as its president. Refused, he pounded the table, then overturned it. Still he did not get his way. Angrily he exiled the colonial attorney-general and two councillors.

In March 1681 Duchesneau's 16-year-old son exchanged insults with one of Frontenac's followers. His father sent the youth to Frontenac to apologize; instead, young Duchesneau demanded that Frontenac apologize to *him*. Frontenac, enraged, beat the boy with a cane and he ran home. The older Duchesneau, afraid his son would be taken by force, armed his servants and

Slaughter in a Hailstorm: The Iroquois Massacre at Lachine

The sky over Lachine was angry with impending storm the night of Aug. 4, 1689. The 77 settlers and their families felt secure nonetheless in their whitewashed farmhouses. In the past, Iroquois raids had forced them to spend much time in nearby stockades but a truce had been signed the previous summer and now Governor Jacques-René de Brisay de Denonville was in Montreal, nine miles away, to seal a lasting peace. He did not know that France and England were at war again—but the Iroquois knew, and their English allies had armed them for new attacks on New France.

A few hours before dawn, Lachine awakened to the drumming of hail, suddenly pierced by the frightful screams of Iroquois slaughter. Fifteen hundred warriors from the Finger Lakes region of present-day New York State descended on Lachine, killed at random with knives and toma-

hawks, dashed out children's brains, and burned houses and barns. Inflamed by the settlers' brandy, they tied captives to stakes and peeled off strips of flesh to be eaten later. Some men shot their wives and children to spare them such torture.

A few survivors stumbled to Montreal. Denonville sent Philippe de Rigaud, Chevalier de Vaudreuil, with 300 soldiers and orders for everyone to take cover in the stockades. Vaudreuil followed orders literally; he refused to allow the rescue of 90 prisoners whose Indian captors were now too drunk to fight.

Later that day the Iroquois retired to the south shore of the St. Lawrence. Lachine watched the smoke of their victory bonfires that night, knowing that captives were being burned alive. Forty-eight of the 90 prisoners escaped; the rest were never seen again.

tacks. The massacre of farmers in their fields, women and children in their homes, drained away the lifeblood of the colony.

Frontenac's response was to wage *la petite guerre* on the English who made the attacks possible, raiding English border settlements with Iroquois-like savagery. The Canadians struck without warning, butchering, burning, taking prisoners, slaughtering livestock. Guerrilla warfare came naturally to habitants eager to revenge their own tragedies, hungry to put the torch to Protestant heretics.

La petite guerre raised the morale of New France and impressed Frontenac's faltering Indian allies but now the English colonies combined for their own assault on the French.

In 1690 an English fleet sailed for New France.

Frontenac got the news in Montreal and headed for Quebec with 200-300 men. He picked up more en route and, when a messenger told him the English were already at Tadoussac, he sent word to Louis-Hector de Callières, governor of Montreal, to rush to Quebec with every man he could find.

"Vive Frontenac!" the people of Quebec shouted when the governor arrived, an old man with fire in his eyes and a sense that this would be his finest hour. To his relief, English sails were not yet in sight.

If Sir William Phips, the English adventurer in command, had attacked earlier, Quebec would surely have fallen. But not one of some 2,000 men in his fleet of 30-odd ships knew the St. Lawrence. As the English ships inched gingerly

Kateri Tekakwitha, a Mohawk baptized at 19 and persecuted for her Christian faith, took refuge in 1677 in a Jesuit mission at Caughnawaga, near Montreal. It is said that when she died at 24 her smallpox-ravaged face took on a miraculous beauty; many claim to have received favors after asking "the Lily of the Mohawks" to intercede for them. She was declared blessed in June 1980, with the likelihood that she would one day be canonized.

The Botanist Who Named a Plant—and Found the Skunk 'Frightful'

The common pitcher plant *(right)*, which catches, drowns and digests insects, got its scientific name—*Sarracenia purpurea*—from an uncommon man, Michel Sarrazin, an army doctor who roamed the woods, fields and bogs of New France and was Canada's first scientist.

Sarrazin was 26 when he came to Quebec in 1685. He practised medicine until his death from smallpox in 1734 but he is best remembered as a botanist who often risked Iroquois ambush to study species unknown in Europe such as the carnivorous pitcher plant and the sugar maple. He

sought to improve the colony's agriculture and is said to have turned maple syrup into a major industry, reducing the need for expensive imported sugar. He sent countless notes, sketches and plants to scientists in Paris as well as specimens of rocks and minerals.

Canada's animal life also came under Sarrazin's scrutiny. With surgical instruments and a magnifying glass, he probed the anatomy of the beaver, the muskrat, the porcupine and the skunk—which, he wrote, had a "frightful smell capable of making a whole canton a desert."

An enemy emissary (in red in this painting by Marc-Aurèle de Foy Suzor-Côté) has demanded that Quebec surrender to an English fleet standing offshore in October 1690. Frontenac replies: "I will not keep you waiting so long. I have no reply to make other than from the mouths of my cannon and muskets." The British were routed.

upriver, habitants and even priests fired on them. When the fleet furled its sails on Oct. 17, Phips saw a fortress prepared to fight, the fleur-de-lis proud on Frontenac's château.

He sent Maj. Thomas Savage under a flag of truce to demand surrender. Chuckling habitants watched as the major was blindfolded, then led a roundabout way up the steep rock and over one palisade after another, while they tramped their feet and clashed weapons to signify armed strength. In the council chamber, Savage's blindfold was taken off and he beheld Frontenac in his glory. The governor had set the scene again: the room was crowded with officials dressed as for a royal levee, in gold and silver lace, in ribbons and plumed hats, their hair curled and powdered.

Frontenac ordered Phips's letter read aloud. It charged that unprovoked raids against English settlers "put them under the necessity of this Expedition for their own Security and satisfaction. Your answer, positive within an hour, returned by your own trumpet, with the return of mine, is required upon the peril that will ensue."

But Frontenac defied the British and a few days later Phips landed 1,300 men downriver on the Beauport flats near the mouth of the St. Charles River, close to Quebec. Frontenac, his main force drawn up in the rear, let them approach until, when they reached higher ground, they were exposed to sharpshooters hidden be-

hind palisades, rocks and trees. French casualties were few as the English advanced, withdrew, then opened fire again. The attack fumbled to a halt.

Phips turned his cannon on the rock but saw his own flag shot away. As it floated downstream, exulting young Frenchmen in a birchbark canoe set out under a hail of fire to get it. One jumped into the river, grabbed the flag and swam ashore.

The two-way cannonade continued. French shells shattered sails, broke masts, splintered hulls, maimed and killed. Phips's shells terrified refugees and the wounded in Quebec's Ursuline Convent but did no harm.

Short of powder, and with his men falling sick with smallpox, Phips realized he could not crack Quebec's defences. Frontenac merely had to hold fast until ice closed the river.

The British spent a bitter night in the mud and brush of the Beauport flats, shivering, soaked, famished, clothes frozen to the ground. But in the morning they began a final attempt to reach Frontenac's main force across the St. Charles River. It was a failure. The attackers were forced to withdraw in chaos, leaving behind five of their six artillery pieces.

Frontenac was hailed as a savior. The captured English flag was paraded in celebrations that were climaxed with a bonfire honoring Frontenac. He had won by sitting tight.

New France's reward for victory was one of its *worst* years. Food, ammunition and wine—Frontenac was afraid he might be reduced to drinking water—were scarce. Spring brought more marauding Iroquois to massacre farmers in the fields.

Frontenac tried again to woo the Indians to peace. Failing, he turned once more to *la petite guerre;* again the Canadians struck at the Iroquois and at English settlements. War had become a way of life.

At his château in Quebec, far from Iroquois wrath, Frontenac maintained a large staff, entertained lavishly, charmed the ladies and put on plays. He feuded with Jean Bochart de Champigny, the intendant, particularly over the fur trade and the west. But as the Ottawas, former French allies, turned to the Iroquois to discuss not only peace but also alliance, Frontenac acted decisively.

Soldiers, militiamen and Indians mustered July 4, 1696, on St. Helen's Island, off Montreal. With the 74-year-old governor in nominal command, more than 2,000 men travelled up the St. Lawrence to Fort Frontenac. They worked for six days to strengthen the fort, then struck out across Lake Ontario and into the lands of the Onondagas, one of the Five Nations. The French portaged canoes and barges around rapids and waterfalls in the Onondaga River until one night

Frontenac's guns fire from the Citadel in this engraving of the battle for Quebec in 1690. Behind them is the Château Saint-Louis (the governor's residence), where now stands the Château Frontenac hotel.

they saw the sky lit up around an Onondaga village a day's march away.

Next day, with Montreal Governor Callières riding a horse he had brought by barge, and the aged Frontenac borne in an armchair, most of the army pushed on. They found the village abandoned, its stockade in ashes. In flight the Onondagas had left just one withered old chief. Frontenac gave his Indians permission to burn the chief at the stake.

Frontenac's force ravaged for three days, burning crops in the fields, destroying caches of food, putting an Oneida village to the torch. *La petite guerre,* famine and disease were taking their toll of the Iroquois, and this destruction of food supplies was a final blow. By 1698 the Iroquois fighting force—2,800 strong in 1689—would number fewer than 1,300. But losses among New France's 13,000 inhabitants were more than offset by the arrival of immigrants. The Iroquois, exhausted and outnumbered, would have to seek peace. What Champlain had attempted 81 years before (see p. 36), Frontenac had at last accomplished. Iroquois power was broken.

By 1701 the master diplomacy of Callières,

Sir William Phips sailed from New England in August 1690 to attack Quebec. Delayed by fog and lack of a pilot in the St. Lawrence River, he arrived Oct. 17 and withdrew, defeated, eight days later.

79

The 14-Year-Old Who Held the Fort at Verchères

Madeleine de Verchères, who led the defence of her father's seigneury against Iroquois in 1692 when she was 14 *(top)*, wrote the best-known account of her feat 30 years later. She claimed she ran in from the fields ahead of 45 Indians, repaired the fort and, with two soldiers, an old man and two younger brothers, held out for seven days *(left)* until help arrived from Montreal, 22 miles to the southwest. In 1699 she had written a more plausible account: she struggled free of one Iroquois who grabbed her neckerchief, and with one soldier she fought off attackers for two days. Whichever story is to be believed, Madeleine remains a heroine. In 1722 when her husband, Pierre-Thomas de La Pérade, was attacked by two Indians, she disabled one and saved her husband's life.

The church of Notre-Dame-des-Victoires is on the site of Champlain's Habitation in Quebec's Place Royale. It was named Notre-Dame-de-la-Victoire after the defeat of the English in 1690 and renamed when a second British invasion fleet was wrecked in 1711.

Frontenac's successor as governor, had achieved not only peace with the Iroquois but also a general ceasefire among Indian tribes from the Atlantic to the Mississippi. Sealed with great and often riotous ceremony in Montreal, the peace pledged the Iroquois to a neutrality they faithfully observed. And for America's English population it stripped away their first line of offence against the French.

Frontenac never saw the peace he helped to win. He had died in 1698 after spending his last days sitting propped up in an armchair, making his mellowed peace with Intendant Champigny and with his Maker. Despite his faults, he had seen New France through its gravest years.

He died without riches and, in Champigny's words, as "a true Christian," and no one grieved more than this rival. Frontenac was buried in Quebec's chapel of the Recollets, with a priest praising those virtues that the storms of his life had long obscured. In Quebec's Basilica, not far away, hung the captured flag of Sir William Phips, a symbol of the survival of Frontenac's colony against a far more populous foe. There it would remain as long as New France lived.

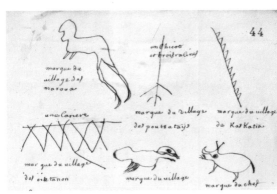

Frontenac's successor, Governor Louis-Hector de Callières, witnessed a treaty at Montreal in 1701. It bore the marks (some are above) of 38 Indian chiefs. The Iroquois promised to keep peace with tribes that were allies of the French.

Heritage Sites

KINGSTON, Ont. The remains of Fort Frontenac, the stone stronghold built by La Salle in 1677, lie within Tête de Pont Barracks and under Ontario Street between Barrack Street and Place d'Armes. The fort replaced a wooden stockade built by Frontenac in 1673. Foundations of the south and east walls, the southeast bastion and a gateway have been unearthed within the barracks (not accessible to the public). The place where Frontenac and the Iroquois conferred is south of the barracks on Ontario Street between Princess and Brock streets.

□ Main site (Ruins) ✹ Multiple attractions ▲ Museum ◆ Monument ■ Ruins ▪ Unmarked site

Other sites

Lachine, Que. (1) A 12-foot stone monument to La Salle, who founded Lachine in 1667, stands outside city hall. Plaques nearby describe the Iroquois massacre of settlers on Aug. 4-5, 1689.

La Pérade, Que. (4) Madeleine de Verchères, who as a 14-year-old held a fort against Iroquois in 1692 (see Verchères), later lived here in a manor with her husband, the seigneur of La Pérade. The ruins of the building are near Sainte-Anne Street and Chemin des Iles.

Montreal (2) Place Royale, Montreal's first market place (1657), was the site of fur-trading fairs during the 17th century. On St. Helen's Island governors La Barre, Denonville and Frontenac mustered their forces in 1684, 1687 and 1696 before invading Iroquois territory in present-day New York State. Exhibits in the Montreal Military and Maritime Museum include a cannon from the British expedition to Quebec in 1690, a military pass (1682) and 17th-century muskets and helmets.

Quebec (5)

BASILICA OF NOTRE-DAME The remains of Frontenac are believed to be in a crypt in this, the church of Canada's oldest parish (1659).

CAPE REDOUBT The city's oldest fortification (1693) stands at the northeast end of the Citadel. In the museum of the Royal 22ᵉ Régiment are one of Canada's oldest documents—a 1679 deed signed by Frontenac—and a French cannon ball from 1682.

JOLLIET HOUSE This house (1683) was the residence of Louis Jolliet who, with Jacques Marquette, discovered the upper Mississippi in 1673. A tablet commemorates the achievement.

MUSÉE DU FORT The siege of 1690 is reenacted with a sound-and-light show and a 450-square-foot model of 18th-century Quebec.

NATIONAL ASSEMBLY Recessed into the façade are life-size statues of Frontenac, Louis Jolliet and Intendant Jean Talon.

NOTRE-DAME-DES-VICTOIRES Built in 1688 as l'Enfant-Jésus, the church was renamed in honor of French victories over the British in 1690 and 1711.

QUEBEC SEMINARY A museum here exhibits a British cannon used in the siege of 1690. The oldest part of the seminary, in the Procure Wing, dates from 1678.

TALON'S VAULTS A museum in the vaults of the first commercial brewery in Canada (built by Jean Talon in 1668) exhibits 17th-century guns and furniture.

URSULINE CONVENT Canada's oldest nunnery (1642) was used as a shelter during the British siege of 1690. In the Madame de La Peltrie Museum are a 17th-century pharmacy, infirmary and schoolroom.

Tobermory, Ont. (not shown) Timbers recovered off Russel Island in Georgian Bay in 1955 may be from La Salle's *Griffon*, the first ship to sail the Great Lakes. The timbers will eventually be displayed in a museum at nearby Dunks Bay.

Verchères, Que. (3) A 20-foot bronze statue of Madeleine de Verchères commemorates her defence of her father's fort against the Iroquois in 1692.

Quebec's Ursuline Convent was founded in 1642 by Madame de La Peltrie and Marie de l'Incarnation. Bishop François Laval lived here for two years after his arrival in 1659. Mementos of him are in the convent museum.

Louis XIV saw himself as the "sun king," an eminence unequalled in brilliance and power.

Children of the 'Sun King'

"The king regards his Canadian subjects, from the highest to the lowest, as his own children," proclaimed Louis XIV's chief minister, Jean-Baptiste Colbert. France's "sun king" was 25 when, in 1663 (although remaining in Paris), he took personal control of New France. He swept away the Company of One Hundred Associates (see p. 40), whose 36 years of rule had left New France with only 3,200 inhabitants, and he set up a sovereign council to impose his royal will. On it were the governor, the bishop, an administrator called an intendant (all from France), and five colonists.

Population must be increased, said the king, and Jean Talon, the first intendant, arrived in 1665 as "head of the family." To encourage immigration, he paid passages and provided land, supplies and tools. He ordered fathers of unmarried girls over 16 and of unmarried men over 20 to report every six months to "explain themselves." Bachelors were denied fishing, hunting and trapping rights, but parents of 10 or more children received 300 livres ($750) a year. By 1673 the population had more than doubled.

"All the necessities of life can be produced in this one country if it is properly developed," said Talon. He encouraged farmers to grow hops for a brewery he started in Quebec (see p. 74), and hemp for thread, cloth, rope and sails.

As the colony prospered, Louis set out rules to ensure order. Women had to be home by 9 p.m.; unmarried girls were permitted to dance only with one another, in their homes, with their mothers present; ships from France were not allowed to bring in rouge. (But Canadian women still shocked Bishop François Laval—see p. 60—who complained in 1682 that they came to Mass "revealing scandalous views of their nude shoulders and bosoms.") Public meetings to discuss politics were forbidden. For continued profanity a man could have his lips seared with a red-hot iron.

But the council was responsible for the people's welfare and security. "The rich must nourish the poor," Colbert insisted. Seigneurs, "persons of rank" who pledged loyalty to the king, were granted waterfront land which they had to clear and fill with tenant farmers. The seigneur had to live on his land, build a flour mill and run it for his tenants. They paid him respect but little rent (about $35 a year for 100 acres)—and impoverished seigneurs went hungry to keep up an appearance of gentility.

Militiamen paid for their own muskets.

Seigneurs divided their land into thin strips so that each tenant had river frontage. (Above: the Richelieu River valley today, near Saint-Denis.) Some Quebec farmers still pay land rent under contracts laid down in the 17th century. Industrious habitants (left) grew wheat, oats, peas and beans, raised sheep, cattle, pigs and chickens—and prospered. They doffed their hats to the seigneur and came to his manor house on New Year's Day for blessings but they often lived more comfortably than he did.

Walls of Stone Four Feet Thick

Stone houses of 17th- and 18th-century New France were cool in summer and warm in winter: their walls, bonded only with lime mortar, had to be about four feet thick for stability. Steep gable or hip roofs limited the buildup of snow. The downstairs was often one big room. Dormers were added when growing families needed top storeys for bedrooms.

18th century, Deschambault

Les filles du roi *(the king's girls)* were farmers' daughters and Paris orphans recruited to be wives and mothers in New France. Intendant Jean Talon requested that they be strong, healthy and *"free from any natural blemish or anything personally repulsive."* Each girl had a certificate from a priest stating she was unmarried and of good moral character, and a dowry from the king (usually a few animals, two barrels of salt meat and 11 crowns—about $85). More than 1,000 girls—up to 150 at a time—reached the colony between 1665 and 1672. As they stepped ashore (left: at Quebec), waiting bachelors *"singled out their brides, just as a butcher does an ewe from amongst a flock of sheep."* The fattest went first—they seemed most likely to withstand Canadian winters. Some marriages were performed on the spot, but more often the girls were looked after by nuns for a week or two before they wed. A girl was permitted to turn down a suitor (once married, she could obtain a separation only if her husband beat her with a stick thicker than his wrist) but most were not too choosy: there was little future in the colony for an unwed king's girl.

La Corriveau's Penalty

Punishment for crime in New France was severe. The story of "La Corriveau" inspired Alfred Laliberté's bronze sculpture (right) at the Musée du Québec. In 1763, Marie-Josephte Corriveau murdered her second husband with an axe while he slept. She was hanged, and her chained corpse was displayed in an iron cage at a crossroads in Lévis. Death—often preceded by torture—was the penalty for robbery, rape and arson.

New France's first professional fighting force—"very wretched soldiers," said Intendant Jean Bochart de Champigny—arrived from France in 1683. They were the Troupes de la Marine, named for the Ministry of Marine and Colonies which administered New France. (Left: students dressed as Troupes de la Marine at the old fort on St. Helen's Island in Montreal.) These soldiers were required only to be 4 feet 10 inches and to have enough teeth to chew army biscuit and dried meat. Short of weapons and supplies, frequently unpaid, they often took jobs on farms. Mobilizing them was difficult. Most of New France's fighting was done by the militia founded in 1669. (Far left: a typical militiaman.) Able-bodied males 16-60 drilled every month. There was no pay and no uniform. Habitants copied the Indian style of guerrilla fighting; some wore paint and feathers into battle.

Jean Talon, the "Great Intendant," had the look of a dandy but his imagination, energy and dedication brought prosperity and hope to New France as he travelled the colony in a birchbark canoe and visited settlers in their homes. "I have denied myself the pleasures of life," he wrote. "I sacrifice everything to my work." Talon, who to encourage population growth decreed that unmarried men could neither fish nor hunt nor trap, died in France in 1694—a bachelor.

17th century, Ile d'Orléans

18th century, Boischatel

Bored with farm life and tired of regulations, many young men in New France donned buckskins and took to the forest as coureurs de bois. They traded for furs and often lived with Indians. Some never came back. Others returned with valuable furs, sold them, and spent the profits on gaudy clothes, drinking, feasting, gambling and women. When their money was gone they returned to the woods. By 1680 there were some 600, and the colony was threatened with an acute shortage of men. Coureurs de bois were accused of corrupting Indians with brandy and of being a bad influence on the colony's youth. Intendant Jean Talon called them "bandits." Government and church decrees made them outlaws. Yet they helped to open up Canada's interior, provided contacts between French and Indians, and enlarged the fur trade. Two of the most famous, Radisson and Groseilliers, helped found the Hudson's Bay Company (see p. 62). Of the coureurs de bois life, Radisson said: "We weare Cesars, being nobody to contradict us."

The building that is the centrepiece of Fort Anne National Historic Park—a reconstructed British officers' quarters that dates from 1797—is set among earthworks built by the French about a century before that. The storied fort, whose proud old guns still watch out to sea, was originally the French Port Royal. It is in the Nova Scotia town that the British renamed Annapolis Royal.

The Reborn Port Royal, Canada's Most Fought Over Place

New life was again throbbing into Port Royal, the colony beside Nova Scotia's lovely Annapolis Basin.

Founded by the French in 1605 (see p. 22), Port Royal had been abandoned, revived, sacked by the English, settled by Scottish privateers—and returned to France by treaty in 1632.

Now, in 1636, Frenchmen were coming back. Charles de Menou d'Aulnay, an aristocratic, 32-year-old former naval officer, was determined to rule not only Port Royal but all Acadia (most of today's Maritime Provinces and part of Maine) and to crush anyone who stood in his way.

He reconstructed the colony on a peninsula across the Annapolis Basin and seven miles east of the old settlement. He gave each of 40 settler families a tract of rich valley land. He built a manor house, two mills, and ships. He labored in the fields with the peasants but ruled the settlement and its outposts along the shore like a feudal lord. He traded furs and friendship with the Micmacs and tolerated the 12 Capuchin friars who sought to convert the Indians to Christianity.

Guarding all were d'Aulnay's ships and his 60 cannon. For his 300 soldiers he built a fort; for his enemies, a dungeon.

The historic enemies of the French were English colonists to the south. But d'Aulnay's chief enemy from the start was his French rival for the fur trade of Acadia: Charles de Saint-Etienne de La Tour of Fort Sainte-Marie, across the Bay of Fundy at present-day Saint John, N.B.

La Tour had been in Acadia for 26 of his 43 years. When the first Port Royal was laid waste in 1613 he took to the woods. He and Charles de Biencourt partially rebuilt Port Royal on the original site. After Biencourt's death in 1623, La Tour built Fort Saint-Louis amid the fog and rocks of Baccaro Point on Nova Scotia's southern tip. Six years later, with France again at war with England, La Tour's was the only French fort in North America that did not surrender.

Charles d'Aulnay sold and mortgaged estates in France to buy ships and cannon and attract settlers and soldiers for his colony at Port Royal. He fought an epic struggle to become unchallenged ruler of Acadia—and won, only to die in a canoeing accident a few years later.

For £1,350, a Clump of Earth and a Nova Scotia Baronetcy

The Scottish poet Sir William Alexander *(left)*, a favorite at the court of England's James I, was piqued. There was a New France, a New England, a New Spain. Why not a New Scotland?

James was sympathetic and in 1621 gave Alexander the huge area that now comprises the Maritime Provinces and the Gaspé Peninsula—land claimed by England after Samuel Argall sacked Port Royal in 1613 (see p. 28). The grant, written in Latin, called New Scotland Nova Scotia.

Two expeditions of Scottish settlers cost Alexander some £6,000. Both failed. In 1624 the king approved a new scheme to find colonists and to help Alexander get out of debt. Ambitious Scottish gentry could become Baronets of Nova Scotia by paying £1,350 toward colonization. A plot of ground at Edinburgh Castle was declared Nova Scotia soil—so it still remains—and each baronet received his title and 16,000 acres by the feudal ceremony of sasine—accepting a clump of earth as a token of possession.

The Scots were slow to respond but in 1629 the first baronets sent "70 men and tua weemen" to the Port Royal that Argall had sacked, and others to Baleine on Cape Breton Island. The settlers doubled as privateers: James's son, Charles I, gave them permission to "make prize of all French and Spanish ships and goods at sea or land."

But four years later the settlers were shipped home. Charles, debt-ridden, had married the sister of France's Louis XIII and exchanged New Scotland and other lands for 400,000 crowns ($240,000)—half of her dowry.

When France regained her colonies in 1632, La Tour was named governor—but only of the areas around Fort Saint-Louis (renamed Fort La Tour) and newly built Fort Sainte-Marie. When the French attacked the English at Fort Pentagouet (present-day Castine, Maine) a few years later, La Tour refused to serve under d'Aulnay. That was the start of a famous feud.

La Tour was pitted against a man as aggressive and ambitious as himself but of higher birth, greater resources and greater influence in Paris. Each had parts of Acadia; each wanted it all.

Paris intervened but, ignorant of Acadian geography, it made matters worse. It gave d'Aulnay land in present-day New Brunswick but land not including Fort Sainte-Marie; it gave La Tour present-day Nova Scotia except Port Royal. Now each rival had his headquarters in an area ostensibly controlled by the other.

D'Aulnay had shown his determination to establish roots in Acadia by marrying the aristocratic Jeanne Motin. La Tour responded by sending for the fiery Françoise-Marie Jacquelin to become his wife. She arrived from France in 1640 and soon was fighting at her husband's side.

Marie persuaded La Tour to ally himself with *les Bostonnais,* the English of Boston. That was too much for Paris, which decided to uphold d'Aulnay's claim to all of Acadia. La Tour was declared a traitor. In April 1645, while La Tour was in Boston seeking help, d'Aulnay attacked Fort Sainte-Marie with ships and 200 men.

Marie, clad in a steel breastplate, her men outnumbered five to one, held the fort for three days.

But, under fire from a 16-gun frigate, and with the enemy, guided by a traitorous sentry, across the palisades, she surrendered. She was promised "quarter to all" but saw the garrison survivors hanged one by one. Heartbroken, she died within three weeks.

D'Aulnay returned to Port Royal the undisputed master of Acadia. La Tour set up in Quebec as a fur trader.

There he might have stayed but for the capsizing of a canoe near the mouth of the Annapolis River in May 1650. D'Aulnay's valet was rescued but d'Aulnay died from exposure. (Legend says he was towed ashore with his head underwater by an Indian to whom he had administered a beating three days earlier.)

With d'Aulnay's death, La Tour's dream was revived. La Tour went to France and was back within a year, a poor man but governor of Acadia. Now he was officially innocent, d'Aulnay guilty, in their epic feud. La Tour entered Port Royal in triumph and, at 60 years of age, married d'Aulnay's widow, the mother of eight children.

When a d'Aulnay creditor pressed for payment, the impoverished couple moved to Fort Sainte-Marie—only to be attacked by New Englanders in 1654. In three days in July, Robert Sedgwick, with 170 men and four ships, took Fort Sainte-Marie and Port Royal.

La Tour went to England, a prisoner, but in 1656 he was back, with English partners, as a fur trader. Eventually he retired to Baccaro Point with his wife and the five children she bore him.

The English now ruled Acadia.

There were two Acadias, historian J. B. Brebner once wrote: the Acadia of the power struggles and the Acadia where people lived and wanted only to be left alone. In 1654 there were some 250 such persons, chiefly around Port Royal.

Marie La Tour pleads with Charles d'Aulnay—in vain—for the lives of her garrison after surrendering Fort Sainte-Marie (at present-day Saint John, N.B.) in April 1645. D'Aulnay ordered every man hanged. Now he ruled Acadia.

Most of these persons had been recruits of d'Aulnay or La Tour, from western France. The English were not much interested in Acadia and brought no settlers there. In 1667 England ceded the area back to France.

And then the French expanded to the Minas Basin, across the fertile marshlands of the Chignecto Isthmus into what is now southeastern New Brunswick. They established communities such as Grand Pré, Piziquid (Windsor, N.S.), Cobequid (Truro, N.S.) and Beaubassin (at the present-day New Brunswick–Nova Scotia border).

The colonists were supposed to be governed from Paris and Quebec. But Paris largely ignored them, and Quebec was fighting for survival against the Iroquois. And so the people became independent in outlook and indifferent to authority. "They live like true republicans," one official reported, "not acknowledging royal or judicial authority." They became, in the words of historian Naomi Griffiths, "a gloriously awkward compendium of exceptions to everybody's rules." In this waif among colonies, they became a new people—Acadians.

A Thousand Misfortunes for Nicolas Denys

In the winter of 1668-69 fire destroyed Nicolas Denys's trading post at Saint-Pierre (St. Peters, N.S.).

Misfortune had dogged La Grande Barbe (for his full beard) since his arrival at La Hève (La Have, N.S.) in 1632. There in 1634 the French-born Denys *(right)* established Canada's first lumber business. A year later his right to export timber was revoked. He built fishing and trading posts at various places in Acadia, but still success eluded him. In 1653 Emmanuel Le Borgne—a merchant claiming Denys's land at Saint-Pierre and Nipisiguit (Bathurst, N.B.)—threw Denys into prison.

The fire was the final blow. Now 70, Denys took up the pen, and made his mark as an author. His *Description géographique et historique des costes de l'Amérique septentrionale,* published in 1672, is an entertaining account of 17th-century Acadia.

Denys is commemorated by cairns at Bathurst and St. Peters (where earth mounds are the remains of the trading post). Its destruction, he recorded, was but one of a thousand misfortunes. Nonetheless, wrote Nicolas Denys, "I believe that I have not altogether lost my time."

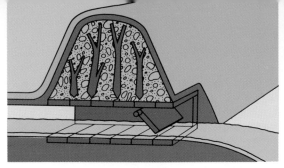

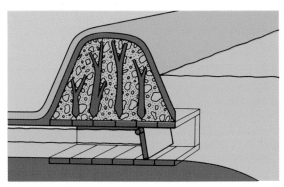

Acadians reclaimed Annapolis Basin marshes with 12-foot-wide dikes in which they built aboiteaux *(wooden boxes) with clappers hinged to seaward. Sea water could not enter; eventually, after many a low tide, the marsh was drained.*

Old French dikes such as this one near Wolfville, N.S., held back Bay of Fundy tides along the Annapolis Basin shore. Acadians built the dikes of stones and logs packed with clay, and used them to rescue thousands of acres from the sea.

They lived in a land of plenty—of fruit, berries, wildfowl and game. Their cattle, sheep and pigs roamed unfenced. They grew grain, flax and vegetables, and found it all good. They made cloth of wool and linen—they loved scarlet cloth—and produced most of what they needed.

They married young and raised large families. They enjoyed homemade cider and spruce beer and were joyful and gregarious. They carried disputes—and there were many—all the way to Paris. They smuggled and traded with the New Englanders.

Some outsiders found the Acadians lazy; abundance freed them to enjoy life. Some found them obstinate; they had their own ways. Some found them poor and backward; they were satisfied with their lot. Some found them ignorant; few could read or write. Others admired their practical skills, their contentment and their hospitality.

Their tragedy was not how they lived but where. As New France and New England grew and collided, Acadia was caught in between.

The French along the St. Lawrence were tormented by the elusive Iroquois, allies of the English. They took revenge in *la petite guerre*—vicious guerrilla warfare against the frontier settlements of New England. The English colonists did not have to go as far as the St. Lawrence for vengeance. They struck at Acadia. For 20 years the Atlantic coast suffered a confusion of attacks on villages, trade depots and forts; pillaging, piracy and privateering.

When a new French-English war intensified hostilities in North America in 1689, Louis-Alexandre Des Friches de Meneval, the gouty governor of Acadia, pleaded for recall to France, preferring "three years in the Bastille rather than one single week" in ill-prepared Port Royal.

A supply ship did come, and an engineer razed the old fort and started to build a larger, bastioned *enceinte* (the earthworks of which are still to be seen). But the new fort had not been finished on the day in May 1690 when seven armed ships and 736 New Englanders under Sir William Phips dropped anchor in the basin. Meneval, who had only 70 soldiers, fired a gun to bring in the Acadians; three came. Meneval surrendered.

Phips's militiamen sacked houses, destroyed crops, burned the fort and slaughtered livestock. When he sailed home, after attacking Quebec (see p. 78), he took Meneval, two priests and most of the French soldiers.

Meneval asked Phips to guard his prized possessions, among them two dressing gowns of linen trimmed with lace, three new wigs and four nightcaps with lace fringes. He never saw most of them again. Acadia, however, was recovered easily. The New Englanders, without men or money to defend it, let it slip back into French hands.

It was 1696 before they tried another major reprisal. That August a force sailed north under Benjamin Church, a 57-year-old soldier and Indian-fighter, so devout that he saw himself as the avenging arm of God, so fat that in time a sergeant would have to help him over fallen trees. His men burned buildings at Beaubassin.

Yet another French-English war was raging when Church came back in 1704 with 14 transports, three warships and 700 men. He burned

Grand Pré, took Cobequid and Piziquid and again laid Beaubassin waste. Then he laid siege to Port Royal.

The fort had been repaired but was only a sodden, timbered earthwork. Yet the governor, Jacques François de Mombeton de Brouillan, with only 200-odd soldiers, refused to surrender. Church sailed away believing "ourselves inferior to the strength of the enemy."

When Brouillan died, Daniel d'Auger de Subercase took over Port Royal in 1706. He found the fort decaying again, its inhabitants feuding, supplies and funds so short that he secretly bought clothing for his officers in Boston. He repaired the fort, built a frigate and appealed for help. Sixty men arrived from Quebec in June 1707, one day before John March, a Massachusetts militia colonel with 20 ships and 1,600 men, anchored in the basin.

When the New Englanders landed, Subercase led sally after sally against them. The New Englanders grew discouraged, burned houses, killed livestock and in July withdrew.

An angry New England sent them back in August but Subercase, now joined by Pierre Morpain, a young Caribbean privateer, beat them off again. They went skulking home to Boston where they were taunted as "wooden swords."

Port Royal rejoiced but its situation was desperate. No supplies had arrived from France. The king threatened to abandon Acadia "if it continues to be such a burden." Subercase sold his furniture and silver to pay his men and repair the fort. He gave his sheets and shirts to the sick. The governor found his officers dishonest, negligent, even mentally unstable. He said he had "as much need of a madhouse as of barracks," and feared the *"mauvais esprit* of this country" would drive *him* crazy.

Les Bostonnais still enriched themselves by trading in Acadia. "Nobody," groaned Subercase, "could suffer more than I do at seeing the English so coolly carry on their trade under our very noses." He took prizes at sea, but raids from Port Royal—this "nest of spoilers"—whipped the New Englanders into a fury. They had long spurned military aid from condescending Englishmen but now they were resolved to drive the French from North America and for this they needed help.

Six English warships and 500 marines were in the 36-ship, 2,000-man force that entered Port Royal's basin on Oct. 5, 1710, under the command of the British Gen. Francis Nicholson.

Subercase had fewer than 300 men, their morale so low that he dared not send them out on sorties because he knew none would come back. The English attacked Port Royal from two sides, dug trenches, mounted batteries and laid siege to the ramshackle fort until they were within 100

Scurvy Chaser

Spruce beer was both beverage and medicine in New France in the 17th and 18th centuries. It contained vitamin C to combat scurvy.

Buds, twigs and branches of spruce were boiled in water. Bark was removed after peeling from the branches; then to the water was added molasses, honey or maple syrup. The mixture was boiled until the syrup dissolved, then cooled, and yeast was added. In less than a week it was ready to drink. Beer was also made from fir, pine and hemlock—and probably from white cedar, which Jacques Cartier simmered in 1536 to treat his men for scurvy (see p. 17).

Newfoundlanders combined spruce beer with rum and molasses to make a powerful drink called callibogus.

Henry Wadsworth Longfellow's stirring poem Evangeline, *about the dispersal of the Acadians, inspired this painting of Evangeline's betrothal to Gabriel. With them (right) is a notary. The dispersal (see p.100) and the fictional Evangeline—based on a real person—are commemorated at Grand Pré in Nova Scotia.*

A powder magazine set into the southwest bastion of Fort Anne survives from the days when this was French-held Port Royal. It was built in 1708 using limestone brought as ballast from Caen, France.

yards of its walls. For seven days Subercase held them off with six guns and two mortars. Finally the Acadians in the fort pleaded to surrender, 55 men deserted and a council of officers agreed capitulation was inevitable.

The French soldiers marched out with drums beating, colors flying, weapons on their shoulders, but so famished, so tattered, mostly so young, that even the victors watched in sadness.

It was the end of French rule in Port Royal, in exhausted Acadia. The fort was renamed Fort Anne after the queen of England, and the town became Annapolis Royal. The French soldiers and officials departed for France. This most

fought over part of Canada would yet hold out against French and Indian attacks and two sieges. But after one last pirate raid in 1781 peace came to Annapolis Royal for good.

Meanwhile, for some 1,700 Acadians, the two Acadias had been reduced to one, and under the 1713 Treaty of Utrecht they faced hard alternatives: an oath of allegiance to the English Crown or exile. The French urged them to settle anew in Canada (Quebec) or on Cape Breton Island, which France had managed to keep.

But the land had worked its loyalties too deeply. Most Acadians stayed where they were. They would pay dearly for that decision.

New Brunswick, the Colony Holland Never Had

Jurriaen Aernoutsz, a Dutch privateer, claimed parts of present-day New Brunswick as New Holland in 1674.

Holland and France were at war. The Dutch governor of Curaçao in the West Indies commissioned Aernoutsz, with his frigate *The Flying Horse* and 50 privateers, to sail north from Curaçao and harass the French in the North Atlantic. In New York a Massachusetts adventurer named John Rhoades persuaded Aernoutsz that the Dutchman could easily oust the French from western Acadia. Rhoades signed on as Aernoutsz's pilot.

They first swooped on French-held Fort Pentagouet (Castine, Maine) and captured the garrison. Then they looted French posts up the coast,

scattering settlers into the woods. They sailed up the Saint John River and seized Fort Jemseg. Wherever they stopped Aernoutsz left a bottle containing a declaration that the territory belonged to the Dutch Crown.

They sold their booty in Boston; their prisoners were held for ransom. Aernoutsz returned to Curaçao and Rhoades tried to administer "New Holland" from Boston, but men he had left in Acadia skirmished with New England traders and he was tried for piracy and banished from Massachusetts. The French returned to their settlements.

For almost 100 years the Dutch protested to Britain that the people of Boston had deprived them of their "colony."

Heritage Sites

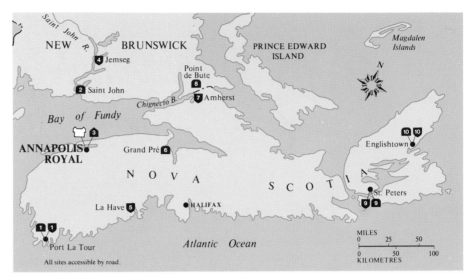

ANNAPOLIS ROYAL, N.S. Earth ramparts built about 1690, when this most fought over place in Canada was French-held Port Royal, are preserved in 31-acre Fort Anne National Historic Park. A powder magazine dating from 1708 (the oldest building in Canada outside Quebec) has a door reflecting a violent history that includes some 15 sieges and numerous raids: the top hinge is French, the other English. Port Royal was moved here in the 1630s from its original location across the Annapolis Basin. In 1710 the English renamed the town and fort Annapolis Royal and Fort Anne. A reconstructed officers' quarters (1797) displays 18th-century pistols, muskets and furniture.

Also in Annapolis Royal (3) The Delancey-Barclay-Banks House, a two-storey clapboard structure, is thought to be the town's oldest dwelling. Its foundations date from about 1709.

Other sites

Amherst, N.S. (7) The Acadian settlement of Beaubassin, laid waste by New Englanders under Benjamin Church in 1696 and 1704 and finally destroyed by fire in 1750, was near here on the Chignecto Isthmus. A plaque on the Government Information Bureau at Fort Lawrence, four miles northwest of Amherst, records the history of Beaubassin.

Bathurst, N.B. (not shown) A cairn honors Nicolas Denys, who in 1652 established a fishing and trading post here when it was called Nipisiguit.

Englishtown, N.S. (10) Earthworks here date from 1713, when the French fortified the settlement of Sainte-Anne and renamed it Port Dauphin. Sainte-Anne, founded in 1629, was Cape Breton Island's first French colony. A cairn marks its site.

Grand Pré, N.S. (6) This small community was a major Acadian settlement in the 1600s and 1700s. Remains from that period, including traces of dikes, are in 14-acre Grand Pré National Historic Park.

Jemseg, N.B. (4) Fort Jemseg (1659), a French-held post on the Saint John River, was captured by the Dutch in 1674. A cut-stone monument locates the site.

La Have, N.S. (5) A cairn marks the site of Fort Sainte-Marie-de-Grâce where Charles de Menou d'Aulnay and Nicolas Denys helped establish a colony in 1632.

Point de Bute, N.B. (8) Two miles north are the remains of La Coupe Drydock, apparently built by the French in the late 1600s or early 1700s to repair ships. Earth dikes up to 20 feet high enclose an area of two-thirds of an acre straddling the La Coupe River.

Port La Tour, N.S. (1) A cairn commemorates Fort Saint-Louis, which Charles La Tour built about 1627 some three miles south of here at Baccaro Point (where earthworks are visible). Traces of Fort Temple, the first English stronghold on the coast of Acadia (1658), are seen at Barrington Bay, northwest of Port La Tour.

Saint John, N.B. (2) A low mound on the east side of the harbor (near Main Street) is the site of Fort Sainte-Marie, built in 1631 by Charles La Tour.

St. Peters, N.S. (9) Earth mounds are the remains of Nicolas Denys's port and trading post, destroyed by fire in the winter of 1668-69. The Nicolas Denys Museum commemorates the trader. A plaque records the settlement's early history.

This museum is on the site of the trading post built by Nicolas Denys at St. Peters, N.S., in 1650, and in the same architectural style.

91

'Impregnable' Louisbourg, Citadel of Shattered Dreams

A three-foot fleur-de-lis, 80 feet above the ground, crowns the tower of the King's Bastion Barracks at Louisbourg. The clock's single hand tells the hour; the bell rings the hours and half-hours.

The fortress of Louisbourg frowned into the mists and fogs and the Atlantic storms, a mighty symbol of a deadly struggle between enemy states 3,000 miles away. This massive fortification in wild Cape Breton was on the fringe of a vast land that still, in the middle of the 18th century, was nearly empty of settlers. Louisbourg had consumed time, energy, materials and armaments in huge amounts. It was ringed with 10-foot-thick stone walls 30 feet high and fanged with 148 cannon. It cost so much that Louis XV said he expected he would one day see the towers of Louisbourg rising over the Paris horizon.

In the Treaty of Utrecht in 1713, France had yielded Hudson Bay, Newfoundland and much of Acadia (most of today's Maritime Provinces and part of Maine) to England. The French were left with a vast area to the west defended by a string of forts and settlements along the St. Lawrence and the Great Lakes and down the Mississippi, and with Ile Royale, present-day Cape Breton Island. They built Louisbourg to guard the Atlantic approach to New France.

Construction started in 1720. Louisbourg was to be both fortress and commercial centre. It had a harbor two miles long and half a mile wide, protected by an entrance only 400 yards wide. The star-shaped stronghold covered 100 acres, took decades to construct and cost the equivalent of $200 million.

Developments in gunnery had made such forts obsolete. Engineers counted on the natural advantages of the remote location to offset this weakness. On an island dominating the harbor entrance they put a battery with 30 guns. On the northeast side of the harbor they erected another (the Grand Battery) with twenty-eight 42-pounders and many smaller guns. There were defences also at Gabarus Bay, two miles south. It was hoped that marshes would prevent cannon from approaching Louisbourg's walls.

The fortress, on a narrow headland, was built

Fortress Louisbourg on Cape Breton Island was an imposing French town with a governor's palace, barracks, houses, a hospital, arsenals and warehouses. Along the shore were earthworks, ponds and palisades, 200 guns and 20 mortars. A $20 million re-creation of one-fifth of the garrison area and enclosed town was undertaken in 1961, to be completed in 1980.

"to stand forever." Warships, and friendly Mic-macs who were paid a bounty for English scalps, increased its strength.

There were problems: hillocks overlooked the site; the humid weather prevented mortar from hardening; contractors cheated; materials and manpower had to be brought from France. There was no good farming land for miles.

Only time could tell whether Louisbourg was impregnable. There was elegance in the wigs and ruffles of high officials and officers, and the jewels and powders of their women; but there was corruption everywhere. French wines, fine cloth, even building materials, were sold amid Louis-bourg's shortages at lavish profits. Two dozen inns and taverns flourished for fewer than 1,200 souls and gambling was rampant. There was one brothel for the well-to-do, another for lesser peo-ple. There was venereal disease, which the hospi-tal's Brothers of Charity refused to treat. There was monotony and boredom and, over all, the stink of drying cod.

Women in 18th-century dress gossip along a street of typical Louis-bourg reconstructions (inns, shops and houses). In the background is Porte Frédéric, the main access from the harbor. The pine arch is roofed with slate.

This well inside the King's Bastion at Louisbourg was rebuilt over the original shaft. The wooden bucket was among two mil-lion artifacts recovered in wells, trash pits and basement exca-vations at the site.

A Tub of Whale Oil, Wicks Floating on Cork

At Fortress Louisbourg stood Canada's first lighthouse, a 70-foot, circular stone tower at the harbor entrance. Its light, from an iron tub of whale oil in which wicks floated on cork, shone through a lantern with 400 panes of glass and could be seen 18 miles at sea.

The lighthouse was built by order of Louis XV to aid shipping and to help make Louisbourg a better naval and military base. It was financed by shipping tolls and went into operation April 1, 1734. It was gutted two years later in a fire so hot it melted the iron tub.

A new tower 68 feet high was completed in July 1738. Wicks were placed far apart to reduce heat, and the fuel reservoir was set in water. English gunners destroyed this structure in 1758.

The next year the British built what now is Canada's oldest lighthouse (paid for by liquor taxes and a lottery), on Sambro Island outside Halifax Harbor. Ship captains complained they often had to fire at the 62-foot stone tower before the lamp was lit and that smoke from its whale oil clouded the lantern. Today the tower has been heightened to 80 feet and illumination is from a 500-watt incandescent light shining through a lens.

On the ruins of the original Louisbourg lighthouse is a concrete lighthouse (right) erected in 1923. Embedded in it is a lead plaque salvaged from the first one.

The common soldiers were treated abominably. Poorly paid and fed, they lived in unheated quarters so verminous that in summer they slept on the ramparts. They supplemented their pittance by hiring out as laborers. Their officers ran supply canteens and took rake-offs from the brothels. The soldiers mutinied in 1744.

Later that year Louisbourg sent 22 officers and 335 soldiers 50 miles southwest to Canso, where they destroyed a small English fort and fishermen's shacks. The force was barely back with its prisoners when mutiny broke out again because the governor authorized the officers to sell Canso codfish at exorbitant prices to the troops who had seized it.

The men looted shops, threatened their officers and at bayonet point forced Intendant François Bigot (see p. 106) to give them their back pay. Officials listened to their complaints, promised improvements, and did nothing.

On April 29, 1745, there was a ball at the splendid palace of Governor Louis Dupont, Sieur du Chambon. The élite danced all night while 560 regular soldiers, 1,400 militiamen and 2,000 civilians slept. Louisbourg awakened at dawn to the sound of guns. After 25 years it faced its first attack.

The 4,000 New Englanders had sailed in a ramshackle fleet of armed trading ships and fishing vessels. They were mostly untrained, among them Harvard students who enlisted for a bumper of rum, and the 70-year-old Puritan preacher Sam Moody with his hatchet to smash Roman Catholic idols. They had brought cannon balls too big for their own 34 guns, confident they would capture the larger French artillery.

They were led by William Pepperell, politician and militia commander from Boston.

The English had been joined at Canso by Sir Peter Warren of the Royal Navy with his flagship, two other warships and some armed auxiliaries. On April 30 they were off Louisbourg.

While Warren set up a blockade, men in whaleboats braved surf, rocks, ice and French fire to secure a beachhead on Gabarus Bay. By nightfall some 2,000 men were ashore and dragging cannon through the mud to one of the hillocks from which they could fire into the fortress.

Du Chambon withdrew his men into the fort and batteries, sank ships to block the harbor—and then made a mistake. He abandoned the damaged Grand Battery without demolishing its cannon. Two days later, New Englanders were using them to fire the outsize cannon balls they

Tourists sometimes complain about the poor posture and scruffy attire of the French soldiers in reconstructed Louisbourg. But literature distributed at the fortress explains that this is genuine. Such convincing portrayals of the ill-paid, undisciplined and mistreated 18th-century garrison are hard work.

The governor entertained in viceregal splendor in this high-ceilinged, richly furnished Louisbourg dining room.

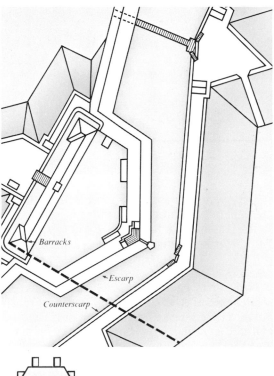

had brought. Their first shot killed 14 inside the walls of Louisbourg. Three hundred New Englanders hauled some of the captured cannon two miles through the marshes, then opened fire from another hillock overlooking the fort.

The French soldiers shouted insults, cried out that women alone could hold Louisbourg against such men. They stood on the walls and raised wine glasses in mock toasts, then ducked.

Inexperience led the New Englanders to overload their guns, and they often paid for it in explosions that maimed and killed. Sickness cut their strength by half. Powder ran short. Barefoot and in rags, they tired of the dampness, the cold, the sparse diet. As the siege went on, their hell-for-leather spirit soured. But their luck held.

The Marquis de la Maisonfort showed up in

These were Louisbourg's formidable defences. Behind the massive parapet, screened from enemy fire, were the broad terreplein (for cannon) and banquettes (firing steps) for individual marksmen. Across the main ditch (deeper at the escarp than at the counterscarp) were the outer defences—a covered way along which troops could move, more banquettes, another parapet and the sloping glacis.

64-gun *Vigilant,* only to be fooled into chasing a smaller frigate straight into Warren's fleet. He lost not only his ship but 1,000 barrels of powder, 20 cannon and four month's supplies for Louisbourg.

Then the decisive piece of good fortune for the New Englanders: someone looked down into the water below a headland and saw 10 cannon, half-buried in the sand. Years earlier they had

fallen off a warship. Within hours, they were out of the water and firing at the island battery. On June 15, when a shell struck its powder magazine, it surrendered.

The fortress was surrounded by fire. Food and powder were running short. Nearly every building had been wrecked or damaged. Louisbourg's walls were badly battered, its strongpoints out of action.

This 1731 view of Louisbourg by Etienne Verrier and his son, now in the Bibliothèque nationale in Paris, includes Canada's first lighthouse (far left) three years before it was erected. The Verriers had worked on plans for the beacon.

The Great Fleet That Fired Not a Single Shot

Sept. 27, 1746. At Chebucto (present-day Halifax) lay a once proud French fleet. The Duc d'Anville *(right),* its 37-year-old commander, was dead. So were 1,135 French soldiers.

The fleet—7,000 men and 800 guns in 71 ships—had been assembled at Brest to aid the Scots' Charles Edward Stuart. But with Prince Charlie's defeat at Culloden, d'Anville, newly appointed lieutenant-general of the navy, sailed for Chebucto. There he would join a French squadron from the West Indies, then recapture Louisbourg from the English and seize Annapolis Royal. With d'Anville went the Marquis de la Jonquière, bound for Quebec as governor.

Storms battered the fleet and the voyage stretched to 100 days. Scurvy, typhus and small-

pox raged. One ship sank; another caught fire; some ships turned back; about half the fleet limped on. D'Anville anchored at present-day Bedford Basin on Sept. 10 to find that the West Indies squadron had sailed for home. The rest of his fleet arrived Sept. 27—and that day d'Anville died. Apoplexy, said his officers. Poison, whispered the men. Surgeons bored into his skull but learned nothing of the cause of death.

On Oct. 13 five ships sailed for France with the sick. Men well enough to stand went in the remaining ships to attack Annapolis Royal—and found English warships waiting for them. La Jonquière returned home with what remained of the great fleet. Some 2,400 men had died, none in action. The fleet had fired not one shot.

97

Du Chambon asked for terms. He accepted conditions that promised the French they would "have their personal estates secur'd to them." Bigot left with the royal treasury of some four million livres among his "personal possessions."

England and New England celebrated with ringing bells and booming cannon. Pepperell was knighted, Warren promoted. He ordered that Louisbourg's French flags be kept flying and ship after ship sailed into his trap.

The invaders had won, in seven weeks, "the greatest Conquest, that Ever was Gain'd by New England."

Three years later, without consulting the colonists, the British ceded rebuilt Louisbourg and all of Cape Breton back to France. New England's pride in its victory turned to bitter disappointment in the mother country that had given the hard-won victory away. Then Britain began to build a strongpoint of her own to counter what she had restored to France. In a great natural harbor on Nova Scotia's Atlantic coast she founded Halifax.

Lt.Col. the Hon. Edward Cornwallis, a 36-year-old bachelor, came to the inlet of Chebucto. He landed June 21, 1749, and within a week had greeted 13 ships bearing 2,576 passengers, building supplies, seeds, salt beef and pork, cannon, powder, a fire engine, hospital equipment and a midwife.

Cornwallis wrote that "the number of industrious active men proper to undertake and carry

The Halifax *Gazette,* a Paper to Remember

Canada's first newspaper, the single-sheet Halifax *Gazette*, was about 6½ by 8 inches, its editor an impecunious printer from Boston. John Bushell's first issue, on March 23, 1752—three years after the founding of Halifax—contained barely 100 words of local news (two deaths; beef at fivepence and sixpence a pound), world news picked up from English papers, and advertisements such as: "Reading school for children kept, and gold and silver lace cleaned; also mournings stiffened, by Elizabeth Render, near Rev. Mr. Tutty's new house on Barrington Street."

In Boston in 1734, Bushell had formed a partnership with Bartholomew Green, son of the printer of North America's first newspaper, the Boston *News Letter*. Green had moved to Halifax in 1751 and, near present-day Grafton and Duke streets, set up Canada's first printing shop. Green died within months and Bushell came from Boston, took over the shop and launched the *Gazette*. He and his paper were frequently in debt but the *Gazette* lasted until 1843. It survives as the Nova Scotia government's *Royal Gazette*.

Nova Scotia Governor Edward Cornwallis (above) directed the founding of Halifax in 1749—portrayed in this watercolor by C. W. Jefferys. Most of Cornwallis's settlers were impoverished Londoners attracted by a year's free rations, but he put his best men in charge of work gangs, cut down the forest and built a fortified town as a counter to the French Louisbourg.

on a new settlement is very small. Of soldiers there are only 100, of tradesmen, sailors and others able and willing to work, not above 200." He built his town at the foot of a hill, two miles from the open sea. Around a 12-street site Cornwallis built a palisade and a ring of forts and blockhouses. One fort near the hilltop was a 200-foot-square stockade with two-storey bastions at each corner and a barracks for 100 men.

By the first snow some 300 houses had been built, with a stone mansion for one rich officer and a simple wooden house for Cornwallis. People were still living aboard ship or in tents. "To see the vast Flakes of Snow," said an inhabitant, "lying about the Tents of those who have been accustomed to warm fires about Newcastle and London, was enough to move the Heart of Stone." Typhus claimed nearly 1,000 lives.

More immigrants arrived: first New Englanders, then Protestants from the Rhineland and France. By September 1750 services were being held in St. Paul's, the first Protestant church in what is now Canada. Governor Cornwallis was presiding over the council which ruled Nova Scotia. Annapolis Royal (see p. 90) had been supplanted. But Halifax had become the capital of a British colony with a unique problem: the French-speaking inhabitants outnumbered the English.

Cornwallis's orders were to populate the colony with British subjects and to command loyalty and seek a conversion to Protestantism from the Acadians. Within three months they must take an oath of allegiance to His Britannic Majesty. Cornwallis, the soldier, expected his orders to be obeyed. He misjudged the Acadians' obstinate sense of place and history, their will to survive between two forces far more powerful than they. The Acadians, in turn, expected to state their case and be heard. They misjudged the new régime.

For more than a century they had thrived, independent of either French or British authority. From their original few hundred they had multiplied almost fortyfold in a network of settlements around the Bay of Fundy. When Acadia fell to the English in 1710, most of them had refused to move to French territories.

For four decades they had been commanded to take the oath and had always given the same answer: they would take an oath only if it were guaranteed that they would never have to take arms against the French or their Indian allies. Cornwallis faced this situation: the Acadians held the best lands, and their Indian friends were happy to scalp any other settlers, at a good price from Louisbourg.

New France, too, claimed Acadian land and allegiance. Priests were encouraged to work in Acadia as agents. "We are here," two told the English at Annapolis Royal, "on the business of France." The most fanatical of all, Abbé Jean-Louis Le Loutre, stirred Acadians and Indians to hatred of the British and bullied the farmers to abandon their land and move to Acadian settlements behind French lines, in present-day New

Tuque, blanket coat, leggings (and an Indian garter): a French soldier of the 1750s, in winter campaign dress. This fusilier of the Compagnies Franches— among the regular troops at Louisbourg—carries iron ice-creepers to tie to his moccasins when walking on ice. His cartridge box is at his waist, as is his colorful ceinture fléchée. In hand-to-hand combat he will use not a sword or bayonet but his hatchet.

A 200-Mile March, Then Winter Victory at Grand Pré

One January day in 1747 an Acadian named Arsenault snowshoed into Beaubassin (at the present-day New Brunswick–Nova Scotia border) with news that rocked the French Canadians wintering there. New Englanders had seized Grand Pré, 200 miles away, and would surely attack Beaubassin in the spring. Two weeks later 240 Canadians and 60 Indians set out to retrace Arsenault's path. *They* would attack *now*, striking a surprise blow for France in the campaign to recapture Louisbourg.

The leader was Nicolas Coulon de Villiers, a grandson of Madeleine de Verchères (see p. 80). His men dragged sleds through a white tangle of trees, suffered the icy sting of the swirling *poudrerie*, gnawed at scant rations, and slept where they could—often in snowdrifts. On Feb. 11, after three weeks travelling, they were in Gaspéreau and ready to make war. The New Englanders were only a mile away.

Their commander was Col. Arthur Noble, a Massachusetts veteran of the Louisbourg cam-paign of 1745. His 500 men were billeted in 24 Acadian houses along a 1½-mile-long ridge over-looking the great meadow that gave Grand Pré its name.

Coulon's force attacked 10 houses at 3 a.m. The first was taken in 10 minutes, although Coulon was gravely wounded. Lieut. Daniel-Marie Liénard de Beaujeu wrote: "All our people did marvels there: 21 corpses and three prisoners were proof of the detachment's courage." Noble leaped from bed, was offered quarter, bellowed "No surrender!" and was killed.

In daylight the New England survivors surrendered and pledged not to bear arms in the region for six months. But before marching away they invited the French officers to dine. The hosts had rum, sugar, lemons and nutmeg and concocted a punch that made the ration pork and biscuits go down very well indeed. The Battle of Grand Pré ended with a party at which, Beaujeu recorded, the Canadians received "many compliments on our polite manners and our skill in making war."

The Clerk Who Sold Beauséjour's Secrets

In 1753, while Acadia enjoyed a shaky peace, there was a kind of no-man's-land eating house at present-day Point de Bute, N.B. Here French and English officers from Fort Beauséjour (Aulac, N.B.) and Fort Lawrence (near present-day Amherst, N.S.) mingled freely. Another patron was the chief clerk of the Fort Beauséjour storeroom, Thomas Pichon *(right)*, liar, lecher, braggart and poseur. It was probably at the restaurant that he met Capt. George Scott, commandant of Fort Lawrence. Soon he was selling Beauséjour's secrets to Scott.

Some he sent by unsuspecting Acadians who went to Fort Lawrence to barter for cheap English goods. Others he slipped to British officers to whom he gave French lessons.

When British and New England forces stormed Beauséjour in 1755, Pichon was inside urging its defenders to lay down their arms. When the fort surrendered, Pichon was among the prisoners taken to Halifax. He told other captives he was soon to be sent to Louisbourg and they entrusted to him letters and reports, some containing escape plans. All these the "prisoner" Pichon turned over to the English.

After this betrayal, Pichon sailed to England. He called himself Thomas Tyrell and collected a £200 annual pension for his treachery.

No Halifax building is older than St. Paul's Church and no structure in the great port city is more storied. The church dates from the founding of Halifax in 1749 (this engraving was done in London in 1764 from a 1761 drawing). Now in the heart of a downtown Halifax of high-rises and expressways, St. Paul's is a repository of Nova Scotia history, from the days of Charles Inglis, first Anglican bishop of the province, to the world wars and the present.

Brunswick. If they refused they faced reprisals from the Indians, as did any who took the British oath of allegiance. In 1750 Le Loutre's Indians levelled Beaubassin (at the present-day New Brunswick–Nova Scotia border).

French troops were sent to the mouth of the Saint John River and to the Chignecto Isthmus, which they claimed was the limit of the territory ceded to the British in 1713. They built a fort at Beauséjour and another across the isthmus. Then English forts were built to face them. The Acadians were once again caught between the enemy forces from Europe.

When the ailing Cornwallis left in 1752, his ears were ringing with British complaints: the Acadians were taking their produce to Louisbourg not Halifax; British settlers would not come to a colony where they faced attack from Indians and the best land was in alien hands. Some Acadians had helped French troops in the past and would do so again; French strength was growing in Louisbourg, creating a "new Acadia" to the north. For two more years the rivals confronted each other in an impasse both knew could be broken only by force. It came in 1754. By then, Lt.Col. Charles Lawrence, a soldier to the core, was lieutenant-governor of Nova Scotia. He decided to drive the French from Chignecto.

In June 1755 Lt.Col. Robert Monckton led 2,000 New Englanders and 250 British regulars in an attack on Fort Beauséjour, commanded by Louis Dupont du Chambon, Sieur de Vergor, son of the man who had surrendered Louisbourg 10 years before. Beauséjour fell in three days.

The second isthmus fort, Gaspéreau, fell without a shot. The 200 Acadians captured at Beauséjour rejoiced over Monckton's promise of a pardon. But to Lawrence "pardon" merely meant they wouldn't be hanged for treason. He told Acadian delegates from Minas they must take the oath. When they refused, they were confined. Then the ultimatum: Acadians who refused the oath would be deported. When, on July 28, more Acadian delegates refused, Lawrence sent out the orders that haunt Canadian history.

At Chignecto, at Grand Pré, at Annapolis Royal and elsewhere, with bayonets glinting in the hot summer sun, British troops herded bewildered, incredulous Acadians aboard ships to be taken south and scattered through the English colonies. Families were broken up; their communities died in flames.

To Col. John Winslow, in charge at Grand Pré, the deportations were "very disagreeable." To Charles Lawrence, they were a military necessity. He was promoted governor.

Early in 1756 a writer reported that "one of the most beautiful countries in the world is now ravaged and empty." But not quite empty.

The expulsions, which continued sporadically

until 1762, uprooted roughly 8,000 of 10,000 persons. Many escaped to join those who were left in the forests with the Indians. Their leader was Charles Deschamps, Sieur de Boishébert. With 600 men he kept up guerrilla warfare until the British dared not stir from their forts.

Then, in May 1758, Halifax reeled with the arrival of 27,000 British soldiers and sailors. When war had officially come in 1756, Prime Minister William Pitt had promised George II an empire no emperor had ever known. Louisbourg must be won, and then the Quebec which it guarded.

Augustin de Boschenry de Drucour, governor of Louisbourg, knew his fort's weaknesses. As the British governor had said in 1748: "the General design of the Fortifications is Exceedingly Bad and the Workmanship worse Executed and so Disadvantageously Situted that almost every rising Ground or little Eminence Commands one part or other, that either a Vast Sum of money must be laid out to Fortifye it properly or it will never answer the Charge or Trouble."

Even so, Louisbourg was stronger than ever. Drucour had 3,000 French regular soldiers, as

Bewildered Acadians who have refused to swear allegiance to England wait to be led aboard ships that will take them into exile. La Dispersion des Acadiens, *an oil painting by Henri Beau, is in the Université de Moncton collection.*

well as militiamen; 2½ miles of ramparts thronged with 219 cannon and 17 mortars; 13 warships with 3,000 sailors and 544 guns. The Grand Battery had been destroyed but the crucial island battery and Gabarus Bay were well defended. There were supplies for a year for the forces and 4,000 civilians.

On June 2 the morning mists parted to reveal

Fort Beauséjour was the first French fort to fall in the British drive that ended with the expulsion of the Acadians in 1755. Above: some of the restored stonework in the national historic park at Aulac, N.B. Beauséjour was renamed Fort Cumberland and the British strengthened it with entrenchments that can still be traced. Cumberland was unsuccessfully attacked in 1776 by settlers sympathetic to the colonists' revolt in the United States.

the first of an enemy armada. A day later some 160 ships were there with 1,842 guns. The soldiers had artillery of every kind.

The English tried for nearly a week to get men ashore through the surf in Gabarus Bay, until an impetuous, 31-year-old brigadier named James Wolfe saw a landing place in an empty cove, free of the devastating French fire, and pointed his cane to divert his troops from their own front to exploit it. Then he led a bayonet charge. Within four hours the French troops were retreating.

The attack was dogged, relentless. It was much more professional than the 1745 siege, although some of the British guns were positioned by several hundred "laundresses"—even an invasion force had its camp followers. The British hammered the French warships in the harbor, and found that only Jean Vauquelin's 36-gun frigate *Aréthuse* fought back. Vauquelin drew the fire as long as possible and then stole through the enemy blockade and out to sea. The other French captains asked leave to fight at sea or run for France. Drucour forbade them to do either.

There was chivalry at Louisbourg. When the intelligent, gracious Madame Drucour and several other women were captured aboard a French vessel they were returned to the fortress. Then the British sent a basket of pineapples as a present for her. A lady in the British lines reported a liaison with a French officer and was escorted into the fort with a gift of lettuce. The French sent out a tub of butter.

Each day Madame Drucour, *La Bombardière*, went to the ramparts to fire three guns. On July 8 her gallant husband sent out troops in the dark to charge British lines with bayonets. It was all useless. The British had encircled the fortress. From as close as 200 yards, they knocked out one bulwark after another. Buildings crumbled. "Not a house but has felt the force of their cannonade," recorded one survivor.

The end came July 26. The British had again taken the strongest fort in America in seven weeks, with a loss of only 200 lives. Drucour had always known that the best he could do was to prolong the siege, to give Quebec time. He surrendered only when one quarter of his men were killed, when his few remaining cannon seemed "more like the minute guns at a funeral than a defence."

While the impatient Wolfe complained of wasting time "gathering strawberries," the British were forced to content themselves with ousting Acadians from Prince Edward Island, the Saint John Valley and the forests to the north, and sending Wolfe on forays into the Gaspé. An attack on Quebec had to wait another day, another year. But it would come.

Somebody's big sister is being teased—or is there really a mouse or a bee or a snake in the grass at her feet? Youngsters are part of the staff that makes reconstructed Louisbourg come alive each summer. Local people make the meticulously accurate 18th-century clothing.

Heritage Sites

LOUISBOURG, N.S. The Fortress of Louisbourg, begun by the French in 1720 to save New France, was destroyed by the English in 1760. Now the world's biggest historical reconstruction and the focal point of 20-square-mile Fortress of Louisbourg National Historic Park, it includes some 50 buildings, the blackened shells of other structures (giving the impression of a city under siege) and extensive stone fortifications.

FORTRESS OF LOUISBOURG MUSEUM Plans and drawings of the original fort and accounts of the sieges of 1745 and 1758 are displayed. Other exhibits show how Louisbourg has been reconstructed.

HÔTEL DE LA MARINE Typical 18th-century meals are served in a waterfront tavern.

KENNINGTON COVE A cairn marks where Brigadier James Wolfe landed during the siege of 1758.

KING'S BASTION BARRACKS Once the New World's largest building, it contains the governor's 10-room suite, officers' quarters, soldiers' barracks, a chapel, a prison and an artillery school.

LOUISBOURG LIGHTHOUSE A lead plaque from Canada's first lighthouse (1734), stating that the beacon was constructed by order of Louis XV, is on a lighthouse built in 1923 on the ruins of the original.

Other sites

Amherst, N.S. (8) A cairn four miles northwest, on the Nova Scotia-New Brunswick border, identifies the site of Fort Lawrence. Built by the British in 1750-52 to counter Fort Beauséjour across the Chignecto Isthmus, it was abandoned after they captured Beauséjour in 1755. The Acadian settlement of Beaubassin was on the isthmus.

Aulac, N.B. (7) Walls, bastions and casemates of the stronghold built in 1750-55 by the French on their side of the Chignecto Isthmus have been restored in 500-acre

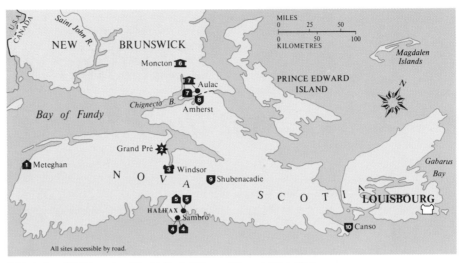

Fort Beauséjour National Historic Park. (The post was renamed Fort Cumberland after its capture by the British in 1755.) A museum displays 18th-century muskets and uniforms.

Canso, N.S. (10) A cairn describes the early history of this town, razed by soldiers from Louisbourg in 1744. English forces grouped here the following year before capturing Louisbourg.

Caraquet, N.B. (not shown) The Village Historique Acadien, portraying the life of Acadians who returned after the 1755 expulsion, has been created near here, using some 40 restored buildings from different parts of the province. Structures include a tavern, school, chapel, five farms, and five miles of restored dikes. Exhibits in the Musée Acadien in Caraquet include 18th-century furniture. An eight-day festival in August features folk songs and dances and a ritual blessing of fishing vessels.

Grand Pré, N.S. (2) A chapel in Grand Pré National Historic Park commemorates the church in which the 1755 expulsion notice was read to the Acadians. Outside is a bronze statue of Evangeline, the heroine of Longfellow's poem. A monument near the 14-acre park marks the site of the 1747 Battle of Grand Pré. An iron cross at nearby Horton Landing commemorates the embarkation of the Acadians.

Halifax (5) In Province House is the table at which Edward Cornwallis and his ad-

Like an echo from an 18th-century French provincial town, this is a typical happy clutter of roofs and chimneys in re-created Louisbourg. Houses are of wood or roughcast masonry; roofs are of bark, board, shingle or slate.

visers sat—in a ship in the harbor—as they planned Halifax in 1749; a plaque commemorates the establishment of Canada's first printing press, on which the country's first newspaper was printed in 1752. St. Paul's Church, built with timbers shipped from Boston in 1749, is Halifax's oldest building. In St. Paul's Cemetery are the graves of some of the city founders. A cairn beside Bedford Basin, in Rockingham, indicates where the Duc d'Anville's storm-battered expedition, sent from France to recover Acadia, anchored in 1746.

Meteghan, N.S. (1) La Vieille Maison, an Acadian house built in the 1760s, is a private museum containing 18th-century sea chests, butter churns and spinning wheels.

Moncton, N.B. (6) Among some 6,000 artifacts in the Acadian Museum at the Université de Moncton are a cornerstone from a church built at Beaubassin (see Amherst) in 1723 and a compass that belonged to a deported Acadian. Interiors of a barn, a schoolroom and a cobbler's shop have been re-created.

Ottawa (not shown) Weapons in the Canadian War Museum include a mortar and a brass cannon used at Louisbourg, and 18th-century muskets and swords.

Sambro, N.S. (4) Canada's oldest lighthouse, built in 1759 and still in use, is on nearby Sambro Island. Its history is outlined on a cairn in the village.

Shubenacadie, N.S. (9) An iron marker indicates where Abbé Le Loutre, who stirred Acadians and Indians against the British, had his headquarters in 1738.

Windsor, N.S. (3) A split-log blockhouse, the oldest in Canada, was built by the British in 1750 as part of Fort Edward.

Decision at Dawn on the Plains of Abraham

A century earlier a retired river pilot named Abraham Martin had pastured his cows on the heights outside the walls of Quebec. The land was still known as the Plains of Abraham as French and English armies faced each other there in an early morning drizzle on Sept. 13, 1759. Wolfe and Montcalm were reviewing their troops—about 3,250 English, 3,500 French.

Worried by the approach of cold weather, Gen. James Wolfe had scaled the cliffs at l'Anse au Foulon in a supreme effort to take Quebec before winter. His army, only two ranks deep, stretched for about half a mile, its right flank near the cliffs, its left under fire from Canadians and Indians concealed in woods to the north.

Opposite the English, on a small rise, were five French regiments flanked by Canadian militia. Astride a black charger the Marquis de Montcalm brandished his sword in exhortation.

"Are you ready, my boys?" Montcalm asked.

"Long live the general!" his men replied. "Long live the king!"

With drums rolling, the French went into battle—a battle that would seal New France's doom.

A British attack on Quebec had been almost inevitable since 1713 when the Treaty of Utrecht acknowledged Britain's mastery of the seas and gave her Hudson Bay, Newfoundland and most of Acadia. To complete her conquest of the New World, she had to defeat the French on Ile Royale (Cape Breton Island) and along the St. Lawrence and Mississippi valleys. English colonists, eager to spread inland from the Atlantic seaboard, contributed men and arms.

To guard the Gulf of St. Lawrence, France built the fortress of Louisbourg on Cape Breton Island (see p. 92). Wooden fortifications at Montreal and Quebec were strengthened with stone. Fort Chambly protected the Richelieu River valley south of Montreal. Old forts were restored and new ones built on the Great Lakes, on the Mississippi and on Lake Champlain.

Meantime, New France's economy flourished. Shipyards were built at Quebec, and tar factories and sawmills began to operate along the St. Lawrence. Canada's first heavy industry, Les Forges du Saint-Maurice near Trois-Rivières, encouraged and financed by Louis XV, was producing stoves, pots, ploughshares, tools and anchors by 1738. In 1734 *le Chemin du Roy* was completed, the first road between Montreal and Quebec. Tobacco was introduced. Production of wheat, hemp and flax tripled between 1721 and 1739. A surge of immigration and a high birthrate pushed New France's population to 74,000 in 1755, and settlement spread to the Lake Champlain region and down the Chaudière River valley toward present-day Maine.

Contemporary accounts describe a Quebec society whose elegance, pleasures and customs were those of France. But *les Canadiens* were distinguished from the French by a spirit of adventure and indiscipline moulded by the rigorous climate and open spaces of the new country.

The fur trade was still the main source of revenue. The trade, once the monopoly of a favored few, had been open to all colonists since 1717 and, with the Hudson Bay hunting ground lost to the English, new sources of pelts were needed. But there was stiff competition from English traders around the Great Lakes and along the

Cape Diamond, where the Citadel now stands above Quebec City, was guarded in 1759 by this armed storehouse known as the Cape Redoubt. Built by Governor Frontenac in 1693, the redoubt has walls which are seven feet thick at their bottom. It was incorporated into the fortifications when the Citadel was built by the British in 1820-32.

The Battle of the Plains of Abraham: a composite engraving in the Public Archives of Canada. An English advance party climbs up a dry streambed at l'Anse au Foulon and overpowers a guard, enabling troops to go up two abreast.

Bigot: Pompadour's Favorite and New France's Biggest Cheat

During the summer of 1759 besieged Quebec lived on a meagre bread ration, plus the meat of dogs and cats. But Intendant François Bigot and a score of cronies feasted, danced and gambled every night. As British troops scaled the cliffs to the Plains of Abraham on Sept. 13, the 56-year-old justice and finance minister of New France was playing cards at his château in present-day Charlesbourg-Est, north of Quebec.

Bigot used his position to steal on a massive scale from both Louis XV and the colonists. A warehouse in which he stored stolen goods was known as *la friponne* (the cheat).

He imported or requisitioned supplies in the name of the king, then sold them to colonists at many times their cost. He charged the king for rations for militiamen who had not been called to duty. He bribed army officers to sign for double the supplies they received, and charged the government 10 times their value. Colonists worked six *corvée* days a year, usually on roads, without pay; it was supposed to be for the king but it was often for Bigot.

The intendant kept accounts with forged vouchers. Paris did not question them for Bigot was a favorite of Madame de Pompadour, Louis's mistress.

It was rumored that she shared the proceeds of Bigot's fraud.

Bigot's own mistress was Angélique Péan, the wife of an army officer. He gave her monopolies on flour and vegetables, and let her husband buy and sell grain at prices decreed by Bigot.

When Quebec fell, Bigot made sure the surrender terms provided for a ship to take him and his loot to France. But he did not retire in splendor. Paris made him the scapegoat for the loss of New France; he was fined $2,500 and ordered to make restitution of $3,750,000. His possessions confiscated, he died in exile in Switzerland.

This bust of Pierre de La Vérendrye is part of a monument in Trois-Rivières on the site of the house where he was born in 1685. La Vérendrye and his sons, in search of furs and the western sea, ranged across what now is northwestern Ontario and onto the prairies. They were the first white men to see the Rockies. Trade generated by the chain of forts they built was vital to New France in the early 1700s.

rivers to the south. The French and the English were bound to confront each other soon in a final struggle for the continent.

The valley of the Ohio, part of the French route to the Mississippi and Louisiana, was the first battleground. British traders, calling themselves the Ohio Company of Virginia, claimed 500,000 acres there in 1749. New France replied by planting markers, stamped with the royal arms of Louis XV, throughout the region and by building four forts. The English then built Fort Necessity, 65 miles southwest of Fort Duquesne (present-day Pittsburgh). A 22-year-old Lt.Col. George Washington and 150 Virginians attacked 31 Frenchmen near Fort Duquesne on May 28, 1755, killing their leader, Coulon de Jumonville, and nine others, then retreated to Fort Necessity. A force led by Jumonville's brother swept into Necessity on July 3 and forced the future first president of the United States to sign a confession to Jumonville's "assassination."

Meanwhile, although nominally at peace, England was decimating French shipping. In 1755 alone some 300 ships were captured. French policy had been to keep New France dependent, so it would continue to send furs in exchange for food and other necessities. Now, with many ships being lost, New France faced serious shortages. England declared war May 17, 1756.

Montcalm was a 44-year-old major-general in command of French regular troops in North America. He had left France for Canada on April 3, 1756, accompanied by his second-in-command, the Chevalier de Lévis, and by colonels Louis-Antoine de Bougainville and François-Charles de Bourlamaque.

He razed Fort Oswego (Oswego, N.Y.) on

Aug. 14 and the next year took Fort William Henry on Lake George. In July 1758 he held Fort Ticonderoga on Lake Champlain against an army four times as big as his own.

William Pitt, British secretary of state, planned to cripple France by striking at her colonies and he increased British strength in North America to 23,000 soldiers compared to New France's 6,800 troops. Louisbourg fell July 26, 1758, and with it Cape Breton Island and Prince Edward Island. Fort Frontenac (at present-day Kingston, Ont.) was taken Aug. 25, isolating Fort Niagara. Fort Duquesne could no longer be defended and the French destroyed it Nov. 23. With the St. Lawrence open to invasion by sea,

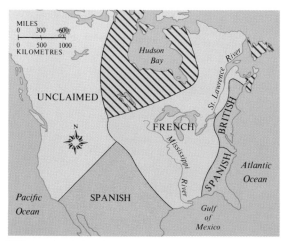

▨ *Land ceded by France to Britain in 1713*

By the early 1700s New France had been extended to Hudson Bay by Pierre Le Moyne d'Iberville and to the Gulf of Mexico by René-Robert Cavelier de La Salle. When lands in Acadia and around Hudson Bay were ceded to Britain, New France looked west and Pierre de La Vérendrye pushed almost to the Rockies.

and supplies scarce, New France was desperate.

Montcalm sent for reinforcements, only to be told by Paris, preoccupied with Europe, that one did not try to save the stables when the house was on fire. The King's Council realized that the colony's survival depended on French naval support but urged that European defence come first. In February 1759 the Marquis de Vaudreuil, governor of New France, was told no warships would be sent to Quebec.

The war destroyed the colony's economy. Every new soldier was one more mouth to feed and every habitant in uniform was one less farmer. Most supply ships sent from France in the spring of 1758 were captured by the English.

By 1759 all French forts on the Great Lakes and Lake Champlain had fallen. New France, which had once included all the present-day Maritime Provinces, which had been extended to Hudson Bay by Pierre Le Moyne d'Iberville, to the Gulf of Mexico by René-Robert Cavelier de La Salle and almost to the Rockies by Pierre de La Vérendrye, was reduced to Louisiana and a toehold in the St. Lawrence Valley.

Wolfe arrived off Quebec on June 25, 1759, with 168 ships and 13,500 sailors (commanded by Admiral Sir Charles Saunders) and 8,500 soldiers. Wolfe, 32, had won this command by his brilliance the year before at Louisbourg.

For a month Quebec had been strengthening its fortifications and thousands of Canadians from 12 to 80 had answered Vaudreuil's call to arms; now there were some 16,200 defenders. On

Place Royale in Quebec will be a 75-building showcase of New France's glory when restoration, begun in 1970, is complete.

July 12 English guns began firing from the heights across the river. But Wolfe doubted he could bombard Quebec into submission; he had to engage the French in open battle and to do that he had to land his army. The best place seemed to be the Beauport Flats, between the St. Charles and Montmorency rivers, downstream from Quebec. But the flats were defended.

On July 26 Wolfe landed 2,000 men east of the Montmorency River opposite the flats. At dawn some 800 Indians attacked the English camp, killing and wounding 200 men, then retreating. On July 31 Wolfe tried to land on the west bank of the Montmorency but was repulsed by Montcalm, this time with 443 casualties. His cannon on the south shore were levelling houses in Quebec but Wolfe knew he was marking time. He must act soon or give up the siege, or his ships would be caught in the ice. As he returned Sept. 9 from an abortive landing at Saint-Augustin, 12 miles upstream from Quebec, he scrutinized the formidable cliffs. Two miles above Quebec he spied a dry streambed descending the rock face near a cove named l'Anse au Foulon.

On the night of Sept. 12 Wolfe ordered diversionary manoeuvres near the Beauport Flats, then at 4 a.m. landed troops near l'Anse au Foulon. An advance guard of 24 redcoats scaled the cliff by way of the streambed. Thirty Canadian guards asleep in tents on the heights above the cove were easily overpowered and British troops were able to march up two abreast. In the first glimmer of dawn they were in formation on the Plains of Abraham.

Montcalm refused to believe—until he saw—that English soldiers were "where they have no right to be." If he had waited for Bougainville's

Stokers on six-hour shifts worked around the clock firing cold-air blast furnaces at Les Forges du Saint-Maurice, a Trois-Rivières ironworks that thrived from 1730 to 1883. By 1741 the forges were the most important industry in New France. At peak production they employed 300 men, using local bog iron and wood.

107

French and English: Into Battle in Style

French and English infantrymen of the 18th century—called fusiliers after their *fusils,* light muskets—went into battle in style.

The French fusilier usually wore a grey-white *justaucorps,* a coat with long tails that hooked up at the sides for easier marching. Underneath was a long-sleeved, thigh-length waistcoat in his regimental colors, a white linen shirt, breeches and woollen stockings. The buttoned gaiters were white canvas. Sword and bayonet were slung on a leather belt. Fusiliers in winter campaigns wore heavy, unbleached wool coats and snowshoe moccasins. Grenadiers, élite troops trained to hurl grenades and to storm barricades, carried sabres and were encouraged to wear mustaches, which were forbidden in other regiments.

The British fusilier usually wore a red coat, waistcoat and breeches. The coat was lined in regimental colors. Grenadiers had tall, mitred caps emblazoned with the white horse of the House of Hanover, and shoulder "wings" of red cloth trimmed with regimental lace.

All were heavily burdened. A British soldier carried 65 pounds—often half his weight. This included clothing (13 pounds); weapons and ammunition (20 pounds); equipment and six days' ration of biscuit, salt pork and peas (32 pounds).

French fusilier, 1755-60

British grenadier, 1758-67

On the Plains of Abraham, French troops with their backs to Quebec (top left) met English soldiers who had scaled the cliffs (right) in the most decisive battle in Canadian history. "What honor belongs to the defenders of Canada," a British officer wrote, "must go to the men who, fighting for their native land in their traditional way, made it possible for the regulars of France to make good their escape."

élite troops, camped at Cap Rouge, he could have taken the enemy in a pincer movement. If he had stayed within the city walls, ice forming on the river would have forced Wolfe to withdraw. But Montcalm would not wait. He ordered the French army forward.

Wolfe waited at the head of his Louisbourg Grenadiers. The British stood motionless in a hail of grapeshot from four French cannon. As Montcalm's troops advanced through meadow and cornfield there was growing disorder. Regular soldiers collided with militiamen, who threw themselves on the ground to reload and who zigzagged from bush to bush for cover.

The armies were 40 yards apart when Wolfe gave the order to fire. The salvo boomed like a cannon blast. The redcoats reloaded and a second volley rang out. They loaded again but when the smoke cleared they could see the enemy lines were riddled with dead and wounded.

Wolfe gave the order to charge and led with his Grenadiers. A bullet apparently had broken his wrist but he had bound the wound with a handkerchief. He was hit again, in the stomach, but was swept forward by the surge of battle. A bullet struck his chest. This time he fell, blood streaming from his mouth. He was carried to the rear but refused medical aid. As he was dying he learned that the French were in full flight.

Montcalm was rallying his fleeing army when he was struck in the thigh and groin as he approached the city walls. He was held in the saddle by his soldiers and taken to the Saint-Louis Gate. Women ran to help.

"It is nothing, nothing at all," said Montcalm. "Do not grieve on my account, my dear friends."

He died the next day and was buried in the chapel of the Ursuline Convent—in a crater dug by an English shell. With him, wrote one of the nuns, New France itself was laid in the tomb.

So it would seem later. But the city of Quebec, its ramparts intact, was not yet lost, New France not yet defeated. And the French army had not been destroyed in the 10-minute battle. While the English laid siege to the city, Bougainville and Lévis prepared to counterattack from Pointe-aux-Trembles (present-day Neuville) and Fort Jacques-Cartier (present-day Cap-Santé). But frightened, starving citizens begged the garrison commander, Lt.Gen. Jean-Baptiste-Nicolas-Roch de Ramezay, to lay down arms. He surrendered Sept. 18 even as Brig. George Townshend, Wolfe's successor, was considering retreat before winter. The British entered the city the next day.

Quebec spent a hungry winter under British rule. It was so cold that nuns took pity on kilted Highlanders and knitted them woollen drawers. Vaudreuil governed from Montreal, where Lévis, the new commander-in-chief, mulled over plans for Quebec's recapture. In spring, hoping that the first ship to reach the colony would be French, Lévis set off for Quebec. There, on April 28, 1760, the garrison commander, Brig.Gen. James Murray, repeated Montcalm's error and

Gen. James Wolfe (top) was scornful of the men he commanded: "rascals and canailles (scum)," he called them. Canada to the Marquis de Montcalm was a place "where rogues get rich and honest men are ruined."

A Common Death, a Common Fame, a Common Monument

James Wolfe, who led the English on the Plains of Abraham, longed only for victory. His opponent, the Marquis de Montcalm, longed for home.

"I am deeply desirous of peace," Montcalm had written to his wife in Provence. "I think I should have given up all my honors to be back with you, but the king must be obeyed. I believe I love you more than ever."

But Wolfe, who had joined his father's regiment at 14, once boasted: "I had much rather listen to the drum and the trumpet than any softer sound whatever." One day, staring across the St. Lawrence River, he said he "would cheerfully sacrifice a leg or an arm to be in possession of Quebec."

Montcalm, whose forebears had long been soldiers of France, deplored the Canadian militia's refusal to fight in the traditional European style. He despised most things "Canadian."

Wolfe was painfully awkward in female company. He was occasionally suspected of madness. "Mad, is he?" George II expostulated. "Then I hope he will bite some of my other generals."

The two generals died very differently. "Now God be praised," Wolfe murmured. "Since I have conquered, I will die in peace." Montcalm told his officers: "I have much more important matters to attend to than your ruined garrison and this wretched country." Wolfe's body was borne to England; Montcalm's was buried in Quebec.

But an obelisk *(right)* in the Governors' Garden at Quebec bears this inscription in Latin: "Valor gave them a common death, history a common fame, posterity a common monument."

Victory at Quebec in 1759 committed British soldiers to a bitter winter of occupation, in weather so severe that sentries froze to death at their posts. Here, wary of harassment by townsfolk, kilted Highlanders escort other troops hauling wood to their barracks.

emerged to meet Lévis at Sainte-Foy, one mile northwest of l'Anse au Foulon. The English were routed in a two-hour battle, then Lévis besieged the city and kept an anxious watch down the St. Lawrence.

A sail appeared May 9 but it belonged to a British frigate. But one ship could scarcely support the occupying force. Then on the evening of the 15th three more English ships dropped anchor before Quebec. Lévis retreated to Montréal and Vaudreuil wrote bitterly: "The sight of a single French flag would have assured the recapture of the City of Quebec."

That summer three British armies—16,000 men in all—converged on Montreal from Quebec, Lake Champlain and Lake Ontario. Fort Chambly fell on Sept. 1. It was useless for the 3,000 soldiers behind Montreal's frail fortifications to resist and Vaudreuil surrendered. The English entered Montreal on Sept. 8. The Seven Years' War was over in mainland North America.

The war in Europe lasted another two years. The Canadians hoped that the land they had toiled on and fought for would be returned to France. But the Treaty of Paris, ratified Feb. 10, 1763, gave France only the islands of Saint-Pierre and Miquelon and fishing rights on the Newfoundland banks. Louisiana had been ceded to Spain in 1762. New France was no more.

The writer Voltaire hailed France's deliverance from responsibility for "a few acres of snow." And Madame de Pompadour, favorite of Louis XV, sighed: "Now the king can sleep."

French Guns on Signal Hill Ended French Hopes in 1762

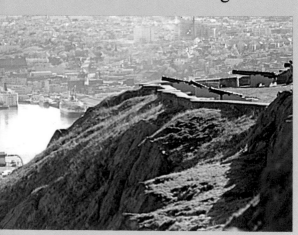

On May 8, 1762, four French ships slipped through the British blockade of Brest in northern France and sailed for St. John's, Nfld. On board were Comte d'Haussonville and 700 soldiers. Their mission: to establish a base in North America for a campaign to retake New France.

The British had batteries on both sides of the harbor entrance to St. John's and had built Fort William on the slope behind the town, but there were no fortifications on Signal Hill (left), the 500-foot rock dominating the settlement. The French landed June 24 at Bay Bulls, 20 miles south, moved against St. John's by land, and captured it three days later without a fight. D'Haussonville promptly put guns on Signal Hill.

But France sent no reinforcements, and in the cold, foggy dawn of Sept. 15 a force of 1,500 British soldiers from Halifax, Louisbourg and New York, which had landed at Torbay two days earlier, reached Cuckold Cove on the north side of Signal Hill. They climbed a ravine, crept past sentries, seized the French guns and trained them on the garrison below. After three days of bombardment, d'Haussonville surrendered. It had been the last encounter between French and English troops in North America.

110

Heritage Sites

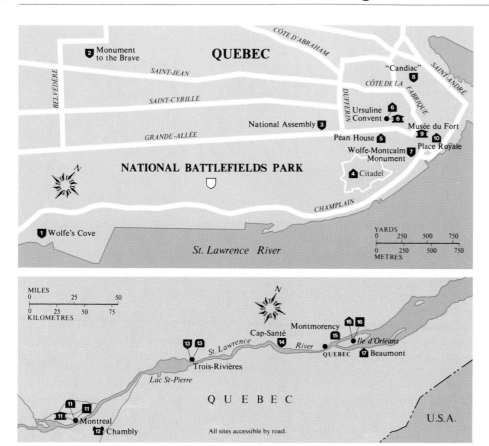

◌ Main site (Monument) ⌂ Historic building(s) ▣ Museum ▼ Monument ⊠ Fort ■ Ruins ▪ Unmarked site

QUEBEC Granite markers in 235-acre National Battlefields Park trace the course of the 1759 Battle of the Plains of Abraham. An obelisk marks where Wolfe died. The St. Joan of Arc Monument honors those who fought on the Plains of Abraham, and at Sainte-Foy the following spring. Outside the park is a statue of Montcalm and an angel, at the place where the general was mortally wounded.

Also in Quebec

"CANDIAC" (8) A plaque at Ramparts and Hamel streets identifies the site of the house in which Montcalm lived from December 1758 to June 1759. The residence was named after his birthplace in France.

CITADEL (4) Fortifications which date from the French régime are the Cape Redoubt (1693), and a powder magazine (1750) which is now a museum.

MONUMENT TO THE BRAVE (2) A stone column at the site of the Battle of Sainte-Foy (now in Park of the Brave) commemorates those who fought there in 1760.

MUSÉE DU FORT (9) The battles of the Plains of Abraham and Sainte-Foy are re-enacted with sound and light on a 450-square-foot model of 18th-century Quebec City.

NATIONAL ASSEMBLY (3) Recessed into the building's stone façade are statues of generals Wolfe, Montcalm and Lévis and explorer Pierre de La Vérendrye.

PÉAN HOUSE (5) The building at 59 Rue Saint-Louis is thought to have been the home of Angélique Péan, the mistress of Intendant François Bigot. Montcalm died here Sept. 14, 1759.

PLACE ROYALE (10) More than 30 buildings have been restored or rebuilt in what was the commercial centre of New France. The Hôtel Chevalier (1752), which has had a cannon ball embedded in a wall since 1759, is a museum of 17th-century furniture. Displays in the Fornel House (1724) interpret military life and colonial administration. Tours leave from the Le Picard House (1763), an interpretive centre.

URSULINE CONVENT (6) Montcalm's skull is preserved in the Museum of Marie de l'Incarnation Centre. Nearby is the chapel where his body was interred in a shell crater and where a funeral service was held for Wolfe.

WOLFE'S COVE (1) A plaque at l'Anse au Foulon, 175 feet below the Plains of Abraham, marks where Wolfe's men made their ascent on Sept. 13, 1759.

WOLFE-MONTCALM MONUMENT (7) A 50-foot stone obelisk in the Governor's Garden honors the two generals.

Other sites

Beaumont, Que. (17) Saint-Etienne-de-Beaumont Church was 26 years old when Wolfe's troops posted a surrender ultimatum on its door. Villagers tore down the notice and soldiers set fire to the door. Only the door was burned. The damage can no longer be seen.

Cap-Santé, Que. (14) A stone at the head of a private road three miles east marks the site of Fort Jacques-Cartier, the last place in New France to surrender (Sept. 13, 1760—exactly one year after the Battle of the Plains of Abraham).

Chambly, Que. (12) Fort Chambly, now in Fort Chambly National Historic Park, was a link in the chain of bastions protecting New France. Its walls date from 1709-11 and have been partially rebuilt.

Ile d'Orléans, Que. (16) Wolfe's campaign headquarters were in a house at Sainte-Pétronille on the island's western tip. The Mauvide-Genest Manor (1734) at Saint-Jean bears the scars of English cannon balls. The Saint-François church (1734) and rectory were requisitioned as a hospital for English soldiers.

Montmorency, Que. (15) Remains of two stone redoubts built by Wolfe's men have been unearthed in Hydro-Quebec Park near the crest of Montmorency Falls.

Montreal (11) A section of the city's stone wall, dating from 1724, is preserved in the Brasserie des Fortifications. In Place d'Armes, 3,122 French officers and men laid down their arms Sept. 8, 1760. The Montreal Military and Maritime Museum on St. Helen's Island has a model of 18th-century Montreal, a paper bearing Montcalm's signature, and French and English drums, swords, boots and helmets of the kinds used in the battle on the Plains of Abraham.

St. John's, Nfld. (not shown) The Battle of Signal Hill, the last meeting of French and English troops in North America (Sept. 15-18, 1762), is partly re-enacted once each summer on Signal Hill.

Trois-Rivières, Que. (13) Remains of Canada's first iron foundry are in Les Forges du Saint-Maurice National Historic Park. A bust of Pierre de La Vérendrye marks the site of the house where he was born.

French Canadians Fight to Keep Quebec British

Guy Carleton, destined to lead the defence of Quebec against American invasion, was Irish born (1724) and a British soldier from the age of 18. He fought at Quebec in 1759 and was wounded about the time that his friend James Wolfe died. Appointed governor in 1768, he worked hard to win French Canadians' goodwill—and won their loyalty when the Americans attacked in 1775.

A blizzard beat against the stone walls of the city of Quebec on the night of Dec. 30, 1775. Guy Carleton, commander of this last British stronghold in the Province of Quebec—the others had fallen to the Americans—peered down into the swirling blackness of Lower Town, where barricades were up and Quebec's defenders waited, in streets such as Champlain and Sault-au-Matelot. Carleton felt certain the invaders would attack the city before dawn.

Short weeks ago he had strolled the streets of Montreal, governor of the province which was His Majesty's largest American colony. But now armies from the 13 rebellious colonies had driven his garrisons from Montreal and the Richelieu Valley. At this moment, he knew, American troops led by generals Richard Montgomery and Benedict Arnold were massing nearby.

In 1760, when New France fell to English armies, 55,000 *Canadiens* came under British rule. By language, religion and nationality, they were traditional enemies of the British, and their way of life could have been brutally changed. But the conquerors saw no point in reorganizing a colony that by treaty might well become French again when the fighting in Europe was over. The army officers who governed spoke French fluently. They maintained French civil law and tolerated the Roman Catholic Church.

But when the Seven Years' War ended in 1763 Britain kept Quebec. British American colonists did not want an old enemy reestablished to the north; and France was happy enough to let her colony go—it had never shown a profit for Paris. It was a stunning humiliation for the French colonists. They had been conquered by the English,

Canadian militiamen (in tuques) and British fusiliers stop the attack on Quebec. Americans have charged down Sault-au-Matelot but cannot surmount a heavily braced two-storey barricade which blocks the end of the narrow street.

This end of Sault-au-Matelot in Quebec's Lower Town is where the invasion of 1775-76 was stemmed. Americans were trapped between a barricade at this corner and British troops charging from the other end of the street.

cast aside by their own king—and bankrupted when France refused to honor the paper money it had circulated in Quebec.

But New England merchants were delighted. They had competed with Canadians for years. Now they could take over all the St. Lawrence trade. By the fall of 1763 many were in Montreal.

Then came the Royal Proclamation of 1763. Quebec, like all English colonies, would have a governor general and an elected assembly. Roman Catholic worship would be tolerated but, in accordance with British law, Catholics could neither hold public office nor sit on juries. The newly arrived Boston merchants celebrated. They were Protestants; they could hold office and dominate the assembly. Quebec was theirs for the picking.

But they reckoned without the man who became governor general. James Murray had been a member of the military government and looked down on the upstart merchants. What is more, he had an affinity with the French ruling class, the Catholic clergy and the seigneurs, whose ideas of order and authority matched his own. He decided to rule without an elected assembly.

But the merchants had powerful friends in London and Murray was recalled in 1764. The next governor was another soldier, Guy Carleton. He too refused to allow the merchants to dominate the French Canadians. He sensed trouble brewing in the other American colonies and reasoned that Canadian support might soon be valuable to the British government.

The merchants bombarded England with petitions urging that Quebec be administered as the other colonies were. They created unrest among the French and agitated against Carleton.

Britain responded with the Quebec Act of 1774, which reflected Carleton's view that the French Canadians should continue to have the laws and

Anglo-Americans in Montreal were angered by the Quebec Act of 1774 and its generosity to Roman Catholic French Canadians. Someone blackened this bust of George III in Place d'Armes (it now is in Montreal's McCord Museum) and hung on it a rosary of potatoes. On the rosary's wooden cross were the words: "Behold the Pope of Canada and the English fool."

government they wanted. Catholics were given full political rights and religious freedom. The Roman Catholic Church was granted the right to collect the tithe—a tax on Catholics which had been illegal since the conquest. Civil law was to be French and seigneurial ownership of land, mostly along the St. Lawrence and the Richelieu, was retained. Criminal law was British.

A Cantankerous Yankee Loses an Ear

Thomas Walker *(left)* moved from Boston to Montreal about 1763 and quickly joined other New England merchants there in denouncing British authorities for protecting French rights.

When a soldier refused to leave a house whose owner (Walker thought) was not required to billet troops, Walker and others had the man jailed. Soon after, six masked soldiers broke into his home, beat him unconscious and cut off an ear. Evidence pointed to men from the 28th Regiment but there were no convictions and Walker accused Governor James Murray of sympathizing with his attackers.

When the Americans invaded Quebec, Governor Guy Carleton (Murray's successor) accused Walker of treason. On the night of Oct. 5, 1775, some 30 soldiers surrounded his farmhouse at L'Assomption, northeast of Montreal, and captured him and his wife.

Walker spent a month chained in solitary confinement before being put on board ship for Quebec City. But Americans captured the ship at Sorel and he was freed. Back in occupied Montreal he was so vengeful and cantankerous—and his wife so meddlesome—that they became unpopular with the Americans too.

The couple fled south with the retreating Americans but apparently settled in London.

Why Nova Scotians Said No to Their Rebel Kin

George Washington's fear of English sea power, a Yankee settler's ridiculous effort to make war, incursions by New England privateers—and the powerful oratory of a young evangelist—all these helped keep Nova Scotia from joining the American Revolution.

In 1776 more than half the 20,000 whites of Nova Scotia (present-day Nova Scotia, New Brunswick and Prince Edward Island) had close relatives in New England. Only the 2,000 in Halifax were openly loyal to Britain. (Their livelihood depended largely on the Royal Navy.)

Col. Jonathan Eddy, a Yankee farmer who had settled at Chignecto (near the head of the Bay of Fundy), urged George Washington to attack Nova Scotia because it commanded the North Atlantic sea lanes. But Washington refused: he had too much respect for the Royal Navy. So Eddy raised a small band of New Englanders, intimidated some Nova Scotians into joining him, then besieged Fort Cumberland (the former French Fort Beauséjour). Three weeks later two companies of Royal Marines from Halifax routed the rebels.

In November 1775, American privateers had looted Charlottetown and throughout the war various ports were raided. When 50 privateers led by one Benjamin Cole landed at Liverpool in 1780, a former New Englander named Simeon Perkins rallied the townspeople. Cole was captured and held at Perkins's house (*left,* now a museum) until prisoners taken by the privateers were released. Perkins then gave the raiders 24 hours to get out. They left.

Evangelist Henry Alline, a Puritan who had moved to Nova Scotia from Rhode Island in the 1760s, also aroused anti-American feeling. From 1775, for eight years, he rode and tramped the countryside holding revival meetings.

Alline thundered that long ago God had directed Alline's English forefathers to New England to do His bidding. When New England turned sinfully rebellious, God led His faithful to "the Apple of His Eye," Nova Scotia; there His church would be reborn. Alline's message, coming when ties with New England were already loosened, offered a new identity and helped create a new people—Nova Scotians.

It was a generous act in an age of religious hatred and it won the support of clergy and seigneurs. But Britain was mistaken in thinking the ordinary people would approve. The French colonists were as infected by New World independence as their English counterparts were—and they bitterly resented the tithe.

There were others angrily eying the Quebec Act. In the autumn of 1774 a Continental Congress was convened in Philadelphia and delegates from the 13 other English colonies protested Britain's restoration of Quebec's frontiers along the Ohio and Mississippi rivers. They criticized Britain also for supporting a people and a church they had fought for a century.

Some Americans endorsed the protests. But many remembered how New France's militiamen had waged years of border warfare against New England. They had no desire to fight the Canadians again. So, while wanting Britain to damn Frenchness and Catholicism, they also supported "A Letter Addressed to the Inhabitants of the Province of Quebec," asking their help against Britain.

In the spring of 1775, New England merchants in Montreal were still debating alliance with the Philadelphia congress when they learned that American militiamen and British troops had clashed at Lexington in Massachusetts. This was war. When Fort Ticonderoga and Crown Point, British posts on Lake Champlain, fell in two American surprise attacks, the gateway to Quebec—the Richelieu River—was open.

Governor Carleton immediately called for volunteers to augment the fewer than 800 British

Fort Chambly (at present-day Chambly, Que.) was captured by the Americans in 1775 and burned when they withdrew the following year. Three of the walls have been rebuilt. This red-roofed administration building is on the site of the guardhouse.

Pierre du Calvet, a prosperous French merchant (and propagandist for the Americans), lived in this house in old Montreal. Du Calvet boasted that he was the only Canadian creditor ever paid by the American Congress—but his collaboration with American forces that occupied Montreal in 1775-76 cost him three years in jail.

This watercolor of Montreal in the late 1700s, from St. Helen's Island, is in the National Gallery of Canada in Ottawa. It is by Thomas Davies, a Royal Artillery officer, one of about 50 soldier-artists among 18th-century British troops in North America. Some of the best watercolorists of the day trained artillery and engineer officers to enable them to make accurate pictorial records of strategic military positions. Their work amounts to a school of early Canadian painting. Davies delighted in the little towns and settlements and his paintings are remarkable for his attention to detail, his feeling for atmosphere and his rich colors.

soldiers in Quebec's widely separated garrisons.

Across the colony, seigneurs and priests urged the people to enlist—and met stubborn indifference. Why join what looked likely to be a losing side? Why get involved in an English family quarrel? Carleton expected thousands of volunteers. He got only a few hundred. And the English merchants openly made plans to welcome an invading American army.

While Carleton raged, Gen. Richard Montgomery led 2,000 New York troops into the Richelieu Valley, where he gathered some Canadian sympathizers. By early September he had reached Fort Saint-Jean, a day's march from Montreal.

But for two wet, cold months 600 British and Canadian soldiers delayed the Americans at Saint-Jean. Maj. Charles Preston and an officer named de Belestre were ordered to hold Fort Saint-Jean to the last extremity, and powder, food and shot were supplied weekly from Fort Chambly, 12 miles north. Then an American force slipped around Saint-Jean and took Chambly, capturing enough powder and guns to take Saint-Jean. On Nov. 2, after 55 days, with supplies exhausted and 20 of the fort's 500 men dead, Preston and de Belestre surrendered. In pressing the siege Montgomery had lost half his 2,000 men to gunfire and disease.

Pierre du Calvet, merchant and justice of the peace, was bustling around his Montreal house on Nov. 12 (it still stands at St. Paul and Bonsecours streets) when sudden explosions rattled the windows. Carleton's army, too small to hold the city, was destroying powder and cannon before fleeing to Quebec. Du Calvet started in surprise, then happily resumed his preparations to greet the victorious Americans.

The first of them entered Montreal just as Carleton's ship sailed for Quebec. Other Americans followed the Richelieu to Sorel and were waiting when Carleton reached there. Carleton's capture would mean the end of Canadian resistance.

But Jean-Baptiste Bouchette, a St. Lawrence River boatman nicknamed *La Tourte* (the Wild Pigeon), slipped Carleton over the side into a small boat. He took the governor—dressed as a farmer—through mist and darkness to within yards of American sentinels. Then La Tourte and Carleton shipped oars and paddled to safety with their hands.

Carleton reached Quebec Nov. 19—with two armies on his trail. Gen. Benedict Arnold had come through northern Maine and down the Chaudière River to Lévis, opposite Quebec, after floundering through swamps and forests that cost him weapons, food and nearly half of his 1,100 Virginians, Pennsylvanians and New Hampshiremen.

Starving survivors ate soap and hair grease and chewed boiled moccasins. They crossed to Quebec on Nov. 14 but, driven off by battery fire, retired to Pointe-aux-Trembles (present-day Neuville), 22 miles west, to wait for Montgomery's troops and artillery. Montgomery arrived Dec. 3 after a week's march from Montreal. Few Canadians joined either force. Many were reluctant to fight for the English—but the Americans hardly seemed preferable.

In fact, Carleton was gaining support. He had 1,800 men, more than half of them volunteers. When American sympathizers were ordered out, most of the English merchants left the city.

The American generals had to act soon. To camp outside the city all winter would be to risk deaths from exposure. Spring might bring the Royal Navy and reinforcements for Carleton. Already there was smallpox in the American ranks.

Carleton knew the American quandary. So when the blizzard struck on Dec. 30 he was on the ramparts, ready. The Americans would surely choose just such a night. Carleton ducked into his quarters and, fully dressed, stretched out on his bed to rest as he awaited the attack.

It came at 4 a.m. Dec. 31. Benedict Arnold led 700 men through drifting snow toward the Palais Gate in the city's northern ramparts.

At the same time, across the city in a darkened house on Rue Champlain, militiamen heard sounds in the street. They rushed into the storm and at Captain Chabot's command fired grapeshot into a line of New Yorkers only 40 paces away. Montgomery fell mortally wounded. His 350 soldiers panicked, dropped their guns, turned and ran, leaving their wounded.

(Montgomery's body was buried later near the Saint-Louis Gate.)

Behind walls and barricades throughout Lower Town were French-Canadian militia, Royal Highland Emigrants (men who enlisted in 1775 to support Carleton: they wore Royal Highland Regiment uniforms), British seamen and regular soldiers. Because Montgomery advanced along Rue Champlain, Chabot's Canadians had struck the first blow in Quebec's defence.

Unaware of the rout in Lower Town, Arnold's Americans were approaching the Palais Gate when the blackness exploded into red musket fire. They ran down de la Canoterie hill and Rue Sous-le-Cap into Lower Town where Arnold fell, a musket ball in his leg.

But his men overran a barricade, seized houses along Sault-au-Matelot and hauled ladders toward a second barricade. They never passed it. Two hundred militiamen spurred by Charles

First American Novel: a Quebec Love Story

Frances Brooke, a writer, came to Quebec in 1763 mainly to keep an eye on her English military chaplain husband. She recorded her impressions of the country in *The History of Emily Montague,* the first novel written in North America. It was published in England in 1769.

The novel is a love story (about Emily and a retired British officer who has land in Quebec) and it is told through letters home and among members of the English community in Quebec. The plot is thin but there is great enthusiasm for the province's "bold, picturesque, romantic" landscape. Thunder, Mrs. Brooke wrote, "is more magnificent and aweful than in Europe, and the lightning brighter and more beautiful." She had mixed feelings about the Canadian "peasants," finding them "brave, hardy, alert in the field but lazy and inactive at home." One of her characters says Quebec's "vile climate is at war with beauty, makes one's hair gray and one's hands red."

Richard Montgomery (top) and Benedict Arnold both fought for and against the British. Montgomery saw service with the British army in America before leading an American invading force north in 1775. "Quebec is ours," he told his men moments before he was killed by Canadian militia fire Dec. 31. Arnold was among the last Americans to flee Quebec the following June, but within five years he was leading British troops against his former American comrades. Later he established a shipping and trading business in Saint John, N.B. He died in London in 1801.

Americans occupying Montreal in 1775-76 made their headquarters in the Château de Ramezay, which had been Governor Guy Carleton's residence. Benjamin Franklin dined here during an unsuccessful visit to rally Quebec support for the American revolutionary cause.

A Trappist monk believed to have been a soldier in Gen. Richard Montgomery's invading army in 1775 carved vignettes of the assault on Quebec on this powder horn. It is in the Canadian War Museum in Ottawa.

Charland counterattacked and retook the houses. Then out through the Palais Gate swept Carleton's troops to attack the Americans from the rear. Within hours some 400 surrendered. Many, including Arnold, escaped across the St. Lawrence ice; about 100 were dead. Arnold's men had inflicted only seven fatal casualties.

Arnold besieged Quebec with reinforcements (about 1,200 arrived between January and March) until spring but he knew the city would never be his. Most of the captured Americans knew it too: 100 joined Carleton.

The Continental Congress was dismayed by the defeat and by rumors that repressive American rule in Montreal was turning Canadians against the revolution. In April 1776 Benjamin Franklin was sent to Montreal to investigate.

Franklin was too late. In May, when Royal Navy ships with 10,000 men and supplies reached Quebec, the Americans fled toward Montreal. A farmer, Antoine Gautier, deliberately guided another party of Americans into a swamp near Trois-Rivières. There they were bombarded by navy guns from the river and by British regulars on land. At Les Cèdres, some 40 miles above Montreal, 400 Americans surrendered with scarcely a fight to 40 British regulars and 200 Indians.

On June 15, Arnold ordered his army to burn Montreal but citizens beat out the flames.

Beaten, tired, ridden with smallpox, the Americans fell back along the Richelieu to Lake Champlain and reinforcements—10,000 men in 16 ships. Carleton, with five warships and 50 gunboats attacked Arnold at Valcour Island on Oct. 11, sank two of his ships and killed or wounded 60 of his men. Two days later, Carleton annihilated the American fleet at Crown Point but Arnold escaped to Ticonderoga. By winter, of all the forts taken in 1775, it alone remained in American hands but it was no threat to Canada.

A Canadian nation had been born in 1774 when the Quebec Act gave men such as Chabot and Charland something to fight for. British regulars and Canadian militia had stood together to hold Quebec against the American armies. Although there had been discontent in all of Britain's American colonies, Quebec alone decided in the end for Britain and fought hard to defend its choice. The people along the St. Lawrence would remain French and Roman Catholic.

Canadians Had No Say in U.S. Independence Terms

The Americans made no conquests during their War of Independence but they gained much at the peace conference that ended the struggle. Britain was ready to make concessions: she wanted to resume trade with her 13 former colonies and her former enemies, France and Spain.

The Treaty of Paris in 1783 gave the Americans all the land between the Great Lakes and the Ohio River—most of present-day Illinois, Indiana, Michigan, Ohio and Wisconsin. Once part of New France and still important in the fur trade, the territory had been made part of Quebec by the Quebec Act in 1774. It had blocked the 13 colonies from expanding west, and now it was sacrificed. The Americans also were given access to the rich fisheries off Nova Scotia and Newfoundland, and the right to go ashore to dry their catches and take firewood. The people of present-day Canada had no voice in deciding these terms of peace.

Heritage Sites

QUEBEC At a barricade across Sault-au-Matelot Street, where it joins Des Sœurs Street, the American invasion of 1775 was finally halted. Buildings lining Sault-au-Matelot are on the foundations of those from which Canadian and British soldiers ousted the Americans and fired down on the invaders. Another barricade at Sous-le-Cap and Saint-Jacques streets was overrun but Benedict Arnold, the American general, was wounded. A plaque at Saint-Pierre and Saint-Jacques streets commemorates Arnold's defeat.

Also in Quebec (13)

CHAMPLAIN BOULEVARD A plaque marks where American Gen. Richard Montgomery was killed.

CITADEL HILL Near the Saint-Louis Gate a plaque marks where Montgomery was buried. In 1818 his remains were moved to St. Paul's Church in New York City.

MUSÉE DU FORT The siege of 1775-76 is re-enacted with a sound-and-light show on a 450-square-foot model of 18th-century Quebec City.

Other sites

Aulac, N.B. (3) The remains of Fort Beauséjour, called Fort Cumberland in 1776 when it was besieged by pro-American settlers under Jonathan Eddy, are in Fort Beauséjour National Historic Park.

Chambly, Que. (9) In Fort Chambly National Historic Park is the stone stronghold which surrendered to invading Americans in 1775 and was burned by them during their retreat the following year.

Charlottetown (4) A granite memorial in the Old Protestant Cemetery marks the grave of Phillips Callbeck who, as acting governor in November 1775, was robbed and kidnapped (with two other citizens) by American privateers. Callbeck was later

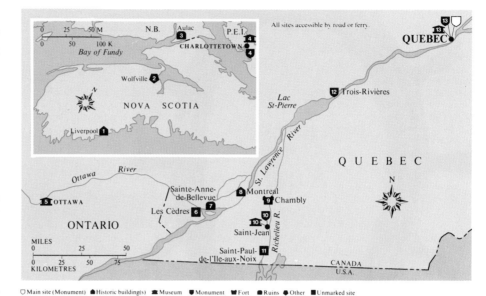

released by George Washington and returned to Charlottetown in May 1776.

Les Cèdres, Que. (6) The Battle of Les Cèdres, at which a British force captured 400 Americans, was fought here in 1776.

Liverpool, N.S. (1) The Simeon Perkins House was built in 1766-67 by a former Connecticut merchant who in 1780 rallied Liverpool citizens against American privateer raiders. Now a museum, the house contains 18th-century furnishings and a copy of Perkins's diary.

Montreal (8) The Château de Ramezay, 280 Notre-Dame Street East, built in 1705, was used by invading Americans as their headquarters in 1775-76. It is now a museum. Exhibits include a snuffbox owned by an American officer, and a portrait of Sir Guy Carleton. The three-storey du Calvet House, 401 Bonsecours Street, was

the home of Pierre du Calvet, who helped supply the Americans. Twice accused of treason, he was eventually banished.

Ottawa (5) Exhibits in the Canadian War Museum include Guy Carleton's carriage and a powder horn with scenes of the Quebec assault carved by a monk.

Sainte-Anne-de-Bellevue, Que. (7) The ruins of Senneville Manor, burned by American troops in 1776, are a mile north. They are on private property but can be seen from the Lake of Two Mountains.

Saint-Jean, Que. (10) A plaque marks the site of Fort Saint-Jean whose defence delayed Montgomery's march on Montreal for 55 days. Weapons, uniforms, medals and documents from the fort are in the museum of the Collège Militaire Royal.

Saint-Paul-de-l'Ile-aux-Noix, Que. (11) Ile aux Noix, one mile southeast on the Richelieu River, was a British stronghold captured by Montgomery in 1775. Retreating Americans regrouped there in 1776. (The island now forms Fort Lennox National Historic Park; its fort dates from 1819-28.)

Trois-Rivières, Que. (12) The site of the 1776 Battle of Trois-Rivières, an American defeat, is marked by a plaque.

Wolfville, N.S. (2) The sermons and journal of Henry Alline, whose preaching helped keep Nova Scotia from joining the Americans, are in Acadia University's Vaughan Memorial Library.

Near Sainte-Anne-de-Bellevue, Que., are the ruins of Senneville Manor. Americans garrisoned it briefly in 1775. Benedict Arnold destroyed the manor as he retreated from Canada.

119

Pirates With Royal Blessing

William Knox of Halifax fitted cannon instead of loading cargo, and took his sloop *Sea Flower* to war in July 1756 against French traders off Cape Breton Island. Only the tacit approval of Nova Scotia Governor Charles Lawrence kept this from being piracy, even though England and France were at war. Three months later, royal instructions arrived from England encouraging Nova Scotians to arm their ships and attack and capture enemy vessels. This was privateering—fully legalized piracy.

Nova Scotians (and, later, New Brunswickers) needed little encouragement. Between 1756 and 1815, in hundreds of ships, from New England to the Caribbean, thousands of them harassed Frenchmen, Spaniards, Dutchmen and Americans. Their first vessels were hastily armed fishing schooners and merchantmen. Fast, light ships were later built specially for privateering, and captured enemy privateers were renamed and taken out again.

A privateer owner had to obtain a letter of marque (a licence), usually good for six months, from the governor. Without it the captain and crew could be hanged as pirates. Even with it, there were strict rules. Only enemy ships or those trading with the enemy could be attacked. Captures had to be taken to Halifax, where the Court of Vice-Admiralty decided whether they were legal prizes. Captains had to keep daily logbooks and, when possible, report enemy ship movements.

Most prisoners were taken to Halifax in the hold of their own ship and jailed until they could be exchanged for captured Nova Scotians. Legal prizes—ships and cargoes—were auctioned off, but court costs were high and an owner could end up with less than a third of the profits, to be shared with the captain and crew. There was no regular pay. But Enos Collins, who had an interest in three privateers, made enough to found Nova Scotia's first bank (the Halifax Banking Company) and when he died in 1871, aged 97, his estate totalled six million dollars. He was the richest man in British North America.

The privateer Rover, *a 16-gun brig from Liverpool, N.S., was trapped—becalmed on Sept. 10, 1800, between the coast of what is now Venezuela and the heavily armed Spanish schooner* Santa Rita, *towed by three armed slave galleys. The 36 Nova Scotians healthy enough to fight hung cutlasses at their belts. Cannon were positioned (right), muskets loaded and primed.* Santa Rita, *firing steadily, her bow crowded with marines, approached* Rover *from astern. But when she was only 15 yards away, and had cast off the galleys in preparation for boarding,* Rover's *24 strongest men, manning oars which had been hidden from the Spaniards, turned the brig broadside to* Santa Rita *and a salvo crashed into her. The oarsmen turned* Rover *another 180 degrees and a second broadside raked the galleys, which crawled away, disabled. For another hour cannon fire thundered between the two ships, until* Santa Rita's *topmast snapped. The Nova Scotians boarded the crippled schooner, and the Spaniards surrendered. Fifty-four of them, including all but one officer, were dead. Not one man in* Rover *had been wounded.* Santa Rita *was patched up and was sailed 2,000 miles to Liverpool.*

...ks Saturday June 5th 1813
...ege and hazy weather standing off and...
...ght of Cape Ann...
...bu of the bacco boats about us —— ...
...ploy a evercuzing great guns and small...
...ood towards the Shore, intending to try...
...t the Pilot Boat schooner in Sandy Bay...
...moderate breeze and hazy close in with...
...t point—...

This logbook of the Saint John, N.B., privateer Dart *records 25 chases and five captures in one month of 1813.*

Privateer cannon, eventually planted muzzle down on street corners like this one in Milton, near Liverpool, N.S., kept carriages to the road and away from front gardens.

More than 200 American privateers were captured during the American Revolution (above, the British brig Observer *takes* Jack *of Massachusetts off Halifax in May 1782) but coastal towns in the present-day Maritime Provinces were attacked frequently. In June 1782 the*

women of Chester, N.S., whose men were away lumbering, donned red petticoats as cloaks, shouldered broomsticks as muskets, and fooled Americans offshore into thinking they were British redcoats. The Americans sailed away.

Many cargoes captured by Nova Scotia privateers were stored before auction in the Privateer Warehouse, now part of Historic Properties on Halifax's waterfront. One cargo included 12 hogsheads of gin, 4,000 sides of leather and 12 marble tombstones.

The most dreaded Nova Scotia privateer ship of the War of 1812 started out as a contraband slaver called Black Joke. *Seized by a British man-of-war, the sleek schooner was bought by Enos Collins, a Liverpool-born merchant and former privateer. He fumigated her and christened her* Liverpool Packet. *Under Capt. Joseph Barss of Liverpool (left) she coasted from Newfoundland to Cape Cod, taking more than 30 American ships in nine months. Eventually captured by the Americans, the* Packet *was retaken by the British and bought again by Collins. Her catches during the war totalled nearly 100 ships, with prize money of more than a quarter of a million dollars.*

A chance at riches and honor—and immediate treats of rum—enticed fishermen, merchant seamen, adventurers and navy deserters to become privateersmen. Advertisements such as this one (right) in the Nova Scotia Gazette *appeared in newspapers and on tavern doors. Men already signed on, wearing cutlasses and beribboned hats and led by a drummer, a piper and the boatswain waving a British flag, marched through the streets to encourage others to join.*
Up to 80 men might be needed on a voyage, for fighting and to take captured ships home. Navigators were required as prize masters, and boys as "powder monkeys," carrying powder and shot from the magazine to the gunners on deck. Men and boys slept in hammocks in unventilated, cramped spaces below decks.

The Privateer **SCHOONER**
Liverpool.
George Young Commander.
Mounts Eight Carriage Guns with Swivels and small Arms.
All British Seamen and others willing to engage in the above Vessel, bound on a Cruize to the Southward for four Months and to return to this Port will meet with every encouragement and have a protection from the Press, ay applying to Capt. Young at Mr. White's Tavern at the Slip.
No Person belonging to the Navy or Army will be taken, and to prevent Deserters from imposing themselves by false pretences, it is requested that their officers will apply to James Greenlow at Mr. Proud's, opposite the Market House and they shall be shewn every person engaged in the above Privateer.

Water became stale, and food (mostly salt pork and biscuit) often went bad. Ships were breeding grounds for disease, and in the Caribbean many Maritimers died of "Yellow Jack"—malaria. Capture could mean years of sickness, privation and torture in a stinking jail far from home.

Exasperation—and a Voyage of Revenge

In 1799, when 23 and privateering in the Caribbean, Tom Freeman of Liverpool was captured, thrown into a Haitian jail, rescued and grabbed by a Royal Navy press gang. He escaped and got home a year later. Then, in 1803, as master of the trading ship *Goodfortune,* he was captured by a French privateer and caught malaria in Antigua. In 1812, as he was peacefully heading home after a trading trip to the Caribbean, the American *Constitution* seized his ship and cargo. That did it. Freeman got back to Liverpool, bought a small warship he called *Retaliation,* and stormed up and down the New England coast, forcing American ships onto reefs and shoals. In a few weeks he brought in prizes worth more than $30,000.

A boulder at the foot of King Street in Saint John, N.B., marks the place where the first Loyalist refugees went ashore in 1783—an historic landing commemorated in this painting by Adam Sherriff Scott. With the growth of Loyalist settlements at the mouth of the Saint John River, the city became, in 1785, the first in Canada to be incorporated by charter.

An Influx of English: The King's 'Traitors'

The Americans who supported the British during the revolution of 1776 called themselves Loyalists. Others branded them Tories, traitors to the cause of independence—and made them pay dearly.

Throughout the fledgling United States, Loyalist homes were sacked and burned, Loyalist properties confiscated. Loyalists were denied the right to vote, to sell land, to sue debtors, to be lawyers or doctors or schoolmasters.

Loyalists were hounded—so much that one Loyalist minister preached with loaded pistols beside him for self-defence. Some Loyalists were tarred and feathered. Many were beaten by mobs, some were lynched, murdered or executed. When the harsh treatment of Loyalists was protested, George Washington replied that, in simple decency, all Loyalists should commit suicide.

Between 1776 and 1783—during the War of Independence—some 40,000 fled north into territory that remained British, most of them to a Nova Scotia that included much of modern New Brunswick and stretched to some uncharted point in today's Maine. Other thousands trekked into the St. Lawrence River valley and beyond to lands bordering the Great Lakes.

In 1783, the fighting over and the rebels victorious, the tide of refugees swelled—aided by Sir Guy Carleton, the British commander-in-chief, who refused to surrender New York until the last Loyalist had left.

Early in May some 3,000 refugees in seven ships were anchored in the Bay of Fundy off the mouth of the Saint John River. They could see dense forest, a few clearings with log huts, and a rocky peninsula where they were to build a town. At low tide they gazed in dismay at Fundy's mud flats.

The first group landed May 18—a boulder identifies the Loyalist Landing Place—and it was early June before everybody was ashore.

Another 11,000 Loyalists would land here before the end of the year. None knew quite what to expect. Taunting rebels had sneered of "Nova Scarcity." Enthusiastic Loyalists had described a land of promise. For those first refugees there was more scarcity than promise.

They faced a forbidding, lonely country. "The roughest land I ever saw," said one. Years later a Loyalist woman recalled the despair that gripped her as the ships left for New York for more refugees. Carrying her infant, she climbed a hill to watch. As she saw the winds fatten the vanishing sails, "such a feeling of loneliness came over me that, although I had not shed a tear through all the war, I sat down on the damp moss with my baby in my lap and cried."

Through that summer and fall, at the site of present-day Saint John, they pitched tents, cleared land and built shanties. They argued over who was to settle where and they complained that surveys had not been made.

These Americans were a varied lot: farmers and lawyers, carpenters and clergymen, craftsmen and clerks, soldiers and slaves, college graduates and men who could not write their own names. They were the first mass influx of English-speaking people to a country of fewer than 150,000 whites, most of French stock. Out of their settlements would grow the provinces of New Brunswick and Upper Canada (Ontario), and, in time, much of the nation called Canada.

The tragic twist of exile was that the Loyalists had had much in common with the fellow Americans they opposed: a love of homeland, a deep sense of belonging there, a respect for Britain as mother country, a distaste for clumsy British efforts to reorganize the colonies after French power in North America had been broken in 1760.

But the revolutionaries were for armed insurrection. Loyalists believed that time, common

This coat of arms of George III, over the west door of Trinity Anglican Church in Saint John, N.B., was smuggled to Canada in 1776 by Loyalists who stole it from the council chamber of the former colony of Massachusetts in Boston.

The pioneer life of men of the disbanded King's American Dragoons has been re-created at Kings Landing Historical Settlement at Prince William, N.B., 23 miles up the Saint John River from Fredericton.

Ward Chipman, a Loyalist from Massachusetts, was deputy mustermaster general of the British forces during the War of Independence. He was solicitor general of New Brunswick from 1784 to 1808 and in 1823 became president and commander-in-chief of the province. He died, aged 69, after presiding at only one session of the legislature.

sense and rational debate could settle differences. Rebels cried that George III had forfeited their loyalty by jeopardizing their liberties, by imposing taxation without representation. Loyalists refused to throw off allegiance to the king.

Thousands of Loyalists sought British protection during the war and lived broken, waiting lives. They were angered by the incompetence of British military leaders, the scorn of Britons for colonials and soldiers without British army training.

Frustrations peaked in 1783 when the Whig party, long sympathetic to the rebels, came to power in London and made a conciliatory peace that afforded scant protection to Loyalists. Congress was to urge the 13 state governments to restore properties and civil rights but Loyalists who tried to go home were persecuted by anti-Loyalist neighbors.

Five of every six Loyalists who came to Canada settled in Nova Scotia, primarily because it was open to the sea—the great highway of the times. Although the Nova Scotia government had tried for years to lure settlers, Governor Sir John Parr was poorly prepared for a sudden tripling of population.

Weeks after the first Loyalists reached the fu-

ture Saint John, Col. Edward Winslow reported people "crowded into one spot without covering, and totally ignorant where they are eventually to settle." When Loyalist regiments landed in the fall they too found their promised lots unsurveyed and unready. Winslow listened to men "addressing me in a language which almost murdered me as I heard it. 'Sir, we have served all the war, your honour is witness how faithfully. We were promised land . . . only let us have a spot of our own.'"

With winter approaching, some Loyalists claimed land on Belleisle Bay, about 30 miles upriver from the mouth of the Saint John, surveyed it and built 17 log houses, a school and a church. Their community became known as Kingston. Deep in the forest, fiery Maj. John Coffin got "busy hutting myself" and was comfortable in about eight days on 6,000 acres he would call Alwington Manor.

People like these were ready for winter. For others, unsuited for frontier life or too late in arriving to make adequate preparations, it was agony. In Saint John, thousands huddled in tents. In Halifax, sheds, stores and even ships' cabins were jammed with refugees. Exiles from the Carolinas, who moved east from Halifax, ran short of food; on a hill that became known as Mount Misery, they watched and waited for a relief ship. Nearly 40 bodies lay under the snow when help arrived.

Up on the Saint John River, Mrs. Lewis Fisher, the wife of a soldier, recorded: "We pitched our tents in the shelter of the woods and tried to cover them with spruce boughs. We used stones for fireplaces. Our tents had no floors but the ground, and we tried to keep the snow from drifting in by putting a large rug at the door. How we lived through that winter I hardly know. Many women and children, and some of the men, died."

To physical torments were soon added envy, doubt, accusation and bitterness. Soldiers looked askance at men who had not fought. In one squabble over land, 55 men stressed their sacrifice and service, and asked for 5,000 acres apiece. In stinging rebuttal, more than 600 others charged that the 55 were "more distinguished by the repeated favors of government than by the greatness of their sufferings or the importance of their services." Loyalists quarrelled not only among themselves but also with those who had preceded them. They spurned earlier Nova Scotia settlers as "Bluenoses," questioned their loyalty to the Crown and described the ruling clique in Halifax as pirates. Governor Parr, in time,

Many Loyalists who fled persecution in the United States during the War of Independence forsook land their families had lived on for generations. Some were seen off by stone-throwing neighbors. Their anguish was captured by American illustrator Howard Pyle in "Tories on Their Way to Canada," painted in 1901.

would castigate Loyalists as "a cursed set of dogs" and "people preying on one another like sharks."

But for the time being he was helpful. Loyalists began to clear land on grants that ranged from 100 to 500 acres. Encouraged by Parr, and with tools, food and supplies provided by the British, they founded such places as Wallace, Parrsboro, St. Stephen and St. Andrews. One group estab-

Loyalist Shelburne's Brief, Elegant Heyday

During the spring and summer of 1783 some 10,000 Loyalists landed in a tiny Nova Scotia fishing village and made it Canada's largest town. In Port Roseway, chosen for its deep, beautiful harbor, they planned a community where they would live in gracious prosperity.

By the end of summer some 800 houses had been built—on surveyed streets—and Governor John Parr had renamed the place Shelburne, after the British secretary of state who negotiated the peace (and the Loyalist exodus) with the American rebels. Some thought the name Shelburne a bad omen—as they did the fact that the British flag was hoisted upside down at the change-of-name ceremony.

Shelburne prospered nonetheless, on government rations and aid. Millions of pounds were invested in fishing, logging and farming. Settlers built shops, taverns and beautiful houses. Many dressed stylishly and entertained freely.

But few were experienced fishermen, loggers or mariners. The land proved too rocky for good farming, and government regulations restricted coastal trade. More settlers arrived, straining the supply of land and food. Unemployment was widespread. Some townspeople, living on credit and dwindling personal fortunes, clung to their dream: they gossiped in coffee houses and entertained at lavish balls. Longtime Nova Scotians sneered at "the dancing beggars of Shelburne."

Government rations—"the king's flour and pork"—were cut off in 1787. Shelburne's population scattered to other communities in the colony. Shops and businesses closed. Fine houses were sold, abandoned or broken up for firewood.

Modern Shelburne is a shipbuilding town of 2,700. A cairn marks where the Loyalists came ashore in '83, and the Ross-Thomson House *(right)*, built that very summer, has been restored and is a museum.

Old St. Edward's Church at Clementsport, N.S., has been little changed since Loyalists built it in 1786. It now is used for worship once a year, on the third Sunday in August.

People of Saint John don 18th-century dress each July to commemorate the arrival of the Loyalists in 1783. A highlight of the five days of festivities is the serving of tea—in memory of settlers who could seldom afford such a luxury.

lished Sydney in 1784, and for the next 36 years Cape Breton Island was a separate province.

Other Loyalists pressed for a colony of their own, hoping to rule themselves, to reward sacrifice with a hierarchy of official jobs. They planned a model colony under the "most gentlemanlike" government on earth. So in August 1784 Nova Scotia was cut off at the Chignecto Isthmus and New Brunswick was born. Loyalist-dominated it was; untroubled it was not. People who settled at Saint John or waited there for jobs protested proposals to develop the interior. To their annoyance the new governor, Col. Thomas Carleton, established his capital 75 miles upriver at Ste. Anne's Point—renamed Frederick's Town (later Fredericton).

From London Carleton brought his own Loyalist gentlemen to run his new domain. In the first election for the House of Assembly, poor-area Loyalists defeated candidates more suited to a government of gentlemen. The sheriff simply disqualified enough votes to get the proper people in. The authorities saw a surfeit of democracy as having helped foment the revolution; now they tried to fashion a society that would curb democracy. The majority fought what they saw as favoritism in land grants. They sought to pry control of the public purse from the hands of the governor and his appointed councillors.

William and Edward, the Halifax Princes

Prince William and Prince Edward, sons of George III, left their mark on Halifax in the late 1700s. William (later William IV) generated mainly scandal. Edward (later Duke of Kent) was known as a military planner—and for his devotion to a French sweetheart.

William was wild and 21 when he came to Halifax as a naval captain in the summer of 1786. For the next three summers he spent his days hunting, fishing and watching cockfights, his nights drinking. He ended many of them in the arms of Frances Wentworth, the ambitious wife of John Wentworth, surveyor general of the king's woods in North America. Wentworth did not object, but respectable Halifax was scandalized. It was even more shocked when in 1791 the prince, who had returned to Europe, named Wentworth governor of Nova Scotia.

Edward, a soldier, was sent to Halifax in 1794, aged 26. He was a churchgoer, an early riser, and a most devoted "husband" to his lovely Julie de St. Laurent, a commoner he therefore could not marry. They spent most of their time together at Prince's Lodge, an estate on Bedford Basin. Julie could walk for miles along landscaped paths that spelled her name, and around a heart-shaped pond. A wooden rotunda *(below)*, where a band played for the prince and his beloved, still stands.

Edward returned to Britain in 1800. His last gift to Halifax was a clock which (with its tower) is a Citadel Hill landmark. In 1814 he was obliged to leave Julie, marry a German princess and produce an heir to the English throne since his brother had no legitimate children. Edward's child was a girl—the future Queen Victoria. Julie died heartbroken in a Belgian convent.

Horse-High, Bull-Strong, Skunk-Tight

A pioneer farmer's first fences were often made from the stumps he had to move off his newly cleared land before he could plough. Neighbors might help him with a stumping bee. Laid on their sides, the stumps made a fence that was "horse-high, bull-strong and skunk-tight."

A farmer might split logs and make a rail fence. A snake rail fence, requiring no posts, was easier to build—especially around obstacles—but weeds flourished in its angles and it wasted land. When a snake fence was replaced with a straight rail fence, neighbors often disagreed over who owned the newly available land. (Disputes might arise when any fence was replaced, because the first surveys were often hasty and inaccurate.)

Boulders could be fitted into a mortarless wall that needed no foundation because the stones shifted when frost heaved the ground. Boulders too big to be manhandled to the edge of a field were hauled on stoneboats—sleds with log runners—by oxen. If there were not enough stones to finish the wall, rails would do as well.

Stump fence

Straight rail fence

Stone fence

Snake rail fence

Stone and rail fence

The Loyalist Burial Ground in Saint John, N.B., is on the Loyalist Trail, a three-mile walk through the historic city. The oldest stone is marked 1784, the newest, 1848.

In New Brunswick, the resulting struggles pitted Loyalist against Loyalist. In Nova Scotia, once Shelburne's collapse ended hopes of a bulwark of Loyalist strength, new settlers and old gradually merged and fought the struggles together, on both sides.

Gradually new lives took shape. On land grants of 100, 200, 1,000, up to 5,000 acres, many created farms. Many lumbered. Along the coast men went into fishing and seaborne trade; near the American border they traded illegally with their former enemies.

From the first many sought fields greener than those they drew by lot. Some went elsewhere along the seaboard. Unknown numbers, among them six members of the first New Brunswick legislature, returned to the United States once word spread that animosities had cooled. Some left when the Royal Bounty (relief for Loyalists) ran out. Some officers departed when they found they could draw their half-pay anywhere. Later, spurred by "Niagara fever," others went west to Quebec—and beyond, to present-day Ontario—where land was good and prospects better.

Apart from scant settlement along the Detroit River, the French régime had never tapped the potential of this future heartland of a nation nor had the English after the French defeat of 1760. Instead, the English had heaped fuel on colonial unrest by adding this area to Quebec as part of a vast Indian reserve denied to white exploitation. Even as the revolution ended, Sir Frederick Haldimand, governor of Quebec, was still not convinced he should make it anything else. But as land-hungry Loyalists crowded in, as their complaints multiplied, he found himself under increasing pressure.

Most of the good St. Lawrence Valley land was in the hands of French Canadians. The future Eastern Townships, Haldimand felt, were too close to the potential taint of republican America. Some Loyalists settled on government property around Sorel or headed northeast to

A house built in 1787 by Loyalist Dr. Frederick Stickles in Gagetown, N.B., is now the Queens County Museum. In a corner of the kitchen are utensils of the period: a bellows, a cast-iron muffin pan, a bed warmer and a goose-feather duster.

Joseph Brant's Plea: 'Have Pity on the Poor Indians'

The Iroquois had been Canada's enemies since the time of Champlain but in 1776-79, led by the Mohawk chief Thayendanegea (Joseph Brant), several thousand came to Canada in peace, as immigrants.

During the long French-English struggle for North America most Iroquois had been allies of the English. Led by Brant, they remained loyal during the American Revolution—and were therefore among the losers.

Brant was born in 1742, was raised in the Mohawk Valley of what now is New York State and went to a Protestant school. He went to London in 1775 and George III assured him Iroquois land rights would be respected.

When the revolution began, many Iroquois favored neutrality but Brant won them over to the Crown. With peace they lost their land and animals and Brant decided their future lay in Canada. They were granted land on the Bay of Quinte, near present-day Deseronto, Ont. Others were given 570,000 acres along the Grand River, which flows into Lake Erie. There in 1785 the Mohawks built St. Paul's, the first Protestant church in Ontario. It still stands at Brantford (Brant's Ford).

Brant made a second trip to England in the mid-1780s to claim more compensation for his people. He refused to kiss King George's hand, saying he was a king in his own country, but he got all he asked for. In 1798 he was granted 3,450 acres for himself at present-day Burlington, Ont. The Joseph Brant Museum is in a replica of his house there.

Brant died in 1807. His last words were "Have pity on the poor Indians."

the Gaspé Peninsula and around the Baie des Chaleurs.

In 1784, with the approval of the Indians, Haldimand threw open the region west of the Ottawa River. After a winter of "discontent, friction and disturbances of many kinds" in temporary camps along the St. Lawrence, nearly 5,000 Loyalists were loaded aboard scows and transported into the "Western Settlements" that were to become Upper Canada. Despite Haldimand's

A settler's first home was often no more than a log hut such as this one at Upper Canada Village, near Morrisburg, Ont. The spinning of wool, here demonstrated at the village, was essential to a self-sufficient pioneer family.

efforts, the land had not been surveyed; the Loyalists had to live in tents until it was. Citing "a general despair," an official reported: "There is scarce any turnip seed. They have no seed wheat and many not so much as a blanket to cover them. Axes and hoes have not yet come up for half of them."

Fortunately, many were frontier farmers, unlettered but tough, skilled in the sort of life that confronted them. They cut down trees and built log cabins, fashioned roofs of bark or logs, stuffed clay and moss between the cracks in the walls, plastered the walls with clay, put oiled paper in most of their windows. With flagstones

for hearths, they built open stone fireplaces. Doors were made of rough boards, or doorways were covered with blankets.

Some had brought furniture and family treasures that contrasted with the rude chairs, benches, beds and chests created on the spot. Each family drew meagre rations of flour, pork, beef, salt and butter. Each eventually got an axe, a spade and a hoe. Other tools were shared: a scythe among five families, a plough between two. It was not easy to fetch livestock through the forests. By 1785 one township boasted only two horses and three cows.

The Indians taught settlers to convert deerskin into boots, petticoats, dresses and trousers. Trade was conducted with promissory notes written on paper or cards—cash was scarce for years. The settlers grew flax to be turned into rough linen for clothes, planted apple orchards and raised sheep. A grist mill had been built in advance at Niagara and another was soon added at present-day Napanee. Some settlers received portable hand-operated mills. Others burned holes in stumps with red-hot cannonballs and worked grain with wooden pestles.

There were many new arrivals that first summer of 1784. Many, too late to plant crops, spent cold, hungry winters. Yet by the summer of 1785 one official wrote that the Loyalists "appear in General to be extreamly well satisfied . . . and have made much greater Improvements than could be expected in so short a time, they are all in Comfortable Houses, and their cleared Lands

sown." In November, the Rev. John Stuart reported from Cataraqui: "The Town increases fast, there are above fifty houses built in it, and some of them very elegant. It is now the Post of Transport from Canada (Quebec) to Niagara. The number of Souls to the westward of us is more than 5,000, and we gain daily new Recruits from the States—we are a poor, happy People, and industrious beyond Example."

For the first few years crops were small. In 1788 came the worst blow: famine, caused by drought, poor crops and the end of government rations. With food and seed all but gone, starving children begged boats' crews for biscuits; people ate horses, dogs, roots. Sometimes a beef bone was passed from house to house to be boiled again and again. Unknown numbers died.

But the settlements survived at places such as

One of Toronto's oldest buildings is the cabin (left and above) built by John Scadding. Friend and farm manager to John Graves Simcoe in England, Scadding came to Upper Canada as his clerk in 1792, settled on the Don River in 1794, and built his cabin. It was moved to Exhibition Park in 1879.

today's Cornwall, Kingston (the former Cataraqui), Adolphustown and Port Rowan. In 1791 the new province of Upper Canada was created and John Graves Simcoe, a dynamic, aggressive Englishman who had led a Loyalist regiment in the war, was appointed lieutenant-governor. He travelled his vast domain by canoe and snowshoe, and set former soldiers to work building roads that still bear the names Yonge (from Lake Ontario to Lake Simcoe) and Dundas (from Dundas to London and, later, York). He fortified defences against possible American attack, planned new towns, and gave new, English names—Newark for Niagara, York for Toronto—to existing ones.

Simcoe insisted on proper ceremony when he took the oath of office in a small, partly finished church in Kingston in July 1792 and when he opened his first legislature at Newark (now Niagara-on-the-Lake). He picked a wilderness site to be the provincial capital and grandly called it

Lieutenant-Governor John Graves Simcoe (here in the uniform of his regiment, the Queen's Rangers) and his wife Elizabeth (in the costume of her Welsh ancestors) moved to York, now Toronto, in 1793. While soldiers cleared land for barracks and government buildings, the Simcoes, a nurse and two children lived in a two-room tent until their house was built. In spite of hardships, the governor's energetic lady loved her life in Upper Canada. Her diary, illustrated with sketches and maps, gives a vivid account of early days in a pioneer community that grew into a great city.

London and its river the Thames, only to be overruled and told to establish the capital at York (renamed Toronto again in 1834—see p. 180).

The trappings of Westminster and the building of roads, forts and towns were not enough for Simcoe. If wheat was to make Upper Canada the granary of England, if its economy was to grow, there was another need: people. The settlers who came in answer to his call were Americans—and Loyalists grumbled that the newcomers' professions of loyalty to the king masked American greed for free land. Some did come solely to speculate in land, got it free, sold it and headed home. Others stayed but were doubted for years.

Soon the Americans and later British immigrants outnumbered the early Loyalists. Within three generations the frontier was half as populous as the 13 American colonies had been on the eve of the revolution. Canadian confederation came about in 1867, only 84 years after the first Maritime Loyalist cut down his first tree.

The Loyalists' important contribution to the settlement of Upper Canada is recognized in Ontario's Latin motto, *Ut Incepit Fidelis Sic Permanet* (Loyal she began, loyal she remains).

Loyalty to the Crown became a central, if paradoxical, pillar of Canadian life. For two centuries it provided resistance to the pull of America. It repeatedly sent Canadians to fight at Britain's side. It bedeviled and confused attempts to assert a national identity for Canada. Nonetheless, wrote historian Leslie Upton, the Loyalists maintained "the tie with Britain that was Canada's guarantee of independence." Said historian W. S. MacNutt: "Because they were Loyalist, we are Canadian."

The Maroons, Exotic Immigrants to an Inhospitable Land

Jamaica had banished the Maroons as a threat to peace in that Caribbean colony. But to Nova Scotia Governor John Wentworth the 600 black men, women and children who sailed into Halifax in July 1796 were a godsend in a province short of manpower.

The Maroons were descended from Spanish-owned slaves who fled into the Jamaica interior during the British conquest of 1655. Maroons had terrorized the island for almost 150 years. But in 1796 they were hunted down and deported to be free men.

Many worked on the fortifications overlooking Halifax harbor. Others farmed on the outskirts of the city. Several joined the Royal Nova Scotia Regiment and some were commissioned. Almost everywhere these arrogant exiles were treated with respect.

Maroon Hall, a spacious house (since demolished) in present-day Westphal, was a den of cockfighting, prostitution and voodoo. Here was the harem of Alexander Ochterlony, one of two white commissioners who accompanied the Maroons from Jamaica. Haligonians soon complained about the Maroons' wild behavior and their polygamy. The Maroons found they could not grow yams or bananas, as they had expected to do, and winter was severe. They refused to work.

Wentworth persuaded the blacks to try one more year. But the second winter was worse. Many Jamaicans suffered frostbite, and even Wentworth conceded the experiment was a disaster. As the cost of subsidizing the Jamaicans increased, Ochterlony was discharged and the other commissioner resigned. In the winter of 1798-99 nineteen Maroons died.

For more than two years the Maroons had petitioned to be sent to a warmer country; never, as one Jamaican put it, could they "thrive where the Pine Apple does not." In 1800 the government relented. The Maroons were shipped to Sierra Leone in West Africa.

Heritage Sites

SAINT JOHN, N.B. The Loyalist Landing Place, where refugees from the American Revolution came ashore in 1783, is marked by a boulder and a plaque. It is on a three-mile walking tour which also passes the Loyalist Burial Ground, restored Loyalist residences, and Loyalist House, built in 1810 and now a museum of period furnishings. In the New Brunswick Museum is a slipper believed worn by the first Loyalist to land. Loyalist Days, a week-long festival in July, commemorates the city's origins.

Other sites

Adolphustown, Ont. (14) A cairn in United Empire Loyalist Memorial Park identifies where some 250 Loyalists landed June 16, 1784. Spinning wheels, butter churns and maps tracing Loyalist settlement are in the park museum. The Hay Bay Methodist Church, five miles north, dates from 1792.
Brantford, Ont. (10) A nine-foot bronze statue by Percy Wood commemorates Joseph Brant, a Mohawk chief who led the Six Nations Iroquois here in 1784. Brant's tomb is at St. Paul's, Her Majesty's Chapel of the Mohawks. A sundial in Lorne Park is at a bend in the Grand River (Brant's Ford) where the Six Nations settled.
Burlington, Ont. (11) The Joseph Brant Museum, in a replica of a house that Brant built here in 1800, has Brant's ring and a silver gorget given to him by George III.
Clementsport, N.S. (6) Old St. Edward's Church was consecrated in 1797 to serve Loyalist settlers. Coins, household effects and a silver communion set from that period are displayed in the church.
Fredericton (2) A campsite where Loyalists wintered in 1783-84 is marked by a granite boulder. The Old Burial Ground contains Loyalist graves. A walking tour leads past restored Loyalist residences including the Jonathan Odell House (1785). Loyalist furniture is displayed in the York-Sunbury Museum.
Gagetown, N.B. (3) The Queens County Museum, in a house dating from 1787, is a national historic site. The kitchen has been restored in Loyalist style.
Halifax (8)
GOVERNMENT HOUSE The residence of the lieutenant-governor of Nova Scotia (closed to the public) was built in 1800-05 for Governor John Wentworth.
OLD TOWN CLOCK This landmark, a gift from Prince Edward (Duke of Kent), was installed in 1803 in a tower on Citadel Hill.
PRINCE'S LODGE A small rotunda (closed to the public) remains from a villa con-

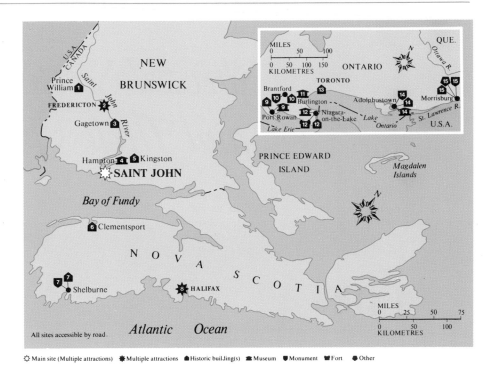

All sites accessible by road.
✩ Main site (Multiple attractions) ✳ Multiple attractions ⬟ Historic building(s) ■ Museum ▼ Monument ⬛ Fort ◆ Other

structed on Bedford Basin by Prince Edward for Julie de St. Laurent, his mistress. A heart-shaped pond and traces of a pathway that spelled her name also remain.
PRINCE OF WALES TOWER A martello tower begun in 1796 has been restored and is a national historic site.
ST. GEORGE'S CHURCH This round, Byzantine-style Anglican church was built in 1800-12.
ST. PAUL'S CHURCH Halifax's oldest building (1750) was the cathedral of Loyalist Charles Inglis, the first Anglican bishop of Nova Scotia. A tablet commemorates him. Vaults in the church contain the remains of governors John Parr and John Wentworth.
Hampton, N.B. (4) Loyalist artifacts in the Kings County Museum include sunglasses and farm and household implements.
Kingston, N.B. (5) Trinity Anglican Church, built by Loyalists in 1789, has the original pews and a record of the first vestry meeting.
Morrisburg, Ont. (15) Loyalist dwellings among some 45 restored or reconstructed buildings in 40-acre Upper Canada Village include a log shanty and the Ross-Boffin House (c.1810), where quilting is displayed. The French-Robertson House was the home of a prosperous merchant. The Loyalist Memorial includes a nine-foot bronze statue of a tattered soldier putting aside his gun and picking up an axe; a cross-shaped garden nearby has walls

made of bricks and timbers from Loyalist homes.
Niagara-on-the-Lake, Ont. (12) Upper Canada's first capital was established in 1792 in what was then called Newark. The McFarland House (1800) is a museum of period furnishings. The Niagara Historical Society Museum displays Loyalist furnishings. Parts of Fort George have been restored or rebuilt as they were in 1796-99.
Port Rowan, Ont. (9) The Backus Mill, built by Loyalists in 1798, is still used to grind flour. The nearby Backus Agricultural Museum displays homemade ploughs and stump-pullers from the early 1800s.
Prince William, N.B. (1) A typical Loyalist farming community, today maintained by artisans in Loyalist costume, has been recreated at 300-acre Kings Landing Historical Settlement. Among some 60 restored and reconstructed buildings are a log shanty, a forge, a carpenter's shop, an inn and an eight-sided, 12-foot-high outhouse.
Shelburne, N.S. (7) A cairn marks where 10,000 Loyalists landed in 1783. The Ross-Thomson House, built in 1784, has been restored and is a museum. Part of the house is a store with period merchandise.
Toronto (13) Scadding Cabin, a squared-log structure built about 1794, is furnished to the period. (Open only on certain days in summer and during the Canadian National Exhibition.)

Shrewd Scottish 'Pedlars' and Tireless Voyageurs

It was a marvel, a palisaded wilderness fort bustling with the energies of an enterprise whose grasp extended from London to the Orient. And more: each summer Fort William became a madhouse of carousing, fighting, lusting voyageurs—and a "parliament" of fur traders whose hearts could be touched only by a beaver skin.

For the North West Company, this great mid-continent entrepôt on Lake Superior was an exchange point where each year partners who had brought trade goods from Montreal met *hivernants* (wintering partners) laden with furs from the far Northwest, the *pays d'en haut*. They paused here for boisterous bacchanalia, swapped cargoes and headed back where they had come from. Between revelries the partners had discussed the trade in the *pays d'en haut*—Indian tribes contacted, prices paid for pelts, competition with the Hudson's Bay Company, and explorations that extended Canada's boundaries to the Pacific.

Fort William was a halfway house, a giant headquarters at the start of the harsh canoe route west. Until 1803 the east-west rendezvous had been Grand Portage, about 45 miles west along the lake (on the border of present-day Minnesota). When Grand Portage was absorbed by the United States in 1794, Nor'Westers rediscovered in British territory the 100-year-old route of the French fur traders, and built Fort William at the mouth of the Kaministikwia (at the site of Thunder Bay, Ont.).

When men first saw it they were amazed. Well

Fort William, the linchpin of North West Company operations in the early 19th century, has been reconstructed at Thunder Bay, Ont. Left: a demonstration of how furs were canvas-wrapped in 90-pound lots for transport to Montreal by canoe. Above: in the Council House, actors portray company partners planning strategy against fur-trading rivals.

they might be—it had taken 1,000 men three years to build.

Fort William was surrounded by 15-foot wooden walls. In the centre of the enclosed square was a great dining and dancing hall. On one wall of the hall was space for a map that eventually would show the extent of company explorations and locate its outposts in the North-west. Near the hall was the Council House where the *bourgeois* (company partners) conducted business. There were two similar buildings, one for wintering partners, the other for Montreal agents. Lining the Kaministikwia River was an Indian village where voyageurs lived while at Fort William.

The North West Company was born in Mon-treal in 1779 when nine rival trading firms united to resist British colonial government restrictions. (Private shipping on the Great Lakes had been

A fiddler and the tunes the voyageurs sang lend authenticity and atmosphere to reconstructed Fort William.

Jean-Marie Boucher's tavern, sanctioned by the North West Company but outside the Fort William palisade, was a first stop for weary voyageurs after the long journey from Montreal or the far Northwest—and a scene of revelry throughout the annual Great Rendez-vous. The men lived in a nearby Indian village.

Barns at Fort William, many weatherproofed with cedar shingles, reflect the building preferences of French Canadians who kept livestock and poultry and grew produce for the fort.

embargoed during the American Revolution for fear trade goods would fall into enemy hands.) With peace, they formed in 1784 an even stronger coalition.

The Nor'Westers relied on French Canadians to man the canoes, and retained the routes of the French fur trade which ended when New France fell in 1760. To justify the great wedge they drove into the domain of the London-based Hudson's Bay Company, they claimed they were Canadian heirs of the French. The North West Company was dominated by shrewd Highland Scots, first Simon McTavish, then his nephew William Mc-Gillivray. They were the chief architects of an enterprise that had agents in London, warehouses in Montreal, markets in Europe and the Far East, and trading posts in a network perhaps the most extensive of any in the world. At the company's peak there were Nor'Westers from the Great Lakes to the Pacific, from the sources of the Mississippi to the Arctic.

The canoes from the east that came annually to Fort William—it was named for William McGillivray—were manned by voyageurs off farms in the St. Lawrence Valley. Each year young men were enticed by tales told by free-spending, hard-drinking men in buckskins, moccasins, silk sashes and red caps—some with the feathers that marked them as *hommes du nord,* Northmen who had wintered in the Northwest. Just before the spring breakup they ranged along the St.

The way it was at Fort William: North West Company partners lived and dressed as they did in Montreal. Here, on the steps of the Great Hall, two partners enjoy the nostalgic offerings of a Scots piper.

"Canoes in a fog, Lake Superior" is by Frances Anne Hopkins, wife of the secretary to HBC Governor George Simpson. Several times between 1858 and 1870 she accompanied her husband on journeys to outlying trading posts. The woman in the centre of the canoe in the foreground is believed either the artist herself or Governor Simpson's wife Frances.

Lawrence on recruiting campaigns, hoping to lure into the company's service young bucks strong enough to perpetuate Nor'Westers legends of endurance, small enough to fit into canoes packed tight with trade goods. Five feet four inches was just right.

By May they were above the rapids at Lachine, nine miles west of Montreal, their 36-foot, 600-pound birchbark *canots du maître* (Montreal canoes) gummed for leaks and gay with paint. Into each went three tons of trade goods packaged into 90-pound *pièces,* canvas-wrapped bales with two ears that let a man lift them easily to his shoulders. Into each canoe, as well, went liquor for each voyageur, kegs of shot, tarpaulins, rope, an axe, a cooking pot, a bailing sponge, and barrels of salted pork. On the day of departure, families, lovers, company officials and relatives lined the shore for the spectacle.

In a scene as close to pageantry as business is ever likely to get, they left in brigades of four to eight canoes, each boasting the company flag, each with a scant six inches of freeboard, each ringing with traditional French songs that gave rhythm to their paddles. At the bow stood an *avant,* the man in charge of the canoe and an expert in shooting rapids. Behind him sat six or eight voyageurs and sometimes passengers.

As traditional as the songs the voyageurs sang was the first stop, a few miles on at Sainte-Anne-

Pointe au Baptême on the Ottawa River (near modern Chalk River, Ont.) is where North West Company brigades bound for Fort William stopped to "baptize" novice voyageurs.

de-Bellevue, on the western tip of Montreal Island. There they prayed at a chapel which was, as explorer-trader Peter Pond wrote, "Dedacated to St. Ann who Protects all Voigers." Then they were off, 350 miles against the current of the Ottawa River, past the site of today's capital, past the graves of voyageurs drowned in treacherous waters. On long, sandy Pointe au Baptême, near today's Chalk River atomic energy plant, they baptized novices as Nor'Westers, regular employees of the company. And they abided by yet another tradition—the novices treated the old-timers to brandy.

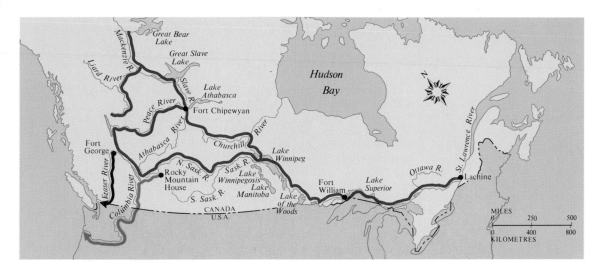

North West Company trade routes covered thousands of miles between Great Bear Lake and Lachine. Explorations by Simon Fraser and David Thompson pushed the company's domain to the Pacific.

———North West Company trade routes
———Simon Fraser (1808)
———David Thompson (1811)

On again, into the 35-mile-long Mattawa River, across Lake Nipissing, into the French River where at last the current was with them.

On they sped through white rapids, on in stretches of up to 80 miles, sometimes paddling all night but usually making camp at twilight. They ate dried peas or beans mixed with the salt pork that gave these voyageurs their name—*mangeurs de lard* (porkeaters). Then pipes and tobacco were brought out and yarns were told of men who carried not the regular load of two

Among the buildings in reconstructed Fort William (at Thunder Bay, Ont.) are two canoe sheds where craftsmen demonstrate how birch-bark canoes were made.

The Symphony of the Portage—But Only If Necessary

Most voyageurs, most of the time, battled *through* rough and dangerous waters. A time-consuming portage *around* shallows and rapids and falls was the last resort.

If the water was shallow and the riverbed firm, poling was the first recourse against a current that made paddling impossible. The voyageurs stood in the canoe and used 8-to-10-foot iron-tipped poles to fight their way upstream. For deeper water, lining (also known as tracking) was the answer: men wore shoulder harness and, with 60-to-100-foot rope lines, strained along the riverbank like canal horses. The *gouvernail* (sternman) stayed in the canoe and steered.

Some rapids were traversed by a *demi-chargé*. Half of a canoe's 60 *pièces* (90-pound bales of trade goods or furs) were unloaded on the riverbank and the lightened canoe was paddled, poled or lined through the rapids. Then the crew went back for the goods left behind.

Rapids with shallows or falls required a *décharge*. The entire cargo was carried and the empty canoe was lined if possible; otherwise the men entered the water to tow it.

A portage, in which canoe and cargo were carried, was a symphony of teamwork. Before the canoe touched shore, some men leaped into the water and held the craft steady as others unloaded it. Each voyageur carried six *pièces*, two at a time, in a leather tumpline (sling); the weight was taken by a broadened section of the tumpline which went across the voyageur's forehead. He trotted (he did not walk) over the often rocky and tangled portage. The 36-foot, 600-pound canoe was carried by the *gouvernail*, the *avant* (bowman) and two paddlers. (Two men carried the 25-foot, 300-pound canoes used west of Lake Superior as in this painting by Paul Kane of a portage at Kakabeka Falls about 22 miles west of present-day Thunder Bay, Ont.)

A portage longer than half a mile was divided into laps of 500 to 800 yards. The canoe and first *pièces* were left at a *pose* (put down)—a guard was posted in case of an Indian attack—and the men returned for a second load. When the entire load was at the *pose*, everything was carried to a second *pose*—and so to the end of the portage.

They Lived on Pork and Pemmican—and a Classic Called Rubaboo

With big appetites and little time to hunt or fish, voyageurs ate as best they could with what they could carry. From Montreal to Fort William it was mostly dried peas and beans, biscuit, flour and salt pork. West of the head of the lakes the great staple was pemmican—buffalo (or caribou or moose) meat dried in the sun, pounded to powder, mixed with animal fat (and perhaps saskatoon berries) and packed in buffalo hide containers which held 90 pounds. Three or four pounds a day fueled the voyageur who was the main cog in the machinery of the fur trade.

Voyageur cooks turned plain pemmican—simply a chunk eaten raw—into rubaboo, a classic of the North-

west. Into a hot flour soup went pemmican slices and perhaps a wild onion or a scrap of salt pork. Another variation was *richeau*—pemmican fried in its own grease and embellished, if possible, with flour, salt and potatoes.

The porkeaters of the east ate the same thick mixture morning and night: peas were boiled to bursting in a 10-gallon kettle, then pork strips and crumbled biscuits were added. Everyone ate from the kettle.

Weather delays might mean a chance to fish, search for honey or eggs, or trap a beaver. The church decreed that roast beaver tail could be enjoyed even on Friday—apparently because, like a fish, a beaver swam.

If food ran short and hunting was poor, voyageurs might have to live on *tripe de roche*, a black leathery lichen that, washed and boiled, "becomes a little slimy but makes a nourishing soup." Sometimes it was either that or a chew of the spruce gum used for patching canoes.

Beaver trapping (see p. 28) became easier with the introduction of iron traps about 1797. They were baited with castoreum, a secretion from beaver glands.

pièces but up to eight. Then they slept in the lee of canoes turned on their sides, ignoring mosquitoes, rain and cold.

They were up before dawn and away without breakfast. That came 15 or 20 miles on and, unless they had a particularly hard day ahead, they knew there would be no midday stop for food.

On they went into Lake Huron, to the Sault Ste. Marie rapids, bypassed by a lock built in 1799, then into stormy Lake Superior, wherever possible hugging the shore out of fear of its violent squalls, its oceanlike expanse. *La Vieille,* the old woman of the wind, was wooed when the weather was fine by casting tobacco and trinkets into the water and singing her a song: "*Souffle, souffle, la Vieille*" (Blow, blow, old woman). And if she was kind they raised makeshift sails of oilcloth or blankets.

A month after Lachine, they stopped just out of sight of Fort William and washed and dressed themselves into dandies. Veterans of the Northwest put bright feathers in their caps. Then, singing as loud as they could, they made shore amid the uproar of Fort William's annual greeting and high wassail.

If the Northmen were not already there from the *pays d'en haut,* they soon would be, men who paddled 3,000 miles from Fort Chipewyan on Lake Athabasca with furs from the valleys of the Saskatchewan and the Assiniboine, the remote Mackenzie and Peace. They had cheated, fought

A wooden lock built in 1799 to enable canoes to bypass rapids on the St. Mary's River at Sault Ste. Marie was destroyed 15 years later. This is a stone replica.

and sometimes killed HBC traders for furs. Each year, for months, the Northmen left behind their Indian wives and the Métis children who would someday form a nation of their own (see p. 164).

In *canots du nord,* canoes half the size of those from Montreal, they came with scathing pride. To be *un homme du nord* was to disdain pork-eaters who scurried back to civilization each fall. To be a Northman was to arrive at Fort William eager for rum, brawling and women and to squander a year's wages in an explosion of holiday exuberance.

By day they gossiped, feasted and drank; at night, in the words of a distraught missionary, "the furies of Hell were let loose" as Indians and voyageurs fought for the favors of Chippewa girls. There were confinements in a jail called the *pot au beurre* (butter tub), and as many as a dozen Indians were murdered in a season. For three weeks the Fort William wilderness marvel was awash in vice and violence.

The partners celebrated with banquets of beef, hams, venison, Indian corn, wine and spirits, then with a ball. The piper and fiddler tuned up as voyageurs, Indian men in vivid paint and Indian maidens in their finery filed into the great hall. In his ruffles and lace and silver-buckled shoes, the senior partner bowed gallantly to a chief's daughter, led her into the first reel, and the dancing began. With pauses for refreshment, the festivities continued until dawn.

At the end of July the porkeaters returned to Montreal with furs, the Northmen to the West with trade goods. Fort William slumped into exhausted quiet.

By September, four months after they left, the porkeaters were back at Lachine. The furs were carted by road to Montreal, then loaded on London-bound ships for the last leg of the 6,000-mile trip from trapline to market.

By then the Northmen were spreading out to the far-flung posts of the company. They observed rituals of their own. The first was an initiation ceremony that took place between Lake Superior and Lake of the Woods, at the height of the land where waters flow north to Hudson Bay, east to the Atlantic and south to the Gulf of Mexico. William McGillivray experienced this ritual in 1784, the year he went west to learn the business as a clerk on the Red River.

He heard the banter and singing die, saw the men assembling, watched the most experienced Northman unsheathe his hunting knife, sharpen it, cut off the bough of a scrub cedar and command McGillivray, the novice, to kneel. Historian Marjorie Wilkins Campbell tells the story:

"McGillivray had doffed his cap. Now he dropped to his knees. Suddenly his head and shoulders were drenched with cold water, dipped

Peter Pond the Dreamer: Was He a Murderer Too?

Peter Pond was an irascible dreamer who opened North America's richest fur trapping area to the North West Company. He may also have been a murderer.

Pond, born in Connecticut in 1740, started trading furs in the Mississippi Valley and had killed a man in a duel when he came to the Canadian Northwest in 1775. His restless spirit led him ever deeper into the wilderness and in 1778 he became the first white man to see the Athabasca River. He wintered 40 miles south of Lake Athabasca and found furs there the finest he had ever seen.

Pond took furs to Grand Portage on Lake Superior the following year and was welcomed into the North West Company. But in the spring of 1782 at Lac La Ronge (in what now is Saskatchewan), Nor'Wester Jean-Etienne Wadin was shot and killed in a quarrel with Pond and a clerk. The widow petitioned to have Pond tried, but the Northwest was outside Quebec's jurisdiction and he was left free to continue exploring and trading.

Pond had little education (he used a strange phonetic spelling in his journal) but he was inquisitive. Endlessly, he questioned Indians about the land to the west of Lake Athabasca. Laboriously, he drew crude maps (sometimes having to thaw his ink). He concluded, erroneously, that the lake drained to the Pacific. (He shared his theories and his knowledge of the Northwest with Alexander Mackenzie—see p. 147.) But Pond would never reach the Pacific. In the winter of 1787 he was implicated in another slaying.

John Ross, a trader with a rival Montreal company, was camped near Pond's Lake Athabasca post. When Ross accused the Nor'Westers of forcing Indians to trade with them, he was shot by one of Pond's men. Two Nor'Westers were tried and acquitted. This time there was no suggestion that Pond had pulled the trigger. But his quarrelsome nature had turned the company partners against him and he was shunned. By 1790 he had sold his company shares and returned to Connecticut. He died in 1807, forgotten and impoverished.

Pond's version of Wadin's death will never be known. The early part of his journal was preserved after his death as a curio because of its language, but the part dealing with his years in the Northwest was used to light a kitchen fire.

North West Company voyageurs swore that a man-eating monster dwelt in the black depths of this cave on the north shore of the Mattawa River. This stretch of the Mattawa, which was part of the canoe route between Montreal and Fort William, is now in Mattawa River Provincial Park.

*"We had to pass where no human beings should venture,"
wrote Simon Fraser (left) of his exploratory journey down the
Fraser River in 1808. John Innes's painting portrays Fraser's
men and their Indian guides clinging to the walls of the river's
Black Canyon.*

from the stream with the cedar bough. The guide commanded him to repeat the ancient two-fold promise. Keeping his voice as firm as he could, McGillivray swore in French never to permit a new-comer to pass the Height of Land without a similar ceremony—and never to kiss a voya-geur's wife without her permission." The ceremony ended with a dozen gunshots and a round of brandy from the new members. William Mc-

Gillivray "realized that only a few hundred men made the long, dangerous trip each year. He felt something of the deep emotion behind each northman's proud boast: *'Je suis un homme du nord!'* Now he, too, was a northman."

Another ritual came after their passage down the swift, turbulent Winnipeg River with its spec-tacular rapids and falls. On Lake Winnipeg they raced one another into exhaustion to establish a hierarchy of their own.

The haughtiest Northmen were the Athabas-cans. On Lake Winnipeg they made their boasts and others going to less remote posts took them up. For hours they raced, as many as 100 canoes. The normal pace of 40 strokes a minute jumped to 45, 50, 55, 65. The longest race lasted 40 hours without interruption and was stopped only when a *bourgeois* so ordered.

The fur trade was as old as Canada; it had drawn men deeper and deeper into the continent as trapping depleted the supply of beaver. The North West Company, in extending its net-work of trading posts, became hostage to fantastic distance.

Repeatedly Nor'West partners bargained with the HBC for use of Hudson Bay to ship furs to Europe and receive supplies from England. It would have finished Montreal and Fort William as hubs of the trade but easier access to the inte-rior would have meant greater savings in money, time and distance.

But the HBC had no intention of sharing its

*These stone chimneys,
dating from 1866, are the
only remains of a series
of forts at Rocky Moun-
tain House, Alta. The
North West Company
built the first Rocky
Mountain House in
1799. The last was in
ruins by 1885.*

Huzza, huzza pour le pays sauvage!

"I could carry, paddle, walk and sing with any man I ever saw."

He was old now, a onetime voyageur, and his memories of life in *le pays sauvage* were recorded by Alexander Ross (1783-1856) in *The Fur Hunters of the Far West:*

"No portage was too long for me and my end of the canoe never touched the ground. I saved the lives of 10 *bourgeois* [company partners] and when others stopped to carry and lost time, I pushed on—over rapids, over cascades, over chutes; all were the same to me. No water, no weather ever stopped the paddle or the song. I have had 12 wives and was once possessed of 50 horses and six running dogs. No *bourgeois* had better dressed wives than I; no Indian chief finer horses; no white man better harnessed or swifter dogs. I wanted for nothing; and I spent all my earnings in the enjoyment of pleasure. Now I have not a spare shirt to my back nor a penny to buy one. Yet were I young I should glory in the same career again. There is no life so happy as a *voyageur*'s life; none so independent; no place where a man enjoys so much variety and freedom as in the Indian country. *Huzza, huzza pour le pays sauvage!*"

century-old advantage with a rival that had challenged its monopoly of all lands drained into Hudson Bay. It had, instead, sent factors inland, abandoning its policy of waiting for Indians to bring furs to its posts along the bay.

Simon McTavish spurred his men on, cut prices and flooded the interior with cheap liquor diluted with five parts of water into "Blackfoot milk" to woo the Indians.

There was competition also from the American John Jacob Astor's Pacific Fur Company with its eyes on the West Coast. To survive, the North West Company would have to exploit the territory west of the Rockies. But this required a route through the mountains.

In 1789 Alexander Mackenzie, another Highland Scot Nor'Wester, paddled to the mouth of the great river that now bears his name, only to find not the Pacific but the Arctic Ocean. On another trip, in 1793, he crossed the Rockies and became the first white man to cross Canada to the Pacific (see p. 144). But he returned without a passable trade route.

In 1805, when an American expedition led by Lewis and Clark charted a route to the mouth of the Columbia, the Nor'Westers thought that river might be a trade route. Posts in the Athabasca district and on the Pacific slope could be supplied with trade goods shipped from England via Cape Horn; pelts could be canoed down the Columbia and shipped directly to England, superseding the expensive 4,000-mile canoe route to Montreal.

Surveying the Columbia became the task of Simon Fraser, the American-born son of a United Empire Loyalist, and David Thompson, educated in an English school for the poor. Both had been in the trade since their teens and both had explored the Rockies, trading and establishing posts.

On May 28, 1808, Fraser left Fort George (present-day Prince George, B.C.) with 23 men in four canoes. They soon encountered rapids impossible to navigate. Fraser and his men portaged along precipitous banks where, in Fraser's words, "our lives hung upon a thread, as the failure of the line or a false step of one of the men might have hurled the whole of us into Eternity."

They realized the river was impassable, and on June 10 erected a scaffold for the canoes and buried unnecessary equipment. They set out on foot for the sea, following the riverbank, scaling wild river gorges sometimes passable only on Indian ladders of roots and bark that swayed in the wind like "the shrouds of a ship."

Tin dishes and trade goods lost in 1800 when a North West Company canoe overturned in the Winnipeg River near what is now the Manitoba-Ontario border were recovered more than 160 years later and are in the Royal Ontario Museum in Toronto. Included are six knife handles, files, two axe heads, musket balls, bird shot, knife blades, glass beads and an ice chisel.

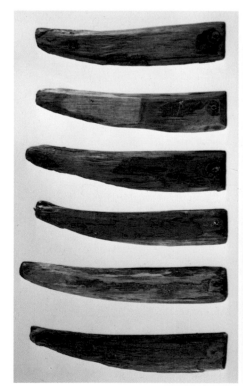

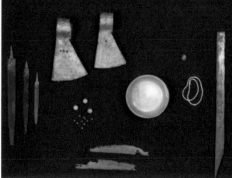

This house (now a restaurant) in Sainte-Anne-de-Bellevue, Que., was the home of North West Company partner Simon Fraser—a distant relative of the Simon Fraser who discovered the Fraser River.

Saskatchewan River in 1807, reached the upper Columbia River and, going upstream, discovered its source. Thompson established trading posts in what now is southern British Columbia and Washington, Idaho and Montana. In 1809 he learned of Fraser's failure. The partners told him to follow the Columbia to its mouth.

He spent a year exploring its tributaries, then on July 3, 1811, with nine men set off down the river. Twelve days later he rounded the last bend only to find that Astor's men had come by sea three months before and established a trading post called Fort Astoria, which the North West Company would purchase in 1814 when the War of 1812 made it impossible for American supplies to arrive by sea. Thompson had extended the Nor'West domain from Montreal to the Pacific. Three years later, in retirement, he completed a map, "The North West Territory of the Province of Canada," which illustrated the company's empire west of Fort William. With appropriate ceremony and celebration it was hung in the space on the wall of Fort William's Great Hall.

On it the partners could trace the aggressive conquest of a continent, the course of the Columbia, the heartbreaking journeys of Fraser and Mackenzie, the location of posts dotting the Northwest, the sinuous canoe routes that bound it all together with the nerve centre of Fort William. Hewn out of wilderness, conquering incredible distance and terrain, the North West Company was, as David Thompson's map so vividly illustrated, one of the most remarkable enterprises Canada has ever known.

On June 14, near present-day Lillooet, B.C., natives told Fraser the river was navigable from there to the sea. Fraser bargained for wooden dugout canoes, and on July 2 he reached the Pacific near today's New Westminster, B.C. He took his bearings and reached a melancholy conclusion: this was not the Columbia. Nor was it a route for trade. Harassed by Indians, his food running short, Fraser rallied his mutinous men and the same day headed back up the river that now bears his name, finding on July 20 the canoes and supplies. They reached Fort George on Aug. 6 without losing a man.

It was left to David Thompson, a man trained in navigation and surveying, to find the Columbia. He left Rocky Mountain House on the North

After *le pays d'en haut,* the Good Life of Montreal

McTavish, Frobisher, Pangman, Chaboillez, McGill, McGillivray . . . the business and social élite of Montreal in the late 18th and early 19th centuries . . . McLeod, Mackenzie, Montour, de Rocheblave, Richardson . . .

They were the fur barons. Most had known the hardships of *le pays d'en haut* (the Northwest), and now, many of them married to French Canadians, they lived the good life of Montreal. Most were hospitable men.

Joseph Frobisher and his wife, Charlotte Joubert, entertained at Beaver Hall, his mansion in the country (where now there is the downtown street called Beaver Hall Hill). A sweeping drive led up to the house with its backdrop of Lombardy poplars (and Mount Royal); below were the bustling city and the

broad St. Lawrence River. Frobisher was an original North West Company partner and later, with Simon McTavish, a founder of McTavish, Frobisher and Company, which controlled Nor'Wester operations. At 43, Simon McTavish married 18-year-old Marie-Marguerite Chaboillez. Their home was a stone house which still stands at 2327 Rue Saint-Jean-Baptiste.

In 1785, nineteen traders who had spent at least one winter in the Northwest formed the Beaver Club. The members (eventually there were 55) were given a gold medal engraved with the member's name and the club's motto 'Fortitude in Distress.' They ate roast beaver, pemmican, sturgeon and wild rice and drank toasts to the mother of all the saints; the king; the fur trade

in all its branches; voyageurs, wives and children; and absent members. On occasion, as the wine flowed, members sat in two rows on the floor, each paddling with a walking stick, tongs or a poker, all singing lusty voyageur songs.

The Beaver Club died as more and more of the fur barons died. Their memory lives on with their names and in the institutions some of them helped create. James McGill bequeathed £10,000 (an estimated $50,000 at the time) and Burnside, his 46-acre estate, to found a college that in 1821 became McGill University. John Richardson, a North West Company partner, was one of the founders of the Bank of Montreal, organized in 1817 as Canada's first permanent bank.

Heritage Sites

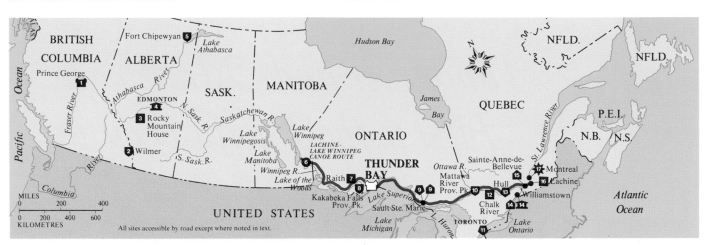

🛶 Main site (Fort) ✳ Multiple attractions ▲ Historic building ◼ Museum ◆ Monument ● Fort ◇ Route ● Other □ Unmarked site

THUNDER BAY, Ont. Fort William, the North West Company's inland headquarters, is re-created in 125-acre Old Fort William. Most of its 48 buildings are inside a palisade beside the Kaministikwia River, nine miles upstream from the original location. They include storehouses, artisans' shops and a jail.

CANOE YARD Fur-trade canoes are displayed and the building of birchbarks is demonstrated. In an outfitting store are bark, spruce gum and roots, and paddles and tarpaulins such as voyageurs used.

CANTINE SALOPE Typical Nor'Wester meals including stew and soup are served in this old-style restaurant.

COUNCIL HOUSE The building in which company partners conducted business has been reconstructed.

Other sites

Chalk River, Ont. (12) On long, sandy Pointe au Baptême, 225 miles after leaving Lachine, novice voyageurs and clerks were baptized as Nor'Westers.

Edmonton (4) Timbers, nails and scissors excavated from company forts are in the Provincial Museum of Alberta.

Fort Chipewyan, Alta. (5) A cairn marks the site of the company's most northerly post. The fort was moved here about 1804 from across Lake Athabasca. *Accessible only by air, boat or winter road.*

Hull, Que. (13) In Saint-Jean-de-Brébeuf Park are stone steps and a low causeway built by voyageurs for a portage.

Kakabeka Falls Provincial Park, Ont. (8) Mountain Portage bypassed these 128-foot-high falls on the Kaministikwia River, the first major obstacle for travellers going west from Fort William. A plaque identifies the portage.

Lachine, Que. (16) The starting point for canoe brigades bound for Fort William was at the head of the Lachine Rapids near present-day Promenade du Père-Marquette.

Lachine-Lake Winnipeg Canoe Route (6) Much of the main artery of waterways and portages travelled by North West Company canoe brigades between Montreal and the Northwest can be traced. The Trans-Canada Highway between Montreal and Thunder Bay stays close to the voyageurs' course; wilderness canoe routes such as those on the Ottawa, French and Winnipeg rivers follow it exactly.

Mattawa River Provincial Park, Ont. (10) A plaque identifies La Porte de l'Enfer (Hell's Gate), a swift section of the Mattawa River, and a cave that voyageur legend said was inhabited by a monster.

Montreal (17) The house to which Simon McTavish, the dominant Nor'Wester, brought his French-Canadian bride in 1793 is at 2327 Rue Saint-Jean-Baptiste. A monument commemorating him stands at the head of Peel Street, in Mount Royal Park. At 1085 Beaver Hall Hill a plaque marks where senior Nor'Wester Joseph Frobisher built a mansion he called Beaver Hall. La Maison Bertrand at 160 Rue Saint-Amable dates from 1815; it is thought to have been a company warehouse. A birchbark canoe, an iron beaver trap and a flintlock musket owned by McTavish are in the Montreal Military and Maritime Museum.

Prince George, B.C. (1) The re-created palisade of a trading post built by Simon Fraser in 1807 is in 90-acre Fort George Park. From here in 1808 Fraser reached the Pacific by descending the river that now bears his name.

Raith, Ont. (7) Height of Land Lake, near which Nor'Westers making their first trip to winter in the far Northwest were baptized as Northmen, is eight miles northwest. *Lake accessible only on foot.*

Rocky Mountain House, Alta. (3) The site of a company post built in 1799 is 2½ miles southwest in Rocky Mountain House National Historic Park. Geographer David Thompson left from the post in 1807 on his trek to the source of the Columbia River. Remains in the park date from a later fort (1866).

Sainte-Anne-de-Bellevue, Que. (15) A two-storey stone house dating from 1798 was the home of company partner Simon Fraser (a distant relative of the explorer of the same name). It is now a restaurant, the Petit Café. The Church of Sainte-Anne-de-Bellevue is believed built on the foundations of a chapel in which voyageurs prayed for divine protection.

Sault Ste. Marie, Ont. (9) A stone reconstruction of a wooden canoe lock erected in 1799 is on the property of Abitibi-Price Inc. Ermatinger Old Stone House, built by a company partner in 1814, is now a museum and national historic site.

Toronto (11) The map of the Northwest which David Thompson hung in the Great Hall in Fort William in 1814 is in the reading room of the Archives of Ontario.

Williamstown, Ont. (14) Exhibits in the Nor'Westers and Loyalist Museum include a desk that belonged to David Thompson, a snuffbox owned by Simon Fraser the explorer, and a fur press. The house in which Thompson lived in 1815-35 is nearby. It is privately owned.

Wilmer, B.C. (2) A cairn marks the site of Kootenay House, a company post built by David Thompson in 1807.

Vancouver and Mackenzie, First to the Pacific Coast

Alexander Mackenzie knew full well what he had given up to live as an explorer of the Canadian wilderness. He wrote on the eve of his incredible journey to the Pacific: "I begin to think it is the height of folly in a man to reside in a country of this kind, deprived of every comfort that can render life agreeable, especially when he has a competency to enjoy life in a civilized society." This portrait by Sir Thomas Lawrence, the only known true likeness of Mackenzie, is in the National Gallery of Canada in Ottawa.

One Indian of the Bella Bella tribe, in what now is coastal British Columbia, was known for his story of being "attacked" by white men—he did not say why—on a spring day in 1793, far up Dean Channel, a long arm of the Pacific Ocean. He said the leader fired a musket at him—whether intending to injure was not clear—and that another slapped him on the back with the flat of a sword.

A strange story. The only whites known to be in that immediate area that spring were Capt. George Vancouver and his crew, peaceful men who wanted to befriend the Bella Bella and their cousins the Bella Coola. Vancouver, a Royal Navy officer, was mapping the tortuous Pacific coastline and trying to determine whether there was a northern route from the Pacific to the Atlantic—the Northwest Passage that other men were seeking from the other side of the continent.

Vancouver had sought the passage before—as a 20-year-old midshipman in an expedition led by James Cook.

It was with Cook in 1778 that George Vancouver first saw Vancouver Island and met the friendly coastal Indians who lived in wooden houses and wore clothes of sea otter and other opulent furs. The Cook expedition, the first from Europe known to have set foot in present-day British Columbia, went north into the Bering Strait, only to be turned back by ice, then sailed to Hawaii. There, in February 1779, Vancouver witnessed Cook's murder by hostile natives.

Cook's journal heightened European interest in North Pacific trade. In 1789, Spanish ships entered Nootka Sound on the west coast of Vancouver Island, captured English trading vessels and built a small gun battery overlooking the harbor. When an angry Britain threatened war, Spain agreed to give up Nootka. The Admiralty sent Vancouver to secure the territory. He sailed from England on April 1, 1791, in the 100-foot

These famous words were embedded with red cement in a rock—believed to be Mackenzie's Rock—near the mouth of the Bella Coola River (below), in British Columbia. The pigment and grease mixture with which Alexander Mackenzie recorded his crossing of the continent was erased by the weather within 50 years.

This picture in the Public Archives in Ottawa depicts the Spanish seizure of English trading ships at Nootka Sound on Vancouver Island, in 1789. To avoid war with Britain over the incident, Spain relinquished her claims to northwestern North America.

Did Drake Reach Vancouver Island in 1579?

Francis Drake, the first European known to have visited the west coast of North America, may have sailed as far north as Vancouver Island.

On his round-the-world voyage of 1577-80 Drake crossed the Atlantic in *Golden Hinde,* became separated from four companion ships after passing through the Strait of Magellan into the Pacific, and looted and destroyed Spanish ships and settlements up the west coast of South America.

In the spring of 1579 Drake pressed northward hoping to find a shortcut to the North Atlantic and home. How far north Drake got is uncertain. His nephew John, a crewman, corroborated his uncle's claim that he reached the 48th parallel, almost the latitude of Long Beach on Vancouver Island. A 7,219-foot peak nearby, which may have been a landfall, has been named Golden Hinde. Drake finally turned back south, anchored near present-day San Francisco to repair his ship, and claimed Nova Albion—all the coast north of there—for Queen Elizabeth.

Drake crossed the Pacific in 1580 and received a hero's welcome in England. His voyage inspired the one by James Cook 200 years later, and laid the basis for British claims to western North America.

sloop *Discovery*, with the tender *Chatham* in company.

A year later he was surveying and mapmaking from one of *Discovery*'s boats—and adding more than 200 names to existing charts. (Cook and Vancouver were among the first navigators to use a chronometer for determining longitude.) He named the Strait of Georgia after George III, Point Grey (near the University of British Columbia) after a navy friend. The inlet to what would be Vancouver harbor became Burrard's Channel (Burrard Inlet), named for a naval officer.

Discovery and *Chatham* put into Nootka Sound in August 1792 and there Vancouver met Capt. Juan Bodega y Quadra, sent by Spain to negotiate the transfer. They became friends and the Englishman named the great island "Vancouver's and Quadra's Island." (Quadra was eventually dropped from the island's name but it is perpetuated in the name of an island north of the Strait of Georgia.) Eventually Spain withdrew from the whole northwest Pacific coast.

Vancouver and his crew spent the winter of 1792-93 in Hawaii, returning in late May 1793 to Dean Channel (which he named for Dean King, the father of a fellow officer). There, if the Bella Bella was to be believed, Vancouver shot at the Indian. He went up fjords as far inland as present-day Bella Coola, then pushed north into what now are Alaskan waters, but found no passage to the Atlantic.

Increasingly disabled by tuberculosis (of which he would die in 1798), Vancouver returned to England in 1794. He had sailed 65,000 miles in 4½ years and had charted 10,000 miles of coastline. Navigators would use his maps for a century.

Vancouver in his ship's boat was surveying the present-day Oregon coast when on May 9, 1793, 10 men clambered into a 25-foot canoe at Fort Fork in what now is northern Alberta. Alexander Mackenzie was starting up the Peace River on a trek he hoped would lead overland to the Pacific.

The blond, 29-year-old Scottish fur trader, strong-willed and determined to reach his goal, was a natural leader. He started in the fur trade at 15, became a partner in a Montreal firm that merged with the North West Company (see p. 132), and was made supervisor of the Nor'Westers' Athabasca district. But transporting furs to Montreal was costly. Profits would be higher if furs were shipped from the Pacific coast; and Mackenzie determined to blaze the trail.

He went to London in 1791 to study navigation and to learn to use a chronometer. In 1792 he was back in Canada. Late that year he left Fort Chipewyan on Lake Athabasca to winter at Fort Fork (near present-day Peace River, Alta.) and

thus be 300 miles closer to the sea when he set out in the spring.

Mackenzie started his 1793 journey with North West Company clerk Alexander Mackay, six French-Canadian voyageurs and two Indian interpreter-hunters. Ten days later they entered the Peace River canyon, in which the river drops 270 feet in 22 miles. (Mackenzie's party, going *upstream*, had to *climb* that 270 feet.)

The canoe was damaged twice on the first day in the 300-foot-deep canyon, and was repaired with bark and melted tree gum.

On the third night the men wanted to turn back. Mackenzie ignored them and next morning sent scouts ahead to determine where the rapids ended. They reported that the river looked *im-*

This wooden sea chest, inscribed G. V. and believed to have been Capt. George Vancouver's, is in a replica of the stern of Vancouver's ship Discovery *in the British Columbia Provincial Museum in Victoria. Above: a chronometer used by both Capt. James Cook and Vancouver. It is in the National Maritime Museum in Greenwich, England.*

River Disappointment: In Failure a Triumph

Alexander Mackenzie tried twice to reach the Pacific Ocean by land. His first attempt failed—but was nonetheless a triumph.

On June 3, 1789, Mackenzie left Fort Chipewyan, a North West Company post on Lake Athabasca in present-day Alberta, to find a route by which furs could be taken to ships on the west coast.

With 13 companions and three canoes he headed north down the Slave River toward Great Slave Lake. Yellowknife Indians told him of a river flowing northwest from the lake's western end, and on June 29 he entered the river, expecting it would lead him through the Rockies. But on July 10, the river widened into its delta—and the Rockies were still to the west. Five days later Mackenzie reached the Beaufort Sea.

He turned back up the river that he called the River Disappointment. When he reached Fort Chipewyan on Sept. 12, Mackenzie felt defeated. But he had travelled nearly 3,000 miles in 102 days, and had discovered North America's second largest river—which now bears his name.

Easy Wealth Fostered West Coast Indian Art

Cedar and salmon were the basis of a rich Indian culture that Europeans encountered along 900 miles of Canada's west coast in the late 1700s. Here lived the Haida, Tsimshian, Kwakiutl, Bella Coola, Nootka and Coast Salish.

Cedar trunks grown huge in the mild, damp climate made dugout canoes up to 75 feet long in which 50 paddlers would range beyond sight of land to harpoon whales or would prowl the coast in search of slaves and booty. Cedar posts and beams framed houses 60 feet wide and 300 feet long that held 10 families. The wood, easily split with stone tools, made planks to sheathe the houses; its shredded bark was woven into cloaks to wear in the rain with conical hats of woven spruce roots.

Salmon were plentiful. A few weeks of spearing and trapping during the summer spawning run provided food for a year. The fish were dried on wooden frames. For variety there were abalone, crab, seal, deer and other game, and roots and berries. Fuel for cooking and for lamps came from the oolichan, a kind of smelt, whose body was rendered into oil—or dried and burned as a torch.

So much wealth so easily obtained left plenty of time for artistic expression. Brightly colored geometric designs and stylized animal forms were woven into capes and carved into masks, and into the totem poles that stood before the houses of chiefs. Ornamentation covered the cedar chests in which chiefs stored their ceremonial garb: blankets of mountain goat wool and shredded cedar bark, and carved wooden headdresses. The wealthy decorated their bodies with tattoos and paint made from oils, berries and earth pigments. Copper and jade

ornaments were worn in noses and ears; women pierced their lower lips to take plugs of polished wood or stone. In summer, Indian men wore no clothes.

In the rainy winter months people watched dramas in which the eagle (representing authority), the whale (the spirits of those lost at sea) and other creatures retold legends of the beginning of the world and histories of great families.

Social rank was based on wealth. Noble families owned the fishing and hunting grounds, and ordinary members of the tribe had to pay to gather food. Prisoners of war became slaves of the chiefs and nobility.

Wealth was displayed at ceremonies called potlatches. The host would kill some of his slaves, burn valued possessions and give expensive gifts to guests. But any gift had to be returned, with interest, at some future potlatch.

These totem poles and cedar longhouses 'Ksan, a village re-created near Hazelton, [ ] it was about 1870.

These Paul Kane paintings portray Coastal Indian life. Above: a Coast Salish woman weaves a blanket edged with vegetable-dyed geometric designs. In a typical village (below), salmon are hung to dry from roof edges and below the raised floors of lodges from which the walls were removed in warm weather.

This map shows the distribution of Coastal I in the late 1700s, based on language.

☐ *Tlinkit language group*
☐ *Haida language group*
☐ *Tsimshian language group*
☐ *Wakashan language group*
☐ *Salishan language group*

History on a Pole

A totem pole was a history, its carved birds and mammals representing tribal emblems or supernatural ancestors. The poles probably originated as supports for the roof beams of houses and later were erected outside chiefs' homes. This one, in Thunderbird Park in Victoria, portrays the totems of four Kwakiutl tribes.

The thunderbird flashed lightning from his eyes, and his beating wings made thunder. After he became a man, his son returned to the sky and resumed these functions.

The grizzly bear, clutching a copper shield to his mouth, indicates wealth. He sits atop the figure which represents him after be became human and, in tribal mythology, the first clan member.

The beaver, usually with a crosshatched tail and a stick in enormous clenched teeth, appeared on many poles. The little face represents a joint in his tail.

Dsonoqua, a giantess, was pursued by a man who saw her stealing drying fish. They married and their son (held by Dsonoqua) later founded the tribe.

Figures on different poles usually had the same principal characteristics; details reflected local myths and legends.

passable for nine miles. Mackenzie gave them all rum and sugar-sweetened wild rice for the long portage ahead.

On May 22 the little expedition started up Portage Mountain (near present-day Hudson's Hope, B.C.). They felled trees but did not cut them from the stumps, thus forming railings the men could grasp. For three days they carried canoe and cargo over the mountain on a course parallel to the river.

By May 31, 22 days after leaving Fort Fork, they had crossed the main chain of the Rocky Mountains but, although they did not know it, they were still 500 miles from the sea. Many mountain ranges still lay between them and the Pacific.

Mackenzie faced a major decision that day, when the expedition reached a fork in the Peace, at present-day Finlay Forks. They could follow, as his men preferred, the wide, slow northwest branch, now called the Finlay, or turn south up the narrow, swift Parsnip. An Indian at Fort Fork had said that the northwest branch led into a maze of mountains, but from the other branch there was a portage to a river "where the inhabitants build houses and live upon islands." Mackenzie chose the Parsnip.

After many days they were close to the head of the Parsnip and despaired of finding the portage. But on June 10 one of a group of Sekani Indians they encountered led them to it. They went up a branch of the Parsnip to Arctic Lake, then—two days later—walked 817 paces to Portage Lake. From there the rivers drained west. They had crossed the Continental Divide.

The Sekanis told Mackenzie of a tribe to the west who lived in houses near a sea which the Sekanis called the stinking lake. The tribe traded with whites who came in boats as big as islands. The Sekanis, Mackenzie concluded, knew about the Pacific Ocean.

Alexander Mackenzie was nearing the end of his journey to the Pacific as he pushed through this verdant British Columbia valley (now called the Mackenzie Valley, in Tweedsmuir Provincial Park). Beyond these mountains lay the Bella Coola River, his route to the sea.

Now their journey was down a stream that Mackenzie named the Bad River (James Creek). The canoe was smashed on rocks and a gravel bar and the men begged Mackenzie to turn back. He waited until they were dry, fed and rested and then talked to them, inspiring them with his determination to reach the Pacific. A day and a half later, the canoe again repaired with tree gum and bark, they went on. That night their Sekani guide deserted.

On June 18, northeast of present-day Prince George, B.C., they were the first Europeans to see the river which would be explored 15 years later by Simon Fraser (and after whom it was named).

In four days they travelled 80 miles south on the swift river. A shower of arrows from a hostile band of Carrier Indians greeted them on June 21. Mackenzie pacified the Carriers with gifts and they warned him that this river to the sea was rough and dangerous. The next day another group of Indians advised him to strike west across the mountains, and on June 23 he chose to leave the Fraser and reach the Pacific overland.

They built a canoe and hid it in woods near present-day Alexandria, B.C., for their return journey. Then they headed west, eating only pemmican and occasionally fish, until they met more members of the Carrier tribe. It took Mackenzie a day to persuade them to act as guides.

They trekked for 12 more days through hail, snow and rain. They crossed the Coast Mountains on July 17. They travelled on until it was dark, crashing through the forest down a steep-sided valley to an Indian village beside a river, the Bella Coola.

The hospitable Bella Coola Indians feasted them on roast salmon, and Mackenzie called their home Friendly Village.

They travelled down the Bella Coola in borrowed canoes past prosperous Indian fishing villages. At last they landed at a village on North Bentinck Arm from where Mackenzie "could perceive the termination of the river, and its discharge into a narrow arm of the sea."

Mackenzie and his men paddled into Dean Channel, the closest they would come to the open Pacific, on July 21. They had travelled more than 800 miles from Fort Fork in 74 days—the first Europeans to cross North America north of Mexico. Next morning, Mackenzie mixed red pigment with melted grease and wrote on a rock: "Alex Mackenzie from Canada by land 22d July 1793."

Mackenzie found the Bella Bella Indians less friendly than their Bella Coola cousins, in part apparently because of an incident one of them described. Other white men had been to Dean Channel that year, the Indian said; their leader—whom he called "Macubah"—had fired a musket at him and another had slapped him with a sword.

Alexander Mackenzie and Capt. George Vancouver had missed each other by seven weeks.

One Man's Shameless Lies Helped England Win the Pacific Northwest

The Pacific coast north of San Francisco Bay became English territory in 1790 in part because of a lying English sea captain named John Meares. *Aita-Aita Meares* the Indians called him—Liar Meares.

Two years earlier, flying the Portuguese flag to avoid expensive English licences, he had begun trading furs illegally on the west coast of Vancouver Island. At Friendly Cove in Nootka Sound he built a small fort on land he later claimed to have bought from an Indian chief for two pistols. The chief said he had sold no land, only otter skins. When two American ships put into Nootka Sound, Meares told the captains horrendous stories of dangers along the Pacific coast and swore he had not collected 50 skins all season.

Spain as well as England claimed the coast and Spaniards seized Meares's post and two ships in 1789. The poacher who had flown the Portuguese flag, who had lied that he could not find 50 skins in a season, went to London and claimed $650,000 from Spain in damages for lost trade. England, glad of an excuse to press its claim to the coast, prepared for war to back him up. But the Nootka Sound Controversy ended peacefully in 1790: Spain returned the ships, paid Meares $210,000 and agreed to open the coast north of California to British subjects.

Meares went on lying. He published a colorful account of his voyages, claiming credit for discoveries made by others. George Dixon, who had been a licensed captain in Nootka Sound, produced a pamphlet exposing Meares's falsehoods. By 1790 Meares was discredited in England—but by then Spain had withdrawn from what now is British Columbia. Aita-Aita Meares had triggered that withdrawal.

Heritage Sites

BELLA COOLA, B.C. The rock on which Alexander Mackenzie is believed to have recorded his crossing of North America— the first north of Mexico—is in Sir Alexander Mackenzie Provincial Park, 25 miles northwest. His words, written July 22, 1793, and long ago erased by weather, have been re-created and embedded in the rock with cement. *Park accessible only by boat.*

Other sites

Campbell River, B.C. (4) Kwakiutl, Coast Salish and Nootka Indian artifacts are displayed in the Campbell River Centennial Museum. They include masks and mortuary poles. Outside the museum is an 18-foot Kwakiutl totem pole, in the rotunda a carved thunderbird. A plaque four miles south records that in 1792 George Vancouver became the first European to circumnavigate Vancouver Island.

Dawson Creek, B.C. (12) Mackenzie's discovery of the Peace River route into the eastern Rockies is commemorated by a plaque 32 miles north.

Duncan, B.C. (5) Outside the British Columbia Forest Museum, a plaque indicates where James Cook cut spars for one of his ships in 1778.

Fort Chipewyan, Alta. (not shown) A plaque here commemorates the North West Company fort, on Old Fort Point, from

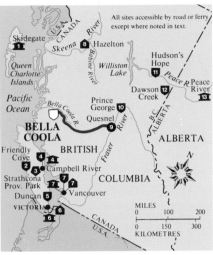

All sites accessible by road or ferry except where noted in text.

♡ Main site (Monument) ♠ Historic building(s) ▲ Museum ◆ Monument
■ Ruins ● Route ◆ Other

which Mackenzie began his two attempts to reach the Pacific. *Accessible only by air, boat or winter road.*

Friendly Cove, B.C. (2) The Nootka Sound Controversy between England and Spain started here in 1789 when Spaniards seized trader John Meares's post and ships. George Vancouver and Spanish Capt. Juan Bodega y Quadra met here in 1792 with the intention of signing a settlement:

a plaque commemorates the meeting. *Accessible only by air or boat.*

Hazelton, B.C. (8) 'Ksan is a re-creation of a 19th-century Gitskan Indian village, with cedar longhouses, smokehouses, totem poles, fishing traps, and displays showing how clothes and utensils were made from bark.

Hudson's Hope, B.C. (11) A plaque at the W.A.C. Bennett Dam, 12 miles west, marks where Mackenzie's 1793 expedition began a three-day portage of a section of the Peace River Canyon.

Peace River, Alta. (13) In the Peace River Centennial Museum is a model of Fort Fork, which was eight miles to the west and where Mackenzie wintered in 1792-93. Also displayed is the fort's fireplace, rebuilt in part with stones from the original.

Prince George, B.C. (10) A plaque commemorates Mackenzie's passage down the Fraser River.

Quesnel, B.C. (9) A 240-mile hiking trail between the Fraser River and Bella Coola follows Mackenzie's route to the Pacific.

Skidegate, B.C. (1) Haida artifacts in the Queen Charlotte Islands Museum include bone and antler tools, blades for sharpening harpoons, and argillite carvings of white explorers.

Strathcona Provincial Park, B.C. (3) Golden Hinde, the highest mountain (7,219 feet) on Vancouver Island, may have been Francis Drake's landfall in 1579. It is named after his ship.

Vancouver (7) A bronze statue of George Vancouver, the first European to navigate English Bay (1792), stands outside city hall. Totem poles and ceremonial masks are among some 10,000 Indian artifacts in the Museum of Anthropology at the University of British Columbia. Outside is a Haida house. At Horseshoe Bay a plaque commemorates pioneer navigators of the northwest coast.

Victoria (6) The stern section of Vancouver's ship *Discovery* has been re-created in the British Columbia Provincial Museum. Furnishings in the main cabin include a wooden sea chest thought to have been Vancouver's. Totem poles and a replica of a Kwakiutl house are in nearby Thunderbird Park. The Maritime Museum of British Columbia has a model of Cook's ship *Resolution.*

Capt. George Vancouver's lack of wealth is reflected in the simplicity of his cabin in the part of his ship Discovery *that has been re-created in the B.C. Provincial Museum in Victoria. The Admiralty in his day did not furnish officers' cabins.*

Struggle Along the Border— and a Sense of Being Canadian

Nowhere in Upper Canada, in the spring of 1812, were the rumors of war more repugnant than in peaceable Queenston, snuggled beside the Niagara River. With America, the "enemy," only 250 yards across the water, Queenston was bound to bear the brunt of any fighting. Yet many of the so-called enemy were friends, even *relatives*, of the 300 Canadian villagers. And war would ruin business, just as Queenston was becoming the liveliest trading centre on the Niagara frontier.

Queenston's 100 frame buildings nestled on a shelf of land. Behind, 350 feet above the river, rose the Heights, part of the Niagara Escarpment extending like a spine into Upper Canada. Below the village, wharves with thickets of masts cluttered the shore. On the main street was James and Laura Secord's clapboard house; Secord was a dealer in flour and potash. And there was Ingersoll's Tavern, run by Laura's father.

On June 18 the rumors came true: America declared war on Britain. From that first day, Queenston was in the front line.

Millions on both sides of the border hated the thought of war. But to others who wanted a fight, there seemed adequate reasons.

The first was Britain's high-handed conduct at sea. At war with Napoleon, Britain forbade neutral America to trade with France, turned back American ships and boarded them on whim to search for British deserters. This infuriated the Americans. The second reason was the growing America's desire for more territory. Canada seemed a logical and easy conquest, and many Americans believed that Canadians yearned to live under the Stars and Stripes.

Canada's half-million people—thinly spread in the Maritimes, Lower Canada and Upper Canada—were not sure what they wanted. Some were United Empire Loyalists, staunchly true to the king. Many were recent immigrants, their homes in Canada but their hearts still in America. Nearly two-thirds of Canada's population was French, with no love for England.

Militarily, Canada was outnumbered. At the start some 8,000 British and Canadian regulars and fewer than 20,000 militiamen faced 35,000 American regulars and a militia of hundreds of thousands. The Canadians needed a leader, and they found him in Maj.Gen. Isaac Brock, since October 1811 administrator of the government of Upper Canada.

Everything about Brock seemed to shout "hero." Six-foot-two, broad-shouldered and muscular, he towered over most men of his time. At 42 he had been a British career soldier for 26 years and had commanded in Canada since 1802. In that decade he diligently shored up Canada's sloppy defences and learned his frontier by heart. Fluent in French, he mingled easily in Lower Canada. He was utterly fearless yet uncommonly kind. He insisted his men have warm greatcoats and he cancelled parades on frigid days. With Brock in command, morale soared and desertions dwindled.

Brock knew that Canada's best hope lay in a quick offensive. He ordered Capt. Charles Roberts to seize Fort Michilimackinac, on an island between Lake Michigan and Lake Huron. By taking Michilimackinac, and then Fort Detroit, Brock would secure his western flank, win over the skeptical Indians, and boost Upper Canada's confidence. Roberts closed in on Michilimackinac

This attendant at Fort Malden National Historic Park in Amherstburg, Ont., wears the uniform of the Royal Newfoundland Regiment which fought in the War of 1812. The corvette Detroit, *flagship of Capt. Robert Barclay, British commander on Lake Erie, was built at Amherstburg in 1813.*

A 184-foot monument to Sir Isaac Brock thrusts high above the heights overlooking the village of Queenston, across the Niagara River from Lewiston, N.Y. (foreground).

Tecumseh the Shawnee 'Shooting Star'—and His Dream That Died

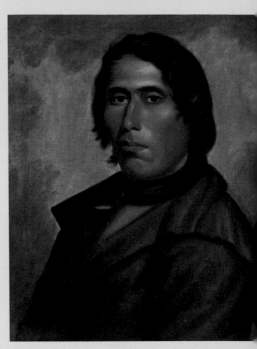

On Aug. 17, 1812, to the boom of saluting British field guns and the victory whoops of 600 Indians, a stately Shawnee chief and a British major-general rode side by side into Fort Detroit. Together they had captured it. Isaac Brock presented his pistols and tasseled sash to Tecumseh. The Shawnee gave his own arrow-patterned sash to Brock.

Tecumseh ("Shooting Star") was the courageous and eloquent leader of a confederacy of Indian tribes between the Ohio and Mississippi rivers. On the Tippecanoe River, near present-day Tippecanoe, Ind., he had built a sprawling town of huts and teepees that he dreamed would become the capital of an Indian state where his people would live in peace. But, in the fall of 1811, American Gen. William Henry Harrison sacked the town and slaughtered most of its inhabitants.

Could Tecumseh turn to the British? His Indians had fought for them during the American War of Independence, yet in the Treaty of Paris (1783) the British reneged on their promise to push for an Indian homeland. But Tecumseh trusted Brock and was confident that he would not permit a second betrayal.

After the capture of Detroit, Brock hastened to the Niagara front—and death. Col. Henry Procter, now in charge at Detroit, proved timid and incompetent and in September 1813 he abandoned the fort and retreated east, pursued by Harrison's Americans.

Tecumseh likened Procter to a fat, frightened dog running with his tail between his legs and shamed him into making a stand at Moraviantown (near present-day Thamesville, Ont.). But in a battle there Oct. 5 Procter's redcoats and Tecumseh's Indians were routed. Tecumseh was killed—and, with him, his dream. The Treaty of Ghent, which ended the War of 1812, gave the Indians nothing.

Tecumseh's grave was never found. The shooting star left no trace.

Sir George Prevost, governor-in-chief of the Canadas, was recalled to Britain in 1815 in disgrace for his misconduct of the war. He demanded a chance to defend himself before a court-martial but died a week before the trial was to have started.

on July 17 with 49 redcoats, 380 Indians and about 200 voyageurs. The American commander, who had not yet *heard* of the war, surrendered.

Small victory though it was, it served Brock's purpose. Five days earlier, American Gen. William Hull had crossed into Canada from Detroit, posing as liberator and friend, offering "peace, liberty and security" or "war, slavery and destruction." The demoralized Canadians were ready to opt for peace. But, with the victory at Michilimackinac, Indians flocked to Brock's side. Their reputation for taking scalps terrified Hull and he retreated to Fort Detroit.

Brock, seizing his advantage, sailed up Lake Erie to Amherstburg where he met the Shawnee chief Tecumseh. "There is a *man*!" Tecumseh cried to his followers, and the admiration was mutual. That night Tecumseh sketched from memory a detailed plan of Fort Detroit. Hull had more than 2,000 men; Brock would march with 700 soldiers and 600 Indians.

He moved up opposite the fort and demanded the Americans surrender. Hull refused. That night the Canadians crossed the river. Hull awoke to find redcoats and Indians at his gate. In front rode Brock, on his magnificent grey charger Alfred, and a glittering Tecumseh. Hull gave up without a shot.

While Upper Canada rejoiced, Brock planned an attack on Sackets Harbor, the naval base opposite Kingston, hoping to reduce American strength on Lake Ontario. But Sir George Prevost, Canada's cautious governor-in-chief, held him back—and the Americans rushed in reinforcements everywhere. By early September, some 6,300 U.S. troops were ranged along the 33 miles of the Niagara River between Lake

Ontario and Lake Erie. Brock's 1,500 soldiers and 250 Indians along the same front waited for the attack.

Brock gambled that the Americans would move against his headquarters at Fort George, near Newark (now Niagara-on-the-Lake). Queenston, seven miles south, was left with only 350 defenders and three cannon. On the stormy evening of Oct. 12, Brock conferred late with his officers, then wrote despatches until midnight. He lay down to rest but at 3 a.m. he was awakened by the boom of guns from Queenston.

Four a.m. The distant gunfire went on. A messenger galloped in with news: 24 American guns in Lewiston were hammering Queenston, and Yankee troops were crossing the river. Brock, already in the saddle, ordered his second-in-command, Sir Roger Sheaffe, to stand ready.

Then he set spurs to Alfred and sped along the river road for Queenston Heights. His ride that wet, blustery night was a race to save Canada.

A second messenger met him. The attack on Queenston was mounting, the soldier shouted. Brock sent him on to Sheaffe; every available man was to be marched to Queenston.

Brock galloped into Queenston before dawn.

A portrait of George III hangs in the restored officers' mess at Fort George, near Niagara-on-the-Lake. The fort was destroyed by the Americans in 1813.

This painting by J. W. L. Forster (in the Public Archives of Canada) is believed the only authentic portrait of Maj.Gen. Sir Isaac Brock. The tunic and sash he wore in the Battle of Queenston Heights are in the Canadian War Museum in Ottawa, along with his watch and telescope. Just below the tunic collar is the hole made by the bullet that killed Brock. The sash was a gift from the Shawnee chief Tecumseh.

155

His old regiment, the 49th, with stinging musket fire and one feeble six-pound cannon, had held the first wave of American invaders to the beaches. The sight of Brock—massive in his crimson tunic, an arrow-pattern sash from Tecumseh fluttering at his waist—lifted their hearts. They cheered.

Halfway up the Heights, gunners with a single 18-pounder hammered at the American shoreline. A mile to the north, the Canadians' third gun, a 24-pounder, methodically thumped the enemy. Across the river some 2,000 unenthusiastic American troops waited for boats. If only the Canadians could hold until Sheaffe arrived. Wild cries and musket fire broke out suddenly behind Brock. Into sight burst 350 American infantrymen. They had scaled the sheer, slippery, unguarded face of Queenston Heights.

"Follow me!" shouted Brock. He rallied 200 men, led them on the run to the foot of the Heights and took cover behind a low stone wall.

"Take your breath, boys, you'll need it presently!" They cheered him again. Brock dismounted, sent his panting horse away with an apologetic pat for the punishing ride, and drew his sword. His men fixed bayonets. They poured over the wall and up the hill, directly at the enemy's centre.

Brock, always in the lead, was a spectacular target. A bullet struck his wrist. He went on. The enemy fell back. Then a rifleman stepped from the trees 30 yards away, took aim and shot Brock through the chest. He died almost immediately.

His friend and aide-de-camp, Col. John Macdonell, took over. Riding Brock's horse, he rallied the troops. Then he, too, fell mortally wounded. The Canadians retreated, carrying dead and wounded comrades. Alfred, Brock's charger, lay dead on the battlefield.

A lull fell over the Heights. Across the river, hundreds of Americans still refused to budge.

Near noon Sheaffe closed in on Queenston with a remarkable cross section of Upper Canada: Indians, 300 regulars, a battery of field guns drawn by farmers' horses, and 250 militiamen including "Capt. Robert Runchey's Company of Coloured Men"—men who had fled slavery in the United States. Sheaffe took an Indian trail and gained the Heights two miles behind the enemy.

Three p.m. The invaders were in trouble. The defenders of Queenston village turned a hail of musket fire on the Heights. Sheaffe's redcoats charged with fixed bayonets; Indians closed in from the flanks. The Americans fired one nervous fusillade, then many turned and ran. The rest threw down their weapons—close to where the Brock Monument stands today.

Some 300 Americans had been killed or wounded, nearly 1,000 taken prisoner. Sheaffe

Sir Isaac Brock's first burial was at Fort George near Niagara-on-the-Lake. In 1824 the body was reinterred in a vault beneath a memorial column on Queenston Heights. That monument was blown up in 1840 by a veteran of the 1837 rebellion and this new column was completed in 1856, paid for by public subscription.

This engraving of the Battle of Queenston Heights is from a painting by Capt. James Dennis, who commanded a detachment of Brock's old 49th Regiment in the battle. The Heights are above the village of Queenston (right).

had more prisoners than men of his own. British and Canadian casualties totalled 112.

Brock and the Battle of Queenston Heights had united the Canadian colonies as never before. That winter 600 men of the 104th Regiment of Foot marched from Fredericton, N.B., to Kingston to fight for Canada. Still, the tide would turn against Canada in 1813.

Canada's most humiliating setback that year—indeed, its worst defeat of the war—was the capture of York, the capital of Upper Canada. It was defended by 300 regulars, 300 militiamen and 100 Indians led by Sheaffe.

Although capable of following Brock's lead at Queenston Heights, he was neither imaginative nor inspiring at York. Brock would have guessed that York was a prime target because the Ameri-

The British government gave Maj.Gen. Sir Roger Sheaffe a baronetcy for his part in the victory at Queenston Heights in 1812. But after the sacking of York in 1813 he was removed from his command and sent home.

After the Battle of Lake Erie, the Bloodless War of the Shipbuilders

Mastery of Lake Erie and Lake Ontario gave Britain the upper hand when the War of 1812 broke out. The armed ships of the peacetime Provincial Marine, a transport service run by civilians, enabled troops, supplies and messages to be moved quickly.

Then the Americans began building warships and arming merchant schooners at Sackets Harbor, N.Y., on Lake Ontario and at Erie, Pa., on Lake Erie.

The Royal Navy had only six warships on Erie and Ontario. The entire squadron clashed with nine American warships at Put-in-Bay on Sept. 10, 1813, and after the two-hour Battle of Lake Erie the British surrendered.

From then on the Americans controlled Lake Erie, using captured ships to supply their troops.

Determined to hold Lake Ontario, the British began building at the Kingston shipyard *(right)* the 2,304-ton *St. Lawrence,* with 112 guns on three decks. She patrolled Lake Ontario during the last weeks of the 1814 navigation season. The Americans started two 120-gun three-deckers, the British two more. But the war ended before any of these last four was completed.

The "shipbuilders' war" had involved no fighting: neither side would risk defeat. Within 20 years the ships were sold, broken up or abandoned.

cans coveted the new battleship *Sir Isaac Brock*, lying almost finished in a shipyard where Toronto's Union Station now stands. He might have used her 30 unmounted guns for Fort York's defences.

Sheaffe, though, was scarcely prepared when on April 26 watchers on Scarborough Bluffs cried the alarm. Twenty-five miles to the east was a 14-ship armada with 1,700 troops. But the American land forces were commanded by old Gen. Henry Dearborn, so fat that he had to travel in a special carriage, and as much a liability to his bright young officers as Prevost had been to Brock.

The first landing party waded ashore at today's Sunnyside Beach. The 100 regulars and militiamen that Sheaffe sent to meet them were raked with a murderous crossfire from ships and shore.

Sheaffe, believing York doomed, decided to withdraw to Kingston. He ordered *Sir Isaac Brock* set afire and a fuse set to the fort's grand

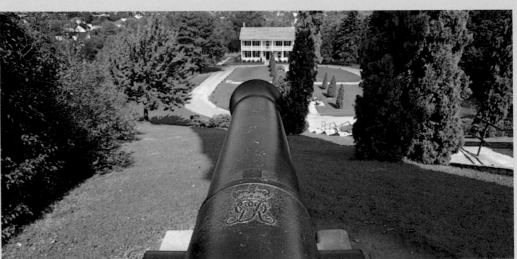

A bronze sculpture of Laura Secord is set in the granite of her monument on Queenston Heights.

Billy and Laura, the Civilian Heroes

In the spring of 1813 the Americans were on the march. If they could take the Niagara Peninsula and Kingston (the British naval base) they could perhaps win the war. British regulars and Canadian militia retreated to Burlington Heights (overlooking present-day Hamilton Harbour), only 10 miles west of the enemy front line. But on June 5 nineteen-year-old Billy Green of Stoney Creek helped turn the tide against the invaders who occupied his town.

Green—called Billy Green the Scout—spied on the Americans. Then he ran into his brother-in-law, Isaac Corman, who had learned the American password (Will-Hen-Har, from the name of their general, William Henry Harrison). Green set out for Burlington Heights with details of the American position—only to forget the password as he approached the American lines. But, as he recorded years later, "I pulled my coat over my head and trotted across the road on my feet and hands like a bear." He reached the British lines about 11 p.m. Col. John Harvey launched an attack that same warm and moonless night, with Green guiding 700 soldiers to the American position on a hill beside James Gage's house (*above*; it is now a museum). By dawn, Green later recorded, "we could see the Americans running in all directions." American casualties were 17 killed, 38 wounded, 100 missing, two generals taken prisoner. British losses were 23 dead, 136 wounded, 55 missing.

During their retreat (eventually to Fort George) the Americans suffered another defeat. Laura Secord, a 36-year-old housewife, overheard American officers in her father's tavern in Queenston planning to attack the British at the house of John De Cew, 12 miles southwest. Shortly before dawn June 22 she set off alone, on foot, and at nightfall she delivered a warning to Lieut. James FitzGibbon. Two days later, in a beech wood near Beaver, Dams, FitzGibbon's force of 50 soldiers and 400 Indians ambushed an American force; 462 Americans were captured.

Laura Secord did not lead a cow on her journey: that was a fabrication of W. C. Coffin, a fanciful biographer. But she *was* a heroine and she *was* the first to warn the British. Her courage won her fame; Billy Green died in obscurity.

magazine—the main ammunition dump containing about 400 barrels of gunpowder.

The Americans, wary of the seemingly abandoned fort, were a few hundred yards away when the magazine went up in one horrendous blast. Timber, stones and other debris rained from the sky, killing 38 Americans. Some of the 222 wounded died later. Altogether the Americans had lost more than 300 dead and wounded, twice as many as York's defenders. Enraged, they ran amok, burning the legislative building and looting houses. Eleven days later they sailed away, leaving York humbled and whipped.

Dearborn, astonishingly, did not capitalize on his military advantage. He left York free—and the lifeline to Niagara intact. Battered York would rise again, and Canada would have its vengeance.

From the beginning of the war the Americans wanted Montreal. With it, they would control the St. Lawrence River, Upper Canada's vital supply route. They finally aimed a two-pronged attack at Montreal in September 1813.

From the south with 4,200 men marched Maj. Gen. Wade Hampton. In the west Maj.Gen. James Wilkinson was mustering 8,000 men.

By late October Hampton was 35 miles west of Montreal along the Châteauguay River. Victory might have been just a brisk march away—had it not been for a small, superbly disciplined force of French Canadians led by Lt.Col. Charles-Michel de Salaberry.

While de Salaberry built a strong defensive position at a bend in the Châteauguay, help was on its way. In Kingston, Governor Prevost—showing more spunk than in 1812—called in Col. "Red George" Macdonell, commander of the crack French-Canadian Select Embodied Militia, as good as any regular army unit of its size.

"When can you start for Châteauguay?" asked Prevost.

"Directly the men have finished their dinners, sir!" said Red George. He and his men, in a gale, raced through dense forest to stand in support of de Salaberry on Oct. 25, the eve of the battle. De Salaberry had thrown up log breastworks and barricades facing the Americans.

A patrol informed Hampton that de Salaberry had only 350 men, mostly militia, on the front line, and could be outflanked. This was the first of a nightmare of American errors.

Hampton sent 1,500 men into the woods that night to encircle de Salaberry. The advance party got lost in the dark. By morning they had blundered not *behind* but *beside* de Salaberry's position. Worse yet, they had lost communication with Hampton. De Salaberry recognized their confusion and opened up on the floundering advance party.

Macdonell, out of range in the rear, set up a din of whoops and bugle calls. The startled Americans believed *they* were caught in a trap. The advance party scattered in panic. Then Hampton's entire force withdrew. The French Canadians had routed an enemy four times as numerous.

Meanwhile, Wilkinson's thousands were lumbering east along the St. Lawrence. Hard on their heels was Lt.Col. Joseph Morrison, only 30 and with no battle experience in Canada, but revered

American ships are close to York in this painting by Owen Staples. They were sighted from Scarborough Bluffs (upper right) as they sailed west to land troops in the small bay on the extreme left. The troops marched east to attack the town of 800 which was capital of Upper Canada.

Should-Have-Been Foes Remained Good Friends

St. Stephen, N.B., and Calais, Maine, across the St. Croix River from each other, should have been enemies in the War of 1812. They chose to remain friends—such *good* friends that gunpowder donated by St. Stephen fired Calais's salute to American independence on July 4, 1813.

In general, Maritimers had no quarrel with New Englanders. Since Yankees and Maritimers wanted to keep trading, Nova Scotia Governor Sir John Sherbrooke issued "import licences" to get American ships through a Royal Navy blockade of the United States coast. (The amiability did not extend to privateers [see p. 120]. Maritimers and New Englanders sailed private ships of war and seized hundreds of the other side's trading vessels.)

In 1814 the British invaded northeastern Maine and were welcomed by many in the conquered territory who were happy to be British subjects again; now they could trade openly.

In less than a year the Castine custom house took in £13,000. When the war ended and the British withdrew they gave the "Castine Fund" to Nova Scotia. It was used to found Dalhousie University at Halifax.

by his men. Although outnumbered 10 to one, they included the cream of the colony's fighting men: Voltigeurs, Fencibles (also French-Canadian regulars) and Brock's 49th Regiment.

By the night of Nov. 10 the armies were close, 20 miles west of Cornwall. Morrison, camped in militia Capt. John Crysler's farmhouse, decided to seize the initiative here. With woods on one flank, water on the other and a reasonably flat clearing ahead, it was, for the first time in the war, a field ideal for British warfare. The redcoats' strength lay in their rigid training to fight shoulder to shoulder in two ranks (see p. 215). Each soldier had to maintain contact with those on either side of him. When iron discipline prevailed, as it usually did, the "thin red line" was almost invincible.

The next morning was bleak and grey. Morrison sent out three companies of Voltigeurs and about 30 Indians to provoke the Americans. When they spotted a patrol about a mile from the main British force, one of the Indians fired his musket. The Americans replied with a volley, forcing back the Voltigeurs and causing Wilkinson to send 2,000 regulars on attack. The thin red line met the Americans at 2 p.m. and poured withering, accurate "rolling volleys"—one platoon firing, the other reloading—into the advance. The enemy was caught in a deadly rain of musket balls. At 4:30 the American attack faltered and turned into a retreat. Darkness and a gathering storm halted pursuit by the British. Even so, the Americans lost 102 killed and 237 wounded—about double Morrison's casualties.

Although Wilkinson's huge army was still rel-

The British and Canadians suffered heavy casualties in the Niagara region in 1814. In the indecisive Battle of Lundy's Lane (right) in July they lost 900 of their 3,000 men; the Americans lost 1,000 of 4,000.

atively intact, he was beaten. As the Quebec *Mercury* summed it up, the American invasion "terminated in their compleat discomfiture and disgrace." Montreal was saved. Upper Canada had a new lease on life.

The war dragged on in a bloody stalemate. The Americans resolved to take the Niagara Peninsula in 1814. On July 25 their Brig.Gen. Jacob Brown, after winning a battle at Chippawa, struck out triumphantly for Burlington where the new Canadian commander, Gordon Drummond, was believed encamped. Hearing that the British had just taken Lewiston, Brown wheeled toward Queenston. Unknown to him, Drummond was coming in the opposite direction.

The advance units met, to their mutual surprise, at a crossroads called Lundy's Lane. Here on a little hill, about a mile from the Niagara River, Drummond mounted seven guns, and here the bloodiest battle of the war raged far into the stifling night. It began at 6 p.m. Again and again the battery changed hands, until both sides fell back exhausted.

A monument near Châteauguay, Que., commemorates this battle (painted by H. de D. Holmfeld) in which Canadian Voltigeurs led by Lt.Col. Charles-Michel de Salaberry defeated Americans marching on Montreal in October 1813.

The American regulars attacked again, guided by the flash of muskets. Again the Americans took the battery. Again Canada won it back. Muskets flamed, bayonets flashed, dying men screamed.

At last, near midnight, the Americans withdrew to Chippawa. The Canadians and British collapsed on the spot and slept. A hush fell over the bloody field, broken only by the moans of the wounded and the distant rumble of Niagara Falls. No one had really won the Battle of Lundy's Lane but, again, Upper Canada had refused to yield.

Now, having finished off Napoleon, Britain turned to deal with the troublesome Americans. In mid-August an English fleet sailed into Chesapeake Bay with 4,000 troops who easily routed a larger force of American militia, and on Aug. 24 marched into Washington. Although they harmed no person or private property, the bitter

From a prison beneath this trap door in the Ancaster Old Mill, 17 traitors were taken to be tried at the "Bloody Assize" of 1814. Eight were hanged.

memory of York was with them. The enemy had to be chastised. President and Dolly Madison's half-finished dinner was on their hastily abandoned table when the British put the torch to the presidential mansion and other government buildings. Then they marched back to their ships. The scorched mansion, repainted to cover the smoke stains, became the White House.

Britain could have been harsher but, after 2½ years of fighting, both sides were ready for a truce. Canada had won the war: the American invasions had been stemmed and Fort Michilimackinac, Fort Niagara (opposite present-day Niagara-on-the-Lake), and part of Maine had been captured. But Canada lost the peace. The Treaty of Ghent, signed by the British and the Americans on Christmas Eve 1814, simply restored the status quo. Not a word was uttered about the causes of the war. Key decisions on fisheries rights, naval forces on the Great Lakes and the international boundary were postponed.

The old boundary, the 49th parallel, prevailed—a victory for the Americans. Britain gave up all the territory she had won.

Canadians wondered: had the 8,600 Canadian and British dead died and the wounded bled for nothing? What of the Indians, decimated by war and disease, and the ruins of Upper Canada? Yet the cruel war left one great legacy. For the first time, a Canadian spirit was tangible and strong. For the first time, Upper Canadians, Lower Canadians, Maritimers—Canadians of every walk of life and political persuasion—had stood united. Now they would go ahead and build a nation.

No Ships Left, the Navy Fights On in a Canoe and Two Bateaux

At sunrise on Aug. 14, 1814, the guns of the American brigantine *Niagara* and schooners *Tigress* and *Scorpion* shattered the stillness along what is now called Wasaga Beach on Lake Huron's Georgian Bay. Their target, moored several hundred yards up the Nottawasaga River, was *Nancy*—the last British ship on the Upper Lakes *(right)*.

Nancy supplied food to Fort Michilimackinac, a key island post between Lake Michigan and Lake Huron. The Americans intended to take *Nancy* and starve the British out of the fort. From a hastily built blockhouse, Lieut. Miller Worsley and his crew fought back. When defeat seemed certain, Worsley burned his schooner. The British fled as *Nancy*'s hissing hulk sank.

But at Willow Depot, a British post nine miles west of present-day Barrie, Ont., Worsley got a canoe and two bateaux. In eight days he and his men paddled and rowed 380 miles to Michilimackinac.

Worsley had sworn to avenge *Nancy*. His chance came Sept. 3. *Scorpion* was patrolling Lake Huron but *Tigress* lay at anchor in False Detour Channel, about 55 miles northeast of Mackinac Island, hoping to intercept North West Company fur brigades. Worsley and 77 men boarded her at midnight, as her crew slept, and quickly captured the ship.

Scorpion came in sight and anchored next evening. At dawn *Tigress,* flying the American flag, sailed toward *Scorpion,* turned suddenly, fired her swivel gun and ranged alongside. Fifty men captured *Scorpion*'s deck in moments. The Union Jack flew from both ships as they sailed to Fort Michilimackinac with supplies for a year. The British would control the Upper Lakes until the war ended.

A hull believed to be *Nancy*'s and a replica of her figurehead *(top left)* are at the Museum of the Upper Lakes at Wasaga Beach.

Heritage Sites

QUEENSTON, Ont. A small stone cenotaph in Queenston Heights Park marks where Maj.Gen. Isaac Brock was killed in action. A 184-foot column stands over his grave. At the base of the column a plaque lists the soldiers and Indians who fell repulsing American invaders. A battlefield walking tour includes Laura Secord's house in Queenston, now a museum containing 19th-century furnishings.

Other sites

Amherstburg, Ont. (1) The remains of Fort Malden, where Brock and the Shawnee chief Tecumseh planned their 1812 attack on Detroit, are in 11-acre Fort Malden National Historic Park. Earthworks and a blockhouse (on Bois Blanc Island) are preserved. So is the rock from which Tecumseh exhorted his warriors and reviled Col. Henry Procter before the Battle of Moraviantown.

Ancaster, Ont. (12) In a mill that dates from 1790 is an underground chamber where persons accused of treason were imprisoned during the War of 1812. (A plaque at Ancaster Memorial School tells the story.) Guided tours take visitors past operating millstones.

Beauport, Que. (11) A plaque identifies the house in which Charles-Michel de Salaberry, victor of the Battle of Châteauguay, was born.

Chambly, Que. (10) A statue of de Salaberry is in a park facing the town hall. His grave is in the Roman Catholic cemetery and the de Salaberry manor house is nearby. In Fort Chambly National Historic Park are the partially rebuilt walls of a stronghold where Americans were imprisoned during the War of 1812.

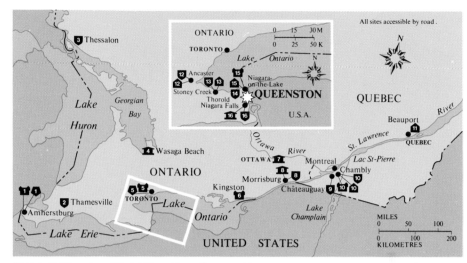

Châteauguay, Que. (9) A monument and interpretive centre southwest of here mark where de Salaberry and 460 Canadian Voltigeurs defeated 1,500 Americans at the Battle of Châteauguay.

Kingston, Ont. (6) The main British naval base in the War of 1812 was on Point Henry, a promontory commanding Kingston Harbour. Naval equipment of the period is at Fort Henry (1832-36).

Morrisburg, Ont. (8) In 2,000-acre Crysler Farm Battlefield Park is a 50-foot mound of battlefield soil topped by a 15-foot obelisk commemorating those killed in the Battle of Crysler's Farm. An interpretive centre describes the encounter.

Niagara Falls, Ont. (16) In Drummond Hill Cemetery, the site of the Battle of Lundy's Lane, are the graves of Canadian, British and American soldiers, and of Laura Secord. In nearby Lundy's Lane Museum are tunics, swords and bayonets from the battle.

Niagara-on-the-Lake, Ont. (15) The bastions, stockade, living quarters, powder magazine and artificer's shop of Fort George, Brock's headquarters in 1812, have been restored or rebuilt in Fort George National Historic Park. Three miles south of the park is McFarland House, used as a wartime hospital by both sides and now a museum of 19th-century furnishings.

Ottawa (7) Exhibits in the Canadian War Museum include the bullet-torn tunic and

Georgian-style McFarland House at Niagara-on-the-Lake was built of handmade bricks in 1800. It was badly damaged in the War of 1812.

the sash (a gift from Tecumseh) that Brock was wearing when he died.

Stoney Creek, Ont. (13) Two plaques and a 100-foot stone tower in Stoney Creek Battlefield Park identify the site of the Battle of Stoney Creek. In Battlefield House, the American headquarters, are an audio-visual presentation and displays relating to the battle. A granite monument in Stoney Creek Cemetery honors Lt.Col. John Harvey, Billy Green and Isaac Corman, all instrumental in the British victory.

Thamesville, Ont. (2) A monument in the town's park commemorates the Battle of Moraviantown and the death of Tecumseh.

Thessalon, Ont. (3) A plaque in Lakeside Park commemorates the capture of the American schooners *Tigress* and *Scorpion* at False Detour Channel, 25 miles southwest.

Thorold, Ont. (14) A monument a mile southeast marks the site of the Battle of Beaver Dams and commemorates Laura Secord.

Toronto (5) Two cannon are all that remains from the original Fort York, attacked by the Americans and blown up by its British defenders in 1813. The present fort dates from 1816. In a blockhouse, slides and a map illustrate the 1813 attack.

Wasaga Beach, Ont. (4) A blackened hull believed to be the remains of *Nancy*, a British schooner scuttled in an attack by American warships, is at the Museum of the Upper Lakes. Also displayed are a 12-foot model of *Nancy* and a replica of her figurehead. A sound-and-light show tells *Nancy's* story and describes the capture of *Tigress* and *Scorpion*, two of her attackers.

The Métis and the Settlers, and Massacre at Seven Oaks

Armed conflict was perhaps inevitable between the Métis, who lived by the fur trade and the wide-ranging buffalo hunt, and the settlers, determined to fence the great, unbroken plain into neat farms. Still, neither side was spoiling for a fight that evening of June 19, 1816. Almost by chance—and because of a few cartloads of pemmican—Métis and settlers came together at a place on the Red River called Seven Oaks (now part of Winnipeg).

The Métis, led by a 23-year-old North West Company clerk, Cuthbert Grant, were running pemmican to the company's fur brigades on Lake Winnipeg—and trying to avoid the settlers. Governor Robert Semple of Assiniboia, with 25 men, marched out from the settlement at the junction of the Red and Assiniboine rivers (the heart of Winnipeg) just to see what was happening. Suddenly the mounted Métis (and a few Indians) were in a crescent formation that outflanked the settlers, who were on foot. Grant raised his musket. In his sights was Semple.

François Boucher, a Métis, rode up to Semple and the two men spoke angrily. Semple grabbed Boucher's reins and his gunstock. Then, when an Indian moved out of the Métis formation and was shot by a nervous settler, Grant fired, strik-

Métis on horseback—and some on foot—charge outmanoeuvred Red River settlers at Seven Oaks in a massacre that was almost an accident. There had been bad blood but apparently no thought of killing—until a fateful encounter on a June day in 1816. The Métis, led by Cuthbert Grant (right, top), suffered no fatal casualties. But Governor Robert Semple (right, below) and 20 settlers were killed.

A Way of Life That Died With the Buffalo

The Plains Indians—Assiniboine, Blackfoot, Plains Cree, Gros Ventre and Sarcee—lived off the buffalo and little else.

Buffalo tongue, liver, brain and hump were eaten as delicacies. Flesh was hung to cure, then cut into strips and dried. Some was made into pemmican (see p. 138). Hides of young animals were tanned to make moccasins, leggings and tunics. Older hides—also tanned—became teepee covers. Hides taken in winter were used as sleeping robes—with the wool left on.

The inch-thick skin of a bull's neck could be dried and hardened over a fire to make a warrior's shield. Rawhide made thongs. The paunch and bladder made bags for food, grease and water. From sinew came thread and bowstrings; from the braided hair of the shoulders and beard, rope. Bones were made into cutting and scraping tools, and toys. Horns became drinking cups or were boiled until soft and carved into spoons. The tail was used as a whip, ornament or fly brush. Dried dung made fuel.

Before the first use of horses in the early 1700s (the buffalo then numbered some 40 million) most of the animals were killed after being stampeded into enclosures called pounds. A fence was built in a circle about 600 feet across, with an opening of some 200 feet. From the opening, two long fences extended out and away from each other, forming a funnel to the pound's entrance. Using small fires, shouts and decoys

Assiniboines and Crees attack Blackfoot ca[...] outside a fort in 1833. The combat was sketch[...] Swiss artist Karl Bodmer.

covered in buffalo skins, Indians direc[...] herd toward the funnel's mouth, [...] goaded the nearsighted animals into cl[...] ing down the funnel into the pound. T[...] they were slaughtered.

Another common hunting method w[...] stampede a herd over a cliff—a bu[...] jump *(left)*.

In winter the buffalo migrated s[...] When dried meat and pemmican ran [...] there was starvation. But in summer, v[...] life was easy, the Indians celebrated wit[...] Sun Dance. All the bands of a tribe w[...] gather for three or four days of religiou[...] emonies and feasting. In some trib[...] young brave would dance while roped [...] pole by thongs threaded through his [...] muscles until the muscles broke o[...] fainted from pain and exhaustion.

For centuries the Indians stayed in s[...] bands, keeping within traditional t[...] boundaries. But when horses (broug[...] Central America by 16th-century S[...] iards) reached the prairie, hunting on [...] gave way to wild chases on horse[...] through stampeding herds. Mounted b[...] attacked other tribes across age-old bo[...] aries. Horses became wealth, horse thi[...] an honorable profession.

Then, half a century after the hors[...] rived, white men brought firearms. Bu[...] had once been killed by the hundred[...] they died in the thousands and the Ir[...] way of life that depended on them died [...] them.

This map shows the distribution of Plains Indi[...] the late 1700s, based on language.

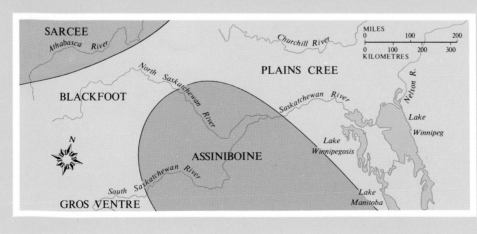

☐ *Algonkian language group*
☐ *Siouan language group*
☐ *Athapaskan language group*

ckfoot shirt (c. 1840), in the National Museum of Man, Ot-
is made of two deer or antelope skins, sewn with sinew, and
ed with quillwork, glass beads and horsehair.

is harnessed to one travois (others are stacked against a
skin teepee) in this painting by Karl Bodmer. Plains Indi-
uled loads on nets strung between the trailing poles.

Fort Douglas, the Red River in the foreground, was painted in
1822 by Peter Rindisbacher. The fort was the headquarters of
the Red River Settlement from 1812 to 1836.

ing Semple in the thigh. As the settlers crowded around Semple they were hit by a volley of musket fire. Some mounted, some on foot, yelling and brandishing skinning knives and tomahawks, the Métis charged.

Semple and 20 settlers were killed in the Seven Oaks Massacre, the West's bloodiest incident in the conflict between old and new ways of life, between Nor'Westers and Métis on one hand, farmers on the other.

Cuthbert Grant was a leader of "the new nation," a people the English called half-breeds, the French *bois-brûlés* (burnt wood, for their dark complexion). They were beginning to call themselves Métis, from the French *métisser* (to mix breeds).

There had been Métis for two centuries. The first were the children of French coureurs de bois and Indian women. Later the half-breed children of English and Scottish traders swelled the population but most of the Métis were French-speaking Roman Catholics. They were buffalo hunters and makers and sellers of pemmican, a staple food of the Northwest.

The interdependence of the Métis and the fur traders who bought the pemmican—the men of the North West Company and the Hudson's Bay Company—was threatened when settlers appeared on the plains early in the 19th century. Farms and fences could not share the prairie with wandering herds of buffalo.

The North West Company, seeking to gain advantage over the rival Hudson's Bay Company, joined the Métis in resisting the threat of settlement. The HBC decided to wait to see what de-

This monument to Thomas Douglas, Earl of Selkirk, is in Winnipeg. The humanitarian Selkirk was moved by the sufferings of crofters turned out of their homes in the Scottish Highlands when the land was enclosed for sheep farming. To save them from starvation or city slums, he established farm colonies in North America.

veloped. Soon the conflict was centred in the Red River Settlement where the Assiniboine meets the Red.

The Red River area (Assiniboia as it became known) was part of Rupert's Land, a vast territory under the absolute rule of the HBC—which nonetheless shared it with the Nor'Westers until 1812 when the first colonists began to appear.

Thomas Douglas, the philanthropic Earl of Selkirk, had taken pity on poverty-stricken highland farmers in his native Scotland. In 1803 he was granted land in Prince Edward Island and what now is Ontario and encouraged Scots to settle there. Then he looked west to the valleys of the Red and the Assiniboine. He bought shares in the HBC and got personal title to a region that included present-day southern Manitoba and adjoining parts of Saskatchewan, North Dakota, Minnesota and Ontario—an area almost as large as Great Britain. The first farmers sailed into Hudson Bay in 1811, bound for the Red River.

They wintered near York Factory, then journeyed by boat some 200 miles up the Hayes River to Oxford House, where they picked up a bull and a cow called Adam and Eve, then down Lake Winnipeg and into the Red River. In the summer of 1812 the boats nosed into the muddy bank at the confluence of the Red and Assiniboine. They called the place Point Douglas, after their patron (soon the HBC would build Fort Douglas there), and on Sept. 4 they pro-

Jean-Baptiste Lagimodière, voyageur and buffalo hunter, arrives at the Montreal home of Lord Selkirk in March 1816, having travelled for five months by canoe and snowshoe with news of attacks on Red River settlers. The astonished Selkirk asks: "Did you walk all the way?" "No," Lagimodière replies, "I ran most of it." The painting is by Adam Sherriff Scott.

The Red River Cart: A Shrieking Do-It-All

The shriek of the Red River cart, wheels turning on ungreased hubs, appalled new arrivals to the prairie in the 1800s.

The all-wood cart was simply a platform and railing, an axle, two big wheels, and shafts for an ox or horse. Dust got in the hubs and would have gummed up grease, so the hubs were left dry. The resulting noise, said one traveller, "makes your blood run cold."

But the carts could carry 1,000 pounds. They provided cheap transportation and were the standard prairie freight vehicle for nearly 100 years. They were built (and repaired) with an axe, a saw, a drill and a knife. The nearest tree provided spare parts. The two-wheel design reduced chances of bogging down on rough ter-

rain. The cart was easily dismantled for use as a raft. Métis on buffalo hunts formed trains of hundreds of carts, divided into brigades of 10, which spread for a mile across the prairie, raising clouds of dust, their axles screeching. "To hear a thousand of those wheels," said a traveller, "is simply hellish."

claimed their leader, Miles Macdonell, governor of Assiniboia.

News of Lord Selkirk's settlement on the Red astounded the North West Company partners at their headquarters at Fort William (Thunder Bay). They concluded the HBC was using colonists to disrupt Nor'Wester fur trade routes. But they would fight back with Métis help. They could use a man like Cuthbert Grant.

Grant's Scottish father had been a North West Company partner. His mother was probably part French, part Cree. Educated in Scotland, he went to Fort Espérance on the Qu'Appelle River at 19 to be a company clerk. With roots in several cultures and an unquestioning loyalty to the company, Grant could surely rally the people. In 1815 the company gave him the title captain-general of the Métis. He would lead the fight against the HBC.

But the HBC did not want a fight. Although company men, as individuals, sometimes helped the settlers, and although farmers attacked by the Métis took refuge at HBC posts, *both* companies held the same view: the settlers were a threat to the fur trade.

The farmers' first years in Assiniboia were

Close to the site of the Seven Oaks Massacre (at Main Street and Rupertsland Avenue in present-day Winnipeg) stands this sombre monument.

hard and hungry. Long cold winters and hot dry summers made it difficult to produce enough food and they too depended on the buffalo. By the winter of 1813-14 their plight was so desperate that Governor Macdonell forbade the export of food—except by licence from him. He also prohibited hunting that drove the buffalo beyond the range of the settlers—and thus heightened the risk of trouble with the Métis. His decree was a direct threat not only to the Métis' livelihood but also to their sense of nationhood in a land they had occupied long before the settlers arrived. Macdonell's order had still another effect: the North West Company, with next winter's fur brigades to provision, believed he would grant licences only to the HBC.

Bands of Métis, incited by Grant and other Nor'Westers, defied Macdonell and terrorized the settlers, finally persuading some that they could never prosper in this harsh land. In June 1815 some 42 farmers in canoes provided by the North West Company left the colony for Upper Canada. Those who stayed were shot at and their cattle were stolen, their barns burned. More and more of them left until only 16 settlers remained. Macdonell surrendered to the North West Company and was taken to Montreal. The last settlers were ordered off their land by Grant's Métis and went to Jack River House at the north end of Lake Winnipeg. As they departed, Métis trampled the young wheat in the fields and put torches to the settlers' cabins. For most of that summer the cabins remained empty, the fields untended.

But in late August they returned with 84 new colonists and 40 laborers. With them came Colin Robertson, a Hudson's Bay Company clerk and former Nor'Wester who understood the Métis.

In the fall and winter of 1815-16, Robertson welcomed Métis to his fireside, served drinks and talked about how the settlers could be a market for Métis pemmican. He won the Métis' friendship and respect and on March 17, when he seized the Nor'Westers' nearby Fort Gibraltar—to keep its pemmican from being sent to the fur brigades in the Athabasca region—not one Métis opposed him. The North West Company had lost control at the Red and Assiniboine. But meanwhile Lord Selkirk had sent a new governor, Robert Semple, to Fort Douglas.

Semple's cold manner quickly destroyed the trust that Robertson had inspired. Robertson still tried to win the Métis away from the Nor'Westers but Semple's aides, acting for the settlers, treated the Métis with hostility. And the hated decree against the export of pemmican remained in effect.

Grant rallied 60 Métis at his headquarters at the junction of the Assiniboine and Qu'Appelle rivers and led them on a lightning raid to

Two of Pierre Falcon's surviving songs of great events in Métis history are about the happenings at Seven Oaks in 1816. His voyageur ballads were sung by fur traders from the St. Lawrence to the Mackenzie but few were written down and only a handful are known today.

The French-Canadian style of building log houses, with horizontal squared logs fitted into grooved upright supports, followed the fur trade across the continent. This example is in the Manitoba Museum of Man and Nature, in Winnipeg.

Chief Peguis and his band of Saulteaux befriended Lord Selkirk's settlers, guiding them and teaching them to hunt. Peguis signed a treaty of peace with Selkirk in 1817, and in 1840, aged about 65, became a Christian. This bust—Peguis holds a Bible—is in Winnipeg's Kildonan Park.

Grand Rapids on the Qu'Appelle to seize HBC canoes loaded with pemmican—food desperately needed by the settlers. He hoped to transport it to North West Company partners waiting on Lake Winnipeg.

On June 19, several miles up the Assiniboine from Fort Douglas, Grant began to move the pemmican overland, bypassing the fort and thus avoiding a clash with Semple.

In the early evening, as the first carts neared Frog Plain, north of Fort Douglas—to be canoed down the Red to Lake Winnipeg—a Métis horseman pounded up to tell Grant that Semple was approaching with a party of armed settlers. Grant and the men not needed to drive the carts rode back to meet Semple. As they broke through the scrub around Seven Oaks, they saw Semple and his 25 men. This was the confrontation nobody had intended.

Only five settlers survived the Seven Oaks Massacre. One of them, John Pritchard, was captured. Next day, Grant sent the terror-stricken Pritchard to Fort Douglas with a horrifying tale of the massacre. That took all fight out of the settlers. On June 22 they abandoned the colony, taking refuge at Norway House, a Hudson's Bay Company post at the north end of Lake Winnipeg.

Lord Selkirk, warned of Métis attacks on his settlement (see p. 168), was already coming west with a private army of soldiers discharged after the War of 1812. Now he descended on the North West Company's Fort William headquarters, captured it, arrested its officers and wintered there. His men took two more North West Com-

pany posts during the winter, and in May 1817 he continued west to the Red River. He rebuilt the settlement beside Fort Douglas and brought back the settlers from Norway House.

In the fall of 1817 he travelled to Montreal with "a cargo of criminals"—Métis and officers and clerks of the North West Company. There were counteraccusations and soon the company and Selkirk had laid nearly 200 charges against each other. In 1819, while the cases were before the courts, draining the finances of the North West Company and of Selkirk (now gravely ill of a lung disease), the Hudson's Bay Company struck a decisive blow: an armed schooner seized all of the North West Company's furs on the Saskatchewan River.

Two years later, the Nor'Westers—whose ruthlessness and daring had captured the West for Canada—agreed to be taken over by the HBC. The Scots from Montreal and their partners from posts scattered across the West sat down in the company's great hall at Fort William to hear the terms of their surrender.

The new company would be called the Hudson's Bay Company. Some North West partners would join it; others who had been lords over river and prairie would settle into obscurity and die in poverty. All furs now would reach the Atlantic by way of Hudson Bay. Not for 60 years would Montreal and the Northwest be linked again. Then the link would be the Canadian Pacific Railway.

Hunting the Buffalo: The Twice-Yearly Harvest of the Plains

This was to be the biggest buffalo hunt yet. Some 1,600 Métis (including 400 children), 1,200 Red River carts, 400 hunting horses and 500 dogs were assembled in June 1840 at Pembina, 60 miles south of present-day Winnipeg.

The Métis' semi-annual hunts produced the pemmican essential for settlers and fur traders. Since the best hunting was in the territory of the hostile Sioux in present-day North Dakota, the hunts were paramilitary operations.

The president, or war chief, and 10 captains were elected. Under each were 10 "soldiers" who kept general order. Ten elected guides took turns setting the day's course. Rules were drawn up against thievery and to ensure that individuals would not frighten off herds before the main party could arrive.

The carts moved off shortly after sun-up each day, following the camp flag carried by the guide, either looking for a herd or following one. After about 10 hours and 15 miles the guide dropped the flag and the carts were drawn into a circle, shafts outward, with tents and animals inside and sentries in rifle pits. (In 1851, at Grand Coteau, N.Dak., 77 Métis hunters beat off 2,000 Sioux with the loss of only one man.)

When buffalo were sighted the hunters mounted and began a charge about 1½ miles from the herd. They "enter the herd with their mouths full of bullets," an observer wrote. "A handful of gunpowder is let fall from their 'powder' horns, a bullet is dropped from the mouth into the muzzle, a tap causes the salivated bullet to adhere to the powder during the second necessary to depress the barrel, when the discharge is instantly effected without bringing the gun to the shoulder."

The hunters fired over and over again, riding miles with the stampeding herd. Four hundred hunters might kill 1,500 buffalo in two hours. (A top hunter could kill a dozen.) Then the hunters reassembled to skin and butcher the carcasses. Carts carried meat and skins back to the camp, where women made pemmican and preserved the hides.

The great hunt of 1840 was one of the most successful ever. In two months it produced 500 tons of meat and pemmican. At least that much usable meat had been left behind.

Would there be a place for Cuthbert Grant and his followers in the new HBC? George Simpson (see p. 226) of the company's northern department believed Grant's influence could be useful and in 1824 he gave Grant a tract of land on the Assiniboine and eventually named him warden of the plains. Grant and his Métis followers built Grantown (present-day St. François Xavier, Man.). The Métis leader who had fought long and hard against the HBC became responsible for enforcing HBC law.

Settlement spread during the 1820s along the Red almost to Lake Winnipeg, and along the Assiniboine to Portage la Prairie. While the Métis continued a way of life based on the buffalo hunt, the settlers farmed along the riverbanks, hunted, or manned heavy York boats for the company. The people of the plains spoke French, English, Gaelic, German or Cree. The Métis far outnumbered the Europeans, yet the struggle to make a homeland of the harsh wilderness united them at last.

With Fish Oil and Soot, an Alphabet for the Cree

Hudson's Bay Company men at Norway House, 400 miles north of Winnipeg, listened disdainfully to the Rev. James Evans. The English-born Evans, 39, superintendent of Northern Missions for the Wesleyan Church, wanted to teach Cree Indians to read, and he wanted the company to import a printing press. The HBC men preferred to keep the Cree illiterate and under their control. They refused Evans's request.

But he was determined and resourceful. In 1840, tired of waiting at York Factory for an HBC boat, he had taught himself to work in metal, built a tin canoe, and paddled 400 miles to the mission he had established at Rossville near Norway House.

Now, equally undaunted, Evans studied the Cree language and reduced it to a syllabic alphabet with nine symbols, each used in four positions. He carved moulds in oak and cast type from melted musket balls and tea-chest foil. Fish oil mixed with soot was his ink, birch bark his paper. In 1841, using a fur press, he printed 100 copies of the *Cree Syllabic Hymn Book,* bound them in deerskin and gave them to Cree hunters. The alphabet is still in use.

Guillaume Sayer was one of four Métis the HBC accused of illegal fur trading in 1849. He was convicted—but freed—and the others were released, an admission of the right of the Métis to trade with whomever they wished.

But life continued hard. Crops were attacked by wind, drought, frost and grasshoppers. Wolves, dogs and blizzards killed the few cattle. Two summers running, in 1818 and 1819, clouds of grasshoppers ravaged crops, their bodies clogging streams and wells. In the terrible winter of 1825-26 buffalo hunters were caught in the worst blizzard in memory. When it cleared, 35 bodies were frozen under the snow and the herd had scattered far to the west.

After that hungry winter the thaw came suddenly in late spring and the Red flooded farms. Cold and hungry, the people huddled on high ground to watch the destruction of their houses and possessions; then, when the waters dropped, they returned to rebuild. Nature was kinder in the following years.

The HBC saw a threat to its own trade from this semi-independent colony. In 1834, the company bought back the Red River Settlement from Selkirk's family. The district was once more part of Rupert's Land and was governed by a council under the presidency of George Simpson. Simpson shrewdly appointed Grant one of the councillors but he built a jail, perhaps as a sign of the way the company intended to rule.

The company was determined to maintain its monopoly. Farmers and Métis who did not deal exclusively with the HBC were jailed for illegal trading. In good years the settlers produced more crops and pemmican than the company could buy. In bad years they depended on the company for help. That help, always grudgingly given, was never adequate.

Needy settlers and Métis looked for new markets and began trading with Americans who offered cheaper goods and the rum and other commodities that the HBC would not supply.

At length the company could no longer stand this defiance of its monopoly and on May 17, 1849, four Métis were put on trial at Upper Fort Garry for illegal fur trading. But more than 300 armed and angry Métis gathered before St. Boniface Cathedral that morning. One of them, Louis Riel (father of rebel Louis Riel, see p. 276), spoke from the cathedral steps, calling to the men to show the HBC they would have their own way in their own nation. Led by Riel, they made their way to the courthouse.

The first verdict was announced: Guillaume Sayer was found guilty. Outside the court were hundreds of Métis, and the company's police force was small. Adam Thom, recorder of the court, pronounced sentence: the court did not wish to be harsh; Sayer was free to go; charges against the other three were dismissed.

As the news spread there were shouts of *"Le commerce est libre!"* (Trade is free). Muskets were fired in the air. The Hudson's Bay Company monopoly was ended.

The years that followed were more tranquil. The West of the fur trader had given way to the West of the farmer. By 1858 an American railway reached St. Paul, Minn., southeast of the Red River country. Men in Montreal were talking of a Canadian railway to the Red River—the railway that was to open the West but hasten the end of the Métis nation.

Heritage Sites

WINNIPEG A nine-foot limestone column marks approximately where Métis killed Governor Robert Semple and 20 Red River colonists in the Seven Oaks Massacre of June 19, 1816.

Also in Winnipeg

FORT GARRY PARK (6) A stone and wood gate remains from Upper Fort Garry, a Hudson's Bay Company post built in 1835 just west of where the North West Company's Fort Gibraltar stood.

GRANT'S OLD MILL (3) A replica of a grist mill built by Cuthbert Grant in 1829 is on Portage Avenue beside Sturgeon Creek.

LORD SELKIRK MONUMENT (4) The founder of the Red River Settlement is commemorated by a plaque on a limestone column.

MANITOBA MUSEUM OF MAN AND NATURE (5) Exhibits include a diorama of a Métis buffalo hunt, a sword owned by Cuthbert Grant, and a silver medal presented to Peguis, a Saulteaux chief who aided survivors of the Seven Oaks Massacre.

PEGUIS MONUMENT (11) A bronze bust atop a granite column in Kildonan Park honors the Saulteaux chief.

ST. BONIFACE CATHEDRAL (9) The present basilica is on the site of western Canada's first church, built in 1818 by Father Joseph Norbert Provencher. On its steps in 1849 Louis Riel (father of rebel Louis Riel) rallied more than 300 Métis in a protest against the HBC trade monopoly.

ST. BONIFACE MUSEUM (8) A building constructed by the Grey Nuns in 1846 as a convent has displays of settlers' belongings of the early 1800s. The sword, sash and pouch of Jean-Baptiste Lagimodière, who canoed and snowshoed almost 1,800 miles to Montreal in 1815 to warn Lord Selkirk of attacks on the Red River Settlement, are displayed.

"SEIZIN' OF THE LAND" (7) A plaque commemorates the formal proclamation of the Red River Settlement Sept. 4, 1812.

SIR WILLIAM WHYTE PARK (10) A cairn identifies the site of Fort Douglas, built by the HBC in 1813 for protection of the Red River Settlement. The log Ross House Museum, in which William Ross opened western Canada's first post office (1855), is in a nearby heritage park.

Other sites

Eldon, P.E.I. (not shown) The Lord Selkirk Settlement contains replicas of shelters and a cabin built by Scottish crofters who came here in 1803. St. John's Presbyterian Church in Belfast was built by the settlers in 1823.

Norway House, Man. (1) The ashes of James Evans, who built a mission at nearby Rossville in 1840-41 and devised a Cree alphabet, are interred in a cairn. A bark-and-skin hymnal printed by Evans is in the E. J. Pratt Library, Victoria College, University of Toronto. *Norway House accessible only by air.*

Selkirk, Man. (2) A museum at Lower Fort Garry National Historic Park contains HBC artifacts. The Fraser House, a typical farmer's dwelling, was constructed about 1835 and is furnished to the period of the 1850s. St. Peter's Dynevor Church (1853) in East Selkirk stands where an Anglican mission was built in 1831 for Saulteaux Indians; Chief Peguis is buried in the churchyard.

A working replica of a mill built by Métis leader Cuthbert Grant (a former North West Company clerk) near Grantown (present-day St. François Xavier, Man.) grinds flour for sale to visitors. Grant's Old Mill, now on the outskirts of Winnipeg, was the first mill west of the Great Lakes. It was erected in 1829 on land granted by the HBC.

Britons Roughing It in the Bush

Grist mills like Roblin's Mill (above) at Black Creek Pioneer Village in Toronto saved settlers the labor of grinding their grain into flour by hand. In 1836 Upper Canada had some 600 grist mills, although many settlers still had to carry their grain 20 miles. Mills became meeting places and communities grew up around them. At busy times, an owner might be at his mill from 2 a.m. Monday until Saturday night, eating as he worked, sleeping on dusty sacks. "Killed in his mill" was a frequent epitaph (many a miller fell or got clothing caught in the huge gears). Candles, oil lamps and friction from the wooden machinery started fires. Spring floods sometimes carried away entire mills.

In 1833, when John Langton settled at Sturgeon Lake, northwest of Peterborough, Ont., he had six fellow pioneers as neighbors. Four were university graduates, another had been to a military college, and the sixth—Langton wrote home to England—"has half a dozen silver spoons and a wife who plays the guitar." Such persons were among Canada's "gentle pioneers"—Britons of moderate means who joined the wave of emigration between 1815 and 1855 (see p. 197). Many came to the forests north of Lake Ontario.

Some women tried to keep up old ways. One would receive no visitors in her one-room log cabin until she had changed into "company" clothes—behind a hanging blanket. Another summoned her maid with a cow bell on an embroidered bell-pull. But most "gentle pioneers," men and women, soon learned about the hard work of converting a forest into a farm.

Many women helped clear land for the log houses. Lacking yeast, they grew hops to make bread rise, then baked the bread in kettles on a fire. They made substitute coffee from dandelion roots, and teas from sage, mint and hickory. They butchered animals, made sausages, smoked hams, salted pork—and saved the scraps to make soap and candles. Soft soap—thick, bright brown and strong—was made in a great iron cauldron by boiling animal fat, entrails and bones with lye (made from water and wood ash). Bars were made by adding handfuls of salt at the end of the boiling process, and cutting up the resulting congealed cake. Tallow candles were made in moulds or by dipping twisted cotton wicks until the layers had built up enough.

Illnesses were treated with home remedies and prayer. The recipe for an ointment to cure sprains and backaches began: "Take four good sized live toads, put into boiling water and cook very soft." Ague—anything from a cold to malarial fever—was the commonest complaint. Some settlers used quinine but whisky and brandy were popular remedies. In 1846 ague was epidemic, and John Langton recorded that "sometimes we had difficulty in finding men strong enough to carry the coffins up to the churchyard."

With little leisure time, pioneers turned work into social events. Neighbors gathered for "bees"—women quilting (right) and sewing; men clearing land, raising barns and ploughing. Logging (land-clearing) bees were most common: men from 15-20 miles around brought tools and oxen, then raced one another to speed the work. Whisky livened the day and much of the night, and such bees ended, according to pioneer author Susanna Moodie, with "unhallowed revelry, profane songs and blasphemous swearing." Week-long Methodist camp meetings (above) also brought settlers together. Regulations for camp life were strict, but scoffers and jokers got in and some took advantage of engrossed worshippers.

Take One Bald Head . . .

Pioneer women combined plant lore and ingenuity to meet household needs. Marigolds *(top right)* were used to treat cuts, burns and gangrene, and to color butter. Yellow bedstraw *(lower right)* became mattress stuffing, and also curdled milk for cheese. Garlic *(left)* was mixed with honey for coughs, colds and asthma—and rubbed into the scalp to cure baldness.

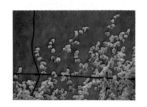

Regular stage coach service between Upper Canada's main towns was established by 1830 but a ride, as one passenger put it, was "a punishment of no ordinary severity." Roads were full of rocks, stumps and holes; corduroy roads—logs laid side by side over swampy areas—were "abominably jolty." Passengers were advised to wear hats to protect their heads but bloodstains on coach roofs were not uncommon. When a coach got stuck, passengers got out and pushed. A journey of 25 miles could take nine hours. At every roadside inn—and there were many—passengers would treat the driver, and the driving got more erratic as the journey progressed. Drivers fell asleep at the reins and horses wandered off the road, sometimes overturning the coach.

When a man found time for the long walk to the nearest post office he might collect mail for his whole district and distribute it after church *(above)*. Postage was usually paid by the recipient of a letter, not the sender. One poor settler who received letters with postage due had them read aloud to him at the post office, memorized them, then said they were not for him. One way of cutting postage costs was to save weight by "crossing"—writing horizontally then vertically on the same side of a sheet of paper.

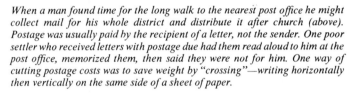

A settler might take three years to clear 30 acres. Trees were cut down or burned or girdled (killed by cutting a broad ring around the trunk, thus stopping the flow of sap). But until they rotted or were pulled out, stumps made one-third of the cleared land useless.

Two English sisters took up backwoods life, then homemade quill pens, and wrote books that became classics. Catharine Parr Traill and Susanna Moodie came to Upper Canada with their husbands in 1832. Catharine adapted cheerfully to life in Douro Township, northeast of Peterborough, and in The Backwoods of Canada *(1836) and* The Female Emigrant's Guide *(1854), gave practical advice—and warnings—to would-be English emigrants. Susanna was less enthusiastic. In* Roughing It in the Bush *(1852) she told of feeling like a "condemned criminal . . . his only hope of escape being through the portals of the grave." But she survived a forest fire and being chased by a bear, and in 1853 produced a more optimistic book,* Life in the Clearings.

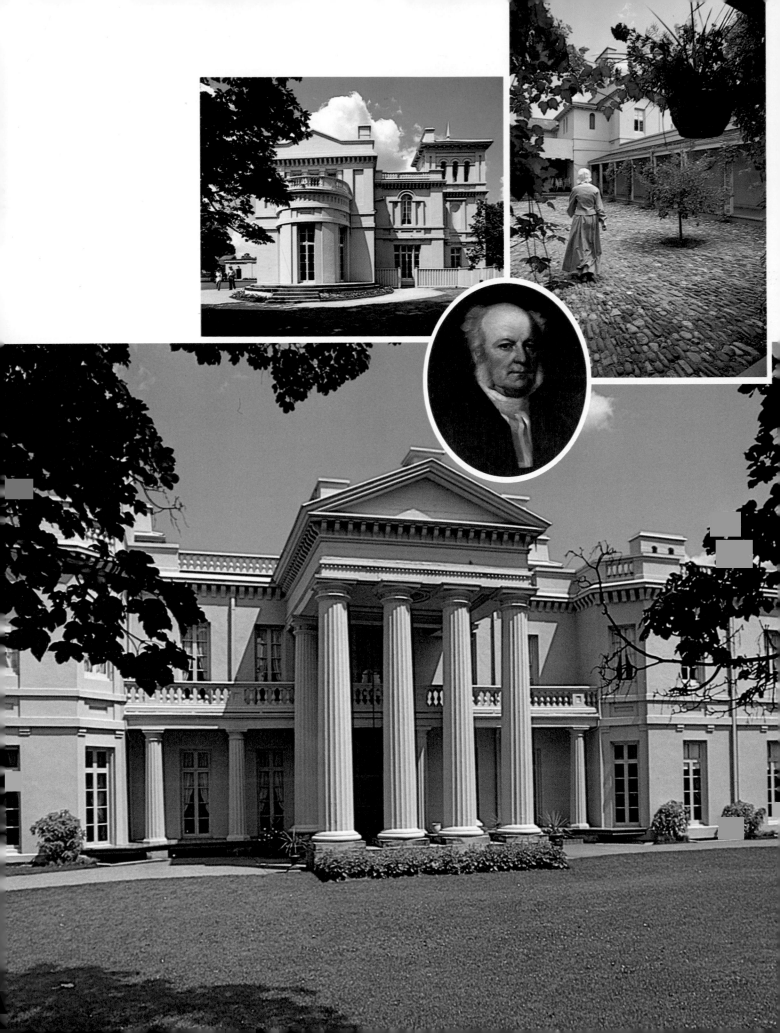

The Arrogant Aristocrats of Upper Canada

Allan Napier MacNab, the laird of Dundurn, surveyed his comfortable world with satisfaction as he gazed down from Burlington Heights one June evening in 1836. The provincial elections were concluded and from his Dundurn Castle, the grandest residence in all Upper Canada, he could see much of Wentworth County, which had just returned him to the Legislative Assembly. To the southeast was Hamilton, where he had made his fortune—as land agent, builder and lawyer.

The voters that June had overwhelmingly elected candidates who supported—or, like Mac-Nab, were members of—the Family Compact, the province's ruling élite. Family connections, wealth and education were required for membership in this self-styled aristocracy, but above all it was necessary to be fiercely loyal to the Crown. The Family Compact distrusted all who might have republican sympathies—middle-class businessmen and farmers, artisans and laborers.

The American Revolution had been recent history and the French Revolution was still being fought when Lt.Col. John Graves Simcoe, first governor of Upper Canada, sailed for the wilderness in 1791 to head a system of government based as closely as possible on that of densely populated Britain.

The governor stood for both king and prime minister. His cabinet was the Executive Council, leading citizens whose advice the governor usually took. There was a Legislative Council modelled on the House of Lords but its members were appointed, not hereditary. The only elected body was the Legislative Assembly, of which Allan MacNab was a member.

Hamilton's restored and refurnished Dundurn Castle epitomizes the elegant, privileged life-style of Sir Allan Napier Mac-Nab (inset), who built it in 1832-34. Left: the main entrance. Top left: a side door. Top right: the courtyard.

Among the pioneer settlers of what became Ontario, only a handful were qualified to hold government positions and these few founded the dynasties that made up the Family Compact. Settling the land was the major government business and land became the main source of Family Compact wealth. The few could make large grants to themselves and thus secure the position of their descendants.

William Jarvis, for example, was an army officer when he came to York, the capital. Simcoe appointed him provincial secretary. One Jarvis son was sheriff of the Home District, the area between York (later Toronto) and Lake Simcoe; another was a court clerk and superintendent of Indian affairs. A cousin was registrar of deeds and thus determined who got title deeds to Crown land.

Another of the élite was D'Arcy Boulton. He arrived in York in 1797 and was successively solicitor general, attorney general and judge. All three positions were later held by his son, Henry John Boulton, as well as by Henry's contemporary, John Beverley Robinson. Robinson, Canadian-born of a Loyalist family from Virginia, first held office at 22 (in 1813) and was chief justice before he was 40.

The undoubted leader of the Compact was John Strachan. Penniless, he came to Upper Canada in 1799 to tutor the children of a rich Kingston family. But he was ordained an Anglican priest in 1804 and was appointed rector of Cornwall and headmaster of a government grammar school there. He married the beautiful widow of a wealthy Montreal fur trader named McGill (and persuaded McGill's brother James, also a fur trader, to bequeath money for a university; that was the inception of McGill University).

Strachan received an honorary doctor of divinity degree from a university in Scotland. This, he told Scottish friends, "would be of great service" in Upper Canada, for "no people are so

This is one of two matching Regency crystal candelabra that grace a gleaming mahogany table in the dining room of Dundurn Castle in Hamilton.

fond of distinctions of rank." Strachan moved to York in 1812 to be rector of St. James' Church, headmaster of the grammar school and chaplain to the garrison.

When American invaders set fire to the parliament buildings in York in 1813 and began looting the town, Strachan spoke for the citizens and threatened military retaliation. The looting was curbed and Strachan's moral leadership was established. In 1839 he became the first bishop of Toronto.

Strachan was a member of both the Executive and Legislative councils and his influence on successive governors was strong. He said of one: "He arrived here with some ideas on the Executive not founded on sufficient evidence, but now sees things more clearly." The Compact usually managed to control elections (see p. 208) to the Legislative Assembly. If a pro-government member was in danger of losing his seat, tavern keepers could be paid to dispense hospitality on his behalf or the town could be promised a post office.

After the War of 1812, the Upper Canada aristocracy was joined by retired British officers. Their farms were not as efficiently run as those of more practical immigrants from Britain and the United States—but such men became justices of the peace, were called squires and supplemented their half-pay incomes with favors from Compact leaders in York. They became part of the Establishment and helped keep the country British.

Allan MacNab, though poor at the start of his career, was acceptable to the Compact. He had been to school in York with the Boultons and the Jarvises and had proved his loyalty in 1813 when, though only 15, he joined Maj.Gen. Isaac Brock's former regiment, the 49th Foot. He fought at Fort Niagara, Sackets Harbor, Plattsburgh and Black Rock, all in New York.

By 1820, still in York, he was buying and sell-

Sir Peregrine Maitland was a soldier, unskilled in civil affairs, when he became governor of Upper Canada in 1818. His 10-year administration was marked by persecution of political reformists and overreaction to any hint of republicanism. He once stopped the pay of a retired British officer who had called for the singing of "Yankee Doodle" at a benefit concert for a touring company of American actors stranded in York (Toronto).

ing land for his former schoolmate and patron Henry John Boulton. He articled in the law office of Boulton's father before moving to Hamilton in 1826. He married a Boulton and ennobled himself by adding "of Dundurn" to his name long before he owned the Burlington Heights property or built his castle. (Dundurn—Gaelic for fort on the water—is the clan MacNab's seat in Scotland.) He made a small fortune selling lots, houses, legal services and government patronage to the settlers.

MacNab had seen three splendid mansions built in postwar York. Strachan's at Front Street and University Avenue, completed in 1818, was called the Palace—particularly appropriate when he became a bishop. It was the town's first brick residence, two storeys high with shade trees and a carriageway. (It was demolished in 1896.) The Grange, built by D'Arcy Boulton, Jr., still stands. It is furnished as a gentleman's residence of 1835, and part of the Art Gallery of Ontario is housed within it. Chief Justice William Campbell's elegant mansion was completed in 1822, seven years before work began on Osgoode Hall. Originally on Adelaide Street, it was moved in 1972 to Queen Street across from Osgoode Hall. It is owned by the Ontario Advocate Society and is open to the public.

MacNab was determined to outdo the mansion owners of York. In 1832, two years after his first election to the Legislative Assembly, he bought the most impressive site in the district. On it he built Dundurn Castle, an ornate villa in Regency and Italianate styles. Mrs. Henry John Boulton, mortified lest her own house be outshone by Dundurn's magnificence, persuaded her husband in 1833 to hire the Upper Canada

This canal fed water from the Grand River (near Port Maitland, Ont.) to the locks at Welland when the Welland Canal was opened in 1829. Government financing of the canal company reduced Upper Canada almost to bankruptcy.

Four Great Fortresses and the Rideau Canal Deterred U.S. Invasion

The War of 1812 (see p. 152) was over but the United States still coveted Canadian territory. To deter further invasions, Britain embarked on a defence program which included the building of four great fortresses:

• On 210-acre Ile aux Noix, 30 miles southeast of Montreal in the Richelieu River, Fort Lennox (1819-28)—to block the historic invasion route down the Richelieu Valley.

• On Cape Diamond in Quebec, a 40-acre citadel incorporating old French fortifications (1820-32)—to defend Britain's North American military and administrative headquarters.

• On Citadel Hill in Halifax, a massive fort, the fourth in a series there (1828-56)—to help guard the entrance to the Gulf of St. Lawrence.

• At Kingston, Fort Henry (1832-36)—to guard the Rideau Canal and the Provincial Marine base whose ships protected settlements along Lake Ontario.

The Rideau Canal, between Kingston and the future site of Ottawa, was also part of the defence system. Built in 1826-32 by Lt.Col. John By of the Royal Engineers, it was part of a water route joining Upper and Lower Canada via the Cataraqui, Rideau and Ottawa rivers.

By the 1850s British North America had attained responsible government (see p. 204); Britain built no more North American defences. But the stone fortresses (all of which survive) were an effective deterrent. The United States grumbled but did not intervene as Canada became a nation in 1867 and expanded to the Pacific in 1871.

Fort Lennox

The Rideau Canal (and Bytown Museum)

Fort Henry

College drawing master, John Howard, to "gothicize" their own Holland House in York.

Keeping up with one another was a continual struggle for this frontier aristocracy. The wife of William Dummer Powell, an earlier chief justice, wrote to a friend in 1819: "In an aristocratical Government, expenses must be incurred according to the station held; it would be improper for me to receive my company in a cotton gown, to give them a joint of meat and a pudding, or to return their visit in a wagon."

The model was life in an English country house; the problem was finding servants. "For God's sake try and bring out a servant or two with you," William Jarvis wrote to an English friend. "The whole country cannot produce one fit to put in 'Hell's Kitchen.'" Large houses such as Dundurn and The Grange required a small army of kitchen and upstairs help to bring water from a well for every room and logs for a dozen fires.

Visitors were frequent, meals elaborate. Dinner often began at 4 p.m. and included fish and game courses and a couple of roasts, served by candlelight with wines and brandies. (Locally made beer, cider and green rye whisky were for the common people.) Silver, china and glass were usually brought from Europe but by the time Dundurn was built, fine furniture was often manufactured by local cabinetmakers.

Many Family Compact marriages were arranged on the croquet lawn at The Grange, under the watchful eye of Mrs. D'Arcy Boulton, Jr. Allan MacNab probably met his wife at a dinner party at The Grange.

The Family Compact's life-style and the

A Muddy Capital Dependent on London's Flour Prices

The capital of Upper Canada was known as Muddy York in the early 1800s. York (Toronto) was built on low land between the Don and Humber rivers and its streets became quagmires each spring.

Merchants cursed the mud; 90 percent of their business was with farmers along the 60-mile cart road called Yonge Street—and it was impassable for weeks on end. They also cursed a system of barter which forced them to trade British cotton, nails and tea for the farmers' flour; profits depended on London's erratic flour prices.

York had been founded in 1793, an administrative centre in the wilderness. There was no bank to provide loans for business. In 1803 the Earl of Selkirk (see p. 168) described it as "an insulated spot almost detached from both ends of the colony." Five years later a lighthouse *(right)* was erected on Gibraltar

Point to make York a safe, attractive port, yet the population was barely 800 when the War of 1812 began.

With a postwar flow of immigrants into York and its hinterland, the merchants in 1817 persuaded the Rev. John Strachan and other members of the Family Compact to establish a municipal government. York got plank roads, and Yonge Street some macadam surfacing. Lobbying in London by Governor Sir Peregrine Maitland and by Compact members secured royal assent for The Bank of Upper Canada, which opened in 1821. The 740-ton *Frontenac,* first Canadian-built steamer on the Great Lakes, had been in regular service between Kingston, York and Queenston since 1817.

By 1830 York had 2,800 inhabitants, and there were 27,000 persons on farms up Yonge Street. The town was incorporated as the City of Toronto in 1834.

A proud sweeping staircase, a great arched window, a statue in its special niche . . . symbols of Family Compact affluence in The Grange in Toronto.

abuses of privilege that supported it offended ordinary folk. A farmer wrote: "The author has been in Canada since he was a little boy, and he has not had the advantage of a classical education at a District School. The greater part of his time has been spent watching over and providing for an increasing and tender family. He had in most instances to make his own roads and bridges, clear his own land, educate himself and his children, be his own mechanic, and except now and then, he had no society but his own family. He had his bones broken by the fall of trees, his feet lacerated by the axe, and suffered almost everything except death. He waited year after year in hope of better days, expecting that the government would care less for themselves and more for the people. But every year he has been disappointed."

In 1817, long before Dundurn Castle but about the time the great houses were being built in York, the people's discontent was given focus by the arrival of Robert Gourlay, a Scot of good family whose wife had inherited 866 acres near London. He disliked the system and its leader. Strachan, he pointed out, had been brought out as a hired "servant" in the household of a relative of Gourlay's wife.

This Georgian mansion in Toronto was the home of Sir William Campbell, a chief justice of Upper Canada. Dating from 1822, it has been restored and is open to the public.

The Bitter Battle Over Church Lands

The Ven. John Strachan, archdeacon of York (later Toronto), long the leader of the Family Compact, was mightily distressed in 1827. He found it "sickening to the heart" that the Church of England was so beleaguered by the clergy reserves issue.

Thirty-six years before, Britain had awarded the church one-seventh of each township in Upper Canada—2.2 million acres. The land was to be sold (when its value increased) to support an established Protestant clergy. But now, when Strachan wanted to sell at least half the clergy reserves, Britain balked, fearing that the sale of more than one-quarter of them would be premature. Meanwhile, Upper Canada's Reform party complained that the clergy reserves—200-acre lots, most still uncleared—impeded settlement. The Reformers also demanded that proceeds from all clergy reserve sales be shared with other religious denominations.

What Strachan needed was a declaration that the Church of England was the established church, with full control over proceeds from the reserves. He wrote to the Colonial Office and *what* he wrote caused an uproar. He had used grossly inaccurate figures to dismiss "dissenting" denominations as a handful of itinerant teachers with republican leanings and few followers. Methodist Egerton Ryerson (see p. 202) then demonstrated that the Church of England itself was a minority, outnumbered by the Methodists, by the Presbyterians and by the Anabaptists. The solidly Anglican Family Compact insisted nonetheless that the Church of England should receive all proceeds.

By 1838 some 400,000 acres had been sold in small lots but the controversy over the revenue raged on, Reformers in the Legislative Assembly now insisting it be used for education. In 1854, with the power of the Compact at last broken, the assembly agreed to give the money to newly established municipalities to set up local administrations.

John Strachan, educationist and pillar of the Family Compact, became the first Anglican bishop of Toronto, in 1839. This marble bust is in St. James' Cathedral there. Strachan also was the first president (1827-48) of King's College, the present-day University of Toronto.

Gourlay wanted to encourage immigration. To collect information to send to Britain he printed and distributed a pamphlet with 31 questions. Question 31 was: "What, in your opinion, retards the improvement of your township in particular, or the province in general?" The replies convinced him that the chief problem was uncultivated land owned by absentees and speculators. These many blocks of vacant land meant the population was scattered and could not support such things as roads. Often the absentee landlord was the Church of England or a member of the Family Compact. Each executive councillor was granted 5,000 acres, each of his children 1,200 acres; similar grants were made to some members of the legislature and others of the élite. Sometimes a whole township was owned by one man.

Gourlay denounced this "paltry patronage and ruinous favoritism," and criticized the governor's power to dispose of land, positions, pensions and licences and "to provide dinners and drinks to all supplicants and sycophants." He summoned a convention at York in 1818 to petition reforms from the new governor, Sir Peregrine Maitland.

The convention was tame and respectable, attended by only 14 delegates, but it reminded the Family Compact of the American and French revolutions. Enraged and alarmed, Strachan and John Beverley Robinson persuaded Maitland to prohibit future conventions. The governor went further: he refused land grants to those who had co-operated with Gourlay, and fired all unrepentant sympathizers.

Archibald McNab—as head of his clan he signed himself The Mc-Nab—*came to Upper Canada in 1823, curried favor with the Family Compact and got title to 80,000 acres in the Ottawa Valley. He enticed settlers there, then tyrannized them, demanding rents in perpetuity and refusing permission to leave the township. After 23 years an order-in-council ended his feudal reign.*

Arrested in December 1818, Gourlay was charged with spreading disaffection and was given 10 days to leave the province. He refused and was jailed until the August 1819 assizes. He was confined in a small cell, frequently without exercise or access to his lawyer and distracted by violent headaches, and his mental and physical health deteriorated. Perjured evidence was presented against him and Chief Justice Powell banished Gourlay from Upper Canada.

The Compact had created a martyr. For 10 years the name of "the banished Briton" was a rallying point for opponents of Family Compact government and by 1829 a Reform party had been formed. It won a majority of the assembly seats in the elections that year and in 1834. The Compact still held most appointed positions.

A new governor arrived in 1836, an opinionated little fighting cock of a man, Sir Francis Bond Head. He was as much annoyed by the Reformers as he was pleased by the company and views of such men as MacNab and Robinson. He embraced the aristocratic style and rule of the Family Compact and preened himself as the embodiment of the Crown.

In the 1836 election Head appealed to the people to elect assemblymen loyal to the Family Compact, calling the Reformers Yankee rabble-rousers. He appointed returning officers who were government supporters and sent agents to the polling booths to bribe voters with land grants—unprecedented interference by a governor. Head and the Compact won an overwhelming victory and he told the Colonial Office in London that he had "saved the Canadas."

It had been rumored that Hamilton radicals were threatening to burn down Dundurn Castle. Now they and their kind had been defeated. But even as Allan MacNab rejoiced at his villa on Burlington Heights, the most radical Reformer was bitterly contemplating his first defeat in eight elections in York County. Perhaps justice could come only through revolution. William Lyon Mackenzie was preparing for rebellion.

The Colonel Was No Saint But He Got Things Done

Col. Thomas Talbot—after whom St. Thomas, Ont., was named—was cantankerous, hard-drinking, arbitrary, unlikable, a member of the Family Compact . . . anything but a saint.

Irish-born, he came to Canada in 1790 as a 19-year-old soldier, was named secretary to Governor John Graves Simcoe, and in 1803 founded the Talbot Settlement on 48,500 acres he had been granted south of London. He lived at Port Talbot on Lake Erie.

Talbot wanted "none other but sound British subjects" on his land. Some would-be settlers were dismissed with "Devil a sod will you get here!"

A Talbot settler received title to only a quarter of his 200 acres until he had cleared and seeded three acres, built a house and cleared half the width of a roadway in front of the lot. Talbot kept township plans in pencil and erased the names of settlers who failed to perform their duties or who broke his restrictive rules about mortgaging and selling lots. He started drinking each morning at 11 and would do no business after noon.

But the colonel got things done and his settlement grew. St. Thomas was founded in 1817. By 1831 Talbot had 6,000 settler families in 29 townships. The Talbot Road (the basis of present-day Highway 3) beside Lake Erie was the best road in Upper Canada.

Eventually, however, Talbot's eccentric behavior became a political issue, and in 1837 the Legislative Assembly ordered him to surrender the township plans. He died in London in 1853, lonely and bitter.

Heritage Sites

HAMILTON, Ont. Dundurn Castle is an Italianate-Regency villa built in 1832-34 by Allan MacNab, a member of the Family Compact. Here he lived in splendor until his death in 1862. Among 35 restored rooms are a black-walnut-panelled library from which MacNab practised law, and a dining room with a mahogany table seating 20, and a chandelier with 720 crystal prisms. Dundurn Castle Museum (in the mansion) depicts the early history of Hamilton. An adjacent building, now the Cockpit Theatre, is thought to have been used for cockfights.

Other sites

Arnprior, Ont. (8) Archibald McNab, a despotic Scot who brought settlers to this area beginning in 1823, is featured in an exhibit at the Arnprior & District Museum. An 1837 map of McNab's settlement is displayed. Nine miles southwest is Waba Lodge, a re-creation of McNab's summer home, with exhibits of 19th-century furnishings.

Cornwall, Ont. (10) Bishop Strachan Memorial Church is named after John Strachan, an arch-Tory and pillar of the Family Compact, who became Anglican bishop of Toronto in 1839. While living in Cornwall he founded one of Upper Canada's first grammar schools in 1803 and later built the town's first Anglican church.

Halifax (not shown) A stone fortress completed in 1856 is in Halifax Citadel National Historic Park. It contains a military museum, a maritime museum and a museum of furniture and farm implements.

Kingston, Ont. (6) Fort Henry, completed in 1836, has been restored as a museum of military history. In summer, students in 19th-century uniforms drill and fire salutes from the fort's original cannon.

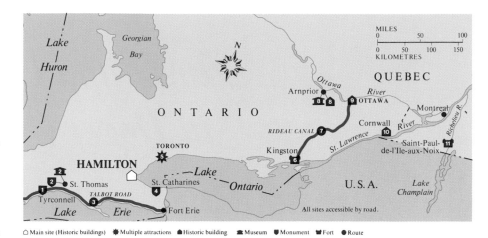

Ottawa (9) The stone building that Lt.Col. John By used as a storehouse, office and treasury during construction of the Rideau Canal is now the Bytown Museum. Displays illustrate the history of the canal and of Ottawa (formerly Bytown).

Quebec (not shown) Most of the present Citadel was erected by the British in 1820-32. A museum in the former powder magazine exhibits an original plan of the officers' quarters.

Rideau Canal (7) This 126-mile link between Ottawa and Kingston follows natural waterways and 12 miles of artificial channel. Built for military purposes, it is now used mainly by pleasure craft.

St. Catharines, Ont. (4) A plaque in Centennial Gardens Park describes the building of the first Welland Canal from Port Dalhousie (now part of St. Catharines) to Port Robinson in 1824-29, and its extension to Port Colborne in 1833.

Saint-Paul-de-l'Ile-aux-Noix, Que. (11) Fort Lennox National Historic Park, covering 210 acres, is on Ile aux Noix in the Richelieu River. Most of the fort dates from 1819-28. A barracks, commissary, guardhouse and canteen have been restored. In the former officers' quarters is a museum of military equipment.

St. Thomas, Ont. (2) A plaque at the Elgin County Court House commemorates the eccentric Col. Thomas Talbot, who settled Kent, Elgin, Middlesex, Oxford and Norfolk counties in the early 1800s. Some of his personal effects are in the Elgin County Pioneer Museum. The Talbot Road, Upper Canada's best in the 1830s, is commemorated by a marker three miles west.

Many Family Compact gatherings were in The Grange, the great house D'Arcy Boulton, Jr., built in Toronto. This is the dining room.

Talbot Road (3) Highway 3, flanking Lake Erie, follows the approximate course of the 300-mile road built by Talbot Settlement inhabitants starting in 1809.

Toronto (5)

CAMPBELL HOUSE This restored Georgian mansion, a typical Family Compact dwelling, was built in 1822 by William Campbell, chief justice of the Court of King's Bench and speaker of the Legislative Council in the 1820s.

COLBORNE LODGE Constructed in 1836 by John Howard, Toronto's first city surveyor, the house contains Howard family furnishings including a bathtub and a wood-and-brass shower. The lodge was named after Sir John Colborne, lieutenant-governor of Upper Canada (1828-36).

GIBRALTAR POINT LIGHTHOUSE One of the oldest lighthouses on the Great Lakes (1808) is on Toronto Island. A plaque on the 82-foot beacon records its history.

OSGOODE HALL The Law Society of Upper Canada erected this building in 1829-32 as a meeting place—on land purchased from Chief Justice John Beverley Robinson, a Family Compact stalwart. It now houses the Ontario Supreme Court.

ST. JAMES' CATHEDRAL John Strachan was the minister of four churches on this site including the present one, built in 1850-53. In 1812, Strachan had become rector of St. James' Church, Toronto's first, which stood here in 1803-31.

THE GRANGE This stately brick mansion, built in 1817 by D'Arcy Boulton, Jr., a prominent member of the Family Compact, has been restored as a gentleman's house of 1825-35. It is part of the Art Gallery of Ontario.

Tyrconnell, Ont. (1) At St. Peter's Church, near the centre of the original Talbot Settlement, is the grave of Thomas Talbot.

Anger and Bloodshed in Lower Canada

Louis-Joseph Papineau's carriage clattered across the square in the small town of Saint-Eustache, 15 miles west of Montreal, a square dominated by the limestone façade of a church whose twin belfries were a landmark for miles around. Two months later, on Dec. 14, 1837, Saint-Eustache and its church would lie in ruins, destroyed by British soldiers and Canadian volunteers.

Papineau was the leader of *Les Patriotes,* a radical reform party supported by most of Lower Canada's French-speaking inhabitants. On this October day, with his son Amédée—a member of *Les Fils de la Liberté,* young militant *Patriotes*—he was travelling to Montreal from the Papineau seigneury of La Petite Nation, on the Ottawa River near Montebello. In Saint-Eustache he stopped to talk with Dr. Jean-Olivier Chénier, *Patriote* leader for the region of Two Mountains.

The countryside was not at peace. About 80 percent of Lower Canada's population was French speaking and a long campaign against British rule was boiling into scattered acts of violence—often against countrymen who supported the British régime. *Vendus* they were called (persons who have sold out to the other side) or *Chouayens,* after French militiamen who deserted at the Battle of Chouagen (Oswego, N.Y.) in 1756.

Papineau told Chénier he hated the escalating violence. *Chouayen* businessmen could find no customers; their houses were being seized, some even destroyed; many had volunteered to fight alongside British regular troops. And now Ché-

Louis-Joseph Papineau was a proud and determined man but always a man of peace. When he lost control of the Pa-triote reform movement in Lower Canada, blood-shed became inevitable. For Papineau himself the rebellion meant exile from the land and the people he loved.

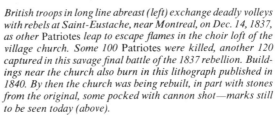

British troops in long line abreast (left) exchange deadly volleys with rebels at Saint-Eustache, near Montreal, on Dec. 14, 1837, as other Patriotes *leap to escape flames in the choir loft of the village church. Some 100* Patriotes *were killed, another 120 captured in this savage final battle of the 1837 rebellion. Buildings near the church also burn in this lithograph published in 1840. By then the church was being rebuilt, in part with stones from the original, some pocked with cannon shot—marks still to be seen today (above).*

Conciliation but no concession to the Patriotes, *said Lord Gosford when he became governor of Lower Canada in 1835. Courteous, convivial, hospitable, he appeased many* Patriotes, *but when Britain rejected constitutional reforms, the assembly refused to pay administrators' salaries. Gosford prorogued the colonial parliament and in February 1838 he resigned.*

nier said the people of Two Mountains planned to remove government-appointed magistrates and militia officers and replace them with men "elected by the people."

Papineau spoke to a crowd that awaited him as he left Chénier's house. And as he drove out of Saint-Eustache he pondered the growing anger of the reform movement he led but could no longer control.

Lawyer Papineau had been a member of the Lower Canada Legislative Assembly since 1809, and for most of those years its Speaker—which then meant party spokesman rather than impartial chairman. He had been given his seigneury by his father as a wedding present in 1818 but spent most of his time in Quebec, the seat of government, or Montreal, the rapidly expanding commercial centre where half the population spoke English. In 1837, at 51, Papineau was a handsome, eloquent man, the idol of most of the people of Lower Canada. He had sought reform ever since entering the assembly, although he had fought for the British in 1812.

The Legislative Assembly was the colony's only elected body. Members of the Executive Council, a kind of cabinet, and the Legislative Council, the upper house, were appointed by and responsible only to the governor, who answered to the Colonial Office in London. Legislation passed in the assembly could be overthrown by the councils; the assembly could raise taxes but revenue from Crown lands was at the governor's disposal, as was the Civil List, the fund from which the salaries of government officials were paid.

The assembly had established French as its working language by electing a unilingual Speaker in 1792. But it had no control over the Bureaucrats, as government appointees (mostly English) were called. Papineau's reform party, which had many non-French members at first, campaigned for an *elected* Legislative Council as part of a truly representative government in Lower Canada.

There were other grievances. The French-speaking middle class—like lawyer Papineau and doctor Chénier—saw posts at the top of their professions and in the civil service granted almost automatically to English Canadians.

For years the assembly debated over Crown revenues, government appointees and the Civil List. Appointments went to a few persons who spoke French but not enough of them to appease

The Hospitable Habitants, Bad Servants and Stubborn Subjects

Visitors to the St. Lawrence and Richelieu valleys in the early 1800s found most French-Canadian farmers mild, polite, hospitable, apparently content with life—if not very ambitious.

Only a few of the habitants were educated, and they only for the church, medicine and law. Most men tilled the soil. Each farm provided necessities such as bread and meat, homespun clothing and cowhide boots.

Neighbors would gather of a winter's day (*below:* Cornelius Krieghoff's oil painting *Merrymaking*), stomping in from the cold wearing bright woollen *tuques* and snug *capotes* (tied at the waist with colorful *ceintures fléchées*), and the house would fill with the squeak of homemade fiddles, the clump of dancing boots and a pungent cloud of *tabac canadien*.

The church, through the authority of the priest, bound each community together. The church steps were the place of political debate.

But a traveller might glimpse another habitant characteristic. "They are bad servants," one wrote. Their pride and independence were bound to make for bad servants—and stubborn subjects. The same traveller recorded that moments of habitant gaiety were bought at the price of brutal work the rest of the year, so that "they soon looked old."

By the 1830s the habitants felt their life-style threatened. English-speaking settlers were arriving. British governors were calling for public education in English, demanding the right to veto curé appointments. When *Patriotes* advocated an end to British rule, the habitants concurred. A proud and independent people was ripe for rebellion.

Five thousand followers of Louis-Joseph Papineau assembled at Saint-Charles, Que., on Oct. 28, 1837. Papineau preached patience but the cheers went to those who cried insurrection.

A plaque identifies this restored house on cobblestoned Bonsecours Street in Old Montreal as the home of the Patriote *leader Louis-Joseph Papineau. It dates from the middle of the 18th century.*

growing French anger, especially when Lower Canada's government was compared to Britain's. (In London an elected Parliament controlled all government revenues and expenditures.)

Papineau was furious when in 1822 a bill to unite Upper and Lower Canada was introduced in the British House of Commons. If it passed, the French would be in a minority in their homeland. Papineau and his friend and ally, John Neilson, Scottish editor of the *Quebec Gazette,* went to London. They won the support of Reformers in Parliament and the bill was shelved. Papineau returned to Lower Canada to continue his bitter fight with Governor George Ramsay Dalhousie and the Bureaucrats, more than ever determined to reform Lower Canada's government—by political means and with help from Britain.

But Papineau's verbal violence and *Patriote* refusal to accept conciliatory appointments to

This replica of the John Molson *(at the Canadian Railway Museum, Saint-Constant, Que.) is similar to locomotives which operated on Canada's first railway, opened in 1836 between Laprairie and Saint-Jean, Que.*

the councils gradually lost him the support of English-speaking. moderates such as Neilson. Animosity increased between *Les Patriotes* and the Bureaucrats. Papineau looked more and more to the American Revolution for inspiration, but he never really faced the possibility that rhetoric might lead to violence.

Violence did come, in a by-election in Montreal in the spring of 1832. One candidate was Daniel Tracey, a *Patriote* journalist who had often attacked the governor and his appointees. He had been imprisoned for breach of privilege of the Legislative Assembly and on his release found himself a popular hero. During the campaign and the month-long polling, supporters of Tracey and Stanley Bagg, the English community's candidate, used every means to recruit voters. Tracey's newspaper, *The Vindicator,* said: "While there was a man in the city who could be bought, no pains were spared to buy him."

The election returning office was in Place d'Armes, in front of Notre-Dame Church, and the square was packed with people when Tracey's victory was announced on May 21. As his supporters formed into a victory procession, both men's hired "whackers" struck out with clubs and campaign volunteers joined in with sticks and stones. Battle raged in the square.

But British troops from the St. Helen's Island fort were on the church steps. They advanced into the mob and when, despite their show of force, the fighting increased, they opened fire. As the crowd dispersed, three French Canadians lay dead, the first to be killed by British bullets in seven decades.

Two years later, in 1834, *Les Patriotes* presented their Ninety-Two Resolutions to the assembly, denouncing partisan judges and government corruption, demanding representative government and impeachment of Governor Matthew Whitworth Aylmer. The assembly adopted the

Passage of the Richelieu by Night, *a lithographed sketch by an army captain, is apparently of the force that marched on Saint-Charles from the south in November 1837.*

This statue of a Patriote *fighter, in a park in Saint-Denis, Que., honors the 12 men killed there Nov. 23, 1837, in the first clash of the Lower Canada rebellion. Two hundred rebels, half of them unarmed, routed 250 British soldiers.*

resolutions, 56 votes to 23—and all 23 men who opposed them were defeated in a general election that year. The resolutions were forwarded to London and the British government sent Archibald Acheson, Earl of Gosford, to replace Aylmer as governor and to head a royal commission on the situation in Lower Canada.

One of Gosford's first actions was to ban private armed groups. This put an end to the Bureaucrats' British Rifle Corps but it was reformed as the Doric Club.

Patriote meetings during the summer of 1836 adopted resolutions inspired by the American Declaration of Independence, including one to boycott British goods. Instead of imported clothes, *Les Patriotes* now proudly wore the habitant's homespun coat and trousers, knitted tuque and *ceinture fléchée* (a gaily colored woven sash), even in the assembly.

The British government gave its answer to the Ninety-Two Resolutions in the House of Commons on March 6, 1837: it presented Ten Resolutions of its own, acceding to few of the *Patriote* demands.

That summer of 1837 there were more stormy meetings in Lower Canada. The *Patriote* movement now had its own flag—a red, white and green tricolor—its own songs and its own hero, Papineau. Liberty poles—tall, white posts topped with the red cap of revolution—were raised at meetings and in front of *Patriote* homes. *Les Fils de la Liberté* formed in response to the Bureaucrats' Doric Club and both groups roamed the streets of Montreal spoiling for a fight. Everywhere there was talk of armed rebellion.

On Oct. 23, two weeks after his meeting with Chénier in Saint-Eustache, Papineau addressed a crowd of 5,000 at the village of Saint-Charles on the Richelieu. Alarmed to see many armed with guns, Papineau spoke against violence. But Dr. Wolfred Nelson, *Patriote* leader in nearby Saint-Denis, cried out: "I say the time has come to melt down our tin spoons and plates into bullets." Dr. Cyrille-Hector Côté of Lacadie, near Saint-Jean, proclaimed: "We must direct not words but lead against our enemies." Before a liberty pole dedicated to Papineau, *Patriotes* swore to conquer or die.

On Nov. 6 the Riot Act was read when Doric Club members and some *Fils de la Liberté* clashed in Montreal. The French group's leader, Thomas Storrow Brown, was beaten up; the offices of *The Vindicator* were raided. On Nov. 16

Governor Gosford issued warrants for the arrest of 26 *Patriote* leaders.

The 26 were dispersed in villages along the Richelieu and in the Two Mountains region. Volunteer cavalrymen with a civilian magistrate captured two at Saint-Jean on the Richelieu. On the way to Montreal they were ambushed near Longueuil. *Patriotes* freed the prisoners and wounded four of the volunteers.

Gen. Sir John Colborne, commander of British forces in Lower Canada, decided to take stronger measures and two expeditions left Montreal on Nov. 22 for the Richelieu. Col. Charles Gore took 250 men down the St. Lawrence by steamer to Sorel; from there they would travel up the Richelieu to Saint-Denis. Lt.Col. George Augustus Wetherall marched 350 men to Chambly, southeast of Montreal, to travel down the Richelieu Valley to Saint-Charles, eight miles south of Saint-Denis. The two forces would crush the rebels between them.

Moving south from Sorel, and hoping to surprise the *Patriotes,* Gore's men plodded through mud, rain and snow during the night of Nov. 22. Early next morning, near Saint-Denis, some *Patriotes* captured a young lieutenant, George "Jock" Weir, who had lost his way when taking dispatches to Gore. His captors, infuriated when he broke a promise not to attempt escape, killed him with bayonet, swords, knives and pistol.

Well before Gore reached Saint-Denis at 9 a.m. on the 23rd, church bells had warned Papineau and Wolfred Nelson. To ensure he would be free for post-battle negotiations, Papineau left for his sister's house at Saint-Hyacinthe 15 miles southeast.

With 200 men, only 109 of them armed, Wolfred Nelson took up position in the thick-walled stone Saint-Germain house. More *Patriotes,* some of them veterans of the War of 1812, most armed only with stakes and pitchforks, took cover in a distillery, in houses nearby, and along the main road. Their sole artillery was an old fieldpiece which fired only scrap iron.

Gore's first cannonball killed four *Patriotes* in the Saint-Germain house. But the cannon caused little damage beyond that. After five hours only one house had been taken and hundreds more rebels were pouring into Saint-Denis from neighboring villages. Gore retreated, his casualties 6 dead and 18 wounded. Another 92 deserted before roll call at Sorel that night. The *Patriotes* lost 12 men killed and 7 wounded.

Wetherall and his force were seven miles south of Saint-Charles when he learned of Gore's defeat. He sent to Chambly for reinforcements and with them on the 25th resumed the march to Saint-Charles. Along the way his men were spattered by occasional fire but at Saint-Charles he

Wolfred Nelson was a wealthy medical doctor and distiller who passionately hated bureaucracy. A man of wild enthusiasms and fierce angers, he was involved in politics all his life. He was exiled to Bermuda for his leading role in the Rebellion of 1837-38, but returned in 1843, was reelected to the assembly, and became inspector of provincial penitentiaries and mayor of Montreal.

A Wave of Immigrants, an Epidemic of Death

Some shivering, some so sick their faces were blue, 200 paupers landed at Quebec on June 7, 1832, from the filthy immigrant ship *Voyager.* Within a week *230* persons were dead—immigrants and townsfolk. It was cholera.

There was a wave of immigrants to Lower and Upper Canada that year. Most, like *Voyager*'s human cargo, were dispossessed Irish tenant farmers and unemployed from the English slums, people that England did not know what to do with. Cholera was sweeping Europe and in April a quarantine station was established at Grosse Ile, 30 miles down the St. Lawrence River from Quebec. But soon it was filled with sick and dying, and overworked doctors passed ships such as *Voyager* after only cursory inspection.

Quebec officials at first denied there was any sickness (but sent their families to the country). Besides immigrants, ships brought goods that Canadian merchants had ordered, and they carried huge cargoes of timber to Britain. Commerce could not be stopped.

Well-to-do immigrants moved on to Quebec's Eastern Townships or Upper Canada. The poor, many sick and dying, streamed into narrow, cobblestoned waterfront streets in Quebec and Montreal, streets dank from abnormally heavy rain, their gutters running with sewage. Quebec's hospitals were filled by the end of June and the sick were put in tents on the Plains of Abraham. The Quebec immigrant shed was renamed L'Hôpital des Emigrés. It had little medicine and no toilets. The sick lay two and three to a sodden mattress. Filth on the floor was ankle-deep.

Doctors experimented with herbs and liquor—even cannon fire (to clear the air)—but found no cure. Day after day the dead were loaded onto carts, buried—often in mass pits—and covered with lime. By the time the horror ended in the dry weather of September, 3,800 persons had died in Quebec and 4,000 in Montreal—about one-tenth of the population of the two cities.

Angry French Canadians blamed the epidemic on the British government for dumping the destitute into Canada, on merchants hungry for profits at whatever cost, and on colonial officials in league with the businessmen. French Canada tended to lump all these villains under one name: "the English."

found only a crude rampart of tree trunks running from the river to the manor house, with barely 200 *Patriotes* behind it. The rebels here were led by Thomas Storrow Brown, still suffering from injuries received in the Montreal riot of Nov. 6.

Wetherall sent Brown a message that if the troops were given peaceful passage through the village they would do no damage. Brown agreed—on condition they lay down their arms. Wetherall's men moved forward and were met with gunfire. The British climbed an undefended hill and trained guns on the rebels below. Said one British soldier: "Them fellers fought well. They waited too long to run." Within an hour 40 *Patriotes* were dead, 30 wounded.

Wetherall returned in triumph to Montreal. He had lost three men but had taken 30 prisoners, two rusty cannon and a liberty pole.

The *Patriotes* disbanded as news of the Saint-Charles defeat spread. Some rebel leaders, including Papineau and Brown, fled to the United States. Wolfred Nelson was captured as he tried to flee and was imprisoned in Montreal. The rebellion was over along the Richelieu.

British garrisons were left at Saint-Charles and Saint-Denis and, on Dec. 4, Jock Weir's muti-

The Patriots' Prison, where rebels were held in 1837 and 1838, is au Pied-du-Courant—at the foot of a current in the St. Lawrence River. It has been classified as an historic site.

This 6½-foot bronze statue of the Patriote *leader Dr. Jean-Olivier Chénier is in Montreal's Place Viger. Chénier, who had sworn to conquer or to die, was 31 when killed at Saint-Eustache in 1837.*

A Secret Society Sworn to End British Rule

A blindfolded man was led into a shuttered and candlelit room and was forced to his knees. Then, in one of thousands of such ceremonies in the spring and summer of 1838, he was initiated into *Les Frères Chasseurs,* a secret society dedicated to ending British rule in Lower Canada.

Rebellions in both Canadas had been crushed in 1837. Dr. Robert Nelson of Montreal had attempted another uprising in February 1838 but it collapsed when informers warned the government. So Nelson planned a secret society for yet another attempt. Its emblem was a rifle crossed by a long dagger. Its name came from what rebel suspects called themselves when found carrying arms: they were *chasseurs*—hunters.

Headquarters was in Montreal; lodge branches were scattered south and east of the city. Hunters' Lodges, English-language counterparts in the United States (see p. 200), attracted American sympathizers and fugitive Canadians. Nelson, a fugitive, directed operations from St. Albans, Vt.

The *Chasseurs* were republican plotters, some who feared coercion if they did not join—and a sprinkling of government spies. The kneeling applicant swore loyalty to the society, its members and its aims, failing which "may my throat be cut to the bone." His blindfold was ripped off and he found himself surrounded by *Chasseurs* pointing guns and knives at his heart—he was expected to take his oath seriously.

Chasseurs eventually numbered some 50,000. They had ranks, starting with *chasseur* and rising to *raquette* (snowshoe), *castor* (beaver) and *aigle* (eagle). The commander-in-chief was *Grand Aigle* Edouard-Elisée Mailhot, a veteran of 1837.

But when Nelson declared Lower Canada independent on Nov. 4, 1838, only a few thousand *Chasseurs*, mostly at Napierville, rose to support him. Only 250 muskets and one cannon got past alerted U.S. authorities and, without guns, membership melted away. Attacks on loyalists by the remainder were put down with little bloodshed and the government arrested the leaders, of whom 12 were executed. Some, Nelson included, escaped to the United States.

lated body was found in the river. With the discovery, the attitude toward the rebels hardened. "Remember Jock Weir!" became a rallying cry for the English troops.

In the county of Two Mountains, the *Patriotes* of Saint-Eustache and Saint-Benoît were far from defeated. Rebels roamed the countryside requisitioning food and arms. Abbé Jacques Paquin, curé of Saint-Eustache, tried to discourage further resistance but Jean-Olivier Chénier kept most of his forces together for whatever might come.

Colborne left Montreal on Dec. 13 with 2,000 men. As the British approached Saint-Eustache next day many of the untrained, poorly armed *Patriotes* fled, but Chénier rallied some 250 men, who occupied the convent, the priest's house and another house near the church. Chénier was inside the barricaded church.

Colborne's forces encircled the village but met heavy fire. For two hours troops and artillery failed to breach the *Patriotes'* stone strongholds. But the house near the church was set afire and, under cover of smoke, Colborne's forces drove the rebels from the convent and the presbytery, then got into the church from the presbytery. Chénier's men had destroyed the stairs and were shooting from the choir loft. The British built a fire, using wood from the altar, then withdrew. Trapped by spreading flames, 70 *Patriotes*

A cairn honors militiamen who were casualties when Patriotes *attacked a loyalist force sheltering in this stone chapel at Odelltown, Que., in 1838.*

jumped from the windows and British soldiers picked them off to cries of "Remember Jock Weir!"

Chénier escaped through a window in the Virgin's Chapel, was struck by a bullet, but ran on through the cemetery. Another shot hit him in the chest and he fell dead.

When the battle ended, nearly 100 French Canadians were dead and some 120 had been taken prisoner. Colborne let his soldiers pillage and burn for an hour. Some staggered drunk through the streets wearing the curé's vestments. A mass of charred corpses lay in the smoldering ruins of the church.

Colborne's army marched to nearby Saint-Benoît next morning and was met by *Patriotes* carrying a white flag. At noon, 300 men in the village laid down their arms. An hour later, more loyalist volunteers arrived from villages along the Ottawa and Colborne left them to finish off Saint-Benoît. They smashed statues in the church, forced open the tabernacle, ground the consecrated Hosts beneath their heels and desecrated the sacred vessels. Then they put the village to the torch.

At the beginning of 1838 there were some 500 *Patriotes* in Montreal prisons. Two hundred were released in January, 100 more on May 1. Meanwhile, in the United States, rebel leaders Dr. Cyrille-Hector Côté and Dr. Robert Nelson, Wolfred's brother, were raising support and accumulating arms. On Feb. 28, Nelson and 300 men entered Canada from Alburg, Vt., and at

Gen. Sir John Colborne—"Old Firebrand," he was called—was commander-in-chief in Canada during the Rebellion of 1837-38. He did nothing to halt the atrocities his troops committed after the fall of Saint-Eustache and the surrender of Saint-Benoît. This portrait is in Toronto's Upper Canada College, which he founded.

This watercolor in the Public Archives in Ottawa was Katherine Jane Ellice's recollection of rebels who seized the Ellice manor at Beauharnois, near Montreal, in November 1838. Canadians must have their rights, they told her, they had suffered long enough. The rebels waited at Beauharnois for guns that never came and skirmished with British troops. But at the approach of 1,500 Glengarry Highlanders from Upper Canada, the rebels fled.

Noyan, five miles north, proclaimed the Republic of Lower Canada. They returned to the United States the next day.

There was a third summer of *Patriote* activity, this time in secret. Lord Durham arrived in May to begin his inquiry (see p. 206) and decreed a general amnesty. But eight *Patriote* leaders, including Wolfred Nelson, were exiled to Bermuda. Sixteen who were in the United States, including Louis-Joseph and Amédée Papineau, Cyrille-Hector Côté and Robert Nelson, were forbidden to return to Canada, under pain of death. But Durham, in failing health, resigned and returned to England in November. Gosford had resigned in February and now Colborne remained as acting governor and commander-in-chief of British forces in Canada to handle a colony still grumbling with rebellion.

On Nov. 3 and 4 there were skirmishes in villages south of Montreal but, for want of arms and competent leaders, there was no general uprising. At Napierville on the 4th, Robert Nelson met Côté, and before some 800 followers repeated his declaration of independence and was proclaimed president of the republic. They had nearly 3,000 men, arms for 600.

There were more arms at the American border but Côté, dispatched with 500 men to collect them, was overwhelmed Nov. 6 by loyalist volunteers at Lacolle. He headed once more for the border; his men scattered, as did many of Nelson's when they heard the news.

On Nov. 9, with about 1,000 *Patriote* followers,

Nelson battled loyalist volunteers at Odelltown, just north of the U.S. border. The loyalists, in the church, held off the rebels for two hours, then rushed out to fight. Volunteer reinforcements, well armed, poured into the village. Nelson disappeared. By dusk 50 *Patriotes* lay dead, 50 were wounded and many were prisoners. Again rebel houses were burned by volunteers. Again Colborne did little to prevent the excesses.

Of more than 800 *Patriotes* imprisoned in December 1838, 99 were condemned to death. Only 12 were in fact executed (at the Patriots' Prison in Montreal). Of those spared, 58 were deported to Australia, 2 were banished and 27 freed. Six years later the exiles were granted amnesty. Louis-Joseph Papineau returned to Canada in 1845, re-entered the legislature, retired in 1854 and finished his days at his seigneury, where he died in 1871. Wolfred Nelson also was re-elected to the assembly and was mayor of Montreal in 1854-55. Robert Nelson made a career as a surgeon in New York. Thomas Storrow Brown became a businessman in Montreal.

Saint-Eustache and Abbé Paquin rebuilt and on Oct. 14, 1841—four years and four days after Papineau's visit to Chénier—the reconstructed church was blessed by the bishop of Montreal. The landmark twin towers and the walls pocked with cannon shot had become—simply by surviving—the greatest monument of all to Louis-Joseph Papineau and *Les Patriotes* and the dreams and defeats of 1837.

Many Patriotes *went into battle armed with only a sword or a pitchfork. A man with a gun carried ammunition in a wooden cartridge box with a leather shoulder strap. This one, worn by a rebel at Saint-Eustache, is in the McCord Museum in Montreal.*

Ranvoyzé! Chunks of Metal Into Works of Art

Some of the world's finest silverware was fashioned in Quebec in the late 1700s and early 1800s—most of it for the colony's churches—and many fine examples are still in regular use.

Church law required that sacred vessels be of silver or gold. In practice that meant silver, and New France's isolation—the craft developed during the French régime—decreed that pieces be made and repaired locally. Silversmiths also worked for wealthy citizens: silver, the standard of exchange, was crafted into dishes and cutlery in good times, melted to make money in hard times. Church silver—the sacred vessels and ornate candlesticks with flowers, cherubs and fluting—was made from lay pieces and from coins.

Most church silver was cast and engraved. But François Ranvoyzé, the master among dozens of artisans at the end of the 18th century, hammered some of his best works out of chunks of metal, giving them an attractive texture and an extra sparkle. The ingot was beaten into a sheet of silver, which was then shaped to the desired form and its edges soldered. Three pieces were shaped into this Ranvoyzé monstrance in the Musée du Québec.

Born in 1739, Ranvoyzé was at his most creative in 1770-90. His apprentice Laurent Amiot (1764-1838), and Montrealer Pierre Huguet dit Latour (1770-1817) continued the tradition of individual craftsmanship into the 1800s.

The work of independent craftsmen is preserved at the Quebec Seminary, the Basilica of Notre-Dame in Quebec, and Notre-Dame Church in Montreal.

Heritage Sites

SAINT-EUSTACHE, Que. The walls of Saint-Eustache Church, scarred by cannon shot, bear witness to the fiercest battle of the Rebellion of 1837. On Dec. 14 about 250 *Patriotes* under Dr. Jean-Olivier Chénier barricaded themselves against some 2,000 British soldiers led by Gen. Sir John Colborne. Nearly 100 were killed, 120 captured. The church was rebuilt in the 1840s: parts of the façade, and the walls of the apse and transept, are original.
Also in Saint-Eustache (2) A monument outside Sacré-Coeur School commemorates Chénier.

Other sites

Grosse Ile, Que. (not shown) A monument marks where an immigrant quarantine station was established at the start of the 1832 cholera epidemic.
Montebello, Que. (1) Louis-Joseph Papineau, who inspired the Lower Canada rebellion, retired in 1854 to the seigneury his father had bought here in 1804. The stone manor house and the chapel in which Papineau is buried are on the grounds of the Château Montebello, a hotel.
Montreal (3)

CHÉNIER MONUMENT A 14-foot granite column topped by a bronze statue of the leader of the Saint-Eustache *Patriotes* stands in Place Viger.

NOTRE-DAME CHURCH MUSEUM An ornate *bénitier* (vessel for holy water) and a processional cross are by silversmith Pierre Huguet dit Latour.

PAPINEAU HOUSE Louis-Joseph Papineau

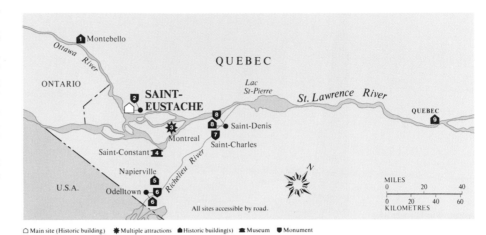

lived here periodically from his birth in 1786 until his flight to the United States in 1837. Built about 1750, the house at 440 Bonsecours Street has been privately restored. It is not open to the public.

PATRIOTES' MONUMENT Dr. Jean-Olivier Chénier is buried beneath a 60-foot obelisk in Notre-Dame-des-Neiges Cemetery. The monument bears the names of more than 100 *Patriotes* and commemorates those who were killed in action, executed or exiled.

PLACE DES PATRIOTES The Patriots' Prison, where 145 *Patriotes* were held after the 1837 uprising and another 816 were held in 1838, is now a Quebec government office-warehouse. Twelve rebels, hanged at the main gate, are commemorated by a monument nearby.

ST. HELEN'S ISLAND Weapons used in the 1837 uprising are in the Montreal Military and Maritime Museum.
Napierville, Que. (5) A plaque on the registry office relates that in front of this building on Nov. 4, 1838, *Patriote* leader Robert Nelson and some 800 men proclaimed the independence of Lower Canada.
Odelltown, Que. (6) Outside Odelltown Chapel, in which 300 loyalists barricaded themselves against *Patriotes* on Nov. 9, 1838, are a cannon captured from the rebels and a cairn commemorating six loyalists who were killed and four who were wounded.
Quebec (9) Sacred vessels and church candlesticks by silversmiths François Ranvoyzé and Laurent Amiot are in the Quebec Seminary and the Basilica of Notre-Dame.
Saint-Charles, Que. (7) A 10-foot stone monument commemorates both the great *Patriote* meeting of Oct. 23, 1837, and the Battle of Saint-Charles 33 days later.
Saint-Constant, Que. (4) The *John Molson,* a replica of a steam engine used on the Champlain and St. Lawrence Railroad—Canada's first railway—is in the Canadian Railway Museum. Louis-Joseph Papineau attended the opening of the line July 21, 1836.
Saint-Denis, Que. (8) A cairn marks the site of Maison Saint-Germain in which some 200 *Patriotes* fought off a superior British force Nov. 23, 1837, in the Battle of Saint-Denis. In Saint-Denis Park a stone statue of a *Patriote* in fighting stance honors 12 rebels killed in the battle. British troops were billeted at the Cherrier House, 190 Cadastre Street, in 1837.

Louis-Joseph Papineau dined here in the manor house of his seigneury at Montebello, Que.

William Lyon Mackenzie, the fiery Scots editor, has been judged an idealist without a plan, a critic without acumen to institute the reforms he advocated. But his vision of government by the people moved other men and he won the admiration and loyalty of many. Friends expressed appreciation of the creditor-plagued rebel with the purchase in 1858 of Mackenzie House (right), on Bond Street in Toronto. Mackenzie died there in 1861 at 66. The house, furnished as in his day, is open to the public.

'Reform!'– and Terror in Upper Canada

Isaac Brock's monument on Queenston Heights was to be torn down! Sir Peregrine Maitland, lieutenant-governor of Upper Canada that summer of 1824, had learned that buried under the cornerstone of the uncompleted memorial to the hero of the War of 1812 (see p. 153) was a bottle containing mementos of the time. One was a copy of the first edition of the newspaper the *Colonial Advocate*. At Maitland's order, the masonry was demolished and the bottle removed. Then the monument was rebuilt, unsullied by anything to do with William Lyon Mackenzie.

Maitland hated the *Advocate* and Mackenzie, its publisher, as much as Mackenzie hated the way Upper Canada was governed. The newspaper expressed widespread discontent and its readership grew. Soon Mackenzie left his stone house at Queenston and moved to York (later Toronto), to be closer to the infamies he denounced.

There in the capital, as muckraking journalist and as politician, he raged for 13 years. Blue eyes blazing under the flame-red wig that hid his baldness, he attacked autocratic rulers for "enslaving Canadians" and dismayed moderates who wanted reform as much as he. Eventually he would lead a tragicomic army against autocracy, and when democracy came he would not like that. Mackenzie, said a biographer, William Kilbourn, was a firebrand with an impossible dream: heaven on earth.

William Lyon Mackenzie was born in Scotland in 1795. By his early twenties he had read nearly 1,000 books, had worked at merchandising and accounting, kept a general store, fathered a son out of wedlock and run up gambling debts. In 1820 he came to Canada, opened a store, first at Dundas, Ont., then at Queenston, and married Isabel Baxter, a former schoolmate.

He started the *Colonial Advocate* in Queenston

Armed with muskets, clubs and iron-tipped staves— looking less like rebels than farmers bound for a duck hunt—William Lyon Mackenzie's followers march to Montgomery's Tavern, the Toronto assembly point for the 1837 revolt in Upper Canada. Mackenzie had called for an armed demonstration; few understood he meant to fight. Left: the desk at which Mackenzie assembled damning dossiers of his opponents' misdeeds, and where he composed his vitriolic editorials, is in Mackenzie House in Toronto.

in 1824 because he found the country "in the hands of a few shrewd, crafty, covetous men under whose management one of the most lovely and desirable sections of America remained a comparative desert." He used the paper to rail at "funguses" who flattered the ruling clique (see p. 176), at graft in the post office, at land reserves that blocked development and benefited the Church of England (see p. 181), at the policies of The Bank of Upper Canada, at clergymen and judges in politics, at antagonism toward Americans—half the province's population.

The acacia trees in front of this house in Queenston, Ont., were planted by William Lyon Mackenzie. He launched the Colonial Advocate *when he lived there in 1823-24.*

The chief target of Mackenzie's anger was a system that kept power in the hands of a British governor and a Family Compact of appointed administrators who could overrule the elected assembly. In a time of reform in Britain, of frontier democracy in the United States, of revolutions in Europe, Mackenzie wanted popular control; he was never quite sure in what form. The Compact's opinion was expressed by Solicitor General John Beverley Robinson: he called Mackenzie a "reptile."

One June evening in 1826, fifteen youths from York's leading families wrecked Mackenzie's Front Street premises, broke his press and threw type into the harbor. The courts awarded him £625 damages. "It may be said that I am proof of the freedom that exists," said Mackenzie. "Far from it: where I have survived hundreds have sunk to rise no more. Trial by jury is in the sheriff's power, the sheriff is in the governor's power, the governor is in the power of his advisors."

The raid made Mackenzie famous and he was elected to the assembly in 1828. He was idolized by the voters of York County but his extreme views and his impatient energy embarrassed

Politics held little interest for Sir Francis Bond Head (a soldier and writer who had never even voted) until his surprise appointment as lieutenant-governor of Upper Canada in 1836. The post, perhaps intended for Sir Edmund Head (later governor general of Canada), may have been offered to Sir Francis in error.

other Reformers—such as physician-lawyer John Rolph and lawyer Robert Baldwin (see p. 207)—who were also working for responsible government (the holding of power by elected representatives). He infuriated the Family Compact; its supporters expelled him from the assembly five times. The first time was in 1831.

On Jan. 2, 1832, York County voted to elect someone to fill his seat. Mackenzie came to the hustings—a wooden platform in the yard of the Red Lion Inn, in the village of Yorkville—atop a two-decker sleigh, bagpipes skirling. The Tory candidate conceded after 119 of 120 voters publicly declared against him. Amid thunderous applause, the re-elected Mackenzie was presented with an immense gold medal and chain worth £250.

With crimson banners flying, he led a parade of 134 sleighs past Lieutenant-Governor Sir John Colborne's residence (Maitland was now lieutenant-governor of Nova Scotia) and the Parliament buildings. Boys in a covered sleigh printed copies of Mackenzie's New Year's message on a small press and threw them to the crowd. They took him home at last by the light of blazing torches. In his joy he flung off his wig and embraced his beloved Isabel and their four children. (The couple had 13 eventually.)

Next day he published a violent attack on Colborne and put on his medal in front of the assembly. He was expelled again on Jan. 7—five days after the by-election—and was immediately re-elected. One day in March he was brutally beaten in Tory Hamilton. Days later he jumped to safety when a York mob ran off with the wagon from which he was speaking; another mob smashed his office windows.

Mackenzie gathered 25,000 signatures on petitions for reform in Upper Canada. He took them to England that April, stayed away for 14 months and won some concessions from London but lost his faith that the British government would help the Canadian Reformers. He was expelled from the assembly while away, won back his seat on his return, but was again ejected, this time by physical force.

York became the City of Toronto and in March 1834 Mackenzie was elected its first mayor. He was a poor administrator, as ready as the Family Compact to reward friends and oust enemies, and the Reformers lost the civic election the next year. The contradictions in his personality were evident. The liberal Reformer was capable of crushing a printers' strike, and he belittled Jews, blacks and Roman Catholics even while leading his moral crusade.

Reformers won an assembly majority in 1834 and named Mackenzie chairman of the Select Committee on Grievances. He confronted and questioned Compact members and assembled a

The Agony of Sealed Hatches, Rats, Rotten Food, Pestilence . . .

For most British immigrants in the early 1800s, getting to Canada was a nightmare. All but the most privileged spent up to two months crowded aboard filthy ships, eating bad food and tormented by sickness and storms.

But thousands came anyway—264,000 between 1829 and 1839 alone—desperate to escape the unemployment and poverty that followed the Napoleonic wars and the subsequent industrialization. This embarcation illustration was in Harper's Weekly in 1858. Some shipowners, anxious to fill vessels sailing to Canada for timber (see p. 308), put as many as 300 persons in the 25-by-75-foot steerage section of a 400-ton ship. A row of double berths ran along each side, and the aisle, only five feet wide, was jammed with immigrants' belongings.

The only daylight and ventilation were from the hatches—which were closed most of the time to keep water

out. Sanitary facilities were primitive, seasickness was common, and the congested quarters could not be cleaned properly. There were hundreds of rats.

Until 1823, passengers had to bring their own food. Often it was not enough. Then ships were obliged to carry provisions for each passenger. But these supplies were often rotten when distributed. Water, stored in wooden casks for up to six months, became murky and rancid. Typhus and cholera (see p. 189) were rampant.

During storms all passengers were herded below deck and the hatches sealed, the only light, if any, coming from a few safety lanterns. The pounding of the waves, the creak of the ship's timbers and the clatter of immigrants' possessions mingled with the cries of the frightened and the groans of the sick. Many ships were driven onto reefs and rocky shores, sometimes with no survivors. Other vessels crashed into icebergs in the fog off Newfoundland.

mountain of information. His 533-page report condemned the patronage governing every appointment—postmasters, magistrates, customs officers, land agents, even clergymen. Britain's Colonial Secretary, Lord Glenelg, read it and dismissed Lieutenant-Governor Colborne—who had not sent him a copy.

Mackenzie, increasingly attracted to American institutions, had already said: "I am less loyal than I was." The new lieutenant-governor pushed him all the way. Sir Francis Bond Head, military engineer and adventurer, was so unqualified for the appointment that it astonished even him—as did banners welcoming him as "A Tried Reformer." Of demands for responsible government, he reported to Britain: "The people of Upper Canada detest 'democracy.'" During the 1836 election he warned people not to "quarrel with your bread and butter," lavishing patronage on those who agreed with him. His supporters won decisively.

Of eight assembly elections contested by Mackenzie, this was his first loss. Eighteen months earlier, overwhelmed by mayoral and assembly duties and the death of a son, he had sold the *Advocate* (the word *Colonial* had been dropped from the title in 1833). Now, on the 60th anniversary of the American Declaration of Independence, he launched another paper, *The Constitution,* to prepare "the public mind for

William Lyon Mackenzie's hand-operated Washington flatbed press—one of the great rebel's most powerful weapons against the Upper Canada Establishment—is the centrepiece of a reconstructed print shop in Mackenzie House in Toronto.

His medical students found Dr. John Rolph a saddled horse for his escape from Toronto when his complicity in Mackenzie's rebellion was discovered. Intercepted by a loyalist posse, he was released when one of his captors, a former student of Rolph's, vouched for his loyalty. Rolph made his way to the United States, was granted amnesty in 1843, and returned to Toronto. He re-established a school of medicine and was re-elected to the legislature.

nobler actions than our tyrants dream of." By mid-1837 Mackenzie was setting up vigilance committees, preaching that oppression "warrants an appeal to force." He was threatened with assassination and followed by Orange Order mobs, and armed bodyguards rode with him. Farmers and clerks dug out weapons. Some made bullets. Others drilled with walking sticks and umbrellas. "There is," Mackenzie warned, "discontent, vengeance and rage in men's minds."

Head dismissed the discontented as lunatics and in October showed his contempt by sending his regular troops to Lower Canada, where French-Canadian *Patriotes* were in revolt (see p. 184). Only two constables guarded the several thousand weapons and the ammunition stored in the Toronto city hall. On Oct. 9, 1837, when a message from *les Patriotes* asked Mackenzie to join them, he met with 10 radicals in a candlelit room at the back of a brewery, urged them to seize Head, take the arms and establish a provisional government, but the meeting broke up without a plot being agreed to. Mackenzie later was sent to find out if there was enough support in the countryside for rebellion; if so, a date could be set.

Mackenzie instead began recruiting for a Dec. 7 uprising. He claimed 5,000 men would assemble at Montgomery's Tavern, four miles north of Toronto near today's Yonge-Eglinton

These prisoners—suspected as supporters of Mackenzie—were lucky: their captors were Dragoon Guards, regular soldiers. Hundreds less fortunate were beaten by volunteers.

A Winter in the Woods for Rebels on the Run

Thousands of men implicated in William Lyon Mackenzie's rebellion took to the snowy woods of Upper Canada in December 1837, hounded by reward-hungry loyalists. Most hoped to find refuge in the United States.

Dr. Charles Duncombe, who had rallied a rebel force at Scotland, south of Brantford, spent one night hidden in a bed between a farmer and his wife. Another night, after friends put him to bed dressed as "Grandma," he received respectful good nights from a posse tramping through the house in search of Dr. Duncombe. After a four-week flight, he reached his sister in London, Ont. Disguised as "Aunt Nancy" he was taken by sleigh to the border post at Sarnia. Militia guards escorted him across the St. Clair River to the American shore—whereupon "Aunt Nancy" shouted: "Go back and tell your commander you have just piloted Dr. Duncombe across the river!"

Samuel Lount, a leading rebel, battled stormy Lake Erie for two days in a small, open boat, only to be blown back to capture—and execution. John Montgomery, original owner of the tavern that was rebel headquarters, was convicted of high treason. "These perjurers," he thundered at the judge, "who have sworn my life away, will never die a natural death; and when you, sir, and the jury shall have died and perished in hell's flames, John Montgomery will yet be living on Yonge Street."

His death sentence was commuted to exile and Montgomery, being held at Fort Henry at Kingston, escaped to the United States. Pardoned in 1843, he *did* return to Yonge Street and built a new inn on the site of his former tavern. He died at 95, long after two of his accusers had committed suicide and his judge, jury and prosecutors were in their graves.

John Montgomery   *Dr. Charles Duncombe*

intersection. They would be led by Samuel Lount, a blacksmith, and Capt. Anthony Anderson, a young man with some military experience. The moderate Reform leaders Thomas Morrison and John Rolph were angry but surrendered to Mackenzie's fait accompli, although demanding a more professional leader. Mackenzie sent for Col. Anthony Van Egmond, an old Dutch soldier who had fought under Napoleon.

In Toronto, Col. James FitzGibbon, a hero of the War of 1812, pleaded with Lieutenant-Governor Head for government action. "I do not apprehend rebellion," Head replied. He blocked FitzGibbon's attempt to enrol volunteers.

On Nov. 24, glorying in reports that *Patriotes* had defeated British troops at Saint-Denis, Mackenzie galloped north with circulars proclaiming: "The promised land is now before us—up then and take it." On Saturday, Dec. 2, FitzGibbon burst into a meeting of Head and leading officials, insisting that a rising was imminent. They laughed him off but ordered two militia regiments organized on Monday—and issued a warrant for Mackenzie's arrest.

Alarmed by militia preparation and rumors that Head knew the precise plans, Rolph sent a message to Mackenzie: if they acted on Monday, Dec. 4, 300 men could take the city hall. Lount got the message instead, took it for an order and called on his troops to assemble at Montgomery's Tavern. On Sunday Mackenzie told him to stick to the original plan. On Monday, with Lower Canada's rebels crushed at Saint-Charles, Rolph wanted to call the whole thing off. It was too late, said Mackenzie.

By 8 p.m., weary men with pitchforks and staves were arriving at the tavern but the muskets they had expected were not there. Mackenzie called for attack but they would not march till daylight. He posted a guard at Yonge Street to prevent anyone alerting the city, and with four men reconnoitred southward. He met and captured Alderman John Powell who was on a northward scouting expedition of his own. Mackenzie believed Powell's assurance that he was unarmed and continued on his patrol, sending Captain Anderson, with Powell as prisoner, back to Montgomery's Tavern.

Meantime, Col. Robert Moodie, riding south from Richmond Hill to warn the city, was mortally wounded by the Yonge Street guard. Moodie's companion galloped on, met Powell and Anderson and yelled: "The rebels have shot poor Colonel Moodie and are advancing on the city." Powell drew a pistol, shot Anderson and galloped back toward the city with the warning. He caught up with the patrol and took aim for Mackenzie but his weapon misfired. He rode on toward Toronto, forced his way into Head's

bedroom and convinced the lieutenant-governor a rebellion was under way.

Mackenzie was in a frenzy of excitement. At noon on Tuesday, Dec. 5, he was bundled in several overcoats—a buffer against bullets—and heading down Yonge Street on a white pony: behind him an army of 800, hats pulled down over their ears, muskets, pikes, pitchforks on their shoulders. While Head bewailed the absence of his troops and the apathy Toronto's 12,000 citizens, 200 armed men, mostly Compact members, waited in the market place.

At Gallows Hill, just below today's St. Clair

Col. Robert Moodie, the only Tory killed in Mackenzie's 1837 rebellion, is hit by rebel fire in this 19th-century drawing of a skirmish outside Montgomery's Tavern in what now is North Toronto.

Navy Island, up the Niagara River from Niagara Falls (at plume of mist), was rebel headquarters (and "seceded" from Canada for a few weeks) after Mackenzie fled Toronto.

Four red and three white stripes, and a strange galaxy of white stars on a blue background . . . this is a sketch of the flag of the short-lived republic that William Lyon Mackenzie proclaimed on Navy Island in the dying days of his rebellion. The significance of the number of stripes and stars—and the stars' arrangement—is not known.

Avenue, Mackenzie met Rolph and Robert Baldwin who gave him a message: the lieutenant-governor, knowing himself outnumbered and unaware of Rolph's complicity, promised amnesty if the rebels dispersed. Mackenzie wanted the promise in writing. It never came. Soon militia reinforcements were arriving in the city from Hamilton and the truce was off.

Rolph advised that quick action could still take the city. Instead Mackenzie wasted time haranguing and threatening in one Tory house, then burned another. Spurred by another message from Rolph, he finally got his army moving again. At dusk he approached a 27-man picket that Sheriff William Jarvis had placed behind a fence in a garden (on present-day Yonge Street, southeast of Maitland Street). They were 100 yards apart when the picket fired. Lount's front-rank riflemen replied, then went to ground to let those behind do the same. But, convinced that the whole front rank had been hit, the second rank fled. So did the sheriff's force. Jarvis and Mackenzie were left shouting at running men. One rebel was killed and two other rebels were mortally wounded.

Next morning, with militiamen still pouring into Toronto, Rolph sent word to the rebels to disband, then rode to exile in the United States.

In the Spirit of '37, the War of the Hunters

The spirit of 1837 lived on, and for a year after William Lyon Mackenzie fled into exile the Establishment that had defeated him was harassed by the bloody Patriot War. Throughout 1838, from Prescott to Windsor, there was gunfire and burning and execution. And, in the trials that followed one battle, a young Kingston lawyer named John A. Macdonald accepted the unpopular task of advising a member of an invading American force. (Because the man was court-martialled, a lawyer could not plead his defence, but merely advise.)

Nearly all the troublemakers of 1838, known as Patriot Hunters, were Americans. A few were idealistic, egged on by Canadian exiles. Some were adventurers. Most simply hated all things British—or loved all underdogs.

In January the schooner *Anne*, out of Detroit, occupied Bois Blanc Island, bombarded Fort Malden (near Amherstburg), then ran aground; the crew was captured. In February Americans occupied Pelee Island for a few days. In June more raiders crossed the Niagara River and got some miles into Canada; and others plundered a store and some houses in Sarnia.

The bloodiest encounter was the Nov. 12-16 Battle of the Windmill, near Prescott. A 400-man raiding force organized by Hunters' Lodges (U.S. counterparts of the *Frères Chasseurs*—see p. 190) set out Nov. 11 from Ogdensburg, N.Y., but half the force deserted, including the commander.

Col. Nils Von Schoultz *(above)*, a 31-year-old Polish army veteran, took over.

The attackers went ashore at Windmill Point and sheltered in the stone mill that still stands there. It withstood shelling by British soldiers and militiamen (some from nearby Fort Wellington) but Von Schoultz was completely cut off from supplies. On the fifth day the British accepted the unconditional surrender of 108 men. Seventeen Americans and 16 Canadians and British were dead.

A Hunter force of 135 raided Windsor on Dec. 3, burning a barracks, delivering republican speeches, then engaging the militia on the François Baby farm. (The farmhouse

This watercolor depicts the windmill near P, Ont., that was the focal point of the bloodies. of the Patriot War of 1838. Left: the rebel Col. Nils Von Schoultz. Below: the windmi ture today. It is not open to the public.

Mackenzie held up a stagecoach, robbed passengers and travellers and ransacked mailbags for money and dispatches. Of 500 men still with him, only 250 had firearms. When Colonel Van Egmond arrived on Thursday, Dec. 7, there were quarrels over strategy. Finally some 60 men were sent to the only bridge over the Don River ravine, to cut off the city from the east. The others waited for reinforcements.

Snow was melting in the early afternoon sun when a sentinel heard music in the distance, then saw armed men cresting Gallows Hill. Colonels FitzGibbon and Allan MacNab (see p. 176), accompanied by Lieutenant-Governor Head on a huge stallion, were advancing with 600 militiamen, two artillery pieces and two bands blaring *Yankee Doodle*.

Within half an hour it was over. Rebels were driven from positions behind trees on the west side of Yonge Street. They fled toward the tavern. A cannon ball smashed through the dining room window and the opposite wall. The rebels scattered. Mackenzie jumped on a horse and joined their flight across the fields, as the triumphant Lieutenant-Governor Head burned Montgomery's Tavern—to mark the death of "that perfidious enemy, responsible government."

Four days later Mackenzie reached Buffalo, N.Y., was greeted as a hero and engulfed with offers of aid. Within a week he had set up a republic on Navy Island, Canadian territory in the Niagara River, three miles above the falls. He created his own seal (a new moon breaking through darkness) and flag (red, white and blue, with stars and stripes) and promised recruits, mostly Americans, land and silver.

In Canada 10,000 to 12,000 militiamen were arresting and terrorizing those who had fought (or sympathized) with the rebels. Property was

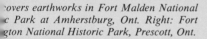

...overs earthworks in Fort Malden National ...c Park at Amherstburg, Ont. Right: Fort ...gton National Historic Park, Prescott, Ont.

Pirate Bill Johnston was "Commodore of the Patriot Navy." He and 13 rebels burned the steamer Sir Robert Peel *near Gananoque, Ont., in 1838.*

...Hiram Walker Historical Museum.) ...iders dispersed after the militia's first ...but drew cheers from 5,000 rooftop ...tors across the river in Detroit. ...ty-five invaders were killed, 44 taken ...er. Four militiamen were killed. ...anwhile, in Fort Henry at Kingston, ...onald's client (Daniel George) and ...Schoultz were cell mates—charged ...ggression (as subjects of foreign coun-...t peace with Britain). Von Schoultz ...ted to Macdonald that the attack had

been misguided but insisted on pleading guilty and was sentenced to hang.

In the week following the trial Macdonald visited Von Schoultz several times, drew up his will, refused payment, and sought to have the former officer given the honor of execution by a firing squad.

The request was denied. But although 10 other men (including George) were hanged at Kingston Jail as common criminals, Von Schoultz went to his death at Fort Henry—as a partial concession to Macdonald's request.

plundered and burned. Neighbors turned on one another. Sam Lount and one Peter Matthews would hang. Close to 100 would be deported. Some 25,000 would leave Upper Canada of their own accord to escape vicious reprisals by triumphant Compact supporters.

Up to 2,500 militiamen grouped at Chippawa on the Niagara River—so close to Navy Island that the enemies shook fists at one another. Mackenzie set up shanties in the woods, barricaded his headquarters with fence rails. American recruits and supplies kept coming in on the paddle steamer *Caroline.* His wife arrived on Dec. 29 and made cartridge bags from flannel, "inspiring with her courage all with whom she conversed." That night, Capt. Andrew Drew of the Royal Navy and about 50 Canadian militiamen cut *Caroline* loose at nearby Fort Schlosser, N.Y., and sent her flaming toward the Horseshoe Falls where she ran aground and burned.

Two weeks later Mackenzie had between 300 and 400 recruits and men to lead them. But their quarrels, combined with bombardment from Chippawa and pressure from the United States (alarmed lest Britain be provoked by American support for Mackenzie), drove him from Navy Island in mid-January. Before him lay 11 difficult years. He spent one year in jail—for breaking U.S. neutrality laws—others as journalist, author, clerk, actuary. The loving father saw hunger dog his family. For nearly four years he covered American politics for the *New York Tri-*

bune. Had he seen the U.S. system sooner, he said, he "would have been the last man" to rebel. In 1849 a Reform government in Canada permitted Mackenzie's return. He came for a visit and then, a year later, he came home to stay.

On his first night in Toronto he was threatened with lynching but two years later he was a member of the Canadian assembly and held his seat for seven years. Canada now had responsible government but, though he had fought for it, Mackenzie the eternal rebel did not like it. He still wanted to reform everything. *Mackenzie's Weekly Message* came out as often as he could find enough money to print it. Friends bought him a two-storey stone house on Toronto's Bond Street in 1858. There he lived his last years, a semirecluse seeking solace in his Bible. In 1861, at 66, he died.

His legend, and reverence for him, grew. Men told of reports that Sam Lount, before his execution, denounced Mackenzie—but that Mrs. Lount informed Mackenzie her husband respected him to the end. They told of how shackled rebels being marched to jail paused before Mackenzie's house to raise their hats. To biographer William Kilbourn, Mackenzie was "the incarnation of impossible loyalties, the secret hope at the heart's core . . . the chief gargoyle on the sober edifice of our public history." But probably no heaven on earth would have satisfied him. He could not have been content, one observer noted, "under the government of an angel."

Egerton Ryerson's Object: 'To Educate All the Brats'

Education was neither free nor compulsory in Upper Canada in the 1830s. A child was taught only if his parents could pay the teacher. The teacher was probably unqualified—an ex-soldier or simply a drifter for whom teaching was preferable to starving or to manual toil. Children's labor was needed at home, so most went to a one-room log schoolhouse (such as this restored school in Upper Canada Village at Morrisburg, Ont.) for only a year or two.

They sat on rough-hewn benches and learned some reading, writing and arithmetic, but books were few and poor, ink was scarce, and most schools had no blackboards or maps.

A Methodist minister, the Rev. Egerton Ryerson *(left),* helped change much of this as Upper Canada's assistant superintendent of education. In 1844-45 he observed education systems in more than 20 countries and in his Report of 1846 called for free, compulsory education for all, for better trained teachers, improved textbooks and expanded curric-

ula. It laid the groundwork for the Common School Acts of 1846 and 1850. These established a system financed largely by local property taxes—payable by everyone.

Many objected to underwriting the schooling of other people's offspring. One taxpayer wrote: "I do not wish to be compelled to educate all the brats in the neighborhood." Ryerson replied that "to educate all the brats in the neighborhood is just the very object."

Heritage Sites

TORONTO Mackenzie House, which admirers bought for William Lyon Mackenzie in 1858, nine years after his return from exile, was the rebel leader's home until his death in 1861. The two-storey gaslit dwelling at 82 Bond Street has been restored as it was in Mackenzie's time. Family furniture, Mackenzie's watch and Bible, and portraits of Mackenzie and his wife, Isabel, are displayed. Copies of Mackenzie's newspaper, the *Colonial Advocate,* are printed on his hand-operated flatbed press in a reconstructed print shop.

Also in Toronto (8)

MACKENZIE'S PRINT SHOP The building where Mackenzie lived and produced the *Colonial Advocate* was at Front and Frederick streets when Family Compact supporters destroyed his press in 1826.

MONTGOMERY'S TAVERN A plaque at Yonge Street and Montgomery Avenue marks the site of rebel headquarters in the 1837 rebellion. Montgomery's Farm, where loyalists led by Lieutenant-Governor Sir Francis Bond Head routed rebel defenders Dec. 7, was just south, near what now is Eglinton Avenue.

NECROPOLIS A 20-foot granite monument with a broken peak (symbolic of life cut short) marks the grave of Samuel Lount, a rebel leader hanged April 12, 1838. Mackenzie's grave is in the cemetery.

SHARPE'S GARDEN The garden from which Mackenzie and a rebel force were ambushed Dec. 5, 1837, by Sheriff William Jarvis and 27 men was at Yonge Street, just southeast of Maitland Street.

Other sites

Amherstburg, Ont. (1) In Fort Malden National Historic Park are the remains of a stronghold attacked by Patriot Hunters—Americans hoping to "liberate" Canada from British rule—during the Patriot War of 1838. A plaque at Elliott's Point marks

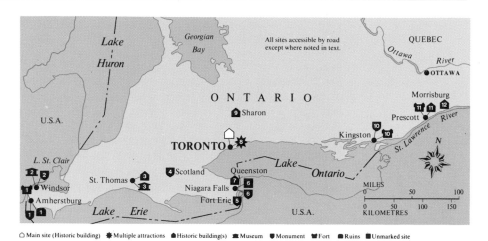

where the invaders' schooner *Anne* ran aground.

Fort Erie, Ont. (5) A plaque beside the Niagara River marks where Mackenzie fled by boat to the United States in 1837.

Kingston, Ont. (10) The section of Fort Henry where John Montgomery, the original owner of Montgomery's Tavern, was imprisoned in May 1838 has been restored as a leatherworker's shop. Montgomery and 14 fellow rebels escaped two months later. In Saint Mary's Roman Catholic Cemetery is the grave of Col. Nils Von Schoultz, leader of a Hunter raid at Prescott, who was hanged at Fort Henry Dec. 8, 1838.

Morrisburg, Ont. (12) Buildings in Upper Canada Village which depict life in the 1820s and '30s include Cook's Tavern, Crysler's Store and a schoolmaster's house.

Niagara Falls, Ont. (6) Navy Island, three miles south, was the headquarters of Mackenzie's provisional government from December 1837 to January 1838. A plaque on the Niagara River Parkway opposite the island recalls the destruction of Mackenzie's supply ship *Caroline* by Canadian militiamen. *Island accessible only by boat.*

Prescott, Ont. (11) A 66-foot stone tower, built as a windmill in 1820 and captured on Nov. 12, 1838, by Col. Nils Von Schoultz and some 200 Patriot Hunters, is part of 13-acre Fort Wellington National Historic Park. After five days and more than 40 casualties, the Hunters surrendered to militiamen and British regulars. An interpretive centre at the mill describes the battle. Earthworks and a blockhouse at Fort Wellington (1813), the target of the Hunters' attack, have been restored.

Queenston, Ont. (7) The house where Mackenzie lived in 1823-24 and published the *Colonial Advocate* has been rebuilt at York and Queen streets.

St. Thomas, Ont. (3) The Talbot Dispensatory, Ontario's first medical school, was started here in 1824 by doctors Charles Duncombe and John Rolph, both rebel leaders in 1837. The Elgin County Pioneer Museum, in a house believed owned by Duncombe, displays medical equipment. Rolph's cottage is a mile west.

Scotland, Ont. (4) A plaque commemorates Dr. Charles Duncombe, who briefly rallied a rebel force here in December 1837, then escaped to the United States.

Sharon, Ont. (9) The Temple of Peace was built in 1825-31 by a Quaker sect known as The Children of Peace. Many members supported the 1837 rebellion.

Windsor, Ont. (2) A plaque on the grounds of the Hiram Walker Historical Museum is across the street from the site of the Battle of Windsor, the last engagement in the Patriot War. In the museum are the diaries and duelling pistols of Col. John Prince, leader of the Canadian militia.

The Children of Peace, a breakaway Quaker sect that built this Temple of Peace at Sharon, Ont., joined Mackenzie's rebellion in 1837.

A Victorian-era fire station, still in use, stands on the site of the parliament building in Place d'Youville that an English-speaking mob burned in 1849. The legislature was in a section of the Marché Sainte-Anne, a market building.

In Anarchy and Riot, the Old Order Dies

This Cornelius Krieghoff portrait of Lord Elgin, governor general of Canada from 1847 to 1854, is in the McCord Museum in Montreal— a city that Elgin found "rotten to the core." But French Canadians respected Elgin for his courageous assent to the Rebellion Losses Bill, a decision for which English Canadians reviled him. The Thistle Curling Club of Montreal rejected his patronage and the St. Andrew's Society revoked his membership.

Lord Elgin's carriage raced across Montreal's Place d'Youville and away from the parliament building of the united Canadas under a hail of insults, rocks and debris. On this April 25, 1849, the governor general had just signed a bill to compensate those who had lost homes and other property in the Lower Canada Rebellion of 1837. That night about 1,500 English Canadians congregated on the windy, starlit Champs de Mars. Bad enough, speakers cried, that the French-dominated assembly would wish to compensate rebels but now a British governor had *approved.* Alfred Perry, Montreal's fire chief, suddenly shouted that the time for speeches was past. The cry went up: "To the Parliament House!"

Rocks struck the vaulted windows where the assembly was in session. Now the mob surged inside. They smashed the gaslights and one man strode to Speaker Augustin-Norbert Morin's chair and announced: "I dissolve this French House." A second man hacked the chair to bits; a third hurled the mace, symbol of parliamentary authority, through a window. Fire Chief Perry ground his heel into a portrait of Louis-Joseph Papineau (see p. 185). Gas escaping from broken fixtures ignited and the velvet drapes caught fire. One of the stunned assemblymen at last moved adjournment and, led by Morin, they filed into the street. There they watched as members of the appointed Legislative Council slid down wooden pillars from the second-storey balcony. Sir Allan MacNab of Hamilton (see p. 177) rescued a portrait of Victoria, the queen whose Parliament had just been destroyed.

Perry's firemen, despite their chief's involvement in the violence, tried to put out the flames. But other men slashed the hoses and the assembly building burned for most of the night, the mob celebrating what it thought was an English victory over French Canada.

It was a bad day for all Canada.

The high-handed rule of British governors and their advisers and supporters had driven both Canadas to rebellion in 1837. Britain had sent Lord Durham to investigate and he recommended union of Upper and Lower Canada. He also recommended what the rebels had demanded—responsible government. The Executive Council (the cabinet), said Durham, should be made up of members of the majority party in the elected assembly.

But Britain believed responsible government was equivalent to independence. She consented to unite the two colonies, with Kingston as the capital (it was later moved to Montreal), but would not approve responsible government.

English-Canadian Reformers welcomed the union. French Canadians saw in it the seeds of their destruction. They had suffered the defeats of 1837-38, Durham's insults (he recommended they be "Anglicized"), and the rejection of French as an official language. Britain was determined that the French must not hold power. But French politicians and journalists who opposed union were forced to admit, in the words of pro-union Reformer Louis-Hippolyte LaFontaine, that "it was impossible to arouse either the town or the countryside, so discouraged were they by events."

LaFontaine had been an ardent supporter of Papineau until the rebellion. Although he had sought compromise not conflict in 1837, he campaigned for amnesty for rebels and compensation for those who suffered property losses.

In 1840 LaFontaine published an historic address to his constituents in Terrebonne, north of Montreal. The French should not give up their rights as British subjects, he wrote, and risk repressive measures which could "leave us with no representation at all." Reformers were in the majority in both Canadas. If they worked together in "peace, union, friendship, and fraternity," they could persuade the colonial authority to grant them responsible government.

LaFontaine was in close touch with English-speaking Reformers. A Toronto journalist, Francis Hincks, wrote that "your countrymen would

The administration led jointly by the Upper Canada Reform leader Robert Baldwin (top) and his Lower Canada counterpart Louis-Hippolyte LaFontaine forged bonds between English and French. LaFontaine failed to win a seat in the assembly in 1841; Baldwin won two and vacated one for his friend. Two years later 25 French-speaking members offered to resign when Baldwin lost a by-election. He was returned for Rimouski, a Lower Canada constituency he had never seen.

Radical Jack Writes a Report on the Canadas

When Upper and Lower Canada broke into rebellion in 1837, Britain asked John George Lambton, first Earl of Durham, to see what had gone wrong. Durham, a brilliant politician who lived in ostentatious luxury, was appointed governor of Lower Canada and governor-in-chief of British North America. In May 1838 he installed himself in the governor's residence at Quebec, with his servants, horses and carriages, the family plate and furniture, and dozens of cases of champagne.

The pomp was misleading, however, for Lord Durham meant business. He had co-authored Britain's Reform Bill of 1832, and was known in England as "radical Jack." His advisers collected detailed information on land use, education and legal systems. Failing health, and lack of support at home, forced Durham's resignation after only five months. His "Report on the Affairs of British North America"—the Durham Report—was issued early in 1839.

Durham argued that the greatest single cause of Canadian discontent was racial conflict, "two nations warring in the bosom of a single state." French Canadians must become a minority and be systematically Anglicized, he contended. To this end, he proposed the political union of Upper and Lower Canada. A second problem, and the one history has shown to be more significant, was government mismanagement by privileged cliques. Durham recommended an administration responsible to the people's elected

representatives just as the cabinet in Britain was responsible to Parliament.

The Union Act of July 24, 1840, adopted Durham's first recommendation but colonial self-government was rejected. Britain was not yet ready to give up control of the colonies. Lord Durham died of tuberculosis five days after the Union Act was passed. He was 48.

François-Xavier Garneau, whose Histoire du Canada *was a response to Lord Durham's insistence that French Canadians had* no *history, lived in this house in Quebec.*

LaFontaine and Baldwin, almost as co-premiers, set about making changes. In the fall of 1843 they proposed that the assembly sit in Montreal. They consolidated their power by appointing their supporters to government posts—and tried to make the new governor, Sir Charles Metcalfe, ask their approval for all *his* appointments. When Metcalfe refused in November 1843, all but one member of the council resigned.

For 11 months the public debate raged. A well-defined two-party system was developing, with the Tories, claiming Metcalfe as figurehead, on one side and the Baldwin-LaFontaine Reformers on the other. The election of October 1844 produced an assembly with a Tory majority from Canada West, a Reform majority from Canada East. Politicians seemed to be dividing on racial as well as party lines.

The new assembly met in Montreal on Nov. 29, 1844. The overall majority was Tory, led by William Draper, a moderate who strove to gain the support of both factions for every measure and who proposed to make French an official language and to grant amnesty to rebels. But LaFontaine, supported by the French-Canadian press and clergy, urged his people to stand together *en bloc* against the predominantly English Tory majority. French Canadians who accepted government positions were *vendus* (sellouts).

To strengthen the government, Governor Metcalfe yielded to Draper what he had denied LaFontaine and Baldwin: control of patronage. Responsible government had *imposed itself*—without British approval. Soon, however, London's policy changed.

Britain, needing foreign markets for her industrial products and cheap food for her workers, had embraced free trade. Tariffs that protected colonial products from competitors in the British market were progressively wiped out between

This painting of Queen Victoria by John Partridge, "Portrait-painter Extraordinary to Her Majesty," was rescued from the Montreal Parliament fire in 1849. It is now in the Centre Block of the Parliament buildings in Ottawa.

never obtain their rights" in a legislature of their own. But in partnership, "as *Canadians*," they could force the autocrats to agree to democratic government. Reformers in Upper Canada were led by Robert Baldwin, a lawyer who had persuaded Lord Durham to advocate responsible government. Baldwin and LaFontaine formed the first of the English-French alliances which helped lead Canada toward Confederation.

The united Province of Canada was proclaimed in 1841 and the first joint assembly met in June that year. Governor General Charles Poulett Thomson, Lord Sydenham, selected his 24-man Executive Council—as London instructed—from among the ablest men. All, as it happened, were elected members of the assembly, but Baldwin resigned his appointment when LaFontaine and other French-Canadian Reformers were excluded. Sydenham's successor, Sir Charles Bagot, realized "you cannot govern Canada without the French," and that responsible government "virtually exists." In September 1842 he appointed LaFontaine—who accepted on condition that Baldwin and two other Reformers be named to the council. To London's horror, Bagot agreed. By November the Executive Council was Reform-dominated, with full French participation.

Men building Montreal's Victoria Bridge in 1859 uncovered the bones of typhus epidemic victims and erected this Irish Stone—from the St. Lawrence River—as a memorial.

1846 and 1849. There was no longer any need to control internal affairs in the colonies to further imperial trade.

The final obstacle to responsible government had gone. But so had the protective walls behind which Canadian business had developed. It was, said historian W.L. Morton, "a shock as violent and a change as revolutionary for English Canada as the conquest and cession of 1759-63 had been for French Canada."

Another new governor, James Bruce, Earl of Elgin, a young political tactician and former governor of Jamaica, arrived in January 1847. The Colonial Office had now accepted that "it is neither possible or desirable to carry on the government of any of the British provinces in North America in opposition to the opinion of the inhabitants." Elgin was to put into effect what his father-in-law, Lord Durham, had recommended.

He tried to remain aloof from party politics. It was not easy. If a man could govern Canada, he wrote to the colonial secretary, he could govern any country. Politics were not Elgin's only problem. The economy slumped under the effects of worldwide depression and the removal of colonial preferences. Bankruptcies increased, property values plunged; Montreal, the commercial capital, was full of bitterness and dismay. News of flourishing radical movements in Europe

A Time of Aches and Pains, When No Man's Vote Was Secret

Before the secret ballot became general in Canada in the late 1800s, elections were so violent that advertisements for liniment listed them as a cause of aches and pains.

The only persons entitled to vote were owners of country property that yielded an income of £12 a year or town property that produced £5—and tenants who paid at least £10 a year rent. A voter needed courage and stamina as much as affluence. First, he might have to travel 50 miles to the polling place (there was only one in each riding). Supporters of the candidates might try to buy his vote by treating him at a tavern or they might threaten him with a beating. In front of a boisterous crowd he had to show his property deed or other proof of qualification to vote and state his choice. His vote was entered in a poll book for all to see; it served as a receipt if his support had been bought. This Joseph Légaré painting is of an election at Château-Richer, northeast of Quebec.

The polls stayed open for days, sometimes weeks. On the first day, candidates delivered speeches from the hustings—high platforms erected near polling places. Then members of the opposing factions retired to taverns to hold open house. Strategy included the formation of club-swinging gangs to harass opponents—and sometimes the forging of deeds.

When rival gangs clashed in the election of 1841 several men were killed in Upper Canada and Lower Canada. In Reformer Louis-Hippolyte LaFontaine's mainly French-speaking riding of Terrebonne, north of Montreal, the governor fixed the polls at the outlying English-speaking hamlet of New Glasgow. LaFontaine and 850 supporters, armed with sticks, knives and pitchforks, arrived to find the polling place blocked off by some 700 men armed with clubs. LaFontaine went back to Montreal (conceding the election) before "the law of the bludgeon." The following year the assembly of the united Canadas passed a law against election violence, bribery and intimidation. The secret ballot was adopted in New Brunswick in 1855, for federal elections in post-Confederation Canada in 1874, and in all the then existing provinces by 1877.

created French-Canadian unrest, and Louis-Joseph Papineau, back from exile in Paris, was urging union with the United States.

In the winter election campaign of 1847-48, Baldwin's opponent, William Boulton, warned that a Reform victory would sacrifice Canada to "Tobacco-smoking, Dram Drinking, Garlick Eating Frenchmen, foreign in blood, foreign in race and as ignorant as the ground they stand upon." But the well-organized Reform party swept into power with decisive majorities in both Canada East and Canada West.

The first true one-party cabinet, "the Great Reform Ministry," took office in March 1848. When the assembly met in January 1849, Elgin drove in from Monklands, his big 18th-century stone house a few miles west of Montreal. White-plumed and splendid in a blue and silver tunic, he sat under a red and gold canopy and read the Speech from the Throne in English and French. "When," asked the newspaper *La Minerve*, "has our nationality been more respected, more honored?"

LaFontaine and Baldwin again led the government as a team. Responsible government by party had arrived. Then came the Rebellion Losses Bill—and anarchy.

Damages totalling £40,000 had been awarded in Canada West and a royal commission had recommended that Canada East victims be similarly reimbursed. LaFontaine's proposal to pay

Monklands, the vice-regal country residence in Montreal from 1844 to 1849, is the main building of Villa Maria, a private secondary school for girls. It is not open to the public.

This 1849 watercolor is one of the last meetings of the assembly of Canada in its Marché Sainte-Anne quarters in Montreal. Rioters burned the building in April of that year.

£100,000 staggered the Tories. He agreed that anyone exiled or convicted of participation in the rebellion would not be compensated—but it was common knowledge that many rebels had never been brought before the courts. Tories predicted civil war. The editor of *The Montreal Gazette* wrote: "If you do not resist, you will submit to anything."

The assembly debated the issue passionately before packed galleries whose interruptions sometimes drowned out the speakers. Finally, the bill was passed with a substantial majority.

Elgin could veto it or refer it to London. But he feared another rebellion if it was rejected. By approving it, he wrote, "whatever mischief may ensue may probably be repaired by the sacrifice of

This bamboo and wicker chair is one of a pair that Lord Elgin brought to Monklands, the vice-regal residence in Montreal. Both are in the McCord Museum in Montreal.

This house at Mount Uniacke, N.S., was the summer home of James Boyle Uniacke, a fiery Tory leader who resigned from the Nova Scotia Legislative Council in 1837 to join Joseph Howe's Reform party. Eleven years later Uniacke became Nova Scotia premier and attorney general—in the first responsible government anywhere in the British Empire. The house is now a branch of the Nova Scotia Museum.

me." That set the stage for the events of April 25. Elgin gave the bill royal assent and fled back to Monklands. That night they burned "the Parliament House"—the Marché Sainte-Anne in Place d'Youville.

Groups of English Canadians in Montreal (more than half its 55,000 population was English-speaking) rioted for four months. On April 26 LaFontaine was rescued by soldiers when attacked outside the Bonsecours Market, now used by the assembly and Executive Council, but another member was injured. That same evening, rioters attacked the police vehicle in which Perry, the fire chief, was being carried to jail. They turned loose the horses and tore the uniforms off the policemen. At the jail, the Tory sheriff set up Perry and other rioters in comfort—with catering by the popular chef of Dolly's Chop House.

Mobs smashed up LaFontaine's house and the home and office of Francis Hincks, now a Montreal newspaper proprietor.

There were violent demonstrations in Toronto, Bytown (Ottawa) and Hamilton. Elgin's effigy was burned by English Canadians in Trois-Rivières. Effigies of Elgin and LaFontaine intended for burning at Montreal were captured by French and Irish shipyard workers who paraded them through the streets singing "God Save the Queen."

The government stood firm, determined to

For Press and People, Without a Blow Struck

After Halifax County elected him to the Nova Scotia House of Assembly—on Dec. 13, 1836, his 32nd birthday—journalist Joseph Howe promised that, in the political struggles ahead, "I will by the blessing of God, endeavor to be a man." He did better than that—he became a *great* man. His surpassing struggle was for government responsible to the people rather than to itself. He won that in January 1848, without, as he said proudly, "a blow struck or a pane of glass broken."

Howe was born near Halifax and at 13 became a print-shop apprentice. Ten years later he bought a small newspaper, the *Novascotian*. In 1835 he was sued for libel when he published an attack on the Halifax magistrates for exacting over-heavy fines. He conducted his own defence in a packed courtroom at Province House. (*Below*: in the room, now the Legislative Library, is a plaster replica of a statue of Howe. The original is outside Province House.) With moving oratory he detailed the suffering caused by official corruption—and insisted on the right of the press to point it out.

The jury acquitted him. A year later he won a seat in the assembly.

He boldly criticized the Executive Council for meeting "in secret conclave to transact the public business." In 1840 he was challenged to a duel by the son of the chief justice whose honesty he had questioned. The other man shot first and missed; Howe fired his pistol into the air and coolly walked away.

The Reform party took power Feb. 2, 1848, and one week later Howe was named provincial secretary of the first British colony to achieve responsible government. Joe Howe was to undertake more great endeavors for the people of his beloved Nova Scotia (see p. 246).

meet violence with moderation. In the governor's official residence, the Château de Ramezay, thousands signed a huge book to show their support for the governor. *Canadiens* by the hundred volunteered for the militia to keep the peace, but Elgin refused their services. "The great object," he told the Colonial Office, "is to prevent collision between the races." To soothe the situation, he had stayed at Monklands. But when the assembly adopted an address affirming its loyalty, Elgin announced he would formally receive it at the château at noon April 30.

Vegetables, dead rats and garbage were rained on the assemblymen and their military escort when they walked to the Château de Ramezay from Bonsecours Market. Elgin, hat over his face, drove with cavalry outriders in a closed brougham along St. James Street through jeering, stone-throwing crowds. When the château's iron gates slammed shut behind his carriage, Elgin ran indoors carrying a two-pound rock that had landed at his feet in the carriage.

The crowds had barricaded Notre Dame Street when Elgin later slipped out by a side gate. His cavalry escort feinted in one direction; he took another. It didn't work. Scores of carriages gave chase, intercepting him at St. Lawrence and Sherbrooke streets. His brougham was damaged by stones, his brother injured as they dashed to Monklands. "We were for a time I believe in great danger," he wrote. "I confess I did not before know how thin is the crust of order which covers the anarchical elements that boil and toss beneath our feet."

Through spring and summer, mobs roamed the streets looking for *Canadiens* to insult. Lawyers left their offices, merchants their stores, women their homes to join the mobs. The Hospital of the Grey Nuns was attacked—and saved by counterattacking *Canadiens.* Gunmen wounded three guests at a hotel where Reformers were dining. A concert became a riot when "La Marseillaise" was sung.

On Aug. 15 LaFontaine's house was attacked again and its gates battered down. LaFontaine and some friends waited inside with guns. As the mob neared the front door shots rang out. One attacker, William Mason, was killed; six of his companions were wounded. Hundreds of mourners were at Mason's funeral and the riots went on for three nights afterward. There were rumors that LaFontaine would be assassinated if he testified at the inquiry into Mason's death. He was not, but three buildings were set on fire. The

Sam Slick: 'Wise Saws' From Here to Etarnity

Sam Slick was irreverent, colorful, boisterous and boorish, with a tongue as sharp as the pen of his creator, Thomas Chandler Haliburton, a Nova Scotia lawyer and author. It was Sam, a fictional Yankee clock vendor, who first said "the early bird gets the worm." He coined "jack of all trades and master of none," "barking up the wrong tree," "as quick as a wink" and "raining cats and dogs." These and Sam's countless other "wise saws" on "human natur" brought Haliburton international fame.

Haliburton wrote humorously but with serious intent. He thought his fellow Bluenoses were lazy so Sam once remarked: "An owl should be their emblem and the motto, 'He sleeps all the days of his life.'" He wanted Nova Scotians to become as enterprising as their New England neighbors—despite his belief that Americans were vain opportunists.

There were 11 Sam Slick books, beginning in 1836 with *The Clockmaker,* which tells of Sam's Nova Scotia travels with his horse Old Clay ("half-horse, half-alligator, with a cross of the airth-quake"). Haliburton lived in this house, now a museum, at Windsor, N.S. A shelf clock of the type which came to be called a Sam Slick is in the study. Haliburton became a judge of the Nova Scotia Supreme Court and moved to England in 1856.

He died in 1865, but Sam Slick lives on, selling clocks "warranted to run from July to eternity."

Bonsecours Market in Old Montreal was still under construction when used by the assembly of the united Canadas after its Place d'Youville building was destroyed in 1849. Bonsecours also was the city hall and police and fire department headquarters until 1878. It was used as a market until 1964, then underwent a $3 million restoration and now houses municipal offices.

rioting petered out as summer ended, with the Reform government still in power and supported firmly by Elgin. The Tories of English Canada felt betrayed. Their desperate response was to turn against Britain.

Tories who in 1837 had accused rebels of treason for trying to introduce an American system of government into Canada now proposed to join the United States. French-Canadian culture would be obliterated by the huge English-speaking majority; vast new markets would open up to Canadian producers. Four Montreal English newspapers supported the Annexation Association and on July 4, 1849, the American flag fluttered over several Montreal buildings.

The Annexation Manifesto published in Oc-

tober was signed by 325 of Montreal's commercial and social élite, including Alexander Tilloch Galt (a future Father of Confederation) and John Abbott (a future prime minister). Elgin put soldiers on guard against an American invasion. But the movement withered and died for lack of support. Manifesto signatories in official posts were dismissed if they did not retract. Elgin moved his government away from Montreal to meet by turn in Quebec and Toronto for seven years until it settled in Ottawa in 1857.

Before his return to England in 1854, Governor General Elgin went to Washington to negotiate a reciprocity treaty. Tariffs were abolished on many commodities, giving Canada access to the U.S. markets and the cheap American raw materials that the annexationists had coveted. The Canadian economy, already recovering from a slump after losing its privileged status in the British market, benefited enormously.

The LaFontaine-Baldwin administration had come to an end in 1851 when both retired into private careers. John A. Macdonald, a young Tory lawyer who had not signed the Annexation Manifesto, was building a new partnership with LaFontaine's successor, George-Etienne Cartier. That partnership would lead the country into Confederation in 1867.

The assembly of the united Canadas met in this building, now part of the Kingston (Ont.) General Hospital, from June 1841 to May 1844, when Montreal became the capital.

Heritage Sites

MONTREAL Place d'Youville is where English-speaking Tories stoned the carriage of Lord Elgin, governor of the united Canadas, and burned the parliament building on April 25, 1849. The Youville Stables—originally warehouses—have been restored to the period 1825-60 and house offices, boutiques and a restaurant.

Also in Montreal (4)

BONSECOURS MARKET This cut-stone building, now housing municipal offices, was used as a parliament building in the spring and summer of 1849 after the Place d'Youville riot.

CHÂTEAU DE RAMEZAY This fieldstone château, dating from 1705 and now a museum of Quebec history, was Elgin's official residence. He received the assembly's address of loyalty here April 30, 1849, and was attacked a second time by a Tory mob.

IRISH STONE A 10-foot-high boulder at the northern approach to the Victoria Bridge commemorates Irish immigrants who died of typhus in 1847-48.

VILLA MARIA Monklands, Elgin's country residence, is now the central building of a girls' private school. Built about 1790, it is visible at the end of a tree-lined driveway facing the east end of Monkland Avenue. Wings were added later.

Other sites

Dartmouth, N.S. (9) The home study of journalist and politician Joseph Howe has been re-created in the Dartmouth Heritage Museum. Displays include his roll-top desk, top hat and Micmac dictionary.

Halifax (8)

HOWE'S BIRTHPLACE A plaque commemorating Howe is at 5956 Emscote Drive, on the gatepost of the house (now demolished) where he was born in 1804.

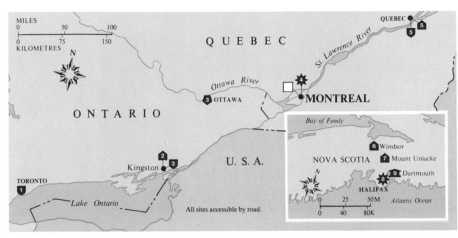

HOWE FESTIVAL High school oratorical contests, with the finals in Province House, highlight the Howe Festival in October.

PROVINCE HOUSE The courtroom in which Howe successfully defended himself in 1835 against a charge of criminal libel is now the library of Canada's oldest (1818) legislative building. The librarian's desk is where the judge's bench stood. Canada's first responsible government, in which Howe became provincial secretary, met in this sandstone building Feb. 2, 1848. A Philippe Hébert statue of Howe, gesturing in debate, stands outside.

PUBLIC ARCHIVES Exhibits include presses on which Howe printed the *Novascotian* between 1827 and 1841, and the desk he used when he was provincial secretary.

Kingston, Ont. (2) A plaque outside the centre wing of the Kingston General Hospital records that the first assembly of the united Canadas met there June 14, 1841.

(The newly built hospital had not yet been opened.) Kingston's domed, limestone city hall was built to house the assembly but in 1844, before construction was finished, the capital was moved to Montreal.

Mount Uniacke, N.S. (7) Uniacke House was built in 1813-15 by Richard John Uniacke, a pillar of the Establishment against which Joseph Howe fought. In the 1830s it became the summer home of Uniacke's son, James Boyle, premier and attorney general in Canada's first responsible government. The house has been restored and is a branch of the Nova Scotia Museum.

Ottawa (3) The portrait of Queen Victoria rescued by Sir Allan MacNab from Montreal's burning Parliament House in 1849 hangs near the entrance to the Senate Chamber in Parliament's Centre Block.

Quebec (5) The house in which historian François-Xavier Garneau lived is at 14 Rue Saint-Flavien. Garneau wrote a four-volume *Histoire du Canada* to refute Lord Durham's assertion that French Canadians were "a people without history." In niches in the façade of the National Assembly are statues of Lord Elgin and Reform leaders Louis-Hippolyte LaFontaine and Robert Baldwin.

Toronto (1) A plaque in the provincial Parliament Building honors Robert Baldwin.

Windsor, N.S. (6) "Clifton," the frame house in which Thomas Chandler Haliburton wrote the Sam Slick stories, is now the Haliburton House, a branch of the Nova Scotia Museum. Built in 1834-36, the house contains Haliburton's desk and a Sam Slick shelf clock.

The Youville Stables, three restored 19th-century buildings, face Place d'Youville in Montreal.

213

Garrison Gaiety and 'Scarlet Fever'

"Thanks in great measure to the garrison and the fleet," wrote an English civilian in Halifax in 1850, "you may have gaiety to a degree undreamed of in towns of the same size at home."

British soldiers and sailors served in Canada from the mid-1700s to the late 1800s. Few fought any battles, but as a group they brought glamor, elegance and excitement to many a fort and town. Mustachioed officers in dress scarlet danced the local belles until dawn (right: a military ball at Halifax in 1869) and military bands played in the streets and the parks.

But there was another side to garrison life. Sham battles, guard duty, endless drill and spit-and-polish chores were supposed to keep men occupied but boredom was inescapable. Unable to afford their officers' social diversions, ordinary soldiers took to the rowdy back streets and bought solace and often oblivion in taverns and brothels. Soldiers and sailors in Halifax frequented Hogg Street (named after a brothel keeper) and Knock Him Down Street (for its fights and murders). Barracks built in Saint John, N.B., in 1821 were soon surrounded by 15 licensed taverns and countless illegal dives. Dance halls in such areas teemed with prostitutes and dolly-mops—girls whose "scarlet fever" made them flock around men in uniform. Rum flowed, and as the dances grew ever more boisterous fights broke out, men swinging their belts, lashing out with the brass buckles and fastenings. A brawl on the Market Wharf in Halifax in 1813 went from fists and belts to worse, and five civilians were bayoneted, one fatally.

British troops were withdrawn from Canada after Confederation. The last (except for a small garrison at the Halifax naval base) sailed from Quebec in November 1871.

Many a British soldier in Canada tried to desert to the United States, although the penalty might be death (left: an execution in 1824) or, after the letter D had been branded on his chest, transportation to Australia, or 14 years' service in West Africa. During the American Civil War soldiers were lured by crimps, men paid to find recruits for the Union army. Some used drugs—or prostitutes trained to use chloroform. The British army offered civilians a £5 bounty for each captured deserter.

British soldiers were flogged for offences from disobedience to "unsoldierlike conduct," a term defined—as they saw fit—by individual commanding officers. (Below: a flogging is specially re-enacted at Fort George, Niagara-on-the-Lake, Ont.) Until 1812 a man could be sentenced to 1,200 lashes. After that the maximum was 300—with 100 strokes considered light punishment. Men of a unit watched as drummers did the flogging with a cat-o'-nine-tails, one relieving another after every 25th stroke. Drummers themselves were beaten for not striking hard enough. Prince Edward, later Duke of Kent (see p. 126), was a particularly stern disciplinarian. It is said that when he was military commander in Halifax in the 1790s the townsfolk were awakened every morning by the screams of soldiers being flogged on Citadel Hill.

A tour of duty in British North America lasted seven years. Most soldiers had enlisted to escape desperate poverty in their homes in England. Others were runaways, idlers, and criminals released from prison on condition they join up. Many were better off than in civilian life. Still, the pay was less than a penny a day and a man in the ranks lived in a barrack room (often unheated) with up to 100 other men, sleeping on a straw mattress in sheets that were changed once a month. A roller towel for about 20 men had to last a week. Toilets were "cesspools or mere reservoirs." (Above: a barrack room, c. 1812, at Fort George, Niagara-on-the-Lake, Ont.) The unvarying daily ration was a pound of bread and half a pound of meat, and cooking was done in the barrack room. Six of every 100 men were allowed to bring their wives. A couple bunked in the barrack room, their only privacy a blanket hung up at night. Women received half rations, and children proportionately less (at 14 they had to fend for themselves). Wives cooked, washed and cleaned for officers and men alike. Army widows were left without support, and many quickly remarried. One woman in 1840 had three husbands within six months.

Students at Fort Henry in Kingston, Ont., demonstrate battle formations. The "British square" (above), formed of two or four ranks, was used against cavalry. The "thin red line" (below) was the main battle formation throughout the 19th century. An entire army, as many as 10,000 men, formed into two ranks and advanced together. Companies (60-80 men) fired individually.

British officers—usually the sons of aristocratic families who had bought their commissions—were not expected to suffer hardship in Canada. Much of their time was spent reading, fishing and hunting (above: Officers' Trophy Room *by Cornelius Krieghoff). Each had his own room, his own furniture, his personal soldier-valet—to serve tea, clean and lay out uniforms, polish equipment and look after the officer's horse. Officers shared a wine cellar and a mess where they dined on such delicacies as venison and fine cheeses. Most kept diaries and many expanded them into memoirs that sold well in Britain. Many diaries did not mention military duties except as an intrusion on social life.*

Five Shillings a Day, 10 Days a Year

The modern Canadian army had its beginnings in 1855—"in a moment of patriotic enthusiasm," as one writer put it—when British troops were being withdrawn for the Crimean War. The legislature of the united Canadas established an "active militia" of 5,000 volunteers—cavalry, artillery and rifles—to be equipped, trained and paid five shillings a day for 10 days a year. By 1864 there were almost 22,000 volunteers. There were drills, firing range practices (sometimes), a sham battle, and speeches by politicians. But in 1866, during the Fenian raids, many of the militiamen called up had never fired even a blank cartridge.

But a soldier's life still seemed glamorous to some. The new Dominion of Canada set up a Department of Militia and Defence in May 1868 and increased to 45,000 the number of volunteers who could receive annual training. Canada's first regular units, two small artillery batteries formed in 1871, occupied the Quebec and Kingston, Ont., fortifications. In the '80s and '90s there was a steady growth in the numbers and efficiency of the militia (below: some full-dress uniforms of 1898) and in 1899 Canada was able to send a well-trained contingent to the South African War (see p. 338).

Long before the Militia Act of 1855, men were subject to call-up in emergencies but most companies did little more than one day's drilling a year. Above: an 1830 militia drill is reenacted at Kings Landing Historical Settlement, Prince William, N.B.

Discovery and Disaster on the Roof of the World

REX WOODS

One day in May 1847, confident they were about to discover the Northwest Passage that had eluded explorers for centuries, eight Royal Navy men trudged across the ice north of King William "Land"—as they called it, not knowing it was an island. Lieut. Graham Gore, Mate Charles Des Vœux and six seamen were an advance party of a superbly equipped expedition led by Sir John Franklin.

Other explorers had charted the north coast of the American mainland from the Bering Strait as far as Queen Maud Gulf and beyond—to the mouth of the Back River (south of King William Island). Franklin, approaching from the east, was less than 100 miles northeast of that gulf, the closest known navigable opening to the Pacific. But getting to it would not be easy.

Although it was May 24, Franklin's sailing ships *Erebus* and *Terror* still lay trapped in the ice at the north end of Victoria Strait when Gore's sled party went ahead to search out a route the ships could take when the ice broke up.

Four days later, following good Royal Navy procedure, Gore left a message in a stone cairn at the tip of King William "Land":

28 of May 1847. H.M. Ships Erebus and Terror wintered in the ice . . . in 1846-7 at Beechey Island . . . after having ascended Wellington Channel . . . and returned by the West side of Cornwallis Island. Sir John Franklin commanding the Expedition. All well. Party consisting of 2 officers and 6 men left the Ships on Monday 24th May 1847. Gm. Gore, Lieut. [and] Chas. F. Des Voeux, Mate.

The ships Erebus *and* Terror *are locked in ice off King William Island as Sir John Franklin (left) bids farewell to Lieut. Graham Gore on May 24, 1847. Gore and seven men, hauling sleds, are to seek a route that the ships can take when the ice breaks up.*

Sir Humphrey Gilbert, an English soldier and navigator, was among the first to believe in the existence of a Northwest Passage. He never went to the Arctic but a book he wrote in 1566, A Discourse of a Discoverie for a New Passage to Cataia *(China), influenced Martin Frobisher to undertake his explorations, starting in 1576.*

The Elizabethans Found Cod, Mutiny and Death But No Route to China

A trade route to the riches of the Orient—around North America but far from hostile Spanish ships and safer than the stormy Strait of Magellan below South America—became a goal of London merchants in the 1570s. Helped by Elizabeth I, they financed early searches for the Northwest Passage. These men led the way:

Martin Frobisher sailed west in 1576. He reached a 150-mile inlet on Baffin Island, now known as Frobisher Bay, which he mistook for an entrance to the passage. He returned to London with a "blacke stone" which he was told was gold ore. In 1577 and 1578, distracted from his original goal, Frobisher led mining expeditions to Kodlunarn Island in the bay. But tons of "ore" he took to England turned out to be worthless pyrite, and Frobisher switched to privateering in the South Atlantic.

John Davis made three voyages in 1585-87, mapping the coasts of Labrador and of Baffin Island and Greenland on both sides of Davis Strait. He reported on the strait's rich sealing and whaling potential, and on the abundance of cod off Labrador. War with Spain in 1588 ended support for his explorations.

Henry Hudson was commissioned in 1610 to follow up Davis's discoveries. In the 55-ton barque *Discovery* he sailed through the strait and bay which bear his name. His ship, trapped in James Bay by ice, was the first to winter in the North. In a mutiny in June 1611 Hudson and eight men were cast adrift (see p. 36). *Discovery* was sailed home by mate Robert Bylot.

William Baffin was a pilot not a captain, but his maps, journals and astronomical observations make him one of the great Arctic navigators. In 1615 he entered Hudson Bay as pilot in Hudson's *Discovery* (still commanded by Robert Bylot) and rightly concluded that a Northwest Passage lay elsewhere. In 1616, again with Bylot in *Discovery*, he circumnavigated Baffin Bay. On the southward journey he discovered Lancaster Sound, later proven to be the entrance to the passage.

But the importance of Baffin's discovery was not recognized and commercial backers of the search for the passage gave up. Two hundred years later the task would be resumed by the Royal Navy—not for profit but for glory.

(The date 1846-7 was an error. Franklin spent the winter of 1845-46 at Beechey Island.)

But all was *not* well. The west coast of King William "Land" would be a place of doom for Franklin's men.

Discovery of the Northwest Passage had seemed imminent for three decades. With the Napoleonic wars ended, Britain had men and ships to spare and by 1818, after several relatively mild winters, Arctic ice conditions were more favorable than usual. In that year Capt. John Ross repeated William Baffin's voyage of two centuries before, through Baffin Bay into the narrow waters between Ellesmere Island and Greenland.

In 1819 Lieut. Edward Parry sailed the ships *Hecla* and *Griper* into Lancaster Sound (at the north end of Baffin Island) and pushed west through Barrow Strait and across Viscount Melville Sound. He was on the great broad sea road through the Arctic but was stopped by ice in McClure Strait (beyond which lay the Beaufort Sea and a clear run to Bering Strait and the Pacific). Still, Parry had gone farther west than anyone before him. He earned a £5,000 reward for crossing 110° west longitude.

Ross went back in 1829, on a privately financed expedition, in the coastal packet *Victory*, the first steam-powered ship used in the search for the passage. Locked in ice, she was abandoned in May 1832 in the Gulf of Boothia.

Ross's nephew and second-in-command, James Clark Ross, on a sled expedition down the west coast of the Boothia Peninsula, in 1831, had mapped as *a bay* the waters now known as Rae Strait, which leads to Simpson Strait, south of King William Island, then to Queen Maud Gulf and the elusive passage. James Clark Ross was probably the victim of a mirage. In any case, his

This cairn (since rebuilt) apparently contained the only surviving document of the Franklin expedition. On one sheet of paper were Lieut. Graham Gore's account of his journey in 1847 and Capt. Francis Crozier's report of Franklin's death.

The Arctic has a "main street" (Viscount Melville Sound, Barrow Strait, Lancaster Sound)—but it is usually heavy with pack ice. Nineteenth-century searchers for the Northwest Passage probed avenues off it but found ice blocking all of them. Successful voyages were eventually made by reaching open water south and east of King William Island.

—— *Thwarted voyages*
❶ *Edward Parry (1819-20)*
❷ *John Ross (1829-33)*
❸ *John Franklin (1845-?)*
—— *Successful voyages*
❹ *Roald Amundsen (1903-06)*
❺ *Henry Larsen (1940-42)*

Parry *Chose* to Stay—and Defeated Cold, Scurvy and Boredom

Edward Parry *(right)* was the first Arctic explorer who *deliberately* spent a winter with his ships locked in the ice.

He was a 29-year-old Royal Navy lieutenant, in command of the ketches *Hecla* and *Griper,* when he sailed from England in May 1819 to probe Lancaster Sound. (Years later, it would prove to be the entrance to the Northwest Passage.) He had determined not to return home after only one short season, but to remain and thus have more time for exploration in the following short Arctic summer. By early October his ships had penetrated some 700 miles west from the mouth of the sound and were frozen in at Winter Harbour on Melville Island. Cold, scurvy and monotony would be winter enemies but Parry had planned carefully.

As the four-month Arctic night closed in, the ships' upper decks were roofed with quilted canvas on wood frames. The hulls were banked with snow up to the gunwales. Heat was piped from the galley stoves.

Unaware that lack of vitamin C caused scurvy, Parry gave his crew lime juice, vinegar, pickles, fresh bread, preserved fruits and soups, and beer brewed on ship. When, despite these precautions, three cases of scurvy oc-

curred, he planted mustard and cress in a box of earth over the heating pipes in his cabin. The seeds sprouted in five days and salads, rich in vitamin C, quickly cured the scurvy.

Parry kept his men busy melting snow for water, taking scientific readings, chipping ice from the ships, building a weather station and hunting.

In bad weather the men jogged on the enclosed upper decks. Once a fortnight the officers staged a London play. Crew members contributed articles and sketches to the expedition's newspaper, *The North Georgia Gazette and Winter Chronicle.* Other men were taught to read and write. Parry practised his violin, helped write an operetta entitled *The Northwest Passage,* and planned an escape route to the nearest trading post—1,000 miles away.

But after 10 months in the ice, *Hecla* and *Griper* sailed free. Parry, his men safe and healthy, arrived home in November 1820 and collected a £5,000 prize for sailing so far west. Other explorers proved later that white men could live off the land as natives did, but Parry's take-it-with-you style—successful *this* time—was adopted by John Franklin for his 1845 expedition. That time every man perished.

219

"bay" was shown on the maps that Sir John Franklin took when he sailed from London with *Erebus* and *Terror* on May 19, 1845. Never had ships been so well equipped for the Arctic. Their bows were iron-plated to withstand ice; they had steam engines to move them in calm weather; they carried food for three years. "It is curious how few wants we find," Franklin wrote. "There is scarcely anything that would be of use that has been neglected."

In late July a whaling captain saw *Erebus* and *Terror* moored to an ice floe in Baffin Bay, awaiting favorable wind and ice conditions. After that only Inuit hunters ever saw the ships or the 130 men aboard them.

In 1847, with no word from Franklin, the Admiralty decided against a search because *Erebus* and *Terror* were equipped for a three-year voyage. But in 1848 two search expeditions were sent, one across the Atlantic, the other across the Pacific to Bering Strait. They found no trace of Franklin.

In the summer of 1850 six naval and several private expeditions sailed in search of *Erebus* and *Terror*. On Beechey Island in Lancaster Sound, where Franklin had wintered in 1845-46, searchers found a rag, a glove, a few pieces of rope, the ruins of several small buildings, and three grave markers. That was all.

During the next four years 38 expeditions searched the Arctic coast and islands (33 by sea, 5 by land) before any clue to the fate of *Erebus* and *Terror* was found.

Dr. John Rae of the Hudson's Bay Company surveyed the east coast of the Boothia Peninsula in 1853-54 and learned from the Inuit that in the spring of 1848 forty men had been seen far to the west, dragging sleds and a boat south over the ice. Later that year 30 corpses and some graves had been found on the Adelaide Peninsula and five bodies on King William Island. To the Admiralty Rae reported what he had been told: "From the mutilated state of the corpses, and the contents of the kettles, it is evident that our wretched countrymen had been driven to the last resource—cannibalism." Rae bought from the Inuit "some silver spoons and forks, an Order of Merit in the form of a star, and a small silver plate engraved 'Sir John Franklin, K.C.B.' " The Admiralty announced that the fate of the lost explorers was "settled" and awarded Rae the prize of £10,000 for solving the mystery.

Five years later, still hoping her husband might have survived, Lady Jane Franklin sponsored an expedition led by Capt. Leopold McClintock, who had been on earlier searches. In the winter of 1859, travelling by sled down the west coast of the Boothia Peninsula, McClintock purchased from Inuit hunters "silver plate bearing the crests or initials of Franklin, Crozier,

The Royal Navy gave its exploring parties printed forms on which to record details of their journeys. The only one ever recovered from Franklin's 1845 expedition was used twice, first by Lieut. Graham Gore on his overland reconnaissance and, a year later, by Capt. Francis Crozier after the expedition's two ships had been abandoned. The document is in the National Maritime Museum at Greenwich, England.

Fairholme and M'Donald . . . bows and arrows of English woods, uniform and other buttons." He was shown "a heavy sledge made of two stout pieces of curved wood, which no mere boat could have furnished."

Inuit on King William Island told McClintock that years before, many white men had dragged sled loads of equipment from two ships marooned in the ice. A search of the island's west coast turned up a 750-pound boat on a 650-pound sled, and tools, furniture, sheets of lead, a lightning rod and many toilet articles—"a mere accumulation of dead weight," said McClintock, "very likely to break down the strength of the sledge crews." There were also two skeletons. An elderly woman told him: "The white men dropped by the way as they went. Some were buried and some were not."

McClintock's second-in-command, Lieut. Robert Hobson, found the message written by Graham Gore on May 28, 1847, after *Erebus* and *Terror* had spent two winters in the Arctic. But around the margin was this message:

April 25, 1848. H.M. Ships Erebus and Terror were deserted on the 22nd of April, 5 leagues NNW of this, having been beset since 12 of

An artist's conception of Erebus *in the ice. François Etienne Musin's painting is in Britain's National Maritime Museum.*

Ross Learned the Inuit Way: Don't Fight the Arctic, Adapt to It

They were in three small boats, 20 gaunt men dressed in animal skins, and for four years they had existed—but only just—in the icy grip of the Gulf of Boothia, off the northwest end of Baffin Island. Now, on Aug. 26, 1833, they were saluted with three cheers and climbed aboard the British ketch *Isabella.* Royal Navy Capt. John Ross and his men, long presumed dead, had survived by *not* keeping a stiff upper lip; they had learned from the Inuit not to fight the Arctic but to adapt to it.

There had been 23. Ross and his nephew, Comdr. James Clark Ross, with 21 men, had sailed from England in 1829 to seek the Northwest Passage. They did not find it—but 20 of them survived in the Arctic longer than any Europeans before them.

Three winters were spent on the Boothia Peninsula, where their steam packet *Victory* lay trapped in the ice. In January 1830 they befriended a band of Inuit. A wounded Inuit hunter was fitted

with a wooden leg and, with two friends, was sketched *(right)* by Captain Ross.

From the natives the explorers learned to build sleds and snow houses. With Inuit guides they hunted seal and bear and explored the Boothia Peninsula. Like the Inuit they ate animal oil and fat.

Ross abandoned *Victory* in April 1832 and headed overland for Fury Beach, 185 miles north, where they would find boats and provisions cached in 1825 by explorer Edward Parry. When his dispirited men grumbled—"the first symptom approaching to mutiny"—Ross drew his gun and demanded obedience. In July 1833 they set out from Fury Beach for Lancaster Sound, north of Baffin Island. There they were rescued.

The Ross party had shown how Europeans could survive in the Arctic. Twelve years later the Franklin expedition would ignore their findings—and perish. Asked to lead that expedition, James Ross refused. At 44 he felt he was too old. Sir John Franklin was 59.

September, 1846. The officers and crews, consisting of 105 souls, under the Command of Captain F. R. M. Crozier, landed here . . . . Sir John Franklin died on the 11th June 1847, and the total loss by deaths in the Expedition has been to this date 9 officers and 15 men. F. R. M. Crozier, Captain and Senior Officer. James Fitzjames, Captain H.M.S. Erebus. And start on tomorrow 26th for Back's Fish River.
No other message was ever found.

What had turned Franklin's well-prepared, well-equipped expedition into this most terrible of Arctic tragedies?

The first summer had gone well for *Erebus* and *Terror.* Gore's note told of voyaging north from Lancaster Sound and circumnavigating Cornwallis Island, and of a relatively comfortable first winter on Beechey Island.

In the summer of 1846 *Erebus* and *Terror* must have sailed west through Barrow Strait and south down Peel Sound, between Somerset Island and Prince of Wales Island.

By early September they were north of King William "Land" only 100 miles northeast of a charted coast and a waterway (Queen Maud Gulf, Dease Strait, Coronation Gulf, Dolphin and Union Strait, Amundsen Gulf) that leads to the Pacific. Franklin seemed close to success.

From here the route *around* King William Is-

A brass cannon from Capt. John Ross's Victory *is in the RCMP Museum at Regina.* Victory *was the first steamship to enter Arctic waters (in 1829) but was abandoned after three years trapped in the ice. Her crew journeyed for more than a year before being rescued.*

Inuit: The People Who Never Said Good-Bye

Motionless, leaning forward, harpoon raised, an Inuit hunter would wait hours for a seal to surface at its breathing hole in the ice. Seals were life itself for Inuit families—the main source of food, clothing and oil for fuel.

A sudden thrust of the harpoon: another kill in the endless struggle for survival. Or, if the hunter was unlucky or miscalculated, the harpoon hit the ice and the seal was gone. "*Ayornamat*" (Can't be helped), he would mutter with a shrug. And he would move off to another breathing hole, another long and lonely vigil.

The migratory inhabitants of the Arctic were called Eskimos (eaters of raw meat) by their ancient enemies the Cree. Inuit was their *own* name for themselves: simply "the people."

Inuit survived by making do. They got fire by striking chunks of pyrite together and catching the sparks in grass. To make a soapstone cooking pot required a month of chipping and smoothing. Clothing of seal or caribou skin was sewn with needles of goose or gull wingbone and thread of animal sinew. Two sets of clothing were worn in winter, the inner layer with the fur toward the skin. A baby was carried in the hood of the mother's parka. A person caught in a blizzard sat with his back to the wind, leaned forward and waited until the storm was over.

Blubber, meat and fish were often eaten when raw (and most nutritious), and partly digested lichen and grass from a caribou's stomach was a delicacy. Driftwood—the

Patience was more than tradition with Inuit fishermen; they fished to live. These men on the ice of an arctic lake spear and jig for trout and char.

only wood available—was carved and pegged to make harpoons and sleds. Where there was no wood, caribou antlers were straightened in hot water and pieced together. With neither wood nor bone, Inuit built sleds of frozen hides, fish or meat strips—sleds which could be eaten if necessary.

The Inuit had 100 words for various types of snow but not one word for chief. Power lay in the community's approval or rejection of its members. There was no war. There were no bad hunters, just "unlucky" ones, and when all luck ran out people died. Cannibalism was viewed with horror but accepted as a last resort in the fight for life.

The Inuit acceptance of fate was such that a man who had killed another would raise his victim's sons as his own—knowing that by the laws of revenge they would eventually have to kill him.

Kayaks were hunting boats but some Inuit used them for travel, especially across rivers and lakes. Some weighed as little as 25 pounds.

Loose-fitting Inuit clothing ensured a layer of air between clothing and skin. This woman (watercolor dated 1570) carries a baby in the h... her parka.

Life was lived one day at a time, w... constant cheerfulness that puzzled I... pean explorers—but for which the Inui... an explanation: "If you knew the ho... we often have to live through, you w... understand too why we are so fon... laughing."

They had many a happy word for ... come. And not one for good-bye.

Inukshuks—piles of rocks in the rough shape ... mans—were built as landmarks, to locate c... migration routes, and perhaps as gods.

low Inuit Made an Igloo

rm, compact snow was cut with an ivory knife into ocks 3 by 2 feet, 8 inches thick. The top of each block

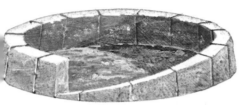

is trimmed to slope inward, then a ramp was cut. Blocks re added to the inward sloping spiral, the angle increas-

g until a dome could be fitted. A temporary igloo was out 7 feet in diameter and 5 feet high. A winter dwelling, out 15 feet across and 12 feet high, usually had an en-

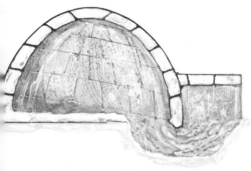

nce tunnel and often a window—a piece of freshwater . Outside cracks were wedged with snow; inside walls re rubbed with snow, then glazed with flame. The rance was excavated to trap warm air inside; cold avier) air remained in the entrance.

Discovery of this medal, Sir John Franklin's Cross of the Guelphic Order of Hanover, was one of the first solid clues to his expedition's fate. Searchers found silverware, watches, guns, skeletons—but no record, until in 1859 they uncovered a written record of Franklin's death 12 years previously. At the same rock cairn was this medicine chest.

land, via Rae Strait, was navigable—but because of James Clark Ross's error the strait appeared on Franklin's charts as a bay with no outlet. The only option appeared to be Victoria Strait, west of the island. But, unknown to Franklin, it is choked year-round with ice. By Sept. 12 *Erebus* and *Terror* were locked in the floes.

Gore may have returned in June 1847 with news that he had crossed the ice as far as the south of King William "Land." Franklin died that month (of what cause is not known) and by then supplies were running low. The ships moved a little with drifting pack ice before being trapped for a third winter. By now 14 men had died. Most of the rest were hungry, many sick from eating the rotting remains of their supplies. (Franklin had relied on food that was canned—a technique not perfected in the 1840s.) In the spring of 1848 the survivors decided to abandon the ships. They apparently planned to drag boats 250 miles across King William "Land" and the Adelaide Peninsula to the mouth of "Back's Fish River" (now the Back River). They would travel up it until they reached a Hudson's Bay Company post. Soon after setting out, they added their message to Gore's.

Weakened by scurvy, many died on the sea ice and on the stony beaches of King William Island. Some reached Chantrey Inlet on the Adelaide Peninsula. There, at a place now called Starvation Cove, they left the horrible campsite that the Inuit later described to Rae.

Lady Jane Franklin petitioned the governments of France, Russia and the United States, as well as Britain, to send ships to the Arctic to look for traces of her husband's expedition. She spent most of her fortune— even selling her house and moving to rented rooms—to finance search parties but abandoned hope when, in 1859, Capt. Leopold McClintock brought to London a document which told of Franklin's death in 1847.

The Agony of Thomas Simpson: Mad Prelude to the Franklin Disaster

Thomas Simpson journeyed down two of the North's great rivers, charted hundreds of miles of Arctic coastline, and was one of the great figures in the long, tragic search for the Northwest Passage. But his pride and impatience and the physical and mental toll of Arctic exploration drove him to insanity and death, perhaps by suicide, at 31.

In the mid-1830s, when the Hudson's Bay Company decided to join in the search for the passage, Governor George Simpson (see p. 226) chose his cousin Thomas to be second-in-command under Chief Factor Peter Warren Dease.

Royal Navy officers had searched by sea and had failed. They had mapped much of the Arctic mainland coastline but there were gaps, one in what now is Alaska, the other between Coronation Gulf and Fury and Hecla Strait far to the east. The easygoing Dease and the driving, impetuous Simpson—the real leader of the expedition—would try in small boats to complete the mapping and find the passage.

In 1836 Simpson walked 1,300 miles from Upper Fort Garry (Winnipeg) to Great Slave Lake to join Dease. The following spring they went down the Mackenzie River and some 500 miles west to Point Barrow. That closed the western gap in the coastline

chart. They wintered at Great Bear Lake. Next year they descended the Coppermine River and into Coronation Gulf, only to be blocked by ice in what became known as Dease Strait. Simpson proceeded on foot for 100 miles, then returned to Great Bear Lake.

In 1839 they reached King William Island, some 600 miles east of the Coppermine, before having to turn back. They knew they were close to Fury and Hecla Strait but they did not know that the Boothia Peninsula blocked the way, and that there *was* no direct route to the strait.

Simpson proposed one more try: down the Back River and east to Fury and Hecla. But Dease was on leave and George Simpson would not trust his cousin with command. Young Simpson appealed to the HBC governors in London; then, anxious for their decision (he never knew it was favorable), he left Upper Fort Garry, intending to go to New York and then England.

In Minnesota the effects of three strenuous years caught up with the moody, frustrated man: it is thought he killed two Métis companions, then shot himself.

His madness may indirectly have caused many more deaths. A fourth journey might have produced chart corrections to save Franklin's 1845 expedition from disaster.

The skeletons of seven members of Franklin's 1845 expedition were found in 1931 by a Hudson's Bay Company search party on an island in Douglas Bay on the southeast shore of King William Island. They were buried where they were found and a cairn was erected on the spot.

Who did discover the Northwest Passage?

Perhaps the honor should go to Lieut. Graham Gore. He may have travelled far enough south to discover that King William "Land" was an island, that no land barrier lay between their position in the ice of Victoria Strait and Queen Maud Gulf—although indeed the ice barrier was as impassable as if it had been land.

Comdr. Robert McClure was the first to travel the Northwest Passage from one end to the other. On a Franklin rescue mission from the Pacific in 1852 he left his ship off Banks Island, walked across the ice to Melville Island, and sailed to the Atlantic in another search vessel.

The first journey through the Northwest Passage entirely by ship was in 1903-06. The Norwegian Roald Amundsen, in the ship *Gjoa,* followed Franklin's route to Cornwallis Island and down Peel Sound, then passed east of King William Island through Rae Strait and Simpson Strait, and went on by way of Queen Maud, Coronation and Amundsen gulfs to the Beaufort Sea.

The first Canadian ship (and second ship ever) to cross the Arctic was the RCMP schooner *St. Roch* under Sgt. Henry Larsen, going from west

to east in 1940-42. In 1944, going east to west, *St. Roch* became the first ship to make the passage in one season and the first to traverse the passage both ways.

Roald Amundsen in *Gjoa* and Sgt. Henry Larsen in *St. Roch* both passed not far from Starvation Cove.

A cenotaph in memory of Sir John Franklin and his officers and men (and paid for by Lady Franklin) was erected in 1855 on Beechey Island close to the graves of three who died there.

Heritage Sites

KING WILLIAM ISLAND, N.W.T. Victory Point, off which the Franklin expedition abandoned its icebound ships April 22, 1848, and where the only known document left by the expedition was found, is about 100 miles northwest of the settlement of Gjoa Haven. A rebuilt cairn is believed the one in which the document was discovered in 1857. It now contains a survival kit. The graves of seven of Franklin's men are in Gjoa Haven. Equipment, skeletons and graves from the expedition have been found on the island's west and southeast coasts. *Gjoa Haven accessible only by air.*

Other sites

Beechey Island, N.W.T. (2) A white stone cenotaph commemorates the Franklin expedition, which wintered here in 1845-46. Beside the monument are the graves of three of Franklin's crew. *Accessible only by special arrangement.*

Calgary (not shown) A two-wheeled wooden cart used by Edward Parry's expedition while wintering at Melville Island in 1819-20 is in the Glenbow-Alberta Institute.

Elizabeth Harbour, N.W.T. (5) A boiler from John Ross's *Victory*, the first steamship in the Arctic, lies where it was abandoned in 1829. *Accessible only by special arrangement.*

Fury Beach, N.W.T. (3) Nails, chains and barrel staves from Parry's ship *Fury*, crushed by ice in 1825, are still here. Traces of a house in which John Ross and his men wintered in 1832-33 also remain. *Accessible only by special arrangement.*

Greenwich, England (not shown) The Franklin expedition document found at Victory Point, one of Franklin's medals

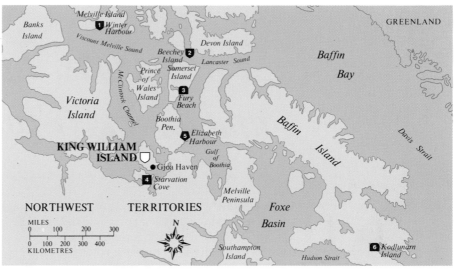

Main site (Monument)   Monument   Ruins   Other   Unmarked site

(obtained from the Inuit by Dr. John Rae), and portraits of Franklin's officers are in the vast Arctic exploration collection of the National Maritime Museum.

Kodlunarn Island, N.W.T. (6) Depressions in the ground are where Martin Frobisher and his men mined what they thought was gold ore in 1577 and 1578. Nearby are the ruins of a stone house they built. *Accessible only by special arrangement.*

Regina (not shown) A brass cannon from John Ross's *Victory* is in the RCMP Museum. Other exhibits include a model of the schooner *St. Roch* (see Vancouver) and her original crow's-nest and telescope.

Starvation Cove, N.W.T. (4) Bones found by Inuit in the 1850s were the remains of about 30 Franklin expedition members who trekked farther south than any of

their fellows. All apparently perished here. *Accessible only by special arrangement.*

Vancouver (not shown) The 104-foot RCMP schooner *St. Roch*, first ship to navigate the Northwest Passage from west to east (1940-42), is in the Vancouver Maritime Museum.

Winter Harbour, N.W.T. (1) A plaque on Parry's Rock, a 10 foot-high sandstone mass, records that Edward Parry and the crews of *Hecla* and *Griper* spent the winter of 1819-20 here. *Accessible only by special arrangement.*

Yellowknife, N.W.T. (not shown) An exhibit in the Prince of Wales Northern Heritage Centre traces the search for the Northwest Passage. Among the displays are supplies from a stone storehouse built in 1853 for the Franklin expedition.

No Mere Sled Dogs, They Were Men's Hope for Arctic Survival

To Arctic explorers (as to the Inuit) the Eskimo dog was essential to survival.

It probably descended from dogs brought from Siberia by migrating Inuit some 10,000 years ago. When Arctic exploration began, Eskimo dogs were 20-28 inches at the shoulder and weighed 60-85 pounds. They sniffed out musk-ox, located seals' breathing holes in the ice and held polar bears at bay. They warned humans away from thin ice and led lost hunters home

through blizzards. A team of a dozen or more could haul twice its weight for up to 60 miles a day.

They had a woolly undercoat up to two inches thick impregnated with waterproofing oils, and guard hair three to six inches long. Broad "snowshoe" feet, thickly padded with fur, enabled them to run easily on snow and ice. They ate about six pounds of fish or meat a day but often worked without food for days at a time.

Three Forts, Three Men and a New Crown Colony

George Simpson, a Scot who drove himself as hard as he did underlings, rose from obscurity to become the all-powerful governor of the largest fur-trading empire in North America—the Hudson's Bay Company.

Three Hudson's Bay Company forts and three remarkable HBC men dominated British Columbia in the 35 turbulent years that led to its designation as a Crown colony in 1858 and set the stage for Canada's extension to the Pacific. The forts were Langley, Vancouver (near present-day Portland, Oreg.) and Victoria. The men were George Simpson, John McLoughlin and James Douglas. One of these—Douglas—became known as the father of British Columbia and his Fort Victoria became the B.C. capital.

In 1824 the HBC still moved all furs to the Pacific at Fort Vancouver by way of the Columbia River. This was the Oregon Territory. It was held jointly by Britain and the United States but the U.S. wanted to colonize it and to establish the border along the 49th parallel—already the frontier east of the Rockies. HBC Governor George Simpson had to find a new river route to a new Pacific headquarters. He sent scouts to explore the Fraser River.

They explored only about 10 miles of the river but found it "a noble and majestic stream" rich with salmon, in a land full of beaver, a land fertile for farming. They identified a likely site for a fort and there, three years later, 25 HBC men built a dwelling and a storehouse inside a 120-by-135-foot palisade with bastions of squared logs eight inches thick. On Nov. 26, 1827, the fort was given the name Langley, after an HBC director. This was to be Simpson's new headquarters.

George Simpson—behind his back they called him the Little Emperor—stood only five-foot-six but he was as tough and scrappy as a fighting cock. Words were his favored weapons but he occasionally resorted to force and flogged wayward voyageurs. He started each day with a dive into icy water and sometimes snowshoed to distant forts to make surprise visits. He seldom spoke of

Fort Langley, the birthplace of British Columbia, has been reconstructed in Fort Langley National Historic Park. One of the original Hudson's Bay Company buildings survives—the large one in the photograph below. Originally a cooper's shop, it has been converted into a warehouse. Left: trade goods and furs are displayed inside the warehouse. Extreme left: at the corner of the fort is a bastion that was both lookout and arsenal and also served as sleeping quarters.

his origins, perhaps because he was illegitimate, born in Scotland in 1786 or 1787. In 1820 he joined the HBC and came to Canada. Within a year he was governor of the northern department, between Hudson Bay and the Rockies, the HBC territory richest in furs.

That same year—1821—the North West Company merged with the HBC and the fur trade became an HBC monopoly. To celebrate, Simpson held a feast at York Factory on Hudson Bay. The Nor'Westers walked into the dining room in silence, at first refusing to mingle with their hosts. Simpson bowed, smiled, shook hands, and persuaded the guests to relax and sit down. Conversation was difficult as Nor'Westers faced HBC factors who had been deadly rivals, but the diplomatic new governor kept the peace.

Not long after that, Simpson proved his worth as a ruthlessly efficient administrator: he dismissed half the men and cut the wages of the rest. He often left his home at York Factory (and a later home at Lachine, Que.) to inspect trading posts across the West, from Lower Fort Garry (present-day Selkirk, Man.) to Fort Vancouver in Oregon. In 1826 he became governor for all of the HBC's North American territory.

In 1827 he was convinced that the Fraser was navigable from the interior (New Caledonia) to its mouth. He had yet to test the waterway. On July 12, 1828, less than a year after Fort Langley was built, he left York Factory to inspect the trading posts in New Caledonia. He led a gaudy

cavalcade in which French-Canadian voyageurs wielding red paddles sang in seemingly endless chorus, and a kilted Highland bagpiper played as the governor made notes about the trip. They travelled every day from 2 a.m. to 8 p.m. with only a 10-minute break at noon for a lunch of pemmican. As they approached each trading post the inspection party put on blue uniforms to impress the Indians, and they arrived to a fanfare of pipes and gunfire. They reached Fort St. James on Stuart Lake, the chief post in New Caledonia, on Sept. 17. Then they travelled about 175 miles down the northern section of the Fraser to Fort Alexandria and rode across country to Fort Kamloops on the Thompson River.

In early October, Simpson and his men descended the Thompson to its junction with the Fraser at Lytton, intending to follow the Fraser to Fort Langley in their hastily constructed light craft. The rock-strewn Fraser squeezed through its steep canyon in a fury of foaming white water, and several times, despite the skill of Simpson's "Iroquois Bowsman who [was] nearly amphibious," threatened to fling the party onto the rocks. Simpson wrote: "I should consider the passage down, to be certain Death, in nine attempts out of Ten."

By the time Simpson reached the Fraser's calmer waters, near the ocean, he realized the river was not "a practicable communication with the interior." Fort Langley could never be the HBC's Pacific headquarters.

A fur press that the Hudson's Bay Company used at Lower Fort Garry (to compress furs into 90-pound bales) is on display in the fort's fur loft building (right). The fort, at Selkirk, Man., is now part of a national historic park.

But Langley's own produce made it a valuable supply depot. Beaver and marten skins were sent to Europe, salted salmon and cedar shingles to the Hawaiian Islands, cranberries to California, even ice to Hong Kong. A 2,000-acre farm up-river made the fort self-sufficient except for clothing, tea and tobacco.

Furs would still have to reach the Pacific via the Columbia River and Fort Vancouver, head-quarters of the HBC's Columbia District. The chief factor there was Dr. John McLoughlin. Simpson had appointed him in 1824 because of his experience in dealing with the company's American rivals when he ran a small HBC post at Lac la Pluie (near present-day Fort Frances, Ont.).

A farmer's son, born near Rivière-du-Loup, Que., in 1784, McLoughlin was licensed to prac-tise medicine at 19 and that same year joined the North West Company as a £20-a-year apprentice doctor. He became a wintering partner (trader) but as the Nor'Westers neared bankruptcy he shifted his allegiance to the HBC. More than six feet tall, with prominent blue eyes and a shock of shoulder-length white hair, McLoughlin was especially formidable when clad in his factor's uniform of beaver hat, frock coat and tartan cloak.

McLoughlin faced fierce competition in Ore-gon from Americans who had recently moved into the Pacific Northwest. A confrontation over

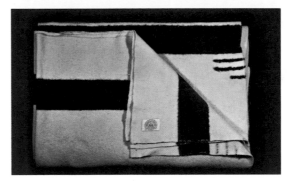

The thin lines (points) on a Hudson's Bay blanket indicate its size and weight. This 2½-pointer is 11 feet by 50 inches and weighs 6 pounds 11 ounces.

Fort St. James, on Stuart Lake about 600 miles north of Vancouver, was built by the North West Company in 1806 and became a Hudson's Bay Company post in 1821 when the companies merged. It was used by the HBC until the late 1940s and is now a na-tional historic park.

Wedded Bliss Was Country Style in the Northwest

White men in the Northwest in the early 1800s were thousands of miles from white women and many took In-dian or Métis wives. A native wife taught her husband the local dialect and customs, repaired his canoe, helped make his traps, skinned the catch and prepared the hides. This earned her food and clothing for her-self and her children, and such luxuries as tea and sugar.

These marriages were *à la façon du pays* (country style), seldom witnessed or recorded, but many couples re-mained together for decades. Eventu-ally, however, most men were trans-ferred or ordered home. Some stayed, taking up new careers as farmers; others left, abandoning their "country" dependants for the company to look after. Many a man found (or paid) an Indian or another white man to take his place.

The Hudson's Bay Company at first forbade such marriages, fearing the ex-pense of children. But when the North West Company encouraged these liai-sons, the HBC was forced to follow suit or lose personnel to its rival. HBC Gov-ernor George Simpson, after fathering three children on his travels, took Mar-garet Taylor, a Métis, as his wife in 1826. Chief factors John McLoughlin and James Douglas also married Métis.

But Simpson went to England in 1829 (leaving what he called his "com-modity" and two children in the care of a chief factor) and returned with an 18-year-old English bride, Frances. Eventually Frances fell ill and returned to England. But she had brought "re-spectability" and *it* stayed on. Country marriages were legalized by mission-aries. And fathers with Indian or Métis wives insisted on proper marriage vows for their daughters.

York boats, first built by the Hudson's Bay Company at York Factory, were used throughout western Canada in the mid-19th century. Boats such as this one in the Saskatchewan River at re-created Fort Edmonton (above) carried as much as several canoes could. Most were 40 feet long, built of wood, with crews of from 8 to 15.

control of the territory was inevitable and McLoughlin, a Canadian, at first seemed unwaveringly loyal. But George Simpson came to distrust McLoughlin. While supposed to be protecting HBC interests in the Columbia District, he was in fact encouraging American immigration.

Fort Vancouver under McLoughlin became the biggest HBC post on the Pacific. But McLoughlin, who sympathized with Reformers in Upper and Lower Canada, came to believe that governments there were despotic. He was sure the American government was just.

Simpson criticized his chief factor for generosity to American colonists but did not dismiss him for fear McLoughlin would set up a rival company. In 1842 their quarrel became bitterly personal when McLoughlin accused Simpson of not making a proper investigation into the murder of McLoughlin's son at a company post.

As McLoughlin raged against his superior, the character of the Columbia District was being changed dramatically. Nine hundred immigrants arrived by wagon train in 1843, bringing the population to 1,200. Some settlers brought

Homicide at Stikine—and John McLoughlin Fights for His Son's Name

Flags were at half-mast at Fort Stikine (near modern Wrangell, Alaska) and there was no sign of the fort commander, John McLoughlin, Jr., as Hudson's Bay Company Governor George Simpson arrived April 25, 1842, on a tour of inspection.

Four nights earlier, Simpson was told by the men at the fort, McLoughlin (son of HBC chief factor John McLoughlin) had gone on a rampage and one had killed him in self-defence. McLoughlin was a heavy drinker, they said, and had regularly abused them.

Simpson knew that McLoughlin had once caroused and wasted money, but believed he had since settled down.

Simpson told the elder McLoughlin his son's conduct was disgraceful and the fort had been mismanaged. It had been a "justifiable homicide" and no charge would be laid.

The grieving father, who disliked the imperious Simpson, launched his own investigation and found that young McLoughlin alone had to control some of the company's rowdiest men. When he tried to stop their nightly revels, they

plotted his death. He knew of his danger but kept at his work. An audit of his books showed everything in order. His liquor allowance had barely been touched.

In 1843, overwhelmed by protests from McLoughlin, Sr., the company cleared the son's name. But the father's dislike for Simpson turned to hatred and his loyalty to the HBC dissolved. Later, he would be accused of subverting HBC interests on the Pacific and encouraging American settlement in what became the state of Oregon.

The Paddlewheeler That Looked Like a Man-of-War

She was small but psychologically huge, a water-borne trading post with a towering smoke stack, churning paddle wheels and wood- and coal-burning engines. She was the Hudson's Bay Company's 101-foot, 109-ton *Beaver*, first steamship in the North Pacific. To Dr. J. S. Helmcken of the HBC, "She had the appearance of a small man-of-war, had four brass cannon, muskets and cutlasses in racks round the mainmast, and hand grenades in safe places."

The London-built *Beaver* arrived at Fort Vancouver (near present-day Portland, Oreg.) in 1836, and became vital in the HBC's struggle to control the North Pacific fur trade. American sailing vessels were no match for her. When the wind dropped, *Beaver* steamed on at up to 8½ knots. And she could enter coves and inlets inaccessible to sailing ships.

Beaver terrified the Coastal Indians. They believed the vessel carried a fire devil or ran by witchcraft. Awestruck Bella Bella fashioned a crude replica: a covered dugout, painted black

and powered by braves with bright red paddles.

Beaver served for more than 20 years, allowing the HBC to reduce the number of its forts on the North Pacific. In 1863 she became a British Admiralty survey ship, then was sold to a towing company. In July 1888 she ran onto rocks at the entrance to Vancouver harbor and was left to rot. Four years later she slipped to the bottom.

prejudice to Oregon, threatening to force out any white with an Indian or half-breed wife. (McLoughlin's wife was part Ojibwa). They heard false reports that the British, through HBC traders and Indian allies, had killed 500 Americans, and some settlers spoke of attacking Fort Vancouver. Even McLoughlin reported to HBC headquarters in London that some Americans, "desperate and reckless characters," had tried to seize company land. American settlers formed a provisional government three years before he retired in 1846. Disillusioned with Americans but even more bitter toward his HBC superiors, McLoughlin stayed in the Oregon Territory when, in 1846, Britain and the United States signed the Oregon Treaty. Under its terms, the United States controlled the mainland south of the 49th parallel and the waters south of the Gulf of Georgia and the Strait of Juan de Fuca. Fort Vancouver was in the United States; Vancouver Island remained British.

John McLoughlin's successor at Fort Vancouver was his former assistant, James Douglas, like Simpson a man of mysterious background. Stout and dark-skinned, he was rumored to be an illegitimate mulatto, born sometime in 1803. Douglas began his career at 16 as a North West Company clerk and survived the merger with the HBC. At 25 he married 16-year-old Amelia Connolly, the daughter of New Caledonia's chief factor.

In 1843 Douglas built Fort Camosun (it was

renamed Fort Victoria that year) on the southeast tip of Vancouver Island. The fort was 300 feet by 330 with a palisade of 22-foot-long pickets cut by Indians who were paid in blankets—one for every 40 pickets.

Douglas worked well under John McLoughlin and as the doctor's successor. He became chief factor at Fort Victoria in 1849. (The British government had ceded Vancouver Island to the HBC in 1849 and Fort Victoria had succeeded Fort Vancouver as Pacific headquarters.) In 1851 Britain made Douglas, still HBC chief factor, the island's governor as well.

Fort Victoria was surrounded by forests of pine and cedar luxuriant in the moist, mild climate. British immigrants in the colony that rose around the fort planted gardens to soften the starkness of their homes. In 1855 Douglas opened a schoolhouse on the HBC's 900-acre Craigflower Farm—which already had a slaughterhouse and a flour mill. A year later Victoria (as it was called by then) had its own House of Assembly. Sixty-eight miles to the north, Colvilletown flourished as a coal-mining settlement and HBC fort. In 1860 it was renamed Nanaimo, from the name of the confederation of Indian tribes in the area.

By 1856 gold had been found on the upper Columbia River and within a year there were reports of finds on the Thompson and the Fraser in New Caledonia.

One Sunday morning in the spring of 1858, as

John McLoughlin, a chief factor of the Hudson's Bay Company, was suspected of pro-American bias. Nonetheless he met the competition of American traders head-on and made Fort Vancouver (near present-day Portland, Oreg.) the biggest HBC post on the Pacific coast in the late 1830s.

Victoria's colonists headed home from church, a ship from San Francisco landed about 450 miners from the played-out goldfields of California. They had been among the first to learn that the HBC had deposited gold in the mint at San Francisco. Now the Fraser River gold rush had started (see p. 235). Twenty thousand people passed through the town of 400 that year, sleeping in tents and in bushes. Within six weeks of the arrival of the first boatload, 200 new stores had opened as the gold-seekers bought supplies for their trek upriver.

Governor Douglas could not wait for instructions from London. As governor of Vancouver Island he had no authority on the mainland, yet he insisted that the flood of newcomers be brought under British law. He set up a police force to patrol the district. He appointed justices of the peace to control lawlessness at the goldfields and revenue officers to collect licence fees from the miners. Soon Britain declared the territory west of the Rockies a Crown colony and ended the HBC trading monopoly. If Douglas would resign from the HBC he would be named the colony's governor.

On a rain-soaked Nov. 19, 1858, James Douglas arrived at Fort Langley from Victoria. He disembarked from the old HBC steamer *Beaver* and stepped onto the muddy bank of the Fraser as an 18-gun salute was fired and the Union Jack was unfurled over the fort.

In the Big House, before an audience of 100, Judge Matthew Baillie Begbie read Queen Victoria's letter appointing Douglas governor of British Columbia. (The queen herself had chosen the name British Columbia.)

James Douglas, long a chief factor of the Hudson's Bay Company, resigned in 1858 to become the first governor of the colony of British Columbia. He was knighted five years later.

Colonial officials prepare to leave Fort Langley after the swearing in of Governor James Douglas in 1858. He became known as the "father of British Columbia."

Dr. John McLoughlin died a year before the birth of British Columbia—he had become an American citizen and would someday be called the Father of Oregon.

James Douglas, knighted in 1863 for his service to the Crown as one of the founders of British Columbia, died at Victoria in 1877.

George Simpson was knighted in 1841 for his service as governor of the Hudson's Bay Company. He died at Lachine, Que., in 1860. His fort still stands at Langley, B.C.

Christmas Bittersweet: Plum Duff and Moose Nose

At Hudson's Bay Company posts from Fort Vancouver to York Factory, Christmas was celebrated with feasting that made lonely Europeans more homesick than ever. With luck a man might taste plum duff as well as buffalo hump, perhaps served this day on bone china instead of a tin plate. But whatever the fare, Christmas was a day rich in sentiment— and tradition adapted to reality.

A wagon ox was sacrificed into passable "roast beef" at York Factory one year, while HBC people at Fort Vancouver dined sumptuously on such fruits of the wilderness as quails, cranes and "swans so fat that they swam in grease." Fort Edmonton's specialty was unborn buffalo, removed from the cow and boiled whole. Another delicacy was moufle, made from dried moose nose.

The Canadian artist Paul Kane, who spent the years 1846-49 painting and sketching the Indians of the Northwest, left also a word picture of the dance that followed the feasting at Fort Edmonton on Christmas night 1847. It was, he wrote, a picturesque mix of Indians with painted faces, voyageurs in bright sashes and decorated moccasins, and Métis "glittering in every ornament they could lay their hands on." One Cree girl "sported enough beads round her neck to have made a [fur] pedlar's fortune." To the boisterous scrape of a fiddle, grave Indians and Métis joined the HBC men in Northwest versions of Scottish reels.

Heritage Sites

FORT LANGLEY, B.C. The Hudson's Bay Company post where James Douglas was sworn in as the first governor of British Columbia on Nov. 19, 1858, has been partially reconstructed in 21-acre Fort Langley National Historic Park. Buildings inside a palisade of split logs are furnished in the style of the 1850s and include a replica of the Big House where company officers lived and where the swearing in took place. Craftsmen in a re-created artisans' building demonstrate the making of barrels such as those used for the export of salmon, and a warehouse–trading store (1840) contains furs, miners' gear and bulk provisions. The fort on this site was completed in 1841. The original Fort Langley (1827) was 2½ miles downstream.

Other sites

Campbell River, B.C. (1) Part of a totem pole with a carved likeness of William McNeill, captain of the HBC paddlewheeler *Beaver*, first steamship in the North Pacific, is displayed at the Campbell River Museum.

Edmonton (not shown) The fifth and final HBC post in this area, built in 1830, is re-created in 158-acre Fort Edmonton Park. Some 10 buildings, furnished in the style of 1846, include replicas of the Big House, a watchtower and the first windmill west of the Red River. York boats are moored in the North Saskatchewan River.

Fort St. James, B.C. (6) A fur warehouse and a clerk's house (c.1880) remain on the site of a North West Company post built in 1806 and taken over by the HBC in 1821 as its headquarters in New Caledonia (mainland British Columbia). James Douglas was an assistant factor here in the late 1820s.

Kamloops, B.C. (7) An HBC trading store built between 1821 and 1843 within Fort Kamloops has been reassembled in the Kamloops Museum. Exhibits include a fur press, traps and a wooden canteen.

Ladner, B.C. (4) A 15-foot granite obelisk at English Bluff, eight miles south, was erected in 1861 to mark the 49th parallel, the Canada-U.S. boundary established by the Oregon Treaty of 1846.

Nanaimo, B.C. (2) The Bastion, a blockhouse with two original cannon, remains from an HBC fort built in 1853 to accommodate Britons brought out by the company to dig coal. The Nanaimo Centennial Museum has trade goods including a blanket and beads from the city's HBC period (1852-62).

Selkirk, Man. (9) The last intact stone fur

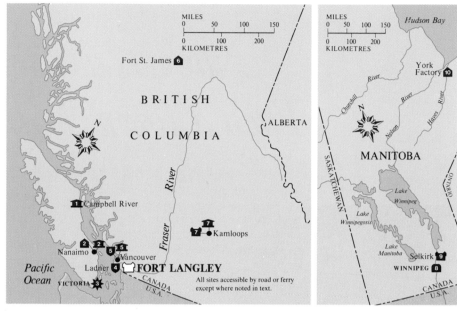

All sites accessible by road or ferry except where noted in text.

⌂ Main site (Fort) ✳ Multiple attractions ⬟ Historic building(s) ▮ Museum ♦ Monument ▮ Fort ● Ruins

trade fort, HBC headquarters in 1831-37, is in 85-acre Lower Fort Garry National Historic Park. Begun in 1830 by George Simpson to replace the original Fort Garry, 20 miles up the Red River at present-day Winnipeg, the new fort proved to be too out-of-the-way, and became a provision depot. The Big House, largest of the fort's 13 buildings, was the home of Simpson and his English bride, Frances. In a fur loft building are traps, axes, bales of wool, whisky casks and the furs of hundreds of animals. York boats and fur presses are displayed. Costumed attendants card and spin wool and make soap and candles.

Vancouver (5) A cairn at Prospect Point records that the paddlewheeler *Beaver* was wrecked near there July 26, 1888. The Vancouver Maritime Museum contains an anchor, pieces of hull and rigging, and coins and medals struck from metal from the ship.

Victoria (3)

BRITISH COLUMBIA PROVINCIAL MUSEUM Displays on the development of British Columbia include a model of Fort Victoria, founded by the HBC in 1843.

CRAIGFLOWER MANOR This two-storey house, completed in 1856, was the headquarters of an HBC farm which supplied Fort Victoria with meat, fruit and vegetables. It is now a museum and a national historic site containing furnishings and possessions of Kenneth McKenzie, the company representative who lived in it.

CRAIGFLOWER SCHOOL The oldest (1855) school west of the Great Lakes, now a museum of pioneer life, has a schoolroom and farm implements.

FORT VICTORIA A plaque at Government and Courtenay streets marks where James Douglas founded Fort Victoria. The Crown colony of Vancouver Island was created seven years later, in 1850, after the fort had consolidated British claims to the island.

HELMCKEN HOUSE Built in 1852 by Dr. J. S. Helmcken of the HBC, this log dwelling is now a museum displaying 19th-century furnishings and Helmcken's medical instruments. Helmcken was the first Speaker of the Legislative Assembly of the Crown colony of Vancouver Island (1856) and helped negotiate British Columbia's entry into Confederation in 1871.

MARITIME MUSEUM Two three-foot models of *Beaver* (one as the ship appeared in 1836, the other as she looked in 1880) are displayed. Cannon and a ship's wheel are believed from *Beaver*.

Winnipeg (8) One gate of Upper Fort Garry, reconstructed by George Simpson in 1835, still stands in Fort Garry Park.

York Factory, Man. (10) A fur warehouse and administrative building (c. 1835) remains from the HBC post where North West Company and HBC men met in 1821 following the merger of the companies. The two-storey building contains an interpretive centre and is a national historic site. *Accessible only by air.*

Nuggets as Big as Eggs, Then a Town Named for Billy

Billy Barker was broke. It was August 1862 and he was digging a crude mine shaft in rock and gravel beside Williams Creek downstream from Richfield Canyon in British Columbia's Cariboo Mountains. He and six partners were at 50 feet and still had not found gold. Perhaps there was none there; perhaps it was all upstream where some miners were daily panning gold worth $2,000 to $3,000. But Billy would not quit. He had a recurring dream in which the number 52 kept appearing. Let's give it a couple more feet, he urged, a few more hours.

Next day, Aug. 21, Barker picked, shovelled and sweated as usual as bucket after bucket of worthless gravel was hauled to the surface. Then, *at 52 feet,* he saw gold nuggets as big as eggs. A mother lode! That night, in the saloons of Rich-field, Billy threw a party that ended only when the liquor ran out.

Prospectors hurried to Williams Creek to stake claims near Billy's. A town of tents, shacks and stores soon sprang up along the creek and in honor of Billy it was named Barkerville, soon to be called Gold Capital of the World.

The Cariboo gold rush had begun in 1858 when news leaked out that prospectors had exchanged B.C. gold dust and nuggets for money at the San Francisco mint. Men from the exhausted California goldfields sailed on every available ship to pick up supplies at Victoria on Vancouver Island (then a separate colony) before heading for the Fraser River on the B.C. mainland. Far up the Fraser they might find El Dorado.

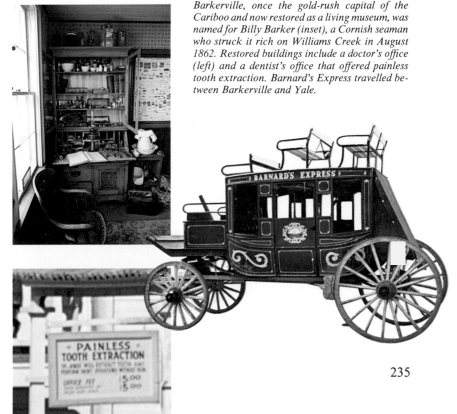

Barkerville, once the gold-rush capital of the Cariboo and now restored as a living museum, was named for Billy Barker (inset), a Cornish seaman who struck it rich on Williams Creek in August 1862. Restored buildings include a doctor's office (left) and a dentist's office that offered painless tooth extraction. Barnard's Express travelled between Barkerville and Yale.

235

This painting of a Cariboo miner is by an artist who himself dug for gold—and found none. William Hind was in the Overlander expedition of 1862 (see opposite page), sketching along the way. After a try at prospecting, he went back to art, opening a studio in Victoria.

Gold-seekers bound for the Cariboo fought their way through the narrow canyon of the often swollen and turbulent Fraser.

Snow had been heavy in the winter of 1857-58 and the always turbulent Fraser River now raced to the sea in a torrent. Many men were drowned, swept from overloaded canoes and scows and tipsy rafts towed by wheezy steamers. At Fort Hope the route turned north into the Fraser Canyon. The stern-wheeler *Umatilla* struggled for five hours to go the 15 miles from Fort Hope to Yale. The downstream return trip took 51 minutes.

Rapids made water travel extremely dangerous beyond Yale. Nor was travel by land easy. Men raged and cursed as pack horses bogged down in the muddy banks. Those unable to afford animals strained under huge loads. When they came to sandbars where they expected to find gold, the high water made it impossible to work them. Thousands of miners turned back, denouncing this gold rush as the Fraser River Humbug. By winter only 3,000 of 25,000 who had come to the Fraser were still there.

Many of the 3,000 moved north, beyond Soda Creek. They climbed sheer rock walls, trekked narrow Indian trails, blazed paths through the forest. Laden with supplies, they crossed chasms on unsteady bridges of poles and branches. By the spring of 1860 most were washing gravel along the shores of Quesnel and Cariboo lakes. A few had ventured as far north as Fort George (present-day Prince George) and east onto the vast plateau inside the loop of the Fraser. Myriad creeks sliced the land into gullies and canyons. Deer and caribou tracks were everywhere and the game had no fear of man. The region came to be called the Cariboo.

One evening in late fall, four partners prospecting on a creek that runs into the Bowron River, in the heart of the Cariboo, found yellow stones

'Cataline' Caux, King of the Cariboo Packers

North of Yale, the head of navigation on the Fraser River, mule trains were the Cariboo miners' lifeline until the Cariboo Road was completed in 1865. One man above all others kept the mules moving: Jean Jacques "Cataline" Caux, king of the packers.

Hydraulic equipment, flour, champagne—whatever the miners ordered, he delivered. Despite forest fires, blizzards and washouts, he never failed to fulfill a contract. His pack trains had 16 to 48 mules, each carrying 250 to 400 pounds. It took about a month to cover the 400 miles from Yale to Barkerville.

Born in the mountainous Béarn region of France, Cataline was nicknamed after neighboring Catalonia in Spain. He always wore a silk kerchief but never socks—even in winter. Before

each trip he bought a new shirt, but attached a collar only on special occasions. On the trail he slept under the stars and lived on bannock, beans, game, and raw herbs and weeds steeped in vinegar.

Cataline was proud of his Canadian citizenship and his friendship with Judge Matthew Baillie Begbie (see p. 239). One time when feelings ran high against Begbie's frontier justice, Cataline was asked where he stood. He drew his long Mexican knife from his boot and replied: "I stand by the judge." Begbie heard and remembered the story. Cataline later squatted on a piece of land in the Cariboo and his right to it was challenged because he was not a citizen. Begbie met Cataline on the trail, held an impromptu court and naturalized him a legitimate "Canada boy."

The 'Fast, Safe Route' to Riches: It Wasn't

The "speediest, safest and most economical route to the gold diggings." That is what the British Columbia Overland Transit Company promised in the spring of 1862. More than 200 men and one pregnant woman with three children set out in May from Quebec and Ontario to seek gold in the Cariboo. They expected to travel by rail to St. Paul, Minn., and by wagon to the Rockies and through the Yellowhead Pass. Then they would drift pleasantly down the Fraser River to the goldfields.

At St. Paul a few of the "Overlanders" turned back. The others went on by foot, oxcart or river steamer to Fort Garry (Winnipeg) and bought ox-drawn Red River carts in which they creaked across the prairie. At the Yellowhead Pass the carts were abandoned and the Overlanders struggled through trackless forest (as shown in William Hind's painting). In late August they reached the turbulent Fraser.

Most elected to run the river with canoes and six 20-by-40-foot rafts they built. One man was drowned. But by Sept. 10 this group reached Fort George.

At Tête Jaune Cache a smaller group had struck off overland to the Thompson River. There they too built rafts; one man was drowned but the rest of the party reached Fort Kamloops on Sept. 13. The following day Mrs. August Schubert gave birth to the first white child born in the interior of British Columbia.

A few Overlanders went on to the goldfields. Only one found gold, but most stayed west, won over by a land that the transit company (accurate for once) had called "unequalled for its beauty and salubrity of climate."

in the gravel. One pan alone yielded nuggets worth $75. The news got out and by January 1861 four hundred miners were camping in holes in the snow along the creek, waiting to work their claims in the spring. By July there was a town of wooden houses and stores along the creek (by now called Antler Creek) and bars and gambling halls were doing a booming business.

More gold-bearing creeks were soon found in the Cariboo, including Lightning, Lowhee, Grouse and the really big one—Williams Creek. But after a good start Williams Creek panned ever more poorly. Soon it became known as Humbug Creek.

Until now gold nuggets had been found close to the surface; no one had dug to bedrock. A prospector named Jourdan decided to try. After 48 hours of digging he emerged from his shaft with gold worth $1,000. Soon Williams Creek rang with the noise of pick and shovel as an army of miners bored through the clay, lifting out gravel and washing it in sluice boxes. Some claims produced 40 pounds of gold in a day and, before the snows came, a town of tents and shacks arose around the diggings. It was called Richfield.

In the spring of 1862 the trail into the Cariboo was alive with prospectors, packers, merchants and ever-hopeful greenhorns. It was a well-trod trail but a heart and bone breaker nonetheless.

B.C. Governor James Douglas had begun to make the miners' way easier, starting construction of a wagon road north from Yale to the goldfields. Road gangs were pushing their way up

Panning for gold was a job for one man. He scooped a pan of dirt and gravel from the streambed, stirred it to break up lumps, and removed rocks and pebbles. Then, swirling the pan in the water, he washed away most of the dirt. He placed the remainder— gold dust, nuggets and fine sand—in the sun or by a fire. When it was dry, he blew away the sand and had his gold.

British army engineers directed construction of the Cariboo Road through the Fraser Canyon. In this painting by Rex Woods, log cribworks are built to form the roadbed and to shore up the canyon wall and prevent rock slides.

the west side of the canyon, engineers in the lead, blasting a path through the rock. Behind them was an army of sweating pick-and-shovel men—mostly Chinese (see below). When they could go no farther on the west side, a suspension bridge was thrown across the canyon near Spuzzum. Then the road edged along the cliffs on the east side. In the autumn of 1862 Douglas went up to inspect the season's work. "Passes of ominous fame, so notorious in the history of the country,

have lost their terrors," he wrote with pride—and exaggeration.

Billy Barker arrived at Williams Creek in the summer of 1862, when the days of easy takings were over. But capital and men were needed to fell trees, dig shafts, mine gold, construct water wheels. Barker and six partners, pooling their resources, formed the Barker Company. The only claims left were downstream from Richfield Canyon. Other miners laughed. The canyon,

Lonely Men Seeking Gold and Celestial Peace

North America was "The Golden Mountain" to thousands of men who left 19th-century China in search of work—and of money to send back to their poverty-stricken families.

Some 25,000 Chinese, most from overcrowded villages around Canton, went to California in the 1850s; many moved on to the Cariboo after 1858. By 1865 there were about 5,000 Chinese in and around Barkerville. Most lived in cabins at one end of town. The centre of their life was the *Chi Gung T'ong*, a secret society whose temple served

as community centre, employment office, medical clinic and court. It still stands.

Most Chinese led lonely lives, saving money to return home. They worked mines and sandbars abandoned by impatient whites or hired out as laborers, cooks and laundrymen. Some became shopkeepers.

About half of those who came to "The Golden Mountain" returned home. Sometimes the bones of those who died in America were sent to China for reburial, so their owners' spirits would find celestial peace.

they said, was a natural sluice box, trapping all the gold. It was a waste of time to stake anywhere else. Barker sank his shaft anyway and, at 52 feet, made history. From a claim just 600 feet long, he unearthed gold worth $600,000.

Soon 4,000 miners were working the 3,000 claims along Williams Creek, producing most of the $3,913,000 taken out of the Cariboo in 1863. But now the creek was devastated, crossed with muddy ditches and diverted into half a dozen channels by flumes (troughs) and sluices. The hills were denuded of trees. Huge banks of tailings (rubble from which ore has been extracted) were dumped on the flats. Over all this devastation was the never-ending din of the mines.

In the midst of the mess was Barkerville, the town that boasted it was the "largest community west of Chicago and north of San Francisco." But a city Barkerville was not. Its only street, 18 feet wide and always muddy, looked as if it had been thrown together by a drunken surveyor. Wooden buildings, crammed together, were on log stilts because sometimes tailings would divert the creek and send it flowing through town. Linking stores and houses were uneven wooden sidewalks, also on stilts.

Yet Barkerville lacked few services. A blacksmith arrived first, quickly followed by bankers, barbers, tinsmiths, brewers, laundrymen and restaurant and hotel men. Tradesmen opened and closed when they felt like it, as this advertisement in the local *Cariboo Sentinel* suggests: "HALLO! OLD JACK'S ALIVE! JUST RETURNED FROM BEING ON A BENDER! Fully prepared to Repair all BOOTS and SHOES. CHEAP FOR CASH."

Wages were $10 a day, compared with $2 on the "outside." Prices were high too: potatoes cost 90 cents a pound, butter $3, nails $1, flour $300 a barrel, a box of soap $20, a pair of boots $50, champagne $16 a bottle and up.

There were plenty of saloons—with gamblers, girls and big spenders. The greatest party of all was when "Red Jack" McMartin spent $44,000 in gold in the Shuniah Saloon. With the help of a crowd called in off the street, he drank or smashed every bottle of champagne in the place. He ended the festivities by hurling the last of his nuggets at his reflection in the $3,000 mirror over the bar. McMartin went out into the night, penniless, and never struck pay dirt again.

With completion of the Cariboo Wagon Road as far as Barkerville in 1865, some miners brought in their wives. In its heyday some 10,000 persons lived year round in the town.

In 1866 eight German women were brought to Barkerville from San Francisco to work in a saloon. They charged $10 a dance and were called Hurdy Gurdy Girls, after the instrument they danced to. At 2:30 p.m., Sept. 16, 1868, as one girl

was ironing a dress in the canvas-roofed kitchen at the back of a saloon, a miner came in and tried to steal a kiss. In the struggle, he knocked over a stovepipe. The canvas caught fire and within minutes the saloon was ablaze.

Barkerville was tinder dry after a summer of drought. The flames leaped from one building to another and across the narrow street. Even as the alarm sounded, the townspeople knew there was no point in fighting. People grabbed what belongings they could and fled to the creek and the

Up the Cariboo Road Came Begbie—and Law

Judge Matthew Baillie Begbie, according to one miner, was "the biggest man, the smartest man, the best-looking man, and the damnedest man that ever came over the Cariboo Road." It was a fair verdict.

Over six feet tall, with the physique of a prizefighter, Begbie brought law and order to the Cariboo. He seemed fearless. One day in Clinton, through the open window of his hotel room, he heard men on the street below plotting to shoot him. He brought his chamber pot to the window and emptied it on their heads.

Begbie was 39 when he came from England in 1858 to be British Columbia's first judge. He roamed the interior on horseback, holding court in cabins, barns, tents and fields—as well as in courthouses such as the one still standing at Richfield, near Barkerville. Sometimes he was prosecution, defence and judge all in one. He cared nothing for the written law, everything for justice.

He sometimes quarrelled with a jury's verdict. With the acquittal of a man clearly guilty of sandbagging another in a barroom brawl, Begbie snarled: "Prisoner at the bar, the jury have said you are not guilty. You can go, and I devoutly hope the next man you sandbag will be one of the jury."

Begbie was unjustly called "The Hanging Judge." Hanging was then the only penalty for murder and he never condemned a man who had not been convicted by a jury. Sometimes he tried to have death sentences commuted.

Begbie's rough and ready justice saved the colony from the wild excesses of the American West, and in 1870 he became its first chief justice. He was knighted in 1875 and died June 11, 1894, having ordered that his grave be marked by a simple cross inscribed *Lord, be merciful to me, a sinner.*

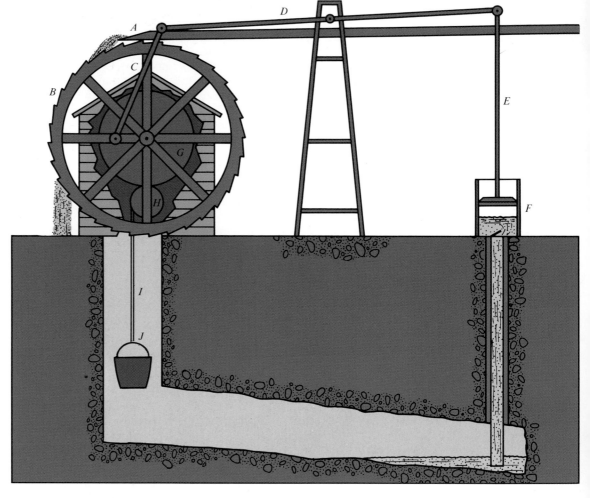

A wheel (below) at Fort Steele, B.C., is typical of water wheels used in the Cariboo. Water from a flume (A) filled individual compartments (B) on the rim of the wheel. The water's weight turned the wheel and activated a connecting arm (C), rocker arm (D) and push rod (E). The wheel thus operated both a pump (F) to draw water out of the mine, and a flywheel (G) and a winch (H) with a rope (I) that hauled an ore bucket (J) to the surface.

hillsides. Someone had the good sense to remove 50 kegs of blasting powder from a store in the path of the fire. In little more than an hour it was over. *The Cariboo Sentinel* reported that only "charred timbers and heaps of rubbish marked the spot where stood the metropolis of Cariboo." The newspaper reported 116 buildings destroyed and estimated the damage at $678,200.

Six days later 30 new buildings had been put up along a now wider street, with level sidewalks and spaces for cross streets. But Barkerville's glory days were over. The gold was harder to get at and small companies and miners' partnerships were being liquidated or sold to large ones able to finance costly equipment. The "free miner" with his pick, shovel and wash pan had moved on to creeks leading into the Kootenay and Columbia rivers to the east, the Stikine and Peace to the north. These new goldfields were not as rich as the Cariboo but they caused the British government to extend the boundary of British Columbia north to the 60th parallel (now the British Columbia-Yukon border).

Governor Douglas had retired in 1864, his dream of a great road to the goldfields a reality.

But it had been costly. In 1866 the combined debt of Vancouver Island and British Columbia was $1,296,681. It was decided, for the sake of economy, to merge the two colonies: united British Columbia came into being Nov. 19. Victoria was named the capital May 24, 1868. Three years later, lured by John A. Macdonald's promise of a railway linking eastern Canada to the Pacific coast, the young colony decided to join the Canadian Confederation. On July 20, 1871, British Columbia became a province.

In just 13 years a land known only to Indians and fur traders had been transformed into a fragile frontier colony, then into a province of a proud new nation. It was the Cariboo miner who had opened up this territory.

Governor Douglas was knighted and settled in Victoria. There he died at 74, the richest man in British Columbia. He had invested not in gold but in Victoria's choicest real estate.

Billy Barker married a widow with expensive tastes. When his money ran out, so did she. Barker, like Douglas, ended his days in Victoria, aged 74, but in an old men's home. They buried poor Billy in a pauper's grave.

Heritage Sites

BARKERVILLE, B.C. Some 75 buildings from the 1860s—when this was the gold-rush capital of the Cariboo—have been restored or reconstructed in 160-acre Barkerville Historic Park. They include hotels, saloons, a gold commissioner's office, a stagecoach depot and the office of *The Cariboo Sentinel*. Among buildings in the Chinese quarter are a trapper's cabin and community centre (the Masonic Hall). Visitors can ride horses and pan for gold.

BARKERVILLE HISTORICAL MUSEUM A watch, gold poke and axe used by Billy Barker, whose strike was the start of Barkerville, are among displays in this interpretive centre.

BILLY BARKER'S SHAFT Here, on Aug. 21, 1862, Barker discovered gold in Williams Creek.

RICHFIELD COURTHOUSE One mile south, along a preserved section of the Cariboo Road, is a restored courthouse where Judge Matthew Baillie Begbie presided. An actor plays Begbie.

THEATRE ROYAL Vaudeville, such as the miners saw, is presented in a wooden playhouse.

WAKE-UP-JAKE Sourdough bread and stew are still served at this "Coffee Saloon and Lunch House."

Other sites

Ashcroft, B.C. (9) The Ashcroft Museum has gold pans, scales and miners' lamps, and Chinese artifacts that include musical instruments, wine bottles and tiles for the game of mah-jong. Nearby Ashcroft Manor, a famous stop on the Cariboo Road, still welcomes travellers.

Cache Creek, B.C. (7) This is the southern end of the modern 260-mile Cariboo Highway to Barkerville. Several miles of the old Cariboo Road can be traced—often by two rows of snake fences that marked the right-of-way. Hat Creek

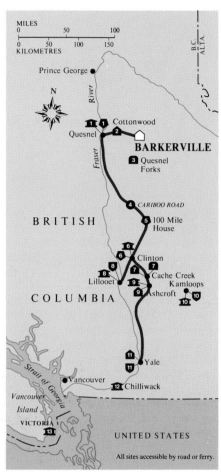

MILES
0   50   100
0   50   100   150
KILOMETRES

Prince George

Cottonwood
Quesnel
BARKERVILLE
Quesnel Forks
CARIBOO ROAD
100 Mile House
BRITISH
Clinton
Cache Creek
Kamloops
Lillooet
Ashcroft
COLUMBIA
Yale
Vancouver
Chilliwack
Vancouver Island
VICTORIA
UNITED STATES

All sites accessible by road or ferry.

⌂ Main site (Historic buildings)   ▲ Historic building(s)   ▲ Museum
◆ Monument   ■ Ruins   ● Route   ◆ Other

House, one of the oldest Cariboo Road stopping places, is 7½ miles north.

Cariboo Road (4) Highway 1 from Yale to Cache Creek, then Highway 97 to Quesnel and Highway 26 to Barkerville follow the approximate course of the 400-mile Cariboo Road, completed in 1865. The earliest section, built in 1861 and later bypassed, ran from Lillooet to Clinton. (Lillooet was at the end of the Harrison Trail from Chilliwack. Many roadhouses—such as 100 Mile House—based their names on the mileage from Lillooet.)

Chilliwack, B.C. (12) A museum at the Royal Canadian School of Military Engineering portrays the building of the Cariboo Road.

Clinton, B.C. (6) Ore samples, a prospec-

A miner's cabin dating from the early 1870s is among the reconstructions at Barkerville. Most cabins were near the miners' claims, far from "downtown." This one is on the re-created community's main street.

tor's griddle and a replica of a Cariboo Road freight wagon are at the South Cariboo Historical Museum. The three-day Clinton Ball in May relives the town's early days at the junction of the earliest Cariboo Road from Lillooet and the later one from Yale.

Cottonwood, B.C. (2) The only complete, preserved roadhouse between Yale and Barkerville is in Cottonwood House Historic Provincial Park. Log buildings dating from 1864 include an inn, stables and a general store (now a museum of farm implements). A working stagecoach transports visitors along the Cariboo Road, in the style of yesteryear.

Fort Steele, B.C. (not shown) The Kootenay gold rush of 1864 is commemorated in 371-acre Fort Steele Historic Park which has a 32-foot water wheel, a ferry office built in 1864, and a museum exhibiting gold pans and sluice boxes. There are traces of gold diggings at Wild Horse Creek, four miles east. Prospectors' graves are in the nearby cemetery.

100 Mile House, B.C. (5) A Cariboo Road stagecoach is displayed outside the Red Coach Inn.

Kamloops, B.C. (10) Gold scales used in the 1850s are displayed in the Kamloops Museum. A plaque on the Yellowhead Highway 40 miles north commemorates the Overlanders of 1862 who reached Fort Kamloops.

Lillooet, B.C. (8) A cairn of stones from placer-mining streams marks the starting place of the earliest Cariboo Road. The Lillooet Museum displays bellows for pumping air into mines.

Quesnel, B.C. (1) Here the Cariboo Road turned east toward Barkerville. A water wheel stands near the Fraser River. The Quesnel Museum displays mining equipment, a gold scale and a Chinese opium bottle.

Quesnel Forks, B.C. (3) Now a ghost town, this was a supply centre and stopping place on the original trail to Williams Creek.

Victoria (13) Exhibits in the British Columbia Provincial Museum include a Cariboo Road freight wagon and a water wheel set against a backdrop of Barkerville. Miners once recovered gold from sluice boxes fed by water from the wheel.

Yale, B.C. (11) A cairn marks the southern end of the 400-mile Cariboo Road to Barkerville. The Anglican Church of St. John the Divine, built in 1860 when miners flocked here after the discovery of gold at Hill's Bar, has the original brass candleholders and urns.

No Going Back, No Standing Still

Sir John A. Macdonald, Canada's first prime minister: "I don't care for office for the sake of money, but for the sake of power, and for the sake of carrying out my own views of what is best for the country."

Nothing, its people often said, could ever happen in drowsy Charlottetown. But suddenly, in August 1864, *too much* was happening and the community of 7,000 was hard pressed to find room for all the visitors.

For the first time in years there was a circus in town—the Slaymaker and Nichols Olympic Circus. Thousands descended on the little capital of Prince Edward Island, some from the mainland on steamers offering excursion rates, and from all over the tiny island in horse-drawn carriages that raised the red dust. Hotels and boarding-houses were jammed.

But the circus was not all. In the stone Colonial Building, citadel of government, there was to be a conference to discuss a proposed union of Britain's North American colonies. The gilded Legislative Council chamber with its big windows, Ionic pillars, long mahogany table and spectators' gallery was ready for delegates from Nova Scotia, New Brunswick and Canada. Few P.E.I. politicians were much interested and, in the circumstances, it was deemed sufficient to have only Provincial Secretary William Henry Pope greet the delegates. He was, after all, the only P.E.I. minister enthusiastic about the conference.

Then, because the steamer *Heather Belle* was late, and Pope gave up waiting, even he missed the Nova Scotians' arrival on Aug. 31—four delegates led by Charles Tupper, the belligerent doctor-premier with the mutton-chop whiskers. The Charlottetown *Examiner* complained that "they were suffered to find out, by rule of thumb, where they could get something to eat and a bed to lie upon."

Pope did show up at 11 that night when the crowded *Prince of Wales* reached Charlottetown. She carried the New Brunswick delegation of five headed by Premier Leonard Tilley, a druggist with a bent for finance and a taste for temperance. Somewhere Pope found lodgings for them.

Still to come were the delegates from Canada. They would be in a vessel of their own.

Late in the morning of Sept. 1 Pope hustled back to the waterfront and was disturbed to see the sleek Canadian government cruiser *Queen Victoria* already anchored in Hillsborough Bay. All he could find to convey him out to her was "a flat-bottomed boat with a barrel of flour in the bow and two jars of molasses in the stern, and with a lusty fisherman" at the oars. Mustering all the dignity he could, Pope set off.

His dignity took a second blow as he drew near the *Queen*. "Seated on an unclean barrel," he was shouted at by the ship's steward: "I say, skipper, what's the price of shellfish?"

Fortunately the Canadians were in their cabins, dressing. Soon they emerged, shining men on a shining summer's day, and were lowered to the harbor waters in the *Queen*'s two boats.

John A. Macdonald was there, the jaunty master of political manoeuvre who drank too much—but not when it mattered; George Brown, the puritanical journalist-politician; George-Etienne Cartier, the tough, eloquent French Canadian; Alexander Tilloch Galt, the financial wizard; D'Arcy McGee, the former Irish rebel with the magic tongue. There were three other cabinet ministers and three aides.

From his flat-bottomed perch, William Henry Pope uttered greetings. He suppressed his surprise at their numbers, knowing the town was so packed that some would have to sleep on the ship. He led them ashore, then along Great George Street to the Colonial Building. They climbed the stone steps to the Legislative Council chamber, and 14 Maritime delegates, including four from P.E.I. besides Pope, rose for introductions.

The impetus to seek nationhood had sprung not from patriotism but from frustration. The rebellions of 1837-38 in Upper and Lower Canada had led Britain in 1841 to bind the two colonies

The first formal meeting to discuss union of Britain's North American colonies was held in the Colonial Building (now Province House) in Charlottetown. The plaque behind the table, in what now is called the Confederation Chamber, records that "In the hearts and minds of the delegates . . . in this room . . . was born the Dominion of Canada."

Bad Equipment, Careless Crews Made Rail Tragedies Commonplace

At the edge of a marsh on the outskirts of Hamilton, Ont., where once there was a bridge, two big stone abutments brood in stark memorial to the victims of one of Canada's worst train disasters *(below)*—59 souls who perished March 12, 1857, in the hazardous early days of Canadian railroading.

They died because an axle snapped as the little steam locomotive *Oxford* approached the Great Western Railway's swing bridge over the Desjardins Canal. Momentum carried the engine forward, ragged steel ripped out the wooden floor of the bridge, and the *Oxford* and three passenger cars plunged 60 feet to the canal ice.

Accidents happened almost every day in the mid-1800s as railways were rushed to completion and went into service with crews that were poorly trained (if at all) and among whom carelessness was common, drunkenness by no means uncommon.

Equipment was badly designed and poorly constructed. Train movements were controlled by hand signal, flag and lantern. Brakemen leaped from the top of one swaying car to another to manipulate hand brakes. Cars were coupled manually and a slip could mean the loss of fingers, a hand or a life. Fencing was poor, cattle roamed many a right of way—and many an engineer *speeded up*, risking derailment as he smashed into an animal and knocked it clear. Level crossings were unprotected, roadbeds badly ballasted, wooden bridges shaky. Coaches were scarce and passengers often rode in boxcars and flatcars, even in winter. Timetables were often ignored.

There were financial problems as well. Promoters hired fast-talking salesmen to peddle railway stock but a large part of the development funds came from the United States. With the American Civil War in 1861, outside funds dried up and railway construction was dormant for 10 years.

The lines quickly became run down. The Great Western, for instance—the pride of Allan MacNab of the Family Compact—was in disrepair by 1860, only six years after it ran its first train.

Accidents continued. Even worse than the Desjardins Canal disaster was an accident—again at a swing bridge—on The Grand Trunk Railway at Beloeil, Que., on June 29, 1864. The bridge was open and a train carried 97 German immigrants to their deaths in the Richelieu River. A stone in Montreal's Mount Royal Cemetery commemorates the victims and marks the graves of 52 Protestants among them.

A greater memorial is a safety device. The Beloeil accident is said to have spurred the American inventor George Westinghouse, who in 1868 demonstrated the automatic air brake which bears his name.

The Canadian delegation to the Charlottetown conference watches from the cruiser Queen Victoria *as William Henry Pope, the P.E.I. colonial secretary, arrives to welcome them on Sept. 1, 1864. The painting is by Rex Woods. Some records indicate that a fisherman rowed Pope out in a scruffy dory.*

into one colony—Canada—with two sections, Canada West (Ontario) and Canada East (Quebec). Unless the government had a majority in each section, issues tended to divide the legislature on cultural lines, in bitter disputes between English and French. John A. Macdonald, leader of the Liberal-Conservative Party (popularly known as the Conservative Party) and the unequalled political tactician of his day, had achieved the necessary broad support in both Canadas, but kept it with ever-increasing difficulty. Finally even he was not able to obtain a clear majority. By June 1864 his government, the fourth in 13 months, fell. The Union was unworkable.

Then, as Macdonald and Cartier tried to build yet another cabinet, Macdonald's longtime political enemy George Brown sent word he would be willing to join a coalition to find a solution to Canada's constitutional problems. He was the moralistic, humorless leader of Canada West's Reformers (a wing of the Liberal Party), an abrasive Scot and editor-owner of *The Globe* in Toronto. Not only had he made a towering political concession, but also he had set aside his distaste for the pleasure-loving Macdonald. To accusations of party disloyalty Brown retorted:

"Party alliances are one thing and the interests of my country another." Now, with a coalition cabinet headed by Sir Etienne Taché, the way was clear to seek a union of the two Canadas and the Maritime colonies of New Brunswick, Nova Scotia and Prince Edward Island or, failing that, a new federation of Canada East and Canada West.

While Canada was contemplating this new political alliance, Arthur Gordon, the ambitious lieutenant-governor of New Brunswick, became convinced that he could find a niche in history by

This Halifax house was Charles Tupper's home—he called it Armdale—*during the Confederation negotiations and while he was premier of Nova Scotia. It is now an apartment building.*

The prince who became Edward VII used this silver trowel (with its beaver handle) in a ceremony in August 1860 marking completion of the Victoria Bridge at Montreal. It was the first bridge to span the St. Lawrence River and, only feet short of two miles long, it was one of the engineering marvels of the time.

promoting a *Maritime* union. No one was greatly interested but the three legislatures did express a willingness to discuss it. They had not even decided where or when to meet when they were shocked into action by Canada's request for permission to send delegates to the Maritime conference—to propose a confederation of *all* the colonies.

As the Charlottetown conference opened on Sept. 1, 1864, Tupper, Tilley and P.E.I.'s J. H. Gray, the premier-chairman, knew there was no desire in the Maritimes for major change. They were, said the Halifax *Morning Chronicle*, "on a full tide of prosperity" in their age of sailing ships (see p. 256). They looked outward to markets abroad, not inland to Canada. But the Canadians knew "we cannot go back. We cannot stand still." They knew as well that an enormous domain beckoned west to the Pacific and, as Macdonald said, "If Englishmen do not go there, Yankees will."

From the gallery, the Canadians watched the Maritimers quickly postpone the question of Maritime union and invite them to state their case. Now, 22 men from four colonies sat close around the long mahogany table and the wooing began.

The Canadians called first on Macdonald and

British North America's first postage stamp, issued May 23, 1851, in the Province of Canada, was gummed but not perforated. Individual stamps (¾ by 1 inch) had to be cut from a sheet. The design was by Sandford Fleming, inventor of standard time—and a friend of Postmaster General James Morris.

This ornate brick house in Toronto was the home of newspaper proprietor George Brown, founder of The Globe *and one of the Fathers of Confederation. Defeated in the election of 1867, he remained a power in the Liberal Party while concentrating his energies on his newspaper.*

Joseph Howe and 'The Botheration Scheme'

Joseph Howe—a journalist, orator and politician fiercely loyal to Britain and to the cause of Nova Scotia independence—was the archenemy of Confederation, the first Canadian separatist. He lost. But he fought a great fight.

Howe had won other battles—for freedom of the press and for responsible government (see p. 210). His Halifax *Novascotian* was as fine a newspaper as any in North America and he had served in the provincial assembly for 25 years (three as premier). In 1865, out of office, he wrote a series of 12 letters denouncing Confederation as "The Botheration Scheme" and within a year was the recognized leader of the anti-Confederationists. A Nova Scotia submerged in a union with other colonies, he argued, would lose all chance of independence and much valuable trade. He was outraged when pro-Confederation Premier Charles Tupper denied Nova Scotians a referendum on joining the union.

Howe, now in his 60s, stumped the province opposing Confederation. He promoted a monster petition and led delegations to London to try to win over British parliamentarians. But Confederation came about despite him.

Now *repeal* became his objective and he joined what he had been unable to beat: in the election of September 1867 he won a seat in the House of Commons in Ottawa (along with 17 other Nova Scotia anti-Confederationists). Howe returned to England, tried again and found the British government opposed to repeal. Back home, he said: "We may confess to final defeat [or] be driven . . . to take up arms." But he was a realist. By the end of 1868 he conceded that cries against Confederation were like "the screams of seagulls round the grave of a dead Indian on the coast of Labrador."

He helped negotiate better Confederation terms for Nova Scotia and in 1869 became a federal cabinet minister. But he never felt at home in Ottawa and in May 1873 he returned to Halifax as lieutenant-governor of Nova Scotia. Three weeks later he died.

Eliza Grimason, a lifelong friend and supporter of John A. Macdonald, ran the Grimason House (now the Royal Tavern) in Kingston, Ont., and after he became prime minister the inn was known as his unofficial political headquarters. Mrs. Grimason once said of Sir John A.: "There's not a man like him in the livin' earth."

Cartier, both lawyers, the one pragmatic, resourceful, a gifted manager of men, the other an 1837 rebel become French Canada's link with railways and industry. They gave the general arguments for confederation. In these two men was a fascinating, crucial balance. Macdonald was deeply alarmed by the powerful states' rights that had helped lead federated America into civil war, Cartier as deeply convinced that French Canada must have a local legislature, its own "states' rights" to protect its heritage.

If the conference recognized that disagreement between Macdonald and Cartier, it also saw the solution in the same two men, in compromise. Years earlier Macdonald had said of the French Canadians: "Treat them as a nation and they will act as a free people generally do—generously." He knew they must have their own legislature, if the major powers were reserved to the central government. Cartier accepted a dominating central government—given the legislature. And when they finished, Galt, the railway promoter, laid down the financial proposals. Then came Brown's Scots burr on the constitutional aspects.

Canada held out to the Maritimers the prospect of a railway to open markets in the West, assumption of their public debts, allowance for new debts, legislatures for local affairs, representation by population in an elected House of Commons, and Maritime representation in an appointed Senate equal to that of the two mainland provinces.

When the daily sessions ended, the wooing moved into a taxing round of parties, dinners and dances. Lieutenant-Governor George Dundas entertained at stately Government House. William Henry Pope entertained. Many others entertained. D'Arcy McGee spun transcontinental visions. Cartier led singsongs. Good fellowship abounded.

On the third day of the conference, while the delegates lunched in style aboard the Canadians' *Queen Victoria,* someone shouted: "If anyone can show just cause or impediment why the colonies should not be united in matrimonial alliance, let him express it or forever hold his peace." No one demurred. "The union," Brown wrote his wife, "was thereupon formally completed and proclaimed."

It was a sweeping statement but it rang true. The conference went on until Sept. 8, the partying too. When the island government gave a ball the last night, the scrubbed and decorated Colo-

247

Far From Any Battle, an Irish Hero Wins the V.C.

Ten years after Queen Victoria instituted the Victoria Cross "for conspicuous bravery in the presence of the enemy," a 20-year-old Irish soldier won the Empire's highest award far from the scene of any combat, at Danville, Que. Pte. Timothy O'Hea was honored "for conspicuous courage under circumstances of great danger"—an almost classic understatement.

On the afternoon of June 9, 1866, a train from Quebec stopped at Danville. Locked in converted boxcars were 800 German immigrants. In another boxcar was ammunition for use against Fenian raiders. O'Hea was one of four men of the 1st Battalion Rifle Brigade guarding the ammunition.

He noticed that the ammunition was on fire but when he shouted an alarm, railwaymen and the other soldiers fled. O'Hea got the keys of the burning car and climbed aboard. He ripped burning covers off ammunition cases and tossed them outside. Then, for almost an hour, making 19 trips to a creek for buckets of water, he fought the flames, the immigrants cheering him on, unaware of their peril.

O'Hea fought alone and he won. By evening the ammunition had been loaded into another car and the train—immigrant coaches still attached—was on its way again. O'Hea's was the only Victoria Cross ever won in Canada.

George-Etienne Cartier (this statue is in Montreal's Mount Royal Park) is best known as a Father of Confederation. But he was also a poet. His "O Canada, mon pays, mes amours" was set to music and was considered a possible national anthem.

nial Building overflowed: the council chamber was a reception room, the lower chamber across the hall was alive with dancers, the legislative library offered tea, coffee, sherry, claret, champagne, and dinner was in the Supreme Court room. Two bands played. The first quadrille began at 10, the governor's wife on Macdonald's arm; supper was well after midnight.

The ball climaxed events in Charlottetown. No resolutions had been passed but the Mari-

Bellevue House, which John A. Macdonald said reminded him of a pagoda, was at one time his home when he lived in Kingston, Ont., before becoming prime minister. One room (right) was occupied by his bedridden first wife, Isabella.

timers, Brown recorded, "were unanimous in regarding federation of all the Provinces to be highly desirable, if the terms of the union could be made satisfactory." The delegates agreed to meet again in Quebec in October to flesh the dream with reality.

Later, speaking at a dinner in Halifax, Macdonald proclaimed: "Everyone admits that union must take place sometime. I say now is the time. We will become a great nation."

The ghosts from 300 years of white men's history watched over the rock of Quebec, temporarily the Canadian capital, as the delegates assembled Oct. 10, 1864. Thirty-three of them now, including two from Newfoundland, crowded into the reading room of another Legislative Council, in a drab brick building that would be a post office once Ottawa's Parliament buildings were ready. Most delegates were confident that at Charlottetown they had reached agreement on most major points. They were wrong. Autumn rain blurred the majestic view of the St. Lawrence and matched the mood as arguments raged day and night. The pivots of discussion were 72 proposals prepared by the Canadians for the structure of government. The pivots of attack were the Maritimers' doubts.

The delegates argued over the Senate, over financial terms, over the division of powers between the two levels of government and—bitterly—over allegations that the provinces would become little more than municipalities. They granted the French language official status in the central Parliament and the federal courts. They made Parliament what they thought Macdonald, the conference chairman, wanted it to be: dominant.

Through it all, Macdonald stalked as the strong man of the hour, genial, firm, knowledgeable, the chief architect of nationhood. He was said to be the author of 50 of the 72 resolutions, yet he wished to lay down only the minimum of conditions for union. The constitution, he argued, "should be a mere skeleton and framework that would not bind us down." Passionately, he carried the case for giving "all the great subjects of legislation" to Parliament. Wrongly, he felt that time would wither what power the provinces got. He found time to flatter the visiting wives and daughters, to dance and talk with them at the parties. "I went to dinner and John A. sat beside me," a young lady said. "What an old humbug he is!"

Then, after 17 days, it was over, the original resolutions virtually intact. Some delegates headed home, others off to rousing receptions in Montreal, Ottawa, Kingston, Belleville and Toronto. All that remained was to get the approval of the various legislatures and then ask

Britain to sanctify in law this new, unique giant among her global possessions. Macdonald urged the legislatures to act "at a bound."

Most delegates left the Quebec conference confident that union would be accomplished within a year, by the fall of 1865. Macdonald moved that the Canadian legislature bring its own debate to a vote and Confederation was carried easily. But in the once pro-Confederation Maritimes, now at the height of their prosperity, opposition was growing. "Confederation will cost too much," cried the critics, led by former Premier Joseph Howe. "Why should our taxes pay for railroads and defence that will benefit Canada and not us?" Elections were called in all Atlantic Provinces to decide the issue of Confederation. Voters believed Howe and other critics, and three pro-union premiers went down to defeat. Only Tupper in Nova Scotia managed to remain in office, by saying that union of the colonies had become "impracticable." The dream of Confederation was falling apart.

Bad News in Ottawa: John A.'s 'Weakness'

"Bad news, Sir John has broken out again." So wrote the governor of the Hudson's Bay Company to the British prime minister in April 1870, near the end of the Red River Rebellion. After weeks of overwork John A. Macdonald had lapsed into one of his periodic drinking bouts.

The Canadian prime minister's "transient weakness" got him into embarrassing situations, but his charm and wit usually got him out. One time, after a dinner party, he was too unsteady to rise. Taking the arm of a Liberal he said: "You've never given me a vote yet, but you've got to support me now." At a rally, rising to speak after a Liberal, he threw up on stage. Quickly regaining his composure, he began: "Ladies and gentlemen, you must forgive me but . . . that man" (pointing to his opponent) "just makes me sick." Macdonald once admonished D'Arcy McGee, a favorite drinking companion: "Look here, this government can't afford two drunkards, so you've got to stop."

In the provincial assembly one time, when teetotalling Liberal leader George Brown criticized him for drunkenness, Macdonald retorted that the honorable members "would rather have John A. drunk than George Brown sober."

No runaway slave gained greater renown than the Rev. Josiah Henson, who escaped to Upper Canada in 1830 and lived in this house at Dresden, a town that became one terminus of the Underground Railroad. Henson later met Harriet Beecher Stowe and his early life in slavery provided material for her 1852 novel Uncle Tom's Cabin. *Canadian acceptance of runaways—right up to the time of the Civil War (as the Canadian Confederation was taking shape)—was a symbol of Canadian independence and, as such, something of an affront to the United States.*

A huge marble statue of Queen Victoria—purchased in 1871 for $10,000—holds the central place of honor under the great dome of the Parliamentary Library in Ottawa. The 16-sided library has a circular interior, with two galleries. It escaped a fire in 1916 that destroyed the rest of the Parliament buildings.

This Northumberland Strait ferry was once the only way to travel in winter between Prince Edward Island and the mainland of New Brunswick and Nova Scotia. In pack ice crew and passengers donned harness and pulled. A steamer service—one of the reasons P.E.I. agreed to join Confederation in 1873—was introduced in 1874.

Then, in April 1865, the threat of annexation by the United States gave the Confederation idea a boost. The American Civil War had just ended. Would the victorious Northern states, with their million idle soldiers, now attack the colonies to rule all of North America?

Macdonald, quick to capitalize on the situation, went to London to seek help for Canada's defence—and Confederation. This, wrote historian Donald G. Creighton, was "the last powerful card the Canadian government could play in a losing game." Macdonald came home with no promise of military aid against the Americans but a promise nonetheless: London would pressure the Maritime colonies into supporting Confederation. Many Maritimers had looked upon union as a first, disloyal step toward breaking away from Britain; now Britain was ordering the union and making it clear that she would do "everything short of coercion" to get her way.

Another threat came from the United States in the spring of 1866. The Fenian Brotherhood made armed border attacks in an effort to foment rebellion against British rule in Ireland. The Fe-

Macdonald's Happy Second Marriage Held Tragedy Nonetheless

In London to promote the union of Britain's North American colonies, John A. Macdonald quipped on the morning of Feb. 16, 1867, that as a conscientious man he felt bound to set an example of union. The occasion: his wedding breakfast.

Macdonald was 52. His bride was Susan Agnes Bernard *(below right)*, 31, of London, the elegant sister of his secretary, Hewitt Bernard. The couple had met in Canada, where Agnes lived for a year. They renewed their acquaintance in the fall of 1866 when Macdonald led the Canadian delegation to the London conference to settle the terms of Confederation. Agnes was well-read, intelligent and witty. She entertained

well and cared tenderly for her husband the rest of his days.

The marriage was Macdonald's second. In 1843 he had married his cousin Isabella Clark *(left)*. Within a year she had contracted an undisclosed illness that left her bedridden until her death in 1857. She bore two sons. The first, John Alexander, died at 13 months. Hugh John, born March 13, 1857, became premier of Manitoba in 1900.

Even in Macdonald's happy second marriage there was personal tragedy. Agnes gave birth to a daughter, Mary *(below left)*, in 1869 but the infant was stricken by hydrocephalus (water on the brain). She lived to 64 but she was never able to care for herself.

nian goal was to "bust Confederation." Nothing, as it turned out, would do more to save it.

The Fenian raids convinced New Brunswick and Nova Scotia (alarmed by threats against New Brunswick) that Confederation was necessary to their survival. Prince Edward Island and Newfoundland, islands and not affected by the raids, refused to join. But a third conference was called, to be held in London. Only Canada, Nova Scotia and New Brunswick would take part.

They met in early December in the Westminster Palace Hotel. For days 16 delegates reconsidered the 72 resolutions and made some amendments; on Dec. 21 they took a firm plan to Lord Carnarvon, Britain's colonial secretary. Their unquestioned leader, Macdonald, dominated the meetings with Carnarvon and impressed Colonial Office officials as "the ruling genius and spokesman."

In London Macdonald met Agnes Bernard, an

D'Arcy McGee, an Irish immigrant journalist who became a Father of Confederation, was assassinated—shot in the head—April 7, 1868, as he entered his lodgings in Ottawa, after a late session in the House of Commons. His funeral (above) in Montreal, where he lived most of the year, drew thousands. Patrick James Whelan, who police suspected was a Fenian, dedicated to freeing Ireland from British rule, was executed for the crime. (His was the last public hanging in Canada.) Later evidence raised doubts as to Whelan's guilt.

old friend, and, after a brief courtship, married her. On Feb. 19, 1867, he took her to the House of Lords to watch Carnarvon move second reading of the British North America bill. They heard Carnarvon declare: "We are laying the foundation for a great state, perhaps one which at a future day may even overshadow this country."

A week later the bill passed the House of Lords. On March 8 it passed the Commons, without enthusiasm or even much interest from the MPs. In 30 months, with three conferences, the Fathers of Confederation had performed a miracle. The name of the new four-province country

was suggested by Tilley, who found it in the 72nd Psalm: "He shall have dominion also from sea to sea." And it became, by royal proclamation, "One Dominion under the Name of Canada."

On July 1, 1867, guns saluted, soldiers marched, exultant crowds watched as fireworks filled the skies. In little Ottawa, with its muddy, potholed streets, its lumber shanties, its glistening Gothic Parliament buildings, a newly knighted Sir John A. Macdonald was sworn in as prime minister with his cabinet. It was done. "Henceforth," said Cartier, "we shall rank among the nations."

The Comic-Opera, 'Nothing Else to Do' Raids of the Fenians

"And we'll go and capture Canada, for we've nothing else to do."

The marching song of the Fenian Brotherhood, a 150,000-strong American secret society dedicated to freeing Ireland from English rule, described its immediate goal—the occupation of British North America as a base for attacks on British ships and as a pawn in negotiations.

Most Fenians were Irish immigrants and U.S. Civil War veterans. The first Fenian attack was planned for April 1866 against Campobello Island in New Brunswick, off Eastport, Maine, but it fizzled when customs seized the vessel carrying the raiders' weapons and ammunition.

Then, on June 1, some 1,000 Fenians crossed the Niagara River just north of Fort Erie (Ont.). The following day, north of Ridgeway, they clashed (*below*) with some 1,000 militiamen,

mainly of the Queen's Own Rifles of Toronto. The Canadians were winning until their commander, mistaking a few Fenians on stolen horses for a cavalry advance, ordered a retreat.

The Fenians occupied Fort Erie but, warned of the approach of 1,700 British regulars, they returned to American soil on June 4.

Another Fenian invasion, at Pigeon Hill, Que., on June 7, was easily turned back by militiamen from Montreal. A final raid came four years later, on May 25, 1870, near Eccles Hill, Que. It was repulsed by militiamen alerted by a Fenian officer who was a British spy.

The comic-opera attacks did nothing for the Fenian cause. But they demonstrated British North America's vulnerability, rallied its citizens in defence, and gave the flagging Confederation movement a vital boost.

Heritage Sites

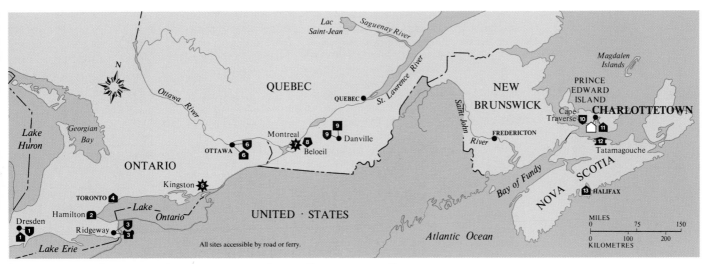

○ Main site (Historic building) ✳ Multiple attractions ⌂ Historic building(s) 🏛 Museum ▼ Monument ◆ Fort ■ Ruins ◆ Other ■ Unmarked site

CHARLOTTETOWN Province House, where the Fathers of Confederation met in September 1864, is at the head of Great George Street, up which delegates walked from the harbor. A high-ceilinged room now known as the Confederation Chamber contains the chairs and green-topped table used by the delegates. The chamber's guest book was signed by John A. Macdonald in 1890, when he gave his occupation as "cabinet maker."

Also in Charlottetown (11) Government House, where delegates were feted during the conference, is the residence of the lieutenant-governor of Prince Edward Island. A plaque outside commemorates the island's entry into Confederation in 1873. Abdgowan House, now abandoned, is at Mount Edward Road and Confederation Street. It was the home of Provincial Secretary William Henry Pope and a gathering place throughout the conference.

Other sites

Beloeil, Que. (8) A railway bridge over the Richelieu River is where a Grand Trunk Railway train plunged off a swing bridge in 1864, killing 99 persons.

Cape Traverse, P.E.I. (10) A 20-foot replica of an iceboat, like those used at the time of Confederation to link Prince Edward Island and the mainland, is at the base of an obelisk commemorating the iceboat service.

Danville, Que. (9) The site of the railway station where Pte. Timothy O'Hea extinguished a fire in an ammunition car in 1866 and won the only Victoria Cross ever awarded in Canada is here. A plaque near the site honors O'Hea.

Dresden, Ont. (1) The two-storey house of the Rev. Josiah Henson, a fugitive slave and the model for the hero of *Uncle Tom's Cabin,* is part of the Uncle Tom's Cabin Museum. Henson's rocking chair, a pulpit from which he preached, and slave whips, handcuffs and a ball and chain are displayed. Henson's grave is near the house.

Halifax (13) Armdale, where Nova Scotia Premier Charles Tupper lived at the time of Confederation, is an apartment house at Tupper Grove and Armview Avenue.

Hamilton, Ont. (2) Two abutments remain from a swing bridge over the Desjardins Canal where a Great Western Railway train crashed in 1857, killing 59 persons.

Kingston, Ont. (5) A two-storey stone house at 110-112 Rideau Street was occupied in 1836-43 by John A. Macdonald, then a young lawyer. Bellevue House, where he lived in 1848-49 with his first wife, Isabella, is at 35 Centre Street. Restored and refurnished, it is a national historic site and contains Macdonald memorabilia. The Royal Tavern at 344 Princess Street, called Grimason House at the time of Confederation and operated by Macdonald's friend Eliza Grimason, is where the prime minister held political meetings and celebrated victories. Macdonald and Mrs. Grimason were buried in adjacent graves in the Cataraqui Cemetery

Montreal (7)

CARTIER HOUSE The three-storey house from which George-Etienne Cartier, leader of the French-Canadian wing of the Conservative Party at the time of Confederation, practised law between 1858 and 1867, is at 460 Notre Dame Street East.

CARTIER MONUMENT A 100-foot stone column with a bronze statue of Cartier is in Mount Royal Park facing Park Avenue.

CÔTE DES NEIGES CEMETERY A vault contains the remains of D'Arcy McGee, a Father of Confederation who was assassinated in 1868.

MOUNT ROYAL CEMETERY A stone marks the graves of 52 persons killed in the Beloeil train disaster of 1864.

VICTORIA BRIDGE This first bridge across the St. Lawrence River (1859) enabled the Grand Trunk Railway to link Toronto and Portland, Maine.

Ottawa (6) The Library of Parliament, a round Gothic structure with four-foot-thick stone walls and a dome 132 feet high, is the only part of the original Parliament buildings (1859-76) to survive a 1916 fire. On Parliament Hill are bronze statues of Macdonald, Cartier, McGee and other politicians of the Confederation period. A plaque at 142 Sparks Street identifies the spot where McGee was assassinated.

Ridgeway, Ont. (3) A plaque marks the site of the Battle of Ridgeway and commemorates militiamen who fought Fenian raiders here in 1866. Six miles east is Fort Erie, occupied briefly by the Fenians.

Tatamagouche, N.S. (12) The Sunrise Trail Museum displays the vote record of the 1867 federal election (without secret ballot) in which Conservative Charles Tupper defeated Liberal William Annand in Cumberland riding. Tupper was the only pro-Confederation member elected to Parliament from Nova Scotia that year.

Toronto (4) A red brick house at D'Arcy and Beverly streets was the 1870s home of George Brown, a Reform leader and Father of Confederation.

Making Fun of Ice and Snow

Nineteenth-century Canadians, especially in Quebec, turned each long, bitter winter into an extravaganza of skating and sleigh-rides, snowshoe parties and—still outdoors—dances, concerts and picnics. Instead of fighting winter, they made it fun.

None were more enthusiastic than the British officers stationed in Canada. Scarlet-coated, they took to Quebec's frozen rivers and raced their blooded horses against the French Canadians' small shaggy animals. Others crewed flat-bottomed, triangular boats in ice regattas. Montreal's Tandem Club (established in 1830) mustered horses and sleighs at Place d'Armes each week for a parade around town and then a picnic in the country.

At gaslit Victoria Rink in Montreal, gallery spectators "like swallows on a cliff" gazed down on men and women skating to waltzes and mazurkas—and a certain diarist once noted of the ladies: "Yes, they wear breeches, a good many of them."

For a ball at a rink in Quebec in 1865, the very proper Frances Monck, sister-in-law of the governor general of the day, wore overstockings and boots and "many warm things under my sealskin coat," preferring to watch in dignity than to risk inelegance as a performer. But one morning before her Canadian visit ended she did go for a romp on a snowy cricket field. "I took off my crinoline," she recorded with some surprise, "and tied myself up in a sheet to keep the snow from my petticoats. I begin to think it very exciting."

The Montreal Snowshoe Club (1840) attracted hundreds to torchlight parades and snowball battles and on tramps to outlying villages for coffee and song and Highland dances. In 1833 Montreal staged North America's first winter carnival—five days of curling, sleigh races, tobogganing, snowshoeing, hockey and fireworks.

It would be many years, though, before skiing became popular. A man using nine-foot skis and one pole drew press attention by skiing from Montreal to Quebec in 1879. But in Ottawa an English lord who tried skiing was met with "universal derision."

Composite photographs of tobogganing, hockey and curling on these pages are by William Notman.

Cornelius Krieghoff's 1853 painting of the Montmorency Falls ice cone near Quebec (right: the cone today) catches the exuberance of carioling, riding at breakneck speed in light sleighs that often spilled passengers and picnic baskets on tight turns. With their "muffins" (female companions) snuggled under buffalo robes and bearskins, officers raced across the snowbound countryside, perhaps to stop at Montmorency, where they could admire ice sculptures, or toboggan down the 100-foot cone. A bar excavated in the cone served whisky and "other strong waters." Nearby were blazing bonfires and picnic tables set on carpets and laden with soup, poultry and roast beef—and a band to play a blood-warming quadrille or two.

The first skating enthusiasts spun and whirled on frozen rivers and ponds, often by moonlight. Large sheds were built to keep snow off these sheets of ice—but, with no moon, romance presumably suffered. The first skates, part wood, were strapped to the skater's boots; all-metal skates were introduced in Halifax in 1861. For many years the Ottawa public could frolic on the grounds at Rideau Hall (below), the governor general's residence.

Tuque, blanket coat and sash (the colorful French-Canadian ceinture fléchée) were the snowshoers' standard garb—and Indian file was their favorite formation. They made seven miles an hour.

Steered then (as now) by hands, feet or sticks, toboggans shot down chutes such as these on Mount Royal in Montreal at what seemed like a mile a minute—and probably was. Ice chutes suited the Victorian sense of order. Tobogganing on natural slopes, said one critic, was "sport gone mad," likely to "scare away or cure blue devils and dyspepsia."

The 1880s were the heyday of the ice palace. This work of art dominated Montreal's Dominion Square in 1885, the year of the Northwest Rebellion and the completion of the CPR. Dominion Square had five such castles—as winter carnival features—between 1883 and 1889.

Wolfe's soldiers introduced curling to Canada in 1759, using gun-carriage hubs. But a century later a Quebec farmer who stumbled on this strange behavior reported: "Today I saw a bunch of Scotsmen throwing huge iron balls, like cannon balls, then yelling 'Soupe! Soupe!' ['Sweep! Sweep!'], then laughing like fools. They are fools!"

Outdoor hockey originally accommodated as many players as wanted to play—and a game ended when one team scored three goals, or when men had to return to barracks, or if a player fell through the ice and was in danger of drowning. Even when hockey moved indoors in the 1870s (left: Victoria Rink in Montreal in 1893), there were no nets and little protective clothing, even for the goaltender. McGill University established rules about 1880; soon there were leagues. Governor General Lord Stanley presented his famous cup in 1893.

Great Ships
and Captains' Captains

Stern, religious, proud, a man unaccustomed to setback, William Dawson Lawrence built one of the world's great sailing ships, launched her in 1874 (named after himself), and saw to it that she made money. He had started his first ship in 1852 with little more than $100. When he died in 1886, at 70, he was a wealthy man.

The year they launched the windjammer *William D. Lawrence*—1874—was the busiest Canadian shipyards had known. In the Maritime Provinces alone, 368 vessels were completed.

William Dawson Lawrence of Maitland, N.S., was already a successful builder and owner of ships when he started construction of a vessel bigger than Nova Scotia had ever seen. She was born in stocks set up in front of Lawrence's house, near where the Shubenacadie River joins an inlet of the Bay of Fundy. He was gambling that he could double a ship's size without doubling her operating costs and he went $27,000 into debt, even mortgaging his home, to meet her $107,000 cost.

Seventy-five men worked for 90 cents to $1.50 a day and for 18 months the air rang with the sounds of hammers and saws, of mauls beating bolts into wood, of mallets driving home the caulking for her seams and joints. Finally her bowsprit and her three masts, the tallest 200 feet, towered over the house. She was 262 feet long and her registered net tonnage would be 2,459. Her deck timbers were 18 inches thick; her sides, with massive, close-spaced ribs and inner and outer planking, were thicker than the length of a man's arm. On Oct. 27, 1874, the great *William D. Lawrence* was launched.

Many believed her unsailable. Everyone knew the risk at launching: you could insure a vessel under construction and you could insure one on the water but not one in between. Would she stick on the ways? Would she topple over? Would she founder in the mud?

She was christened not with champagne but with cider; Lawrence was a teetotaller. Then axemen began knocking out the keel blocks that held her 3,800 tons in place, 400 of those tons made up of stone ballast in her belly. With one keel block still to go, she began to move down the greased timbers of her cradle and slowly gathered speed.

The windjammer William D. Lawrence (with 8,000 square yards of sail set in this painting in the Nova Scotia Museum at Halifax) was built virtually at the doorstep of her owner's house beside the muddy Shubenacadie River at Maitland, N.S. The elm-shaded W.D. Lawrence House, which dates from about 1870, is a national historic site. It has been restored by the Nova Scotia Museum and is open to the public.

Square-Riggers and Fore-and-Afters

Ships of the 19th century carried great clouds of sail. Square rigging (hung from transverse yards) caught lots of wind but required big crews working aloft. Fore-and-aft-rigged ships needed fewer men (working on deck) and were more manoeuvrable near shore. Designs of various ship types changed over the years. These examples (not to scale) are typical of the years indicated.

Brig (1865) Two square-rigged masts; for frequent medium cargoes.

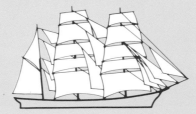

Barque (1870) One mast rigged fore and aft; a good whaler.

Ship (1870) Three or more square-rigged masts; a vessel built for speed.

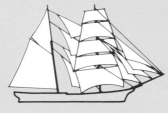

Brigantine (1870) Mainsail (unlike the brig's) is rigged fore and aft.

Barquentine (1875) One mast square-rigged; fast, manoeuvrable.

Schooner (1890) Two or more fore-and-aft-rigged masts; a fishing craft.

Lawrence saw her shadow vanish from his home, heard the crowd give a thundering roar as she was finally afloat. "She went off like a rowboat," someone shouted.

On her first voyage, with widower Lawrence a passenger, she was gone two years, seven months and seven days, carrying lumber to Britain, coal to the Middle East, fertilizer from Peru to Europe. Lawrence came home with gold enough to pay his debts. Soon his great ship would make him rich.

Early in the 19th century Britain looked to North America for wood to build ships for her navy. In Lower Canada and the Maritimes it was seen that there was profit in carrying lumber as well as in producing it. Little shipyards on the St. Lawrence River, and later those around the Bay of Fundy and in Prince Edward Island, began to build huge, clumsy timber droghers, softwood craft made to be stuffed with boards and planks. Some were little more than organized piles of wood to be broken up in England and sold. They served their purpose but were despised by the shipbuilders of Europe, accustomed to superbly crafted ships of teak and oak. But at mid-century a ship was built that changed the reputation of the Maritime shipbuilders.

James Smith of Saint John, N.B., asked himself one day in 1850: If there was a market for timber droghers, would there not be a market also for a ship that would take anything anywhere, a ship that would carry a lot of cargo and move it fast? He began to build such a ship at the east end of Saint John, in "the most Godforsaken hole possibly discovered"—Marsh Creek in Courtenay Bay, a muddy, swampy

Great ribs of spruce rise from the oaken keel of a ship on the stocks at Saint John, N.B. Men work all winter and their creation will be launched on the high spring tides.

'Strange to Say': The Saga of Sarah

"My only help," Capt. John Wren of St. Andrews, N.B., would write when the 72-day ordeal ended, "was the woman"—English-born Sarah Farrington, who later settled in Digby, N.S. Her husband was cook and she was stewardess in the Saint John barque *James W. Elwell,* which sailed from Cardiff in 1872 with Welsh coal for Valparaiso—but never made it.

About the time the barque rounded Cape Horn the mate and Sarah's husband both died of injuries suffered in shipboard accidents. Then, 14 days up the coast of Chile . . . the coal was ablaze! They fought the fire for six days but had to abandon the ship. Wren, 11 seamen and Sarah took to a lifeboat and watched as the barque sank.

Battered by gales, they sailed south, then east into the Strait of Magellan, hoping for rescue. After three weeks, two men died; a few days later, two more. Other men went mad or lay sunk in apathy. One by one *they* died.

After 10 weeks, only Wren, Sarah and two seamen were left. When one more sailor died, the captain lost hope. But Sarah refused to give in, finally rousing Wren from despair. He launched the boat into the strait again. Suddenly, unbelievingly, he croaked: "Ship in sight!" It was the White Star liner *Tropic.*

"Strange to say," Wren recorded with the Victorian male's amazement at such female accomplishments, "the woman stood it better than any. She would have been the last to succumb."

place with little or no water until Fundy's tides came rolling in.

The conventional timber drogher was fat, roomy, slab-sided, built to crash and wallow through the seas. Smith's *Marco Polo,* her ribs tapered sharply to her keel, looked like a cross between a cargo carrier and a yacht. She carried, as author Joseph Schull would put it, "the belly of an alderman on the legs of a ballet dancer."

Saint John watched her grow, this triple-masted triple-decker of 1,625 tons, at 184 feet the longest ship yet built there—and did not like the looks of her. Then, as her frame was completed and the timber for her hull lay ready, a gale whipped in from Fundy and collapsed her. Here, they said, was a ship that did not want to be born. James Smith cleared the wreckage and began to rebuild her, better and stronger than before.

He waited until the high spring tides to launch her. The yard was crowded on April 17, 1851, as champagne splashed over the bow with the figurehead of the celebrated traveller for whom the ship was named. Workers removed the blocks—and she stood there, motionless. A rumble of doubt rippled into laughter. Then someone found one small cleat the workers had missed. With it knocked away, she was moving, her black hull shaking. But as she hit the water excitement turned to dismay. On the falling tide, she had ended up in the mud of this "most Godforsaken hole." It took two weeks to work her free, the ship that did not want to go to sea.

On her maiden voyage she made the English port of Liverpool with a cargo of lumber in a sensational 15 days and a broom was tied to her mainmast to signify she was for sale, as Smith

The passenger ship Marco Polo, originally a cargo vessel built in Saint John, sailed from England to Australia and back in record time in 1852—under six months. On her next trip her captain vowed "to astonish God Almighty"—but, although unquestionably the fastest ship in the world, she failed to beat her record. Eventually Marco Polo reverted to carrying cargo, but seamen still spoke of her with awe and lined the rails of steamers to salute her sailing past.

From the cupola of this mansion, builder James Yeo, Jr., watched ships taking shape in the Yeo yard at Port Hill, P.E.I. Twenty-three vessels were launched there in the great days of sail. The house, Green Park, was once the centre of business, political and social life in the area. It has been restored and furnished as in the 1860s.

had intended when he built her. It was said her keel had been twisted in the launching accident and, although some claimed such a ship sometimes sailed *all the faster,* at first no buyers came. She was sold at last—cheap—to one Paddy McGee. Then great events, far away, determined her future. Thousands were wild to get to the goldfields of Australia, and James Baines of the Black Ball Line needed a ship to take them.

McGee brought Baines to see his ship and next day Baines brought his chief captain, 31-year-old James Nichol Forbes. The tall, swarthy, tyrannical Scot, nicknamed Bully, spent five hours going over every inch of her and his initial doubt turned to conviction. Not only would he take her, but also he bet the captain of the steam packet *Australia* that he would beat him to Melbourne. Forbes went further: on a 29,000-mile round trip that normally took eight to nine months, he would have *Marco Polo* back in Liverpool in six! Baines winced at the laughter provoked by Forbes's boasts but by the time *Marco Polo*

Fast and Beautiful, the Workhorse of the Banks

The beauty of *Bluenose II (right)* dates from the great days of sail, when the schooner was perfected not as a racer or a rich man's plaything, but as the workhorse of the offshore fishery.

A schooner of the 1880s was rigged so that it required relatively few men to handle her—even in freezing weather—and so she could tack close into the east coast's prevailing offshore winds. She had to be fast to get her catch to market quickly. She had a deep belly—mostly hold—a tiny galley ahead of the hold, and crew's bunks crammed into the forecastle. The biggest schooners, up to 145 feet long, carried 20 to 30 men.

Schooners appeared in the early 1700s when settlers who had previously fished near shore in small boats ventured to offshore banks that teemed with cod. From New England to Labrador, the design was

similar. By the 1880s Newfoundland had some 330 fishing schooners and Nova Scotia 200. Lunenburg, N.S., was a great fishing port, its harbor often thick with masts.

Fishing voyages, between March and October, lasted from four to eight weeks. The fisherman's day began by lamplight as he helped bait some 2,000 hooks on a trawl up to two miles long, then coiled the line in a wooden tub. At dawn, dories stacked on deck were swung over the side. One or two men in oilskins and leather seaboots cast off in each dory, anchored one end of the trawl line and laid the rest of it along the sea bottom. After an hour or two the line was hauled up. The fish were unhooked, pitchforked onto the deck of the mother ship, cleaned and put in the hold. Then it was more of the same, until dusk. A good voyage might yield 50 tons of fish, but many dories

were lost forever in fog or sudden stor the 1940s schooners had given way t ships with engines and big scoop ne era of the bankers ended in 1963 wh last of them, *Theresa E. Connor,* was to go to the banks for lack of a crew. now restored and berthed at the Lune Fisheries Museum.)

The greatest schooner of all was *Bl* launched April 26, 1921, in Lunenbur won the International Fishermen's T that October and in four subsequent *Bluenose* was also a working ship. C trip she brought home more than 3 pounds, the largest catch landed in L burg. In 1942 she was sold to ferry fre the Caribbean, and four years lat perished on a reef off Haiti. *Blueno* replica, also built in Lunenburg, berth Historic Properties wharf in Halifax.

sailed she was the talk of England. Baines had turned the timber carrier into an elegant floating hotel, her black paint covered with white, her holds converted into panelled cabins and lounges.

She quickly pulled ahead of *Australia* as Forbes, a master in his element, sailed her through the South Atlantic and around the Cape of Good Hope into the Indian Ocean. Sweating, swearing men swarmed aloft into the rigging to carry out his barked orders. Day after day Forbes climbed out on one of the booms that held the sails and stood there, gripping a rope, black hair flying in the wind. Sails burst with noise like cannon shots and were immediately replaced—a ship took three full sets on an Australia voyage. *Marco Polo* did the last 1,350 miles in four days, mountainous seas clawing at her, the exhausted crew sullen, the 930 passengers fearful, Forbes shouting "Hell or Melbourne." She arrived on the morning of Sept. 18, 1852, only 76 days out of Liverpool, one full week ahead of *Australia*. The crew went unrewarded. Instead, Bully Forbes had them thrown into jail on fake charges of insubordination. He wanted no desertions to the goldfields.

Three weeks later they were released and *Marco Polo* sailed again, this time into ice, blizzards and pounding seas that cascaded over her sides. As she pushed eastward across the South Pacific, Forbes stood on the poop deck with a pistol in each hand, driving the men as they slipped on icy decks and hauled on ropes with half-frozen hands. They rounded Cape Horn in a

Royal William, a sail-equipped paddlewheeler built at Quebec, was the first vessel to make an entire Atlantic crossing under steam power—from Pictou, N.S., to London in 1833.

gale, logging 353 miles in a single day. Then they pointed north.

On Boxing Day 1852, James Baines was drawn to Liverpool's docks by a ridiculous rumor: *Marco Polo* had been sighted down the coast. Round the last bend in the Mersey River he saw his transformed cargo ship, her spars bare, her hull crusted with salt, loafing into harbor behind a tug. She had circled the world in five months and 21 days. Strung between her masts was a banner: "*Marco Polo, Fastest Ship in The World.*"

It was easier to sell Canadian ships after *Marco Polo*'s exploit but Canadians were beginning to see that they could profit from keeping and operating the ships they built. Australian and California gold, the Crimean War, mutiny in India, Europe's Industrial Revolution and, in the sixties, the American Civil War, all added to the flood of people and goods to be carried about the world. Maritime ships and seafarers competed for cargoes. Nova Scotia took the lead. She had been building small ships for years and now she began to build them over 1,000 tons. Foreign sailors called them the Bluenose Fleet.

There seemed to be a ship abuilding in every creek and river. The typical shipyard had large areas for storing and drying its lumber: spruce for planking, durable yellow birch for keels, white pine for cabin work, yellow pine for decking. The woods were searched for the curved surface roots of the tamarack, or hackmatack, to make the knees—deck support braces. There

The eyes of this turbaned Turk—the figurehead of the British barque Saladin (at the Nova Scotia Maritime Museum in Halifax)—seem haunted by the memory of piracy and slaughter in the ship in 1844. Of 14 men aboard, 8 were butchered in mid-Atlantic. The remaining 6 ran Saladin aground in Nova Scotia. Four were hanged for murder (on the South Common in Halifax).

261

The full-rigged ship Research *(Capt. George Churchill of Yarmouth, N.S.) was en route from Quebec to Greenock, Scotland, in the winter of 1866-67 when caught in a storm that swept away most of her canvas—and her rudder. One substitute rudder after another was manhandled into position at the stern (left, in this painting); seven rudders were carried away but the eighth was a success.* Research *reached Greenock after an 88-day voyage, her crew and cargo safe—and her captain destined to be known forever as Rudder Churchill.*

were workshops for blacksmiths and joiners, and sheds for carvers—who made figureheads and wheel and rail decorations—and for storage. There was a steam box or pit and perhaps a shed for refits and repairs.

A ship was not built from engineers' blueprints but from a "half model," a scale model of half the hull. It was carved out of many layers of wood stacked together until the right shape was found, one that would sail well and carry a large cargo. Then the model was taken apart. Each layer was measured, then scaled up to the actual size of the ship. Then its lines were drawn on the thick floor of the stocks to give the shape of the ribs, timbers and keel.

As the frame rose, it was clad with planks, steamed and curved to fit. Then oakum, thinly tarred rope fibre, was forced into the seams and joints to make them watertight. The deck was covered with planking, the masts were fitted,

usually with a silver dollar under each base for luck. When the rudder was hung, the ship was launched. Then cabins, the galley, the spars and rigging were fitted and she was ready for sea, perhaps with pleasant quarters for the captain's wife and children. Children were born at sea; some lived on it for years.

The captains were tough, efficient men with a passion for cleanliness, proud of their worldwide reputation for hard but fair discipline. Most officers were Canadians. The crews were mostly foreigners, picked up wherever their last ship left them, often from crimps—boardinghouse keepers who "sold" their customers for crews. These were the worst, drunks and troublemakers. The captains looked to their ships' officers to tame them, man to man, fist to fist.

The first Nova Scotian to build and operate his own, well-constructed ships instead of cheap and inferior craft for sale was Capt. George McKenzie of New Glasgow. He became a shipyard foreman in his teens and in 1821, at 22, built a schooner of his own. When he died at 78 he had built and owned some 34 ships of up to 1,465 tons. McKenzie founded the tradition that a master and a mate should be able to do anything—be seamen, navigators, carpenters, sailmakers, riggers, stevedores, ships' agents. He trained many Nova Scotia farmers' sons to be shipmasters. They were called "the Captain's captains."

Yarmouth, N.S., became rich. In 1876 its fewer than 6,000 persons owned 282 ships. Wealth flowed into its two banks and its insurance companies, and to sailmakers and ship chandlers. It was the home of such men as Capt. David Cook of the barque *Sarah* who, in an Atlantic gale in 1849, saved hundreds of passengers and crew members from a burning American packet.

Yarmouth was the home also of Capt. Stanley Hatfield, slain with two of his officers in a mutiny in the barque *Lennie* in 1875. The Belgian steward, an experienced seaman, sailed her to the French coast and sent messages ashore in bottles. The four ringleaders were hanged and the Belgian handsomely rewarded.

In 1878 nearly 4,500 ships were registered in the Maritimes, two-thirds in Nova Scotia. But the decline had begun. It became part of Maritime tradition to blame it on the Confederation that most Nova Scotia shipping men had opposed. But the true causes lay elsewhere. The issue of the Halifax *Morning Chronicle* that announced the launching of *William D. Lawrence* carried half a dozen advertisements for steamer services and a report of the first train to arrive in Yarmouth. Iron and steam were revolutionizing transportation and driving the wooden sailing ships from the seas.

Since 1830 this lighthouse on Seal Island, 18 miles off the south extremity of the Nova Scotia mainland, has been an important beacon for inbound ships making for the Bay of Fundy. It was built at the insistence of two families who had settled on the island to aid distressed mariners. Appalled by the number of shipwrecks, Edward Crowells and Richard Hickens and their wives petitioned for a lighthouse, and Sir Edward Kempt, governor of Nova Scotia, ordered construction of the massive structure. Crowells and Hickens were paid £30 a year to man the circular cast-iron lantern. It was fired by seal oil, then mineral oil, then petroleum vapor, and was electrified in 1959. It is a fine example of colonial frame lighthouse construction.

George McKenzie of New Glasgow, one of the great builders, skippered his ships under all the sail they could carry, day and night, storm or shine—and never lost a man overboard. (He once leaped into the sea to save a sailor who had tumbled in.) When his brother died at sea, McKenzie brought the body home preserved in rum.

The Wrecks and the 'Wrackers' of Cape Sable

Cape Sable, the rocky southern tip of Nova Scotia, has for centuries been one of the graveyards of the Atlantic. Submerged, ship-killing ledges extend almost a mile to sea, powerful tides sweep around shoals and islands. Hundreds of vessels have been lost in the area.

The worst wreck was on Feb. 20, 1860, when the steamship *Hungarian,* en route from England to Portland, Maine, foundered on a rocky shoal. All 125 passengers and 80 crewmen died. Much of *Hungarian*'s cargo was saved, and Cape Sable people, like poor folk on rocky shores everywhere, considered a rich wreck a gift from Providence. As soon as a ship was in trouble, "wrackers" would launch boats—to save lives, but also to save food and furnishings. Before radar and modern rescue techniques, scarcely a Cape Sable area home was without dishes or apparel from some wreck.

Cape Sable's biggest windfall was the "great cheese wreck" of Dec. 30, 1881. Times had been hard, and several residents had died of malnutrition, when the SS *Moravian,* bound from Portland to Halifax and Liverpool, England, hit Mud Island, 20 miles west. Passengers and crew were saved—and so were 350 tons of cheese, 169 tons of bacon, 54 tons of butter, 1,108 quarters of fresh prime beef, 116 barrels of pork, 448 barrels of apples, 29,285 bushels of wheat, and peas, flour, lard, canned meat and mutton.

By the seventies Britain was already buying fewer wooden ships, and turning to sailing ships with iron hulls and to steamships. They cost less to insure, lasted longer, carried more.

Some Maritime yards tried to survive by building better wooden ships than ever. Some tried to build with steel but, without a local steel industry, they could not compete with the shipyards of Belfast and the Clyde. Many wooden vessels were sold for little more than their salvage value, often for the Norwegian lumber trade. In 1900 the tonnage under Canadian registry was half what it had been in 1878.

Marco Polo, 29 years old when sold to Norway in 1880, was no longer the fastest ship in the world. In 1883, leaking badly, heavy with lumber, her pumps overwhelmed, she was run ashore and her bones still lie off Cavendish Beach in Prince Edward Island. She had spent 15 years on the Australian run and she had come home to the Maritimes to die.

That same year the nine-year-old *William D. Lawrence* was sold to the Norwegians. Lawrence, remembering his critics, wrote a letter to a newspaper telling in detail what she had done for him: after all costs were paid she had made a profit of $140,000. She made more money for her new owners over the next 15 years, and once, in 1890, before she ended her days as a lowly barge, she came home briefly. She put into Parrsboro, N.S., to load lumber and the people of Maitland organized an excursion across the Minas Basin to have a last look at her. Then she sailed again. It is not known where she ended her days.

As a youth in Halifax he drove the family cow to pasture, sold vegetables on market days—and knitted socks. He later operated a government soup kitchen for immigrants (and helped settle them), and auctioned tea (which he imported from China). By 1840 he had made a fortune in lumbering and shipping. Then he got a contract to deliver mail between Halifax and Liverpool. That was the start of Samuel Cunard's transatlantic steamship line.

Sealing: A Rowdy, Risky Month on the Ice

Going "to the ice"—to the seal hunts of the late 1800s—was many a Newfoundland man's only chance in each long year of poverty to earn some cash money. But to make his few dollars he had to live a rowdy month with as many as 200 other men in a stinking ship that lacked heat, sanitation and medical facilities. He worked brutal hours, ate uncooked food, got drinking water from pools in the ice floes, and daily risked his very life—if not from drowning, perhaps from nicking himself with a bloody knife. This caused "sealfinger," for which the treatment was a soaking in carbolic acid. If that failed, it was amputation—or death.

Each captain sailed his own course to the great rafts of pack ice off Labrador where every March hundreds of thousands of newborn "whitecoats" were slaughtered for their oil and skins. (*Below:* the 1881 hunt.) When swiles (seals) were sighted it was all hands onto the ice with clubs for the killing, knives for the skinning and ropes for the hauling. Soon the deck was knee-deep in slippery skins, and sweaty men reeked with blood and fat. It went on for days and each pelt was worth a dollar.

The greatest hunt of all, in 1884, saw 360 ships carry 11,000 men to the ice; they brought back 700,000 pelts. But most years the loss of men and ships was appalling. Between 1810 and 1870 more than 400 ships were sunk, well over a thousand men were lost—drowned, crushed or frozen to death, or dead of "sealfinger."

Heritage Sites

MAITLAND, N.S. The W.D. Lawrence House (c. 1870) near the mouth of the Shubenacadie River, was the home of the man who designed and gave his name to 2,459-ton *William D. Lawrence*, built in front of the house in 1872-74. She was the biggest wooden ship ever launched in the Maritimes. The portico of the house, with twin curved stairways, is reminiscent of a ship's bridge. In the house, a national historic site restored and operated by the Nova Scotia Museum, are most of its original furnishings as well as shipbuilding equipment and a seven-foot model of Lawrence's great ship. Maitland was a major shipbuilding centre in the late 1800s.

Other sites

Arichat, N.S. (14) The LeNoir Forge Museum is a restoration of a stone smithy that produced anchors, chain and other hardware for sailing ships. The LeNoir shipyard was just west; logs used in launchings can sometimes be seen at low tide.

Basin Head, P.E.I. (13) The inshore fishery of the 1800s and early 1900s is depicted at the Basin Head Fisheries Museum by replicas of fishing shacks and by a display of small craft, a disused cannery and an interpretive centre.

Cape Sable Island, N.S. (4) The rocky southern tip of Nova Scotia, Cape Sable, lies just offshore. Hundreds of ships have been wrecked in the area. Artifacts from them, including a quilt made of cloth salvaged from the SS *Hungarian* (a liner which sank in 1860 with the loss of 205 lives) are in the Archelaus Smith Museum in Centreville.

Cavendish, P.E.I. (11) The remains of the ship *Marco Polo*, once "the fastest ship in the world"—launched at Saint John, N.B., in 1851—lie where she ran aground in 1883, about a quarter of a mile off Cavendish Beach. The hulk can be seen by divers.

Charlottetown (12) Beaconsfield, a three-storey mansion erected by shipbuilder James Peak in 1877, houses the Prince Edward Island Heritage Foundation. One of the last of the great shipowners in the Maritimes, Peak had lost his fortune—and Beaconsfield—by 1885.

Grand Harbour, N.B. (1) Artifacts including tableware and ships' fittings from wrecks in the Grand Manan Island area, and the original lens from the nearby Gannet Rock lighthouse (1832), are in the Grand Manan Museum.

Halifax (9) *Bluenose II*, a replica of the famous fishing schooner that won many international races in the 1920s and 1930s,

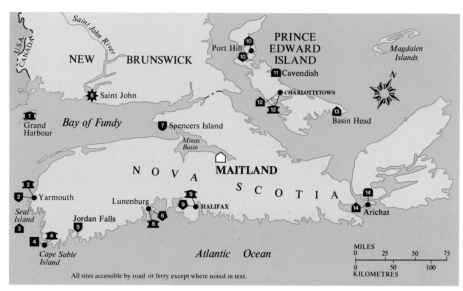

All sites accessible by road or ferry except where noted in text.

○ Main site (Historic building) ✿ Multiple attractions ▲ Historic building(s) ▬ Museum ♥ Monument ■ Ruins ◆ Other ■ Unmarked site

berths at an Historic Properties wharf. Harbor tours aboard the vessel may be arranged. The Nova Scotia Maritime Museum has exhibits on shipbuilding and on fishing and sailing vessels.

Jordan Falls, N.S. (5) A cairn of beach stones, topped by an anchor, honors Donald McKay, builder of some of the finest American clipper ships of the mid-1880s. McKay was born here Sept. 4, 1810.

Lunenburg, N.S. (8) *Theresa E. Connor*, the last Canadian schooner to fish the banks (in 1962) is among restored vessels moored at the Lunenburg Fisheries Museum, a branch of the Nova Scotia Museum. Built by the shipyard of Smith and Rhuland (as were *Bluenose* and *Bluenose II*), she contains exhibits on the history of the offshore fishery, and *Bluenose's* wheel and trophies she won. The Lunenburg Fisheries Exhibition each summer includes contests in fish filleting and scallop shucking, and races for dories. The Fishermen's Memorial Room at the exhibition grounds is dedicated to men and ships of Lunenburg lost around Nova Scotia.

Port Hill, P.E.I. (10) Shipbuilding on Prince Edward Island in the mid-1800s is depicted in 200-acre Green Park Provincial Historic Park, 1½ miles northwest. A re-created shipyard includes functioning blacksmith and carpenter shops, sawpits, a steam box for bending planks, and the keel and some ribs of a ship under construction. Green Park, the mansion erected by shipbuilder James Yeo, Jr., in 1865, has been restored and refurnished. An interpretive centre describes ship construction.

Saint John, N.B. (6)

MARSH CREEK *Marco Polo* was launched near the present Courtenay Causeway, at the head of Courtenay Bay.

NEW BRUNSWICK MUSEUM Displays include a stern carving from *Marco Polo*, a telescope, lantern and dinner bell from the vessel, ship paintings, and explanations of how wooden ships were built.

PARTRIDGE ISLAND The world's first steam foghorn was installed here in 1859 by Robert Foulis (who is honored by a plaque on Prince William Street in Saint John). *The island is accessible only with permission from city authorities.*

"STRAIGHT SHORE" The Saint John Harbour shore below Chesley Drive, between the Reversing Falls and the east end of the Harbour Bridge, was an important shipbuilding area known as the Straight Shore in the late 1800s.

Seal Island, N.S. (3) The island's octagonal timber lighthouse was built in 1830. *Accessible only by boat (charter).*

Spencers Island, N.S. (7) A cairn records that the brigantine *Mary Celeste*, found under sail in the Atlantic in 1872 with no one aboard, was built in this village as *Amazon* in 1861.

Yarmouth, N.S. (2) Ship paintings and models in the Yarmouth County Museum reflect Yarmouth's prominence as a shipbuilding and shipowning centre during the late 1800s, and a chart locates the 20 shipyards in the area at that time. A monument about a mile south commemorates shipbuilding in Nova Scotia; another across the harbor honors Yarmouth seamen.

265

Fort Walsh, a North West Mounted Police post in southwestern Saskatchewan, was vital to the maintenance of peace when Sitting Bull and his Sioux fled from the United States in 1876 and took refuge here in the territory of their traditional enemies the Blackfoot. The fort was demolished in 1883, mainly because food at the post enticed Indians to leave their reserves. It was partially rebuilt in 1942 and is the centrepiece of a national historic park.

The Mounties Bring Law to the Whisky West

At the whisky forts, they said, a man's life was worth one live horse—and a horse could be bought for a gallon of whisky. So much for human values in the Northwest Territories (present-day Alberta and Saskatchewan) in the years soon after Confederation.

At places called Slideout, Robbers' Roost, Whiskey Gap and (most notorious of all) Fort Whoop-Up, traders from the United States would sell a rifle for a pile of skins as high as the gun was long. But mostly they peddled "whisky." A buffalo skin would buy one drink of a concoction that was one part alcohol to three parts water, colored with tobacco juice, laced with vitriol and spiced with peppers and Jamaica ginger. To get this the Plains Indians (see p. 166) sold not only buffalo robes and furs but also their horses, their food and their women.

Brutality and murder were commonplace in the whisky forts and no settlers would go to the lawless territories. Politicians in the East had proposed creating a force to be called the North West Mounted Rifles, but Ottawa lacked funds to establish it. But in May 1873 a gang of 10 wolf hunters from Fort Benton in Montana rode north across the border into the Cypress Hills, and the Canadian West was changed forever.

The hunters, as was their practice, left a strychnine-poisoned buffalo on the prairie and took the skins of the wolves it attracted. Then they rode back to Montana, little caring that Indians' dogs would also feed on the carcass. They camped five miles from Fort Benton. Next morning their horses were gone.

The 10 followed horse tracks as far as the Cypress Hills and camped near a trading post run by Abe Farwell, a whisky vendor, beside Battle Creek (40 miles south of present-day Medicine Hat, Alta.). Also camped there were Assiniboines led by Chief Little Soldier. The Assiniboines said they did not have the stolen animals but they had

With only a few men, but with courage and fairness, NWMP Insp. James Walsh kept the peace when American Sioux camped in the Cypress Hills in the late 1870s. He and Sitting Bull were friends but Walsh gloried in press references to him as the great chief's "boss."

seen a Cree with several horses pass through the day before.

It was Saturday night. The hunters and the Indians drank heavily. About midday Sunday, from a shallow gravel gully overlooking the Indian camp, the wolf hunters began firing rapid-fire repeating rifles into the teepees. Three times the Assiniboines charged—with muzzle-loading, single-shot buffalo guns. One wolfer was killed; the others kept firing until dusk when the surviving Assiniboines fled. Thirty-six Indians were reported killed. One was Little Soldier.

The story that appeared June 11 in the *Herald* at Helena, Mont., soon spread. American newspapers treated the wolfers as a kind of advance guard of civilization; Canadian writers called them American scum and claimed 200 dead (there may have been as few as 15).

Eastern Canada was outraged. The problem at the whisky forts was more than mere lawlessness: Canadian sovereignty had been challenged. Now Prime Minister Sir John A. Macdonald acted. On Aug. 30 the North West Mounted Police was established—"Police" instead of "Rifles" to persuade the United States that it was a civilian, not a military, force.

Recruits numbered 150—clerks, tradesmen, telegraphers, bartenders, lumberjacks, policemen and soldiers from Ontario, Quebec, New Brunswick and Nova Scotia. It was planned that they would train all winter in the East but, under pressure from Lieutenant-Governor Alexander Morris of the Northwest Territories, Macdonald decided to send them west at once.

They assembled in October at Collingwood, 70 miles north of Toronto, and travelled 500 miles by steamer through Lake Huron and Lake Superior to Port Arthur (now Thunder Bay). Then, battered by blizzards, their tents and boots

Lt.Col. George Arthur French, a British artillery officer who was the NWMP's first commissioner, neither inspired love nor sought popularity. One time when Mountie recruits complained of saddle sores, French ordered an extra issue of salt—to rub in their wounds. But he battled to improve conditions for his men and he won their respect. When he resigned in 1876—to rejoin the British army—Mounties who made about $1 a day chipped in to buy him a $200 gold watch.

Eighteen days out from Fort Dufferin on their 1874 trek west, the NWMP held church services in southern Saskatchewan near Roche Percée, a wind-eroded rock venerated by the Indians.

Before the days of whisky forts, traders peddled liquor at Indian camps, making "seductive offers" such as this one portrayed in Frank Leslie's Illustrated Newspaper *in 1871.*

frozen, they trudged 450 miles to Lower Fort Garry, a Hudson's Bay Company post 20 miles north of Winnipeg. A, B and C divisions paraded at the fort on Nov. 3. Among those sworn in that day was Samuel B. Steele, a former army gunnery officer, now in charge of breaking the horses and of riding instruction. "Our work was unceasing from 6 a.m. until after dark," he wrote. "I drilled five rides [groups] per day the whole of the winter and the orders were that if the temperature were not lower than 36 below zero [-38°C] the riding and breaking should go on."

Farwell's Trading Post, near which Assiniboine Indians were killed by American wolf hunters in 1873, in the Cypress Hills Massacre that prompted formation of the NWMP, has been reconstructed in Fort Walsh National Historic Park. Inside (above) are the sorts of goods that Abe Farwell traded (along with bad liquor) for the Indians' furs.

A 32-year-old Royal Artillery Officer, Lt.Col. George Arthur French, on loan to the Canadian government, had been named commissioner in October at a salary of $2,600 a year. He arrived at Lower Fort Garry to find that few of his "Mounted Police" could ride.

When French learned that the whisky forts were armed with cannon and that the Blackfoot alone could muster 2,000 warriors, he asked Ottawa to double the force to 300 men, "the lowest number consistent with any degree of safety." He wrote: "If the outlaws and desperadoes in the forts deserve the character given them, we shall doubtless have to use our guns and may possibly have some hard fighting." Ottawa agreed and in February 1874 French went east to recruit more constables aged 18 to 40, of "sound constitution, able to ride, active and ablebodied and able to read and write either the English or French language." They went from Toronto to Fargo, N.Dak., by rail and after a five-day march reached Fort Dufferin (a Boundary Commission post, near present-day Emerson, Man.) on June 19. The 100 men of A, B and C divisions (50 had deserted or been discharged) had marched from Lower Fort Garry to meet them.

The new recruits' splendid horses were corralled inside a ring of loaded wagons, and A, B and C divisions' broncos were kept at a distance. In a storm the night of June 20 lightning struck among the Toronto horses and they bolted. Steele described what happened: "The maddened beasts overturned the huge wagons, dashed through a row of tents, scattered everything, and made for the gate of the large field in which we were encamped. [They] were between

30 and 50 miles into Dakota before they were compelled by sheer exhaustion to halt." Next morning the NWMP mounted their broncos and within two days rounded up all but one of the runaways.

A 2½-mile-long procession left Fort Dufferin July 8, 1874, bound for Fort Whoop-Up (near present-day Lethbridge, Alta.). Behind French came A Division and 13 of the 73 wagons, B Division with portable forges and field kitchens, then C Division with two nine-pounder field guns, two mortars, artillery and munitions wagons. D, E and F divisions were followed by 114 creaking Red River carts. In all there were 310 horses, 142 oxen and a large herd of cattle.

One horse died and a dozen men deserted on the third day. Supply wagons could not keep up and soon hunger tormented the cavalcade—as did thirst, dust and mosquitoes.

On July 24 the Mounties reached Roche Percée, an outcrop of rock on the Souris River near present-day Estevan, Sask. "What a change since our departure," wrote Jean d'Artigue. Now the force "resembled a routed army corps. For a distance of several miles the road was strewn with broken carts and horses and oxen overcome with hunger and fatigue."

French set up a four-day rest camp and decided to split the column. One division—the "barnyard contingent" of sick men and horses, and cattle—headed for Fort Ellice, 85 miles northeast. There the men would recuperate before marching 800 miles northwest to Fort Edmonton for the winter.

The remaining five divisions moved off July 29.

Charming, tough, a hard drinker—that was James Macleod. A friend called him "a happy combination of the gentleman of the old school and the man of the world and affairs." As NWMP assistant commissioner he built Fort Macleod, the Mounties' first post in the Far West; later he became commissioner. He resigned in 1887 and was a judge in the Northwest Territories until his death in 1894, at 58.

Fort Whoop-Up, the NWMP's first objective in 1874, has been reconstructed near Lethbridge, Alta. The original flew its own flag, designed to resemble the American Stars and Stripes.

Horses and oxen soon weakened again, and the men dragged carts and artillery. At Old Wives Lake on Aug. 13 the Mounties met their first Indians, a bedraggled and verminous band of Sioux. They held a pow-wow and smoked the peace pipe, and when they parted every Mountie was infested with lice. They scrubbed themselves with juniper oil and put their clothing on ant hills—the ants devoured the lice.

Near Old Wives Lake, at what came to be called Cripple Camp, French left seven invalids, 28 horses, 14 wagons and some cattle, then pushed on. By Aug. 24 they could see the Cypress Hills. They encountered their first buffalo Sept. 2 and killed five. They found the buffalo had trampled water holes into stinking bogs of mud, urine and water. But thirsty policemen filled their canteens nonetheless, boiled the liquid, threw in tea and drank.

On Sept. 10 they reached the junction of the Bow and South Saskatchewan rivers. Here, 800 miles from Fort Dufferin, they had been told they would find Fort Whoop-Up. It was *not* there. (It was 75 miles west at the junction of the Oldman and St. Mary rivers.) The Mounties were lost.

The column desperately needed food, water and wood, so it went south to the Sweet Grass Hills, just across the U.S. border. There the men pitched camp five days later. One wrote: "A glance around the camp would reveal very little to remind us of the brilliant parade of the force at Dufferin a few months ago. The sentry in front of

Jerry Potts: No Great Interpreter, Best Damn Scout

It was powerful oratory—and long-winded—as Blackfoot chiefs assembled to thank the Mounties for running the whisky traders off the plains. Assistant Commissioner James Macleod listened to a torrent of words, then turned to Jerry Potts for a translation. The bowlegged little Métis shrugged. "Dey damn glad you here," he said.

Potts was no great interpreter but he was the best scout the Mounties ever had. Macleod had hired him at Fort Benton, Mont., in 1874, to lead 150 bedraggled policemen on the last lap of their long march to Fort Whoop-Up, the whisky fort near present-day Lethbridge, Alta.

In the 22 years he worked for the Mounties, he never used a map or a compass. Yet he could find a landmark he had never seen and track down a whisky trader or a lost patrol in the foulest weather.

Potts's Scottish father was a fur trade clerk, his mother a Blood Indian. He taught the police Indian customs, and reassured the Indians about the Mounties' good intentions. He wore a jacket, trousers and a hat like a white; leggings, moccasins and a knife belt like an Indian. He once dreamed that a cat would protect him from evil. He awoke, spied a cat sleeping in the sun, killed it and wore its hide next to his skin till the day he died.

As a young man he fought in Indian tribal wars and took 16 scalps in one fight. After drinking bouts, Potts and another Métis, George Star, would stand 25 paces apart and try to trim each other's mustaches with bullets from their six-shooters.

He had an unquenchable thirst. When he could not get whisky he drank medicinal painkiller. When his first wife, a Crow, returned to her people, he married two Piegan sisters and lived with them in a teepee near Fort Walsh. He died in 1896 at 56. The Mounties gave him a full military funeral and fired a three-gun salute over his grave.

Promises at Blackfoot Crossing, 'For as Long as the Rivers Run'

Since 1871, in six treaties with the white man, all of Canada's Plains Indians except the Blackfoot Confederacy had signed away their lands. Now, in September 1877, at a great gathering at Blackfoot Crossing on the Bow River (near present-day Cluny, Alta.) came Treaty No. 7. This time, if all went well, 50,000 square miles of rich land between the Cypress Hills and the British Columbia border—virtually all of southern Alberta—would be ceded to the government of Canada in exchange for some small cash and some big promises.

More than 4,000 Blackfoot, Piegans, Stoneys, Blood and Sarcees raised a thousand teepees in a three-mile-long meadow stretching a mile back from the Bow. The Mounties arrived. So did Queen Victoria's representative, Lieutenant-Governor David Laird of the Northwest Territories, a Prince Edward Islander known to the Indians as The Man Who Talks Straight.

Government agents distributed flour, sugar and tea, and there were games and dancing to the throb of Indian drums. There was also an un-dercurrent of discontent. In a half-fun-half-serious demonstration, war-painted Indians galloped their horses around the whites, screaming and firing bullets past spectators.

Treaty discussions started Sept. 19. Laird warned that the buffalo soon would be destroyed. He promised the Indians rights and privileges "for as long as the sun shines and the rivers run." There would be reserves of choice land, one square mile for each family of five. An annual payment of $25 would go to each chief, $15 to each sub-chief. All others—men, women and chil-

dren—would get $12 each on the signing of the treaty, $5 a year thereafter. Each chief would receive a medal, a flag and new clothes every three years. There would be ammunition, cattle, implements and seed—and teachers.

The parley went on for three days. Finally Crowfoot *(left)*—greatest of the Blackfoot chiefs—announced the decision the others had awaited. He said the honesty and the efforts of the police had helped him decide. He would sign the treaty. He did, and others of the confederacy followed.

Two police nine-pounders boomed a salute and the Mountie band played God Save the Queen. Then $52,954 in treaty money was paid out to 4,392 Indian men, women and children.

Now traders selling food, horses and buffalo robes moved in—eager to get at the Indians' money. Some cheated, giving food tin labels as change. And again the policemen who had so influenced Crowfoot's decision stepped in. Each time a label was "passed," wrote NWMP Sub-Inspector Cecil Denny, "We had then to hunt up the culprit and deal with him."

At the town of Fort Macleod, Alta., the oldest community in southern Alberta, is a stylized reconstruction of the original Fort Macleod. It was the first fort built by the NWMP.

the commissioner's quarters has gunny sacking wrapped around his feet, his rags of clothing fluttering in the breeze."

With a few men and some empty wagons, French and Assistant Commissioner James Macleod struck out for Fort Benton, 80 miles south. French returned with supplies; Macleod came soon after, with a Métis guide named Jerry Potts.

French had decided to split the column once more. Macleod and 150 men were to find and destroy Fort Whoop-Up, then establish their own fort nearby. French and the others, including the men at Cripple Camp, would spend the winter in new headquarters—the Swan River Barracks—being built near present-day Pelly, Sask. When the force arrived there on Oct. 21 the barracks were not ready. French left only E Division in the unfinished post and continued southeast. On Nov. 7, four months and close to 2,000 miles since the proud departure from Fort Dufferin, French led D Division into Winnipeg.

Jerry Potts led Macleod to Fort Whoop-Up on Oct. 9. It was a massive fort surrounded by a 14-foot stockade topped by sharpened stakes. There were two corner bastions for cannon. Doors, windows, even chimneys, were barred with iron.

Macleod positioned his two nine-pounders and two mortars. Then he and Potts rode forward and banged on the main gate. They were greeted by Dave Akers, a tall, cadaverous, goateed Confederate Army veteran. The Mounties were expected, he said. Would they care to stay for a meal with him?

Indians had warned of the Mounties' approach and the other traders had sold the fort to Akers and cleared out. There was not a drop of whisky in Akers's fort. So there was buffalo steak for dinner that night in the fort that these Mounties had marched almost 1,000 miles to destroy.

Macleod tried to buy Whoop-Up—he wanted it as the force's headquarters—but Akers refused his $10,000 offer. The column moved almost 30 miles west and built Fort Macleod on an island in the Oldman River. (It was moved to the mainland four years later because of flooding.)

The first attack on the whisky trade came before the fort was completed. Three Bulls, a Blackfoot, told Macleod he had sold two ponies for two gallons of whisky to a trader at Pine Coulee, 50 miles north of the fort. Insp. Leif Crozier and 10

men were sent there with orders to seize all furs and robes which he suspected had been traded for whisky. They returned with five prisoners, 16 horses, rifles, revolvers, buffalo robes and two wagonloads of alcohol—which was dumped.

There were many raids on whisky forts that winter of 1874-75. The Mounties were grateful for the skins they confiscated: they used them as bedding and to make winter coats and caps.

It became obvious that a second post was needed to control the liquor traffic. In May 1875, with B Division, Insp. James Walsh built Fort Walsh 160 miles east of Fort Macleod—on Battle Creek near the site of the Cypress Hills Massacre of 1873.

By late fall a 14-foot log stockade enclosed a cluster of dirt-floored log buildings including a commanding officer's residence, officers' and sergeants' messes, barracks and stables.

Sitting Bull vowed, "as long as there is gopher to eat," not to lead his Sioux back to the United States. But in 1881, four years after entering Canada following the Battle of the Little Big Horn in Montana, his people were starving and the great warrior did return, surrendering meekly to the Americans. NWMP Insp. James Walsh, who had become his friend, said Sitting Bull "is the shrewdest and most intelligent living Indian, has the ambition of a Napoleon and is brave to a fault."

More Voyageur Than Charge of the Light Brigade

The Mounties looked like crack British cavalry as they headed west out of Fort Dufferin on the great trek of 1874. They were bound for Fort Whoop-Up to bust the whisky traders—but in style, which meant the elegance of gold-braided pillbox hats, white breeches and gauntlets, and (when deemed appropriate) white pith helmets and glittering swords. The red of their coats symbolized friendship and fair dealing to the Indians. Some believed the red was the blood of enemies of the Great White Queen.

Nine months later the uniforms were in tatters. The pillboxes and helmets were discarded, replaced by slouch hats. Coats and trousers were of crudely tanned deerskin. Buffalo coats were popular in winter. What Commissioner George

French saw lined up before him when he returned to the Swan River Barracks after several months was more voyageur than Charge of the Light Brigade. "Good God!" he exclaimed. Quickly he rode away.

The slouch hat not only kept off the sun but also was used to carry water, hold horse feed and stow tobacco. It was the forerunner of the Stetson that became the trademark of the Royal Canadian Mounted Police. The Stetson gained official approval in 1901 and the heavy broadcloth of the tunics was replaced by the scarlet serge the Mounties still wear on formal occasions. The cut of the everyday uniform—a brown jacket—was changed. The Mountie attire had become practical as well as impressive.

1874   1878   1901

Far left: the first Mountie uniforms, like those of the British cavalry, included Norfolk jackets and tight breeches.

Centre: as regulation clothing wore out, Mounties adopted informal garb.

Left: Stetson, yellow-striped breeches, and brown boots and gauntlets—still in use today—were not adopted until the 20th century.

In the spring of 1875 warrants were issued for the arrest of men suspected of the Cypress Hills Massacre. Seven were taken at Fort Benton but two escaped. The other five were tried by an American court in Helena—with anti-Canadian feelings running high—and were acquitted. Three more suspects were picked up in Canada, tried at Winnipeg in June 1876 but eventually acquitted for lack of evidence.

No one was punished for the massacre but Indians across the plains were impressed by the Mounties arresting white men for the murder of Indians.

Gradually the whisky trade was wiped out. Tribal conflicts waned as admiration and respect for the Mounties grew. Red Crow, a Blackfoot chief, said of Macleod: "When the police first came to the country, I met and shook hands with Stamix Otokan [Bull's Head]. He has made me many promises. He kept them all." "If the police had not come," Crowfoot, chief of the Blackfoot Confederacy, told his braves in September 1877, "very few of us would have been alive today. The Mounted Police have protected us as the feathers of a bird protect it from the frosts of winter."

In September 1877, leaders of the Blackfoot Confederacy, the last of the Plains Indians to surrender their lands, signed Treaty No. 7 and ceded 50,000 square miles of what now is southern Alberta. The Mounties had led the Blackfoot to expect justice from Ottawa. A battle in Montana a year earlier had showed them they needed protection as well as justice.

On June 25, 1876, at the Little Big Horn River, Sitting Bull and the American Sioux had wiped out five companies of Gen. George Custer's 7th U.S. Cavalry. The United States was enraged

Roughing it was a Mountie way of life, as for these men in the Cypress Hills in 1879. An outbreak of illness put them under canvas for two months while Fort Walsh was fumigated.

Ah, Life in Barracks! Few Books, No Women, and Beans at 21 Below

The average temperature in January 1875 at the new North West Mounted Police Swan River Barracks, near present-day Pelly, Sask., was 21 below (–29°C) and Insp. Jacob Carvell, a Southerner who had fought on the Confederate side in the American Civil War, formally requested a supply of thermometers: "When the men go to bed I think they should know if it is cold enough to freeze their ears if left exposed."

Swan River, NWMP headquarters, was a disaster of badly built barracks strung out along a treeless hill that was endlessly ravaged by north winds. But it was all too typical of police posts in the early days. Food was heavy and dull—buffalo, beans, pork, flapjacks, tea. Liquor was banned, except perhaps at Christmas (although bootlegged year round). Books were few. There was little if any sports equipment and hardly any contact with women.

Letters from home were like pure gold—and this advertisement appeared in the *Montreal Star*: "Two lonely Mounted Policemen desire to correspond with a limited number of young ladies for mutual improvement."

Men did their best. There were dances, with "all the available halfbreed girls" invited. R. B. Nevitt, a young doctor at Fort Macleod, wrote modestly to his fiancée in Toronto that "I was the Belle of the Ball, the only one who could dance [the lady part] with anything like decency, and consequently my hand was sought after." Sports at police posts ranged from horse races and cricket to snake-killing (1,110 one day at Swan River).

On their worst days, some of the men who marched west to break up the whisky trade turned to the same kind of rotgut that renegade traders had fed the Indians. Raw alcohol and Jamaica ginger perhaps. Or bay rum diluted with water and flavored with painkiller. In a pinch, a Mountie might down a swig of his horse's "mustang liniment."

Inspector Carvell presumably went back to mint juleps. After that miserable first winter at Swan River he went on leave—and deserted. He did it nicely enough, with a formal letter of resignation from Boulder, Colo., but the Force never laid eyes on him again.

One of the NWMP's first officers was Insp. Francis Dickens, a son of novelist Charles Dickens. He had served with the Bengal Mounted Police in India before joining the NWMP in November 1874.

and some of the Sioux, traditional enemies of the Blackfoot, moved into Canada. By December about 2,000 were camped at Wood Mountain, 150 miles east of the Cypress Hills. When Sitting Bull arrived in May 1877 there were 4,000 north of the border. Inspector Walsh feared an Indian war.

With only four constables and two scouts, he rode into Sitting Bull's huge encampment and warned the great chief that he must obey the Queen's law. Walsh and his men slept at the Indian camp that night.

The very next morning the Sioux saw the Mounties in action.

White Dog, a warrior of the Assiniboine tribe (a branch of the Sioux) came into camp with three horses that he and two companions had sto-

len. Walsh disarmed White Dog and told him he would be taken in irons to Fort Walsh unless he admitted the theft and surrendered the animals. White Dog said he had found the horses wandering on the prairie but relinquished them anyway. Angry at losing face, he muttered: "I'll meet you again." Holding up leg irons, Walsh insisted that White Dog withdraw the words or be arrested for threatening an officer. The humiliated Indian took back the threat. Walsh's courage won Sitting Bull's respect and the two became close friends.

Although Sitting Bull's people lived peacefully in Canada, the government in Ottawa feared a war between the Sioux and the Blackfoot. By 1879 the buffalo had been slaughtered almost to extinction and the Indians were starving. Many Sioux went to reservations in the United States but Sitting Bull and some others remained in Canada. Walsh was suspected of encouraging them to stay.

In June 1880, in a dispute over police expenditures, Sir John A. Macdonald forced Macleod to resign. A month later Walsh was transferred to Fort Qu'Appelle, Sask. He retired under pressure in 1883, taking with him his horse—for which he paid the government $150.

Sitting Bull had crossed the border and surrendered to the U.S. army on July 21, 1881. Fewer than 200 followers were with him. His last pathetic threat to peace on the plains (and it had been fading just as surely as the buffalo were dying out) had now been removed.

In only seven years the Mounties had brought law and order to the West.

Fort Battleford, established in 1876 (near present-day North Battleford, Sask.), was the fifth North West Mounted Police post and was the capital of the Northwest Territories until 1883. These officers' quarters are in one of five original buildings at Battleford National Historic Park (right).

Heritage Sites

FORT WALSH NATIONAL HISTORIC PARK, Sask.

The North West Mounted Police post established in 1875 to end the whisky trade in what is now southwestern Saskatchewan has been partially reconstructed in this 2½-square-mile park. The buildings include a barracks, commanding officer's residence, workshop and stable. Firearms, saddles, bridles and NWMP uniforms are displayed.

CYPRESS HILLS MASSACRE A plaque 1½ miles south of Fort Walsh marks where Assiniboine Indians were massacred by American wolf hunters in 1873. The killings spurred formation of the NWMP.

FARWELL'S TRADING POST This re-creation of a store at which Abe Farwell traded whisky is stocked with whisky kegs and patent medicines and staffed by guides in 1870s dress. The exterior of Solomon's Trading Post, a similar store, has been reconstructed nearby.

NWMP CEMETERY A stone marks the grave of Const. Marmaduke Graburn, murdered in 1879—the first Mountie slain on duty. (A Blood Indian named Star Child was tried two years later but acquitted because of insufficient evidence.) A cairn 12 miles west is where Graburn's body was found.

Other sites

Calgary (1) A cairn in Central Park commemorates the establishment in 1875 of Fort Calgary, the NWMP post that was the beginning of Calgary. The Horseman's Hall of Fame depicts the signing of Treaty No. 7 in 1877, when Crowfoot and other chiefs of the Blackfoot Confederacy ceded 50,000 square miles of what is now southern Alberta. Life-size figures include Crowfoot, NWMP guide Jerry Potts and NWMP Commissioner James Macleod.

Cluny, Alta. (2) A cairn three miles south identifies Blackfoot Crossing where Treaty No. 7 was signed in 1877. A metal cross marks the grave of Crowfoot.

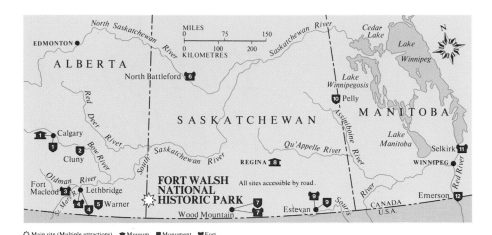

Emerson, Man. (12) A cairn 1½ miles north identifies the site of Fort Dufferin, the Boundary Commission post from which 275 men of the NWMP began their march west July 8, 1874.

Estevan, Sask. (9) A restored barracks in Woodlawn Regional Park, a mile south, remains from a post used by the police about 1886-92. NWMP uniforms are displayed. A cairn at Roche Percée, 15 miles southeast, marks where the Mounties rested four days and held divine services on their march west.

Fort Macleod, Alta. (3) A stylized version of the first fort built by the NWMP is at the edge of town. The original Fort Macleod, built in 1874 after the march west, was on an island in the Oldman River, about a mile east. A museum has weapons and uniforms, and a diorama of the original fort.

Lethbridge, Alta. (4) A cairn at the junction of the St. Mary and Oldman rivers marks the site of Fort Whoop-Up, the first and most notorious whisky fort put out of business by the Mounties. A reconstruction is in Indian Battle Park, along with an original Fort Whoop-Up cannon.

North Battleford, Sask. (6) Five buildings remaining from Fort Battleford, a NWMP post founded in 1876, have been restored in 45-acre Battleford National Historic Park four miles south. The buildings, erected between 1877 and 1898, include the commanding officer's house, officers' quarters, a barracks and a guardhouse.

Pelly, Sask. (10) A cairn about three miles northwest marks the national historic site where Fort Livingstone, also known as the Swan River Barracks, was built in 1874 as the first NWMP headquarters.

Regina (8) The history of the Royal Canadian Mounted Police, from its founding as the NWMP, is portrayed in the RCMP Museum at the Depot Division. Exhibits include one of the muzzle-loading cannon taken on the march west, and a revolver believed owned by Ed Grace (the only wolfer killed during the Cypress Hills Massacre). Also in the museum are flags that flew above Fort Walsh in 1875-80.

Selkirk, Man. (11) The Hudson's Bay Company post where the first NWMP recruits wintered in 1873-74 before the march west is in Lower Fort Garry National Historic Park.

Warner, Alta. (5) A plaque nine miles north commemorates Métis scout Jerry Potts, who led the NWMP through this area on the last leg of the march west, and was their guide for 22 years.

Wood Mountain, Sask. (7) A barracks and mess hall of Wood Mountain Post, a key Mountie station when Sitting Bull and his Sioux moved into Canada in 1876-77, have been re-created in Wood Mountain Historic Park. The place where the Sioux camped is marked by a cairn in nearby Wood Mountain Regional Park.

This museum in Woodlawn Regional Park near Estevan, Sask., is a restored NWMP barracks built between 1886 and 1892.

The Dying of a Dream
in a Battle at Batoche

It was May 12, 1885, and for four days the village of Batoche—on the South Saskatchewan River some 50 miles north of Saskatoon—had been a battleground as about 850 white militiamen from Eastern Canada engaged fewer than 300 Métis sharpshooters. The Métis, of mixed Indian and European blood, seemed invulnerable in the three-to-four-foot-deep pits they had dug, drawing fire with dummies.

The military leader of the rebellious Métis—men fighting for their dream of nationhood (see p. 167)—was 47-year-old Gabriel Dumont, a ferry operator who had learned battle tactics in the days of the great buffalo hunts. But striding among the rifle pits and in front of them, paying no heed to the enemy fire, was another man, the overall leader of the Métis. He wore a black suit and moccasins. He was unarmed. He carried a cross. He was Louis Riel.

Unknown to the militia force, led by Maj.Gen. Frederick Middleton, the Métis were nearly spent. Their ammunition had run out; now they shot stones and nails. That afternoon, against Middleton's orders, impatient soldiers charged. Outnumbered, the Métis could scarcely defend themselves. The Battle of Batoche was over. Dumont escaped into the United States. But Middleton had his prize: Louis Riel, who had not fired a shot, was a prisoner.

Louis Riel, one-eighth Indian, was born in 1844 in St. Boniface—now part of Winnipeg—in the prairie section of the vast territory the Hudson's Bay Company called Rupert's Land (all the land

"The Capture of Batoche," a lithograph from a war artist's sketches, looks west. The Métis' first line of defence (foreground, near stretcher-bearers) has been over-run but other marksmen led by Louis Riel (in happier days, left) hold rifle pits between here and the village. The house (6) with a fence is that of Xavier "Batoche" Letendre, operator of the ferry (3). The Church of Saint-Antoine-de-Padoue and its rectory, not in the battle picture, survive (above) in present-day Batoche.

277

The Commander-in-Chief From Gabriel's Crossing

The fighting was over at Batoche and the rebellion was smashed but Gabriel Dumont refused to quit—despite a promise from Maj.Gen. Frederick Middleton that every Métis would receive justice. "Tell Middleton," said Dumont, the illiterate sharpshooter who was Louis Riel's military commander-in-chief and brilliant strategist, "that I am in the thickets in the woods, and that I have 90 cartridges to spend on his people." Then he learned that Riel had surrendered. That *was* the end. Dumont fled to the United States.

This fearless Métis leader, one of the great buffalo hunters, was a realist too. Long before 1885 he had accepted the end of real freedom on the plains. And yet in Riel he had seen the Métis' one last desperate hope—and had done his best, always bowing to Riel's wishes. His military talents, as it turned out, were all but wasted.

Born in 1837 at St. Boniface, Man., Dumont fought his first battle at 13: for two days he and fewer than 100 Métis held off some 2,500 Sioux. Like all Métis hunters, he could ride into a herd of buffalo, shooting from the hip and reloading

at full gallop. But he was a crack shot, and knew the prairies, one hunter said, "as a sheep knows its heath." Legend says that he once told a band of hostile Blackfoot—in their own tongue: "I am Gabriel Dumont! I have killed eight Blackfoot!" They so admired his reckless courage that they did him no harm.

In 1872, with the buffalo almost depleted, Dumont turned to farming about seven miles south of Batoche. He was elected president of the local Métis government and operated a store and the ferry at Gabriel's Crossing (Sunday crossings free for churchgoers) on the South Saskatchewan River where Gabriel's Bridge now stands. Then, in the tragedy of the Northwest Rebellion, he took up his Winchester and stepped into Canadian history.

For some years after his escape to the United States he toured with William "Buffalo Bill" Cody's Wild West Show as the sharpshooting "Prince of the Plains." The Canadian government granted him amnesty in 1886. In 1893 Dumont returned to Batoche where he died in 1906, aged 68. A plaque in a big stone that marks his grave tells the story of his life.

draining into Hudson Bay). He grew up in a deeply religious home and at 13 went to Montreal to prepare for the priesthood. But at 20 he joined a law office. His employer, Rodolphe Laflamme, was opposed to Confederation and Riel became steeped in Quebec nationalist politics and in constitutional law. In 1868, after living in the United States for several years, he returned home.

Much had changed. The HBC's Upper Fort Garry still faced St. Boniface across the Red River but now just north of the fort was the village of Winnipeg, its population swelled by immigrants from the Canadian province of Ontario. Even yet, however, there were only 1,500 whites on the Prairies—among 10,000 Métis, three-fifths of whom were French-speaking Catholics.

In April 1869 the HBC accepted the terms under which the new Dominion of Canada would buy Rupert's Land. Canada particularly wanted the fertile prairie, but by October Britain still had not transferred sovereignty. Canada, impatient, sent surveyors to the confluence of the Red and the Assiniboine.

Since 1849 the Métis had lived at peace with

Outside Winnipeg's St. Boniface Museum—built in 1846 as a Grey Nuns convent—are four grinding stones imported from Scotland and used by Louis Riel's father, a miller.

Métis traders posed for this photograph (c. 1872) at their bleak camp in mid-prairie. Such groups hauled goods from the railhead at St. Paul, Minn., to the Red River Settlement.

the HBC, farming, trading and hunting buffalo. Now their homeland was to be handed to a new and foreign power. They had not been consulted and they feared that their rights to the land—and their way of life—would not be respected.

Métis farms, like Quebec farms, were laid out in narrow, two-mile-long strips, each fronting on a river, well suited to raising livestock. But the surveyors were staking out the land in square sections of 640 acres, well suited to raising crops. Worse, they had not learned the custom of the hay privilege, which gave the farmer grazing rights to another two-mile strip at the end of his farm. When André Nault found a survey crew on his farm on Oct. 11, 1869, he tried to explain that their line would run between his buildings. The Canadians spoke no French and Nault sent for his 24-year-old cousin, Louis Riel, to translate. Riel arrived with a party of about 18 and, in English, told the surveyors to go no farther. When the Métis stood on the survey chain, the crew went away. No more surveying was done on Métis land.

Soon the well-educated and articulate Riel became a spokesman for his threatened people. When the Métis met on Oct. 16 at St. Norbert, just south of St. Boniface, to form the National Committee of the Métis, Riel was elected secretary. Meanwhile, William McDougall was on his way west to become lieutenant-governor of Rupert's Land. Riel wrote to McDougall that he must not enter Métis territory without the committee's permission. McDougall waited just north of the Canada-U.S. border at Fort Dufferin (an abandoned HBC post later used by the Boundary Commission) but his aide, Capt. D. R. Cameron, drove on. At St. Norbert, at a roadblock, he ordered Métis guards to "remove that blasted fence" but they turned his gig around and sent him racing back to the border.

Cameron's fury was shared by a few English-speaking Canadians in Winnipeg (whose headquarters were in a store owned by Dr. John Christian Schultz). But they were greatly outnumbered by the Métis and on Nov. 2, with 120 men, Riel occupied the HBC's Fort Garry.

Riel, undisputed leader of the French-speaking Catholic Métis, felt he must also win over the English-speaking Protestant Métis and English-speaking white settlers. On Nov. 6 he invited all English-speaking parishes to send delegates "to consider the present political state of this Country, and to adopt such measures as may be deemed best for the future welfare of the same."

Ten days later they met, the first Convention of the People of Rupert's Land. On Nov. 26

Even as a youth (here he is 14) Louis Riel was aloof and egotistical. A classmate at the Sulpician Seminary of Montreal wrote: "To offer an opinion contrary to his was to irritate him. He did not understand that everyone could not share his views, so much did he believe in his personal infallibility."

John Schultz, leader of a small group of English-speaking Canadians who opposed Louis Riel, was imprisoned when the Métis captured Fort Garry in 1869. He escaped in January 1870, fled to the United States, then went to Toronto. There he helped turn English Canada against Riel by talking at public meetings about the Métis' execution of a fellow prisoner, Thomas Scott.

Donald Smith of the Hudson's Bay Company (in red), just arrived at Fort Garry in December 1869, argues the Ottawa government's case as he tries to make peace with the Métis.

Prime Minister Sir John A. Macdonald cabled London halting the Canadian takeover of Rupert's Land unless the Hudson's Bay Company could guarantee peace.

Neither Riel and the 12-man council nor Lieutenant-Governor-designate McDougall knew about the cable, and on Dec. 1, in a simple ceremony at Fort Dufferin, McDougall formally took possession of the country for which Canada had suspended dealing. He named Col. John Stoughton Dennis conservator of the peace and went back to Pembina, just across the U.S. border, and then to Ottawa.

But that same day, in Fort Garry, the Métis council was drawing up a List of Rights to be respected when their country was annexed to Canada. The most important were that the people elect their own legislature; that English *and* French be spoken in the legislature and the courts and that all "privileges, customs and usages existing at the time of the transfer be respected."

Schultz—his store in Winnipeg now an armory—wanted to attack the Métis in their fort but was restrained by Colonel Dennis, who had not mustered enough men to take on Riel. Riel moved first. On Dec. 7, with 200 men, he surrounded Schultz's store, aimed two cannon at the door and gave the Canadians 15 minutes to surrender. Soon after, some 45 Canadians were

marched into Fort Garry as prisoners, Schultz among them. Another was Thomas Scott, a laborer who had come from Ontario with a road-building gang. He was well known for his brawling and for his hatred of Catholics and Métis.

The next day Riel issued a declaration soundly based on his knowledge of constitutional law. It stated that when a people has no government it may choose its own; that his council, the only lawful authority in Rupert's Land, was willing to negotiate with Canada on such terms "as may be favorable for the good government and prosperity of this people." Colonel Dennis made a hasty withdrawal toward Ontario.

Rupert's Land was still nominally under the control of the Hudson's Bay Company. Its chief officer in Canada, Donald Smith (later Lord Strathcona), agreed with Prime Minister Macdonald that an attempt should be made to make peace with the Métis. Smith arrived at Fort Garry Dec. 27, 1869. He reported to Macdonald: "Nothing can be more serious than the present state of affairs here, the power being entirely in the hands of Mr. Riel and his party."

Smith talked with Riel for many hours. On

The Viscount Counts on Canadian Boatmen

Viscount Wolseley had quelled the Red River Rebellion in the Northwest in 1870 and he knew Canadian voyageurs were white water specialists. Fourteen years later, half a world away in Egypt, as he prepared to push up the Nile into the Sudan and lift the siege of Khartoum, Wolseley relied on Canadian boatmen to move his troops through the 860 miles of rapids and cataracts above Aswan.

He had 378 boatmen aged 18 to 64—French, English, Indian and Métis. Most were experienced but a few (not carefully screened) were adventurers who could not be relied on in dangerous water. All were promised $40 a month, a daily ration of rum, and return home in six months; boats were built for them in England.

From above the Second Cataract, 200 miles beyond Aswan, the progress of Wolseley's force depended on the Canadians. On calm stretches of the Nile the soldiers rowed under voyageur supervision; in rough water the boats were tracked from shore while Canadians stayed aboard to pole them clear of rocks. Some voyageurs were drowned.

The rescue mission was a failure. Advance troops reached Khartoum two days too late to save the besieged Britons from slaughter by the Sudanese. But the Canadians earned high praise for their part in the expedition. Their presence, Wolseley wrote, showed "the bonds which unite all parts of our great Empire."

On the downstream return trip they had the suicidal job of shooting the Nile cataracts. Despite the Canadians' skill, 10 boats were smashed and more voyageurs were drowned.

The 378—and five officers—were the first Canadians to serve in an overseas war.

Feb. 7 he extended Canada's invitation to have at least two *residents*—not delegates of the provisional government—go to Ottawa and present the views of the people.

Three residents went at the end of March to discuss the List of Rights with Macdonald. They were worried about preparations for a military expedition to territory that was not yet part of Canada but were assured its intentions were peaceful. Troops would have been sent to a new province in any case, if only to build roads as soldiers had done in Ontario. Two residents returned to the Red River well satisfied. (The third went to England.)

But, meanwhile, Thomas Scott had escaped from the fort and on the night of Jan. 23 so had Dr. Schultz. With a knife that his wife had concealed in a pudding, he sliced a buffalo robe into strips, braided them into a rope and went through a window and over a wall.

On Feb. 10 Riel formed a second provisional government. Thomas Scott was caught on Feb. 17 and Riel made his first mistake. Scott, who had attacked his Métis guards, was sentenced to death. "We wanted to make sure," Riel wrote, "that our attitude was taken seriously." Instead, the execution on March 4 won him the hatred of English Canada. The escaped Schultz toured Ontario calling on loyal Protestants to avenge

Thomas Scott, an Ontario laborer, was executed at Fort Garry in 1870 (by a Métis firing squad, not as in this sketch). His death turned English Canada against Louis Riel.

Col. Garnet Wolseley, commander of the force that crushed the Red River Rebellion in 1870, was a British army veteran of wars in China, India and the Crimea.

This 3¾-inch brass crucifix (in the RCMP Depot Division Museum in Regina) was carried to the scaffold by Métis leader Louis Riel on Nov. 16, 1885.

Scott. Posters in Toronto proclaimed: "Men of Ontario! Shall Scott's blood cry in vain for vengeance?" Col. (later Viscount) Garnet Wolseley left Toronto on May 21 with 800 volunteers in his force of 1,200.

The force took four days to go by boat to the Lakehead, and 91 days to cover the forest, swamp and rock between there and Fort Garry. Wolseley arrived Aug. 24 to find that Riel had taken flight. Wolseley wrote: "I was glad that Riel did not come out and surrender, for I could not then have hanged him." Riel, in flight, said, "Tell the people that he who ruled in Fort Garry only yesterday is now a homeless wanderer with nothing to eat but two dried fish."

But Riel had won. On July 15, 1870, the Red River district became the province of Manitoba. Its name, chosen by Riel and the provisional government, means "the spirit that speaks." One million four hundred thousand acres were set aside for the Métis; the English and French languages were to have equal status.

The Ontario government offered a reward for Riel's capture.

In 1873, he was elected to Parliament by acclamation in a by-election in the Manitoba constituency of Provencher. But he was afraid of arrest and never took his seat.

In the 1874 election he retained the seat without appearing in Provencher. He went to Ottawa and managed to sign the register of members and take the oath of allegiance but fled immediately into Quebec. Ottawa was on fire with rumors that he had been seen and when the session opened it was said that "in the crowd in the public galleries this evening there were over one hundred revolvers."

When he did not appear in the House, Parliament expelled him.

Riel was forced to travel constantly, living off charity. He won another by-election in September 1874 and was expelled again in 1875. He was granted amnesty on condition he remain outside the country for five years.

CPR Salmon (and Misery) En Route to Saskatchewan

For most of the eastern militiamen who put down the Northwest Rebellion in 1885 the worst part was getting there by CPR—and worst of all was a brutal, 253-mile stretch north of Lake Superior between Dog Lake (near present-day White River, Ont.) and Red Rock, where gaps in the track totalled 85 miles. But the railway did its magnificent best and, as it had promised, none of the 3,000 men took longer than 12 days to reach Saskatchewan.

For some the trip started well enough. When the Queen's Own Rifles reached the end of track at Dog Lake on April 1, the CPR greeted them with beef, salmon, lobster, mackerel, vegetables, fruit, bread, cakes and pies. Then, with the temperature plunging to 25 below (−31.5°C), they boarded horse-drawn sleighs for a miserable 36-mile journey over a boulder-strewn tote road to Birch Lake and the next section of track. There they were crammed aboard flatcars and bumped along 96 miles of temporary track *laid on snow*. The temperature dropped to nearly 35 below (−37°C) and there were frequent derailments. Then came a 20-mile trip on the ice of frozen Lake Superior to McKellar's Harbour, another 20 miles by flatcar to Jackfish Bay, a 22-mile march or sleigh ride to

Winston's Dock, then still another journey by flatcar—52 miles this time, without food and in sleet and rain—to Nipigon Bay. The men were exhausted—but had done 246 miles. The last seven miles, on April 5, was a slushy trudge across the frozen bay to Red Rock, where they boarded heated coaches. Ahead lay unbroken track.

By July 2, with Louis Riel and his

rebels crushed, the troops were going home. There were comfortable coaches for the men, sleepers for the officers—and no gaps in the line. The Lake Superior section had been completed May 28. No militiaman had died on the trip west but it had put more men out of action—through pneumonia, bronchitis and tonsillitis—than the campaign itself in Saskatchewan.

The Governor General's Body Guard chose to ride 62 miles on frozen Lake Superior.

Nearly 10 years were to pass before Riel reappeared on the Canadian political scene. These were years that saw an influx of English-speaking Protestant settlers and the end of the great buffalo herds on the Red River. Many Métis settled along the north and south branches of the Saskatchewan in the Northwest Territories (part of Canada since 1870). There the remnants of the herds could be hunted for a few more seasons. Under the leadership of Gabriel Dumont, once a famous leader of the hunt, the Métis struggled for self-government and recognition of their title to the land.

Louis Riel was now 39 and an American citizen, married and working as a teacher. He was still passionately religious. On Sunday, June 4, 1884, he was called from a service in a mission church on the Sun River in Montana. Gabriel Dumont and three other Métis had ridden more than 600 miles to ask him to return to Canada. The federal government was too occupied with building the Canadian Pacific Railway to heed the grievances of the Métis. They needed a leader who would be heard. They needed Riel.

A few days later, with his wife, two children and all his possessions, Riel set off for what he expected to be an absence of only a few months. On the four-week journey he had a vision of a gallows on a hill.

Through the last half of 1884 Riel worked on a petition listing the needs of whites, Métis and Indians and by Dec. 16 it was on its way to Ottawa.

The secretary of state acknowledged receipt but Riel got no reply. Prime Minister Macdonald denied receiving the petition.

Certain segments of the population withdrew their support of Riel. The clergy feared he would undermine their authority with his claim to be the "prophet" of the Métis. The English-speaking settlers feared that his talk of forming a provisional government would lead to rebellion.

On March 5, 1885, Riel and other Métis leaders took a revolutionary oath. They pledged to "Save our souls by making ourselves live in righteousness night and day [and] to save our country from wicked government by taking up arms whenever it shall be necessary."

On March 18 Riel rode into Batoche at the head of a mounted party, occupied the Roman Catholic Church of Saint-Antoine-de-Padoue, and proclaimed a provisional government in "the Saskatchewan." The district already had a legally constituted government in Ottawa, remote and indifferent though it might be. Riel's act was rebellion.

The first act of Riel's provisional government was an ultimatum on March 21 to the North West Mounted Police at Fort Carlton on the North Saskatchewan River: leave the country or face a "war of extermination." On the 26th, the fort commander, Superintendent Leif Crozier, sent a dozen sleighs to bring in supplies from a store at Duck Lake, on the trail from Carlton to Batoche. Gabriel Dumont, to whom Riel had

The Mounties and settlers defeated by Gabriel Dumont's Métis at Duck Lake on March 26, 1885—in the first engagement of the Northwest Rebellion—were from Fort Carlton. (Above: a reconstruction at Carlton, Sask.) Two days later an apparently accidental fire razed much of the fort and it was abandoned. What remained was looted and destroyed by the Métis.

Markers overlooking Steele Narrows, Sask. (hidden, left), describe the final skirmish of the Northwest Rebellion (and the last military engagement in Canada). Big Bear's Crees retreated to the far side of Tubilee Lake on June 3, 1885, and fired on troops led by NWMP Maj. Sam Steele, in position on the near (foreground) side.

At the outbreak of the Northwest Rebellion in 1885, the Rev. Albert Lacombe had been in the West for more than 35 years—a man loved and respected as peacemaker between the Cree and the Blackfoot, as mediator between the Blood and the CPR, as friend and savior in a smallpox epidemic. He was called the man with a good heart. Some Indians, notably the Cree, joined the Métis revolt, but Father Lacombe, in perhaps his greatest contribution to peace on the plains, persuaded the Blackfoot to remain at peace.

delegated military command while he worked on plans for a great Métis society, intercepted the supply party and turned it back at rifle point. Crozier, with 98 men, marched after Dumont into a shallow valley ringed by about 300 Métis sharpshooters. Dumont, master of the buffalo hunt, had made a military tactic of the buffalo "pound" (see p. 166). Four Métis, one Indian and 12 whites were fatally wounded at Duck Lake and Dumont suffered a head wound. Riel looked on, holding aloft a crucifix two feet high.

On March 30, two hundred Crees under Chief Poundmaker attacked Battleford on the north branch of the Saskatchewan. They looted and burned for four days. On April 2 Big Bear's band of Crees (led by his war chief, Wandering Spirit) massacred nine whites at Frog Lake. Along the North Saskatchewan River and as far away as Edmonton, white settlers took shelter in HBC and NWMP forts.

Dumont's scouts kept him informed of every movement in the territory around Batoche. A single cable line ran across his land. Once it was cut, settlers and police on the Prairies could not know that help was on its way. From Fort Qu'Appelle (the railhead) Maj.Gen. Frederick Middleton led some 800 militiamen northwest toward Batoche. From Swift Current, with about 700 men, Col. William Otter advanced on Battleford. From Calgary, Maj.Gen. Thomas Bland Strange, with 600 men, moved north to Edmonton to ensure Blackfoot neutrality.

On April 24 Colonel Otter entered Battleford.

Life on the Reserves: Starvation, Massacre, Rebellion, Oblivion...

By 1880 most of Canada's Prairie Indians had settled into a new life on reserves—peaceably if reluctantly. There they attempted to farm, but they survived only because of government rations. In 1883 the rations were cut back severely and that winter thousands of Indians starved or froze to death.

When Métis leader Louis Riel returned to the Prairies in June 1884 he promised to restore Indian lands and freedom. The Indians listened eagerly, and some—mostly young men in the bands of Cree chiefs Poundmaker and Big Bear—became belligerent. Crops failed and during that winter thousands more perished.

Then, like a prairie fire, news spread that the North West Mounted Police had been defeated at Duck Lake. The white police were *not* invincible!

Poundmaker and a group of followers approached Battleford on March 29 to demand food. When terrified white settlers fled to Fort Battleford, an NWMP post a mile northeast, the Crees sacked and burned the settlement.

On April 2, Big Bear's war chief, Wandering Spirit, led a raid on the Hudson's Bay Company store at Frog Lake, massacring nine whites and taking five others prisoner. Thirteen days later he pillaged Fort Pitt and took some 50 more civilians prisoner. Poundmaker's band, armed only with old muskets, beat off a strong militia and NWMP force at Cut Knife Hill on May 2. Small parties raided trading posts and plundered farms. A wagon train of militia supplies was captured. Police patrols were ambushed. Two farm instructors were killed.

Riel's Métis rebellion was crushed at Batoche on May 12, 1885. Two weeks later Poundmaker surrendered at Fort Battleford. Wandering Spirit attempted suicide, but recovered and stood trial. Big Bear, exhausted and starving, gave himself up July 2. In the trials that followed, Big Bear and Poundmaker were sent to prison; both died within a year of release. On Nov. 27, outside Fort Battleford, Wandering Spirit and seven other Indian warriors were hanged for murder. The concrete slab over their grave, near Battleford National Historic Park, bears no inscription.

Poundmaker surrenders himself and his band to Maj. Gen. Frederick Middleton at Fort Battleford. "You did not catch me," said the Cree chief. "I gave myself up. I wanted peace."

On the same day General Middleton marched into another of Dumont's buffalo pounds. Fish Creek runs into the South Saskatchewan River 17 miles south of Batoche. Advancing into its shallow valley Middleton's men were encircled by Métis firing from higher ground. Dumont, with 150 men, delayed their arrival at Batoche by two weeks.

Fifteen years before on the Red River, Riel had been decisive and quick to act. Now he was preoccupied with religion. He had declared Bishop Ignace Bourget of Montreal pope and administered the sacraments himself. While the people he led were fighting, he worked on new names for the days of the week that did not refer to pagan gods. Dumont was a brilliant military commander and knew that, using guerrilla tactics and the techniques of the buffalo hunt, he could demoralize the Canadian troops while they marched. Riel restrained him and on

First all his ammunition was gone, then all hope, then all life, and he lies where he fell, a warrior at Batoche, on the day that Métis dreams of nationhood died there too.

285

Louis Riel, Prophet With a Mission: Sane He Was Guilty

Regina teemed with journalists and sightseers in July 1885. They had come for the trial of Louis Riel, accused of high treason for his leadership of the Northwest Rebellion that spring. They filled the three hotels and overflowed into a store where beds were set up. Fearing trouble, the North West Mounted Police dressed Riel in a Mountie uniform to smuggle him into a makeshift courtroom.

Riel's three lawyers, all from Quebec, decided his only hope was to plead insanity. Riel stubbornly objected but was forced by the judge to remain silent while doctors analyzed him. One thought "his mind was unsound," another that he "was quite capable of distinguishing right from wrong."

Then came public disclosure that in 1876-78 Riel had been in insane asylums in Quebec: he had called himself "Prophet, Infallible Pontiff and Priest King," chosen to be the savior of the Métis people. For months he had careened between violent uproar and humble submissiveness. On his release he had been advised to live quietly, "outdoors as much as possible."

Riel's lawyers reviewed the grievances of the Métis but they continued to stress his mental illness. At last the prisoner was permitted to speak. None of the six jurors understood French so Riel had to use English. For over an hour he spoke eloquently of his "mission," of his efforts to unite the Métis with the settlers and Indians of the Northwest. "I worked to better the condition of the people on the Saskatchewan at the risk of my life," he declared.

He convinced the jury of his sanity. But sane he was guilty. And on Nov. 16, 1885, Louis Riel was hanged for treason.

Like some awful milestone on the bitter road to Métis oblivion, this stark monument lives in the shadow of Winnipeg's St. Boniface Cathedral: just the man's name, the date he was hanged—and a cross.

April 29 made this entry in his diary: "O my God, for the love of Jesus, Mary, Joseph and Saint John the Baptist, grant me the favor of speedily reaching a good arrangement, a good agreement with the Dominion of Canada. Guide me, help me to secure for the Métis and Indians all the advantages which can now be obtained through negotiations."

Colonel Otter had driven Poundmaker's Crees out of Battleford on the day the fighting started at Fish Creek.

Then, on May 2, at Cut Knife Hill, 38 miles south of Battleford, sharpshooting Indians surrounded Otter's men, killing 8 and wounding 15. Otter retreated to Battleford but Middleton was already close to Batoche.

The final assault came by both land and water. The steamship *Northcote,* armed with a Gatling gun (a new weapon like a machine gun, first used in the American Civil War), headed downriver from Gabriel's Crossing at 7 a.m. May 9. An hour later, as the boat passed the Church of Saint-Antoine-de-Padoue, Dumont's men dropped the ferry cable—normally high above the river—and sheared off *Northcote's* mast and stacks. The boat slipped past Batoche out of control. She was finally anchored about two miles downstream—out of action.

The battle in the village lasted four days. Each morning Riel held religious ceremonies for his men. Middleton's land forces also had a Gatling gun but it was ineffective against the Métis in their rifle pits.

Then, on May 12, the soldiers charged. The battle and the dream were ended.

Riel surrendered to Middleton on May 15. In the first rebellion he led, on the Red River, only Thomas Scott and two others had died. In the second, on the North and South Saskatchewan rivers, at least 105 persons lost their lives. Riel never fired a shot. He was tried for high treason at Regina and sentenced to death on Aug. 1. After three reprieves and an inquiry into his mental health he was hanged on Nov. 16. One of his jurors said in 1925: "We tried Louis Riel for treason but he was hanged for the murder of Thomas Scott."

The Métis nation had lost its general, Gabriel Dumont, and its prophet, Louis Riel. The Indian chiefs were in jail.

Now the vast, rich Prairies belonged to white Canadians.

Heritage Sites

BATOCHE, Sask. Louis Riel, Gabriel Dumont and fewer than 300 Métis, making their final stand in the Northwest Rebellion, were overwhelmed here May 12, 1885, by Maj.Gen. Frederick Middleton and about 850 militiamen.

BATOCHE NATIONAL HISTORIC SITE Panels beside the remains of Middleton's trenches explain the Battle of Batoche. Métis rifle pits are visible despite years of ploughing. In the bullet-scarred rectory of the Church of Saint-Antoine-de-Padoue are Riel's pen case and inkwell, and Dumont's .44 revolver and his bridle of leather and horsehair.

BATOCHE VILLAGE Amid the ruins of the Métis capital are foundations of the house and store of Xavier "Batoche" Letendre, who gave his name to the community.

CHURCH OF SAINT-ANTOINE-DE-PADOUE The church that was Riel's headquarters has been preserved. The graves of Dumont and of some of the Métis killed in the battle are in the adjoining cemetery.

Other sites

Calgary (1) The Glenbow-Alberta Institute displays medals and a saddle of Col. Garnet Wolseley, who led troops sent to suppress the Red River Rebellion in 1870.
Carlton, Sask. (9) Four buildings of Fort Carlton, a Hudson's Bay Company post from which 99 North West Mounted Police and settlers marched to defeat at Duck Lake in the first battle of the Northwest Rebellion (1885), have been reconstructed in 250-acre Fort Carlton Historic Park.
Cumberland House, Sask. (13) The boiler and other parts of the SS *Northcote*, a stern-wheeler used against the Métis at Batoche, are in Cumberland House Historic Park.
Cut Knife, Sask. (6) A cairn in the Poundmaker Reserve, 10 miles north, marks the site of the Battle of Cut Knife Hill, at which Crees led by Chief Poundmaker repulsed soldiers and police in 1885. A stylized teepee nearby marks Poundmaker's grave. The Clayton McLain Memorial Museum at Cut Knife displays Poundmaker's medicine bundle, a collection of objects used in religious ceremonies.
Duck Lake, Sask. (10) A cairn two miles west marks the site of the Battle of Duck Lake (March 26, 1885). Exhibits in the Duck Lake Historical Museum include a cane and gold watch owned by Dumont, and a hunting gun owned by Riel.
Emerson, Man. (16) A cairn 1½ miles north marks the site of Fort Dufferin where on Dec. 1, 1869, Lieutenant-Gover-

nor-designate William McDougall prematurely proclaimed Canadian sovereignty over the HBC territory of Rupert's Land.
Fish Creek, Sask. (8) Depressions in the ground, used by Métis sharpshooters when they ambushed Middleton's force in 1885 in the Battle of Fish Creek, can be traced on a hill. There is a cairn on the battlefield.
Frenchman Butte, Sask. (5) One building of Fort Pitt, an HBC and NWMP post surrendered to Crees in 1885 and sacked by them, has been reconstructed in 15-acre Fort Pitt Historic Park, 14 miles west.
Frog Lake, Alta. (3) Black metal crosses in a cemetery two miles west mark the graves of nine men killed by Plains Crees in the Frog Lake Massacre of 1885.
Loon Lake, Sask. (4) Four plaques in 25-acre Steele Narrows Historic Park, six miles west, describe a clash June 3, 1885, between scouts under Maj. Sam Steele of the Mounties, and Plains Crees led by Big Bear. It was the last military engagement on Canadian soil.
North Battleford, Sask. (7) Five buildings in Battleford National Historic Park, four miles south, are from the NWMP post where some 400 settlers took refuge in 1885 and where Poundmaker surrendered after the Battle of Batoche. Displays include Poundmaker's war club and Winchester rifle, and guns used in the rebellion. A concrete slab nearby identifies the graves of eight Indians hanged for murders committed during the rebellion.
Prince Albert, Sask. (11) In the cemetery of St. Mary's Church is the grave of "Gentleman" Joe McKay, a Métis who was an NWMP interpreter and was reputed to have fired the first shot at Duck Lake.

Regina (12) A play based on Riel's trial for treason is presented three times weekly during the summer at Saskatchewan House. In a museum at RCMP Depot Division (where Riel was executed) are a crucifix he carried to the scaffold and pieces of rope believed used at his hanging.
St. Albert, Alta. (2) A log chapel-residence built in 1861 by the Rev. Albert Lacombe, an Oblate missionary who served in the West for 67 years, is sheathed in brick and is now the Father Lacombe Museum. Some of Father Lacombe's books and his breviary and CPR passes are displayed. The priest's grave is behind St. Albert Church, which is next to the museum.
Selkirk, Man. (14) Men of the 2nd Battalion of the Quebec Rifles, part of the force sent to suppress the Red River Rebellion in 1870, were stationed in the stone HBC post which is now Lower Fort Garry National Historic Park. The names they carved in the wooden gates are still visible.
Toronto (not shown) Handcuffs used on Riel, and what are believed the hood he wore when hanged and samples of his hair, are at Casa Loma in the regimental museum of the Queen's Own Rifles.
Winnipeg (15) A stone gateway is all that remains of Upper Fort Garry, the HBC post which Riel made the headquarters of his provisional governments of 1869 and 1870. Riel's grave is marked by a stone column at St. Boniface Cathedral. His tuque, bridle and stirrups, and the coffin in which his body was brought from Regina, are in the St. Boniface Museum. At 330 River Road in St. Vital is a house (originally owned by Riel's mother) where he planned the Red River Rebellion.

An Ordinary Iron Spike in the Fog at Craigellachie

Craigellachie today: where Canadian history was made in 1885. The trees at the right are apparently on the same spot as those in the famous photograph (opposite page) of the CPR's Donald Smith hammering home the last spike.

On the foggy morning of Saturday, Nov. 7, 1885, a photographer focussed his cumbersome, tripod-mounted view camera on a group of about 50 men in British Columbia's Eagle Pass and took what would become Canada's most famous photograph.

There were no flags, no bands, no orations. Nor did the public participate at the driving of the last spike—the completion of the Canadian Pacific transcontinental railway. It was an ordinary iron spike. The central figures in the photograph, however, were far from ordinary men.

Holding the hammer was Donald Smith, a senior director of the Canadian Pacific Railway and the representative of its president, his cousin George Stephen. Some 12 years earlier, as a Conservative Member of Parliament, Smith had bolted party ranks over the Pacific Scandal and had helped bring down the first administration of Sir John A. Macdonald. To the left of Smith stood Sandford Fleming, another CPR director. He had made the first detailed plan (in 1864) for a railway "from Canada to the Pacific Ocean on British Territory" and had been put in charge of its construction in 1871. William Cornelius Van Horne (to the left of Fleming) was the CPR's vice-president, hired to complete the building of the transcontinental. He had accomplished in 46 months what others had failed to do in more than 10 years.

Metal clanged on metal as Donald Smith hit the spike. His blow, a glancing one, bent the spike. A new one was fitted in its place and Smith drove it home. As the echoes died, Arthur Piers, one of Van Horne's assistants, looked at his watch: it was 9:22 Pacific Standard Time.

For a moment, the only sound was of the Eagle River, rushing toward Shuswap Lake, 17 miles to the west. Then a cheer went up. Van Horne responded: "All I can say is that the work has been well done in every way." The onlookers stood aside as locomotive 148 and its cars headed west-

The great moment (9:22 a.m. Pacific Time) at Craigellachie on Nov. 7, 1885: Donald Smith holds his historic last-spike pose for the photographer. Soon the CPR's first transcontinental train will push on west through the mountains to Port Moody on the Pacific.

ward across the historic join of steel. The directors and senior officers reboarded their train and, the following day, 340 miles from Eagle Pass, reached the Pacific terminal, Port Moody in British Columbia. They were the first men to travel entirely by rail from Montreal to the coast.

The political union of British North America (see p. 242) was hastened by the end of the American Civil War in 1865. Thousands of young veterans sought new adventure. Some found it in the American West, but some Northerners talked openly of conquering British territory in retaliation for Britain's support of the South during the war. In March 1867 the British Parliament passed the British North America Act, creating the Dominion of Canada. A few weeks later the Legislative Council of British Columbia resolved "without delay to secure the admission of British Columbia into the Canadian confederation."

British Columbia did join Canada on July 20, 1871, the two governments having agreed to construction of a railway linking the eastern Canadian railway network with the Pacific coast. It was to be started from both ends within two years and to be completed in 10 years. It would be financed by private capital, aided whenever possible by Canadian government grants of land and money. Sandford Fleming was appointed engineer-in-chief. "Until this great work is completed," said Macdonald, "our Dominion is little more than a 'geographical expression.'"

Vice-President William Cornelius Van Horne said the CPR's thanks to Sapomaxicow. Chief Crowfoot kept his Blackfoot peaceful as the railway pushed west across Indian lands. As a result, he got to ride free on all CPR lines.

The Pacific Scandal of 1873 has brought down the Macdonald government. But, says Sir John A. in this cartoon by J. W. Bengough: "I admit I took the money, and bribed the electors with it. Is there anything wrong about that?"

A Railway 'Fat and Bulgy Like Myself'

"I eat all I can," William Cornelius Van Horne once said, "I drink all I can, I smoke all I can, and I don't give a damn for anything."

Nothing except the Canadian Pacific Railway. He cared so much for it that he got it built in four years when everybody said nobody could do it in 10.

Van Horne was born in Illinois in 1843 and went to work at 14 as a telegraph operator. At 38, when he was hired as general manager of the CPR, he was said to know more about railroading than any man on the continent. In the 10 years up to 1881 the Canadian government had spent millions to lay less than 300 miles of track. Van Horne confidently predicted construction of 500 more miles before the end of 1882—and saw that the work was done, pushing his men to work nights and on Christmas. He gave no less himself.

Concerned with passenger luxuries, Van Horne insisted on hand-carved woodwork. He liked things "fat and bulgy like myself" and personally designed long, wide sleeping-car berths. He planned CPR hotels and set them in some of Canada's most spectacular scenery.

Van Horne was a man of great artistic sensibility. His art collection reflected his varied tastes, ranging from Japanese porcelain to French Impressionist paintings. He took great pleasure in his own drawing, painting and architectural design, and in music and horticulture.

The CPR boss was known for his hospitality and for his delight in elaborate practical jokes. Van Horne hated to leave a game of poker or billiards until he had won, and would play all night. His view on sleeping: "It's a waste of time; besides, you don't know what's going on."

He completed his railway in 1885, and in 1894 was knighted. Even after his retirement the CPR was known as "Van Horne's Road." He died in Montreal on Sept. 11, 1915. On the day of his funeral, at an appointed hour, every wheel in the CPR system stopped for five minutes.

Ravenscrag (now the Allan Memorial Institute) in Montreal was the home of Sir Hugh Allan (above). He owned the Montreal Ocean Steamship Company (the Allan Line) and was a key figure in the Pacific Scandal of 1873.

Two rival groups—one in Toronto, the other in Montréal—applied in 1872 for a charter to build the railway. Macdonald proposed that they merge into one "strong company of Canadian capitalists" but the Toronto group refused. Macdonald then asked Sir Hugh Allan, leader of the Montrealers and the richest man in Canada, to form a company. He agreed to support Allan for president of the company in return for Allan's financial aid to the Conservative Party in the election that year. The Conservatives were returned to power and early in 1873 the Canadian Pacific Railway Company (not today's CPR) was incorporated with Allan as president.

Then came disaster for the Conservatives. A clerk in the office of John Abbott, Allan's confidant and attorney, sold to Montreal Liberals—for $5,000—copies of documents recording the Conservatives' demands for election funds. On April 2 the Liberal opposition in the House of Commons accused the government of corruption. There followed a committee inquiry and a royal commission, with the credibility of the Macdonald government steadily crumbling amid the sensational disclosures of what became known as the Pacific Scandal.

Deserted by his supporters and convinced he would eventually be defeated in the House, Macdonald resigned on Nov. 5, 1873, ushering in a Liberal government under Alexander Mackenzie.

Macdonald's resignation meant the end of Allan's company: Liberal policy called for *public* financing of railway construction. It also came at a time of worldwide depression and major work on the railway was delayed. Some contracts were let in 1874 but the sod-turning ceremony at Fort William (now Thunder Bay, Ont.) was not until June 1, 1875.

In 1878, with the Conservatives back in office, British Columbia threatened to withdraw from Confederation unless railway construction was started in B.C. by May 1879. Contracts were quickly let for the building of 212 miles of line—from Port Moody, at the head of Burrard Inlet (now Greater Vancouver) to Savona's Ferry at the west end of Kamloops Lake.

The successful bidder was Andrew Onderdonk, an American. He had to find a precarious foothold for the railway above the wild Fraser and Thompson rivers where 20 years earlier the Cariboo Road (see p. 238) had been carved out.

This commemorative arch is at the summit of Rogers Pass, deep in the Selkirk Mountains. The Abandoned Rails Trail leads east from the summit, through rugged terrain (right) that itself commemorates the achievement of the builders of the CPR.

Building a railroad was more exacting than building a wagon road. There were limits to curves and grades, requiring more rock excavation and trestle building. Powder men were lowered on ropes to drill explosives holes in sheer rock faces. Along the 20 miles upstream from Yale, past the boiling cauldron of Hell's Gate, 14 tunnels were blasted through the rock. At Cisco Flat, nearly 50 miles above Yale, the railway crossed the Fraser 140 feet above the water. Farther east it penetrated the arid Thompson Valley, where unstable terrain caused landslides and collapsed tunnels.

With work under way in British Columbia, Macdonald sought sponsors to complete the remaining 1,900 miles of track. He found them: George Stephen and Duncan McIntyre of Montreal. They were Scots, both wealthy, both self-made men. McIntyre had begun his career in 1829 as a merchant's clerk, and had risen to be managing director of the Canada Central Railway. Stephen had come to Canada in 1850 as a draper's apprentice and now was president of the Bank of Montreal.

The Canadian Pacific Syndicate—as Stephen, McIntyre and their associates were called—undertook to complete and equip the railway and to operate it efficiently forever. The government agreed to pay the syndicate $25 million and to give it 25 million acres of prairie land as well

The Spirited Place That 'Gassy Jack' Built

Thirsty lumberjacks worked for nothing to erect the first building in what is now downtown Vancouver—a saloon. Its owner was John "Gassy Jack" Deighton *(left)*, a Yorkshireman (nicknamed for his verbosity), who had been an unsuccessful gold prospector and river pilot. He chose the site of the Deighton House carefully—a few feet from the limits of Hastings Mill, a lumber camp and sawmill on English Bay. While the saloon was going up in 1867, Gassy Jack sold spirits from a wagon; after 24 hours the building was complete. Six years later there were three more saloons, an assortment of shacks and 65 inhabitants in what was officially Granville but better known as Gastown. Hard drinking and brawling were a way of life, and stabbings were common.

In contrast was Port Moody, 12½ miles east at the head of Burrard Inlet. It was a model mill town, where liquor was banned and families were en-

couraged. In 1884 when CPR General Manager William Cornelius Van Horne decided to make Burrard Inlet the railway's western terminus, Port Moody was sure it would get the station. But Van Horne chose Granville, where there was less development and more space for docks, where oceangoing ships could navigate more easily, and where he got 6,000 acres free from the British Columbia government. Port Moody tried to deny Van Horne a right of way but backed down when he threatened to "run the railway down the middle of the inlet on a trestle."

Van Horne renamed Granville after explorer George Vancouver (see p. 144). The first transcontinental train did not arrive until May 23, 1887, but settlers flooded in and property values tripled within months of Van Horne's decision to build a port there. The original 1865 Hastings Mill company store still stands; Gastown became a slum but has been refurbished.

as the 700 miles of railway already completed or under construction. On Feb. 15, 1881, the syndicate formed the Canadian Pacific Railway Company.

McIntyre soon assumed overall direction of the company but it became apparent that an experienced railroader was needed to take charge of construction and operation. The man chosen to be general manager of the CPR was 38-year-old William Cornelius Van Horne, general superintendent of the Chicago, Milwaukee & St. Paul Railway. He took up his duties at the beginning of 1882 and built 500 miles of railway that year, in contrast to the company's meagre 135 miles the year before.

Van Horne achieved this through organization, efficient use of men and equipment and frequent visits to construction sites. He insisted on daily reports and demanded explanations for all delays. Supply trains ensured steady progress. Each carried all the material and hardware needed for one mile of track: 352 thirty-foot rails weighing 560 pounds apiece; 2,640 softwood crossties; 704 splice bars; 1,408 bolts, washers and nuts; 10,560 iron spikes.

Most of the workers came from the American Midwest. Many were career railway laborers who returned home each winter. Some built the subgrade, excavated, cut and built embankments to keep the roadbed level. Others laid track, up to 2½ miles a day.

As a supply train arrived, the ties were placed on the subgrade every two feet. Two rails at a time were unloaded and carried to position, then bolted in place with splice bars and spiked to the newly laid ties at the standard railway gauge of 56½ inches. The supply train then was moved forward one rail length and the operation was repeated—this happened 176 times in each mile. Ballast trains dumped fine pebbled rock atop the track; then laborers jacked the track up through the ballast, packing it under and around the ties to bring the track to level.

As the rails crept across the flat prairie between Medicine Hat and Calgary in the summer of 1883, the pace quickened. On July 3 nearly 4¾ miles of track were laid near what now is Brooks, Alta. On July 7 exactly 6 miles was put in position a few miles east of Bassano. Even that was topped. On July 28 a record 6 miles plus 2,000 feet was laid in the Strathmore area.

It was tougher building a permanent roadbed over the swampy muskeg of the Laurentian Shield. The fill there was composed of rocks, earth, tree trunks and stumps, all covered with ballast. Where the muskeg was unusually deep and liquid, huge mattresses of interwoven logs and tree branches were assembled to help consolidate the fill. Unstable muskeg sometimes sank, swallowing an embankment days or weeks later.

Four Miles of Trouble They Called the Big Hill

The Rockies were the greatest natural barrier faced by the builders of the CPR, and the worst of a hundred major trouble spots was a fearsome four miles called the Big Hill, in the Kicking Horse Pass west of the Alberta–British Columbia border.

The original survey proposed a route that would have required a 1,400-foot tunnel through Mount Stephen. The alternative was to snake back and forth across the turbulent Kicking Horse River and that meant, between Wapta Lake and Field, a grade of 4.5 percent (232 feet to the mile)—double the maximum allowed. It was nonetheless approved as a temporary measure to save time, the biggest challenge of the 50½-mile Kicking Horse route between Laggan, Alta. (now Lake Louise) and Golden City, B.C. (now Golden).

Men toiled 14 hours a day, boulders crashing down on them as they chipped out a ledge for the rails. The river had to be bridged eight times. Finally, on Nov. 5, 1884, the line reached Golden City.

Three safety spurs (such as the one below) enabled runaway trains to be switched *uphill* and quickly stopped. Passenger trains had to halt at the top for brake checks. Pulling and pushing *up* the Big Hill was as great a problem. Some trains required four of the powerful locomotives especially built for this task.

The Big Hill, a temporary measure, was used for 25 years. A permanent solution came in 1909 with completion of the CPR's two Spiral Tunnels. The line now followed an eight-mile-long figure 8. The Trans-Canada Highway, just west of Wapta Lake, is built on the original roadbed.

Candlesticks and an ornate Victorian clock are reflected in a huge mirror encased in mahogany in the second-floor foyer of Montreal's Mount Stephen Club. The house, at 1440 Drummond Street, was built in 1880-83 by George Stephen, a CPR president. It has been a private club since 1925.

Now, How to Make the Trains Run on Time?

When construction of the Pacific railway began in 1875, Canadians—like people around the world—set their clocks by the sun. How then could the railway schedule its trains?

Sandford Fleming, the railway's chief engineer, solved the problem by inventing standard time. In Toronto on Feb. 8, 1879, in a lecture (depicted here by Rex Woods) to the Royal Canadian Institute for the Advancement of Scientific Knowledge, he proposed dividing the world into 24 equal zones. Within each zone the time would be the same. The standard would be 12 noon (when the sun was at its peak) at Greenwich, England. The idea was adopted by 25 countries at a conference in 1884. It went into effect on New Year's Day 1885.

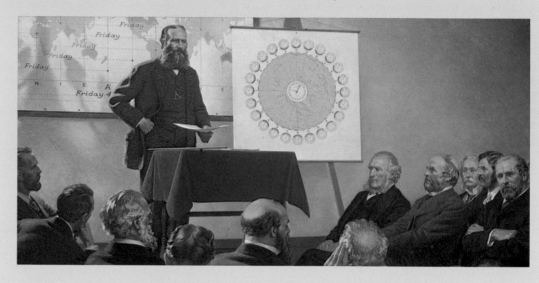

The snowblower, invented by J. W. Elliott of Toronto, made the CPR line through the Rockies usable all year. During the first three winters after completion of the line in 1885, snowslides and drifts up to 20 feet deep blocked the track for months. Snowsheds provided some protection against slides (below, left) and drifts (right). But blowers (like this one in Rogers Pass in the early 1890s) were introduced in 1888. They cleared not only packed snow but also rocks and small trees caught in avalanches.

But the cost was enormous and by 1885 the CPR was in deep financial crisis. The entire project—the transcontinental dream itself—was in jeopardy, at a time when the CPR was only one of Macdonald's pressing priorities. Another crisis saved the CPR.

On March 26, Métis led by Louis Riel (see p. 276) defeated a North West Mounted Police force in a battle at Duck Lake in what now is Saskatchewan. Macdonald's minister of militia contacted the CPR: could it move troops west from Ontario in time to put down the rebellion? Of course, said Van Horne—and the CPR did, despite four gaps in the rail (totalling 85 miles) north of Lake Superior. The CPR had demonstrated its indispensability and the government gave it the much-needed money.

Now it was apparent that the railway could be completed before the end of 1885. The site for the driving of the last spike was determined at the end of September when Onderdonk's crews ran out of rails 17 miles east of Shuswap Lake. Crews working west were 43 miles away at Albert Canyon. On the evening of Nov. 6 they sighted the end of the track from the west.

But, after the strain of four years of unstinting effort, there was no enthusiasm for a lavish ceremony. Who would drive the last spike? Van Horne told a Winnipeg reporter: "It may be Tom Mularky or Joe Tubby, and the only ceremony that I fancy will occur will be the damning of the foreman for not driving it quicker."

As construction bosses, foremen and workmen gathered for the photographer on Nov. 7, Van Horne suggested the place be named Craigellachie. It was Gaelic for Rock of Alarm, the rallying place in Scotland of the Grant clan, from which both George Stephen and Donald Smith were descended.

Observers remained in British Columbia's Selkirk Mountains that winter to determine the effect of snowfall and avalanches on the railway. (Rogers Pass has an average annual snowfall of 342 inches.) Early in 1886 the workmen were back again, ballasting and levelling the track, constructing stations and snowsheds and putting things in order for the first scheduled trains.

"Going over some of the trestles," a CPR passenger wrote in 1886, "we seemed to be veritably floating in the air, especially so when crossing the Horse Shoe Trestle." It was close to Lake Superior a few miles west of Schreiber, Ont.

The $10-a-Week Men at the End of Track

They worked 10 (sometimes 14) hours a day, seven days a week, in temperatures that ranged from well over 100 degrees (38°C) to almost 40 below—digging, drilling, blasting, laying ties and rails—and hammering the spikes that held them together. These were the laborers—called navvies—who built the CPR.

They slept in tents, boxcars, log bunkhouses or CPR boarding cars with three tiers of bunks. They ate mostly salt pork, beans, corned beef, potatoes, oatmeal, molasses and tea. Fresh bread was a luxury. (A stone oven—*right*—that served a CPR construction camp in 1884 can still be seen in Yoho National Park.)

Avalanches, mudslides, cave-ins and blasting accidents were commonplace. Navvies carried on their backs 10-gallon tins of nitroglycerin—which could be set off by the slightest jolt. In one 50-mile stretch 30 men died in nitroglycerin accidents.

The average wage was $10.50 a week. Some men sent most of their pay home; others spent heavily on bootleg drink. (The sale of liquor—except for hop beer—was forbidden in construction camps.) Alcohol was canned and labelled as fruit or vegetables. It was put in barrels marked oatmeal or kerosene, in the hollow soles of boots and in imitation Bibles. Eggs were blown and filled with spirits. One bootlegger dressed a keg in baby clothes and pretended it was a sleeping child.

At dawn, hung over or not, the navvies were expected to shoulder shovels, picks, hammers and explosives, trudge to the end of track and extend once more the iron road that was binding Canada together.

Regular service was inaugurated on the evening of June 28, 1886, when the Pacific Express left Montreal for Port Moody. The affluent rode in the sleeping car *Honolulu* and took meals in the dining car *Holyrood*. Other passengers occupied a first-class coach and two colonist cars.

The train arrived at Port Moody without incident sharp at noon on July 4, 1886, six days and 2,891 miles from Montreal. Nine days later, Sir John A. Macdonald, accompanied by Lady Macdonald, left for Port Moody by special train. When it arrived at Laggan, Alta. (now Lake Louise), Lady Macdonald asked to ride on the front of the locomotive. A box and a cushion were immediately provided. "I don't know how I am going to ride in a car, like a Christian any more," she confided in a letter to Van Horne, "after the delights of a cushioned cowcatcher!"

Macdonald quipped on arrival at Port Moody that he had not expected to live to see the railway completed. He had expected, instead, "to look down from another sphere." "The Opposition," he continued, "kindly suggested that I would more likely be looking up from below."

Around the World on Just One Red Route Ticket

To help keep the CPR busy after completion of the transcontinental line in 1885, General Manager William Cornelius Van Horne made it a link in a system joining Europe and the Orient. Steamships completed this "All-Red Route," which used only British territory and vessels and was speedier than the Suez Canal route.

Regular Pacific service began in 1887. At dawn June 14 the SS *Abyssinia*, under CPR charter, docked in Vancouver after a two-week voyage from Yokohama. Sixty-five bales of perishable raw silk were rushed to a waiting CPR train, sped to Prescott, Ont., ferried across the St. Lawrence to Ogdensburg, transferred to New York by train, and put on a transatlantic liner. They reached London June 29.

Two years later, to the chagrin of American ports and railways, Van Horne (now CPR president) signed a contract with the British and Canadian governments for a monthly rail and ship service "for conveyance of Her Majesty's mails, troops and stores between Halifax or Quebec and Hong Kong," with stopovers at Yokohama and Shanghai. By 1891 the CPR was operating its own ships in the Pacific—*Empress of China, Empress of India* and *Empress of Japan*—built in Glasgow under Royal Navy supervision.

But the CPR wanted its own All-Red Route, so the Beaver Line of Montreal (with 15 ships on the Atlantic) was absorbed in 1903 and the 18-ship Allan Line of Montreal in 1915. (Sir Hugh Allan, a former owner, had offered to build the CPR in 1872.)

Hotels, a telegraph system and an express service had been added during the years. By 1924, when CPR ships began annual cruises from Quebec to Vancouver via the Suez Canal, "the world's greatest travel system" could, as Van Horne had hoped, "send a traveller around the world on one ticket."

Heritage Sites

CRAIGELLACHIE, B.C. A cairn in Eagle Pass marks the spot where Donald Smith, a CPR director (representing his cousin George Stephen, the company president), drove the last spike in the railway's transcontinental line Nov. 7, 1885. A plaque beside the Trans-Canada Highway nearby records that now "A nebulous dream was a reality: an iron ribbon crossed Canada from sea to sea."

Other sites

Calgary (5) CPR 76, one of the passenger cars that transported officials to the driving of the last spike, and a log station (1885) from Lake Louise, Alta., are in Heritage Park.

Glacier National Park, B.C. (3) Remains of snowsheds, bridges and the CPR roadbed supplanted by the Connaught Tunnel in 1916 are in the Rogers Pass area. An interpretive centre illustrates the history of avalanche control. Abandoned Rails Trail, a mile long, follows part of the original CPR line at the summit of Rogers Pass. Two miles west are the foundations

of Glacier House, a CPR hotel built in 1886. The Avalanche Crest Trail follows the path taken by Maj. A. B. Rogers in 1881 when he sighted Rogers Pass.

Montreal (11) The Mount Stephen Club at 1440 Drummond Street was built in 1880-83 as the home of George Stephen. Ravenscrag, once the home of Sir Hugh Allan, a central figure in the Pacific Scandal, is now the Allan Memorial Institute at 1025 Pine Avenue West. Shaughnessy House, a limestone mansion purchased by CPR General Manager William Cornelius Van Horne in 1882, is at 1823 Dorchester Boulevard West. The original section of Windsor Station, Canada's oldest (1889) major station, is at Peel and La Gauchetière streets.

Portage la Prairie, Man. (8) CPR 5, Van Horne's first official car, is displayed at the Fort la Reine Museum and Pioneer Village.

Port Moody, B.C. (2) A cairn commemorates the arrival here July 4, 1886, of the first through train from Montreal. The town was the CPR terminus only until 1887, when the line was extended to Vancouver.

Saint-Constant, Que. (12) Among 30 locomotives at the Canadian Railway Museum is CPR 144. Built in 1886 and similar to the locomotive that hauled the first through train into Port Moody, 144 operated until 1959—one of the last steam engines in regular service. Rolling stock includes Van Horne's official car *Saskatchewan*, which in 1915 formed part of his funeral train, and official car 1, which arrived in Vancouver in 1886 on the first transcontinental train.

Saskatoon, Sask. (7) Saskatoon Station,

a two-storey brick structure, was built in 1907 as a CPR divisional administrative centre. It is a national historic site.

Savanne, Ont. (10) Poland Swamp, 6½ miles east, is one of the muskeg areas that CPR construction crews "mattressed" with logs and branches.

Strathmore, Alta. (6) A Canadian track-laying record—six miles plus 2,000 feet of track in one day—was established here July 28, 1883.

Vancouver (1) Gastown, a downtown area of boutiques, restaurants and restored buildings, was a grubby collection of shacks (named after saloon-owner "Gassy Jack" Deighton) when chosen in 1884 as the CPR's western terminus. The Old Hastings Mill Store, the city's oldest building (1865), remains from the lumber camp whose men built Deighton's saloon: it is a museum of local history. A statue of Deighton stands on Maple Tree Square near the site of his saloon. Under restoration is CPR 374, the locomotive that hauled the first transcontinental passenger train into Vancouver.

Winnipeg (9) The *Prairie Dog Central*, a vintage CPR train pulled by an 1882 steam engine, takes passengers from St. James Station to Grosse Isle in summer.

Yoho National Park, B.C. (4) Walk Into the Past hiking trail follows parts of the Big Hill, a 4.5-percent grade on the original CPR line in the Kicking Horse Valley. Safety switch spur lines can be seen. The Trans-Canada Highway at the western tip of Wapta Lake is built on the Big Hill roadbed. A stone oven (1884) remains from the first construction camp in the valley. An 1885 Alberta mining company locomotive, used during construction of the Spiral Tunnels which eliminated the Big Hill in 1909, is preserved. The tunnels can be seen from lookouts on the Trans-Canada.

Eagle Pass was discovered in 1865 when surveyor Walter Moberly followed a flight of eagles into the valley that the CPR would use 20 years later.

In the peace of the Bell Homestead at Brantford, Ont., amid its Victorian opulence (right: the parlor), Alexander Graham Bell in 1874 conceived the idea of the telephone. This was his first, the Gallows Frame Telephone, which he built in Boston in 1875.

Independence and a Future of Cities and Industries

The last three decades of the 19th century were a time of vast industrial expansion in Canada—in coal and iron and oil, in copper and nickel, in hydro-electricity and cheese-making and shipping, in hundreds of new and exciting fields. Most of it was helped and encouraged by government policy, and much of it was possible only because of the enormous riches that lay in the soil and the rock of Canada. Some of it was due to the inventive genius of individuals, and one invention perhaps more than most others came to typify the dynamic growth of those 30 years. The telephone.

Alexander Graham Bell (here at 29) recorded years later: "Of this you may be sure, the telephone was invented in Canada. It was made in the United States. The first transmission of a human voice over a telephone wire, where the speaker and the listener were miles apart, was in Canada. The first transmission by wire in which the conversation was carried on reciprocally over the same line was in the United States."

Alexander Graham Bell had left Scotland with his parents at 23 to move to Tutela Heights, overlooking the Grand River near Brantford, Ont. In the summer of 1874, home on a visit from Boston, where he worked as a speech therapist, the 27-year-old Bell had the idea that became the basis of the telephone. The Bell Homestead at Tutela Heights is now a national historic site, a monument in a way not only to the inventor of the telephone but also to the many who made the 1870s, '80s and '90s so remarkable a chapter in the Canadian story.

It took Bell two years to build his telephone. On Aug. 3, 1876, in a Dominion Telegraph Company office at Mount Pleasant, Ont., he heard his uncle David—two miles away in the telegraph office in Brantford—recite Shakespeare's "To be or not to be . . ." This was the first intelligible telephone transmission from one building to another. One week later the first long-distance call was made—from Brantford to Paris, eight miles northwest. The Bell Telephone Company of Canada came into being and by November 1877 it had four subscribers.

The fifth was Prime Minister Alexander Mackenzie, who wanted a telephone link between his office and the governor general's residence. It was done—and the company obligingly predated the prime minister's application to make him officially the first subscriber.

Alexander Mackenzie may also have been the first Bell subscriber to scowl at his phone. Lady Dufferin, the governor general's wife, was in the habit of sending a friend to Mackenzie's office *to sing to her over the phone*. Not the phone's fault, but he was desperately wrestling with problems of state. Ever since Mackenzie and his Liberals had come to power in 1873 Canada had been suffering the effects of a worldwide depression. People blamed him. And soon, sometime in 1878, he would have to fight an election.

Mackenzie had asked the United States to eliminate tariffs (import duties) on Canadian goods by renewing the reciprocity treaty of 1854 for the enlarged Canada that had resulted from Confederation. High American tariffs made Canadian goods expensive in the U.S. market—and low Canadian tariffs on goods from the States offered little protection to Canadian manufacturers. Worse, American goods were being dumped in Canada—at a loss—to prevent the development of manufacturing which would compete with American industry.

Mackenzie's request for free trade was turned down. The railway to the West, which despite the United States could have encouraged settlement on the Prairies and opened new markets, had not yet been built, and every year thousands of Canadians emigrated to the United States. But in the words of the latest budget speech in Parliament: "This is no time for experiments."

Not much of an election slogan.

On an overcast July 1, 1876, the people of Uxbridge, near Toronto, had gathered in Elgin Park for a Dominion Day picnic. Sir John A. Macdonald, leader of the Conservatives, was to attend but no one expected him to add sparkle to the festivities. Macdonald had been in the political wilderness since his government's defeat three years before over the Pacific Scandal (see p. 291).

But Macdonald radiated enthusiasm on the ride to the park past welcoming banners and through a triumphal arch labelled "Victory." This was not the Sir John A. of scandal and disgrace but the exuberant, confident man he had been in 1867.

His amazing memory for names and faces pleased the farmers and townspeople clustered around tables laden with roast ducks and hams, pickled preserves, mince pies, cheeses and jugs of lemonade, cider and dandelion wine. He greeted the children who scrambled for candy kisses, and applauded their fathers as they fought a tug of war. When the band struck up "Our Dominion" the picnickers surged to the platform to hear him. He scored heavily.

It was Sir John A.'s first step back to power and so successful that he spent the summer touring Ontario's picnic grounds, polishing and developing the fighting message that had filled the Uxbridge crowd with pride and enthusiasm.

He blamed Mackenzie's Liberals for the slow growth of manufacturing industries and the massive emigration but most of all for begging the Americans for free trade. "We are not beggars," said Macdonald. If the United States could protect its industries with tariffs, so could Canada. Canadian cities would grow and provide markets for the farmers. Tariffs would subsidize a railway to carry immigrants to the Prairies and create a huge domestic market for Canadian goods.

It was a declaration of economic independence and he called it the National Policy. It worked. In the 1878 federal election, the first by secret ballot, Macdonald's Conservatives swept into power on a wave of national pride. The following year, high protective tariffs were imposed and business improved. Even though the economy slumped again in 1883, the National Policy survived. Canada was being transformed into an urban, industrial nation.

An 1891 election poster: farmer and industrial worker reflect Macdonald's confidence that he and his National Policy (plus the British connection) would win. They did.

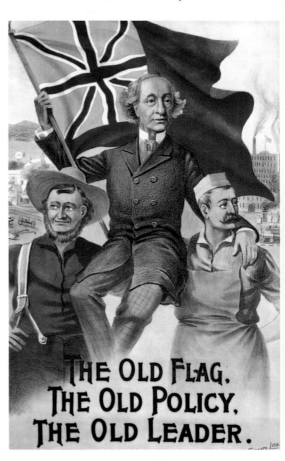

THE OLD FLAG.
THE OLD POLICY.
THE OLD LEADER.

Scots-born Alexander Mackenzie came to Upper Canada in 1842 (aged 20), was a builder and contractor, then editor of the Lambton Shield, *a Reform newspaper. He supported Confederation and in 1873 formed Canada's first Liberal administration. He was prime minister until the Conservatives' return to power in 1878. Mackenzie three times refused a knighthood.*

Much older now, the same elm trees look down where John A. Macdonald strolled—as Conservative opposition leader and friend of the people—at a rally in Elgin Park at Uxbridge, Ont., on July 1, 1876. It was the first of the great political picnics and the beginning of Macdonald's return to power.

(But too late for Alexander Graham Bell and his associates. Bell had been unable to find Canadian financial backing. In 1879, only three years after the first call was made, the development of the telephone industry was in the hands of an American company. Bell himself went to the United States and became an American citizen in 1882, although he maintained a home and laboratory at Baddeck, N.S.)

The first Canadian natural resources to be developed had been Nova Scotia coal (1672) and Quebec iron (1730), but neither had reached its full potential when the National Policy was introduced. North America's first commercial oil well had been sunk in 1857 by James Miller Williams at what became Oil Springs, Ont. Williams went on to build North America's first refinery. As the Quebec Central Railway was being built in the 1870s the strange rock revealed by blasting at present-day Thetford Mines was analyzed and found to be asbestos. Mining began in 1875 and soon the Eastern Townships of Quebec were producing most of the world supply.

Railway construction also uncovered northern

The Rising Risk of Fire in Fast-Growing Cities

A conflagration on June 20, 1877, destroyed two-fifths of Saint John, N.B., and left homeless 13,000 persons—a quarter of the population. It was the city's 10th major blaze in only 50 years—at a time when bad fires were common in Canadian cities. It started in a shed (near where the east end of the Saint John Harbour Bridge is now) and raged for nine hours.

Burgeoning cities (of mainly wooden buildings) often outgrew the rudimentary water systems and fire-fighting services of the 19th century. Quebec City lost many historic buildings, including, in 1834, Governor Frontenac's Château Saint-Louis, which dated from 1694. Two fires in Montreal in 1852 destroyed 1,200 houses. Virtually all of Vancouver was reduced to ashes in 1886. Saint John rebuilt, as other communities did, mainly with brick. The fused remains of what is believed to have been a hardware store were moved to the Loyalist Burial Ground as a reminder of the disaster.

Calixa Lavallée of Verchères, Que., was conductor and artistic director of the New York Grand Opera House before returning to Quebec—to fame as composer of the music of "O Canada." It was first performed on the Plains of Abraham in Quebec in 1880. The words were by Mr. Justice (later Sir) Adolphe-Basile Routhier. English lyrics were written later.

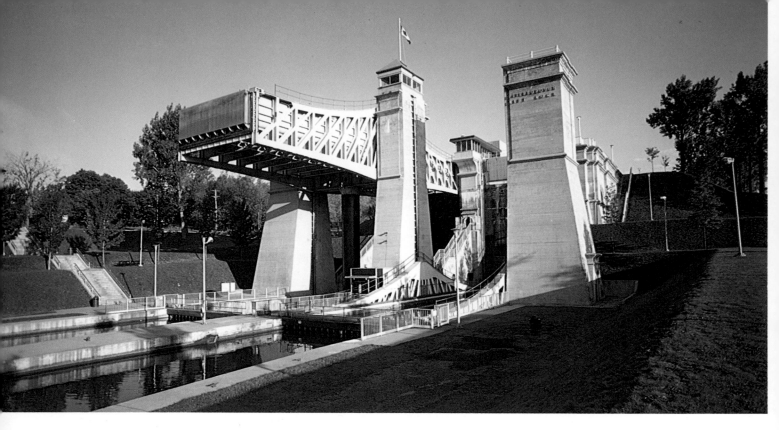

Ontario's copper and nickel. By the early 20th century Sudbury was the world's largest pro-ducer of nickel.

In 1894, iron was found along the Ontario shore of Lake Superior and the Algoma Steel Company came into being in 1901.

By 1896 a copper smelter was in production at Trail, B.C. A few miles away Rossland had grown around the LeRoi mine—a claim that Eu-gene Topping, an ex-railway hand, had bought for $12.50 in 1891. LeRoi's lead went to the United States for processing until 1901, when Canada instituted a subsidy for home-smelted lead. Today the Cominco lead-zinc smelter at Trail is one of the largest in the world.

The Hope Ironworks of New Glasgow, N.S., had been set up in 1872 with a capital of $4,000

and had merged with other companies to form the Nova Scotia Steel Company in 1894. It used Newfoundland iron and Nova Scotia coal to make steel that would have been priced out of its central Canadian markets without the tariff that kept out American competition. Under protec-tion of the National Policy it grew to employ 6,000 persons by the end of the century.

In 1892 Thomas Willson of Hamilton, Ont., became the first to produce carbide, the raw ma-terial for making acetylene. Willson's "bottled sunlight" illuminated construction sites around the clock, fuelled lighthouses, buoys and the lamps on early automobiles. Although electricity replaced acetylene for lighting, the industry sur-vived through the invention of the acetylene torch for cutting and welding steel. But, like Bell, Willson found Canadian investors timid and an American company, Union Carbide, developed his discovery.

Canada's rivers had made exploration possi-ble by providing routes through the heart of the country. They made large-scale industrialization possible by providing power—hydro-electricity. When the first Canadian hydro plant opened at Niagara Falls, Ont., in 1905, industries flocked to the region.

Adam Beck, mayor of London, Ont., and a member of the Ontario legislature, saw that the owners of the Niagara Falls generating plant either could provide cheap power for home and industry or could hold their customers to ransom.

This coal-fired steam carriage built in 1867 by Henry Seth Taylor of Stanstead, Que., was Canada's first automobile. It is displayed in the Ontario Science Centre at Toronto.

James Miller Williams brought in North America's first producing oil well—at Oil Springs, Ont., in 1857. This replica is where he drilled the original and built a refinery.

In 1906 he won a bitter political fight for public ownership. The Ontario Hydro-Electric Power Commission became the model for publicly owned power systems around the world.

The larger cities had had horse-drawn streetcars for many years when first attempts were made to build electric-powered systems. Power lines were buried along the routes but whenever it rained the whole system short-circuited. John J. Wright of Toronto solved the problem. At Toronto's 1883 Canadian National Exhibition people lined up for rides on an electric streetcar powered from an overhead cable.

Wright changed the shape of the world's major cities. Now, people no longer had to live within walking distance of their jobs. Residential districts developed away from the factory dirt and noise.

There had been dairy processing plants in Canada West (at Ingersoll, Ont.) since 1864 and in Canada East (at Missisquoi, Que.) since 1869 but before the National Policy Canada imported dairy products. With the help of the tariff and of Canadian inventions (such as the automatic butter-wrapping machine) Canada soon produced more than enough for its own needs and became a major exporter. By 1900 it was ninth in the world in butter production and first in cheese. Britain, home of cheddar cheese, was so far behind that it asked Canadian experts to help modernize its industry.

Canadian cities were proud of their new fac-

Half-Tone and Bovril: The Unsung Inventors

The first periodical in the world to reproduce a photograph was the *Canadian Illustrated News,* published in Montreal by Georges-Edouard Desbarats. The front page of the first issue (Oct. 30, 1869) was nearly filled with a photo of Prince Arthur, third son of Queen Victoria (and in 1911-16, as Duke of Connaught, governor general of Canada). Prior to that, illustrations in periodicals and most books had been limited to drawings and engravings—which lacked photography's subtle tones. Desbarats invented a process called halftone in which a photograph is re-photographed through a screen, turning the picture into a mass of dots which give the same image as the original. The dots are easily printed, and the technique—basically unchanged—is standard today.

Desbarats is one of many unsung Canadian inventors. Another is John Patch of Yarmouth, N.S., who developed a screw propeller in 1833 (when steamships used paddle wheels). He apparently went to the United States for a patent and was cajoled out of his rights to the device. He died destitute.

A Quebec City dentist, Henri-Edmond Casgrain, devised the first snowmobile (*below*) in the winter of 1897-98. He replaced the front wheels of his three-wheeled Leon-Bollée *voiturette* with steel skis, and the rear tire with a wood rim studded with conical points.

An unknown nutritionist in Montreal developed a hot drink made from beef extract to warm revellers at the city's winter carnivals in the 1880s (see p. 254). But the merrymakers preferred stronger stuff and the drink was a flop. The inventor took it to England where it was an instant hit. Its name: Bovril.

Dr. Abraham Gesner, a Nova Scotian, was doctor, geologist, flautist, sailor, author and, in 1846, inventor. From coal he distilled a light, clear oil that burned with a bright yellow flame. He called it kerosene. Eight years later he patented a process for making kerosene from petroleum; that was the start of the petrochemical industry.

Pre-Confederation, pre-industrial Canada in London in 1851, at the Great Exhibition of man's "useful arts": moose heads and Indian artifacts, fur-draped sleighs, a voyageur canoe . . .

tories and machines, their streetcar lines and paved streets. But most of all they were proud of their municipal waterworks. (A waterworks built in Kingston, Ont., in 1849 is now the Pump House Steam Museum.) Hamilton, Ont., celebrated the Queen's birthday on May 24, 1859, with firehoses shooting jets of water from its new waterworks clear over one of the town's higher buildings. The system could pump 1.6 million gallons of water a day. And those gallons made Hamilton a leading industrial city. With no means of fighting them, fires had often destroyed large sections of cities and the high cost of fire insurance discouraged industrial growth. Its

A Tipperary Legacy: Vigilante Murders in Biddulph

Just after midnight on Feb. 4, 1880, some 30 vigilantes invaded James Donnelly's farmhouse near Lucan, Ont., and bludgeoned to death the 63-year-old man, his wife, a son and a niece. They set the house afire with kerosene, then hurried to the village of Whalens Corners intending to kill another son, Will Donnelly (*right*). He escaped; his brother John, who was visiting, answered the vigilantes' knock and was shot to death.

The slayings climaxed two decades of violence in Lucan and surrounding Biddulph Township. Like many inhabitants of the farming community north of London, James Donnelly came from Tipperary, Ireland, where times had been hard, men proud and life cheap. Immigrants from such areas often brought not only hopes and dreams, but also a dark legacy of sectional feuding which complicated Canada's task of establishing national programs and national loyalties.

At Lucan, Donnelly soon quarrelled with a neighbor over title to 50 acres of land. The community took sides—the Roman Catholics backing Donnelly, the Protestants his neighbor. In 1857, impatient with the pace of the judicial process, Donnelly drove a handspike into the neighbor's head at a barn raising. For two years he hid from the law; for seven he was imprisoned for murder.

Donnelly's seven sons quarrelled with people over land, business, politics and women. They apologized to no one, and boldly avenged slights to the close-knit family. Horses were mutilated, stables and crops burned. Two Donnelly sons were killed during the 1870s—one in a brawl, the other shot while allegedly setting fire to a hotel. Will Donnelly twice tried to abduct one girl, then eloped with another. A vigilante committee hoped to force the family to move, but open harassment of the Donnellys, and lawsuits for assault and vandalism, brought no results. Then the five Donnellys were killed.

The victims were buried in St. Patrick's Cemetery in Lucan under a stone monument that called their deaths murder. (In 1964, because of vandalism, the stone was replaced by one with conventional wording.) Despite eyewitness testimony nobody was convicted. Jurors who acquitted one man said they feared a guilty verdict "would have resulted in the hanging of half a township."

The outside staircase of rural Quebec became an ornate trademark of Montreal in the 1880s. It saved space by eliminating inside stairs and served as a fire escape.

waterworks made Hamilton safe for industry; clean drinking water and flush toilets were side benefits.

The cities were wrapped in cocoons of wire—telephone lines, electric wires and streetcar lines. Most had crowded railway yards. The National Policy got much of the credit—and the blame.

Urban and industrial growth had a heavy price. In the Maritimes, railway expansion destroyed coastal shipping just as the region's wooden sailing ships were being ousted by iron steamers. Industrial Cape Breton benefited from tariff protection but all Maritimers paid the cost in high prices for manufactured goods. Thousands migrated in search of jobs. Those who stayed felt they were being exploited to make profits for central Canada's industry. By the 1880s, Nova Scotia was considering separation.

On the grain-exporting Prairies, tariffs did not help sell wheat but, at a time of poor harvests, they did force farmers to buy more-expensive farm machinery from Toronto and clothing from Montreal by keeping out cheap U.S. goods.

The workers in the cities paid their own price for the growth of industry. As late as the 1890s, Montreal's poor still drew drinking water from

wells beside privies in slum yards. Factory workers still lived in factory districts: the streetcar fare to the suburbs was too high for a laborer who took home only $12 after six 12-hour days of work. There were no paid holidays and there was no insurance against unemployment, accident or sickness.

The great fortunes made by industrialists and railway builders under the National Policy were built on high prices and the cheap labor of the poor—men, women and even children. A government of lawyers and businessmen was not in favor of labor reforms.

Labor organizations, mostly in the skilled trades, had existed in Canada since 1812, and for six decades they were illegal. Strikes too were illegal and the militia was often used to force men back to work.

When Toronto printers went on strike in 1872, the publishers, led by George Brown of Toronto (see p. 245), had the strike leaders arrested for conspiracy. Much as he disliked strikes, Macdonald disliked Brown even more. Brown, a Liberal, regularly attacked the Conservatives in his newspaper, *The Globe.* This was Macdonald's chance to get even and his government made unions legal. The printers won their strike and Canada's first national labor organization, the Canadian Labor Union, was formed the next year.

Several American companies had branches in Canada to qualify as Canadian manufacturers and evade tariffs. Their employees were organized by American unions. One of these, the Knights of Labor, organized unskilled workers and campaigned for compulsory education and safer working conditions as well as better wages.

But the unions had a long way to go. In 1891, sawmill workers in Hull, Que., went on strike for $1.25 for a 10-hour day—a nine-cent increase and a 1¾-hour reduction. Fighting broke out when strikebreakers arrived and Mayor E. B. Eddy, a mill owner, sent in police and called for—and got—troops to keep the mills working.

Montreal's first electric streetcar—the street railway company's No. 350, dubbed the Rocket—*went into service in 1892, with a trolley pole that was a Canadian invention. The* Rocket *is at the Canadian Railway Museum at Saint-Constant, Que.*

Christmas greetings, c. 1880: a card full of Victorian clutter but proudly Canadian in every detail. Nearly all cards of the era were strongly nationalistic, portraying everything from snowshoeing to lacrosse to voyageurs shooting rapids. One Montreal publisher boasted in 1881 that his cards were "all Canadian workmanship, Canadian in sentiment, in design and execution." The Halifax Herald *commented in 1882: "A handsome card is in much better taste than a cheap-looking 'boughten' present." About that time, though, The Montreal Gazette wondered whether the whole Christmas card idea might not peter out once the novelty wore off.*

A small stone cross in Kingston's Cataraqui Cemetery—under a speckled alder, beside a buff memorial obelisk—marks the grave of Canada's first prime minister. It says simply, "John Alexander Macdonald 1815-1891 At Rest."

Some workers settled for a 10-hour day with no pay increase; others for 11 hours and an extra dollar a week.

Few middle-class Canadians were sympathetic to the unions. Most agreed with George Brown that the root of poverty and all urban problems was drink. Pioneer millers such as William Gooderham and Hiram Walker had used surplus grain to distill cheap whisky. In 1870, Toronto had 500 saloons selling it at two cents a glass.

During the 1870s temperance societies demanded legislation and in 1878, at the end of Mackenzie's Liberal government, the Canada Temperance Act was passed. It permitted local governments to regulate retail liquor outlets—as they still do. In 1880 George Brown was shot by an employee he had fired for drunkenness. Brown died six weeks later and at his funeral there were sermons on temperance.

By 1891, an election year, Canada had new industries and growing cities but it also had crushing problems and the depression continued. The National Policy had protected markets but it had not made it easier for inventors like Bell to raise capital at home. The Liberal Party was gaining support with its old demand for free trade.

Macdonald was 76 and ailing in 1891, but he gathered his strength to fight for the course he had set. But how? He could not defend the profits made by the tariff-protected corporations nor claim that farmers and city workers were well off.

Then he remembered the 1876 picnic grounds, when a demoralized country had answered his appeal to national pride. He came out for his last fight.

Free trade, he said, would destroy Canadian industry and Canada would be absorbed into the United States. As for himself, "A British subject I was born and a British subject I will die."

Corporations built on the National Policy poured money into the Conservative election fund. Railway, mine and factory workers, whose jobs depended on the tariff, got time off to vote. Farmers who wanted cheap American manufactured goods realized that they wanted to be Canadians in an independent nation even more. Money, jobs, and loyalty won the election for the Conservatives. Three months later, on June 6, 1891, Sir John A. Macdonald died at his home in Ottawa.

The Canadian Pacific Railway, keystone of the National Policy, draped its stations in mourning and a CPR train carried him to his funeral in Kingston. His grave is in Cataraqui Cemetery. Wilfrid Laurier (see p. 330), leader of the Liberal Party, said "the life of Sir John Macdonald is the history of Canada." Macdonald's election of 1891 decided the future of Canada, a future of cities and industries. Five years later Laurier led the Liberal Party to power and abandoned the old free trade policy.

The prosperity of the Laurier years was built on the National Policy.

After John A., Four in Five Years—Then Defeat

The Conservative Party's search for a worthy successor to Macdonald gave Canada four prime ministers in the five years after Sir John A. died.

Senator John Abbott, 70, an authority on commercial law and former Member of Parliament for Argenteuil (Que.), became caretaker prime minister June 16, 1891, because, in his words, he was "not particularly obnoxious to anybody." His health was poor and he resigned Nov. 25, 1892.

Sir John Thompson, 48, MP for Antigonish (N.S.), whom Macdonald had called "the greatest of all my discoveries," took office Dec. 5, 1892. Thompson had been a Supreme Court judge and premier of Nova Scotia. As federal justice minister he had revised and codified Canada's criminal law. On Dec. 12, 1894, in England to become a member of the Privy Council, he collapsed and died during a luncheon at Windsor Castle.

Senator Mackenzie Bowell, former MP for North Hastings (Ont.), and grand master of the Orange Order, was sworn in Dec. 21, 1894. His vacillation over the Manitoba schools question (see p. 334) led to seven resignations from his cabinet and his own resignation April 27, 1896.

Sir Charles Tupper, 74, the flamboyant veteran statesman from Nova Scotia, who had fought for Confederation alongside Sir John A. in the 1860s, returned home after eight years as high commissioner in London and took office May 1, 1896, but was prime minister for only a few weeks. He introduced a bill to protect separate schools in Manitoba but the Conservative Party was badly beaten in the general election of June 23, 1896.

John Abbott

John Thompson

Mackenzie Bowell

Charles Tupper

Heritage Sites

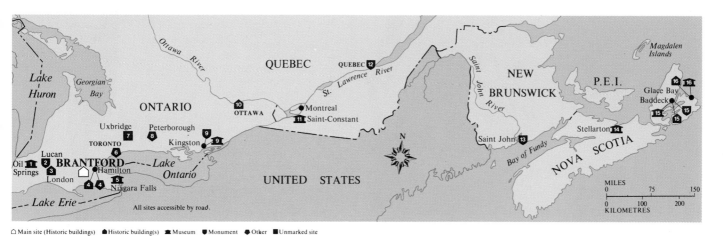

△ Main site (Historic buildings) ▲ Historic building(s) ☒ Museum ♥ Monument ◆ Other ■ Unmarked site

BRANTFORD, Ont. The Bell Homestead, where Alexander Graham Bell lived as a young man and where, in 1874, he conceived the idea of the telephone, is on Tutela Heights Road. The two-storey house, a national historic site, contains many original furnishings and a replica of the apparatus used for the first long-distance telephone call (between the Brantford office of the Dominion Telegraph Company and Paris, eight miles away, on Aug. 10, 1876). The Henderson House nearby, moved from downtown Brantford, was Canada's first (1877) telephone office. It has a typical early telephone exchange with a 50-line switchboard.

Other sites

Baddeck, N.S. (15) A museum in 25-acre Alexander Graham Bell National Historic Park displays replicas of early telephone equipment, and examples of Bell's lesser-known inventions including an original iron lung and a replica of a hydrofoil. Beinn Bhreagh, the mountain estate where Bell summered from 1893 until his death in 1922, can be seen from the park; his grave is on the mountain's summit. The estate is private.

Glace Bay, N.S. (16) A 19th-century coal miner's house and a mining company store have been re-created at the Cape Breton Miners' Museum. Exhibits include early lamps, shovels and augers. An interpretive centre traces the history of coal mining and retired miners guide visitors through workings that extend under the ocean.

Hamilton, Ont. (4) Blast Furnace "A," Canada's oldest (1893), can be seen on bus tours of the Steel Company of Canada plant. The Hamilton Waterworks (closed to the public) was built in 1857-60. It accelerated Hamilton's growth by providing

factories with ample supplies of water.

Kingston, Ont. (9) A small stone cross beside a buff granite obelisk in Cataraqui Cemetery marks the grave of John A. Macdonald. Two steam engines which once helped supply the city with water are among 26 operating engines in the Pump House Steam Museum.

London, Ont. (3) The London Brewery, a predecessor of John Labatt Ltd., has been re-created to show brewing techniques of the 1800s. Exhibits include kegs and brew kettles. A plaque at Headley House commemorates Sir Adam Beck, founder of Ontario's public hydro-electric system, who lived here from 1902 until his death in 1925.

Lucan, Ont. (2) A granite stone in St. Patrick's Cemetery marks the graves of five members of the Donnelly family murdered Feb. 4, 1880, in one of Canada's most notorious crimes.

Niagara Falls, Ont. (5) A Hydro Hall of Memory, in the Sir Adam Beck generating station six miles north, traces the development of hydro-electric power in Ontario.

Oil Springs, Ont. (1) A replica of North America's first commercial oil well, drilled on this site in 1857, is outside the Oil Museum of Canada; inside are pumps and geological displays.

Ottawa (10) Earnscliffe, the three-storey house on Sussex Drive where John A. Macdonald lived from 1883 until his death in 1891, is now the residence of the British High Commissioner.

Peterborough, Ont. (8) The world's highest hydraulic lift lock—able to raise and lower vessels 65 feet—was completed in 1904. There are boat tours of the lock.

Quebec (12) A plaque in the sunken gardens of the Plains of Abraham commemorates the first public singing of "O Can-

ada." The anthem was sung here during the first Congrès Catholique des Canadiens-Français on Saint-Jean-Baptiste Day, June 24, 1880.

Regina (not shown) Working replicas of early telephones, including the one first used by Alexander Graham Bell (March 10, 1876, in Boston, Mass.), are in Telorama, a Saskatchewan Telecommunications historical exhibit at 2121 Saskatchewan Drive. Visitors can hand-crank old wall phones and operate early switchboards.

Rossland, B.C. (not shown) The Rossland Historical Museum displays mining equipment and provides underground tours of the abandoned LeRoi mine, started in 1891. The mine was a predecessor of Cominco, the world's largest producer of zinc and lead, whose smelter is at Trail, six miles east.

Saint-Constant, Que. (11) Montreal's first electric streetcar (1892) is among 20 urban transit vehicles at the Canadian Railway Museum.

Saint John, N.B. (13) A clump of fused metal, believed the remains of a hardware store destroyed in the great fire of June 20, 1877, is a memorial in the Loyalist Burial Ground.

Stellarton, N.S. (14) Coal miners' helmets, hand-mining equipment, an 1854 mining railway locomotive and a representation of a mining tunnel are in the Stellarton Miners Museum.

Toronto (6) Canada's first automobile, a steamer built in Stanstead, Que., in 1867 by Henry Seth Taylor, is in the Ontario Science Centre.

Uxbridge, Ont. (7) Five-acre Elgin Park is little changed since July 1, 1876, when John A. Macdonald spoke to several thousand persons at the first of the great political picnics.

From Freeze-Up to Quebec

Joseph Montferrand (called Joe Mufferaw) was six foot four and the toughest logger of all. Legend said he single-handedly scattered a mob of 150 Shiners and, with the kick shown above in an old wooden sculpture at Montreal's Château de Ramezay, hobnailed his heel mark onto tavern ceilings.

A camboose (from the French cambuse, a storeroom)—like this one in Ontario's Algonquin Park—was a windowless dwelling with no chimney. A fire was kept going night and day, smoke escaping through an opening in the roof.

Lumbering was British North America's biggest industry during most of the 19th century—mainly because of the Royal Navy and a British shipbuilding boom. For decades the RN had made its masts from tall New Brunswick pines but the ships themselves had been built of European timber. When the Napoleonic wars cut off that supply, Britain turned to Canada's great forests; the durable, arrow-straight white pine of the Ottawa Valley became king. By 1864 there were 25,000 lumbermen in the valley—and more in other valleys in Ontario, Quebec and New Brunswick. Whole forests were rafted to Quebec for shipment to Britain.

The men who felled the logs and squared them into timbers also shepherded them on the long river drives—and so were hired each year "from freeze-up to Quebec." "Cruisers" picked the best timber stands, "swampers" broke trail and cleared the camp area, and other men built a camboose (left) in which 50 would live all winter long. Each dawn the cook would shout: "Daylight in the swamp!"—awakening men to a breakfast (like each day's other two meals) of bread, pork, beans and tea—or a cup of melted pork fat to combat the winter cold. Whisky was forbidden.

Axemen worked in pairs, taking alternate swings at a tree and felling it with often remarkable accuracy. The top was abandoned and the trunk cut into 40-foot lengths. Skillful men using razor-sharp 12-pound axes squared the logs into "Ottawa sticks"—big and sound enough to be floated to Quebec, shaped for easy stowage in oceangoing ships. They were hauled to a river's edge on skids pulled by oxen and were stacked there for the spring drive.

It was dangerous, exhausting work in a world with no liquor and no women, and lumbermen in town after being paid off were like "a roistering plague." Many a man's pay—up to $300—was lost in a few wild nights of drinking, wenching and brawling. At least the brawling lumberman seldom used a gun or a knife. He kicked instead. The scars his boots left were called shantyman's smallpox.

Right: Lumbering in the forests of New Brunswick—a hand-colored woodcut at the New Brunswick Museum in Saint John.

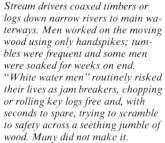

Stream drivers coaxed timbers or logs down narrow rivers to main waterways. Men worked on the moving wood using only handspikes; tumbles were frequent and some men were soaked for weeks on end. "White water men" routinely risked their lives as jam breakers, chopping or rolling key logs free and, with seconds to spare, trying to scramble to safety across a seething jumble of wood. Many did not make it.

Logs squared into timber in the woods during the winter were piled alongside hundreds of streams and started for Quebec at the spring breakup. They moved into the St. Lawrence from Lake Ontario in 300-by-60-foot "drams" held together with birch saplings. "Cribs" were used in the Ottawa—25 to 35 timbers fixed with wooden pegs and laced with chains—for shooting slides around falls at such places as Calumet, Que. (right). In broad, quiet stretches (above: the Ottawa at Hull, Que.) as many as eight drams or 200 cribs were chained into a raft of up to 100,000 cubic feet. Men guiding the rafts lived "on board."

Holocaust Along the Miramichi

The summer of 1825 had been unusually hot and dry and the 1,300 persons of Newcastle, N.B., and nearby Douglastown were in sudden peril on Oct. 7 when fire started in the Miramichi Valley forest to the north. Within a few hours, as flames roared into the two communities, some 160 persons died and 400 were injured; 600 buildings were destroyed and 2,000 persons were homeless; 6,000 square miles of standing timber was consumed. Townspeople ran to the Miramichi River to escape and many were drowned. It rained heavily that night; next day there was "nothing except ruin and desolation and death." No one ever determined how many lumbermen died in their camps in the forest.

Sometimes 20 feet above the ground, British Columbia axemen stood on springboards (below) to clear the swollen butts of giant Douglas firs—like those (right) in Cathedral Grove in Macmillan Provincial Park on Vancouver Island. After being notched, the firs were felled with eight-foot saws.

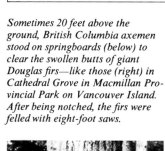

A City of Gold at the End of the Trail of '98

George Carmack was not interested in gold. He was a white man who lived as an Indian, fishing and logging; like most Indians, he considered prospecting a white man's game. Yet on Rabbit Creek in the Yukon one summer day in 1896, he was indeed searching for the stuff, prodded by his Indian friends Skookum Jim and Tagish Charlie.

Jim had detected traces of gold in the gravel of the creek; now he and California-born Carmack were panning for more. They found a nugget as fat as a thimble, then enough surface gold to pack a shotgun shell—enough to make them think this could be the richest strike in the whole territory. Carmack convinced Jim that no Indian would be acknowledged as the discoverer, so on Aug. 17 he declared himself the first man on the site. That entitled him to a double claim—1,000 feet of the creek.

George Carmack had caught the gold fever. He would carry it, spread it, until it became an epidemic infecting thousands around the world. It would be the wildest, gaudiest gold rush in history, three years of astounding good fortune and much bad luck, of greed and hardship and starvation and lavish spending.

Another man shares credit for the discovery. Robert Henderson, a Nova Scotian who had hunted gold around the world for a quarter-century, had directed Carmack into the promising area around Rabbit Creek. Henderson had been panning a nearby creek he called Gold Bottom. Like Rabbit Creek, it ran into a river the Indians called Throndiuck (Hammer-Water), for

In modern Dawson (left, from Midnight Dome, the hill behind the town) gold bricks are weighed at the Canadian Imperial Bank of Commerce in a gold room manned by actors in '98 dress. Pretty girls dance down from the stage at Diamond Tooth Gertie's, whose gambling-table profits are spent to restore Dawson's historic buildings.

311

the stakes they hammered in at its mouth to hold salmon nets. The guttural Indian word became "Klondike" on the tongues of whites.

Henderson invariably obeyed the prospector's code: if a man found gold, he informed others. The philosophy was less generous than practical. Having others around lessened the loneliness of working in the wild; competition was no consideration because even the discoverer of a site could stake no more than two 500-foot claims. So Henderson, happening upon Carmack and his Indian friends earlier that month while going for supplies, had urged Carmack to make a claim on the Gold Bottom. But he offended Carmack by adding: "I don't want any damn Siwashes [Indians] staking on that creek."

Several days later Carmack told Henderson he planned instead to try nearby Rabbit Creek, where he and the Indians had already found some gold. He agreed to let Henderson know if they had any luck. But Henderson again offended Carmack: he refused to sell the Indians tobacco. His slights would cost him a fortune.

On Aug. 17, when Carmack staked his double claim as discoverer, the Indians each staked a 500-foot claim on the Rabbit—soon to be renamed Bonanza. Carmack and Tagish Charlie left Skookum Jim on guard and set off down the Yukon River to the community of Forty Mile to register their claims. At first nobody believed them but within days prospectors descended on the creeks around the Klondike River. A few weeks later, when Henderson learned of the spectacular find, the best of Bonanza Creek had been staked.

Fortunes flourished and waned. A miner named Charles Anderson was tricked by two gamblers into paying $800 for a claim on unproven Eldorado Creek. They thought they had swindled him; three months later the Eldorado was yielding more than the Bonanza.

There was some claim-jumping but officials maintained good order in the Klondike. William Ogilvie, a Dominion government surveyor (and in 1898 commissioner of the Yukon), seldom allowed the letter of the law to stand in the way of good sense.

Ogilvie once resurveyed an Eldorado claim being worked by a miner named Clarence Berry and found it 41½ feet too long. Berry had spent the winter on land not legally his. Ogilvie knew it was immensely fertile ground, perhaps as rich as any in the history of gold mining: a single pan—two shovels of dirt—held as much as $500 in gold.

Forty Mile, 52 miles down the Yukon River from Dawson, predated the "City of Gold" by 12 years and it was there that George Carmack registered his Rabbit Creek claim. It is now a ghost town, a smattering of abandoned shacks and wagons where once a thousand persons lived.

Robert Henderson (top) lost his chance for a share of Bonanza Creek gold because his attitude toward Indians offended George Carmack (below).

312

Stern-Wheelers Battled Sand, Mud and Moose

The stern-wheelers carried out Klondike gold and carried in everything the Yukon needed—food, mining gear, fancy lamps for the dance halls, Bibles and uniforms for the Salvation Army, and liquor, 120,000 gallons in 1899 alone. They were flat-bottomed and high-stacked and looked strangely top-heavy as they plied the 1,700 miles of the Yukon River between Whitehorse and the Bering Sea.

There had been steamers on the Yukon since 1869 but the great era of Yukon River shipping came with the gold rush. Fifty-seven boats carried some 12,000 tons of supplies to Dawson in the summer of 1898. The following year there were 60 steamboats, eight tugs and 20 barges on the river. Passengers on some vessels had to provide their own food and bedding. Other boats boasted snowy linen, accomplished waiters and mahogany-panelled dining rooms.

Almost all the 250 steamers that eventually saw service on the Yukon were stern-wheelers. They had no keel and because the stern-mounted paddle wheel functioned in only 6 to 18 inches of water, they were ideal for the tortuous river with its sudden bends and shifting currents, its rocks, deadheads, mud flats, sand bars—and herds of swimming moose.

The stern-wheelers were of similar design, most with three decks. The giants among them were over 200 feet long, carried 300-400 tons of cargo and burned five cords of wood an hour. The riverboats of the gold-rush years bore such names as *Dusty Diamond* and *Gold Star, Pilgrim, Quickstep* and *City of Paris*. Two later stern-wheelers have been preserved—*Klondike* at Whitehorse, *Keno (below)* at Dawson. Another, *Tutshi,* is beached at Carcross, at the north end of Bennett Lake.

As Ogilvie measured the claim, miners wondered aloud what was wrong. He tactfully suggested that he and Berry go for dinner. After telling him the bad news, Ogilvie asked if Berry had a trustworthy friend. Berry had, and brought the man to stake the 41½-foot claim in the dead of night. The friend then transferred his rights to Berry in return for a slice of another of Berry's claims on the creek.

As prospectors converged on the area, trader Joe Ladue shrewdly guessed that land would become almost as valuable as gold. He staked out a townsite on swampy level ground where the Klondike flows into the Yukon River and named it Dawson, after a government geologist. The next summer (1897), as the population passed 1,500, his house lots sold for thousands of dollars apiece.

That first winter, when Dawson was still a chaos of tents, there was virtual famine. "Food got scarcer and scarcer," A. T. Walden recalled in his autobiography, *A Dog-Puncher on the Yukon*. "The sharing of food was remarkable. Food was priceless, but there was no price on it. This was the Starvation Camp that the people on the outside never heard of." By May 1897 the camp had no food but flour. More prospectors came in by boat when the Yukon River broke up that month, but not until early June did the stern-wheeler *Alice* arrive with food—and with liquor

Sluicing was easier and more efficient than panning for gold. The miner shovelled dirt into a dump box (top) and poured water on it. The water carried the dirt between the rods of the triangular grizzly—which stopped big pieces of gravel. Riffles on the floor of the sluice box below the grizzly caught whatever gold was in the dirt.

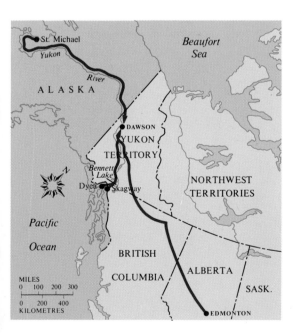

Most of the thousands who flocked to the Klondike came up the Yukon River from Alaska's Bering Sea port of St. Michael—a 1,300-mile trip to Dawson by steamer—or hiked over the White Pass trail (from Skagway) or the Chilkoot Trail (from Dyea). But some struggled into the Yukon along an all-Canadian route from Edmonton through the Peace River country and across northeastern British Columbia. Sam Steele of the Mounties found it "incomprehensible that sane men" would try to cut through this tangle of muskeg and bush. More than 750 did; only 160 made it to Dawson.

that was served free the day the saloons re-opened.

Scarcely a month later the steamship *Excelsior* landed in San Francisco. Her cargo was Klondike prospectors and their embarrassment of gold. Their arrival jolted the continent—indeed, the world—and confirmed rumors that had been trickling out of the Yukon for months. The miners dragged ashore sacks and suitcases swollen with nuggets and dust. In Seattle another shipload of sourdoughs landed with more than two tons of gold. One miner had to hire men to carry his haul. Together the two ships delivered a million and a half dollars' worth. GOLD! GOLD! GOLD! GOLD! headlined the Seattle *Post-Intelligencer*.

The Klondike strike came at the end of an economic depression in North America and men eagerly deserted homes and loved ones to follow the Trail of '98. The records brim with stories of gold-mad barbers deserting their shops, streetcar drivers abandoning their passengers, doctors forsaking their practices. The romantic name for such men was stampeders. In fact most were tenderfoots, greenhorns—cheechakos in the Yukon jargon—and their inexperience would cause them incredible hardship.

A few could afford to go by ship to the Bering Sea port of St. Michael, in western Alaska, then by boat about 1,300 miles up the Yukon River to Dawson. But most trudged into the Yukon over the Coast Mountains, through the White Pass or the Chilkoot Pass.

The White Pass trail began in the Alaska Panhandle at Skagway, a seaport town controlled by several hundred thugs and gamblers led by Jefferson Randolph "Soapy" Smith, a con man from Georgia. Some posed as ministers and newspapermen to direct cheechakos to Soapy's crooked gambling casinos and dance halls.

That fall of 1897 about 5,000 gold-seekers, including some women, attempted the 45-mile trek through the White Pass hills. The slippery trail was so narrow in places that pack teams could not pass; traffic jams lasted for hours. The treacherous path became littered with discarded packs and the remains of most of the 3,000 horses that were forced up into the hills. Novelist Jack London, who took this "Dead Horse Trail," reported that the animals died like mosquitoes in the first

Somewhere under this snowy swarm of fortune seekers on the Chilkoot Trail in 1898 is the boundary between Alaska and the Yukon. Here they were checked by the NWMP and cleared Canadian customs. Supplies that were manhandled along the 35-mile trail included many a $68.69 pack from Eaton's catalogue, a "Klondike special" that would keep a man going for a year on, among other things, 500 pounds of flour, 200 pounds of bacon and one pound of pepper. Right: the rugged, inhospitable Chilkoot Pass today.

frost and were left to rot in heaps. It took only a few hours for a carcass to be mashed underfoot. In the White Pass, wrote Robert Service, "there is no mercy, no humanity, no fellowship. All is blasphemy, fury and ruthless determination." The climbers' watchword seemed to be "mind your own business." They would pass a murdered man without a pause.

Most cheechakos reached the Klondike in 1898 over the awesome Chilkoot Trail—which one cheechako, Martha Black, later a Canadian Member of Parliament, called "the worst trail this side of hell." Raw rock in summer, slick ice and snow in winter, the Chilkoot was 600 feet higher than the White Pass and all but impenetrable by animals—in some places the trail climbed at a 35-degree angle. Its base was Dyea, an Alaska town four miles north of Skagway. At the foot of the pass lay Sheep Camp, also in Alaska, its floating population of 1,500 living in tents, cabins and the odd exotic dwelling, such as a hut woven of branches by New Zealand Maoris.

Meals at Sheep Camp cost $2.50. Whisky was 50 cents a shot and tent hotels overflowed with cheechakos paying a dollar or more to sleep on floors, tables and sometimes bunks. Lawlessness throve, from robbery to the sophisticated shell game, but Sheep Camp established its own rough justice. Some thieves got 50 lashes; others were executed.

A lake of water behind a glacier burst into the Chilkoot Pass that fall, sweeping away scores of tents and drowning three men. In the spring an avalanche suffocated 60 persons under 30 feet of snow.

Through the winter and into the summer of '98, about 22,000 men and women clambered up the pass in what seemed an endless string of humanity. It was four miles from Sheep Camp to the Chilkoot summit—and Canadian territory. The NWMP insisted that each person entering the Yukon have a year's food and equipment—a ton in weight. That meant making the climb 30 to 40 times, sometimes in blizzards and at temperatures of minus 50 (-58°F). Much of each load was food, but luxuries too went over the Chilkoot on men's backs: pianos, a grindstone, newspapers, 10,000 bottles of mosquito lotion.

Ingenuity gradually softened the trail. Steps were carved in the ice and tolls were charged to use them. Rope and cable tramways were built to lift cargo up the steepest slopes. One was driven by horses, another by gasoline, a couple more by steam; one transported 300-pound loads for 14 miles. Yet even the machines were useless when snowstorms roared—stiff enough to lean against, thick enough to blind.

Gold! This 6½-ounce nugget, about three inches long, was found near Hunker Creek, a tributary of the Klondike River. Some nuggets weighed nearly two pounds, but all such giants apparently were melted down years ago.

A stampeder might take three months and trudge 2,500 miles to move his gear—and a year's food—up over one of the passes to Bennett Lake, where boats and rafts were built for the journey down the Yukon River to Dawson. Seven thousand craft and 28,000 persons made the 550-mile trip in 1898. This church at Bennett Lake was built in 1900.

The NWMP arrived on the Canadian side of the White and Chilkoot passes in February 1898, wearing buffalo coats and bringing law and order to the stampede. Their commander was Supt. Sam (later Sir Samuel) Steele, a Mountie "original" with an impressive record of facing down rioters and outlaws. Steele's headquarters was at Bennett Lake, the bottom of both trails. There prospectors built or bought boats or rafts and at spring break-up set off for the Yukon River and Dawson. Near Whitehorse, at the boiling rapids of Miles Canyon, 150 vessels were wrecked and 10 men were drowned before Steele stepped in and enforced safety rules.

At Bennett Lake he and his men served as magistrates, municipal clerks, coroners and executors of estates. The Mounties kept up English traditions, even arranging a sports program to celebrate Queen Victoria's birthday. (The Mounties beat the cheechakos in a tug-of-war.) But their most important job was to maintain order, which they did admirably. In mid-1898—he now was responsible for law enforcement in all of the Yukon and British Columbia—Steele could boast that there had been only three murders in his territory.

Dawson, meanwhile, had endured a second starvation winter. Flour went from $6 a sack to $100. Beans brought $1 a pound. Whisky—watered—was $50 a gallon. Rich miners had almost nothing to buy. In an auction at the Monte Carlo Saloon, a dance-hall girl in a Parisian gown offered herself for the winter—with the stipulation that she could refuse the highest bidder if she didn't like him. She strolled along the bar like a fashion model and the bidding soared to $5,000. She presumably got the money after completing her winter stint.

But after the supply boats arrived in the summer of 1898, Dawson boomed anew. The population reached more than 20,000 and the "City of Gold" was the biggest town west of Winnipeg, with telephones, electricity and running water. Yet it looked primitive: tents, shacks and log

The Bar-Room Origins of Service's 'Dan McGrew'

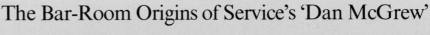

It was Saturday night and as Whitehorse bounced with bar-room revelry a line popped into Robert Service's head: "A bunch of the boys were whooping it up." The young bank teller—and sometime entertainer, renowned for dramatic recitations of such things as "Casey at the Bat"—thought it might make the start of a poem about the Klondike. But he needed a quiet place to work: he went to his cage in the Bank of Commerce—and a surprised guard took a shot at him. With "a bullet whizzing past my head," Service was to recall, "the ballad was achieved." It was his first and probably most famous, "The Shooting of Dan McGrew."

Robert Service went on to immortalize a gold rush he had never seen. When he arrived in Whitehorse in 1904, the big stampede was long over. Service had just begun. "The Yukon was the source of my first real inspiration," he said, "I bubbled verse like an artesian well." *Songs of a Sourdough* (containing "The Shooting of Dan McGrew") was published in 1907. *Ballads of a Cheechako* (tenderfoot), appeared two years later, after the bank had transferred Service to Dawson.

With *Ballads,* Service was financially independent. He resigned from the bank and in a log cabin *(left)* on a Dawson hillside wrote a novel, *The Trail of '98.* The cabin is now a national historic site.

buildings were on permafrost that became a bog in spring. And it *was* primitive: a man won a bet that he could travel Front Street by jumping from one dead horse or dog to another.

Nonetheless, Dawson was unlike such unruly settlements as Skagway. On Sundays the town slept. Saloons and theatres were shut and workmen were required to rest from their labors. (Two men were fined merely for examining their fishnets.) The worst offenders were given a "blue slip" that ordered them out of Dawson on the next boat. The town's 51 Mounties enforced laws that banned the carrying of firearms and the selling of liquor to minors.

Not lawless but not very nice either. In the dance halls and saloons and gambling casinos the motto was "never refuse a drink or kick a dog." The proprietors of these places prospered. So did many a female dancer-actress—some with such colorful names as Glass-Eyed Annie and Overflowing Flora. One miner went through $28,000 in a single night of exuberance—and left town next morning to dig more gold.

Behind the dance halls, the prostitutes of Paradise Alley worked from 70 shacks called cribs and most of their money went to the pimps who had paid their way to the Yukon. The Dawson currency was gold dust, carried in sacks, and signs in the gambling dens warned: "Don't overplay your sack." Two thousand dollars in dust could ride on the turn of a card. Silent Sam Bonnifield lost $72,000—and his Bank Saloon and Gambling House—in a poker game, then with borrowed money won it all back. Diamond Tooth Gertie, a dance-hall girl who wore a diamond between her upper front teeth, said it best:

A Whirl for a Dollar With Snakehips Lily

Gold-rush impresarios struck it rich with the likes of Deadeye Olga and Snakehips Lily on the payroll. The Olgas and the Lilys sang and danced and imitated Bernhardt—few did any of this very well—but between shows they really turned on the charm, enticing miners up to the bar for cheap whisky, or champagne at $40 to $80 a quart. A drink and a dance (another $1) with, say, Moosehide Kate—what more could a man ask on a cold winter's night?

Dawson's first theatre/dance hall, the Opera House, was a log structure whose stage was curtained with blue denim and lighted with candles. The lone survivor, the magnificent Palace Grand Theatre *(below)*, dates from 1899. It sat 2,200.

In Dawson, the theatre entertainment ranged from variety to melodrama or maybe *Macbeth*. The ice floes in *Uncle Tom's Cabin* were newspapers; Simon Legree's pack of bloodhounds was a lone husky dragged across the stage on a wire.

After each show they cleared away the benches, the orchestra struck up for dancing, and the girls went to work—for a commission on every bottle a man bought. A redhead named Cad Wilson once persuaded a miner to unload $1,740 on champagne in a single night. After one season she left Dawson with $26,000—and the memory of a man who filled her bathtub with wine at $20 a bottle. No one knew whether Cad in fact bathed in the wine. But none doubted that somebody surely rebottled it.

Many a photograph out of the Klondike bore the simple caption "One of the girls." Dawson's singing, dancing belles performed in such posh establishments as the Pavilion (which took in $12,000 on opening night in '98), the Tivoli, the Novelty and the Amphitheatre.

Naughty Dawson Counted a 'Saint' Among Its Characters

Over the Trail of '98 they came, ordinary folk most of them—but, oh, the characters among them!

Swiftwater Bill Gates was an adventurer who reached Dawson after all claims had been staked. He ignored superstition, helped develop Eldorado 13, struck it rich, went into the saloon trade and became a specialist in exotic ways to spend money. Jealousy overcame him one day when he saw Gussie Lamore, his favorite dance-hall girl, in a restaurant with another man. She had ordered eggs, an expensive luxury in the Klondike. Before she could be served, Swiftwater Bill bought every egg in the restaurant—for $600. He had them fried one by one—and one by one he tossed them to the dogs in the street.

Belinda Mulroney was a quick-profit specialist. As a stewardess on a coastal ship, she had bought supplies for the vessel at a 10-percent commission and sold hats and dresses to the Indians. When she heard of the gold rush, she invested $5,000 in cotton goods and hot water bottles, got them to Dawson and sold them at a 600-percent profit. Another Mulroney venture was the Fairview Hotel. It offered electric light, chamber music, fine linen, china and silver—and 22 steam-heated bedrooms where the tenderest whisper could be overheard, because all interior walls were canvas.

William Judge, his one-dog sled loaded with medicine, came up from Circle City in Alaska, a sick and emaciated man of 45 who looked 70. He guessed Dawson would need a hospital; so he built one—a church too, for he was a Jesuit—and he worked tirelessly through long months when scurvy, dysentery and typhoid wracked the community. He took little food, was clothed in a torn, patched cassock—no matter what the weather—and gave away most of his few possessions. He became the town's conscience, "the saint of Dawson." Soon after Christmas 1898 he came down with pneumonia and people sensed he would not recover.

On the day of his death, Jan. 16, and until his funeral three days later, the ramshackle town he had loved so selflessly draped itself in black. Even the bars and dance halls shut down until sinful Dawson had buried its saint—in a $1,000 casket.

"The poor ginks have just got to spend it; they're that scared they'll die before they have it all out of the ground."

Two fires levelled the core of Dawson in the winter of 1898-99. After the second, which destroyed 117 buildings, the town took on a different tone. Houses were built with finished lumber, sidewalks and roads were laid in macadam, schools were opened.

The bubble of development would soon burst, but not before some latecomers, among the luckiest cheechakos, struck it rich—by disregarding the conventional wisdom that all gold was close to the creeks. Beginning in 1898, new arrivals with no creeks to stake went into the hills and discovered broad veins with nuggets weighing half an ounce and more.

Great dredges worked the creeks of the Klondike after panning and sluicing became unprofitable and the rush of '98 ended. Giants such as No. 4 (inset), on Bonanza Creek, finally were abandoned and became part of the landscape they had furrowed and scarred. No. 4 extracted 800 ounces of gold daily.

In the summer of '99 news of a gold strike at Nome lured Dawson people to Alaska—8,000 left in one week. The population continued to dwindle as mining by hand became harder. Most Yukon gold lay on bedrock, deep under muck and frozen gravel. The miners couldn't scoop it up in pans; they reached it in winter by burning wood—or, later, by driving steam through steel pipes—to thaw the ground. Then they tunnelled laterally, setting aside the precious gravel until spring. During run-off, creek water was used to wash the gravel through sluice-boxes where the heavier gold settled to the bottom.

Eventually, big companies began to buy up small claims and work them with mechanized dredges. At the turn of the century a year's hand-mining produced $22 million in gold; in 1907 the yield was about $3 million. That year the last of the dance halls closed in Dawson.

The pioneers of the gold rush had long since left the Klondike. Clarence Berry, one of the first to dig on Eldorado Creek, made $1.5 million before moving on to a rich claim in Alaska and later buying oil property in California. Joe Ladue, Dawson's founder, had come to the Klondike to earn enough to impress the parents of his girl friend in Plattsburgh, N.Y.; he went home with $5 million, married her and within a couple of years died of tuberculosis.

George Carmack, Skookum Jim and Tagish Charlie all died wealthy. Robert Henderson, the unlucky man who learned about the Bonanza too late, left the Klondike to look for gold elsewhere in the Yukon and in British Columbia. When he died in 1933, he was still looking.

Heritage Sites

DAWSON, Y.T. Saloons, dance halls, theatres and hotels from the town's heyday (1897-98) have been restored. Museums exhibit gold-rush locomotives and stagecoaches. Visitors stroll along wooden sidewalks that echo with Dawson's colorful past. Outside the town are abandoned workings and prospectors' shacks. A post office (1900) is an information centre for Klondike National Historic Sites.

DIAMOND TOOTH GERTIE'S GAMBLING HALL Cancan girls entertain at Canada's only legalized casino, named for a dance hall queen of 1898.

GOLD ROOM Assay instruments, scales and a smelting furnace are displayed in this room where gold and ore were washed and weighed, and the metal was melted into bars.

PALACE GRAND THEATRE Dawson's most elaborate showplace, now restored, stages the Gaslight Follies in summer.

ROBERT SERVICE'S CABIN Here the poet lived from 1909 to 1912 and wrote *The Trail of '98*. Service's "ghost" gives daily poetry readings.

SS KENO This restored stern-wheeler, typical of vessels in use during the gold rush, was once a common sight on the Yukon River. It is now a national historic site.

Other sites

Bennett, B.C. (6) Gold-seekers who had crossed either the Chilkoot Pass or the White Pass converged at Bennett Lake and built boats and rafts to carry them to the Yukon River and Dawson. A church here was built in 1899 and abandoned in 1900.

Bonanza Creek, Y.T. (2) On this tributary of the Klondike River, George Carmack, Skookum Jim and Tagish Charlie struck gold Aug. 17, 1896: a plaque marks the Discovery Claim. Wooden-hulled No. 4 Dredge, the biggest of its kind in North America, lies where it was abandoned half a mile south.

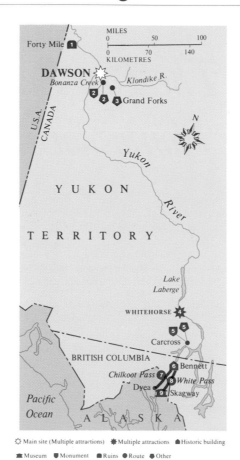

Main site (Multiple attractions)   Multiple attractions   Historic building
Museum   Monument   Ruins   Route   Other

Carcross, Y.T. (5) Skookum Jim (whose headstone is marked "James Mason"), Tagish Charlie ("Dawson Charlie") and George Carmack's wife, Kate, are buried here. The stern-wheeler SS *Tutshi* is preserved in dry dock.

Chilkoot Pass (7) Gear abandoned by gold-seekers lies along a 35-mile hiking route which follows the Chilkoot Trail from Dyea, Alaska, to Bennett Lake. A plaque at the summit commemorates the cheechakos (newcomers) of '98.

Forty Mile, Y.T. (1) This is where George Carmack registered the Discovery Claim. It is now a ghost town, four miles from the nearest road. *Accessible only on foot.*

Grand Forks, Y.T. (3) Visitors pan for gold at the junction of Upper Bonanza and Eldorado creeks, where 10,000 persons lived in 1898.

Skagway, Alaska (9) The Trail of '98 Museum displays railway equipment, prospectors' gear and photographs of miners.

Whitehorse, Y.T. (4) From here, just below some of the Yukon River's worst rapids, gold-seekers had a relatively easy 400-mile trip downstream to Dawson. Traces of the first settlement, Canyon City, can be seen.

MILES CANYON Horse-drawn cars on log rails bypassed the rapids here in 1898; traces of the route are still visible. The MV *Schwatka* cruises the canyon daily from June to September.

OLD LOG CHURCH Built in 1900, this was the Yukon's cathedral until 1959. It is now a museum of Yukon religious history.

SS *KLONDIKE* The last stern-wheeler to operate on the Yukon River has been restored to its original appearance.

W.D. MacBRIDE CENTENNIAL MUSEUM Sam McGee's log cabin, relocated from Lake Laberge, was the home of the prospector whose name Robert Service used in his poem *Cremation of Sam McGee*. Exhibits include a car from the Miles Canyon rail line.

White Pass (8) A 110-mile narrow-gauge railway completed in 1900, the White Pass and Yukon Route follows the former White Pass trail between Skagway and Whitehorse. An extension of the Klondike Highway parallels the railway. (This stretch of the highway is passable only in summer.) A plaque at Inspiration Point commemorates the thousands of pack animals that died on the trail.

The restless ghosts of a gold-rush past seem to prowl Dawson, where Robert Service once found inspiration amid the deserted buildings and "the midnight melancholy of the haunted streets."

The Last Best West: Homes for Millions

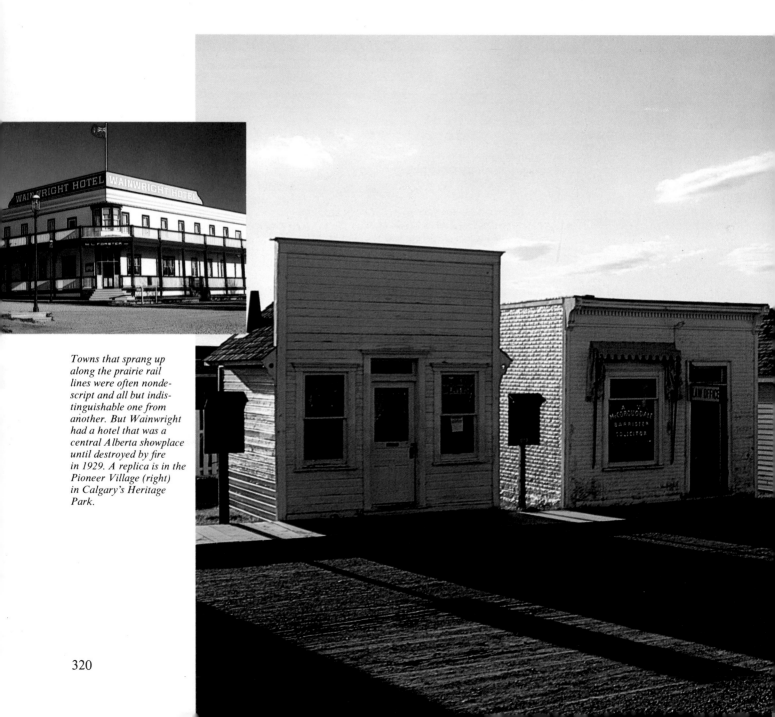

Towns that sprang up along the prairie rail lines were often nondescript and all but indistinguishable one from another. But Wainwright had a hotel that was a central Alberta showplace until destroyed by fire in 1929. A replica is in the Pioneer Village (right) in Calgary's Heritage Park.

The train that has brought him to this prairie depot is chuffing on west again and soon the vibrations in the station platform die under the homesteader's feet. Now there is silence and his gaze shifts from the low buildings of the budding town to the great emptiness rolling unbroken to every horizon. Somewhere out there is his quarter section. He's come half a world to claim it. . . .

It was the Canadian Pacific Railway that breached a thousand miles of rock and swamp north of the Great Lakes and opened the Canadian West. The railway had land to sell—nearly 40,000 square miles granted by the federal government as an inducement to go on laying track—and it had trains to fill. Getting there would be half the fun, the CPR suggested in an 1888 brochure. Colonist cars, it said, were like first-class coaches except that "the seats and berths are not upholstered."

In fact, settlers were often boxed for days in overcrowded, unheated cars. Facing seats pulled out into hard beds that slept two; upper berths swung down from the wall like hinged shelves. "Upholstery"—mattress, pillow and blanket—could be purchased from the railway for about $2.50. Each car had a cook stove (but not always fuel), washbasins and drinking water. Food was whatever the settlers brought with them. There were no toilets—but many places a train might stop.

Sidings identified by number or letter were spotted every seven or eight miles. Most developed into towns, some into cities. The Grand

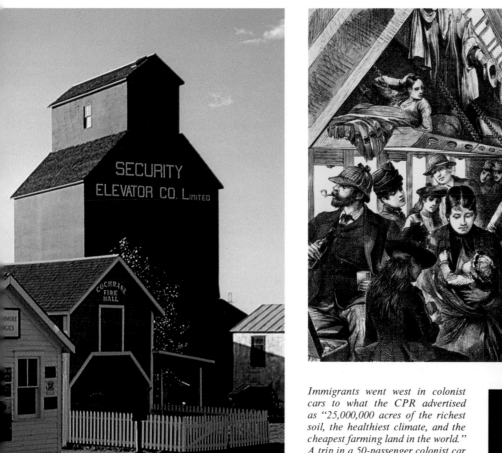

Immigrants went west in colonist cars to what the CPR advertised as "25,000,000 acres of the richest soil, the healthiest climate, and the cheapest farming land in the world." A trip in a 50-passenger colonist car was not nearly as pleasant as suggested in this sketch from an 1888 advertisement in the Illustrated London News. *But at least it was inexpensive: Montreal to Winnipeg, $8; Winnipeg to Vancouver, $12. Right: a colonist car at Heritage Park in Calgary.*

GERMANS ICELANDERS SCOTCHMEN ENGLISHMEN   AMERICANS   FRENCHMEN   SCANDINAVIANS
    BELGIANS   RUSSIANS   AUSTRIANS IRISHMEN

THE MAPLE LEAF FOR EVER

"NOW THEN, ALL TOGETHER"!

Johnny Canuck leads the chorus in this 1912 cartoon in praise of the Canadian West. Each of the wheatfield singers is from another land. So was Scots-born Alexander Muir, the immigrant who wrote the song that John Bull and Uncle Sam are holding.

Trunk Pacific went from A to Z—many times over—to identify its sidings: Atwater, Bangor . . . Young, Zelma, then over again: Allan, Bradwell, Calvet . . . . Sometimes a town that predated the Grand Trunk was towed to the nearest siding and took its place in the alphabetical parade. Thus, as the railway pushed into Alberta, Equity was moved three quarters of a mile and became Ryley.

Prairie towns were almost identical. Each had a wide main street, a grain elevator siding, and building lots for a church, general store, livery stable, blacksmith shop, bank, lumberyard and pool hall. Many a community eventually had a weekly newspaper that regularly proclaimed the town's superiority over all others—and a baseball team ready to prove the paper's claim any summer Sunday afternoon.

In 1885, when the CPR was completed, there were perhaps 150,000 people on the Prairies. When the stream of migration was broken by the First World War there were over a million and a half.

Land was the lure. It cast a spell on farm lads from Ontario and the Maritimes for whom there was no land at home, and on Americans whose own West was filling up. It beckoned British city dwellers fired by a spirit of adventure, Mennonites fleeing Russian oppression, and Ukrainians

Remittance Men Sowed Only Wild Oats

Albert "Bertie" Buzzard-Cholomondeley, formerly of Skookingham Hall, Leicestershire, England, lately of High River, Alta., was always writing home for money—with dire predictions of what would happen if the money wasn't forthcoming. Once he asked for funds to hire a lawyer to defend him on a murder charge. "Should I hang, the papers will bristle with lurid descriptions," he declared, and English papers would pick them up.

Bertie was fictional, the creation of irreverent editor Bob Edwards (see p. 326). But real remittance men, supported by money remitted from home, became notorious on the Prairies. Arriving with expensive wardrobes, polished hunting guns, a taste for high living and only the vaguest idea of doing "a bit of ranching," they often squandered their money and became expert at appealing for more from home.

One man, sent to Canada to buy a ranch, learned his father was coming to inspect it. He'd bought no land at all; so he borrowed a friend's ranch and had its cattle driven repeatedly to new locations. Father and son then rode out to watch a succession of roundups. The father gave his son £1,000 to buy "more" livestock.

Some remittance men behaved better, including those who gravitated to Cannington Manor, eight miles north of present-day Manor, Sask., where a colony of English aristocrats enjoyed cricket, racing and black-tie dinners.

With the outbreak of war in 1914 almost all the remittance men—good and bad—enlisted. Even Bob Edwards dropped his usual caustic tone. "Those fellows were green," he wrote, "but, by God, they're not *yellow.*"

Fur-clad and heavily armed, snowshoes at the ready, his English bulldog straining at the leash—a remittance man's arrival in Canada as satirized by A. G. Racey of the Montreal Daily Star.

escaping intolerable political and economic conditions. It was land that could be bought cheaply from the railway or a colonization company, or federal government land that could be earned by three years' clearing, breaking and residence. It was land to which Canada gave a glittering guarantee of irrevocable title.

A few settlers arrived in rented Pullman cars, with capital for large-scale ranching and farming, but the majority came in colonist cars. Most Europeans were in family groups but many a Canadian or American family went west only after

Interior Minister Clifford Sifton (above) paid hard cash to recruit settlers. An immigration agent who signed up families like these Doukhobors (below) would collect $21—$5 for the farmer, $2 for each of the others. The government magazine Canada West *described the West's golden opportunities for farmers.*

A Stray Cow, a Feast and Then a Murder

On Oct. 20, 1895, on a reserve near Batoche, Sask., a Cree named Almighty Voice shot a stray cow. Nineteen months and four murders later he too was dead, after a manhunt in which field guns were used in action for the last time in Canada.

Food had been scarce and the Cree subsisted on government rations. The cow was for Almighty Voice's wedding feast.

One guest, Dubling, was sullen. His sister, already married to Almighty Voice, had been abandoned for the new bride. Dubling reported who had butchered the cow, and Almighty Voice was jailed. (The jail now is part of the Duck Lake Historical Museum.)

Almighty Voice escaped, but a week later a North West Mounted Police sergeant caught up with him 40 miles northeast of Batoche. Then the Cree who had killed a cow killed a Mountie. He disappeared until May 1897 when, with two Indian companions, he was surrounded by police and civilians in a poplar grove in the Minichinis Hills.

Two Mounties were wounded in the first skirmish. Then a NWMP corporal and the Duck Lake postmaster fell mortally wounded. When still another Mountie was killed, the police pulled back. Amid rumors of an impending Indian uprising, they brought up a seven-pounder cannon from Prince Albert. Twenty-five reinforcements arrived from Regina with a nine-pounder.

Heavy shelling began early Sunday, May 30. The attackers rushed the grove at 9 a.m. and found Almighty Voice and his cousin dead from the cannon fire. Near them lay the body of Dubling, the man who had betrayed Almighty Voice but later joined forces with him. There was a bullet through Dubling's forehead.

Many a homesteader gathered and sold buffalo bones for $5 to $8 a ton. The bones, remains of the great slaughter between 1820 and 1874, were a major export to the U.S. from 1884 until 1893 when the supply ran out. They were used in fertilizer and for refining sugar.

Many a prairie settler built his first house of the most abundant, and often the only, material available—sod. It was held together by the long fibrous roots of plants such as wheatgrass (left: a wheatgrass root display at the Manitoba Museum of Man and Nature at Winnipeg). Sod was cut into "prairie shingles," four-inch-thick slabs 15 by 30 inches. They were piled, narrow side out and grass side down, to form the walls of a "soddy." More sod was laid over a framework of boards to make a roof—as on this sod house (made of commercial sod) in Heritage Park at Calgary, Alta. A sod house was cool in summer and warm in winter and some were elaborately furnished. Right: the interior of a 20-by-24-foot soddy built in 1965 adjacent to a museum at Elbow, Sask.

Isaac Barr's Dream Was a Colonists' Nightmare

There were seven near mutinies on the 13-day voyage to Saint John, N.B., in April 1903. The 2,000 Britons on the steamship *Lake Manitoba,* bound for a new life on the plains of Saskatchewan, were hardly out of sight of Liverpool when most realized that the Rev. Isaac Montgomery Barr *(inset)* and his dream were not entirely as advertised.

Barr, a Canadian-born Anglican clergyman, was a colonizer ("Canada for the British!"), a would-be Cecil Rhodes, apparently a basically good man but shockingly naïve. He seems to have been neither con artist nor cheat—as some insisted—but he was inexplicably ingenuous. *Lake Manitoba's* passengers, in their agony of seasickness and deprivation, remembered that back home, with marvellous understatement, Isaac Barr had told them: "Many of the comforts of England you must leave behind."

They finally reached Saskatoon *(right)* on April 18, gnawing at bread that most believed Barr had sold them at an indecent profit. It was cold and wintry and, despite Barr's promises, their reception was dismal. Women and children made do in bleak immigration sheds and tents; their menfolk unwittingly bought bad horses, broken-down wagons and provisions of all kinds, often at wildly inflated prices. There was trouble over the allotment of home sites, trouble over the lack of supplies and hospital equipment, trouble everywhere. Finally, led by the Rev. George E. Lloyd, the settlers formed a committee to challenge Barr as leader. Lloyd was asked to take over. He did. Barr lamely signed away his leadership, relinquishing even his own homestead. Barr's colonists, having become Lloyd's, settled where now Lloydminster stands on the Alberta-Saskatchewan border. And they prospered.

the husband and father had made the long trip alone, found his land and built a house.

Surveyors had worked their way across the Prairies long before the settlers. From east of Winnipeg to the Rocky Mountains a vast checkerboard had emerged. The land was divided into squares, six miles to a side, called townships. Each township was split into mile-square sections and these were further divided into quarter sections of 160 acres—homesteads. At the southeast corner of every section were a mound and a three-foot iron pipe. On the flattened end of the pipe was chiselled the number of the section.

Land agents sketched maps for homesteaders but often did not make clear the distances involved. One Austrian family, with no English and unable to check, read the four "squares" on a map to mean their land was four *miles* west of Edmonton. Papa left the family in the station while he went to look. He returned two days later to announce the farm was four *townships* (24 miles) away.

The railways were among the first to recruit settlers but other promoters did some hard selling too. One in Ontario advertised homesteads at $2 an acre in what it called the Great Temperance Colony. Buyers were not told that the territory was "dry" by law anyway and that adjacent 160-acre homesteads could be purchased from the government for a mere $10! But when they learned the truth the temperance colonists laughed it off—and founded Saskatoon.

In 1896 the federal government made the recruitment of settlers a national priority. Prime Minister Wilfrid Laurier (see p. 330) named Clifford Sifton minister of the interior with the task of filling the Prairies. One place Sifton looked was the United States. He sought American farmers experienced with conditions similar to those in Canada. Prairie land was advertised at American county fairs and journalists were taken on train junkets to dispel the myth of "the frozen north."

In Britain the Canadian government sponsored trips to Canada for immigration agents, prospective settlers and influential persons— such as David Lloyd George, a future prime minister—in the hope they would preach the emigration gospel. Agents in Europe were paid $5 for each farmer they recruited, $2 for each family member. But Sifton's proposal to recruit farmers in eastern Europe raised a storm from Anglo-Saxons who thought "peasants in sheepskin coats" lacked "quality." Said Sifton: "I think a stalwart peasant in a sheepskin coat, born on the soil, whose forefathers have been farmers for ten generations, with a stout wife and a half-dozen children, is good quality."

Colorful government posters portrayed "Canada West—The Last Best West." A government

Prairie Ukrainians by William Kurelek: plastering the house and painting pysanky *(Easter eggs). Children mix clay, water, straw and horse or cow dung; adults apply it to the walls, inside and out. The walls later were coated with a lime solution to which skim milk or bluing was added to make it white. Legend says the world will end if the art of painting* pysanky *is lost.*

Bob Edwards' Barbs: More Fun Than Fact

If *The Eye Opener* was short on hard news and long on barbed comment, if editor Bob Edwards sometimes happily refused to spoil a good story by sticking to the facts, if you couldn't tell the gospel truth from the Edwards fiction . . . it was still the best five-cent read in the West.

Scots-born Robert Chambers Edwards was the most colorful of a brilliant, flamboyant lot, the Prairie newspaperman of the early days. He founded *The Eye Opener* in Calgary in 1902, and every Saturday (more or less) for 20 years he blasted away at monopolists, the Establishment, the clergy, the Senate and—his favorite target—the CPR.

An *Eye Opener* campaign for safe level crossings led the railway to ban the paper from CPR trains. Edwards retaliated by reporting every CPR accident in detail, perhaps with a picture captioned "Sample of Ordinary Everyday CPR Wreck." When the CPR withdrew Edwards' complimentary pass, Edwards ran a picture of CPR lawyer R. B. Bennett—a future prime minister—over the caption "Another CPR Wreck."

The Eye Opener served up this sort of social note: "Miss Maude De Vere of Drumheller arrived in the city Wednesday afternoon and was run out of town Wednesday night." When the paper did not appear, Edwards would eventually announce in print that his old enemy, drink, had been to blame. He campaigned against hard liquor and for mild beer and obviously believed, despite his own example, in moderation. When challenged to a duel, he declined, because "in the present state of western Canada a frequently sober editor can do more good than a permanently dead hero."

magazine, *Canada West*, distributed to immigration agents and colonization companies, showed bumper crops beneath a kind autumn sun. It spelled out the opportunities of the Last Best West: ranching, dairying, grain raising, fruit raising, mixed farming, and the supreme attraction: "FREE HOMES FOR MILLIONS."

In the belt of poplars that stretched northwest from Manitoba to the Rockies, a skilled axeman could build a log cabin in three days and chink the cracks in a couple more. His watertight, windtight dwelling would keep out the worst of the cold for two or three winters until a frame or brick house could be built and the cabin made

The bronc Buttons has just thrown a California cowgirl named Hazel Walker in this historic photograph of action at the first Calgary Stampede, in 1912. The big show was the brainchild of an eastern cowboy, New Yorker Guy Weadick. He called Canadian cowhands second-raters—and Canadian cattle barons put up $100,000 so Weadick could be proven wrong. Tom Three Persons, a Blood Indian from Alberta, won the saddle bronc championship that first year.

into a toolshed. A man inexperienced with the axe could hire a skilled neighbor for 75 cents a day, or could show the cautious determination of an Englishman who, to protect his feet, learned to swing an axe while standing in a washtub.

On the treeless grasslands near the U.S. border, most settlers built houses of sod—"prairie shingles." Thick pieces about one foot by three were stacked, with holes for windows and a door, to form the walls. The roof too was often sod, over a wood frame and sometimes supplemented by canvas or thatch. Roof sod kept growing.

A man alone might build a house but making a home, as long as he remained alone, was something else. A Methodist preacher, the Rev. Wellington Bridgman, once remarked: "Three things men won't take time to do—sweep the floor, cook meals and wash dishes." The feminist Emily Murphy said of a journey with her missionary husband: "Most of the farmhouses we see are inhabited by bachelors. Where the one Incomparable She holds sway there is a clothesline in the yard and a curtain at the window." C. H. Stout, a homesteader and editor, wrote: "It was the men who had the pioneering urge, but it was the women who finally made western pioneering a success." The homestead housewife made meals of an endless round of rabbits, ducks, dried apples and corn syrup. She converted flour sacks into clothes. And she provided the strength her family needed when conditions fell far short of the government's advertising promises.

The benign sun on a *Canada West* cover could turn sinister and mocking during a drought.

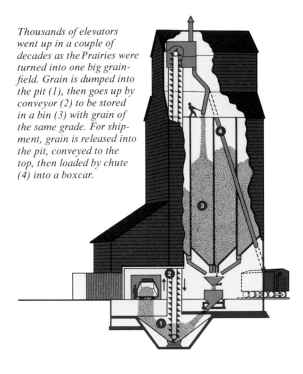

Thousands of elevators went up in a couple of decades as the Prairies were turned into one big grain-field. Grain is dumped into the pit (1), then goes up by conveyor (2) to be stored in a bin (3) with grain of the same grade. For shipment, grain is released into the pit, conveyed to the top, then loaded by chute (4) into a boxcar.

Through the dust, wrote Prairie novelist Sinclair Ross, the sun "looks big and red and close. Bigger, redder, closer every day. You begin to glance at it with a doomed feeling." Grass fires, started by lightning or human carelessness, raced across the prairie in late summer and fall, riding the very winds they created. Flies and mosquitoes sometimes swarmed so thickly that they hid a horse's color in a grey cloud. An early frost could blight a season's hopes, and a summer storm could bring hailstones big enough to kill a man or destroy his crop. On July 8, 1890, Alexander Kindred of Moffat, Sask., had "wheat standing to the chin on every acre I could cultivate." A sudden hailstorm beat it to the ground "and my hair turned grey that night."

Many homesteads were abandoned, sometimes because the settlers didn't measure up: they were townsfolk, unsuited to farm life. They soon went to new Prairie communities where their skills were needed. Sometimes the land didn't measure up: riverbeds, lakes, ravines, hills, dales, black soil and grey—all had been charted by the surveyors. In the grasslands a few years of plentiful rain brought bumper crops; as rainfall reverted to normal and one crop failure followed another the settlers drifted away.

But those who passed the test and had good land stood tall and secure—the youth from New Brunswick on a farm larger than his father had ever dreamed of owning; the "stalwart peasant in a sheepskin coat" on his 160 acres; the Englishman who had swung his axe from a washtub. And having stood up to the land and its climate, they were ready to stand up to powerful men.

Settlers saw in the telephone a marvel that would end their isolation and they wanted one for every farm. Bell Telephone said it couldn't be done. So the governments of the three Prairie Provinces, at the urging of the settlers, forced the giant off the plains and between 1906 and 1908 founded the only state-owned telephone systems in North America.

Then the settlers took on the grain barons—the bosses of the elevator companies and the Winnipeg Grain Exchange. From the start, together, farmers had planted seed, harvested crops and hauled grain to the privately owned elevators. But almost from the start they shared a suspicion that they were being exploited by those who controlled the market—the railways, politicians and elevator owners. Now they decided to fight for their interests.

On Dec. 18, 1901, farmer William Richard Motherwell—later federal minister of agriculture—founded the Territorial Grain Growers' Association. This set the stage for the wheat-pool movement which by the mid-twenties the three Prairie governments had backed with not only rhetoric but also cash. The bosses were not driven out but they had to compete with the upstarts.

The First World War closed the book on 30 seasons of western immigration. By then the newcomers were taking firm control of their destiny. They would be tested again, but they did not fear the future, they banked on it. They kept in their hearts the image of golden harvests on the covers of *Canada West*. If this year's crop should fail, there was always the vision of a bumper crop next year. They had built three provinces on the prairie. They had also created a country. They called it Next Year Country.

Steam tractors such as this one at a threshermen's reunion at Austin, Man., broke prairie sod and powered harvest equipment in the early days of western settlement. A 30-hp giant required four operators; it used 2,000 gallons of water each day— and a ton of coal or two cords of wood.

327

Heritage Sites

CALGARY In a turn-of-the-century Prairie town re-created in Heritage Park are some 60 buildings that include a log opera house, a livery stable and a one-man North West Mounted Police post. Near the town are Indian teepees. *Moyie,* a half-size replica of a Canadian Pacific stern-wheeler, makes excursions on Glenmore Reservoir. A steam locomotive hauls passengers around the 60-acre park in coaches that include a 1905 colonist car.

PRINCE HOUSE A grand piano graces this elegant home, built in 1894 by Peter Prince, who five years earlier had introduced electricity to Calgary.

MIDNAPORE STATION Transported from Midnapore, once eight miles south of Calgary, this restored CPR depot features a telegraph office dating from 1910.

SHONTS ELEVATOR A 25,000-bushel grain elevator built in Shonts, Alta., in 1909 has a hand-cranked mechanism for tipping wagons.

SOD HOUSE This reconstructed soddy has glass windows, a wooden door and typical pioneer furnishings.

WAINWRIGHT HOTEL A replica of a famous Wainwright, Alta., hotel that was destroyed by fire in 1929. Attached by a catwalk is a two-storey outhouse from the mining town of Lundbreck, Alta.

Also in Calgary (1) The Calgary Stampede, a 10-day rodeo and pioneer festival, is held each July. Western Canadiana in the Glenbow-Alberta Institute, an eight-storey museum-archive, includes paintings, taped interviews with pioneers, and more than 25,000 reference books and pamphlets. A collection of nearly one million artifacts ranges from teapots to a horse treadmill.

Other sites

Abernethy, Sask. (15) A 10-room cut-stone house near here, once the home of the father of the Prairie co-operative movement, is a national historic site. William Richard Motherwell came from Ontario in 1882.

Austin, Man. (19) The Manitoba Agricultural Museum exhibits steam- and gasoline-powered tractors, threshers and binders from the 1880s and '90s. Many of the vehicles are operated each July at the Manitoba Threshermen's Reunion and Stampede.

Cardston, Alta. (2) The home of Charles Ora Card (Brigham Young's son-in-law), who led 10 Mormon families here from Utah in 1887, is a museum. A cairn honors the settlers.

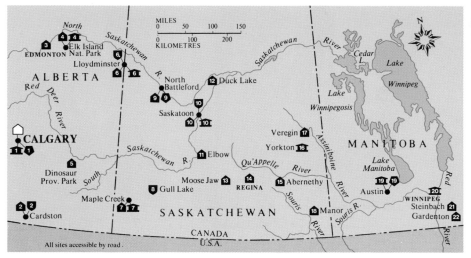

○ Main site (Historic buildings) ▲ Historic building(s) ▨ Museum ▼ Monument ● Other

Dinosaur Provincial Park, Alta. (5) A cabin lived in by John Ware, an ex-slave who was one of Alberta's early cowboys, has been relocated here. Exhibits include saddles and Ware's branding iron.

Duck Lake, Sask. (12) At the Duck Lake Historical Museum is the restored jail from which a Cree named Almighty Voice escaped in 1895, triggering a 19-month manhunt. Exhibits include a photograph of Almighty Voice, a proclamation for his arrest, and two rifles used by pursuers.

St. Michael's Ukrainian Orthodox Church at Gardenton, Man., dates from the late 1890s. It was erected by immigrants from northern Bukovina (the western Ukraine).

Edmonton (3) Fort Edmonton Park, a 158-acre outdoor museum, has two small-town streets re-creating the periods around 1885 and 1905. Its 35 buildings include the first house of A. C. Rutherford (Alberta's first premier) and the original 1878 office of the *Edmonton Bulletin,* the

This 72-foot, four-storey windmill at the Mennonite Village Museum at Steinbach, Man., is a replica of one built in 1877. Below: the Grosse Stube (living room) in a Mennonite dwelling at the museum. A corridor connects the family's living quarters with the barn where livestock and poultry were kept.

White plastered walls and a thatched roof with a pronounced overhang were features of early Ukrainian houses in the West. This example is in Elk Island National Park in Alberta.

province's first newspaper, founded by Frank Oliver.

Elbow, Sask. (11) A re-created 20-by-24-foot sod house adjoining the Elbow Museum has elaborate furnishings such as a wrought-iron stove and an organ.

Elk Island National Park, Alta. (4) A thatched cottage houses the Ukrainian Folk Museum, displaying clothing and household effects. Near the park, in the Ukrainian Cultural Heritage Village, are some 25 buildings from the 1890s including a hardware store and a schoolhouse.

Gardenton, Man. (22) St. Michael's Ukrainian Orthodox Church, consecrated here in 1899 in Manitoba's first Ukrainian settlement, is the oldest Orthodox church in Canada. It displays hand-carved candelabra and Russian icons.

Gull Lake, Sask. (8) Three cairns about 30 miles west at a former headquarters of the "76" Ranch (1888-1920) salute the province's ranching industry.

Lloydminster, Alta./Sask. (6) Barr Colony mementos include a marker at the settlers' first campsite and a log church built in 1904. The Barr Colony Museum contains pioneer furniture and machinery.

Manor, Sask. (18) The remains of Cannington Manor, where English aristocrats settled starting in 1882, are in 25-acre Cannington Manor Historic Park. A museum has a model of the colony and a muzzle-loading walking stick for shooting pigeons. The silver chalice in All Saints Anglican Church used to be a racing trophy.

Maple Creek, Sask. (7) Buildings in Frontier Village include an office-bunkhouse of the "76" Ranch. The Old Timers' Museum has a brass branding iron and a 14-seater lazy Susan table from the "76."

Moose Jaw, Sask. (13) The Museum of Saskatchewan Pioneer Village honors Finnish settlers. One of its 17 buildings is the 100,000th house in Saskatchewan wired for electricity.

North Battleford, Sask. (9) A branch of the Western Development Museum is a pioneer village. Some 35 buildings include a Dominion Lands Office, a Canadian Northern Railway station, and a dentist's office with a treadle-operated drill. At Fort Battleford is the press that printed Saskatchewan's first newspaper, the *Saskatchewan Herald,* in 1878.

Regina (14) The frame house in which John Diefenbaker lived as a boy is in the Wascana Centre. Among its exhibits are the family Bible and a sewing machine.

Saskatoon (10) A plaque marks where the Barr colonists camped while en route to Lloydminster. Exhibits in the Ukrainian Museum of Canada include pottery and decorated eggs; the Museum of Ukrainian Culture displays embroideries and costumes. The Western Development Museum has re-created, indoors, a 1910 village street. Among its 26 buildings are a hotel, a bank and a Chinese laundry.

Steinbach, Man. (21) The Mennonite Village Museum has a typical farmhouse with attached barn, and a replica of an 1877 windmill. Mennonite food is served at a restaurant in a converted livery stable.

Veregin, Sask. (17) A museum in a 1917 prayerhouse displays handmade Doukhobor clothing and farm tools.

Winnipeg (20) Exhibits at the Manitoba Museum of Man and Nature trace Prairie development and include replicas of a teepee, sod house and settler's cabin.

Yorkton, Sask. (16) Re-created in a Western Development Museum branch are a Ukrainian kitchen, a German dining room and an English parlor.

The Buoyant, Bountiful Sunshine Years

There is still something of straw hats and blazers and croquet about the big house on Laurier Avenue in Ottawa, something of bicycles leaning against the steps on a summer evening, of an ice-cream party on the veranda. Laurier House has a secure and gracious Victorian look, its cream brick outline softened by the years, its lawn and trees as green as ever.

Wilfrid Laurier must have been pleased that day in 1897 when he first walked through the comfortable rooms of the three-storey mansion he had just received from his supporters, rooms where he would entertain—and deal and compromise with—men who would help him shape Canada through brilliant, hopeful years. Here would sit the promoters Mackenzie and Mann who strung a patchwork of railways into one of the world's great rail systems. Here would sit the members of one of the strongest cabinets in Canada's history, men such as Oliver Mowat, who had ruled Ontario like a fiefdom, and Clifford Sifton (see pp. 323, 325), a Prairie businessman with an aristocratic taste for riding to hounds.

Upstairs was a study well suited to the loneli-

ness of Laurier's task and to his reflective nature. Here he would plan the endless compromises that Canada demanded—between French and English, Roman Catholic and Protestant, farm and city. Here he would puzzle over the difficulty of governing a country in which it was said the English were more English than the Queen and the French more Catholic than the Pope.

Wilfrid Laurier had now been prime minister a year, a tall and slim man, elegant almost to the point of foppery, radiating grace and charm. He possessed Sir John A. Macdonald's mastery of men and exerted it with a style Sir John A. never had. Macdonald's was the roughness of a nation building, Laurier's was the confidence of a nation established. In later years, as his hair turned shining white, he could still inspire young men with a phrase and a gesture.

Beneath his easygoing manner lay a strength as solid as the Laurentian rock on which Laurier House stood. Laurier was a tolerant man but he knew that tolerance alone could not govern Canada.

The world in the mid-nineties was struggling out of a 20-year depression, and Canada was still only a rudimentary nation. Years of disappointment had bred quarrels that threatened to break up Confederation. Farmers were bitter about tariffs that increased the cost of machinery. Some were threatening to join the United States.

There was endless squabbling over language and religion. The Roman Catholic Church in Quebec contained an influential minority, led originally by Bishop Ignace Bourget, that claimed the clergy had authority above both government and law.

Protestant extremism was sometimes expressed through the Orange Order, a lodge pledged to support of the Protestant monarchy and destruction of Catholicism. It was strong enough to sway elections in much of English Canada, so strong that Macdonald had found it prudent to join the order. Curiously, both Protestant and Catholic extremes tended to support the Conservative Party.

The depression had intensified these quarrels, but Laurier could face them because of yet another essential political gift: he was lucky. He came to power in 1896 and within a year the sun broke through the gloomy clouds—the depression ended. Britain once more could buy Canadian products and invest in Canada. Settlers poured in from Europe and the United States. Gold was discovered in the Yukon (see p. 310). Laurier captured the buoyant mood of Canadians when he said that the 18th century had belonged to Britain and the 19th to the United States but the 20th century would belong to Canada.

Wilfrid Laurier was born in 1841 some 35

Wilfrid Laurier was a man of dignity and intellect, a charmer, a coaxer, a compromiser—but ruthless when he had to be. This portrait is from a full-length painting by Marc-Aurèle de Foy Suzor-Côté.

The mansion on what now is Laurier Avenue was 18 years old when presented to Wilfrid Laurier by political supporters in 1897. That same year, in Normandy, the prime minister and his wife Zoë bought the suite (above) that graces the salon with its portrait by Georges Delfosse. Laurier mementos in the house, a national historic site, include his desk (left) from his office on Parliament Hill, and a 1906 photograph.

331

Ignace Bourget, bishop of Montreal from 1840 to 1876, had built Mary Queen of the World Basilica on Dorchester Street, in the heart of English Montreal, as a warning that the Church of Rome ruled in Canada's largest city. The basilica, modelled on St. Peter's in Rome and originally named St. James Cathedral, was started in 1875. Covering one-quarter of the area of the Roman basilica, it is 333 feet long and 150 feet wide; its 75-foot-wide dome rises 252 feet above the floor. The high altar is of ivory, marble and onyx.

Railroading for the Sheer Fun of It

Railways, it was said, were built by Americans to develop their country, by Germans to make war, by Canadians for the sheer fun of it.

Two who had great fun, largely at public expense, were entrepreneurs William Mackenzie and Donald Mann. In 1915 they and their Canadian Northern gave the country a *third* transcontinental railway—after the Canadian Pacific and the Grand Trunk Pacific—when only two lines at most were needed.

Mackenzie and Mann were smooth talkers with immense energy and no shame. They started in Manitoba in 1896, building several short lines. Settlers were so grateful for the first line that they gave the railway their labor for free. The partners kept adding to the Canadian Northern on the Prairies, then pushed east, finally (in 1918) tunnelling under Mount Royal to downtown Montreal.

Eventually, they built or acquired 10,000 miles of rail and piled up huge personal fortunes. They and their railway were so in debt to the federal government that Ottawa could only avoid bankrupting them by granting more subsidies.

The Canadian Northern's first through train from Toronto steamed into Vancouver in September 1915, some 17 months after the Grand Trunk Pacific had reached the coast at Prince Rupert.

A Royal Commission recommended that both new transcontinentals be nationalized, and Canadian National Railways, formed in 1919, absorbed them. Mackenzie and Mann—now Sir William and Sir Donald—built no more railways. But they were wealthy. And they'd had real fun.

This is the brick house—perhaps a little bit beyond their means—that Wilfrid and Zoë Laurier built in Arthabaska, chief town of Quebec's Bois-Francs region southeast of Trois-Rivières. Laurier practised law in Arthabaska, ran a weekly newspaper and was elected to Parliament. The house is a museum, furnished as in his day.

Below: this 24-by-26-foot brick veneer cottage in Laurentides, Que. (formerly Saint-Lin), 35 miles north of Montreal, was Wilfrid Laurier's boyhood home. Left: the kitchen of the house, which is a national historic site.

miles north of Montreal in the village of Saint-Lin (now Laurentides). Part of his schooling was among the Scots Presbyterians of nearby New Glasgow. But he returned to the French-Canadian tradition, following classical studies at L'Assomption College. This combination instilled an intellectual discipline and a feeling for language that would help make him the outstanding orator in Canadian public life. A lifelong enthusiasm for British history gave him a deep sympathy for the liberal and democratic traditions of the parliamentary system.

These years of preparation ended with a law degree from McGill University in Montreal and a shy proposal of marriage to Zoë Lafontaine. In 1868, Wilfrid and Zoë Laurier were living in Arthabaska in Quebec's Eastern Townships.

Quebec was solidly Conservative and the young Liberal lawyer found himself opposing the ultraconservatives who dominated the Catholic Church in his area. Laurier also grew to oppose the extreme nationalism of the *rouges,* a wing of the Quebec Liberal Party. The voters of Drummond-Arthabaska were attracted by

Laurier's moderation and in 1874 elected him their Member of Parliament. For the next 13 years, Laurier's eloquence and ability won the respect of a Liberal Party largely English and Protestant. In 1887 the Liberals made him national leader.

At the same time, Canada's extreme factions were gaining power within the Conservative Party and Laurier faced them in the federal election of 1896. The burning issue was the Manitoba schools question.

D'Alton McCarthy, a fire-breathing Orangeman from Barrie, Ont., had set out to halt any spread of the French language or the Catholic faith in Canada. In the peculiar language of the

bigots who supported him, this was called equal rights.

McCarthy took his cause to Manitoba's English Protestants. His major target was the schools belonging to the French-Catholic minority and in 1890 the government of Manitoba abolished them. Manitoba's French Catholics would have to attend English-language state schools. Liberal Premier Thomas Greenway knew the few French schools were neither a threat nor an inconvenience. Their abolition was a political stunt to distract attention from government scandals. But the act undermined the trust upon which Confederation was built.

Manitoba Catholics appealed to the Conservatives in Ottawa, and the government, led by Sir Charles Tupper, agreed to restore their schools. Tupper thought that Laurier, as a Catholic, would have to support him. That was the biggest mistake Tupper ever made.

Laurier, pressed to state Liberal policy, answered with a fable about a contest between the North Wind and the Sun to make a man remove

Soldier-industrialist Sir Henry Pellatt built 98-room Casa Loma in 1911-14, insisting it be fit for a king (or any other royalty who might visit Toronto). It was, although no crowned head ever slept under Pellatt's roof. In 1923, soon after his wife's death—and with the great castle (North America's biggest) costing a king's ransom to run—Pellatt abandoned Casa Loma. A Kiwanis club took it over in 1937 as a tourist attraction. Visitors tour rooms finished in teak, oak and marble, slip along hidden passageways and down secret staircases, and walk through an 800-foot tunnel to palatial stables. Left: Lady Pellatt's suite and the Great Hall.

The First Modest Goal: To Be Called a Person

He was Edmonton's leading criminal lawyer, she the Empire's first woman magistrate, and they battled off and on for years. "You're not even a person!" Eardley Jackson would shout at Emily Murphy, arguing that, in law, women were not "persons."

Emily Murphy was a parson's wife, a leader of the "new womanhood" that struggled into being during the sunshine years. Like Nellie McClung, who became her ally, she campaigned tirelessly for women's rights.

She was Ontario-born (1868) and went to Edmonton in 1907. "Whenever I don't know whether to fight or not," she once said, "I always fight." In 1916, when a magistrate excluded women observers from a prostitution trial, Mrs. Murphy crusaded for a woman magistrate to hear cases involving female offenders—and found herself appointed. Before long Eardley Jackson was shouting: "You're not even a person!"

Eventually, in 1929, with Nellie McClung and others, Emily Murphy took that issue to the Privy Council in London. She won: women, said the Empire's highest court, *are* persons.

Like Mrs. Murphy, Nellie McClung was born in Ontario, in 1873. She grew up in Manitoba, rebelliously aware of disparities between men's and women's rights. If morning sickness during pregnancy had been a man's disease, she once said, "it would have been made the subject of scientific research and relieved long ago."

She taught school in southern Manitoba in the 1890s (a log cabin she lived in is at a museum at La Rivière) and became an author, temperance leader and suffragette. She was a fiery public speaker. Her motto: "Never retract, never explain, never apologize—get the thing done and let them howl." She led parades, buttonholed premiers, formed the Political Equality League, and demanded the vote—which Manitoba gave to women in 1916.

By then Mrs. McClung had moved to Alberta and was fighting alongside Emily Murphy. Their woman/person victory in 1929 came none too soon: Emily Murphy died in 1933. Among those who filed past her coffin were two prostitutes. They placed a rose on the old crusader's hands.

Militant feminists Emily Murphy (above) and Nellie McClung were also lively authors. Mrs. Murphy used the pseudonym Janey Canuck. She defended Canada against English critics and attacked slums and drug abuse. To Mrs. McClung writing was "a fire in the blood." Her first book, Sowing Seeds in Danny, *was published in 1908. It ran to 17 editions and sold 100,000 copies.*

---

his coat. The stronger the North Wind blew, the tighter the man wrapped himself in his coat. Then the Sun shone and the coat came off. Laurier went on: "Well, sir, the government are very windy. They have blown and raged and threatened and the more they have raged and blown, the more that man Greenway has stuck to his coat. If it were in my power, I would try the sunny way ... Do you not believe that there is more to be gained by appealing to the heart and soul of men rather than by compelling them to do a thing?"

Thus the election of 1896 became a contest between Sir Charles Tupper's North Wind and Laurier's sunny ways.

The North Wind blew its hardest. Quebec bishops threatened Catholics with damnation if they voted Liberal. Said one French Canadian: "Then I'll be damned but I'll vote for Laurier." Many English Protestants had been reluctant to vote for a French Catholic. Laurier once told them: "Yes, you cheer for me but you won't vote for me." This time, they voted as they cheered.

Prime Minister Laurier promptly negotiated with Greenway to provide language rights for non-English-speaking children in the public schools and to permit religious instruction each day. It was a compromise, but more than Tupper's coercion would have achieved.

Canada was complex in more than language and religion. Maritimers were adjusting from old connections across the seas to a new connection, inland across Canada. The change was symbolized when in 1906 the last British troops in Canada, the Halifax garrison, were replaced by Canadian soldiers. For Maritimers the future now seemed to lie in the West; many, like R. B. Bennett (a future prime minister), followed the rails to the booming Prairies.

Quebec and Ontario profited by the Prairie boom but their people didn't have to leave home. Eastern factories supplied the manufactured goods, eastern wholesalers distributed them, and eastern banks and railways dominated western development.

In Montreal, factory chimneys sprang upward past steeples. The Catholic Church was uneasy at the emergence of an industrial world that had little to do with the faith and seemed owned largely by the English.

Toronto's growth was more commercial than

It was The Farmer's Bible and The Wishing Book. Eaton's catalogue appeared in 1884, soon offered everything from patent medicines to ploughshares, and became a national institution.

The Sailor Who Put Canada in the High Arctic

Bernier is a name to rank with Cabot, Cartier and Mackenzie. It was Capt. Joseph-Elzéar Bernier, a 20th-century explorer from L'Islet-sur-Mer, Que., who established Canadian sovereignty over the islands of the High Arctic.

Bernier was a ship's boy at 12, a master at 17. He sailed to all continents and crossed the Atlantic 269 times. He was a 50-year-old master mariner when he ensured that Canada did not lose the Arctic islands by default.

Americans, Norwegians and Danes were exploring and whaling in the Canadian Arctic; Norway claimed several islands; some U.S. politicians wanted Washington to claim the entire archipelago. Ottawa seemed indifferent.

Bernier spent $21,000 of his own in a long campaign. Finally the Laurier government sponsored four expeditions (1904-5, 1906-7, 1908-9, 1910-11) in which Bernier, in the barquentine *Arctic*, visited most of the islands. On each he erected a cairn bearing *Arctic's* name and containing Canada's claim sealed in a bottle. RCMP posts were established. Canada's presence in the islands could be *seen*.

In a museum at L'Islet-sur-Mer are instruments from *Arctic* and the template used to cast a plaque that Bernier erected on Melville Island on July 1, 1909. A nearby monument honors this man, whose name is all but forgotten in the land he loved.

---

industrial but Protestant leaders there were also concerned over the effects of the new prosperity. They pressured the Laurier government into passing the Lord's Day Act which—throughout Canada—made most business activity and entertainments illegal on Sunday. Toronto was the headquarters for the major Protestant churches. It had Massey Hall for respectable plays and uplifting lectures. Its university was the centre of English Canada's intellectual life. And it had Eaton's, which covered its display windows on Sunday so not to desecrate the Sabbath with advertising.

Montreal and Toronto were arrogant about their wealth—but most of it depended on the West. Prairie wheat became Canada's prime export in the Laurier years, and Winnipeg became "The buckle of the wheat belt." Settlement of the West (see p. 320) was so rapid that by 1905 Ottawa had to create the provinces of Saskatchewan and Alberta. Vancouver, only recently a small lumbering town, became a major port for

Men like these (in the Cochrane district about 1910) took part in the great Northern Ontario mining boom of the early 20th century. It was touched off at Cobalt in 1903 by discovery of the world's richest vein of silver. Exploration and drilling in surrounding districts led to gold strikes in the Porcupine in 1909 and at Kirkland Lake in 1912.

prairie wheat and British Columbia coal, and the commercial centre of a province of mines and farms and timber and fisheries that was rich, and getting richer.

Vancouver was new, raw, and hustling after money. Victoria rather looked down on it, and governed the turbulent province with a genteel aloofness: the wealthy congregated each day at the Empress Hotel for high tea.

There was an explosion of gadgetry. Hydro-electricity provided cheap power for manufacturing and made millionaires such as Sir Henry Pellatt, who built Casa Loma in Toronto.

City dwellers awakened to alarm clocks, punched into work on time clocks, wrote letters with fountain pens or had them done by male secretaries who used the new typewriters. Some far-sighted businessmen adopted the telephone. There were the delights of the soda fountain, the phonograph and the movies. Although moral reformers were shocked at the idea of men and women sitting together in a darkened room, one of North America's first cinemas (named the Ouimetoscope by its manager L. E. Ouimet) opened in Montreal on New Year's Day, 1906.

The low-wheel or safety bicycle was invented. It too raised moral questions, and in 1890 women cycling around Winnipeg in bloomers provoked an angry debate in city council.

And there was the glamor of motoring. In 1897 Quebec City dentist Henri-Edmond Casgrain bought a three-wheel car from France and drove it at a "dizzying" 18 mph along the Chemin Sainte-Foy. Soon after, John Moodie in his Winton raced a steamboat from Hamilton to Toronto and won—in just under three hours. But the champion motorist of the era was probably U. H. Dandurand of Montreal who drove a 26-foot, six-ton monster with sleeping room for 11.

As improved machinery made it possible to farm more land with fewer farmers, there was a steady drift to the cities. There, new machines and methods demanded large-scale organization. Small businessmen were squeezed out by the likes of Dominion Steel, Dominion Canners and Imperial Tobacco. Massey-Harris of Toronto, a leader in the agricultural machinery field, helped form Canada Cycle and Motor in 1899 to corner the bicycle market and build cars.

Canadian economic life fell under the domination of a handful of corporations and wealthy individuals. Many companies were branches of large U.S. corporations, so Canada was in danger of losing control of the economy.

A factory hand could buy a dozen eggs, a pound of sausages, a can of corn, six pounds of apples, a tin of syrup and a bar of soap—*all this*—for only $1. But he earned only $1 a day. Unemployment was widespread and there was no unemployment insurance.

Laurier's accomplishment was not in solving the problems created by religious strife, by industrialization, by American investment, and by poverty. It is doubtful he *could* have found solutions. He inherited a country divided by years of disappointment; it might have been shattered in the years of growth. Laurier's great work was to hold the elements together and to develop in them a common sense of nationhood.

He began in 1897 as Canada's representative in London at Queen Victoria's Diamond Jubilee.

Louis Cyr, a turn-of-the-century strongman (whose statue is in Montreal's Elizabeth Square), weighed 365 pounds and sometimes ate a 30-pound pig for lunch. He was at various times a Montreal policeman, a tavern keeper, and a sensation ("the world's strongest man") with P. T. Barnum's circus. Once he lifted 4,537 pounds on his back; another time, 553 pounds with one finger. A New York promoter offered $5,000 to anyone who could outlift Cyr: no one could. When Cyr died of kidney disease in 1912, age 49, a weeping Montreal gave him a hero's funeral.

Orillia Frowned—Now It's The Sunshine Town

For Stephen Leacock the writing of "humorous nothings" was hard work.

"Solid, instructive stuff fortified by facts and figures is easy enough," said Canada's leading literary figure, who was also head of the Department of Economics and Political Science at McGill University in Montreal. "But to write something out of one's own mind, worth reading for its own sake, is an arduous contrivance only to be achieved in fortunate moments, few and far between."

Many of those few moments of inspiration, which brought Leacock world fame and considerable fortune, were at his summer home on Lake Couchiching's Old Brewery Bay, near Orillia, Ont.—a fine old house that now is a museum of Leacock memorabilia. Among his papers is the handwritten manuscript of *Sunshine Sketches of a Little Town,* published in 1912.

Orillia, which recognized itself in Leacock's "mythical" Mariposa—and disliked the man at Old Brewery Bay for exposing its idiosyncrasies—now proudly calls itself The Sunshine Town.

Leacock was born in England in 1869 and came to Canada at the age of six. At McGill, where he taught for 36 years, he was known not only for his wisdom and his humor but also for his tattered gown, missing buttons and faded hat. But the campus character's *Elements of Political Science* (1906), the first of some 60 books (only 35 were humor), became a standard text. *Literary Lapses* (1910), a collection of humor he'd had "too little courage" to publish earlier, launched Leacock as a humorist. His style was sharp but not vitriolic. "The very essence of good humor is that it must be without harm or malice," he asserted.

He was a prolific and versatile writer of biographies, popular histories and economic and political treatises virtually until his death in 1944. But Leacock once said: "I would sooner have written *Alice in Wonderland* than the whole *Encyclopædia Britannica.*"

© Karsh, Ottawa

THE THOROUGHLY CANADIAN CAR

Canadian Material
Canadian Labor
Canadian Capital

The
Russell

3 MODELS 5 TYPES

Newspapers covered motoring on their sports pages when this two-cylinder 1906 Russell ($1,500) was new. The car's wheels fitted wagon tracks, and ground clearance was nine inches.

Of the lavish entertainments, Laurier groaned: "I am not sure whether the [British] Empire needs a new constitution, but I am certain that every jubilee guest will need one."

Laurier, second only to the queen, was the hero of the jubilee. Sixty years before, when she came to the throne, Canada had been in rebellion. Now, this eloquent French Canadian was the leader of a loyal colony and he was, as he assured her, "British to the core." British newspapers called him the first outstanding colonial statesman and the queen awarded him a knighthood.

But the empire could divide Canadians as well as unite them. Joseph Chamberlain, Britain's colonial secretary, wanted the colonies to agree to something called Imperial Federation, with economic and military control centralized in Britain.

When Laurier refused to surrender Canadian powers the Colonial Office called him Sir Won't-frid. In 1899 Britain went to war against the Boers and Chamberlain put pressure on the colonies to send troops to South Africa. Many English Canadians were enthusiastic but French Canadians, who had no homeland but Canada, were opposed. They found their spokesman in Henri Bourassa, the dynamic grandson of Louis-Joseph Papineau (see p. 184) and a flaming orator in his own right. Like Laurier, he admired British democracy but was repelled by British imperialism.

Laurier recognized the danger signs; but, as a French Canadian, vulnerable to charges of being anti-British, he knew he would have to compromise. He told Chamberlain the Canadian government would call for volunteers, but once in South Africa they would have to be financed by the British government.

The Canadian volunteers fought well against the Boers. But Laurier's compromise had its price. Imperialists called him a slacker who had not done enough. Bourassa accused him of doing too much. He became the spiritual leader of the Nationalist League and Laurier's bitterest opponent in Quebec.

Imperial sentiment was tested again in 1903 during a dispute over the border between Alaska and British Columbia. Britain, responsible for

Canadian foreign affairs, suggested that three British and three American representatives decide who owned the Alaska Panhandle.

Britain appointed two Canadians and one Englishman. Predictably, the three Americans voted for the American claim and the two Canadians for the Canadian claim. President Theodore Roosevelt had warned that if the decision went against the United States he would take the region anyway. The Englishman's vote might force Britain into a confrontation with the United States over a matter of no importance to Britain, so he voted on the American side. The Americans won the Alaska boundary dispute and Canada lost its water route to the Yukon.

Canadians were outraged. The Canadian Club proposed that "O Canada" replace "God Save the Queen." Laurier resolved that Britain would never again give away Canadian territory and the International Boundary Commission was established in 1908 to settle future disputes.

But Imperial Federation was not dead. In 1909, pointing to the threat posed by the German Navy, Britain asked the colonies to contribute money for Royal Navy ships. Canada would pay for three dreadnoughts, the largest battleships of the time, and Canadian Imperialists demanded that Laurier agree.

Laurier felt the only threat to Canada came from the United States, and Britain had shown that Canada could expect no British help against the Americans.

Still, the English were the majority in Canada and their imperial sentiment was strong. Another compromise. Laurier's 1910 Naval Service Bill envisaged a navy of small ships suited to Canadian needs which could be placed at Britain's disposal in case of war. The old cruisers *Niobe* (see p. 345) and *Rainbow* were procured from Britain to train Canadian sailors at Halifax and Esquimalt.

This was one compromise too many and both sides launched furious attacks on Laurier. Conservative leader Robert Borden ridiculed the two cruisers as a "tin-pot navy." Only British dreadnoughts would do. There must be, as the *Ontario Fourth Reader* taught, "One Flag, One Fleet, One Throne." Bourassa's nationalists wanted no fleet at all.

Laurier had aged greatly during the years of conflict and was desperately tired—physically tired and tired of Protestant bigots, tired of Catholic bishops "who handle the holy water sprinkler as though it were a club," tired of those English who still called Britain home, tired of Bourassa nationalists who could not understand the need to compromise in a country as varied as Canada. He then made one of the few blunders

Guglielmo Marconi received the first transatlantic radio signal Dec. 12, 1901, from an aerial on a kite on Signal Hill at St. John's, Nfld. The transmission was from Cornwall, England, 1,700 miles away.

The first controlled flight in the British Empire—on Feb. 23, 1909—was at Baddeck, N.S., by J. A. D. McCurdy in the Silver Dart. *This painting and a replica of the plane are in the National Museum of Science and Technology in Ottawa.*

339

of his career: he called a by-election in his old seat of Drummond-Arthabaska.

Bourassa put forward a nationalist candidate. "Those who disembowelled your fathers on the Plains of Abraham," he cried, "are asking you to go and get killed for them."

The nationalist won after a bitter campaign and Borden saw how to defeat Laurier. His Conservatives would ally themselves with the Quebec nationalists. Borden would fight Laurier in English Canada, Bourassa would fight him in Quebec; together they would destroy him.

A general election was called in the summer of 1911 and Laurier faced it without enthusiasm. Then, like a thunderbolt, came an American offer of reciprocity, a goal of Canadian governments since Confederation. If Canada would eliminate tariffs on American natural products and reduce tariffs on some manufactured goods, the United States would do the same for Canada. When Laurier announced the offer, the Conservatives were dismayed.

But as the terms of the agreement became known, Conservative hopes revived. Farmers were angry that only a few manufactured products were included. Manufacturers were afraid that someday there might be more. Most railways, geared for east-west traffic, opposed greater trade with the United States. Eighteen prominent Liberal businessmen signed a manifesto denouncing reciprocity and the CPR's pugnacious Sir William Cornelius Van Horne vowed he would "bust the damned [reciprocity] thing."

Reciprocity's opponents capitalized on the Ca-

nadian pride that Laurier had nurtured. They accused him of selling out. An American politician helped them. "I hope," he said, "to see the day when the American flag will float over every square foot of the British North American possessions clear to the North Pole."

In English Canada, Borden spoke from platforms covered in British flags and wore a vest made from a Union Jack. But in Quebec he supported Bourassa's campaign of accusation that Laurier was too pro-British. An exasperated Laurier could well complain: "I am branded in Quebec as a traitor to the French, and in Ontario as a traitor to the English. In Quebec I am branded as a jingo, and in Ontario as a separatist." And he could honestly add: "I am neither. I am a Canadian."

It was not enough. Laurier held a majority in Quebec but the Conservatives and nationalists took 27 seats. The Conservatives won 72 seats in Ontario, the Liberals only 14. Conservatives and nationalists together held 133 seats across Canada and the Liberals 88.

Laurier heard the verdict in Quebec. It was as well he was not in Ottawa, for in the street outside the stately mansion on Laurier Avenue a hundred men pulled Borden's carriage triumphantly through the crowds.

Laurier was beaten but his accomplishments were indisputable. In 1896 he had become Prime Minister of a dispirited people. In 1911 there was a confident nation. Whatever the perils ahead, Canada would find that Wilfrid Laurier had used the sunshine years well.

Henri Bourassa, founder (1910) and editor of the Montreal newspaper Le Devoir, *was for four decades the strongest voice of French-Canadian nationalism. He strove for unity between French and English in an independent Canada.*

In a Midnight Fog, an *Empress* Dies

A red buoy bobbing in the St. Lawrence River 10 miles east of Pointe-au-Père, Que., marks where the Canadian Pacific liner *Empress of Ireland* sank May 29, 1914, with a loss of 1,015 lives. Only 464 persons survived this worst marine disaster in Canadian history. The ship's bell *(left)* is among remnants in the Bernier Maritime Museum at L'Islet-sur-Mer, Que.

Although the *Empress* went down in only 150 feet of water, many bodies were not recovered. In Empress of Ireland Cemetery near Pointe-au-Père is but one monument—to the 88 victims buried there, 68 never identified. In Toronto's Mount Pleasant Cemetery is a monument to 167 Salvation Army victims, members of a group of 200 who were to have attended a Salvationist congress in London.

The 14,000-ton *Empress,* bound for Liverpool, had sailed from Quebec the previous afternoon. Now, at 1:26 a.m., six minutes after the pilot had been dropped at Pointe-au-Père,

the crowsnest reported: "Ship's masthead light on the starboard bow." Then low fog suddenly enveloped both ships. *Empress of Ireland* and the 6,000-ton Norwegian collier *Storstad* were only six miles apart, approaching fast and, in those pre-radar days, unable to see each other. The *Empress* wailed her siren, *Storstad* desperately sounded her whistle.

They collided at 1:55 a.m., looming out of the fog at such close range that no reversal of engines, no helm order had any effect. Like *Titanic* before her, the *Empress*—a floating palace with her own cricket pitch—had been thought unsinkable. But *Storstad*'s bow sliced her open. Ruptured boiler rooms flooded. Dynamos failed, plunging the ship into darkness. SOS messages died. The liner was gone within 14 minutes. The awful cries of the drowning, said *Storstad*'s captain, were "like one long, moaning sound." All the collier's crew survived.

Heritage Sites

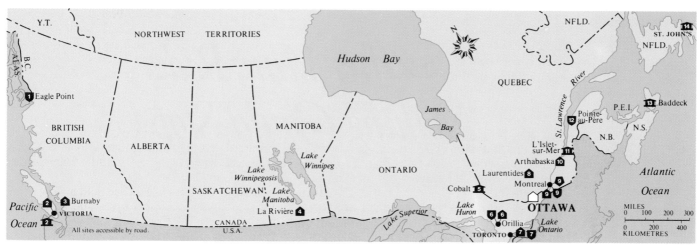

⌂ Main site (Historic building) ● Historic building(s) ■ Museum ▼ Monument ● Other

OTTAWA At Laurier House, in what was Sir Wilfrid's study, are his portrait by Georges Delfosse, his wife's silver toilet set, and the couple's Louis XVI-style settee and four chairs. In an adjoining room are Laurier's desk, inkwell and blotter, and political mementos such as medals and a silver ceremonial spade. (Much of the house, a national historic site, reflects the career of Mackenzie King, who took possession of it in 1923.)

Other sites

Arthabaska, Que. (10) The house where Laurier lived from 1876 to 1897 is a museum, furnished as in his day.

Baddeck, N.S. (13) *Silver Dart,* the airplane that made the first flight in the British Empire, is commemorated by a stylized model atop the museum in Alexander Graham Bell National Historic Park. A replica of the craft is in the National Museum of Science and Technology in Ottawa.

Burnaby, B.C. (3) Heritage Village Museum has some 20 restored buildings reflecting turn-of-the-century small-town life. They include a blacksmith's shop, dress shop and dentist's office.

Cobalt, Ont. (5) Mining tools, machinery and a 1,250-pound piece of unprocessed silver in the Northern Ontario Mining Museum commemorate the boom that began in 1903.

Eagle Point, B.C. (1) A bronze pyramid, erected in 1904 at the south end of the Alaska Panhandle, marks the border which resulted from the Alaska boundary dispute.

La Rivière, Man. (4) A log cabin in which Nellie McClung lived when a teacher is at the Archibald Historical Museum. The furnished cabin dates from 1878.

Laurentides, Que. (8) Laurier's boyhood home, a national historic site, is restored and furnished as in his youth.

L'Islet-sur-Mer, Que. (11) An aluminum globe honors Capt. Joseph-Elzéar Bernier, born here, whose voyages established Canadian Arctic sovereignty. His octant, a model of his ship *Arctic,* and the matrix of a plaque he placed on Melville Island in 1909 are in the Bernier Maritime Museum. It also displays remnants of *Empress of Ireland,* including an anchor and a bell.

Montreal (9)

  ELIZABETH SQUARE   Robert Pelletier's statue of Louis Cyr stands in the district the strongman patrolled as a policeman.

  MARY QUEEN OF THE WORLD BASILICA Patterned after St. Peter's in Rome, the cathedral was built to symbolize Roman Catholic power in Montreal.

  MOUNT ROYAL TUNNEL Railway magnates Mackenzie and Mann completed this three-mile tunnel in 1918, enabling the Canadian Northern to reach Montreal.

Orillia, Ont. (6) The Stephen Leacock Memorial Home on Lake Couchiching, once the author's summer residence, displays his manuscripts, correspondence and some of his furniture. The Orillia Public Library has a bronze bust of Leacock by Elizabeth Wyn Wood.

Pointe-au-Père, Que. (12) A red buoy in the St. Lawrence River marks where *Empress of Ireland* sank in 1914. In Empress of Ireland Cemetery lie 88 unclaimed bodies from among the 1,015 victims.

St. John's, Nfld. (14) Atop Signal Hill on Dec. 12, 1901, Guglielmo Marconi received the first transatlantic wireless message. Illustrations in Cabot Tower explain his work and early signalling devices.

Toronto (7) Casa Loma, North America's largest castle, has 98 rooms, secret staircases and a mahogany-lined stable. In Mount Pleasant Cemetery a pink granite monument commemorates the 167 members of the Salvation Army who perished in the sinking of *Empress of Ireland.*

Victoria (2) The waterfront Empress Hotel has been the city's social centre since 1905. The provincial museum re-creates a turn-of-the-century main street, mine shaft and fish-packing plant.

Elaborate lawns and gardens surround the imposing Empress Hotel in Victoria. There have been major renovations over the years, but tea in the lobby is still an afternoon ritual.

341

After Vimy Ridge
'Nothing Could Stop Us'

There was no love and little patience for "slackers" in 1914-18. Posters were direct and to the point: if you were not in uniform, you probably were letting the side down.

Dominating a low, whale-backed ridge near the town of Arras in northern France are two great white stone pylons, Canada's most eloquent memorial to her dead of the First World War. The ridge is Vimy.

Cut deep into the stone at the base of the memorial are 11,285 names—about 19 percent of the 59,544 men who died in Canada's battles on the Western Front. The 11,285 have no known graves.

The Vimy Memorial is in a 250-acre park that France deeded to Canada in perpetuity—it is part of Canada. Canadian trees and shrubs cover the slopes up which Canadian troops attacked on Easter Monday, April 9, 1917. In a reopened tunnel, one of 12 built to facilitate the concentration of units for the assault, are the scribbles of men who were soon to die—and men who survived:

103234, James Burton, A Company,
Royal Canadian Regiment, May 8, 1917.
Still alive and kicking.

Aug. 3, 1914. Germany and Austria-Hungary had gone to war with Serbia, France and Russia, and Canadians excitedly discussed the possibility of Canada joining in. What would Britain do? Col. Sam Hughes, the blustering militarist who was Canada's defence minister, feared Britain would "skunk it." He ordered the Union Jack removed from the defence headquarters flagstaff.

But that day 750,000 Germans smashed into Belgium, whose neutrality was guaranteed by Britain. Britain's ultimatum to Germany to withdraw brought no reply and on Aug. 4 Britain too was at war. So was Canada. Cheering demonstrations of loyalty swept the country as Canada mobilized under the direction of Sam Hughes.

The erratic colonel had been a schoolteacher. He made money in canal and railway speculation, bought a weekly newspaper in Lindsay, Ont., and became a Conservative Member of Parliament, a colonel in the militia and grand

342

Canada's most imposing memorial to her war dead, a mighty monument created by sculptor Walter Allward, is at Vimy, the long, low ridge whose capture is commemorated in this oil painting by Richard Jack. The Canadians who stormed Vimy Ridge—after almost three weeks of bombardment to soften up the German defenders—gave the British Empire its first major victory of the war.

master of the Orange Order of Ontario. He served with the British as a transport officer in the war against the Boers in South Africa, and did well—but not well enough to justify the decorations he felt he had earned. He claimed at least one Victoria Cross, and perhaps two. The War Office said he had not earned even the war gratuity.

This was the controversial man selected by Prime Minister Robert Borden for the defence portfolio in 1911. Hughes accomplished much. With energy and self-confidence he brought excitement and impetus to military reform. He secured larger defence funds, increased the militia, got more drill halls, rifle ranges and weapons.

Hughes tossed aside the official mobilization plan. He substituted a personal call to arms: volunteers only, no regiments as such, and a centralized concentration of men where no camp existed—at Valcartier near Quebec. There, from scratch, he would form new "numbered" battalions, thus destroying long traditions and honored names.

(An exception was the Princess Patricia's Canadian Light Infantry. This regiment stayed away from Valcartier and was the first Canadian unit to fight in Flanders.)

Recruiting was brisk. Entire militia units joined up. Volunteers signed "for the duration" at $1 a day. The age requirement was 18-45 but many men concealed both their years and their medical disabilities. At railway stations across Canada bands played and women wept as men clambered aboard wooden coaches. Few were in uniform. At Valcartier they were sorted into units, medically examined and sworn in.

Hughes took up residence at Valcartier to preside grandly over what he considered his personal empire. Splendidly uniformed and usually mounted, he made appointments and promotions like a *seigneur,* without reference to the Militia Council or his colleagues. "A fine unit you have here, major," Hughes remarked on one of his many inspections. "Pardon me, sir," corrected the embarrassed officer, "I'm only a captain." "You're a major now," returned the infallible Hughes.

By Hughes's count, 32,665 men reached Valcartier that year. The first contingent—31,200—went overseas in September.

(Hughes was promoted and knighted but Lt.Gen. the Honorable Sir Sam Hughes did not last out the war in office. Borden summoned up the courage to fire him in 1916, in part because at times his "conduct and speech were so eccentric as to justify the conclusion that his mind was unbalanced.")

George V, accompanied by Queen Mary, inspected the 1st Canadian Division on Salisbury Plain in February 1915—a sure omen of the Canadians' imminent departure. The men were drawn up in the rain in two lines two miles long and it was obvious that the raw material of Valcartier had been transformed. Swords and 25,000 bayonets flashed and the king walked down the double line, all two miles of it, wishing good luck to each commander and his men. Five days later the division embarked for France.

Near Armentières, west of Lille, the Canadians took over a four-mile section of a defensively wired trench system that stretched from the North Sea to neutral Switzerland. But trenches in these low-lying fields of Flanders, where France and Belgium meet, were little more than slimy ditches.

The ground had been fought over and digging

The 22ᵉ Battalion (French Canadian)—later the Royal 22ᵉ Régiment—leaves for overseas in May 1915. The Van Doos fought at Ypres and the Somme, at Courcelette, Vimy, Hill 70 and Passchendaele. Breaking through the Hindenburg Line in 1918 the 700-man unit was reduced to 39.

Sam Hughes, Canada's minister of defence, felt "destined to live and die without a single doubt." He bullied his boss, Prime Minister Borden—in Hughes's words "a most lovely fellow, gentle-hearted as a girl."

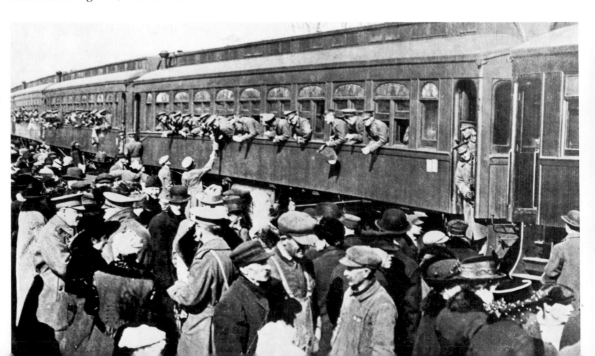

Scandal: Boots, Kickbacks and a Balky Rifle

Greedy contractors had a field day in the early days of the First World War. When soldiers' boots got wet "the paper from which the heels were made returned to its primitive pulp." Greatcoats absorbed rather than shed water. Canadian-built wagons were too wide for the narrow roads of France. Many of 8,150 horses purchased for the army, at $175 each, were so weak they had to be destroyed; 500 were auctioned for an average of $54; 60 of the worst fetched $1 a head. There was profiteering in drugs, trucks, bicycles and jam.

But the public raised little outcry until in 1916 a royal commission found that a munitions committee set up by defence minister Sam Hughes was guilty of misbehavior and that a friend of Hughes had taken a $220,000 kickback. But, as Ralph Allen wrote in *Ordeal by Fire,* "Everyone

was guilty, so in fairness to all everyone was acquitted."

Many a Canadian soldier went into battle with an inferior weapon—the Ross rifle that Hughes insisted was better than the British Lee-Enfield. The Ross tended to jam and the bayonet had "an unfortunate habit of jumping off the rifle when firing is being carried on with bayonets fixed."

Said one soldier: "To hell with the gun, I'll take a club." But Hughes insisted.

It was the 1st Division at Ypres in 1915—superb troops holding against enormous odds (and history's first gas attack)—that rendered the verdict. Of 5,000 infantrymen who survived, 1,452 had thrown away their Ross rifles and used the Lee-Enfields of British casualties. In July 1916 the Ross that Sam Hughes had championed was officially withdrawn.

Sam Hughes paid up to $28 for the Ross rifle (left), $7 more than a Lee-Enfield cost.

uncovered rotted cloth, human bones and putrescent flesh. The filth, the stench, the cold, the snow and sleet and rain made for a grim existence. The men endured, helped by the solemnly measured daily solace of 2½ ounces of dark, overproof Jamaica rum. Six days in the trenches, six days out, six days back, six days in support. There were no hot meals up forward, just bully beef and hard biscuits.

The Canadians were near the Belgian town of Ypres where in October and November 1914 the

Niobe and Rainbow, *cruisers purchased from Britain in 1910, saw limited war service,* Niobe *mainly as a depot ship in Halifax,* Rainbow *on west coast patrol. They and smaller antisubmarine vessels bought or built for the RCN were the forerunners of the hundreds of ships that in the Second World War made Canada the third biggest Allied naval power.*

British and Germans had fought a savage three-week battle (known to history as First Ypres). Now, in the first week of April 1915, the Canadian division moved north through Saint-Julien to the centre of the line holding the Ypres salient, which thrust into enemy territory. This was one of the few parts of Belgium still in Allied hands; politically it was important to hold it.

On the morning of April 20 the Germans began shelling Ypres with 42-cm siege guns that hurled 1,800-pound shells nine miles. Two nights later, some four miles to the northeast and on the Canadians' left, there appeared a yellow-green cloud scarcely higher than the head of a man. It moved gently, said one who saw it, like "mists seen over water meadows on a frosty autumn night." It was chlorine gas and its effect was deadly.

It drifted toward breastworks manned by French colonial troops. Choking and gasping, hundreds of Algerians died of suffocation. Others lay helpless, nauseated, froth on their lips, their lungs seared. Everywhere dark figures ran blindly in the gas cloud, dropping into ditches, vomiting convulsively, sucking at drainage water to obtain relief.

The first significant use of gas in "civilized" warfare—contrary to the rules of war—had opened a four-mile gap on the Canadian left. A German push to Ypres—only four miles away—would trap 50,000 Canadian and British troops and mean the loss of the salient. Bucking a retreating stream of gas-attack victims, Canadian reserves moved up.

The 13th Battalion, the Canadian unit closest to the gap, had been heavily hit by bombardment

The Saint-Julien Memorial is a 35-foot column surmounted by "The Brooding Soldier," head bowed, shoulders weary, hands folded on his reversed rifle. This, the memorial records, is "where 18,000 Canadians on the British left withstood the first German gas attacks. Two thousand fell and lie here buried."

but had stood firm. Nor had it given ground in the gas cloud. A medical officer passed the word that to urinate on a handkerchief and put it over the mouth would help. It did: ammonia in the urine neutralized the chlorine. But the 13th was outflanked and its position was precarious. Canadian reserves dug in and four battalions counterattacked, confusing the enemy. Unexpectedly, the Germans did not advance at daylight and by nightfall on the 23rd the gap was closed; Canadian troops barred the way to Ypres.

On the 24th there was a violent bombardment and another cloud of death rolled directly at the Canadians holding the blunt apex of the salient. Incredulous Canadians saw groups of Germans, wearing what looked like miners' helmets, thrusting out long hoses that emitted the gas. Out of the chlorine fog emerged waves of infantrymen in spiked helmets and hideous mouth protectors, fixed bayonets at the ready. The ill-protected Canadians—coughing, choking, eyes streaming, bleeding hands sometimes tearing at jammed rifle bolts—repelled one German rush after another until relieved April 26. "These splendid troops," wrote Gen. Sir John French, the British commander-in-chief, "averted a disaster." But the price was more than 6,000 Canadians killed and wounded.

By April 1917 no one had any illusions about an early end to the war. Men had died by the thousands in one senseless attack after another, especially at Verdun and on the Somme. Each side's artillery and small-arms fire, combined with trenches and barbed wire, could stop almost any offensive.

There now were four battle-hardened Canadian divisions in France, welded into a corps commanded by Gen. Sir Julian Byng, an Englishman. Three of his divisional commanders were Canadians, the fourth was a Briton. The troops wore steel helmets instead of caps, and carried respirators. Gas was commonly used by both sides.

The corps had spent a relatively quiet winter, fighting mainly cold, rats and lice. (One man made a body-count of lice: undershirt, 400; drawers, 380.) The soldiers made the best of a miserable life. Some fashioned oil drums into stoves, brass shell cases into vases—or dinner gongs. Many made weapons for a war of stealth—clubs and daggers that were useful at close quarters. Ahead of the corps loomed Vimy Ridge, one of the most formidable German positions on the Western Front. From the ridge the Germans controlled the Douai plain and the coal fields of northern France.

Byng, entrusted with taking the ridge, left nothing to chance. He appointed Canada's finest gunner, 30-year-old Lt.Col. A. G. L.

Canadians repel an attack during the Second Battle of Ypres. (One soldier is in hand-to-hand combat with a spike-helmeted German at the far left of this painting by Richard Jack.) France's Marshal Foch said of the Canadians: "They wrote here the first page in that Book of Glory which is the history of their participation in the war."

McNaughton, as the corps' counterbattery staff officer. He had command of the heavy guns and the task of holding the German artillery in check when the assaulting troops were in the open and in the greatest danger. The Canadian Maj.Gen. Arthur Currie, commander of the 1st Division, developed flexible infantry tactics; these, too, Byng adopted. Then the men trained, interminably, over a full-scale model of the ridge constructed behind the lines.

The French, with greater resources, had tried twice to take the ridge in 1915, and had failed, with 140,000 casualties. The German defences had been stiffened immeasurably since then. Byng ordered four miles of tunnels built, through which troops could move to and from the front line in safety; they had piped water and electricity and would shelter the wounded later. There

On a Sunny Day in Halifax, the Biggest, Worst Explosion Ever

A mass grave, the shank of an anchor, a broken window in an historic church, and the few who remain of the many who were blinded in a storm of flying glass that day in 1917 ... Halifax still bears the scars of an explosion that was the biggest and the worst the world had known.

At 7:30 a.m. Dec. 6—a frosty, sunny Thursday—the French freighter *Mont Blanc*, newly arrived from New York with a cargo of high explosives, moved slowly into the Narrows, bound for Bedford Basin, Halifax's inner harbor.

At 8 a.m. the Norwegian tramp steamer *Imo*, bound for Belgium with relief supplies, headed out of the basin and into the Narrows. *Mont Blanc* signalled she would steer to pass *Imo* star-

board to starboard. But *Imo* signalled for a port-to-port passing. Suddenly the ships were on a collision course and at 8:40 *Imo*'s bow ripped into *Mont Blanc* amidships. Benzene on deck caught fire and the flames spread to picric acid and TNT below.

The explosion came at 9:05. In a few awful seconds it killed almost 2,000 persons, injured some 9,000 and destroyed schools, factories and block after block of houses. More than 10,000 persons were homeless. A great wave caused by the blast tossed ships and railway cars like toys. The earth shook. Flying glass blinded some 200 persons—almost as many as the number of Canadian soldiers blinded in battle in the First World War.

The shank of *Mont Blanc*'s anchor was found three miles from the Narrows. It is still there. A hole in a window of St. Paul's Church was thought to resemble the profile of a man's head; was a head blasted through that window? The profile is preserved between double panes of glass. Throughout the city are the graves of the dead; in Fairview Cemetery are the common graves of 249 never identified.

347

Billy Bishop, V.C., scored half of his 72 victories while flying a Nieuport, a French plane with a top speed of 107 mph. Right: three Fokker D VII fighters. Manfred von Richthofen, the Red Baron, flew a Fokker triplane.

was a network of roads—even light railways—to bring up ammunition, stores and rations. Men of the corps dug graves for soldiers who would be killed in the coming action.

The bombardment began March 20, almost three weeks before the date chosen for the assault, and built to a crescendo heralding what the Germans called "the week of suffering." On April 8, the eve of battle, men of the four Canadian divisions moved quietly forward through the tunnels to assembly areas and jumping-off positions in no man's land.

At zero hour—5:30 a.m.—"a continuous sheet of lightning, like a prairie fire," crashed out along the line—the barrage that would roll ahead of the men and provide a sheltering curtain for their advance. The long first wave of 21 battalions sprang forward, sleet at their backs. Up the gentle open slope they went, a slope torn by shells and laced with broken barbed wire.

There had been no slackening of artillery fire at the moment of attack—hence no warning—and the Germans were taken by surprise. Once the forward defences were overrun, however, resistance stiffened. Now, using Currie's tactics, men dropped to engage machine-gun nests frontally while others, using broken ground, sneaked round to tackle them with grenade and bayonet from flank and rear.

By eight o'clock the issue was no longer in doubt. The sun shone for a moment through a sudden rift in the overcast sky. The Germans saw infantry in khaki, with gleaming bayonets, swarming over the crest. They had lost the ridge.

On a four-mile front, in a single day, the corps had overrun enemy positions from foremost defences to gun-line. They had captured 4,000 prisoners and had seized 54 guns, 124 machine guns and 104 trench mortars —but at a cost of 3,598 fatal casualties.

Four Canadian Aces, Three Canadian V.C.s—and the Red Baron

Of all the aces in all the armies of the First World War only 12 shot down more than 50 enemy aircraft. Four were Canadians: Billy Bishop (72 kills), Ray Collishaw (60), Donald MacLaren (54) and Billy Barker (53). Britain awarded the Victoria Cross to only 10 airmen. Three were Canadians: Bishop, Barker and Alan McLeod. And

it was the Canadian Roy Brown who shot down the Red Baron, Manfred von Richthofen, the war's ace of aces (80 Allied planes).

Canada had no air force but more than 22,000 Canadians served in the Royal Flying Corps (renamed Royal Air Force in 1918). They were about a quarter of its fighting strength.

Richthofen was gunning for Wilfred "Wop" May when Brown, in a tiny Camel, dived to the rescue near Amiens at noon April 21, 1918. He saved May's life—May became a legendary bush pilot—and the Red Baron crashed to his death. The seat retrieved from Richthofen's gaudy red Fokker triplane is displayed at the Royal Canadian Military Institute in Toronto.

Billy Bishop won his V.C. on June 2, 1917, when he flew deep into enemy territory and destroyed a German squadron on the ground. Twelve months later, on his last day of active duty, he took his Nieuport up over the German lines and shot down five aircraft in 12 minutes.

Billy Barker survived a battle with 60 German planes. His V.C. citation records that on Oct. 27, 1918, he destroyed a German plane, was attacked by another and, although wounded in the right thigh, shot it down too. Then he "found himself in the middle of a large formation of Fokkers, who attacked him from all directions, and was

severely wounded in the left thigh but succeeded in driving down two of the enemy in a spin." Barker lost consciousness and came to, still surrounded by German planes. Singling out one, he "charged and drove it down in flames." In this fight his left elbow was shattered. Again he fainted. Again he came to, still surrounded. Then he "dived on the nearest machine and shot it down in flames." "Being greatly exhausted," says the citation, Barker "dived out of the fight to regain our lines . . . where he crashed on landing."

Alan McLeod, attacked by eight Germans, manoeuvred his slow reconnaissance plane so that his observer was able to shoot down three. "Then, although wounded in five places, when his petrol tank was set on fire he climbed out on one of the wings and by tipping the machine in descent kept the flames at one side while he continued to control it so that his observer could continue his battle with the machine gun." McLeod crashed the burning plane "and before dropping from loss of blood, he saved the life of his equally gallant observer, helpless from six wounds, by dragging him out of the flaming wreckage, and this too under enemy fire."

McLeod wore his V.C. home to Canada in the spring of 1918. He died of influenza, aged 19, five days before the armistice.

Remembering it all 50 years later, one old veteran proudly said: "From Vimy we were invincible. Nothing could stop us." Another soldier who stormed the ridge: "I think that was where Canada was born."

Front-line units rotated to rest areas where wine and food could be bought. There were barns in which concert parties such as the Dumbells— named for the 3rd Division's insignia of a red dumb-bell—mocked themselves and the war: "Over the Top, a Screaming Farce" or "Mined, a Most Uplifting Performance."

The original Dumbells were eight soldiers who had some stage or musical experience. Capt. Mert Plunkett, the manager, had seven days to put a show together. "We'll joke about what soldiers gripe about," he decided. And, just as sensibly: "If you want to entertain the troops you've got to have girls." Horsehair from furniture

made wigs; women's clothes were scrounged. They rehearsed a scene in which Ross Hamilton, soldier, made passes at a French "girl." "You know something?" remarked one of the party. "*He's* better looking than *she* is!" So the switch was made. Hamilton, in a dress, was transformed. He was promoted to "leading lady."

The first performance started badly. The troops were paraded and resented losing one night of their six out of the line. There were insults and a shower of potatoes. Plunkett decided to bring on his secret weapon: "Marjorie" Hamilton was pushed onto the stage while a pianist played "If You Were the Only Girl in the World." The soldiers stared in disbelief and were suddenly quiet. For "Marjorie" in an expensive gown was convincingly beautiful. The song went to the end. Cheers. Pandemonium.

There was no more trouble. The Dumbells moved up and down the front and, in London,

The French Nieuport 17 had but one speed: full out. Pilots controlled landings by turning the ignition on and off.

played for a week at the Victoria Palace, two weeks at the Coliseum. They gave command performances for King Albert of Belgium and the Prince of Wales. After the war an enlarged Dumbells troupe toured Canada and the United States and had a smash success on Broadway.

The Canadian Corps added to its reputation with two more great victories in 1917: at Hill 70 and at Passchendaele Ridge, which British and other Commonwealth troops had repeatedly failed to capture.

These battles were won under Currie (now Sir Arthur), who succeeded Byng and became the corps' first Canadian commander.

Currie was born in 1875 at Napperton, in Ontario's Middlesex County. He taught primary school and tried insurance and real estate. Early in 1914 he took command of a militia training battalion, a task for which he had little training, and now, three years later, he was a lieutenant-general, the first Canadian nonregular to reach that rank and the first Canadian to command a corps.

He was about six feet two, weighed about 300 pounds and looked too big for his uniform and his horse. He was no inspiring commander but a remarkably intelligent one who never went into a battle that was not carefully planned. When the British cut brigades from four battalions to three, Currie refused to follow suit. Instead, he bolstered his existing battalions, which went into the final year of the war the finest corps on the Western Front.

By August 1918 the Germans' last major offensive had been turned back and it was the Allies' turn. The place: Amiens.

It was essential to conceal the presence of the Canadians. "Regarding them as storm troops, the enemy tended to greet their appearance as an omen of a coming attack," wrote historian Sir Basil Liddell Hart. Currie detached some battalions to Flanders and prepared a mock attack on the Arras front. The Germans suspected Flanders was a feint but strengthened the line at Arras. At the last possible moment and moving largely by night, the corps slipped south to Amiens. Now there was an immense concentration of Allied men, with 420 concealed tanks, and massive artillery emplacements under the command of McNaughton.

At 4:20 a.m. Aug. 8, guns flashed along the 14-mile front and the Allies moved off into a mist, bayonets high—British, Australians, Canadians and French. "We were the spearhead," said Currie, "the centre of the attack.... We made the plan; we set the time and pace in that battle."

The surprise was total. "We went by guns with the muzzle caps on and the crews just laying around," recalled a man of the 19th Battalion. "We simply lit cigarettes, shouldered our rifles and walked behind the rolling barrage to our objective. There was porridge warm on the table...." The tanks had flattened the wire and "we just sailed through that morning: no trenches, *no trenches,* blazing sunlight later and absolute gaiety among the troops." The Amiens victory is commemorated by a block of granite in a park beside the Amiens-Roye road near the village of Le Quesnel.

As a farm boy, Arthur Currie learned resourcefulness and a deep sympathy for the kind of men who were to form his Canadian Corps. He commanded firmly, but challenged his own superiors whenever he thought Canadian lives might be wasted. George V knighted him in a field near Vimy.

Men lived like rats—with rats—in filth and degradation. For weeks at a time the soldier's world was a nauseous funk hole in the hell of a slimy ditch in a dismal land stripped of trees and hope alike. Sleep was fitful and tormented, the rations were cold, death was at every man's elbow. Sixty years later the battlefields are treed and green again (right: the south slope of Vimy Ridge). But the green is veneer; shell holes and mine craters and trenches mark all the Vimys for all time.

A Wonderful Experience in Vimy Village

We left the Ridge and went to Vimy village. That night I found two men who had dug a bivvy into the railway embankment. I snuggled in and in seconds was dead to the world.

A firm warm hand seized one of mine and pulled me to a sitting position. I was face to face with my brother Steve, who had been killed in '15! "Get your gear," he said. We headed into the ruins of Petit Vimy.

My equipment slipped from my shoulder just as Steve went into a passageway. I retrieved it and hurried to catch up. "Steve!" No answer. I searched and called but could not find him. I sat down, tired and excited. I dozed.

Suddenly I was shaken awake. Tommy had me by the arm and was yelling, "He's here! Bill's here!"

"What's all the row?" I asked.

"Don't you know a big shell landed in that bivvy? All they've found is Jim's helmet and one of Bob's legs. They've been trying to find something of you."

An officer asked: "What made you leave the bivvy? The boys say you got in there with Jim and Bob."

"I did. I was there till daylight."

"What made you leave?"

I told my story. He made notes in a book he carried, asking my name and all about Steve. He shook my hand.

"You've had a wonderful experience," he said.

A true story by Will R. Bird
From *Ghosts Have Warm Hands*

It had been the first day of Canada's "Hundred Days" (actually the last 96 of the war) that would take the corps to its final victory at Mons. On Aug. 26, it drove east astride the Arras-Cambrai road. By Oct. 9 it had broken the Hindenburg Line, had surprised the Germans at the Canal du Nord, and had captured Cambrai, the hub of the German defensive system on the British front. With the help of British divisions temporarily under Currie's command, the Canadians had met and overcome a quarter of the remaining German strength in the west. Those battlefields

are seen from a massive Canadian memorial overlooking the village of Bourlon, just south of the Arras-Cambrai road.

The retreating Germans demolished bridges, tore up railways, cratered roads. With bands playing, the corps marched through liberated villages to the cheers of French civilians. At Valenciennes the Germans showed their teeth and Currie paused for a set-piece attack. It was a McNaughton classic—an example of what the power of artillery could do—and as a result one brigade overran the German defences. Only 80 Canadians were killed. There were 800 enemy dead and 1,800 prisoners.

On Nov. 10 the Canadians reached the outskirts of Mons, where British and German troops had first fought in 1914. The long-awaited armistice came the next day.

The Canadian Corps ended the war as the finest fighting body of its size in any army on the Western Front. Its record, ever since the Somme in 1916, was one of unbroken victory—often after other troops had failed. King Albert of the Belgians stated flatly that it was "unsurpassed by any corps in Europe." German Field Marshal Paul von Hindenburg called the corps "the élite" of "English" troops.

On Dec. 12 the Canadians reached Bonn, and Currie stayed in Kaiser Wilhelm's suite in the Palais Schaumburg. Next day, after "a very comfortable night in His Majesty's bed," Currie took the salute as Canadian troops crossed the Rhine.

Currie's corps, wrote Sir Charles Lucas in *The Empire at War*, was "the greatest national achievement of the Canadian people since the

"The boys" called them bluebirds, the 3,000 Canadian nursing sisters who served overseas in the First World War. Many got to France and Belgium, some to live and work in tents and huts, many to experience bombing raids and shellfire, most to see the true horror of the war, all to play a vital role in the success of the Canadian Corps.

Passchendaele in 1917 was Belgian mud so thick that men drowned in it. Passchendaele was 16 days of senseless slaughter (the dead included 2,700 Canadians) for two square miles that mattered nothing. A staff officer who saw it for the first time broke into tears: "Good God," he cried, "did we really send men to fight in that?" Next spring, long after the battle, "corpses rose out of the softening ooze," historian John Swettenham wrote. Two bodies, one Canadian, one German, were "grappling still in death. They had fought desperately and, sucked into the swamp, had died in one another's arms. All efforts to part them failed and so a large grave was dug in which to bury the pitiful remains."

The Victoria Cross, Highest Honor of All: For Valour

The Somme, Oct. 8, 1916: An 18-year-old boy carrying only bagpipes is about to win the Victoria Cross. . . .

The 16th Battalion, almost on its objective, was held up by barbed wire and, in the language of Pte. James Richardson's citation, "came under intense fire, which caused heavy casualties and demoralized the formation for the moment." Then: "Realizing the situation, Piper Richardson strode up and down outside the wire, playing his pipes with the greatest coolness. Inspired by his splendid example, the company rushed the wire with such fury and determination that the obstacle was overcome and the position captured."

Canada had 68 V.C. winners in the First World War, more than in all her battles before and since. Jimmy Richardson was one of that valorous 68.

Another, Gordon Flowerdew of the Lord Strathcona's Horse, won the V.C. March 30, 1918, in a cavalry charge to cut off the German retreat from a strategic wood. Suddenly two lines of Germans, 60 in each, opened fire. Flowerdew's

A crimson ribbon, a clasp with branches of laurel, a Maltese cross of bronze from Russian cannon captured at Sevastopol in 1855.

force lost about 70 percent killed or wounded but broke the German lines.

Gen. Sir Arthur Currie himself described the "superhuman deed" of Sgt. Hugh Cairns of the 46th Battalion on Nov. 1, 1918: "A machine gun opened up on his platoon. Without a moment's hesitation, he seized a Lewis gun, and single-handed in the face of direct fire, killed the crew of five and captured the gun. Later, when the line was held up again, Sergeant Cairns rushed forward alone and killed 12 of the enemy, captured 18 prisoners and took two machine guns. [Still later he] broke open the door of a yard and came upon 60 Germans. They threw their hands up, but as the officer filed past he shot Cairns through the body."

Cairns and Flowerdew, like all too many of the V.C.s, died of wounds. Richardson, in his 10 minutes at the wire, was not wounded. Later he was detailed to take a wounded comrade and prisoners out from the line. He'd gone about 200 yards when he remembered his bagpipes.

He went back for them and "has never been seen since."

Dominion came into being." But the cost of achievement had been high. In all, 619,636 Canadians served in the army, about 10,000 in the navy and more than 22,000 in the air force. Of Canada's 60,661 dead—roughly one in 10 of all who enlisted—59,544 were army.

During the war Canada completed the transformation from a basically agricultural society to an industrialized nation—largely due to the manufacture of munitions.

Sir Robert Borden was a strong prime minister. He built on the reputation of the corps and won a new position for Canada in the empire and in the international sphere. He called for "full recognition of the Dominions as autonomous nations of an Imperial Commonwealth." Autonomy had to wait, but the name "Commonwealth" was substituted for "Empire."

Borden accompanied British leaders to Versailles and took an active part in the peacemaking of 1919. At his insistence, Canada signed the peace treaties separately. With that she achieved the status of an autonomous nation-state. Again through Borden's efforts, Canada became an original member of the League of Nations and occupied a seat as a nation.

Such was the record of the Valcartier recruits of 1914, and of the men who followed. It was justly said of them, in the words of Rudyard Kipling inscribed in the Chapel of Remembrance in the Peace Tower at Ottawa:

They are too near to be great but our children shall understand when and how our fate was changed and by whose hand.

Unity the Real Victim in the Crisis of 1917

Nobody really wanted conscription in 1917. It came nonetheless, because of the ugly statistics of a war whose scope the world had never imagined possible. Canada's one-corps "army," battle after battle, took heavy casualties. At Vimy alone there were more than 10,000. Canadian losses were outstripping enlistments, sometimes by as much as two to one. To provide reinforcements, said Prime Minister Borden, there must be conscription.

Most Québécois were opposed. So were many English Canadians, especially farmers and labor unionists. Wilfrid Laurier, the Liberal leader and main spokesman for Quebec—but a statesman who served all Canada—believed conscription would help little, and merely "take in a few farmers and schoolboys." Labor leaders in western Canada demanded conscription of wealth before manpower. Three thousand Ontario farmers joined in a protest against cancellation of draft exemptions. They argued that a reduction in the already small farm labor force would result in a decrease in food production.

Borden called an election—for which the rules were changed: Canada had no female suffrage but this time soldiers' mothers, wives and sisters voted. Most presumably opted for Borden—for conscription—and his Union government won 153 seats to the Liberals' 82.

Conscription was a failure. There were appeals and exemptions in all provinces. Everywhere men of draft age took to the woods or fled to the United States. Conscription had produced fewer than 25,000 reinforcements when, on March 29, 1918, rioting broke out in Quebec City. For three days anti-conscriptionists battled the military (a battalion sent from Ontario); in a bitter climax of rifle and machine-gun fire and a cavalry charge, four civilians were killed, five soldiers and many civilians wounded and 58 persons arrested.

Canadian unity too lay severely wounded, a victim of the conscription nobody had really wanted. Mason Wade, in *The French Canadians,* wrote that "English Canada overestimated Quebec's rebelliousness, while Quebec made too much of 'Anglo-Saxon brutality' in enforcing conscription and repressing the riots."

The myth took shape that only Quebec had opposed conscription. That is myth, not history.

Robert Borden, prime minister in the First World War, lived in this house in Grand Pré, N.S., as a child and a teenager, from 1858 to 1873. It is a private home but rooms are sometimes rented when the owner's nearby motel has no vacancy.

Heritage Sites

VIMY, France The Vimy Memorial honors all Canadians who fought in the First World War and pays tribute to the French and English troops who also battled the Germans for possession of Vimy Ridge. Trenches and tunnels from 1917 are preserved. Commonwealth cemeteries nearby contain 6,000 Canadian graves.

Other sites

Beaumont-Hamel, France (6) A bronze statue of a caribou, emblem of the Royal Newfoundland Regiment, stands where the 800-man unit suffered 710 casualties during the Battle of the Somme.

Bourlon, France (8) A granite block commemorates the seizure of the Canal du Nord by Canadian troops in 1918.

Dury, France (7) A monument honors the Canadians who smashed an extension of the "impregnable" Hindenburg Line in the Second Battle of Arras.

Le Quesnel, France (5) A granite block acclaims the breakout at Amiens which started Canada's "Hundred Days."

London, England (2) The Tomb of the Unknown Warrior in Westminster Abbey is a memorial to all who fell while serving with the Commonwealth forces in the First World War. The tomb contains the

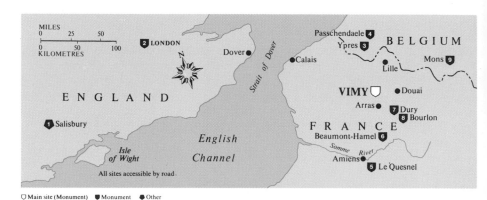

remains of an unidentified body taken from a battlefield in France.

Mons, Belgium (9) A bronze tablet at City Hall recalls the Canadian liberation of Mons at the end of the war.

Passchendaele, Belgium (4) A block of Canadian granite, set in a grove of maples, commemorates the 1917 Battle of Passchendaele in which nine Canadians won the Victoria Cross and 15,654 were killed or wounded.

Salisbury, England (1) The first 30,000 recruits from Canada were trained at British military bases on nearby Salisbury Plain. They were formed into the 1st Canadian

Division and were dispatched to France in February 1915.

Ypres, Belgium (3) The Saint-Julien Memorial, a 35-foot column topped by a brooding soldier, commemorates the Second Battle of Ypres (1915), in which Canadians withstood history's first major gas attack. The Sanctuary Wood (Hill 62) Memorial, a 14-ton block of white Quebec granite atop three landscaped terraces, pays tribute to the Canadian defence of Ypres in 1916. The Menin Gate Memorial honors the 55,000 Commonwealth soldiers missing in action in Belgium. Their names are inscribed in a Hall of Memory.

If ye break faith with us who die . . .

Col. John McCrae (*below:* his birthplace at Guelph, Ont.) was a gunner in the South African War and practised medicine (and occasionally wrote poetry) in Montreal before going overseas in the First World War. The slaughter he witnessed as an artillery brigade surgeon during the Second Battle of Ypres inspired him to write the classic "In Flanders Fields." It was first published in December 1915 by the English magazine *Punch.* McCrae died of pneumonia in January 1918 and was buried in a military cemetery at Wimereux in northern France.

In Flanders fields the poppies blow
Between the crosses, row on row,
That mark our place; and in the sky
The larks, still bravely singing, fly
Scarce heard amid the guns below.

We are the Dead. Short days ago
We lived, felt dawn, saw sunset glow,
Loved, and were loved, and now we lie
    In Flanders fields.

Take up our quarrel with the foe:
To you from failing hands we throw
The torch; be yours to hold it high.
If ye break faith with us who die
We shall not sleep, though poppies grow
    In Flanders fields.

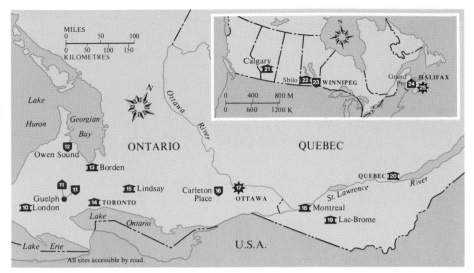

★ Multiple attractions   ▲ Historic building(s)   ▟ Museum   ▮ Monument

Borden, Ont. (13) Armored vehicles displayed at CFB Borden include a First World War Whippet tank.

Calgary (21) In the Princess Patricia's Canadian Light Infantry Museum is the Ric-A-Dam-Doo, the bullet-riddled, original regimental flag sewn by Princess Patricia of Connaught.

Carleton Place, Ont. (16) A plaque in Memorial Park honors native son Roy Brown, credited with shooting down Manfred von Richthofen, the Red Baron.

Grand Pré, N.S. (24) A marker identifies the boyhood home of Sir Robert Borden, prime minister during the First World War.

Guelph, Ont. (11) The John McCrae House, birthplace of the soldier-poet who wrote "In Flanders Fields", is a national historic site. Some of McCrae's manuscripts and pencil sketches are displayed. In adjacent McCrae Memorial Gardens a marble book is engraved with his famous poem and a light burns in his memory.

Halifax (25) The Halifax North Memorial Library is a monument to victims of the 1917 explosion. Outside, a Jordi Bonet sculpture, incorporating a fragment from the munitions ship *Mont Blanc*, symbolizes the explosion and subsequent reconstruction. The shank of *Mont Blanc*'s anchor lies where it landed; a window of St. Paul's Church has a hole the shape of a man's head; 249 unidentified victims are buried in Fairview Cemetery.

Lac-Brome, Que. (19) The Brome County Historical Museum has a German Fokker D VII fighter plane, a trench periscope and German mortars.

Lindsay, Ont. (15) The Victoria County Historical Museum has the dress uniform of Sam Hughes, a local newspaper publisher and controversial First World War defence minister. A portrait of Hughes and two albums of military photographs are also displayed.

London, Ont. (10) The Royal Canadian Regiment Museum displays medals, field equipment and First World War uniforms.

Montreal (18) The Military and Maritime Museum exhibits models of the Ross rifle.

Ottawa (17)

CANADIAN WAR MUSEUM Exhibits include a Vickers machine gun and a German mortar, Billy Bishop's medals, and the fuselage of the Sopwith Snipe in which Billy Barker won the Victoria Cross.

NATIONAL AVIATION MUSEUM First World War exhibits include a Sopwith Snipe, a Nieuport 17 (the type flown by Billy Bishop) and a Sopwith triplane with the markings of Ray Collishaw's "Black Maria."

NATIONAL WAR MEMORIAL Twenty-two bronze statues by Vernon and Sydney March, representing every branch of war service, stand at the base of a granite arch in Confederation Square. Two winged figures atop the arch symbolize peace and freedom.

PARLIAMENT BUILDINGS A Memorial Chamber in the Peace Tower contains four Books of Remembrance with the names of Canadians killed in overseas wars; the pages are turned so that each name is seen once a year.

Owen Sound, Ont. (12) A plaque honors Billy Bishop, born here in 1894.

Quebec (20) The Citadel is the home of the Royal 22e Régiment—the Van Doos—and the burial place of former Governor General Georges Vanier, who became the unit's commander in 1925. The regimental museum displays First World War gas masks, bombs and machine guns. CFB Valcartier near Quebec is still operational.

Shilo, Man. (22) The Royal Regiment of Canadian Artillery Museum exhibits sketches by John McCrae and the plate with which *Punch* first printed "In Flanders Fields" in 1915.

Toronto (14) The regimental museum of the Queen's Own Rifles, in Casa Loma, displays First World War rifles, machine guns and gas masks. In the Royal Canadian Military Institute are uniforms and decorations, and the seat of the Fokker triplane flown by the Red Baron.

Winnipeg (23) The Great Stone of Remembrance, a 12-foot-long granite block in Brookside Cemetery, was placed near the centre of Canada as a memorial to all the dead of the First World War.

The great Book of Remembrance for the First World War has the place of honor in the Memorial Chamber in Ottawa. Plaques tell "how free men throughout this land kept faith in the hour of trial and in the day of battle, remembering the traditions they had been taught, counting life nothing without liberty."

355

The Canadian Way, Something to Cherish

The Canada created by Confederation in 1867 was barely a nation. It was formed not by a surge of popular feeling but by a handful of politicians who were seeking stable government. Common sense prevailed, not passion. Many English-speaking Canadians still regarded Britain as "home." French Canadians knew they were at home but they felt uneasy about the new country's overwhelming English majority. Canada was, in the words of historian A. R. M. Lower, "carpentered together, not smelted."

In many ways, the new country was still a British colony. It had no citizenship of its own, no supreme court, no flag. Britain dictated foreign policy, and any "repugnant" Canadian legislation could be disallowed by the British parliament. But the people's loyalty (rational and calm to be sure) would come. In 64 years would come autonomy too—thanks mainly to the awesome contribution of Canada's fighting men in the First World War and the determination with which Conservative Prime Minister Sir Robert Borden turned that record to Canada's advantage. Final independence was spelled out by the British parliament when it passed the Statute of Westminster in 1931.

Canadians finished the war of 1914-18 outwardly united and proudly conscious that Canadian sacrifice had earned Canada a new place on the world stage. When the League of Nations was formed in 1920, Canada insisted on a seat of its own—and eventually was elected to the League's governing council. It acted independently *within* the League, and was instrumental in changing a rule that obliged all member countries to come automatically to the defence of any one of them that was attacked.

Canada stayed aloof during the Chanak Crisis of 1922 when Britain and Turkey were on the brink of war (despite Opposition Leader Arthur Meighen's cry that Canada should be "Ready, aye ready"). The following year Canada broke protocol in a treaty with the United States. Heretofore the British ambassador in Washington had signed treaties on Canada's behalf. But when he showed up for a ceremony concluding a fisheries agreement (the Halibut Treaty) he was told he need not have bothered. A *Canadian* had signed for Canada.

The British lion's tail was tweaked thus by the quintessentially grey Canadian— Mackenzie King. But although the Liberal prime minister lacked heroic presence, he was quietly determined that Canada should cut her ties of dependence on Britain. At the 1926 Imperial Conference in London, King found that other British Empire leaders had the same goal for their countries. The Balfour Report which grew out of the conference acknowledged the existence of "autonomous communities . . . freely associated as members of the British Commonwealth of Nations." The governor general—in Canada as in Australia, New Zealand and South Africa—became a representative of the Crown rather than of the British parliament. The Canadian and British governments began dealing with each other directly, through their own diplomats (called, then as now, high commissioners, since countries with the same head of state cannot exchange "ambassadors").

The final details were worked out at the next Imperial Conference, in 1930, with Britain resigned (not unhappily) to the inevitable. The Statute of Westminster (taking the informal name of the parliament that passed it) became law Dec. 11, 1931. Canada, Australia, New Zealand and South Africa had obtained—peacefully—everything the rebellious 13 colonies had demanded in 1776.

But Canada was troubled. The First World War had done nothing to unite it internally. Conscription had soured French-English relations. The cost of living had soared. Veterans returning to Prairie farms found that the "big vested interests" of central Canada (so called, it was quipped, because their owners needed big vests to cover their big paunches) still made it excessively expensive to mortgage a farm, buy equipment and ship wheat. Veterans seeking city jobs found wages low, working conditions poor and collective bargaining by no means assured. Worse—they were angrily certain that some employers exploiting them had been profiteers during the war.

The anger boiled over in Winnipeg on May 15, 1919, when the moderate unionists of the Winnipeg Trades and Labour Council called a general strike over the right to collective bargaining. The walkout quickly became a demand for general reform. It was peaceful, and essential services such as milk and bread deliveries were maintained, but citizens began to fear anarchy. (The Russian Revolution was not yet two years old, and a Red scare that swept the United States had reached Winnipeg.) The strike was smashed on June 21 when 50 Mounties, armed with clubs and pistols, broke up a strikers' illegal parade. Two strikers were killed.

The avenues for change seemed closed. Direct action had failed, and existing political parties were strongly suspected of being partners of the "big vested interests." Consequently, many Canadians, particularly in the West, began to speak through new so-called third parties.

The United Farmers of Ontario swept to power in October 1919. The Progressive Party won 65 seats in the House of Commons in 1921, second only to the Liberals' 116 and ahead of the Conservatives' 50. (Lacking firm leadership and internal discipline, however, the party collapsed in a few years.) Farm parties took office in Alberta and Manitoba, and provincial governments became the main voices of discontent with federal policies. By 1929, when the Great Depression struck, British Columbia was relying increasingly on Pacific trading partners, the Prairies were still fighting the high tariffs that industrial Ontario was trying to maintain, Quebec was anxiously guarding its language and culture, and the Maritimes were bitterly contemplating how the prosperity that *had* come in the late 1920s had passed them by.

The Depression aggravated regional discontent—and spawned new, more lasting, third parties. J. S. Woodsworth, a Methodist minister, former longshoreman and veteran of the Winnipeg strike, took the lead in founding the Cooperative Commonwealth Federation (CCF—forerunner of the New Democratic Party) in 1935. He led the grouping of farmers, workers and intellectuals for eight years, becoming known as "a kind of political saint." William Aberhart, a high-school principal and fundamentalist preacher, led the Social Credit Party to power in Alberta in 1935 after campaigning in a patched coat that he said represented Canada's worn-out money system. Quebec's traditional nationalism found new expression in the Union Nationale Party of Maurice Duplessis, who formed his first government in 1936.

Ottawa, of course, was not helpless—particularly because the provinces looked there for financial help in hard times. Prime Minister R. B. Bennett, a dyed-in-the-wool capitalist who had led the Conservatives to victory in 1930, modified his *laissez-faire* principles in 1932 and launched the predecessor of the Canadian Broadcasting Corporation as a bulwark against the fragmenting effects of regionalism. The following year, fighting the Depression, he set up the Bank of Canada to manage the public debt, guarantee bank deposits and take over (from private banks) the right to issue paper money.

The Second World War ended the Depression, lifted Canadian eyes from regional problems, and put Canada back on the world stage. Britain declared war on Germany on Sept. 3, 1939. Canada declared war too—but a week later, after Mackenzie King (back in power) had summoned Parliament to debate the issue. There was never any doubt where Canada stood, but King insisted that a declaration of war be on Canada's terms—a clear expression of the autonomy won at the League of Nations and in the Statute of Westminster.

At first, munitions were perceived as Canada's main contribution to the war effort. By 1942 production had reached 400 aircraft, 4,000 rifles and a million shells a month, and a 10,000-ton cargo ship was being launched every four days. But production was only one part of the Canadian effort. In five years the British Commonwealth Air Training Plan graduated 131,553 men, from pilots to gunners, at 97 flying schools across Canada.

The corvettes, minesweepers and destroyers of the Royal Canadian Navy (the "sheepdog navy") helped convoy merchant ships through a North Atlantic infested with U-boats. The Royal Canadian Air Force became one of the Allies' biggest, and starting with the Battle of Britain it flew in almost every theatre of the war. Canadian soldiers fought in Hong Kong, Italy, France, Germany. At Dieppe in 1942 the 5,000 Canadians in a 6,000-man force suffered nearly 70 percent casualties (including 907 killed) in a raid that was a valuable rehearsal for the invasion of Normandy two years later. In 1945 the First Canadian Army liberated a Holland that was scant weeks from mass starvation. (The tulips in Ottawa each spring are from Holland— an expression of thanks.)

During the war Canada became one of the world's industrial giants. With peace, it quietly took on the remaining attributes of nationhood. Canadian citizenship (as opposed to British) was proclaimed in 1947. The Supreme Court of Canada became the court of last resort when appeals to the Privy Council of Great Britain were abolished in 1949. The Canadian Bill of Rights became law in 1960. A Canadian flag was adopted in 1965. Newfoundland had become the 10th province in 1949 and the North became Canada's new frontier as aerial reconnaissance and development of natural resources reaffirmed sovereignty in the Arctic.

Canada was widely respected at the United Nations and served in all UN specialized agencies. A Canadian, Dr. Brock Chisholm, was the first director of the World Health Organization. Canada's greatest international contribution was her conciliation during the Suez Crisis of 1956 when External Affairs Minister Lester B. Pearson played a decisive role in persuading Israel, Britain and France to end their invasion of Egypt. Canadians served on the first United Nations Emergency Force (itself Pearson's idea), which maintained the fragile truce and forestalled possible intervention by Russia. From then on, Canada kept armed forces available for similar duty.

Conciliation, not confrontation, has been the Canadian way. From Champlain seeking alliances with Indians ("Our sons shall wed your daughters, and henceforth we shall be one people"), to the Fathers of Confederation burying their differences at Charlottetown, to the Statute of Westminster itself, Canadians have sought agreement through good will. There has of course been confrontation—on the Plains of Abraham, in the troubles of 1837, at Batoche in 1885. . . . But compromise has often followed. French Canadians, after the fall of New France, were deliberately *not* assimilated. The rebellions of 1837, although crushed, led to responsible government. There was no accord with the Métis, but the merit of their cause has been recognized—and the hanging of Louis Riel haunts English Canada. Lawlessness such as marred the California gold rush was *not* tolerated in the Cariboo or the Klondike. Racial bigots who sought to deny Prairie land to East European "peasants in sheepskin coats" were *not* indulged. The record is not spotless, but it is clearly and cleanly on the side of decency and tolerance.

In a world torn by strife, this is something to cherish—and to preserve. And despite defeatists at the start of the War of 1812, despite Nova Scotia separatists in the 1860s, despite countless other criers of doom and gloom, it has been preserved. Canada remains independent and intact. With roots that go back nearly 450 years to Jacques Cartier's exploration of the St. Lawrence River, with forefathers who opened a vast, often frozen, wilderness and protected it dauntlessly in war, Canadians share a vast and stunningly beautiful land, an enormous wealth and a society that is as open and free as any on earth.

Problems remain. Canada has been called the perpetual colony—first French, then British, now American. But French and British colonial influences have receded, and Canada—so rich in natural and human resources—is well able to resist economic and cultural influences from the United States. The question of Quebec's future has moved from the battlefields of 1837 to the arena of public debate, and this alone is a mighty tribute to the degree of accommodation already reached between Canada's two founding nations. Debates and referendums are sophisticated substitutes for civil war.

Historian J. M. S. Careless affirms that "the very core of Canadian history is the fact that a separate Canadian community has always survived in North America, and still continues to grow." If Canada, with all its diversity and all its challenges, can survive and flourish, why not mankind?

Chronology

c. 40,000 B.C. Ancestors of Indians and Inuit come to North America across a land bridge from Siberia.

A.D. c. 1000 Norse settle at L'Anse aux Meadows, Nfld.

1497 June 24: John Cabot claims New World territory (either Newfoundland or Cape Breton Island) for England.

1534 July 24: Jacques Cartier, on the Gaspé Peninsula, claims the area for France.

1541 August: Cartier founds France's first New World colony, at Charlesbourg-Royal, Que.

1576 August: Martin Frobisher, seeking the Northwest Passage, discovers Frobisher Bay.

1579 Spring: Francis Drake establishes Britain's claim to the west coast of North America (perhaps landing on Vancouver Island).

1598 Summer: Troilus de La Roche founds a colony on Sable Island, off Nova Scotia.

1605 August: Pierre de Monts founds Canada's first successful colony, at Port Royal, N.S.

1608 July 3: Champlain founds Quebec City.

1609 July 30: Champlain is the first European to use firearms against Indians (Iroquois).

1610 August: John Guy founds Canada's first English colony, at Cupids, Nfld.

1611 May 22: First Jesuits arrive in New France (at Port Royal).

1611 June 24: Henry Hudson cast adrift in James Bay by mutineers.

1613 Early November: Port Royal sacked by Samuel Argall from Virginia.

1629 July 20: Champlain surrenders Quebec to Kirke brothers from England. (Port La Tour, N.S., is the only part of New France to avoid capture by English.)

1632 March 29: Treaty of Saint-Germain-en-Laye returns New France to French.

1635 Dec. 25: Champlain dies in Quebec, aged about 65.

1636 Port Royal re-established at present-day Annapolis Royal, N.S.

1642 May 17: De Maisonneuve founds Ville-Marie (Montreal).

1643 June 9: Three settlers killed in first of countless Iroquois attacks on Ville-Marie.

1649 Spring: Jesuits burn and abandon Sainte-Marie among the Hurons, following Iroquois attacks on other missions and martyrdom of Brébeuf, Lalemant and Daniel.

1659 June 16: François de Laval arrives at Quebec as de facto bishop of New France.

1660 May 2: Iroquois attack Dollard des Ormeaux near Carillon, Que.

1665 Sept. 12: With New France under the personal control of Louis XIV, Jean Talon arrives at Quebec as first intendant.

1666 Sept. 14: Carignan-Salières Regiment leaves Quebec on raids into Iroquois territory that will end Iroquois harassment of New France for 23 years.

1668 Sept. 29: English ketch Nonsuch reaches Rupert River in James Bay, where crew will build first Hudson's Bay Company post.

1670 May 2: Hudson's Bay Company receives royal charter in London.

1673 July 12: Frontenac awes restless Iroquois at Kingston, Ont.

1682 April 9: La Salle claims Louisiana for France.

1689 Aug. 5: Lachine Massacre starts new series of Iroquois raids.

1690 Oct. 21: Frontenac victorious as Sir William Phips lifts four-day siege of Quebec.

1692 Oct. 22: Madeleine de Verchères defends family fort against Iroquois.

1696 July 4: Frontenac and 2,000 men leave Montreal on raid that will permanently end Iroquois harassment of New France.

1697 Sept. 5: Iberville in Pélican wins control of Hudson Bay.

1701 Aug. 3: Iroquois sign lasting peace with New France.

1710 Oct. 12: Port Royal surrenders for the last time to the English.

1713 April 11: Treaty of Utrecht cedes Hudson Bay, Newfoundland, New Brunswick and mainland Nova Scotia to England.

1743 Summer: La Vérendrye reaches foothills of the Rockies.

1745 June 15: Fortress Louisbourg surrenders to the English (but will be handed back three years later).

1749 June 21: Halifax founded by the English to offset Louisbourg.

1752 March 23: Canada's first newspaper, the Halifax Gazette, appears.

1755 July 28: Acadians ordered deported.

1758 July 26: Louisbourg surrenders to the English for second time. (Now it will be destroyed.)

1759 Sept. 13: Wolfe defeats Montcalm on Plains of Abraham.

1760 Sept. 8: Montreal surrenders to the English.

1763 Feb. 10: Treaty of Paris seals the fall of New France.

1774 June 22: Quebec Act, guaranteeing civil, language and religious rights to French Canadians, comes into force.

1775 Dec. 31: American rebels' invasion stemmed at Quebec.

1779 Summer: Montreal fur traders form the North West Company.

1783 May 18: First Loyalists land at Saint John, N.B.

1783 Sept. 3: A second Treaty of Paris ends the American War of Independence and cedes fishing rights and land to the United States.

1784 Aug. 16: Province of New Brunswick formed.

1791 June 19: Provinces of Lower Canada (Quebec) and Upper Canada (Ontario) formed.

1792 Aug. 28: Captains Vancouver and Quadra meet at Nootka Sound to settle British and Spanish claims to the Pacific coast.

1793 July 22: Alexander Mackenzie, first man to cross North America north of Mexico, records his arrival at the Pacific on a rock near Bella Coola, B.C.

1793 Aug. 27: York (Toronto) founded.

1808 July 2: Nor'Wester Simon Fraser reaches the mouth of the Fraser River.

1811 July 15: Nor'Wester David Thompson reaches the mouth of the Columbia River.

Provinces and territories joined Confederation, or were created from existing parts of Canada, on these dates:

July 1, 1867	New Brunswick, Nova Scotia, Ontario, Quebec
July 15, 1870	Manitoba, Northwest Territories
July 20, 1871	British Columbia
July 1, 1873	Prince Edward Island
June 13, 1898	Yukon Territory
Sept. 1, 1905	Alberta, Saskatchewan
March 31, 1949	Newfoundland

1812 June 18: United States declares war on Britain (the War of 1812).

1812 Sept. 12: Selkirk settlers reach Winnipeg.

1812 Oct. 13: Americans defeated (but Sir Isaac Brock killed) in the Battle of Queenston Heights.

1813 April 27: Americans capture Fort York at present-day Toronto.

1813 June 22: Laura Secord warns British troops of impending American attack. (Seventeen days earlier, scout Billy Green had revealed details of American troop positions. Both reports lead to British victories.)

1813 Oct. 26: Americans defeated at the Battle of Châteauguay, near Montreal.

1813 Nov. 11: Americans defeated at the Battle of Crysler's Farm, near Morrisburg, Ont.

1814 Dec. 24: Treaty of Ghent ends the War of 1812, returns captured territory to the Americans.

1816 June 19: Métis and a few Indians massacre Selkirk settlers at Seven Oaks (Winnipeg).

1819 Sept. 26: Edward Parry anchors for a 10-month stay off Melville Island. (He is the first searcher for the Northwest Passage to winter in the Arctic by choice.)

1821 March 26: Hudson's Bay Company absorbs North West Company.

1825 Oct. 7: Miramichi Fire kills more than 160 persons and consumes 6,000 square miles of forest in New Brunswick.

1826 June 6: Reform editor William Lyon Mackenzie's printing shop in York (Toronto) is wrecked by Family Compact members.

1832 May 21: British troops kill three French Canadians in street riot following Patriote by-election victory.

1832 June 7: Immigrants with cholera land at Quebec. By September the disease will kill 3,800 there, 4,000 in Montreal.

1835 March 3: Reform newspaper publisher Joseph Howe's oratory wins him acquittal on a libel charge and establishes freedom of the press.

1836 June 19: Hudson's Bay Company paddle-wheeler Beaver, the first steamer in the North Pacific, enters service.

1836 July 21: Canada's first railway, the Champlain and St. Lawrence, starts service between Laprairie and Saint-Jean, Que.

1837 Nov. 23: Patriote rebels defeat British troops at Saint-Denis, Que.

1837 Nov. 25: British troops defeat Patriotes at Saint-Charles, Que.

1837 Dec. 5: Mackenzie and Upper Canada rebels marching on Toronto are stopped by a militia ambush.

1837 Dec. 7: Upper Canada rebels scatter after militiamen attack and burn Montgomery's Tavern (rebel headquarters).

1837 Dec. 14: *Patriotes* crushed by British troops at Saint-Eustache, Que.

1837 Mid-December: Mackenzie sets up a short-lived republic on Navy Island in the Niagara River.

1839 Jan. 31: Durham Report urges responsible government and political union for Lower and Upper Canada, and assimilation for French Canadians.

1841 Feb. 10: Upper Canada becomes Canada West, and Lower Canada becomes Canada East; they are united into the Province of Canada.

1843 March 15: Work starts on the Vancouver Island HBC post that will become Victoria.

1846 June 15: Oregon Treaty sets the 49th parallel as the western Canada/U.S. boundary.

1847 May 24: Lieut. Graham Gore's sledge party leaves the icebound ships of the Franklin Expedition to seek the last link in the Northwest Passage.

1848 March 11: The Province of Canada's first responsible government by party — the Great Reform Ministry led by Louis-Hippolyte LaFontaine and Robert Baldwin — takes office.

1848 April 22: Franklin expedition ships *Erebus* and *Terror* abandoned. All 130 expedition members will perish.

1849 April 25: English Tory mob burns the parliament buildings in Montreal after Governor General Lord Elgin signs the Rebellion Losses Bill.

1851 April 17: *Marco Polo*, to be the fastest ship in the world, launched at Saint John, N.B.

1851 May 23: Province of Canada issues British North America's first postage stamp.

1855 Militia Act establishes the beginnings of the modern Canadian army.

1858 Nov. 19: James Douglas, already governor of Vancouver Island, sworn in as governor of British Columbia.

1862 Aug. 21: Billy Barker strikes gold on Williams Creek in the Cariboo country of British Columbia.

1864 Sept. 1: Charlottetown Conference opens to discuss the confederation of British North American colonies.

1864 Oct. 10: Quebec Conference opens to continue confederation talks. (It will settle the fundamentals upon which the British North America Act will be based.)

1866 June 2: Battle of Ridgeway climaxes biggest Fenian raid into Canada.

1866 June 9: Pte. Timothy O'Hea extinguishes a fire in a boxcar of ammunition at Danville, Que., and wins the only Victoria Cross ever awarded for an act in Canada.

1866 Nov. 19: Colonies of Vancouver Island and British Columbia are combined into one colony named British Columbia.

1867 March 8: British parliament passes the British North America Act.

1867 July 1: Dominion of Canada comes into being: Sir John A. Macdonald sworn in as prime minister.

1867 September: Canada's first automobile, a steamer built by Henry Seth Taylor, demonstrated at Stanstead, Que.

1869 June 22: Canadian parliament agrees to buy Rupert's Land — all the Hudson's Bay Company territory.

1869 Nov. 2: Louis Riel and Métis occupy Lower Fort Garry. The Red River Rebellion has begun.

1869 Dec. 8: Riel establishes a legal provisional government in Rupert's Land.

1870 March 4: Thomas Scott executed on orders of Riel.

1870 July 15: Métis rights recognized, as Manitoba becomes a province. (But Riel will have to flee Canada because of Scott's execution.)

1871 The last British troops (except for small garrisons which will stay at Halifax and Esquimalt, B.C., for another 35 years) leave Canada.

1873 April 2: The Pacific Scandal erupts: Prime Minister Macdonald accused of corruption in negotiations over a transcontinental railway. (His government will be forced to resign.)

1873 May: American wolf hunters massacre Assiniboine Indians in the Cypress Hills. (The North West Mounted Police will be formed as a result.)

1874 July 8: The Mounties leave Fort Dufferin on their march west to wipe out the whisky trade.

1874 Oct. 27: *William D. Lawrence*, the biggest wooden ship ever built in the Maritimes, launched at Maitland, N.S.

1876 Aug. 3: The first intelligible telephone call between two buildings is made from Brantford, Ont., to Mount Pleasant, two miles away.

Canadian prime ministers since Confederation took office on these dates (party affiliation in brackets):

July 1, 1867	John A. Macdonald (Cons.)
Nov. 7, 1873	Alexander Mackenzie (Lib.)
Oct. 17, 1878	John A. Macdonald (Cons.)
June 16, 1891	John Abbott (Cons.)
Dec. 5, 1892	John Thompson (Cons.)
Dec. 21, 1894	Mackenzie Bowell (Cons.)
May 1, 1896	Charles Tupper (Cons.)
July 11, 1896	Wilfrid Laurier (Lib.)
Oct. 10, 1911	Robert Borden (Cons.)
July 10, 1920	Arthur Meighen (Cons.)
Dec. 29, 1921	Mackenzie King (Lib.)
June 29, 1926	Arthur Meighen (Cons.)
Sept. 25, 1926	Mackenzie King (Lib.)
Aug. 7, 1930	R. B. Bennett (Cons.)
Oct. 23, 1935	Mackenzie King (Lib.)
Nov. 15, 1948	Louis St. Laurent (Lib.)
June 21, 1957	John Diefenbaker (Cons.)
April 22, 1963	Lester B. Pearson (Lib.)
April 20, 1968	Pierre Trudeau (Lib.)
June 4, 1979	Joe Clark (Cons.)
Mar. 3, 1980	Pierre Trudeau (Lib.)

1877 Sept. 22: Treaty No. 7 cedes the last big section of Prairie land to the government of Canada.

1878 Sept. 17: Secret ballot used for the first time in a federal general election.

1879 Feb. 8: Sandford Fleming proposes the idea of standard time.

1885 Jan. 28: More than 300 voyageurs, the first Canadians to serve in an overseas war, reach Khartoum after guiding a British expedition up the Nile River.

1885 March 18: Louis Riel proclaims an illegal provisional government at Batoche, Sask. The Northwest Rebellion has begun.

1885 May 12: Batoche falls, Riel taken prisoner.

1885 June 3: Crees, and whites led by Mounties, fight the last military engagement on Canadian soil (near Loon Lake, Sask.).

1885 Nov. 7: Last spike of the CPR driven at Craigellachie, B.C.

1885 Nov. 16: Riel hanged at Regina.

1891 June 6: John A. Macdonald dies aged 76.

1896 Aug. 17: George Carmack stakes a claim after striking gold on Rabbit Creek in the Klondike.

1896 Nov. 17: Clifford Sifton named minister of the interior with the task of filling the Prairies with settlers.

1899 Oct. 30: First Canadian troops embark for the South African War.

1906 Aug. 31: Roald Amundsen's *Gjoa* reaches Nome, Alaska, after becoming the first ship to sail the Northwest Passage.

1909 Feb. 23: J. A. D. McCurdy makes the first manned flight in the British Empire, at Baddeck, N.S.

1909 July 1: Joseph-Elzéar Bernier affirms Canadian sovereignty in the High Arctic by erecting a plaque on Melville Island.

1910 May 4: Royal Canadian Navy formed.

1914 May 29: *Empress of Ireland* sinks in the St. Lawrence; 1,015 perish.

1914 Aug. 4: Britain declares war on Germany. Canada is automatically at war too.

1915 April 22: Canadian troops in the Second Battle of Ypres hold against history's first major gas attack.

1917 April 9: Canadians capture Vimy Ridge.

1917 Dec. 6: Halifax explosion kills nearly 2,000 persons.

1918 March 29: Anti-conscription riots break out in Quebec City.

1918 Nov. 11: Armistice declared, one day after the capture of Mons has climaxed "Canada's Hundred Days" of unbroken advance.

1919 June 21: Mounties smash 37-day-old Winnipeg General Strike.

1931 Dec. 11: British parliament passes the Statute of Westminster, giving Canada final independence.

1939 Sept 10: Canada declares war on Germany after approval by the Canadian parliament.

1942 Aug. 19: Dieppe raid leaves 907 Canadians dead, 1,946 captured.

1942 Oct. 11: RCMP ship *St. Roch* reaches Halifax after becoming the second ship ever (and the first going west to east) to sail the Northwest Passage.

1956 Nov. 6: United Nations General Assembly adopts Lester B. Pearson's Suez peace-keeping plan.

Index

Page numbers indicate references in the chapter essays, highlight features, captions, closeup features and epilogue. Numbers in **boldface** indicate major references. Numbers followed by the letter P mean the subjects are pictured on those pages.

G

374

Picture Credits

The abbreviations used here are these:

CH	Chic Harris
DW	Daniel Wiener
FP	Freeman Patterson
GA	Glenbow-Alberta Institute
HBC	Hudson's Bay Company
HK	Henry Kalen
JdeV	John de Visser
JR	Jules Rochon
MCM	McCord Museum, Montreal
MF	Menno Fieguth
MTL	Metropolitan Toronto Library
NMC	National Museum of Man, National Museums of Canada
NS	Nova Scotia Communications and Information Centre
PAC	The Public Archives of Canada
PvB	Paul von Baich
ROM	Royal Ontario Museum, Toronto
RS	Rod Stears
RV	Richard Vroom
WNB	Webster Pictorial Collection, New Brunswick Museum

Credits are left to right, top to bottom, with supplementary information as needed. When the number of pictures exceeds the number of credits, the remaining pictures should be credited to the last source named. A single credit means that all pictures on that page are from the same source.

3 MF; **5** Boris Spremo; **10-11** DW; **11** Parks Canada; **12** RV; **12-13** DW; **13** University Library, Heidelberg (West Germany); **14** CH; Viking Ship Museum, Roskilde (Denmark); **15** The National Gallery, Oslo; from *The Quest for America*, courtesy Phaidon Press, Oxford; **16** DW; Mary Evans Picture Library, London; DW; **17** Audio Visual Programs Division, Environment Canada; **18** British Museum/photo © Aldous Books, London; **18-19** Photo Musées nationaux, Paris; **19** PvB; **20** PAC C-21255; **21** Parks Canada; **22** PAC C-23089; **22-23** DW; **23** DW; **24** courtesy Archives of the Commonwealth of Massachusetts, Boston; NS; **25** RS; **26** Department of Tourism, Parks and Conservation, P.E.I.; Lazare and Parker, Toronto; **27** DW; **29** DW; **30** courtesy of the Newfoundland Museum; Nancy Douglas; **30-31** Conception Bay Museum; from *Canada: The Heroic Beginnings*, courtesy MacMillan of Canada; **31** Collections of the Geography and Map Division, Library of Congress, Washington; **33** Ontario Ministry of Industry and Tourism; **34** PAC C-5750; C-6643; **35** National Map Collection, PAC C-22389; New York Historical Society, N.Y.C.; Confederation Life Collection; **36** (detail) by John Collier, Tate Gallery, London; **37** RV; **38** JR; PAC C-5749; **39** *Hélène de Champlain arrive à Québec* by Frank Craig, PAC; **40** Musée du Québec; JR; **41** PvB; **42-43** RV; **43** RV; **44** Archives de la Compagnie de Jésus/photo by Armour Landry; Confederation Life Collection; **45** RV; RV; Archives de la Compagnie de Jésus/photo by Armour Landry; **46** Musée du Québec; Lazare and Parker, Toronto; **47** RV; **48** RV; **49** Archives nationales du Québec; Musée de Besançon (France)/photo by Schwartz; **50** Library of Congress, Washington; **51** courtesy Huronia Historical Parks; **52** PvB; **52-53** Musée des Religieuses Hospitalières de Saint-Joseph de Montréal/photo by PvB; **53** PvB; **54** PvB; Sœurs de la Congrégation de Notre-Dame/photo by Armour Landry; **55** CH; Musée des Religieuses Hospitalières de Saint-Joseph de Montréal/photo by PvB; **56** Centre Marie de l'Incarnation et Musée des Ursulines; (left) courtesy of Marion C. McDougall/photo by PvB; **57** Montreal Municipal Library/photo by Graetz; **58** MCM; photo by PvB; PAC C-3018; **59** Carol Priamo; **60** Archives du Séminaire de Québec; CH; **62** HBC/photo by Max's Studio; **63** photo by HK; **64** HBC; Gerry Kopelow; **65** photo courtesy of Remington Art Museum, Ogdensburg, N.Y.; **66** HBC; HBC; HBC Collection, Lower Fort Garry National Historic Park; **67** Fred Bruemmer; PAC C-1349; **68** HBC; **69** CH; **70-71** Agnes Etherington Art Centre, Queen's University; **71** RV; **72** *The Fur Traders at Montreal* by G. A. Reid, PAC; Department of National Defence; **73** Château de Versailles (France); **74** Montreal Municipal Library, Gagnon Collection/photo by Graetz; PvB; **75** PAC C-1225; PvB; **76** Historical Picture Services, Chicago; MCM/photo by Karen Coshof; **77** St. Francis Xavier Mission Museum/photo by Armour Landry; Betty Greenacre; **78** courtesy of M. and Mme Saint-Jean/photo by Mike Haimes; **79** PAC C-6022; Historical Picture Services, Chicago; **80** *Madeleine de Verchères* by Gerald S. Hayward, PAC; Montreal Municipal Library, Gagnon Collection/photo by Graetz; Quebec Government courtesy of the Tourist Branch; Archives nationales, Paris; **81** Marc Hardy; **82** PAC C-34183; Osprey Publishing Ltd., London; PAC C-20482; Surveys and Mapping Branch, Department of Energy, Mines and Resources; Alain Bienvenue; **82-83** Archives nationales du Québec; Montreal Military and Maritime Museum; Alain Bienvenue; **83** Musée du Québec; Archives du monastère de l'Hôtel-Dieu de Québec/photo by W. B. Edwards; Alain Bienvenue; **84** NS; **84-85** DW; **85** WNB; **86** Historical Picture Services, Chicago; **86-87** *The Fate of the Defendants of Fort Latour* by A. Sherriff Scott, PAC; **88** NS; **89** WNB; **90** Parks Canada, Atlantic Region; **91** Tim Randall; **92** FP; **92-93** DW; **93** FP; **94** FP; DW; **95** DW; **96** FP; **96-97** Bibliothèque nationale, Paris; **98** Nova Scotia Public Archives; Art Gallery of Ontario; **99** Osprey Publishing Ltd., London; **100** *Thomas Pichon* by Henri Beau, PAC; NS; **101** RS; Moncton University/Reid's Photo Centre; **102** DW; **103** Jean-Claude Hurni; **104-105** PAC; **105** JR; **106** PvB; **107** PAC C-82808; JR; **108** Osprey Publishing Ltd., London; Quebec Government courtesy of the Tourist Branch; **109** *General James Wolfe* by Joseph Highmore, PAC; *Louis-Joseph Marquis de Montcalm* by Antoine François Sergent, PAC; PvB; **110** WNB; Eric Woolgar; **112** *Sir Guy Carleton* by Mable B. Messer, PAC; **113** JR; **114** MCM/photo by Karen Coshof; Château de Ramezay; **114-115** FP; **115** PvB; **116** City of Montreal; The National Gallery of Canada, Ottawa; **117** Archives nationales du Québec; Astor Lennox Tilden Foundation, New York Public Library, N.Y.C.; **118** Frank Prazak; Canadian War Museum, NMC/photo by John Evans; **119** PvB; **121** courtesy William Inglis Morse Collection, Killam Memorial Library, Dalhousie University; Historical Picture Services, Chicago; Gary N. Corbett; DW; Images/photo by Peter Barss; Nova Scotia Legislative Library; **122** New Brunswick Tourism; courtesy City of Saint John/photo by Clifford Hodgson; **123** New Brunswick Tourism; **124** RS; WNB; **125** Delaware Art Museum, Wilmington; Ted Spiegel/Black Star, N.Y.C.; **126** FP; RS; DW; **127** JdeV; JdeV; Tim Randall; JdeV; JdeV; RS; **128** *Portrait of Joseph Brant* by William Berczy, The National Gallery of Canada, Ottawa; RV; **129** JdeV; **130** MTL; WNB; **132-133** JdeV; **133** JdeV; **134-135** JdeV; **135** JdeV; **136** GA; RV; **137** JdeV; ROM; **138** *Voyageurs At Dawn* by Frances Ann Hopkins, PAC; Montreal Military and Maritime Museum; D.E. Caufield; **139** RV; **140** Native Sons of British Columbia, Post No. 2; J. Ross Robertson Collection, MTL; Parks Canada; **141** ROM; **142** PvB; MCM; **144** The National Gallery of Canada, Ottawa; **144-145** Daniel Conrad; **145** British Columbia Government Photo; **146** PAC C-5536; Trustees of the British Museum, London; **147** British Columbia Provincial Museum; National Maritime Museum, Greenwich (England); **148** PvB; ROM; **149** A. Niemann; Dr. R. R. Haering; **150** Provincial Archives of British Columbia; **151** HK; **152-153** JdeV; **153** JdeV; **154** Field Museum of Natural History, Chicago; MCM; **155** Canadian War Museum, NMC; PAC; JdeV; **156** JdeV; **156-157** PAC; **157** Historical Picture Services, Chicago; by George Cuthbertson, courtesy of Canada Steamship Lines Collection; **158** JdeV; **159** J. Ross Robertson Collection, MTL; **160** Historical Picture Services, Chicago; **161** Château de Ramezay; PvB; **162** JdeV; RV; courtesy of Richardson, Bond and Wright; **163** JdeV; **166** GA; *Buffalo Rift* by A. J. Miller, PAC; **167** (right) HBC; NMC; C. C. Cruikshank; GA; **168** HBC; Lorne Coulson; **169** Saint-Boniface Museum; Parks Canada, Lower Fort Garry National Historic Park; **170** Manitoba Museum of Man and Nature/photo by C. Douglas Smaill; HK; **171** ROM; **172** Victoria University Library, Toronto; Saint-Boniface Museum; **173** Gerry Kopelow; **174** Pauline Reaburn; Public Archives of Ontario; *The Quilting Party* by Harold W. McCrea, Art Gallery of Ontario; **175** CPS Film Productions; (centre top) CH; *The Postman* by A. Sherriff Scott, PAC; ROM; The Bettmann Archives, N.Y.C.; Trent University Archives, Edwin C. Guillet Papers; Historical Picture Services, Chicago; **176** JdeV; JdeV; Hamilton Historical Board/photo by JdeV; **177** JdeV; **178** J. Ross Robertson Collection, MTL; Pauline Reaburn; **179** Parks Canada; St. Lawrence Parks Commission, Old Fort Henry; RV; **180** Ontario Ministry of Industry and Tourism; JdeV; **181** JdeV; **182** *The McNab* by Sir H. Reaburn, PAC; WNB; **183** JdeV; **184-185** MCM/photo by Karen Coshof; **185** Pierre Gaudard; PAC; **186** Château de Ramezay; courtesy of Mrs. W. C. Pitfield/photo by Mike Haimes; **187** Bibliothèque nationale du Québec; Frank Prazak; Fred Angus; **188** MCM/photo by Karen Coshof; PvB; **189** Archives nationales du Québec; **190** DW; PvB; **191** DW; courtesy of Upper Canada College/photo by Ron Vickers; PAC; **192** MCM/photo by Karen Coshof; Musée du Québec; **193** Canadian Government Office of Tourism; **194** Collection of the Province of Ontario/photo by JdeV; JdeV; **195** PAC Jefferys IC-23; JdeV; **196** JdeV; J. Ross Robertson Collection, MTL; **197** from Harper's Weekly/photo by Graetz; JdeV; **198** Public Archives of Ontario; Radio Times Hulton Picture Library, London; J. Ross Robertson Collection, MTL; PAC; **199** MTL; JdeV; **200** (detail) *View of the windmill at Prescott, Upper Canada, and the adjacent house as it appeared after the action* by Henry Francis Ainslie, PAC; RV; **201** JdeV; George F. Long; **202** J. Ross Robertson Collection, MTL; J. M. Mackenzie/Miller Services; **203** courtesy of Imperial Oil Ltd.; **204** Frank Prazak; **204-205** MCM; **205** MCM/photo by Karen Coshof; **206** Château de Ramezay; Château de Ramezay; PAC; **207** JR; photo by John Evans; CH; **208** Musée du Séminaire de Québec; **209** courtesy Warnock Hersey International Ltd. Canadiana Collection/photo by Mike Haimes; MCM/photo by Karen Coshof; PvB; **210** DW; **211** Department of Rare Books and Special Collections, McGill University; DW; **212** John Hinde Ltd., Belfast; RV; Frank Prazak; **214** PAC C-9161; Anne S. K. Brown Military Collection, Providence, R.I.; JdeV; Parks Canada; **215** ROM; St. Lawrence Parks Commission, Old Fort Henry; St. Lawrence Parks Commission, Old Fort Henry; courtesy of Kings Landing Corporation; MTL; **218** Radio Times Hulton Picture Library, London; R. S. Pilot; **219** National Portrait Gallery, London; **220** photo © Aldous Books, London; **220-221** National Maritime Museum, Greenwich (England); **221** courtesy of Rare Books and Special Collections, McGill University Libraries/photo by Mike Haimes; HK; **222** Trustees of the British Museum © Aldous Books, London; Fred Bruemmer; National Film Board; Fred Bruemmer; **223** National Maritime Museum © Aldous Books, London; National Maritime Museum © Aldous Books, London; National Portrait Gallery, London; **224** Radio Times Hulton Picture Library, London; HBC; Fred Bruemmer; **225** William J. Carpenter/Eskimo Dog Research Foundation; **226** HBC; **226-227** HK; **227** HK; **228** Parks Canada, Lower Fort Garry National Historic Park; MF; **229** Carol Moore-Ede Myers; British Columbia Provincial Museum; Joslyn Art Museum, Omaha; **230** HK; B. A. Johnstone; **231** Maritime Museum of British Columbia; Provincial Archives of British Columbia; **232** Franklin Arbuckle for HBC; Provincial Archives of British Columbia; HBC; **234-235** MF; **235** Vancouver City Archives; PvB; HK; PvB; **236** Allan Harvey; **237** Provincial Archives of British Columbia; **238** MCM; Confederation Life Collection; HK; **239** Provincial Archives of British Columbia; **240** Carol Moore-Ede Myers; **241** HK; **242** PAC C-8735; **243** MF; Department of Tourism, Parks and Conservation, P.E.I.; **244** PAC C-1530; **245** Confederation Life Collection; PAC; DW; **246** JdeV; Canadian Postal Museum/photo by Richard Garner; PAC C-44304; **247** RV; Dr. W. A. Newlands; **248** (right) RV; PvB; RV; JdeV; **249** JdeV; **250** Public Archives of Prince Edward Island; RV; **251** PAC C-4813; PA-25746; PA-26376; **252** PAC C-83423; C-18737; **254** MTL; GA; MTL; **254-255** MCM; Dr. Jules Levesque; Notman Photographic Archives, MCM; **255** Notman Photographic Archives, MCM; **256** Nova Scotia Museum; **256-257** NS; **257** Nova Scotia Museum; **258** Wilson Studio Collection; **259** WNB; **260** FP; **261** Musée du Québec; Nova Scotia Maritime Museum/photo by Terry Waterfield; Bob Brooks; **262** Yarmouth County Museum; **263** Bob Brooks; **264** Nova Scotia Public Archives; courtesy of the Newfoundland Museum; **266** MF; **266-267** MF; **267** RCMP Archives; **268** GA; New York Historical Society, N.Y.C.; Gary W. Seib; **268-269** HK; **269** MF; GA; **270** Canadian Government Office of Tourism; RCMP Archives; **271** collection of the Edmonton Art Gallery, gift of the E. E. Poole Foundation; MF; **272** GA; **273** GA; **274** MF; **275** Gordon D. Knight; **276-277** PAC; **277** PvB; PAC C-86515; **278** Provincial Archives of Manitoba; HK; **279** Provincial Archives of Manitoba; Saint-Boniface Museum; **280** Bruce Johnson for HBC; Provincial Archives of Manitoba; **281** PAC C-20658; GA; Mary Evans Picture Library, London; **282** photo by Joe Thauberger; courtesy of The Governor General's Horse Guards/photo by Ron Vickers; **283** HK; **284** Saskatchewan Historic Parks; Corporate Archives, Canadian Pacific; **285** PAC; PAC C-4523; **286** GA; JdeV; **288** Tina Dornbusch; **289** Corporate Archives, Canadian Pacific/photo by Ross Best and Co.; **290** PAC C-78604; Corporate Archives, Canadian Pacific; Corporate Archives, Canadian Pacific/photo by William Notman and Sons of Montreal; **291** Photo Librarium; PAC C-26668; **292** HK; HK; Allan Harvey; **293** PvB; Corporate Archives, Canadian Pacific/photo by Prof. Buell; **294** Confederation Life Collection; **295** Corporate Archives, Canadian Pacific/photo by J. F. Cooke; Bruno Engler; **296** Brian Stablyk; Corporate Archives, Canadian Pacific; **297** HK; **298** JdeV; **298-299** JdeV; **299** Telephone Historical Collection, Bell Canada; **300** Canada Wide; MCM; **301** JdeV; Archives du Séminaire de Québec; **302** RV; Owned by Richard M. Steward, courtesy of the Automobile Quarterly Magazine, Princeton/photo by Stan Rosenthall; **303** JdeV; Imperial Oil Collection, PAC C-103280; courtesy Library of Congress, Washington; **304** MTL; courtesy of Ray Fazakas; **305** DW; courtesy of Rare Books and Special Collections, McGill University Libraries/photo by Graetz; Fred Angus; **306** RV; Canada Wide; **308** Château de Ramezay; Lyle McIntyre; **308-309** WNB; **309** Ontario Ministry of Natural Resources; British Columbia Forest Service; MTL; Dave Looy/Image Finders Photo Agency; British Columbia Forest Service; **310-311** Clifford A. Fenner; **311** George Hunter; Yukon Government; **312** PAC PA-16875; Crombie McNeil; **313** Yukon Government; **314** National Film Board; **315** Alan Todd; **316** Gillis Collection, Reney-Photographer, Yukon Archives; James Quong; **316-317** Alan Todd; **317** PAC PA-13444; PvB; **318** James Quong; Richard Harrington; **319** Alan Todd; **320** Sig Bradshaw; **320-321** © Toby Rankin/The Image Bank of Canada; **321** GA; HK; **322** from *To Canada, Ottawa, Department of the Interior, 1903*/MTL; courtesy of Rare Books and Special Collections, McGill University Libraries/photo by P. Léveillé; **323** PAC PA-25966; Provincial Archives of Alberta; Provincial Archives of Manitoba; Saskatchewan Archives Photograph; **324** MF; courtesy of Manitoba Museum of Man and Nature; **324-325** MF; PAC C-14974; (inset) Saskatchewan Archives Photograph; **325** Ukrainian Women's Association of Canada/photo by Carol Moore-Ede Myers; **326** Provincial Archives of Alberta, H. Pollard Collection; GA; **327** HK; **328** Lorne Coulson; **329** HK; HK; MF; **330** PAC; **331** Collection du Musée Laurier, Arthabaska; PAC; **332** Sœurs de la Congrégation de Notre-Dame/photo by Armour Landry; **332-333** E. Otto/Miller Services; **333** Collection du Musée Laurier, Arthabaska; Parks Canada; Quebec Government courtesy of the Tourist Branch; **334** M-H Specialty Sales; M-H Specialty Sales; George Hunter; **335** PAC C-89581; GA; Archives Eaton's of Canada Ltd.; **336** PAC C-25960; Rev. W. L. L. Lawrence Collection, Public Archives of Ontario; **337** Canada Wide; © Derek Caron/The Image Bank of Canada; **338** Glenn Baechler Collection; **339** Telephone Historical Collection, Bell Canada, courtesy of Canadian Marconi Company; courtesy of the National Museum of Science and Technology, painted by R. W. Bradford; **340** PAC C-27360; Association des marins de la vallée du Saint-Laurent; **341** Nancy Douglas; **342** courtesy of the Université de Montréal; **342-343** Canadian War Museum, NMC-8178; **343** courtesy of the Canadian Department of Veterans Affairs Minister, The Hon. Daniel J. MacDonald; **344** PAC PA-5314; Musée du Royal 22e Régiment; **345** Montreal Military and Maritime Museum; courtesy of E. J. S. Smith/photo by R. V. Killick; **346** courtesy of the Canadian Department of Veterans Affairs Minister, The Hon. Daniel J. MacDonald; **346-347** 8179—Canadian War Museum, NMC; **347** PAC C-19948; **349** courtesy of the National Museum of Science and Technology; **350** 8673—*Sir Arthur Currie* (detail) by Sir William Orpen, Canadian War Museum, NMC; PAC PA-1326; **350-351** JIPE-CEDRI, Paris; **352** NMC; **352-353** PAC PA-40138; **353** DW; **354** JdeV; Col. John McCrae Birthplace Society/photo by Jerome Knap; **355** RV.

Illustrators:

Tom Bjarnason (page 120), Jim Bruce (11, 66, 87, 97, 165, 200, 201, 223, 248, 263, 272, 294, 308, 312, 348), George Buctel (31), Alan Daniel (32, 113, 165, 289), Réal Lefèvre (88, 96, 240, 327), Merle Smith (351), Gordon Rayner (27, 28, 83, 237, 313), Elaine Scars (31, 74, 120), Rex Woods (217).

Lyrics from *Jesous Ahatonhia* by permission of the Frederick Harris Music Co. Ltd., Oakville, Ont.
Excerpt from *Ghosts Have Warm Hands* by permission of Clark, Irwin & Company Limited, Toronto.

Color separation: Prolith Incorporated
Typesetting: The Graphic Group of Canada Ltd.
Printing: Montreal Lithographing Ltd.
Binding: Harpell's Press Co-operative
Binding material: Boise Cascade (Pajco Products)
Paper: Rolland Paper Company Limited